Y0-BDC-397

In Pursuit of Meaning

Vol. II: Law, Society, and Language

In Pursuit of Meaning
Collected Studies of Baruch A. Levine

Volume 2: Law, Society, and Language

Baruch A. Levine

Edited by
Andrew D. Gross

Winona Lake, Indiana
Eisenbrauns
2011

Printed in the United States of America

www.eisenbrauns.com

Library of Congress Cataloging-in-Publication Data

Levine, Baruch A.
In pursuit of meaning : collected studies of Baruch A. Levine / edited by Andrew Gross.
v. cm.
Includes bibliographical references and index.
ISBN 978-1-57506-206-8 (hardback; 2-vol. set : alk. paper) — ISBN 978-1-57506-207-5 (hardback; vol. 1 : alk. paper) — ISBN 978-1-57506-208-2 (hardback; vol. 2 : alk. paper)
1. Bible. O.T.—Criticism, interpretation, etc. 2. Sacrifice—Biblical teaching. 3. Ugarit (Extinct city)—Religious life and customs. 4. Inscriptions, Aramaic—Jordan—Dayr ʿAlla, Tall. 5. Canaanites—Religion. 6. Balaam (Biblical figure). 7. Temple scroll. 8. Cosmography. 9. Hebrew language—Lexicography. 10. Hebrew language—Grammar. I. Gross, Andrew. II. Title.
BS1171.3.L48 2011
221.9—dc22

2010045563

The paper used in this publication meets the minimum requirements of the American National Standard for Information Sciences—Permanence of Paper for Printed Library Materials, ANSI Z39.48-1984.♾™

To my wife,
Corinne
A "support-group" of one.

Table of Contents
Volume II: Law, Society, and Language

Abbreviations

References to Assyriological publications follow the abbreviations lists in *CAD* and *AHw*. Note also that some individual articles include their own abbreviations list.

AASOR	*Annual of the American Schools of Oriental Research*
AB	Anchor Bible
ABD	D. N. Freedman (ed.), *Anchor Bible Dictionary* (6 vols.; New York: Doubleday, 1992).
AHw	W. von Soden, *Akkadisches Handwörterbuch* (3 vols.; Wiesbaden: Harrasowitz, 1965–1981)
AJSL	*American Journal of Semitic Languages and Literatures*
ANET	J. B. Pritchard (ed.), *Ancient Near Eastern Texts Relating to the Old Testament* (3rd edition; Princeton University Press, 1969)
AOAT	Alter Orient und Altes Testament
AOS	American Oriental Series
AP	A. E. Cowley, *Aramaic Papyri of the Fifth Century B.C.* (Oxford: Clarendon Press, 1923)
BASOR	*Bulletin of the American Schools of Oriental Research*
CAD	*The Assyrian Dictionary of the Oriental Institute of the University of Chicago* (Chicago: The Oriental Institute, 1956–)
CCPA	*A Corpus of Christian Palestinian Aramaic*, C. Müller-Kessler and M. Sokoloff (5 vols.; Groningen: Styx Publications, 1997–).
CHANE	Culture and History of the Ancient Near East
DJD	Discoveries in the Judaean Desert (of Jordan)
DSA	Abraham Tal, *A Dictionary of Samaritan Aramaic* (2 vols.; Leiden: Brill, 2000)
DNWSI	J. Hoftijzer and K. Jongeling, *Dictionary of the North-west Semitic Inscriptions* (2 vols.; Leiden: E. J. Brill, 1995)
DUL	G. del Olmo Lete and J. Sanmartín, *A Dictionary of the Ugaritic Language in the Alphabetic Tradition* (2 vols.; Leiden: Brill, 2003)
EA	J. A. Knudtzon, *Die El-Amarna Tafeln* (2 vols.; Leipzig: J. C. Hinrichs, 1908–15)
GKC	*Gesenius' Hebrew Grammar, as edited and enlarged by the late E. Kautzsch*. 2nd English ed., rev. in accordance with the 28th German ed. (1909) by A. E. Cowley (Oxford: Clarendon Press; New York: Oxford University Press, 1910)
HALAT	L. Koehler and W. Baumgartner, *Hebräisches und Aramäisches Lexikon zum Alten Testament* (5 vols.; Leiden: E.J. Brill, 1967–1990)
HAR	*Hebrew Annual Review*
HdO	Handbuch der Orientalistik
HTR	*Harvard Theological Review*
HUCA	*Hebrew Union College Annual*
IEJ	*Israel Exploration Journal*
JANES	*Journal of the Ancient Near Eastern Society* (*of Columbia University*)

JAOS	*Journal of the American Oriental Society*
JBL	*Journal of Biblical Literature*
JCS	*Journal of Cuneiform Studies*
JDS	Judean Desert Studies
JNES	*Journal of Near Eastern Studies*
JSOTSup	Journal for the Study of the Old Testament. Supplement series
KBL	L. Koehler and W. Baumgartner, *Lexicon in Veteris Testamenti Libros* (2 vols.; Leiden: E. J. Brill, 1953)
KTU	M. Dietrich, O. Loretz, and J. Sanmartín, *The Cuneiform Alphabetic Texts from Ugarit, Ras Ibn Hani and Other Places* (*KTU* 2nd ed.) (Münster: Ugarit-Verlag, 1995)
LS	C. Brockelmann, *Lexicon Syriacum* (2nd edition; Halle: M. Niemeyer, 1928; reprint: Hildesheim: Georg Olms, 1966)
NEB	New English Bible
NJPS	New Jewish Publication Society Version (*Tanakh: The Holy Scriptures, The New JPS Translation According to the Traditional Hebrew Text* [Philadelphia: Jewish Publication Society, 1985])
PIHANS	Publications de l'Institut historique et archeologique neerlandais de Stamboul
RB	*Revue Biblique*
SAA	State Archives of Assyria
ScrHier	Scripta Hierosolymitana
TAD	B. Porten and A. Yardeni, *Textbook of Aramaic Documents from Ancient Egypt* (4 vols.; Jerusalem: The Hebrew University, 1986–1999).
UF	*Ugarit-Forschungen*
VTSup	Supplements to Vetus Testamentum
ZA	*Zeitschrift für Assyriologie*
ZAW	*Zeitschrift für die alttestamentliche Wissenschaft*
ZDPV	*Zeitschrift des deutschen Palästina-Vereins*

A. Law

Capital Punishment*

Normally defined, capital punishment is the imposition of a penalty of death on one convicted of a crime deemed sufficiently grave to warrant depriving the criminal of life. As a legal act, capital punishment is pursuant to a sentence of a court, though in some societies it may be imposed by executive decree.

In biblical terminology, the concept of capital punishment is conveyed by a Hebrew term meaning "a sentence of death" (Deut. 19:6, 21:22; Jer. 25:11, 16). We also find reference to "a capital offense" in Deuteronomy 22:26. Interestingly, the Hebrew word for "blood" connotes both the crime itself—the shedding of human blood—and the guilt and punishment incurred by that act. One finds such usage in Leviticus 17:4, Numbers 35:27, and Deuteronomy 17:8. Since the plural form of words can have an abstract connotation in biblical Hebrew, we also find plural forms of the word for "blood" referring to capital crimes in Exodus 22:1–2 and Deuteronomy 19:10, 22:8, and 2 Samuel 16:8.

We would not regularly include in the category of capital punishment legitimate retaliation against the perpetrator of a homicide. In the biblical system, however, avenging the blood of a murdered clan relative figures prominently in legislation governing the death penalty, and we will discuss it on that basis.

The purpose of this study is to describe the way the Bible views capital punishment. Primarily this consists of legal provisions, but we also encounter normative statements referring to crimes that *should* be punished by death. Certain persons, so we read, deserve to die for their crimes. Such references, often couched in narrative, prophecy, and wisdom, reveal the postulates of biblical criminal law and do a lot to characterize the ethos of biblical society.

I.

Given the nature of the biblical evidence, it is easiest to begin with its legal sources and then continue our discussion with nonlegal materials in an effort to understand what underlies the provisions of biblical law. The Torah preserves several collections of laws, *all* of which demonstrate that capital punishment was integral to biblical justice. The first of these collections to be encountered by the reader, and the earliest historically, is the Book of the Covenant (Exodus, chapters 21–23). It is true that the Decalogue of Exodus, chapter 20, actually precedes the Book of the Covenant; though its categorical pronouncements clearly bear on the subject of capital punishment, they refrain from stipulating

---

* Originally published in Morton Smith and R. Joseph Hoffmann (eds.), *What the Bible Really Says* (Buffalo: Prometheus Books, 1989), pp. 11–32. Reprinted with permission from Prometheus Books.

specific penalties, which is characteristic of commandments, as distinct from laws. The provisions of the Decalogue will be discussed in due course.

Exodus 21:12–14 mandates the death penalty for one who premeditatively deals a death blow to another. If the homicide was *not* premeditated—that is, if the killer did not "stalk" his victim, or was not intent on doing him evil—that killer was allowed to seek refuge at a designated place of asylum. We read further that the deliberate murderer was emphatically denied asylum, and he would be seized even from the altar of a sanctuary and sentenced to death. The Hebrew Bible actually records two instances of persons who feared retaliation and clung to the horns of the altar in the sanctuary of Jerusalem, seeking asylum. Both incidents relate to the Davidic succession. In the former, Adonijah, David's own son, clung to the altar after rebelling against his brother, the king. Solomon had him forcibly removed from the sanctuary, but spared his life after the renegade swore fealty to his king (1 Kings 1:50–53). In the second instance, Joab, David's longtime general, clung to the same altar after having supported Adonijah in his sedition. When Joab refused to withdraw, Solomon ordered him slain on the spot. We note, however, that in the ensuing verses the biblical writer justifies denying Joab asylum. He had often committed murder and actually deserved to die for shedding innocent blood (as recounted in 1 Kings 2:28–34).

In fact, the right of asylum presupposes the right of retaliation. One who has killed another should fear retaliation, which was customary, and seek asylum, at least until he could establish that his killing was either unintentional or justified.

The precise formulation of the opening statement of law on the subject of murder is significant. The Canaanite petty king Abimelech tells his people, "Anyone who harms this man [Isaac] or his wife [Rebecca] shall be put to death" (Gen. 26:11). The conjugated form of the Hebrew verb "to die" used here consistently connotes execution by human agency, never simply that someone deserves to die. Nor does it merely predict someone's death, as do other forms of the same verb. There is no question that Abimelech would have had any such person executed. Similarly, in Exodus 19:12–13 we read the admonition delivered to the Israelite people just prior to the theophany at Mount Sinai: "Anyone who has contact with the mountain shall be put to death.... For such a one will be stoned or shot (with an arrow)," etc. So much for legal formulation.

Chapter 21 of Exodus describes additional circumstances in which capital punishment is demanded. In most cases, when the death penalty is prescribed it is mandatory, not optional. Only rarely do we find allowance for discretionary sentencing. Let us review the specific contents of this chapter.

One who "strikes" either of his parents will be put to death. Although the Hebrew verb employed here is ambiguous, we can assume that the present law does *not* refer to one who kills a parent, only to one who intentionally injures a parent. The death penalty is mandated because of the special relationship between the perpetrator and the victim. (This is one of several laws that emphasize the seriousness of all forms of disrespect toward parents.)

A kidnapper receives the death penalty whether the victim is in his custody when he is apprehended or has been sold by him. One who shows extreme disrespect for his parents shall be put to death. The precise sense of the Hebrew verb used in this case is difficult to establish. At times it means “to curse, blaspheme,” as in Exodus 22:27, and in Leviticus 24:14, 23; 1 Kings 2:8, and elsewhere. But it can also mean “to degrade, shame,” reflecting its primary sense of treating *lightly*. This appears to be the sense in the present law, but because this statement is less than legally precise, one assumes that the courts were obliged to define certain acts as being sufficiently grave to warrant the death penalty, while excluding others.

If one beats his slave to death, the slave “shall be avenged” (Exod. 21:20f.) the verb “to avenge” here denoting the death penalty, in retaliation, against the life of the master. Such is the force of this verb in similar contexts. If the slave does not die instantly but lingers on for a day or two, however, the master “is not to be punished, for the slave is his property.” Some compensation was sometimes allowable in such cases, though.

This law delivers a double message. By allowing mitigation of punishment, it reflects extreme social stratification. In other words, slaves did not have the same rights their owners did. And yet, the law does insist on the death penalty when death is instantaneous, notwithstanding the inferior status of the slave.

Exodus 21:22–25 addresses a situation in which a pregnant woman in killed by men fighting close by. The loss of the embryo could be compensated for by an appropriate payment, but the loss of the woman’s own life could not. The principle of retaliation is explicitly invoked: “a life for a life.” In fact, it is in this very passage that we first encounter the classic formulation of the law of retaliation: “an eye for an eye, tooth for a tooth, hand for a hand, foot for a foot, burn for a burn, wound for a wound, stripe for a stripe....” No allowance is made for the likelihood that the woman’s death was accidental; the death penalty is mandated unequivocally, probably because of the gross negligence and indifference to human life exhibited by the fighting men.

Capital punishment figures, at least indirectly, in the well-known law of the goring ox in Exodus 21:28–32. One who leaves his ox unrestrained, after there is clear evidence that the ox in question had gored a person to death previously, is liable to the death penalty if the ox kills someone else. If “its owner has been warned but has not kept [his ox] in, and it kills a man or woman, the ox shall be stoned, and its owner shall also be put to death.” There could be a way out for the owner, though, if the deceased’s family lays “a ransom on him”: “He shall give for the redemption of his life whatever is laid upon him.” This emphasized the crucial distinction between a human act that directly caused the death of another person, and death brought about indirectly through the agency of one’s property. (Again, slaves are a special case. If an ox gores a slave, “The owner shall give the master thirty shekels of silver, and the ox shall be stoned.”)

Capital punishment also figured in the laws governing theft, at least theoretically. Exodus 22:1 states that one who kills a man caught in the act of breaking into his house would not be charged with a capital crime. We should understand that this applies only if the intruder was caught by night, since 22:2 says that if he was caught after sunrise, the killer would be charged with a capital crime (this is indicated by the words, "A blood claim applies to him"). It is doubtful whether this law actually mandates the death penalty. More likely, the case could be disposed of in less severe ways.

Such latitude hardly applied, however, to other dicta forthcoming in the Book of the Covenant. A sorceress is not to be allowed to live (Exod. 22:18), nor are those caught having sexual relations with a beast (22:19). One who worships or offers sacrifice to a god other than Yahweh, the God of Israel, "shall be condemned to destruction." Though somewhat ambiguous, the Hebrew verb used in this context denotes capital punishment, as it does in the Books of Leviticus and Deuteronomy.

To summarize the provisions of the Book of the Covenant, we list the death penalty as mandatory in the following cases: premeditated murder; striking a parent with resultant bodily injury; kidnapping; beating a slave to instant death; killing a pregnant woman in the course of a physical struggle between men; sorcery; having sexual relations with a beast; and offering sacrifice to any god other than the God of Israel.

In the following cases, one could be charged with a capital offense, but allowances would sometimes be made and substitute penalties given: certain forms of disrespect toward parents; the goring to death of a person by one's ox, in cases where the ox had done so previously and the owner had been warned to take proper precautions; killing an intruder caught by daylight.

II.

In addition to the Book of the Covenant, the Torah contains two other major collections of laws: the Deuteronomic legislation (contained in Deuteronomy, roughly chapters 12–26), and the priestly codes of law, concentrated in the Book of Leviticus and in parts of Exodus and Numbers. These collections add several new categories of capital crimes and further extend the provisions of the Book of the Covenant. Let's discuss the Deuteronomic laws first. For the most part, their promulgation seems to have been more ancient than that of the priestly laws, which, indeed, often synthesize the Deuteronomic laws with the Book of the Covenant.

According to Deuteronomy 17:6 and 19:15f., the death penalty may only be imposed pursuant to the valid testimony of at least two corroborating witnesses. "A person shall not be put to death on the evidence of one witness" (Deut. 17:6). Also, Deuteronomy 10:15–21 deals with the question of adequate—or false—testimony. In a case where a witness, by testifying falsely, would have brought about the execution of an innocent person, the law mandates retaliation against the life of the conspiring witness; no quarter would be shown: The conspirator should suffer the very penalty of death he sought to have imposed on another. "You shall do to him as he meant to do to his brother; so you shall purge the evil from the midst of you" (Deut. 20:19).

Deuteronomy 22:20–29 incorporates a series of laws governing a variety of serious sexual crimes. Some background is required to understand what underlies these regulations. In biblical society marriage, as a legal relationship, took effect in two stages: Initially, a woman was pledged to a particular man who "sought" her as his wife and entered into a contract to marry her. At that point, sexual access to the woman in question was prohibited to other men on penalty of death, just as if she were fully married. Custom may have varied as to whether the intended husband was himself allowed to consummate the marriage in advance, but the prohibition was absolute as regards all other men. Now, if a man who had pledged to marry a woman, represented to him at the time as a virgin, subsequently claimed at the final marriage that she had lost her virginity to another man, he was required to substantiate that claim conclusively. If he was able to do so, the woman was guilty of adultery and was to be stoned to death at the gate of her father's house. If, however, the man's allegations proved to be unfounded, he was penalized for shaming a daughter of Israel.

Chapter 22 continues with further legislation governing adultery. Sexual relations between consenting partners, in a case where the participating woman was pledged or married to another, condemned both partners to the death penalty. In cases of rape, where the female victim was pledged or married to another, only the rapist was condemned to death; the woman was regarded as an innocent victim. It should be clarified that rape, as such, was not a capital offense. When a man raped an unattached woman, he was obliged to "give the father of the woman fifty shekels of silver, and she shall be his wife, because he has violated her, he may not put her away all his days" (Deut. 22:29).

In several cases, Deuteronomy elaborates on already-stated cases of capital crime:

Worship of other gods

Deuteronomy, chapter 13, is devoted to the subject of pagan worship. The false prophet who advocates worshiping other gods is to be put to death. A relative or an associate of an Israelite who urges him to worship other gods is to be executed by stoning. In fact, the principle of collective punishment is invoked: The entire population of an Israelite town that had taken to worshiping other gods in response to the incitement of evil men was to be wiped out. In a more brief statement, Deuteronomy 17:2–7 mandates the death penalty by stoning for any Israelite who worships other gods. Deuteronomy 18:20 reiterates the death sentence for the false prophet who advocates pagan worship: "But the prophet who presumes to speak a word in my name which I have not commanded him to speak, or who speaks in the name of other gods, that same prophet shall die." A priestly narrative, preserved in Numbers 25:1–15, records that those Israelites who worshipped Baal-Peor were put to death at God's specific command.

Retaliation and the right of asylum

Deuteronomy 19:1–13 presents a major statement on capital punishment and its relation to the ancient institution of "blood restoration." We are provided with hypothetical examples of both accidental and premeditated homicide as a way of clarifying exactly when the right of asylum was in force. It is here that we find reference to "the restorer of blood," a designation applied to a clan relative of a victim of homicide, who bore the responsibility to avenge his death. Three towns were to be set aside as cities of asylum, with three more to be added when the settlement of the land would extend to broader areas. The law is emphatic in denying the right of asylum to actual murderers. The elders of the town from which a murderer came were required to extradite him from any place of asylum and deliver him for execution. The determination of guilt was made by the court, but the customary prerogative of the clan relative to take the life of his relative's murderer was respected. The "restorer of blood" actually participated in the execution of the murderer.

Disrespect for parents

Deuteronomy 21:18–21 mandates the death penalty for a son who is defiantly disobedient toward his parents, who is gluttonous, or who is habitually drunk. If all efforts at disciplining him fail, the elders are to condemn such a son to death: "All the men of the city shall stone him to death with stones" (Deut. 21:21). This statement of law has been recognized as elusive, and the terms of reference it employs are either unique to it or rare in biblical usage; so it is very possible that the death penalty was not mandatory.

Extreme negligence

Deuteronomy 22:8 orders Israelites to install protective fences around the roofs of their houses to prevent loss of life. As in Exodus 22:13, the word "blood" here connotes the claim against the life of the negligent homeowner from whose roof someone had fallen to his death. Once again, we sense that the case could be disposed of without imposing the death penalty.

Kidnapping

Deuteronomy 24:7 mandates that a kidnapper be put to death, in much the same terms as were used in Exodus 21:16.

Before leaving the Deuteronomic laws, we should take note of a general principle of law that has far-reaching implications for our understanding of capital punishment in biblical Israel. Deuteronomy 24:16 states that parents are not to be put to death for the crimes of their children, nor children for those of their parents. This principle disallows "substitution," the penalization of someone other than the guilty party. Undoubtedly, this statement means to exclude retaliation against members of a murderer's family—a practice well known in antiquity, not to mention recently. At times, substitution has been a function of social stratification, whereby a slave or subordinate would be punished in place of the actual offender.

We may now proceed to discuss those *priestly* laws that cover capital punishment. The first new category introduced is Sabbath violation. Exodus 31:12–17 and 35:2 mandate the death penalty for an Israelite convicted of intentionally violating the Sabbath. The tasks forbidden on the Sabbath are not fully specified, subsumed as they are under the category "assigned tasks," and the act of violation is conveyed by a Hebrew verb that means "to desecrate."

In Numbers 15:30–36, we find a priestly "story" of sorts. While the Israelites were in the desert they apprehended one of their group gathering firewood on the Sabbath. They placed him under guard and awaited instructions as to his punishment. "And the Lord said to Moses: 'The man shall be put to death; all the congregation shall stone him with stones outside the camp.' And all the congregation brought him outside the camp, and stoned him to death with stones, as the Lord commanded Moses" (Num. 15:35–36).

Priestly law also introduces the crime of blasphemy as a capital offense. In the Book of the Covenant (Exod. 22:27), cursing God is prohibited, but no specific penalty is stated there. A brief priestly narrative in Leviticus 24:10–13 relates that an Israelite of mixed parentage (his mother was an Israelite and his father an Egyptian) committed public blasphemy and was placed in detention. As was true in the account of Numbers, chapter 15, this incident also served as background for a statement of law mandating the death penalty, by stoning, for blasphemers. This applied not only to Israelites, but also to aliens living in Israelite communities. The act of blasphemy is expressed in a specific formula: "uttering the [divine] name explicitly, in the act of cursing [God]."

An understandable concern of priestly law, in particular, was preserving the purity of the sacred precincts of Israelite sanctuaries, especially of the Temple of Jerusalem. In Numbers, we find repeated a key formula: "Any alien who intrudes shall be put to death" (Num. 1:51, 3:10, 17:38, and 18:7). It was the duty of certain of the Levitical clans to guard the Tabernacle against intruders, in the traditions of Numbers.

Priestly law also elaborates on some of the capital crimes already mentioned. A major priestly source is Leviticus, chapter 20, whose principal subject is incest and other sexual crimes. Example: "The man who lies with his father's wife has uncovered his father's nakedness; both of them shall be put to death, their blood is upon them" (Lev. 20:11).

On penalty of death, Israelites as well as aliens are admonished against sacrificing their children to Molech. Verse 9 of chapter 20 restates the provisions of Exodus 21:17 regarding any person who treats his parents with extreme disrespect. That person shall be put to death. Verses 10–16 of Leviticus list a series of sexual crimes for which the penalty is death. As stipulated in Deuteronomy 22:20–29, both partners to adultery are to be put to death. Ezekiel dramatized the penalty when prophesying the destruction of Jerusalem for infant sacrifice and the worship of alien gods:

> O harlot, hear the word of the Lord. Thus says the Lord God, Because your shame was laid bare and your nakedness uncovered in your har-

> lotries with your lovers, and because of all your idols, and because of the blood of your children that you gave to them, therefore, behold, I will gather all your lovers, with whom you took pleasure, and all you loved and all you loathed; I will gather them against you from every side, and will uncover your nakedness to them, that they may see all your nakedness.... And I will give you into the hand of your lovers, and they shall throw down your vaulted chamber and break down your lofty places; they shall strip you of your clothes and take your fair jewels, and leave you naked and bare. They shall bring up a host against you, and they shall stone you and cut you to pieces with their swords (Ezek. 16:35–37, 39–40).

Male homosexuality and intercourse with a beast, by man or woman, were punishable by death. (Even the participating beast was to be executed!) We may add here the law of Leviticus 21:9, which condemns to death by stoning a priest's daughter who became a harlot.

Numbers 35:9–34 contains major statements of priestly law on the subject of murder and the right of asylum. Examples of both premeditated murder and unintentional homicide are enumerated. Amnesty is introduced as a factor mitigating the administration of criminal justice. When the incumbent High Priest died, those who had been confined to the cities of refuge were to be released in safety.

We conclude the summary of priestly law with a cryptic statement disallowing commutation of the death penalty: "Any condemned human being, who is marked for elimination, may not be ransomed; he shall be put to death!" (Lev. 27:29). This statement immediately follows another, which, in contrast, allows compensation in the case of condemned property. The language of condemnation used here suggests that reference is to an Israelite who had been condemned to death for worshiping other gods (compare Exod. 20:19 and Deut. 13–19).

The above review more or less exhausts the explicit legal provisions of the Torah on the subject of capital punishment. We may now look beyond legal evidence to other biblical sources that clarify, in their own ways, the postulates of biblical criminal law.

III.

In both of its versions, the Decalogue categorically prohibits certain acts that elsewhere are classified as capital crimes. There are also positive pronouncements in the Decalogue relevant to capital offenses, including commands to honor one's parents and keep the Sabbath. Worship of other gods is emphatically forbidden, as are false testimony, murder, adultery, and perhaps kidnapping, if it is correct to subsume that crime under the commandment prohibiting theft, in line with traditional Jewish interpretation.

Leviticus, chapter 19, echoes the Decalogue and rephrases six, or possibly seven, of the Ten Commandments. Even in the Book of the Covenant we find, alongside laws formulated casuistically, categorical prohibitions of acts elsewhere classified as capital crimes. An example already noted is the crime of blasphemy (Exod. 22:27). These statements reinforce the role of the death penalty.

Biblical literature, as a whole, tells us little about the operation of the criminal justice system in ancient Israel. We know that stoning, burning to death, and impalement were standard methods of execution. (We refer the reader to the following sources: Deut. 13:11, 22:21, 24; Lev. 20:9, 24:14; Num. 15:35; Lev. 21:9; and Deut. 21:22f.). We read of executions conducted outside the encampment or town (Num. 15:35; 1 Kings 21:13, etc.). In some ways, this practice reflects magical attitudes and concepts of purity. Witnesses whose testimony had been instrumental in convicting criminals at times participated personally in their execution (Deut. 17:7).

Some students of biblical law have suggested that the mode of execution prescribed for particular offenses is significant. Certain methods of execution are normal for particular crimes, but precise correlations are difficult to determine. So, we remain with unanswered questions about both the operative details of criminal justice and more basic matters, such as the source of judicial authority. Who, for example, were these judges, and how were they chosen? How great was the authority of heads of families and clans? Upon hearing that his daughter-in-law, Tamar, was pregnant at a time when her status made sexual relations tantamount to adultery, Judah summarily condemned her to death by fire (Gen. 38:24–25). One assumes that Judah possessed traditional authority, as head of the family, to decide such matters and impose sentence.

Still another set of questions pertains to the realism of the canonical laws of the Torah. Are they a reliable index of actual practice? Did kings, for instance, honor these laws? Are the laws of the Torah rooted in commonly held notions of crime and punishment? It is hard to know for sure, but we do possess windows that look in on the life of biblical society and afford us a glimpse of its reality. One biblical narrative with this function is the account of Naboth, the Jezreelite, and his confrontation with Ahab, king of northern Israel, and his queen, Jezebel. As recounted in 1 Kings, chapter 21, the story is set in Samaria of the ninth century B.C.E. Naboth possessed a vineyard located near Ahab's palace. Ahab approached Naboth with an offer to purchase the vineyard or trade for it another parcel of land, even a better one, located somewhere else.

Naboth emphatically refused to part with his property, invoking his inalienable right to it as a family homestead. Ahab's initial response was resignation to failure in his bid to acquire the vineyard. This suggests that there was no legal recourse left to the king. But Jezebel, Ahab's wife, subverted the law. She arranged with the leaders of Samaria to proclaim a public fast, and seated Naboth at the head of the people so that evil men could later accuse him of blasphemy against the king. The charge leveled against Naboth was precisely that he had cursed both God and king. This charge combines, in effect, the two crimes of Exodus 22:27: "You shall not curse God, nor damn a chieftain among your people." As a result of the perjured testimony of bought witnesses, Naboth was condemned to death and stoned outside the city. Ahab promptly expropriated his vineyard, but the prophet Elijah denounced Ahab's crime as murder. As it turned out, God commuted Ahab's sentence because the king had shown contrition. The death sentence was deferred to Ahab's son, Jehoram, who would later be put to death in a dramatic manner for his father's crime (2 Kings 9:22–26).

Of particular interest are the legal predications of this narrative. Naboth could be condemned only on the testimony of witnesses; the king could not simply issue a decree ordering his execution. The story adds yet another insight: God may establish the guilt of a criminal without recourse to testimony, whereas human agencies may not.

The cycle of stories about David and Bathsheba (1 Samuel, chapters 11–12) similarly suggests that kings were bound by the rule of law, at least with respect to certain heinous crimes like adultery and murder. This conclusion emerges logically from the lengths to which David went to conceal his liaison with the wife of another man, going so far as to conspire to have Uriah, Bathsheba's husband, killed in battle in order to keep his crime from becoming known. Ultimately, God spared David's life—sentencing his son, the product of his adultery, to death in his stead.

Both of these narratives endorse the principle of substitution in deferring the death penalty from father to son. This principle contradicts what we have seen established in Deuteronomy 24:16 and reinforced in Ezekiel, chapter 18, for instance, that only the guilty may be punished. "But if this man begets a son who sees all the sins which his father has done, and fears, and does not do likewise … he shall not die for his father's iniquity; he shall surely live" (Ezek. 18:14, 17). Yet it also calls to mind this well-known pronouncement of the Decalogue: I the Lord your God am a jealous God, visiting the iniquity of the fathers upon the children to the third and fourth generation of those who hate me" (Exod. 20:5).

Leaving aside this apparent paradox, let's look more deeply into the concept of deferral of punishment. Is it regarded as merciful, or unjust? In biblical literature, we find the interaction of two tendencies. Notions of justice disallow substitution through deferral. Other attitudes do affect justice, however: mercy and forgiveness, on the one hand, and vengeance and wrath, on the other.

Two aspects of the incident concerning Naboth (the unlucky landowner), require further comment: the crime of sedition and the subject of loyalty to king and country. This issue dominates the trial of the prophet Jeremiah, recorded in Jeremiah, chapter 26, which speaks of "a sentence of death," the very language used in the legislation of Deuteronomy.

As the chapter opens, Jeremiah is speaking in the Temple courtyard in Jerusalem. This was at the beginning of the reign of Jehoiakim, king of Judah, soon before the destruction of Jerusalem by the Babylonians in 586 B.C.E. Jeremiah's message is blunt: Obey God, who communicates his will through his true prophets, or the Temple will be destroyed. Jeremiah was seized by the priests and court prophets, and the "people" threatened him with death: "You shall die! Why have you prophesied in the name of Yahweh saying: 'This Temple shall be as Shiloh, and this city shall be in ruin and uninhabited?'" (compare Jer. 7).

Jeremiah's trial began. The "princes" of Judah took their seats at the entrance of the New Gate of the Temple. They acted as judges, by virtue of their position of leadership among the people. The court prophets and priests demanded the death penalty for Jeremiah. The prophet appealed on the grounds that he was merely delivering God's message and that condemning him to death would be shedding innocent blood. The elders, who were also representing the people of Judah, cited the precedent of an earlier prophet who, in the days of Hezekiah a century or more earlier, had similarly warned the people of impending destruction. At that time, Hezekiah had heeded the prophet's warning and entreated God sincerely, and Jerusalem was spared. To put Jeremiah to death would therefore constitute a great evil.

The account of Jeremiah's trial includes reference to a contemporary of his, Uriah, a prophet who said pretty much what Jeremiah was saying. His words were cited as corroboration of the truth of Jeremiah's prophecy. Uriah had fled to Egypt, but Jehoiakim, the king, had him extradited and returned to Jerusalem, where he was put to death at the king's command. The chapter concludes by reporting that Jeremiah, who was also sought by the king, was rescued by an official of the well-known scribal family of Shaphan.

In addition to yielding information on the administration of justice in biblical Israel, the account of Jeremiah's trial clearly indicates that sedition was a capital offense under the monarchic system. The issue in Jeremiah's case was whether or not words of prophecy, uttered publicly by a prophet, constituted sedition when they were subversive of royal authority. In the narratives about David, we also find statements indicating that Saul, when accusing David of sedition, marked him for death (1 Sam. 20:31), condemning those who gave him aid and comfort as well (1 Sam. 26:16).

There are other biblical statements on the judicial process that are harder to place in an historical setting. For instance, Deuteronomy 16:18–21 ordains the establishment of local courts "in all your gates," with appointed justices. These courts were to adjudicate all cases brought before them without prejudice or favoritism. Judges were not to be bribed! In Deuteronomy 17:8–13, we read of the establishment of a central court, located in the temple complex of the religious capital. There, Levitical priests and a judge would together decide cases brought before them by local courts, on capital as well as civil matters. The decisions of this superior court were final and binding, and any who blatantly disobeyed them faced the death penalty themselves.

Based on recent studies, there is reason to trace such provisions as we read in Deuteronomy to the northern Israelite kingdom of the eighth century B.C.E. Subsequently, these doctrines were transmitted to Judah as well. What we read in Exodus, chapter 18, as advice given to Moses on the administration of justice may reflect a similar background.

References to judges lead us to other indications of how the judicial process operated in biblical Israel, especially as regards the judicial role of the king. Royal authority is fully taken for granted in the accounts about Naboth and Ahab, David, and Jeremiah that have been discussed above. Deuteronomy

17:14–20 insists that the king of Israel is bound by the laws of Deuteronomy. There are, however, other more realistic indications of a customary role for kings, one which gave them greater sanction, even in capital cases. One theory of the kingship in ancient Israel places considerable emphasis on the judicial role of leaders, especially military leaders. Perhaps the main basis of the authority that accrued to such leaders as David, in his early years, was their ability to secure for the defenseless redress for grievances. It is on this basis that the charismatic leaders who governed Israel prior to the rise of the monarchy were known as "judges." It is also on this basis that in Hebrew a king is called *melek*, which derives from a verb meaning "to counsel, deliberate." So, there is a real framework for the judicial role of the king, and any Israelite could appeal to him for justice, as in 2 Kings 6:26.

Kings probably had the right to impose the death penalty for crimes traditionally regarded as of a capital nature. One could only hope that kings would be wise and just. "Give the king thy justice, O God," begins Psalm 72, "and thy righteousness to the royal son." And one proverb warns, "By justice a king gives stability to the land, but one who exacts gifts ruins it" (Prov. 29:4; Ps. 72:1).

IV.

The right of duly constituted authorities to impose the death penalty reflects certain perceptions of life and death, family and community. These perceptions go beyond legality, bringing us face to face with myth and magic, ritual and drama.

In Genesis 9:1–7, we find a significant statement on the ritual meaning of blood. God has blessed Noah and his family after the flood: "Be fruitful and multiply, and fill the earth…. Every moving thing that lives shall be food for you; and as I gave you the green plants, I give you everything" (Gen. 9:1, 3). But this permission is immediately qualified: "Only you shall not eat flesh while it is alive—its blood" (Gen. 9:4). The unusual formulation of this statement has been a problem in biblical interpretation since late antiquity. Inevitably, it must be understood as combining two thoughts. Humans must slaughter creatures before eating their meat, and, in any event, they may not eat the blood (compare Deut. 12:23; Lev. 17:10–13). The text then shifts attention away from considerations of diet to the subject of murder, as if to anticipate the inference that once humans have been permitted to slaughter animals they might assume license to kill other humans too. The text reads: "Moreover, your blood, to the extent of your lives, shall I requite; from every beast shall I requite it, and from human beings, each from the other, shall I requite human life. Whoever sheds human blood, from among mankind, his blood shall be shed; for He [God] fashioned human beings in God's form."

I have given a stilted translation on purpose, as a way of bringing out the underlying concepts of this singular statement. Humans enjoy a special status in God's creation because they resemble God in form. Beasts who kill humans must be put to death, as is the law for humans who kill one another. But, humans may kill beasts with impunity.

Deuteronomy 21:1–9 prescribes a communal ritual relevant to the subject of capital punishment. When a murdered corpse was discovered in the open field, outside the jurisdictional limits of any town, and the murderer could not be found, it became necessary to deal with the unsolved crime in special ways. The matter could not simply be neglected or ignored. The Levitical priests were to slaughter a female calf near a perennial stream and pour its blood into the stream. The elders of the nearest town were summoned, and they would wash their hands, literally, of responsibility for the homicide, reciting a formula of clearance: "Our hands have not shed this blood nor have our eyes seen [the act]. Grant expiation to your people, Israel, whom you have ransomed, Yahweh, and do not allow innocent blood to remain [unrequited] in the midst of your people, Israel. Let the blood be expiated on their behalf!" This ritual, with its accompanying formula, projects the return of blood to the earth. An animal's blood is substituted for the blood of the murderer.

"Innocent blood" is a complex concept. Most simply, it characterizes victims of homicide as being innocent. It is used most often, perhaps, in speaking of the death of the innocent resulting from the miscarriage of justice. (See Deut. 19:10). Thus, the passengers and sailors on the ship heading for Tarshish prayed that in casting Jonah overboard they would not be guilty of shedding innocent blood (Jonah 1:14). Whenever the Hebrew Bible speaks of innocent blood in this sense, it expresses the unquestioned consensus that taking a human life unjustly would bring down God's wrath. Deuteronomy 27:25 pronounces a curse on those who take bribes to shed the blood of the innocent. Jonathan was once able to persuade his father, Saul, not to attempt killing David, for to do so would be to shed innocent blood (1 Sam. 19:5). "Innocent blood" must be requited; someone must pay for it!

We recall the words God addressed to Cain, recorded in Genesis 4:10: "Hark! The blood of your brother cries out to me from the earth!" So long as Cain, the fratricide, remained alive, the lost blood of his brother Abel had not been requited. Although God commuted Cain's sentence, the story attests to the anathema of unrequited blood. Another example is that of the murders of the family of Ahab. Someone would have to pay for "the blood of Jezreel" (Hos. 1:4; 2 Kings 9:26).

There is a clear difference, however, between condemning a murderer to death and executing an adulterer, for example, just as there is between executing a false witness who has threatened the life of an innocent person and condemning an idolator to death. What is the underlying principle that allows the death penalty to be imposed when no one's life has been either lost or threatened?

In these cases, we are dealing with *tabu*, with fear of punishment when norms of behavior held sacred by the group are flagrantly violated. In the monotheistic context of biblical Israel, the operative principle is disobedience to the God of Israel. When we consider that the biblical theory of law attributes all law to God, directly, not to kings or intermediaries, we understand how all violations of law constitute actual disobedience to God. Biblical traditions about the God of Israel place considerable emphasis on death as a divine punishment and as a feature of his relationship to humankind, and to Israel in particular.

One need not read very far into Genesis to encounter this theme. God forbade Adam to eat of the Tree of Knowledge on penalty of death (Gen. 2:16f.). Adam and Eve's sentences were eventually commuted, or perhaps suspended, but the Eden narrative established the principle that disobedience to God is punishable by death.

Ten generations later, God brought a flood upon the earth, sparing of all humankind only one man and his family (see Genesis, chapter 6, and following). In the story of Moses, God drowns Pharaoh's army, after having slain the firstborn of Egypt as punishment for disobedience (see Exodus, chapters 1–15). When the God of Israel becomes angry at a disobedient Israel (or at its enemies), he strikes out at them with plagues, pestilence, and other forms of deadly punishments. The sanctions of God's admonitions sound like ancient Near Eastern execrations, calling down death on covenant breakers. Capital punishment, as a legal sentence, correlates with ancient Israelite conceptions of God. God mandated capital punishment in his revealed law, and he also demonstrated this commitment, one might say, by punishing wrongdoers with death, acting as the divine judge.

The validity of our conclusion about death as a punishment may be tested by asking whether biblical literature ever voices an objection to capital punishment. Does any biblical spokesman ever protest that it is wrong for a duly constituted jurisdiction to impose the death penalty for prescribed crimes, under proper judicial procedures? We often read of mercy and forgiveness, but legally speaking, is there an objection to taking the life of a convicted criminal?

Perhaps the closest we come to this is in the notion of *repentance*. In Ezekiel, chapter 18, we read that God, the divine judge, does not really desire the death of the sinner. God would prefer that a guilty person "turn back" from evil ways and go on living. The theme of repentance is epitomized in the parable of Jonah.

As important as the idea of repentance became in biblical teaching, there is no indication that it enjoyed legal status. Moreover, there is no suggestion that a convicted premeditated murderer could have his sentence commuted by the court through repentance. Some argue that there is a message in the fact that God is said to have commuted the sentences of certain murderers and otherwise guilty persons when they showed remorse and submission to his will. Some note that repentance figured meaningfully in projections of Israel's destiny as a people. This message actually relates to ideals more than legality, however, and does not mean that the biblical criminal system ever renounced capital punishment, or that in practice biblical spokesmen ever advocated its suspension.

V.

The New Testament contains no codes of law of the kind found in the Torah of the Hebrew Bible. Yet the subject of capital punishment nonetheless figures in the career of Jesus and his disciples. Jesus was accused of blasphemy, a capital crime, by certain Jewish authorities in Jerusalem; and Stephen, one of Jesus' disciples, was stoned to death in Jerusalem for the same crime. Jesus acted on behalf of an adulteress who would have been stoned for her crime. Generally, the tone of narrative and discussion in both the Gospels and Epistles indicates that the categories of capital crimes defined in the Hebrew Bible were normative within the Jewish communities of Palestine during the time of Jesus and his followers.

The account of Jesus' action in the case of an adulteress is a good starting point for our discussion. This passage, in John 7:53–8:11, has often been cited as evidence that Jesus questioned the death penalty for adultery. This is certainly an unwarranted inference.

Jesus had been teaching in the Temple of Jerusalem to a large audience. Some scribes and Pharisees sought to entrap him by requesting him to rule on a case of law. Were he to rule in contradiction to the accepted law, they would be able to accuse him of deviation from authoritative teaching, which was a capital offense according to Deuteronomy 17:8–13. So they brought before him an adulteress caught in the act; there was no doubt concerning her actual guilt. After evading the question of her proper punishment, Jesus challenged the scribes and Pharisees by questioning their right to execute judgment: "He that is without sin among you, let him first cast a stone at her!"

Not one of the scribes and Pharisees could, in good conscience, state that he had the moral right to execute the woman, and one by one they departed. Jesus dismissed the woman, adjuring her to sin no more, and thereby suggesting the efficacy of repentance.

There are, of course, questions about the realism of this account, and this passage is not present in the oldest manuscripts of John. For our purposes, its legal predications are of primary interest. The penalty for adultery was stoning, as ordained in Deuteronomy 22:20–21. What happened here? Those who were about to bring the woman to trial thought better of the matter after their attempt to entrap Jesus had failed.

The most dramatic references to the death penalty in the New Testament pertain to the accusation of blasphemy leveled against Jesus by a Jewish council. In the version of this encounter preserved in John there is no explicit reference to blasphemy, but in the other three versions the charge of blasphemy is explicit (Matt. 26:59–68; Mark 14:55–66; Luke 22:66–77). The interrogation of Jesus by the Jewish authorities proceeded in two stages: Jesus was first asked to confirm that he said he could destroy the Temple of Jerusalem (or would, in fact, destroy it) and rebuild it in three days. This accusation, which is more explicit in Matthew and Mark, misconstrues what Jesus had really said. According to Matthew 24:2, Mark 13:2, and Luke 20:43f., Jesus had predicted (or prophesied, if you will) the destruction of the Temple of Jerusalem on account of the historic sins of Israel, in much the same manner as Jeremiah prophesied in an earlier age. This misconstruction is significant, because it changed a prediction into an arrogation of more-than-human power on the part of Jesus. In turn, this set the stage for the charge that Jesus had identified himself as the Christ, the son of God, an arrogation interpreted as blasphemy.

On the first charge, Jesus stood mute. When pressed with the second accusation, he responded. In Matthew and Luke, he tacitly concedes what his accusers had charged, whereas in Mark (14:62) he actually replies in the affirmative. Jesus follows up by predicting that he would take his place at the right hand of God. Hearing these things, the council members determined that Jesus had confessed his own crime, and there was no further need for testimony. He was guilty of blasphemy, and he should be put to death. In the course of the legal process we find, in some of the versions, references to false witnesses and the lack of corroboration of testimony. All of these references correlate with the Deuteronomic laws and recall the perfidy of Jezebel.

What transpired after Jesus responded to the Jewish authorities need not concern us, except to point out that Gospel accounts indicate that Jewish courts at the time could not actually execute convicted criminals; they could only deliver them to Roman jurisdiction.

In Acts 6:8–8:2, we read the account of Stephen, a disciple of Jesus, who preached his master's teachings and performed wonders in Jerusalem. Stephen was likewise accused of blasphemy and brought before a Jewish court. We find reference to what Jesus had said about the destruction of the Temple, as well as criticism of what Stephen himself was preaching in Jesus' name. These teachings were said to demonstrate a lack of respect for the law. Jesus is accused of having advocated altering the law of Moses.

After a lengthy jeremiad on the sins of Israel throughout its history, Stephen reports his vision of Jesus at the right hand of God. This persuades the council that Stephen is indeed guilty of blasphemy, and he is taken outside the walled city and stoned to death. Here the Jewish authorities carry out the actual execution of Stephen themselves, an action some have found puzzling. In any event, this account was surely modeled after those of the Gospels pertaining to Jesus himself.

Reference to altering the law of Moses again recalls the Deuteronomic statements on the crime of the false prophet (Deut. 13). Execution of the criminal outside the city recalls the provisions of Leviticus 24:10–13. What we observe in Acts, and throughout the New Testament, is a composite of various charges, and attempts at incrimination, involving such capital crimes as violation of the Sabbath (or its advocacy), promoting disobedience to law and authority, blasphemy, and so forth. Superimposed on the legalities of these charges is the unique identity of Jesus as the Christ, the son of God. Jesus' identification as "a divine man" takes us beyond law, so that the charge of blasphemy leveled against Jesus had no legal precedent, strictly speaking.

The right of earthly rulers to impose the death penalty is upheld by Paul in Romans, chapter 13, in the well-known passage that speaks of rendering to civil authorities the obedience due them. The principle that earthly, temporal power is valid later became the dominant policy of the Christian church. As for the definition of capital crime, little had changed since the time of the Hebrew Bible. One senses from reading the New Testament that contemporary Jewish interpretation of criminal law was severe in first century Palestine. It has been debated as to whether this impression is accurate, since Jewish sources like the Qumran documents and later Rabbinic literature have been cited to prove that the imposition of capital punishment was infrequent in the last phase of the period of the Second Temple.

In our discussion of capital punishment in the Hebrew Bible, we made the point that pronouncements about divine behavior correlated in the judicial context to attitudes toward death as a proper punishment. Quite clearly, the New Testament carries on the earlier mentality. Obedience will be rewarded with life; disobedience will be punished with destruction. As Jesus says in the Sermon on the Mount:

> Everyone, then, who hears these words of mine and does them will be like a wise man who built his house upon a rock; and the rain fell, and the floods came, and the winds blew and beat upon the house, but it did not fall, because it was founded on the rock. And every one who hears these words of mine and does not do them will be like a foolish man who built his house upon the sand; and the rain fell, and the floods came, and the winds blew and beat against the house, and it fell; and great was the fall of it" (Matt. 7:24–27).

This polarity is reiterated throughout the New Testament.

A God who rewards with life and punishes by death is one whose laws provide for death as a judicial punishment.

For Further Reading

Albrecht Alt, "The Origins of Israelite Law," *Old Testament History and Religion* (trans. R. Wilson; Oxford: Blackwell, 1966), pp. 79–132.

David Daube, *Studies in Biblical Law* (New York: Ktav, 1969).

Moshe Greenberg, "Some Postulates of Biblical Criminal Law," *Jubilee Volume, Yehezkiel Kaufmann*. Edited by Menahem Haran (Jerusalem: Magnes Press, 1960), pp. 5–28.

Jacob J. Finkelstein, *The Ox that Gored.* Transactions, American Philosophical Society. Vol. 71, part 2, 1981.

Anthony Phillips, *Ancient Israel's Criminal Law* (Oxford: Blackwell, 1970).

Mayer Sulzberger, *The Ancient Hebrew Law of Homicide* (Philadelphia: Julius Greenstone, 1915).

A. Sherwin White, *Roman Society and Roman Law in the New Testament* (Oxford, 1963).

Tracing the Biblical Accounting Register: Terminology and the Signification of Quantity*

No economy can grow in scope and complexity unless adequate accounting methods are developed to record its activity, and to communicate accurate information about the extent of its wealth. *The Economist* of April 26, 2003 contains a special report entitled "The future of accounts" (pp. 61–63), which discusses "the crisis in accounting" in the United States, and what is being proposed to correct for the loss of faith in current procedures. Alongside those who merely seek to fix what is wrong in the current system are others who propose more pervasive change:

> Looking further into the future, however, some see the crisis in accounting as an opportunity to change the shape and content of accounts more fundamentally (page 61; italics mine).

The report goes on to say that present-day economies, on a global scale, have become too complex for the existing accounting systems, which seem unable to record with clarity and accuracy such factors as revenue recognition, market value, the reliability of estimates, and the like. When this happens, new forms and methods must be put in place so as to manage further economic development.

The generative role of written accounts in antiquity was succinctly analyzed by C.C. Lamberg-Karlovsky (1999), in a study of some of the earliest Mesopotamian household economies, showing how the utilization of accounts contributed to urban growth, both economic and political. Long before the invention of writing, as a matter of fact, the use of figurative seals had made extended communication and recording possible. Over the millennia, the great economies of the ancient Near East, those of Egypt, Syria and Mesopotamia, produced myriads of administrative records and fiscal accounts, and even the smaller societies of the West Semitic sphere, operative during the Late Bronze and Iron Age, left financial records that are highly informative.

In a broader sense, information about ancient economies can be retrieved across generic lines, not only from records specifically fashioned for this pur-

* Originally published in R. Rollinger and Ch. Ulf (eds.), *Commerce and Monetary Systems in the Ancient World: Means of Transmission and Cultural Interaction: Proceedings of the Fifth Annual Symposium of the Assyrian and Babylonian Intellectual Heritage Project, Held in Innsbruck, Austria, October 3rd–8th 2002* (Melammu Symposia 5; Wiesbaden: Franz Steiner Verlag, 2004), pp. 420–443. Reprinted with permission from Franz Steiner Verlag. Attempts to contact the copyright holder for Figure 4 were unsuccessful.

pose. One can glean such information from epics and chronicles, treaties and law codes, and rituals and narratives. To do so makes it necessary, however, to perfect proper methods for evaluating the realism of such sources, so as to correct for ideological *Tendenz* and imaginative depiction. Thus it is that we can approach biblical texts, as an example, with economic questions in mind, if we have reliable methods to distinguish between history and tradition. An excellent paradigm is the study of Ezekiel's oracles against Tyre and Sidon (Ezekiel 26–28) by Igor Diakonoff (1992), in which that scholar verifies, in historical terms, that the Phoenician city-states traded in the very commodities enumerated in the biblical prophecies during the contemporary period. In the same vein, my former student, Martin Corral (2002), inspired in large measure by Diakonoff's example, accomplished an informative doctoral dissertation, in which he elucidates the economic background of these same prophecies of Ezekiel. For my own part, I have investigated the economic aspects of land tenure and urbanism in biblical Israel, endeavoring to evaluate the realism of the biblical references (Levine 1996, 1999). In the present study it is my purpose to explore biblical accounting terminology, as well as the systems of quantity signification employed in biblical reports, as we have them.

My interest in ancient accounting stems from the comparative study of biblical cult and ritual, directing my attention to Near Eastern temple records and economic texts, which often tabulate allocations for cultic use. This interest was first expressed in a study of the priestly Tabernacle texts of the Pentateuch (Levine 1965), and has since informed much of my work. It should be borne in mind that there are virtually no original records in the Hebrew Bible; all have been adapted in some degree to narrative style, making it necessary to visualize what their original form might have been. The challenge is to establish a correlation between biblical terminology and formats, and those employed in epigraphic texts discovered in archeological excavations. Because the extent of Hebrew epigraphy is so limited, and because inscriptional materials in the most proximate Canaanite languages of the biblical period are also scarce, it becomes necessary to reach out to comparative sources, principally to Aramaic and Phoenician-Punic epigraphy, but also to a wider range of western sources in several languages and scripts. My ultimate objective is to identify the "register" of adapted biblical accounting texts, and their constituent formulas. In a recent study of Egyptian writing systems, my colleague, Ogden Goelet, defined "register" as follows:

> Register is a term used to describe the variety of language employed according to such social factors as class and context. For example, the way in which people speak and write in academic discourse, in religious contexts, or in legal documents are all considerably different from each other and different from how those same individuals might speak in their daily lives. Each situation represents a different register (Goelet 2003:4).

In earlier studies, I have been able to trace some biblical cultic terminology back to the royal administration. Thus, the term תמיד "regular, daily offering" (Exod 29:42) essentially means "daily ration, allocation" (2 Kings 25:29), specifically, what royal captives of the Babylonian king received. The cult of the First Temple of Jerusalem was sponsored by the royal establishment, and the same was true in northern Israel, and the Second Temple served as the central administrative agency in the post-exilic period, under Persian imperial rule. It should be no surprise, therefore, coming from the other direction, to find that most biblical accounting terms, and numeration sequences are concentrated in courtly and priestly texts. This is their "register."

Selected Biblical Accounting Terms

Note: The list of terms to follow will not include numbers and fractions, or weights and measures, both of which are of importance in comprehending biblical accounting procedures. The reader is referred to two recent, and informative entries in the *Anchor Bible Dictionary*: "Numbers and Counting" by Joran Friberg (1992), and "Weights and Measures" by Marvin A. Powell (1992). These articles provide extensive bibliography, and are comparative in scope.

1) אחז (= *ʾāḥūz*) "(amount/unit) withheld" (Num 31:30, 47; 1 Chron 24:6). The Hebrew verb *ʾ-ḥ-z* means "to hold, take hold" so that the Qal passive participle, *ʾāḥūz* would mean "held, taken," hence, in context: "held apart, withheld." 1 Chron 24:6 yields a clear meaning, even though the Massoretic text probably reflects a scribal error. This reference comes within a register of priestly "divisions," and the listing of their respective assignments. Thus, we read: בית-אב אחד אחז לאלעזר *ואחד* אחז לאיתמר "One patrilineal family 'held' for Eleazar, and *one* 'held' for Ithamar." (The error was undoubtedly triggered by the similarity of the word for "one" and the verb "to hold." The Aramaic cognate of Hebrew *ʾ-ḥ-z* is written with a *daleth*, as *ʾ-ḥ-d*, in later phases of that language). The sense of אחז in the passage from Chronicles is best defined as: "reserved, held apart; selected." This meaning is attested for the comparable Palmyrene Aramaic Peʿil form: *ʾḥyd* (*PAT*, Glossary, 336). As an example: *ʾ*[*t*]*r ʾḥyd* "a place reserved" for a certain person (*PAT* 51, s.v. BS III, 68:1).

As for Numbers 31, it is a war narrative belonging to the priestly stratum of Pentateuchal literature. Within this chapter, verses 25–54 ordain the division of the spoils of war, a large portion of which were to be donated in support of the cult. The formulation of the text is discrete: "And from the half-share (וממחצית) assigned to the Israelite people you shall appropriate one (unit) withheld out of fifty (אחד אחז מן החמשים)," and so forth (Num 31:30). Further on, in Num 31:47, where the fulfillment of this instruction is acknowledged, the word order is reversed: את-האחז אחד מן החמשים literally: "the (unit) withheld, one out of fifty." Quite possibly, this set of meanings goes back to Akkadian *leqû* "to take," which in mathematical texts can mean "to subtract, take off; extract a square root" (*CAD L*, 136, s.v. *leqû*, meaning 1d). It bears notice that Old Aramaic *ʾ-ḥ-z* at times functions as a loan translation of Assyrian *laqāʾu* in the sense of "to receive, acquire by purchase," and that this meaning in fact establishes the functional equivalence of the two verbs (Fales 1986:179). In turn, Biblical Hebrew אחז would represent a back-formation of the Aramaic, not at all improbable during the Late Biblical period, to which both of the biblical references belong, in our view.

2) Verbal Piʿʿel חשב (= *ḥiššēb*) "to reckon, keep an account" (Lev 25:27, 50, 52, 27:18, 23; 2 Kings 12:16). This specialized connotation derives from the basic sense of the root *ḥ-š-b*, namely, "to figure out, conceive." It turns out that the chronicle of temple renovations, 2 Kings 12, is the locus of technical usage conveyed by the Piʿʿel *ḥiššēb*. The relevant passage reads: "And they do not keep an accounting of the men (ולא יחשבו את האנשים), through whom they remit the silver to be paid to the craftsmen, for these perform under terms of trust" (2 Kings 12:16). For the rest, we have only the 3rd masculine singular, in the inverted perfect, occurring in priestly laws governing land tenure. Thus, Lev 25:27: "He shall compute (וחשב) the years since its sale." Or, Lev 27:18: "The priest shall compute for him (וחשב לו הכהן) the silver according to the years remaining." The term חשבון occurs three times in Koheleth (7:25, 27; 9:10), where it seems to mean "a reasoned calculation." In his search for wisdom and meaning, the Sage arrives at such awareness in steps: "One by one to arrive at a reasoned calculation (אחת לאחת למצא חשבון" Koh 7:27). In Post-biblical Hebrew usage, the term חשבון was taken to mean "account, calculation" (Kasovsky 1957, 2:737–738), and Piʿʿel forms continued to be used with the same Biblical Hebrew connotation. Later dialects of Aramaic also attest nominal forms. Thus, the term *ḥšbn* occurs in the great Tariff from Palmyra, line 155 (= *PAT* 1259 = *CIS* ii 3913), and see *ibid.*, Glossary, 369, s.v. *ḥšb* v., and *ḥšbn*, and *DNWSI* 411, s.v. $ḥšbn_1$. In the same Tariff, line 53 we read: *mksʾ dy qṣbʾ ʾpy dnr ḥyb lmtḥšbw* "The tax on butchers must be computed in dinars". The form *lmtḥšbw* represents the Ithpaʿʿal, a reflex of the Paʿʿel. Also note the form חושבנא "account, calculation" in Jewish Babylonian Aramaic (*DJBA* 443). The term חשבן occurs in an Aramaic signature to a Greek legal document from the Babatha archive at Naḥal Ḥever:

די קבלת מן ... לחשבן פקדון כסף דנרין תלתמאה

> "That I have received from PN ... on account; a deposit of silver (in the amount of) 300 dinars" (Greenfield 1989:141, s.v. no. 17, line 41).

Important evidence also comes from Punic sources, which attest the title, or office known as מחשב plural מחשבם "accountant, treasurer; the exchequer" (*PhPD* 277–278, s.v. *MHŠB*). Thus *KAI* 160 lists various officials associated with the sodality, including: מחשב שעת "the treasurer/accountant of the sodality (*apud PhPD* 277, and cf. *ibid.*, 476, s.v. *ŠʿT*). More specifically, the plural מחשבם (cf. Latin *quaestores*), taken as a collective, can designate the exchequer, the agency that imposes fines, and collects taxes." The legend on some Carthaginian coins from Sicily attests this title.

3) כל (= *kōl*) "total." The technical meaning is restricted to contexts in which quantities are tallied, and where it would be insufficient merely to translate "all, all of-." Our attention is directed, therefore, to the very types of biblical texts that give evidence of having been adapted from records. We may compare Sumerian ŠU.NIGIN, Akkadian *napḫāru*, Ugaritic *tgmr* (*DUL* 861–862), all of which mean "total." Clear examples of this technical sense include the following: (a) The absolute form כל (= *kōl*): [a1] Jos 21:37: כל ערים ארבע "Total: towns, four." [a2] 2 Sam 23:39: כל שלשים ושבעה "Total: thirty-seven" (following the list of David's elite warriors). [a3] 2 Chron 26:12: כל מספר ראשי האבות לגבורי חיל אלפים ושש מאות "Total number of the heads of the patrilineal (households), of elite warriors: two thousand and six hundred." (b) The construct form כל (= *kol*): [b1] Gen 46:22: כל-נפש ארבעה עשר "Total of persons: fourteen." (cf. Gen 46:26–27, Exod 1:5). [b2] Num 2:9: כל-הפקדים למחנה יהודה מאת אלף ושמנים אלף וששת-אלפים וארבע-מאות לצבאתם "Total of the musters of the Judahite encampment: 186,400, by their divisions." Numbers 7, the record of the Tabernacle dedication, attests both the absolute and construct forms. Also note הכל מאה שלשים ותשעה "The total: one hundred thirty and nine," concluding a list of personnel (Ezra 2:42, and see below, "*The Signification of Quantity*").

4) מכס (= *mekes*) "customs, tax rate" (Num 31:37–41); cf. feminine מכסה (= *miksāh*) "quota, calculated amount" (Exod 12:4, Lev 27:23). In the war narrative of Numbers 31, this term refers to the rate of taxation to be applied to spoils of war, so as to determine what percentage of the spoils was to go to the priests and Levites (see above, no. 1, אחז). On the precise meaning of the feminine form, מכסה in Lev 27:23, see below, no. 8, under ערך. In Exod 12:5, במכסת נפשות is best translated "according to the quota of persons," namely, according to the number of persons in the household, so many sheep shall be offered. The connection to accounting is indicated by use of the verb *ḥiššēb* "to reckon, keep an account" in Lev 27:23. The priest was to calculate the value of the field depending on how many years remained until the Jubilee. Punic attests a likely cognate, *MKS* (= *mōkēs*?) "customs official" (*PhPD* 281, s.v. *MKS* II). Akkadian attests *mākisu* "tax collector" (*CAD M*/I, 129–130), and verbal *makāsu* "to collect a tax, a share" (*CAD M*/I, 127–128), and the term *miksu* "tax, share of the yield" (*CAD M*/II, 63–65). Of considerable interest is the fact that Aramaic also attests the term מכס in two actual accounts, one a brief record from Saqqara, dated 416 B.C.E. (*TAD* III, C3.11), and the other from Elephantine (*TAD* III, C3.28), an extensive record pieced together from many fragments, and dated to the 3rd century B.C.E.

TAD III, C3.11 contains two headings: כספא זי קים בשנת 6 "silver/funds 'on hand' in year six" (line 1), and: הוה יתרן כסף זי קים בשנת 6 "The surplus of funds 'on hand' in year 6 was-" (line 6). One entry under the latter heading reads: כספא זי אתוסף על מכס פטאסי בר] "The sum that was added on the tax of PN, son of PN" (line 8). A second reads: 6 מכס גבריא זי יתוספו בשנת "Tax of the men who will be added in year 6" (line 10). *TAD* III, C3.28, records several types of transactions, including sales of wine and wheat, and deposits of various sorts. Column 4 (consisting of lines 47–50) is not entirely comprehensible; it lists quantities of unidentified items in the house of a person named Yashib, and "in our house," as well as נחושים, presumably "objects of bronze," and then in line 50 we read:

4 ש 8 שנתא זא במכס כרשן "This year, (owed) in tax: *karš* 8, shekels 4."

The most elaborate Aramaic source relating to the term *mks* is the great Tariff from Palmyra (*PAT* 0259 = *CIS* ii 3913), variously preserved in Greek and Palmyrene Aramaic. The Tariff is dated 147 C.E. and was written on stone slabs. It was issued by the council (Greek *boulē*, Aramaic *bwlʾ*), and provides us not only with a Greek equivalent for Aramaic *mks*, namely, *telos*, but with composite terminology, including: *nmwsʾ dy mksʾ* "the law of taxation" (col. II, line 1), the formulas *mksʾ gby* "the tax shall be levied" (col. II, line 14), *mksʾ ḥybʾ* "liable for tax, owes tax" (col. II, line 146, and cf. the negative: *mksʾ lʾ ḥybʾ* "not liable for tax"), and more. The determined plural, *mksyʾ* "taxes" is also attested (col. II, line 194), and the *nomen agentis*, participial *mks* (= *mākēs*) "tax collector."

It is clear that Aramaic *mks* derives from Akkadian *miksu* (Kaufman 1974:72), but the question remains as to the derivation of Hebrew *mekes*, fem. *miksāh*. In our view, the priestly Torah texts in which these terms occur exclusively are post-exilic, and date from the Achemenid period, which dating, if correct, would suggest that this terminology may have entered Hebrew via Aramaic, not directly from Akkadian. In any event, the term *mekes* is connected to the Aramaic accounting system, as evidenced by its frequent occurrence in later Aramaic dialects. Note the rare occurrence of feminine מכסה in a Hebrew tenancy agreement from Murabbaʿat (Yardeni 2000 A:107, s.v. Mur 24, col. VI, line 11; originally edited in Milik 1961:122–134).

5) מרבית (= *marbît*), also: תרבית (= *tarbît*) "interest, increment" (Lev 25:36–37, Ezek 18:8, *et passim*; Prov 28:8). All attested forms derive from the Common Semitic root *r-b*-3rd-weak—*rabû* in Akkadian, *r-b-y* (secondarily Hebrew *r-b-h*) in West Semitic "to grow, increase." The primary law in Lev 25:36–37 pertains to indebtedness incurred by a fellow Israelite, in which case it is forbidden to charge interest, or to take a "bite," (Hebrew נשך). More specifically, the term מרבית applies to foodstuffs that are supplied to one in need, in which case no increment could be demanded in repayment (see Levine 1989:178, s.v. Lev 25:36). The formula is: נתן במרבית "to give out with interest." In a sort of "Holiness Code," presented as a wisdom mashal, Ezekiel 18 includes among the virtues of the righteous person the avoidance of תרבית (Ezek 18:8), whereas the proverbial, wicked son is guilty of this very offense (Ezek 18:13). Finally, Prov 28:8 cautions the greedy that their unjust gain will ultimately be lost to a truly generous person: "He who aggrandizes his wealth by 'bite' and interest (בנשך ובתרבית), will have amassed it to (the benefit of) one who is gracious to the needy."

The Aramaic cognate מרביתה/א "interest, increment," is well-attested in Aramaic loan documents from Elephantine (*DNWSI* 690, s.v. *mrby*, and *TAD* II, xxxiv, Glossary, s.v. *mrby*). In no. 9, below, it is explained that this term contrasts with ר(א)ש "capital, principal sum." In Elephantine Aramaic we find the formula: יהב במרביתה "to give out (= to lend) with interest," parallel with the Hebrew נתן במרבית (Lev 25:37, cf. *TAD* II, B3.1:2–3). In another loan document from Elephantine (*TAD* IV, D2.18:1–2), we read that the obligation of paying interest was considered part of the overall debt, so that one's heirs inherited the interest obligation as well as the principal. The same terminology is evident in Judaean Desert documents from the 1st and 2nd centuries C.E. Late Hebrew and Aramaic attest the form ר(י)בית "interest." Thus, in a Nabatean-Aramaic debenture, P. Yadin 1, line 19, we read: ומשכון נכסיא דנה ורביתה "And the mortgage on these properties, and its interest" (*JDS* III:178; and cf. in JPA and JBA: *DJPA* 513, s.v. רבי; *DJBA* 1073, s.v. ריביתא).

In the Commentary to P. Yadin 1 (*JDS* III:192–193, s.v. lines 16–18) the specialized sense of the verb *r-b-y*, namely, "to accrue as interest" is explained against the background of the Elephantine Aramaic material. We may add that this provides the most direct link to Akkadian usage of the cognate verb *rabû* "to grow, increase." *CAD R*, 43–44, under *rabû* A, mng. 4, cites many sources, from various periods, where this verb refers specifically to the accrual of interest. Also see Muffs 1969:185 for a discussion of the functional equivalence of the Aramaic and Akkadian formulas. Thus, Akkadian KÙ.BABBAR *ina muḫḫija i-rab-bi* = Aramaic וירבה עלי כסף "The silver of will accrue (as interest) against me / to my debit" (cf. *TAD* II, B4.2:2).

6) Aramaic נפקה, determined: נפקתא (= *nipqətāʾ*) "expenditure, costs; what was paid out" (Ezra 6:4, 8), literally "what goes out," from the Aramaic verb *n-p-q*. This term has a long and full history in the Official Aramaic of Elephantine (*DNWSI* 743–744, s.v. *npqh*). It is also attested at Palmyra, in the masculine plural *npqyn*. The most recent Nabatean evidence comes from Naḥal Ḥever, in P. Yadin 1:40: וכל דרא ונפקה "And any return or expenditure (or: "any 'scattering' or expenditure)." See *JDS* III:198–199, where there is reference to Arabic *nafaqatun* "expense, maintenance" at Ḫirbet Mird. Also see *DJPA*[2] 358.

7) עדף, in העדף (= *hāʿōdēp*) "which is in excess; surplus." (Exod 16:23, 26:12–13, Lev 25:27, Num 3:46, 48–49; Hiphʿil העדיף "to exceed" in Exod 16:18). Biblical Hebrew usage refers to excess of number and quantity, namely "surplus," which is our interest here, and also to measurements, such as greater length. The provisions of Lev 25:27 may be explained as follows: All sales of ancestral land were functionally equivalent to long-term leases, which would terminate at the next, scheduled Jubilee year. One who wished to redeem land he had sold under stress was obliged to compute (the Piʿʿel *ḫiššēb*; see no. 2, above) the value of the crop years since its sale, "and pay (only) the excess (והשיב את-העדף) to the one to whom he had sold it." In other words, the redeemer of the land could deduct for the years that the purchaser had already benefited from his

purchase, and didn't have to pay the entire purchase price to get his land back. Numbers 3 ordains that the tribe of Levi is to be devoted to Tabernacle service in payment to the God of Israel for having spared the firstborn of the Israelites in Egypt. A census indicated, however, that there were 273 more firstborn Israelites than there were adult, male Levites, so that five shekels a head, totaling 1,365 shekels, had to be collected from the firstborn of Israel and remitted to Aaron, the priest. Those 273 firstborn are referred to as העדפים על הלוים "who were in excess of the Levites" (Num 3:46). We also find formulas such as פדוי העדפים בהם "the redemption payments of those among them who were in excess" (Num 3:48), and העדפים על פדוי הלוים "those in excess of the redemption payments of the Levites" (Num 3:49). Imagine an account like the following:

Total firstborn males among the Israelites.

(one month of age and over) :	22,273
Subtract total males among the Levites	
(one month of age and over):	20,000
העדפים "those in excess:"	273
פדוים "redemption payments"	
(at 5 shekels a head × 273) :	1,365 shekels

Comparative evidence on the root *ʿ-d-p* is elusive. All we have are later Hebrew and Jewish Aramaic forms based on this root, and a very rare, though often cited Arabic cognate, *ǵadafa* "to be profuse" (Lane 2232). Later Hebrew preserves interesting connotations reflecting the theme of abundance, profusion and surplus, but I have not found usage as an accounting term until quite late (Ben-Yehudah, *Thesaurus* V:4343–4346; and see *DJBA* 846, s.v. עודפא). The origin of the Biblical Hebrew forms remains unknown.

8) ערך (= *ʿērek*) "assessed value, equivalent" (Lev 27:3, *et passim*; 2 Kings 12:5; cf. the bound form ערכך, and verbal Hiphʿil העריך "to assess, assign a value." It is probable that all meanings share a semantic field, and derive from a common root *ʿ-r-k* "to set up, arrange." Specialization would account for the connotations "to fix a value, to assess; to offer (as a sacrifice); to array (for battle)," and more. Forms of this root are attested in Ugaritic (*DUL* 182–183), in Classical Hebrew and Phoenician-Punic, but only rarely in Aramaic (*HALAT* 837–838, *DNWSI* 887–888). Speiser (1960:30–33) explained the suffixed ערכך, literally "your assessed value" as a bound form, on the analogy of באכה "your coming, as you arrive" hence: "as far as, all the way to-" (Gen 10:19, 1 Kings 18:46, etc.). He also notes Akkadian *mimma šumšu* "whatever be its name," which can be declined as *mimmušunšu–ya* "my 'what's-its-name'," namely, "anything of mine." One may add (if the Massoretic text is accepted) the Hebrew השוק והעליה "the thigh-section and the 'what's on it'," namely: "its covering" (1 Sam 9:24). Once bound, the form ערכך can be determined, yielding: הערכך "the 'your value'," hence: "your value," and it can also be prefixed: בערכך "in/according to the value" (Lev 5:15, 18), and the like.

This terminology is discussed briefly in my Leviticus commentary (Levine 1989:30–31, s.v. Lev 5:15, and *ibid.*, 192–200, on Leviticus 27). For the most part, the context pertains to the votary system of biblical Israel. It was customary, as an act of piety, for Israelites to devote their established value (ערך) to the Temple, a value scaled according to age and gender. They also donated animals and property to the Temple, whose values were fixed by the priesthood for this purpose. In most cases, the Temple wanted cash, so that the donors would pay the Temple the value of what they had donated, with a surcharge added, according to the laws of Leviticus, and thereby "redeem" it. This system is outlined in detail in Leviticus 27. In several instances, one guilty of certain offenses was required to bring a sacrificial offering, with the option of paying for the animal "according to the fixed value" (בערכך) in silver shekels (Lev 5:15–26).

Technical usage of the verb *ᶜ-r-k* and related forms with the meaning "to assess" is not limited to priestly texts; it was part of the administrative vocabulary. Pertaining to the votive system we read in 2 Kings 12:5: "All of the silver brought into the House of YHWH, in silver currency, as sacred donations, the silver of each person's 'life equivalent' (איש כסף נפשות ערכו), all silver that a person may be minded to bring to the House of YHWH." In 2 Kings 23:35 we read that Jehoiakim, after having been installed by Pharaoh Neco "made an assessment on the land (העריך את-הארץ)," and that "he exacted from the people of the land the silver and gold to be paid Pharaoh Neco, according to each man's assessment (איש כערכו)."

There is additional West Semitic evidence bearing on forms of the root *ᶜ-r-k*. We will begin with Ugaritic usage, citing *KTU*[2] 4.728:1–3: *ᶜrk. bᶜl. ḫlb dt. l ytn. šmn* "Prepared account of citizens of ḪLB (Aleppo?) who did not deliver oil" (*DUL* 182, s.v. *ᶜrk* I, n.m.). Although this source does not attest the specific meaning "value, equivalent" for the term *ᶜrk*, its occurrence in and list of persons who have not met required deliveries makes it relevant to the biblical term under discussion. Later Punic evidence demonstrates the survival of the old West Semitic vocabulary, but it is relatively sparse, and at times difficult to interpret confidently. In a Neo-Punic statuary inscription from Tripoli in North Africa, dated to the early 1st century B.C.E., we read: "The senate and the entire nation of Lepcis mutually resolved to pay back to that gentleman, to Aderbal, for his contributions at the expense of the city, in accordance with the full valuation (לפי כל ערך אמלא) of [the statue <that Aderbal made>, as is] incumbent upon them" (*KAI* 119:4–6, *apud PhPD* 387). Under a separate entry, Krahmalkov (*PhPD* 387) lists the feminine form *ᶜrkt* which he renders "bureau of public works, following a suggestion by M. Dahood that ערכה means "building." An alternative interpretation, followed by others (cf. *DNWSI* 888, s.v. *ᶜrkh*) would take the form ערכת to mean: "bureau of assessment." One Phoenician and two Punic sources attest this form. Thus, *RSF* 7 (1979), no. 48, col. I, lines 1–2 (from Nebi Yunis): "This is the Molk-offering table that the bureau of assessment (הערכת) … devoted and presented to their lord, Ešmun." A Punic text from Malta (*KAI* 62:1–4), dated to the 2nd century B.C.E., reads as follows: "The people of Gaulos rebuilt these three sanctuaries during the time of the chief of the bureau of assessment [Latin *Censor*] (בעת ר אדר ערכת), PN son of PN." Finally, *KAI* 130:5–6, also from Tripoli, tentatively dated 180 C.E. reads: "The bureau of assessment in charge of the ports (ערכת אש על המחזם) made four of the benches with (funds derived from) fines."

In summary, the specialized meaning of *ʿ-r-k* "to assess," and related nominal forms, belong to the West Semitic vocabulary, not specifically to the Aramaic vocabulary, as is true of many of the accounting terms examined here. Biblical terminology is utilized extensively in Rabbinic Hebrew sources, where legislation governing priestly activity is a major concern, and even rarely in JBA and in Syriac (*DJBA* 881, s.v. 1# ערך; *LS* 548) for the same reason.

ADDENDUM: The Hebrew term ערך, in its specialized form ערכך "assessed value, equivalent" has now turned up in a Hebrew inscription from the Hebron hills dating from late 7th to early 6th centuries B.C.E. This is the first extra-biblical attestation of this term from the biblical period. See Eshel 2003.

9) ראש (= *rōʾš*) "capital, principal, original amount" (Lev 5:24, Num 5:7). Biblical usage is limited to two priestly Torah texts (in Rabbinic Hebrew "head" is replaced by "horn," Hebrew קרן). Operative verbs are Piʿʿel שלם "to pay out, repay," and השיב "to make restitution." Thus Lev 5:24, speaking of one who had taken a false oath regarding the misappropriation of assets: "And he shall repay it equal to the amount of its principal (ושלם אתו בראשו), adding to it one fifth of the amount." Or, Num 5:7, speaking of one who misappropriated sancta: "And he must make restitution for his liability equal to the amount of its principal (והשיב את אשמו בראשו), adding to it one fifth of the amount." In 1911, the Assyriologist Arthur Ungnad first noted the equivalent connotation of the Akkadian term *qaqqadu* "head, principal sum" (*CAD Q*, 109–111, under mng. 6). The correspondence of Akkadian and West Semitic usage is quite remarkable; in both, "principal" is contrasted with "interest," *ṣibtu* in Akkadian, and the accompanying verbs in Akkadian also mean "to pay, repay" (*apālu*, *mullû*, and the like).

There is considerable comparative evidence from Aramaic sources, where ר(א)ש similarly means "principal, capital," and מרביתא means "interest" (cf. no. 5, above) Quite possibly, the biblical usage of Hebrew ראש to mean "principal" is Aramaistic. Thus, in an Aramaic loan document from: Elephantine (5th century B.C.E.) we read, regarding the compounding of interest:

הן מטת מרביתא לרשא ירבה מרביתא כרשא חד כחד

> "Should the interest reach the (amount) of the principal, the interest (on the interest) shall increase at the same rate as the (interest on the) principal" (*TAD* II:54, B3.1:6–7, and see above, in no. 5, מרבית, for additional references).

A similar clause appears in a broken loan document, *TAD* II, B4.2:4–5:

וירחא זי לא אנתן לך בה מרבית יהוה ראש וירבה ואשלמנהי לך ירח בירח

> "And any month in which I do not pay you interest, it shall become principal, and shall accrue (as interest), and I will pay it to you month by month."

In a business letter from Elephantine (3rd century B.C.E.), we read: שלמת על ראשי עקרן "I completed payment covering the principal sums of the real property" (*TAD* IV:36, D1.17:5 = Cowley 82). The same formula, ראש עקרן "the principal sum of the real property" occurs in a later Nabatean-Aramaic legal document from Naḥal Ḥever, P. Yadin 1:15, dated ca. 103 C.E., (*JDS* III:178). In a deed of pledge from Wadi Daliyeh (late 4th century B.C.E.) we read: יתיחט לראש כספא שקל "It shall be weighed out as the principal amount of silver; shekel, 1" (Gropp 2001:98, s.v. WDSP 10:7 [text broken]).

10) תכונה (= *təkûnāh*) "weighted, measured currency; convertible wealth" (Nah 2:10; [for different nuances see Ezek 43:11, Job 23:3], and cf. הכסף המתכן "the weighted silver" in 2 Kings 12:12). The term תכונה has been studied in depth by J.C. Greenfield (2001:258–262, and literature cited), and we may review his findings in the context of biblical accounting terminology, adding some considerations of our own. Speaking of the flooding of Nineveh at the time of its siege, the prophet declares:

> Plunder silver! Plunder gold!
> There is no limit to the ready currency (תכונה);
> It is a weighty (hoard) of every precious object! (Nah 2:10).

The etymology of תכונה, a term also occurring in Aramaic legal documents from Elephantine (see further) warrants clarification. Ultimately, this form may go back to *k-w-n* "to stand"; more immediately, it derives from a probable secondary root *t-k-n* "to contain; to measure, weigh." In Isa 40:12, the Piᶜᶜel תקן is parallel with *mādad* "to measure," and in Ezek 43:10 they measure the תכנית "plan" of the Temple. Other forms exhibit related meanings (*HALAT* 1596–1597, s.v. תכן v., תכן s.). The form תכונה is one of many *Taw*-preformatives in Hebrew and Aramaic (cf. תמורה, no. 11, below), and literally means: "that which has been weighed, measured." Functionally, תכונה compares with כסף עבר לסחר "silver transferable to/current with merchants" (Gen 23:16), namely, in a form that merchants will accept, such as ingots, or weighted coins. Earlier in the account of 2 Kings 12 (v. 5), we find the designation כסף עובר "silver currency" (see above, no. 7, s.v. ערך).

In 2 Kings 12:12, the form מתכן (= *mətukkān*) is denominative of תכונה, namely: "made into weighted units." As noted by Greenfield, the parallel passage recording payments to craftsmen in 2 Kings 22:4 reads: "Go up to Hilkiahu, the chief priest, and let him melt down (read: ויתך = *wəyattēk*) the silver that has been brought into the Temple of YHWH." Once the silver had been converted into ingots, or weighted coins, it was dispensed as payment to the craftsmen. Applying this to the statement in 2 Kings 12:12, we read, with Greenfield and others: *wayyiṣrûhû* "they cast it" (in place of Masoretic *wayyôṣî'ûhû* "they brought it out)." Namely, they cast the silver that had been collected from the people.

The term תכונה occurs in two Aramaic legal documents from Elephantine (*TAD* II, B2.6 and B3.8) in both the note absolute form and in the determined form (תכונתה, תכונתא). *Pace* Greenfield, there is no reason to regard it as a Hebraism. It is more likely a common Hebrew-Aramaic term, which actually draws our attention to Aramaic accounting terminology. *TAD* II, B2.6 and B3.8 are both contracts of marriage, wherein the items of dowry "brought in" by the wife include: תכונה זי כסף "weighted coins/ingots of silver," followed by the specification of value as *karš* and *ḥallur*, both measures of weight, along with shekels. This silver was in addition to clothing and other commodities made of cloth, as well as bronze objects.

In summary, both the biblical and the Elephantine contexts pertain to accounting. In renovating the Temple in Jerusalem, funds had to be provided in negotiable form to pay the craftsmen. In fact, 2 Kings 12:16, 22:7 both employ the key verb *ḥiššēb* "to reckon, keep an account" (see above, no. 2). In the Elephantine marriage contracts the value of the "cash" contributed by the bride is designated "*təkûnāh* of silver." Greenfield directs the reader to important sources of information on methods of casting and minting weighted coins in the Achemenid period, and refers to hoards of such coins and ingots from all over the ancient Near East (Greenfield 2001, notes 13, 16).

11) תמורה (= *təmûrāh*) "item of exchange" (Lev 27:10, *et passim*). The form with *Taw*-preformative connotes the result of the Hiphʿil המיר "to exchange, replace" (for cultic usage, cf. Lev 27:10, 33, Ezek 48:14), namely, that which was exchanged. This term is widely used in Rabbinic sources, in laws dealing with cultic materiel. The underlying verb, Hebrew *m-w-r*, may be cognate with rare Neo-Babylonian *māru* "to buy," which, in context, functionally connotes "to barter, exchange" (*CAD M*/I, 317, s.v. *māru*), and is listed as an Aramaic loanword. Although it is attested in Syriac (*LS* 377, s.v. *mr*), it is not a typical, Aramaic word.

The above accounting terms, when studied in comparative perspective, indicate that procedures operative in ancient Israel were representative of a West Semitic system, especially evident in Aramaic and Phoenician-Punic records.

The Signification of Quantity

Accounts register quantities with cardinal numbers (and fractions), sequenced in different ways. Certain languages employ dual forms to register two of an item. In the ancient Near East, as in other systems, ancient and more recent, we find two primary sequences: (1) quantity + item [Example: "five (5) cows"], and (2) item + quantity [Example: "cows – five (5)"]. A second factor is the type of numeral employed in a given record. In ancient Near Eastern records we find two primary types: (1) ideographic numerals, in which case what is written signifies a certain number [Example: "1," "2", "3"], (2) non-ideographic, or word numerals, in which case what is written spells out the word for that number [Example: "one", "two", "three"]. There are variations on these primary categories, representing specific formats. For example, in certain types of administrative lists numerals may not function as direct modifiers of nouns, but merely to record quantities, or totals of commodities, personnel, and the like, that have been identified in the title of the record. In other words, instead of registering: "Personal Name – cows, 5," the record will be look something like the following:

> Archers:
> Place Name A – 5,
> Place Name B – 6
> Place Name C – 7, etc

It needs to be said that of the two features under discussion, sequence is more significant than the type of numeral used. Whereas it is possible that unrelated cultures would have independently fixed certain forms as ideographic numerals (as for example, a single, vertical marking to signify "1"), the preference for identifying the person, place, or item first, and then the quantity, reflects a discrete perception, or disposition, and may even demarcate between one *Kulturkreis* and another, as will be seen. And yet, there is a close correlation between the utilization of ideographic numerals and the sequence "item + quantity," so that the two features are best considered together.

Anticipating the discussion to follow, we can say that in the cuneiform writing system (with the exception of the Ugaritic alphabetic cuneiform), "quantity" precedes "item" in accounting records; in other words, the numeral comes before the noun. In contrast, accounts and administrative records from the Aegaean and Eastern Mediterranean, both alphabetic (Ugaritic, Hebrew, Aramaic, Phoenician-Punic) and ideographic-syllabic (Linear A and B) exhibit the sequence "item + quantity," variously utilizing both word numerals, and ideographic numerals of various shapes.

a) The sequence "item + quantity" in biblical records

In manuscripts of the Hebrew Bible there are no ideographic numerals, but it may be that some, or all biblical records which employ the rather abnormal sequence "item + quantity" were modeled after accounts that registered ideographic numerals. The Ugaritic evidence suggests, however, that word numerals might have been employed originally in such records, because there we find exact examples of this pattern (see just below, and under *The Signification of Quantity*, c). In any event, as regards sequence, it is more normal in the Hebrew Bible to find quantity preceding item, meaning that the numeral comes before the noun. This sequence can be formulated in two ways: a) with a word numeral in the construct: שבעת כבשים literally: "seven of sheep" (Lev 23:18); b) with a word numeral in the absolute: שבעה כבשים "seven sheep" (Num 28:27). When item precedes quantity, however, only the word numeral in the absolute is employed, as we would expect.

It is precisely in texts which exhibit the features of accounts or records that we find the sequence "item + quantity" most often. To illustrate, let us begin with Joshua 12, which preserves a list of thirty-one kings of Canaanite city-states conquered by the Israelites.

מלך יריחו	אחד	מלך העי אשר מצד בית-אל	אחד
מלך ירושלם	אחד	מלך חברון	אחד
– –			
כל-מלכים שלשים ואחד			

King of Jericho	one; King of the Ai, which is near Bethel	one
King of Jerusalem	one; King of Hebron	one, etc.
– –		
Total of kings: thirty and one (Jos 12:9–24, with omissions)		

In this record, the numerals do not serve as direct modifiers of nouns, but merely to register quantities. Otherwise, this list, as it is formatted in printed Bibles, is probably the least adapted of all biblical records, once we get past its title, which is part of the introductory narrative (Jos 12:7–8). Another example of the sequence "item + quantity" is to be found in the report of the donations of the tribal chieftains (Hebrew נשיאים) at the dedication of the wilderness Tabernacle. (Num 7:12–88). We find repetitive entries that are formulated as follows:

ולזבח השלמים:	For the sacred gifts of greeting:
בקר – שנים	oxen – two
אילים – חמשה	rams – five
עתודים – חמשה	he-goats – five
כבשים בני-שנה – חמשה	yearling lambs – five

Here we have word numerals being utilized as direct modifiers of nouns. Still another example is Ezra 1:9–11, a list of Temple appurtenances returned to the Judean Premier, Sheshbazzar, by Cyrus pursuant to his edict:

Following is their quantity (ואלה מספרם):
golden sashes – thirty
silver sashes – one thousand
suits of clothes – nine and twenty (תשעה ועשרים)
golden bowls – thirty
silver bowls (of various types) – four hundred and ten
other vessels – one thousand
Total of vessels (כל-כלים) of gold and silver: five thousand four hundred [incorrect]

Additional examples of biblical records and accounts employing the sequence "item + quantity" are to be found embedded in the festival calendar of Numbers

28–29; in the genealogies of Genesis 46; in the town lists of Joshua 15, 18, 19; and 21; and in many of the genealogies of 1 and 2 Chronicles.

b) The sequence "item + quantity" in 1st millennium West Semitic epigraphy:

We can identify near-contemporary models of the type of texts we are positing as the *Vorlage* of the above biblical reports. The closest in time and place are Hebrew ostraca, such as those found at Lachish, and at Arad in the Negev, largely dating from the end of the 7th to the early 6th centuries B.C.E. As an example, we take Arad ostracon no. 1, written in Paleo-Hebrew script. It is a brief letter to one in charge at Arad, instructing him to provide foreign mercenaries from Kition, on Cyprus, with wine and flour. We provide a hand copy, taken from the *editio princeps* by Yohanan Aharoni (1975:12), and his transcription into the customary Hebrew script, followed by our English translation.

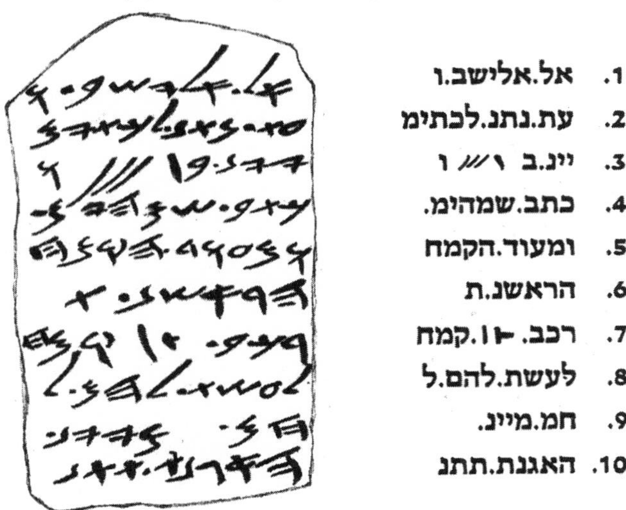

Figure 1: Arad Ostracon no. 1 (From Aharoni 1975:12; reprinted with permission from the Israel Exploration Society)

Translation of Arad, no. 1:

> (1) To Eliashib: And (2) now then: Provide the Kittim (3) wine; *bat* 1, (*hîn*) 3, and (4) register the date. (5) And from the remainder of the flour (6) of first grade you shall (7) mix *ḥōmer* 1 of flour (8) to make for them (9) bread. From the wine (10) in bowls you shall provide.

Notes: For our purposes, it is most relevant to take note of the markings used as ideographic numerals. In fact, the Arad ostraca attest two different sets of ideographic numerals, one West Semitic and the other Hieratic. We are concerned only with the West Semitic markings. In line 3, we have the abbreviation ב, for Hebrew: בת (= *bat*), a liquid measure containing approximately 22 liters. The horizontal marking following the letter ב signifies the numeral "1", of course, and we assume, from similar designations in other ostraca, that the three following markings, signifying the number "3," refer to the Hebrew liquid measure הין, of which six constituted one בת. Hence: "wine, *bat* 1, (*hîn*) 3," as translated. In line 7, the first marking is usually taken as an ideograph representing *ḥōmer*, or *kûr*, a measure containing approximately 220 liters, avoirdupois. On the markings, themselves, see Naveh (1992).

Most importantly, in this ostracon item precedes quantity, although this is not consistently the case in the Hebrew ostraca from Lachish and Arad. Furthermore, there is an observable flexibility in sequence. Thus, in line 7, we do not find: "flour, *ḥōmer* 1," which would be entirely consistent with the formulation of line 2, but rather: "*ḥōmer* 1 of flour." And yet, we do not find "1 *ḥōmer* of flour!"

The same markings are employed in Aramaic ostraca from Arad, dating from the Persian period, edited by Joseph Naveh (Aharoni 1975:196), which leads us directly to the Aramaic papyri from Elephantine, dating to the 5th century B.C.E., where one likewise encounters the sequence "item + quantity" (see further). We begin with a brief example, merely to show graphically how this type of record appears. *TAD* IV, D3.26 dates from ca. 400 B.C.E., and is an inventory of some sort. The papyrus is fragmentary, but the three lines that are preserved should suffice as illustration. It preserves a partial list of boards, or planks, with their length, width and thickness specified. We provide Ada Yardeni's hand copy, with the transcription given in *TAD* IV:101, accompanied by our translation.

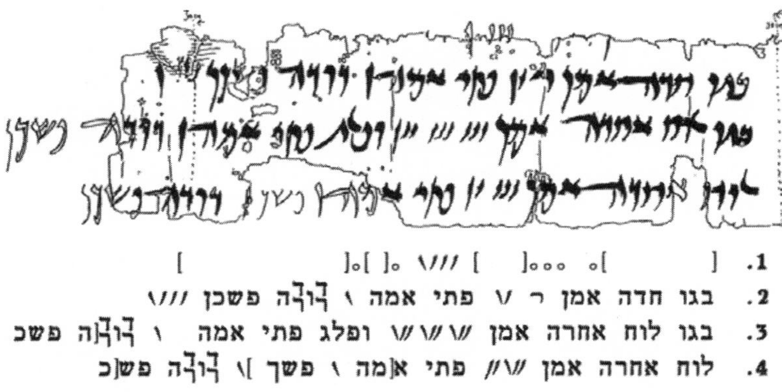

1.]   [o]ooo   [\/// o[ ]o[[
2. בגו חדה אמן ר V פתי אמה \ דֻ֯ו֯ה פשכן ///\
3. בגו לוח אחרה אמן ///\///\ ופלג פתי אמה \ דֻ֯ו֯[ה פשכ
4. לוח אחרה אמן ///\// פתי א]מה \ פשך [\ דֻ֯ו֯ה פש]כ

Figure 2: Fragment of an Aramaic Papyrus from Elephantine, dated ca. 400 B.C.E. (From *TAD* IV:101; reprinted with permission from Ada Yardeni)

Translation:

(2) Inside: a [board]: cubits 12; width: cubit 1; thickness: handbreadths 4.
(3) Inside, another board: cubits 9, and a half; width: cubit 1; thickness: handbreadth[

(4) Another board: cubits 5; width: cu[bit 1 + handbreadth] 1; thickness: handbreadth[

Notes: The noun לוח is common West Semitic, and has a variety of meanings. The rendering "board" is only conjectural. In line 2, the word for "thickness" is most likely written with a *resh*, and is to be read דורה (= consonantal *dwrh* = *dûrāh*) (*DNWSI* 243–244). The word for handbreadth, פשך, is cognate with Akkadian *pušku* (*DNWSI* 946). In line 2, we have in addition to the usual markings for 1, a marking for 10, so that "12" is registered as "10 + 2."

By far, the most elaborate example of the "item + quantity" sequence is the so-called "Ahiqar Palimpsest" from Elephantine (*TAD* III, pp. 82–193; C3.7) discovered and ingeniously restored by Ada Yardeni. It is an extensive customs record, dated ca. 475 B.C.E., and composed of numerous columns. I have selected several lines from a relatively well-preserved section (*TAD* III, pp. 184, 186, D2, verso, cols. 1 and 2). These are provided with Ada Yardeni's hand drawings, with the given transcription, and our translation. The bracketed restorations in the transcription are fairly certain, being based on recurring, conventional entries.

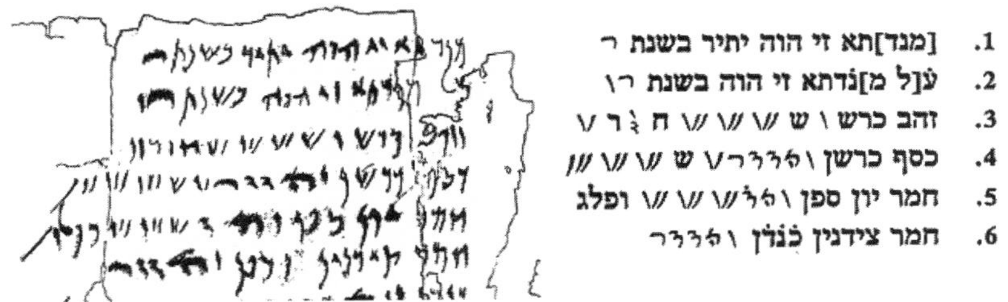

Figure 3: From the "Ahiqar P alimpsest" dated ca. 475 B.C.E. (From *TAD* III:186; reprinted with permission from Ada Yardeni)

Translation:

1) The [duty] accrued as surplus in year 10,
2) Ov[er and above the du]ty that accrued in year 11:
3) gold: *karš* 1, *š* (= *šəqālîn*) 9, *ḫ* (= *ḫallûr*) 1, *r* (= *rəbāʿîn*) 2.
4) silver: *karšîn* 100 + 40 + 10 + 2, *š* 9.
5) Ionian wine: bowls 100 + 20 + 9 and a half.
6) Sidonian wine: jugs 100 + 40 + 10, etc.

Notes: The acronym ר (= *r*) signifies רבען "quarters," a fraction. Two types of containers are mentioned: (1) ספן (=*sappîn*) "bowls," and כנדן (= Hebrew כדים – *kaddîm*) "jars, jugs." It has been observed that utilization of the same vessels for particular commodities is not consistent. The sequence "item + quantity," using ideographic numerals persisted in Aramaic records long after the Achemenid period. It occurs in the great Tariff from Palmyra, to which reference has already been made.

The sequence "item + quantity," using ideographic numerals persisted in Aramaic records long after the Achemenid period. It occurs in the great Tariff from Palmyra, to which reference has already been made.

It also bears mention that some of the same ideographic markings for numerals are to be found in Phoenician-Punic records of the Achemenid period, and thereafter, where we also encounter the sequence "item + quantity." Thus, in the famous tariffs from Marseille, dated ca. 4th century B.C.E., we find entries such as the following: לכהנם כסף שקל 1 זר 2 באחד "For the priests: shekel 1, *zar* 2, for each one" (*CIS* i 165, line 7; Cooke 1903:112);

c) Early western evidence bearing on the sequence "item + quantity."

Whereas the sequence "quantity + item" is a standard feature of cuneiform records, our search for the origins of the sequence "item + quantity" takes us to the Aegean and Eastern Mediterranean of the Middle-to-Late Bronze Age, first to Linear A, the ideographic-syllabic script of the Minoan language of Crete (ca. 1660–1450 B.C.E.); then to Linear B, the proto-Greek ideographic-syllabic script of Mycenae (ca. 1450–1200 B.C.E.); and finally, to Ugaritic of the Syrian coastal region (ca. 1400–1200 B.C.E.), with its particular kind of alphabetic cuneiform.

Michael Ventris and John Chadwick (1956) deciphered the Linear B script and decoded its language, and they have analyzed script development in the Cretan languages, generally. They conclude that the system of numeral markings used in Linear B is the same as that of Linear A, only more developed (Ventris and Chadwick 1956:53). What is more, the sequence "item + quantity" in the Cretan scripts harks back to the earlier Cretan "hieroglyphs," such as those of the tablet from Phaistos (see the hand copy in Ventris and Chadwick 1956:30). This sequence is also evident in Egyptian hieroglyphic writing (Gardiner 1957:192, s.v. no. 261). Whatever the putative influence of Egyptian models on the Minoan scripts, it is clear that the sequence "item + quantity" is a western convention, which contrasts with the eastern, cuneiform convention of registering quantity first, followed by item.

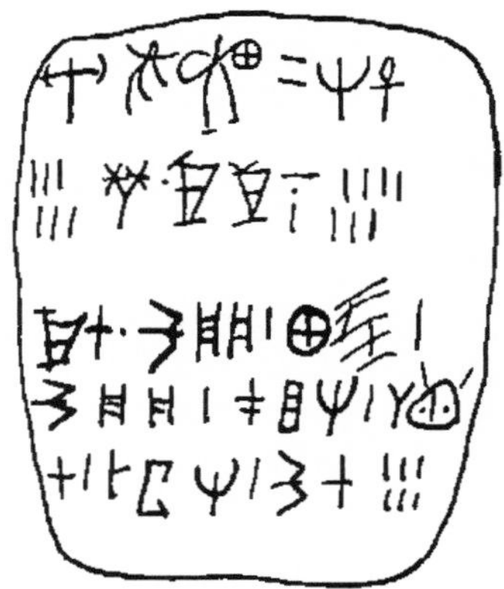

Figure 4: A Linear A inscription (From Gordon 1966, no. 88, Plate VIII)

To be specific: C.H. Gordon (1966:26–27, and Plate VIII) cites two Minoan inscriptions from Hagia Triada (nos. 88 and 122) that exhibit markings signifying numerals. There are verticals for single digits, and horizontals for "10." In no. 88, we find a list of six personal names, each followed by the vertical marking for "1", followed by a total, which Gordon reads: *ku-ro* 6 "Total: 6," shown as two rows of three verticals, one on top of the other. Gordon associates Minoan *ku-ro* with Hebrew כל "total," and actually cites Jos 12:24, as well as determined הכל "the total" in Ezra 2:42 (see discussion above, and under *Selected Biblical Accounting Terms*, no. 3). The Linear A material is sparse and difficult to decipher with certainty, whereas we possess a sizable corpus of economic and administrative texts, including lists of ritual offerings, in the proto-Greek of Linear B. The consistent pattern is "item + quantity," indicated by an ideographic numeral. The Linear B accounting system is actually quite sophisticated, and it exhibits ideographic numerals to signify large quantities, weights, and volumes (Ventris and Chadwick 1956:53–60). On the primary level, the sequence in Linear B is "item + quantity:" "MAN 1, OXEN 6," not: "1 MAN, etc." To cite a simple example, we reproduce the transcription of no. 206 = Gg705 (D 1), appearing in Ventris and Chadwick 1956:310, with our translation. It records a ritual offering.

1)] *a-mi-ni-so* / *e-re-u-ti-ja* ME+RI AMPHORA 1
2)] *pa-si-te-o-i* ME+RI AMPHORA 1
3)]-*ke-ne* ME+RI AMPHORA 1
1) Amnisos: To Eleuthia – honey, jar 1
2) To all the gods – honey, jar 1
3) [broken] – honey, jar 1

Notes: The Linear B script is ideographic-syllabic. Amnisos is a known site near Heraklion, and Eleuthia is the name of a goddess. Vocabulary: *me-ri* = Greek *meli* "honey" and *pa-si-te-o-i* = Greek *pānsi theoi'i* "to all the gods," a frequent formula of address in the ritual tablets (see Ventris and Chadwick 1956:303, note 'P').

Now, to contemporary Ugarit, where we encounter a particular kind of alphabetic cuneiform used to write a West Semitic language. The signification of quantity is complex in economic documents, where three systems are in evidence: (1) Quantity + item, using a word numeral. Example: *KTU*[2] 4.63.III:34: *ṯṯ. qštm w. ṯn . qlʿm* "six archers and two slingers." This sequence predominates in Ugaritic, and parallels the normal conventions of Biblical Hebrew. (2) Item + quantity, using a word numeral. It appears that this sequence is not attested in Ugaritic where the numeral serves as a direct modifier of the noun, but only for registering quantity. Example: *KTU*[2] 4.48:1–4, in a list of towns either receiving or delivering wine, as the list's total indicates. The units of content are not given.

1) *ḫlb ʿprm. ṯṯ*	Place Name A – six
2) *ḫlb qrd. ṯn. ʿšr*	Place Name B – twelve
3) *qmy . arbʿ . ʿšr*	Place Name C – fourteen
4) *ṣʿq . arbʿ . ʿšr*	Place Name D – fourteen

(3) Item + quantity, using an ideographic numeral. This sequence is also limited to registering quantity in Ugaritic, but is more frequent than the utilization of word numerals for this type of record. Example: *KTU* 4.93, entitled: *spr ytnm* "a record of cultic servitors," listing the names of those who received rations of

wine, as the total indicates. Once again, the units of content are not given. Lines 2–5 read:

2) *bn . ḫlbym*	2	Son of A	2
3) *bn . ady.*	2	Son of B	2
4) *bn . ʿṯtry*	2	Son of C	2
5) *bn . ḥrẓn*	2	Son of D	2

To summarize the comparative evidence: We observe in certain biblical records signs of a system of quantity signification known in the Aegean and Eastern Mediterranean since early times, and which is most evident in Aramaic accounting during the Achemenid period and thereafter.

Summary

We have attempted to investigate aspects of the accounting system of biblical Israel in West Semitic perspective by focusing on specific features: terminology, and the signification of quantity. It turns out that biblical terminology is thoroughly realistic, and that accounting terms as well as formulas used to signify quantity fit in well with what is known from West Semitic and other non-Semitic, western languages, such as Mycenean Linear B. The accounting terminology connects most closely with records in Aramaic and Phoenician-Punic, as does the sequence "item + quantity." Most immediately, this sequence is evident in contemporary Hebrew epigraphy. With respect to sequencing, we observe a cultural divide. In cuneiform cultures, one apparently wanted to know quantity first, whereas in the western sphere, one wanted to identify the item first. It's a contrast between "What?" and "How many/much?" This is not a script-specific distinction. It is not determined by the direction of writing or the type of script employed, nor is it driven by the syntactic character of any particular language, or language family. All we can say is that it is a distinction expressive of a difference in mentality, perhaps of a different perspective on the organization and presentation of data.

Reference Bibliography

Ben-Yehudah, *Thesaurus* — E. Ben-Yehudah, *Thesaurus Totius Hebraitatis*, New York: Thomas Yoseloff, 1960, 8 vols.

CIS — *Corpus Inscriptionum Semiticarum*

DJBA — M. Sokoloff, *A Dictionary of Jewish Babylonian Aramaic*, Ramat-Gan & Baltimore, Bar Ilan University Press & Johns Hopkins University Press, 2002.

DJPA[2] — M. Sokoloff, *A Dictionary of Jewish Palestinian Aramaic*, 2nd edition, Ramat-Gan & Baltimore and London, Bar Ilan University Press & Johns Hopkins University Press, 2002.

DUL — G. del Olmo Lete, J. Sanmartin, *A Dictionary of the Ugaritic Language in the Alphabetic Tradition*. Leiden: Brill, 2003, 2 vols.

HALAT — L. Koehler, W. Baumgartner, *Hebräisches und Aramäisches Lexikon zum Alten Testament*, Leiden: E.J. Brill, 1967–1990.

JBA	Jewish Babylonian Aramaic
JDS III	A. Yardeni, B.A. Levine, et al., *The Documents from the Bar Kokhba Period in the Cave of Letters; Hebrew, Aramaic, and Nabatean-Aramaic Papyri*, Jerusalem: Israel Exploration Society, 2002.
JPA	Jewish Palestinian Aramaic
KAI	H. Donner, W. Röllig, *Kanaanäische und Aramäische Inschriften*, Wiesbaden: Otto Harrassowitz, 1954, 2 vols.
KTU[2]	M. Dietrich, O. Loretz, J. Sanmartín, *The Cuneiform Alphabetic Texts*, 2nd edition, Munster: Ugarit Verlag, 1995.
Lane	E. W. Lane, *An Arabic-English Lexicon*, Beirut: Librairie du Liban, 1980, 8 vols.
PAT	D., Hillers, E. Cussini, *Palmyrene Aramaic Texts*, Baltimore and London, The Johns Hopkins University Press, 1996.
PhPD	Ch. R. Krahmalkov, *Phoenician-Punic Dictionary*, Leuven: Peeters, 2000.
RSF	*Rivista di Studi Fenici*
TAD	B. Porten, A. Yardeni, *Textbook of Aramaic Documents from Ancient Egypt*, Jerusalem: The Hebrew University, 1986–1999, vols I–IV.

Aharoni, Y.
1975 *Arad Inscriptions* (Hebrew). Jerusalem: Bialik Institute-Israel Exploration Society.

Corral, M.A.
2002 *Ezekiel's Oracles Against Tyre: Historical Reality and Motivations*. Biblica et Orientalia 46. Rome: Editrice Pontificio Isituto Biblico.

Cooke, G.A.
1903 *A Textbook of North-Semitic Inscriptions*. Oxford: Clarendon Press.

Diakonoff, I.M.
1992 The Naval Power and Trade of Tyre. *IEJ* 42:168–193.

The Economist
2003 True and Fair is Not Hard and Fast: The Future of Accounts. Vol. 367, no. 8321, dated April 26th 2003, pp. 61–63.

Eshel, E.
2003 A Late Iron Age Ostracon Featuring the Term לערכך. *IEJ* 51:151–163.

Fales, F.M.
1986 *Aramaic Epigraphs on Clay Tablets*. Roma: Università degli Studi "La Sapienza."

Friberg, J.
1992 Numbers and Counting. *ABD* 4:1139–1146.

Gardiner, A.
1957 *Egyptian Grammar*, 3rd edition, London: Oxford University Press.

Goelet, O.
2003 Ancient Egyptian Scripts: Literary, Sacred, and Profane. Pages 1–21 in *Semitic Papyrology in Context*, ed. L.H. Schiffman. Leiden: Brill.

Gordon, C.H.
1966 *Evidence for the Minoan Language*. Ventnor, NJ: Ventnor Publishers.

Greenfield, J.C.
2001 The Meaning of *Tkwnh*. Pages 81–85 in Biblical and Related Studies Presented to Samuel Iwry, ed. A. Kort, S. Morschauser. Winona Lake, In: Eisenbrauns. (Reprinted in Sh. M. Paul et al. (ed.), *ʿAl Kanfei Yonah: Collected Studies of Jonas C. Greenfield on Semitic Philology*. 2 vols. Leiden: Brill, pp. 258–262).

Gropp, D. M.
2001 *Wadi Daliyeh II: The Samaria Papyri from Wadi Daliyeh*. DJD 28. Oxford. Clarendon Press, pages 3–116.

Kaufman, S.
1974 *The Akkadian Influences on Aramaic*. Chicago: University of Chicago Press.

Lamberg-Karlovsky, C.C.
1999 Households, Land Tenure, and Communications Systems in the 6th – 4th Millennia of Mesopotamia. Pages 167–201 in *Urbanization and Land Ownership in the Ancient Near East*, ed. M. Hudson, B. A. Levine. Cambridge, MA: Peabody Museum of Archaeology and Ethnology.

Levine, B.A.
1965 The Descriptive Tabernacle Texts of the Pentateuch. *JAOS* 85:307–318 {*VOL 1, PP. 55–72*}.
1989 *Leviticus*, JPS Torah Commentary. Philadelphia: Jewish Publication Society.
1996 Farewell to the Ancient Near East: Evaluating Biblical References to Ownership of Land in Comparative Perspective. Pages 223–242 in *Privatization in the Ancient Near East and Classical World*, ed. M. Hudson, B. A. Levine. Cambridge, MA: Peabody Museum of Archaeology and Ethnology {*VOL 2, PP. 187–208*}.
1999 The Biblical "Town" as Reality and Typology: Evaluating Biblical References to Towns and their Functions. Pages 421–453 in *Urbanization and Land Ownership in the Ancient Near East*, ed. M. Hudson, B. A. Levine. Cambridge, MA: Peabody Museum of Archaeology and Ethnology {*VOL 2, PP. 209–33*}.

Milik, J.T.
1961 Textes hébreux et araméens. Pages 67–205 in *Les Grottes de Murabbaʿât*. DJD 2. Oxford: Clarendon Press.

Muffs, Y.
1969 *Studies in the Aramaic Legal Papyri from Elephantine*. Reissued in 2003, with Prolegomenon by B.A. Levine. Leiden: E.J. Brill.

Naveh, J.
1975 Aramaic Inscriptions. Pages 165–203 in Y. Aharoni, *Arad Inscriptions* (Hebrew). Jerusalem: Bialik Institute-The Israel Exploration Society.
1992 The Numbers of *Bat* in the Arad Ostraca. *IEJ* 42:52–54.

Powell, M.A.
1992 Weights and Measures. *ABD* 6:897–908.

Speiser, E.A.
1960 Leviticus and the Critics. Pages 29–45 in *Yehezkel Kaufmann Jubilee Volume*, ed. M. Haran. Jerusalem: Magnes Press-the Hebrew University.

Ventris, M., and J. Chadwick
1956 *Documents in Mycenaean Greek*. Cambridge: at the University Press.

Yardeni, A.
2000 *Textbook of Aramaic, Hebrew, and Nabataean Documentary Texts from the Judaean Desert*. Jerusalem; Ben-Zion Dinur Center for Research in Jewish History, 2 vols. (Hebrew, with English appendix).

In Praise of the Israelite *Mišpāḥâ*: Legal Themes in the Book of Ruth*

For all its charm, the book of Ruth produces a certain *malaise*. Students of Israelite law and society have found it difficult if not impossible to reconcile the many references to legal institutions contained in Ruth with the evidence of other sources, both biblical and comparative. There is an extensive literature dealing with these legalities, for their very elusiveness seems to have stimulated the scholarly imagination.[1]

Methodologically, the challenge is to establish, if we can, the attitude of the author of Ruth toward those laws and customs to which he refers directly, or alludes indirectly. How precise was he in utilizing legal themes?

This question has been addressed in recent years by D. R. G. Beattie, in a study entitled: "The Book of Ruth as Evidence for Israelite Legal Practice." Beattie postulates that the author of Ruth was committed to credibility, and that he would not "create a legal situation which his audience will know to be impossible." In another statement, Beattie speaks of the author's mandate to be "intelligible" to his readers.[2]

A comparison of Beattie's study with an earlier treatment of the same subject by Millar Burrows shows the difference between a legal and a literary approach to an ancient narrative. Burrows, an authority on Israelite marriage, keenly analyzed the legal problems hypothetically raised in the story of Ruth, and his determinations in this regard were predictably accurate. And yet, one senses the extent to which he forced this tale of devotion and virtue into a legal mold, alien to its essential character.[3]

Although I find Beattie's discussion to be an advance over most recent studies, which inevitably assume a high degree of legal precision in Ruth, I also find that it does not take into account some literary features and narrative devic-

---

* Originally published in H. Huffmon, et al. (eds.), *The Quest for the Kingdom of God: Studies in Honor of George E. Mendenhall* (Winona Lake, IN: Eisenbrauns, 1983), pp. 95–106. Reprinted with permission from Eisenbrauns.

[1] In the past decade two new commentaries on the book of Ruth have appeared. We have Edward F. Campbell's volume (*Ruth* [AB 7; Garden City: Doubleday, 1975]), and that of Jack M. Sasson (*Ruth, A New Translation with a Philological Commentary and a Formalist-Folklorist Interpretation* [Baltimore: Johns Hopkins, 1979]). Campbell's discussion of the legal themes in Ruth is on pp. 27, 132–33, and Sasson's on pp. 228–29, respectively.

[2] Beattie, "The Book of Ruth as Evidence for Israelite Legal Practice," *VT* 24 (1974) 251–67.

[3] Burrows, "The Marriage of Boaz and Ruth," *JBL* 59 (1940) 445–54.

es characteristic of the book as a whole. Beattie argues that the author takes great care in presenting legal details; as, for instance, in describing the removal of the shoe as a symbolic act of conveyances (Ruth 4:7–8). But the mere presence of legal detail, expressed in technical language, does not prove the applicability of the actual legal instruments referred to in the story. The question that should concern us is whether the circumstances of the story, as the author himself fashioned it, call for those legal actions, or not. We shall have occasion to observe that the author of Ruth was capable of legal leaps, of glossing over the prerequisites for invoking certain Israelite laws, while at the same time exploiting the very dynamics of those laws to enhance the intricacy of his plot.

Beattie also attaches considerable importance to dating. In his view, Ruth is predominantly a pre-exilic creation, containing some few ingredients of late language appropriated in the course of transmission.[4] I must disagree with this assessment, and insist that greater emphasis be placed on late language. A composition should be dated on the basis of its latest linguistic components, if language is being used as the basis for dating, whether or not these ingredients are statistically extensive. One could, of course, discount elements blatantly identifiable as later interpolations, of which I doubt any occur in the main body of Ruth. There are also many clear indications of a literary-historical kind which bring us to the brink of the exile, and most probably take us into the early post-exilic period. I refer to biblical sources with which the author was decidedly familiar, and which are paraphrased and played-upon in Ruth.

The importance attached to dating has another implication, less apparent in Beattie's study than in most others. I refer to the notion of development. In the literature of the last century or so, scholars have interpreted the legalities in Ruth as variously representing very early or very late stages in the development of Israelite legal institutions. In this way, discrepancies between Ruth and other biblical sources are circumvented by positing that the author was privy to facts of law and life unknown to us, because he flourished in a period of biblical history otherwise undocumented.

This sounds good, in theory; but when we get down to cases, we encounter problems with tracing developments in biblical law. The levitate law provides a good example: there can be no doubt whatsoever that the author of Ruth was familiar with the Tamar episode in Genesis 38, for he evokes it in the marriage blessing (Ruth 4:12). Nor can there be any doubt that he knew the precise wording of the levirate law in Deut 25:5–10, for he ingeniously paraphrases its formulation in Ruth 4:5b, 10.

Now, if there is evidence of a trend in the performance of the levirate, it is definitely in the direction of mitigating this duty, not of expanding it, or broadening its application. This emerges from a comparison of the early Yahwistic narrative of Genesis 38 with the law of Deuteronomy 25. The Tamar episode makes the point that neglect of the levirate once endangered the continuity of Judah's line. To set matters right, all sorts of unusual, and normally reprehensi-

[4] Beattie, "The Book of Ruth," 253–54.

ble acts had to be undertaken. The Deuteronomic law, on the other hand, presents the levirate as an institution which still retained its traditional authority, but which had already begun to clash with the Israelite way of life and the organization of the family. The *levir* now has an option, and may refuse to unite with the childless widow of his deceased brother. A symbolic humiliation is imposed, which satisfies the tradition; but there is nothing illegal about releasing the widow to marry outside the family. One suspects in a majority of cases this was the option exercised, rather than levitate union, at least by the time that the Deuteronomic law was promulgated.

Now, if it was true that relatives other than a *levir* were obligated to marry the childless widows of their clan relatives, as is explicitly predicated in Ruth 4:5b, such would have been the case before the Deuteronomic law; and what is more, that practice would have antedated the Tamar episode as well. In neither one of these sources is it ever intimated that the *levir* could be replaced by anyone except another brother of the deceased, should the *levir* have been unable or unwilling to perform his duty, or have passed away. The Tamar episode can hardly be cited as evidence that at one time fathers-in-law united with their childless, widowed daughters-in-law![5]

It is my understanding that the author of Ruth entertained a meta-legal attitude. His purpose was to extol the spirit, rather than the letter of Israelite law, as it functioned in the family and larger clan. He created a story in which the ultimate purposes of several interlocking legal institutions, all expressive of collective, clan responsibility, were amazingly fulfilled; but their fulfillment came in a manner that exceeded the strict limits of legal applicability.

This assessment of the author's mentality requires some clarification prior to engaging the specific legalities projected in the book of Ruth, primarily the levirate and the system known as *gĕʾullâ* "redemption."

An important consideration in the study of Ruth is George Mendenhall's emphasis on "policy" as reflected in law. I agree with E. F. Campbell, who applies Mendenhall's analysis to the interpretation of Ruth, that our author was interested in law as a set of policies—the policy of assisting the widow and the poor, of accepting a stranger who sought refuge among the Israelites; the policy of rewarding devotion to the clan and family, and of recognizing loyalty on the part of wives to their husbands' families. The line of Judah, destined for royalty and for eschatology, survived because such "policies" were implemented all along the line. The term "policy" thus focuses our attention on norms and atti-

---

[5] This is virtually assumed by Robert Gordis ("Love, Marriage and Business in the Book of Ruth: A Chapter in Hebrew Customary Law," *A Light unto My Path: Studies in Honor of Jacob M. Myers* [ed. H. N. Bream *et al.*; Philadelphia: Temple University, 1974] 241–64, esp. 249). But, Gordis' logic is convoluted: since incest is forbidden by the law codes of the Torah, Judah's act would have been illegal, and would have rendered Perez illegitimate. Ergo, the levirate was not limited to the *levir*; otherwise, how could Perez' line have been accepted, even ennobled? The heroic literature of the Bible was hardly bound by the laws of the Torah!

tudes; on objectives, purposes and motivations, as they operated in biblical Israel, rather than depleting our attention by a static description of the requirements imposed by specific legislation.[6]

And yet, the author of Ruth recognized in the very detail of law a reflection of its lofty purposes. His statements are not of the prophetic variety, or even of the sort encountered in the Deuteronomic law codes, which often voice broad concepts endemic to the specific commandments. His interest is in the subtleties of law, and he is, in a sense, closer to the spirit of the priestly tradition and its detailed codes of practice. Our author was an artful manipulator of legalities! He transposed *laws* into *legal themes*. He utilized the formulas and technicalities of the legal *dicta* in a meta-legal way; and in so doing, successfully confounded generations of scholars!

The story of Ruth is cast against a social backdrop every bit as significant for the character of the story as its legalities. The social parameter of the story of Ruth is the *mišpāḥâ*, which I regularly translate "clan," for lack of a better term. By this I mean a patrilineal unit considerably larger than the immediate family, or even the "nuclear" family as defined by the incest code (Leviticus 18, 20, and Deut 27:20–21). Endogamous marriages often occurred within the same *mišpāḥâ*, usually between cousins. In fact, such marriages were encouraged, based on what we are told in certain biblical traditions. The system of *gĕʾullâ*, so basic to the literary framework of Ruth, was also a function of the Israelite *mišpāḥâ*.[7]

With this background in mind, we can now proceed to examine the passage that has been central to most scholarly debates on the legalities in Ruth:

> He (Boaz) said to the redeemer (*gôʾēl*): The section of field which belonged to our kinsman, Elimelech, Noami is *offering for sale* (*mākĕrâ*)—she who just returned from the territory of Moab. I intend to serve notice on you as follows: Purchase [it] (*qĕnēh*) in the presence of those seated, and in the presence of the elders of my people. If you agree to redeem, then redeem (*gĕʾāl*)! But if you will not redeem—tell me, so that I may be so informed; for there is no other except you to redeem, and I succeed you.
>
> Thereupon he (the redeemer) responded: I will, indeed, redeem (*ʾegʾāl*)!
>
> Boaz then continued: *At the same time as you purchase* (*bĕyôm qĕnôtĕkā*) the field from Naomi—Ruth, as well (read *wĕʾet*), the Moabite woman, widow of the deceased, you must 'purchase'

[6] See literature cited in n. 1.

[7] In Ruth, as in many other biblical sources, the term for the immediate family which shared a common domicile is *bayit*, "household." Thus, Naomi expresses the hope that her daughters-in-law will find security, each in "the household of her husband" (*bêt ʾîšāh*, Ruth 1:9; and cf. Num 30:11). Likewise, she urges each of them to return to "the household of her mother" (*bêt ʾimmāh*, Ruth 1:8; and cf. Song 3:4; 8:2). In Ruth 4:11 the designation: *bêt yiśrāʾēl* probably means "the household (= family) of Israel (= Jacob)," and in 4:12 we find *bêt pereṣ*, "the household of Perez."

> (*qānîtā*), so as to confirm the title of the deceased over his estate (Ruth 4:3–5).[8]

The above translation is intentionally stilted, so as to focus attention on the textual problems of this passage. A scribal error is assumed in the word *ûmēʾēt* immediately following the Etnah in v. 5. Our translation takes the *mēm* in that word as a dittography, induced by the *mēm* in the name *nāʿŏmî*, the preceding word. On this basis read: *wĕʾet*. Less likely is the suggestion to follow the Vulgate reading *quoque* and read *gam ʾet*, which is what we find in v. 10.

Most important, of course, is the question of Kethibh *qnyty*, versus the Qere, *qānîtā*, in v. 5b. In my opinion, the Qere is to be sustained on text-critical, as well as exegetical grounds. The Qere is an attempt to correct an error, induced by the occurrence of two 1st-person forms, *qānîtî* "I have purchased," in v. 10, which rephrases the words of Boaz' charge. Recently, the Kethibh has gained new adherents, making it necessary to focus on the textual question.[9]

In Ruth 4:3–5, and continuing through v. 10 of that chapter, two significant verbs are employed: *gāʾal* "to redeem," and *qānâ* "to purchase, acquire." I begin with the latter because its occurrence in these passages of Ruth directly links them to the language in Jeremiah 32. That source preserves a unique account of an act of *gĕʾullâ* with respect to the field of a clan-relative. The prophet Jeremiah undertakes the legal process of *gĕʾullâ* for a symbolic purpose, which is stated in technical, legal language:

> Then Jeremiah said: The word of Yahweh came to me as follows: Hanamel, son of your uncle, Shallum, is about to come to you, and he will state: Purchase (*qĕnēh-lĕkā*) my field in Anathoth, for you have *jurisdiction over the redemption by purchase* (*mišpaṭ haggĕʾullâ liqnôt*).
>
> And, indeed, Hanamel, my cousin, came to me pursuant to the word of Yahweh ... and said to me: Pray, purchase (*qĕnēh-nāʾ*) my field in Anathoth ... for you have *jurisdiction over* [*preserving*] the ancestral estate (*mišpaṭ hayyĕruššâ*), and you bear *the* [*duty of*] *redemption* (*haggĕʾullâ*)....
>
> So, I purchased (*wāʾeqneh*) the field .... (Jer 32:6–9)[10]

In this passage the essential verb is *qānâ* "to purchase," and of *gāʾal*, "to redeem," only the nominal form *gĕʾullâ* is used. These two verbs, *gāʾal* and *qānâ*,

---

[8] The perfect form, *mākĕrâ* in v. 3 need not refer to an action taken in the past, but may, as it does here, designate an action which merely began before the moment of speech. There is no need to point the word as a participial form, as once suggested by J. A. Bewer, "The Gᵉʾullah in the Book of Ruth," *AJSL* 19 (1902–3) 143–48.

[9] See the extensive discussion by Sasson, *Ruth*, 121–22, and Beattie, "The Book of Ruth," 263–64.

[10] Hebrew *yĕruššâ* always connotes land or some other form of property, and never, in biblical usage, refers to a legal process. If *yĕruššat pĕlêṭâ* in Judg 21:17 is correct, the sense would be that some number of the persons belonging to the tribe of Benjamin remained alive.

are far from being synonymous. Hebrew *gāʾal* invariably connotes the retrieval of something lost, taken away; or about to be lost. This verb says nothing about the legal status of that which is redeemed, or about who then owns it. On the other hand, *qānâ* necessarily connotes possession, certainly so in legal contexts.[11]

Jeremiah 32 represents the classic act of redemption, in which purchase is material. The redeemer gains title to the field he has redeemed, a fact made explicit in Jer 32:7b: "For you have jurisdiction over the redemption by purchase." In Ruth 4:3–7, both nominal (*gĕʾullâ*, "redemption," vv. 6, 7), and finite forms of the verb *gāʾal* occur alongside the verb *qānâ*. In Ruth, the verb *gāʾal* describes the overall process, whereas *qānâ* specifically refers to the element of purchase.

To indicate the significance of usage, I refer to Leviticus 25, a priestly code governing land tenure, in which forms of the verbs *gāʾal* and *qānâ* are prominent. In that code usage of the two verbs is, however, carefully differentiated. The verb *qānâ* is reserved exclusively for normal business transactions, but never for any act involved in redemption, *per se*. There is a reason for this: Leviticus 25 perceives of *gĕʾullâ* in different terms. The redeemer from the clan *restores* what he redeems to his needy relative and does not gain title to the land for himself, so that one could say that he "purchased" it.[12]

This is the only interpretation that makes good sense out of the provisions of Lev 25:25–26. One who had been compelled to pledge or sell part of his holdings had the option of buying back his property, if he subsequently acquired the means to do so on his own. Or, he could await the advent of the Jubilee year, when his holding would revert to him automatically. A more fortunate solution would be for his *gôʾēl*, of the same clan, to restore his property to him. The interest upheld in the code of Leviticus 25 is that of the individual landowner, not of his whole clan. In this respect, the provisions of Leviticus 25 represent a basic departure from the classic pattern, reflected in Jeremiah 32. There we read that the prophet weighed out the price of the field in silver and had a deed of sale written registering Jeremiah as the new owner of Hanamel's field.

The author of Ruth, by using the verb *qānâ* as he does, clearly demonstrates that his reference is to the classic system of *gĕʾullâ*, in which purchase was a central act. This explains why the unnamed redeemer reneged on his earlier willingness to "redeem" the field in question. He had been willing to purchase Elimelech's field, thereby alleviating Naomi's plight, but he was unwilling to agree

---

[11] In late Biblical Hebrew, the verb *qānâ* occasionally replaces *gāʾal*, as in Neh 5:8, "And I said to them: Did we not buy-back (*qānînû*) our Judean kinsmen who had been indentured to the gentiles." Cf. Lev 25:47 where the verb *gāʾal* is used in a similarly worded statement of law.

[12] Contrast usage of the verb *qānâ* in Lev 25:14–15 as a term of reference for normal buying and selling, with usage of *gāʾal* in vv. 25–26, in the context of the redemption system, where *gāʾal* functions as a reflex of *mākar* "to sell," just as *qānâ* does in general transactions.

to any arrangement that would require him to forfeit his title to what he had redeemed. To do so would "ruin" his own estate (Ruth 4:6).

Here, then, is a clear instance of our author's method in utilizing legal themes. He could be very precise, indeed, if by such precision he succeeded in making his plot revolve around a point of law.

Some scholars have been concerned about usage of the verb *qānâ* in Ruth 4:5b, 10, to designate acquisition of a wife, since that specialized meaning is not attested elsewhere in Biblical Hebrew. The first point to be emphasized is that no deductions are warranted by the use of this verb, as far as the legal nature of marriage itself is concerned. No notion of marriage as purchase may be imputed to the author of Ruth. The fact is that usage of the verb *qānâ* in Ruth is restricted to two passages, where its function is stylistic, not technical. In 4:5a, the words: *bĕyôm qĕnôtĕkā*, "At the same time as you purchase" (the field), produce the reflex: *qānîtā*, "You must purchase" (the woman) in v. 5b. Similarly, *qānîtî*, "I have purchased" (the property) in v. 9 produces the reflex: *qānîtî*, "I have purchased" (the woman) in v. 10. In v. 13, the verb which designates acquisition of a wife is the conventional one, *lāqaḥ*, "to take" a wife.[13]

Thus far in the discussion of our author's attitude toward the system of *gĕʾullâ* it has been my purpose to illustrate how Israelite law was utilized to enhance the plot of the story. I doubt very much, however, if the system of *gĕʾullâ*, in any of its known forms, was at all applicable to the circumstances of the story as the author himself fashioned it. After all, it is he who projected so many deaths into the life of a single family within a short span of time. In so doing, he created an ideal situation for applying the law of inheritance, not for invoking the duty of redemption!

These two legal systems, inheritance and redemption, shared the same social parameter, the *mišpāḥâ*, and had similar objectives. But in any given situation defined by law they were, nevertheless, mutually exclusive. If redemption applied, this meant that an owner of land needed assistance from a clan relative. If no such owner was alive, how could redemption take place?

Technically, Elimelech's field would have fallen to his sons, Mahlon and Kilyon, who apparently survived him. When they died, leaving no heirs, the provisions of Num 27:8–9 would have gone into effect. That priestly code, set forth in the context of "the daughters of Zelophehad," seems to embody widely held views on the succession of inheritance in biblical Israel. When one died without surviving heirs, his brothers became his heirs; but Mahlon and Kilyon had no brothers, or else the levirate would have applied to both Ruth and Orpah, theoretically. The next in line would have been the uncles of Mahlon and Kilyon, i.e., the brothers of Elimelech. But he had no brothers. Those who claim, quite transparently, that Boaz and the other redeemer were Elimelech's actual

---

13 David Halivni Weiss ("The Use of קנה in Connection with Marriage," *HTR* 57 [1964] 244–48) makes a good point about usage of the verb *qānâ* in early Rabbinic texts, such as the Mishnah. He finds that it is not used there to connote the acquisition of a wife *per se*, but only when marriage is associated with other legal actions involving purchase.

brothers, and who translate *ʾaḥînû* in Ruth 4:3 as "our brother," are deliberately forcing the text. One actual brother would hardly be described as more closely related than the other (Ruth 3:12–13; 4:4). Moreover, if Boaz and the other man were Elimelech's actual brothers, they would have inherited the field on this basis, so what need was there for redemption? Finally, as clan relatives, more likely cousins of Elimelech, Boaz and the unnamed redeemer would have inherited the field in due course.

Some scholars have proposed that Naomi enjoyed special rights to the field of her late husband, such as might have been the case had the field in question been granted to Naomi by her father or brothers at the time of her marriage to Elimelech. Normally, such property was for the benefit of her children, but since these had died without surviving heirs, the land might have reverted to Naomi.

Such hypothetical constructions result from the effort to reconcile what is related in Ruth with Israelite law, and even with what is only presumed to be Israelite law! Had the author of Ruth truly intended to represent the legal situation faced by Naomi precisely and accurately against the background of the law codes, he would have told quite a different story.

When Naomi returned to Judea with Ruth and informed the good people of Bethlehem of all the tragedy that had befallen her family, it would have been determined that the abandoned field of Elimelech belonged to the relative who was next in the line of inheritance. That may have led directly to the unnamed redeemer, and to Boaz himself. After all, if they were the only redeemers around, they might well have been the only clan-relatives as well! I would go so far as to agree with those who suggest that the duty of *gĕʾullâ* extended to support of a childless widow like Naomi; but this would not imply any change of legal status as far as she was concerned. Widows did not inherit their husbands' wealth in biblical Israel.

The initial preconditions for invoking the duty of redemption are not present in our author's story. Our author merely utilized the precise legalities of the system of *gĕʾullâ* in order to epitomize the laudable motivations and purposes of that system. His meta-legal attitude is perhaps revealed most clearly in the fact that he proclaims the son born to Ruth and Boaz as the ultimate *gôʾēl* of Naomi:

> Blessed be Yahweh, who has not deprived you of a redeemer (*gôʾēl*) today, and may his name be perpetuated among the Israelites![14] He shall restore your vitality and maintain you in your dotage. For your daughter-in-law, who showed her love for you, bore him—she who has become more valuable to you than seven sons! (Ruth 4:14–15)

[14] H. Ch. Brichto ("Kin, Cult and Afterlife," *HUCA* 44 [1973] 1–54) proposed this translation for the formula *wĕyiqqārēʾ šĕmô bĕyiśrāʾēl*, in the context of a discussion of the continuity of the family and clan as a major concern in biblical Israel. This rendering in Ruth 4:14 was adopted in *The Five Megilloth and Jonah* (Philadelphia: Jewish Publication Society of America, 1969).

In Ruth, the system of *gĕʾullâ* functions as a structure, a framework for the story. What is remarkable about our author is that he fashioned a plot that virtually obviates the legal applicability of *gĕʾullâ*, as he certainly understood the system, while at the same time utilizing its legal principles to stimulate magnanimous acts on the part of Boaz. He adroitly introduces the theme of redemption by having Naomi inform Ruth, relatively early in the story, that Boaz is *gōʾălēnû*, "our redeemer" (Ruth 2:20).[15] When he subsequently activates the legalities of that system, the reader is less likely to question his major premise, i.e., that *gĕʾullâ* actually applies. Once this legal leap is accomplished, our author invests his story with legal detail which encourages credibility.

A similar approach should enable us to perceive how our author uses the theme of levirate marriage. He took his cue from Ruth's predicament as the childless widow of one of Elimelech's sons. Officially, there was nothing to tie Ruth to the family of her late husband, whose only brother had also died childless. A levitate union was out of the question. And yet, Ruth insists on sharing the fate of her mother-in-law, Naomi. As noted long ago by J. A. Bewer, there is a veiled allusion to the levirate in the taunting words of Naomi to her daughters-in-law near the beginning of the story.[16] Naomi bitterly laments her inability to bear additional sons whom her daughters-in-law might marry someday (Ruth 1:11–12). One is reminded of Tamar, patiently waiting for little Shelah to reach maturity (Gen 38:11).

A more obvious reference to the levirate is, of course, the mention of Tamar in the marriage blessing.

> May your household be as the household of Perez, whom Tamar bore to Judah (Ruth 4:12).

This suggests a parallel between Ruth and Tamar. Tamar was a woman who took bold initiatives on her own behalf, which resulted in preserving the family line of Judah when it was threatened with extinction. Her acts were a risk to her own life and compromised her father-in-law, but they achieved the effective goal of the levirate, through a substitution. Ruth also took initiatives that were bold, in their own way. Whether or not a sexual liaison occurred between Ruth and Boaz at the threshing-floor, and the sexual allusions in the text certainly allow for this conclusion, Ruth's action in going to Boaz at night and placing

---

[15] Naomi may have been following custom in referring to Boaz as a redeemer, because the term *gôʾēl* may have been part of the nomenclature of the clan. A relative would be so called because of his potential function, based on his clan relationship. I am thinking of the enigmatic term *mĕsārĕpô*, "his burner," in Amos 6:10, referring to a relative whose duty it would be to burn incense for the dead, if this interpretation is correct. The point is that this was the traditional duty of a certain relative. I wish there were some certainty as to the meaning of the rare term *môdāʿ* (Kethibh, *mydʿ*) in Ruth 2:1. Intuitively, I prefer to see it also as a relational term, with a specific meaning in the nomenclature of the clan, rather than as merely a way of referring to a friend or acquaintance.

[16] Bewer, "The Gᵉʾullah in the Book of Ruth."

herself at his feet while he slept was compromising and had to be kept secret.[17] She, too, achieved the purposes of the levirate with one who was not her *levir*, though her marriage to Boaz represented a highly laudable form of endogamy.

There is also a possible allusion to the levirate in the words Boaz spoke to Ruth at the threshing-floor:

> May you be blessed before Yahweh, my daughter. By your latter kindness (*ḥasdēk hāʾaḥărôn*) you have outdone your former one—by not attaching yourself to the young men, whether poor or rich (Ruth 3:10).

The "former" kindness refers to Ruth's initial commitment to her mother-in-law, with all this entailed. I take the reference to a "latter" kindness to mean that Ruth had kept herself available to Boaz and had not sought marriage with a man outside the clan. I find this interpretation preferable to the more romantic view that Boaz was praising Ruth for preferring him, personally, over a younger man. Throughout the story, Boaz' attentions toward Ruth are expressed in a subdued tone, and though they undoubtedly bespoke personal feelings they were not expressed as such, but rather as admiration for her virtue.[18]

If this interpretation is correct, we are reminded of the restriction stated in the levirate law, which prohibits the childless widow awaiting the *levir* from marrying outside the family (Deut 25:5). In a similar way, though the circle of relationships has been widened, Ruth awaited Boaz.

The clearest reference to the levirate occurs, of course, in Boaz' charge to the unnamed redeemer in Ruth 4:5b, and again in v. 10, in a statement of Boaz. In both verses, the relevant words are: *lĕhāqîm šēm hammēt ʿal naḥălātô*, "to confirm the title of the deceased over his estate."

The sense of *hēqîm* in this formula differs from its meaning in the levirate law. Here, *hēqîm* means: "to fulfill, confirm," the opposite of *hēpēr* "to annul, void." This meaning is elsewhere attested in legal contexts, as well as occurring in covenant language.[19]

This is hardly the sense of *hēqîm* in the levitate law of Deut 25:5–10, where it is merely the reflex of *qûm*. Thus, in Deut 25:6 we read: *yāqûm ʿal šēm ʾāḥîw hammēt*, "he shall 'stand' for the name of his deceased brother," and in v. 7 we read: *lĕhāqîm lĕʾāḥîw šēm*, "to 'raise up' a name for his brother," i.e., to produce an heir.

---

[17] See the extensive discussion in Sasson's commentary, 66–67, which provides valuable comparative material.

[18] This approximates the view of Ruth 3:10 conveyed in *The Five Megilloth and Jonah*, with p. 26, n. b.

[19] On legal usage of *hēqîm*, "to confirm, fulfill," see Num 30:14–15, relevant to the confirmation of vows already pronounced. On the synonymity of *hēqîm* and *ʿāśâ* "to accomplish," see Jer 23:20; 30:24.

The author of Ruth evoked a clear association with the levirate law, while, at the same time, putting over on his readers a semantic transaction and a syntactic shift!

The system of *gĕʾullâ* and the levitate law are the author's building-blocks. He assigns to his characters multiple roles. Most notably, Boaz functions both as *levir* and *gôʾēl*, though neither role was mandated by the actual circumstances of the story. The laws of ancient Israel served to highlight the overriding concern of the author of Ruth—the history of the royal line of Judah. From the very start, women played an important part in preserving Judah's line. The tradition of self-help which operated within the Israelite *mišpāḥâ* provided the context for the efforts of these exceptional women, from Rachel and Leah, through Tamar, and reach to Ruth, whose adventure is cast into the generations just preceding the establishment of the Davidic dynasty. *Ḥesed* was the virtue of the Israelite *mišpāḥâ*, and human acts of kindness were fully rewarded by God's *ḥesed*. This was the experience of Ruth, the Moabite woman.

On the Origins of the Aramaic Legal Formulary at Elephantine*

The late E. Y. Kutscher, writing in 1954 soon after the publication of the Brooklyn Museum Aramaic Papyri lamented the neglect of the Egyptian Aramaic materials by scholars, and pointed to several areas of inquiry, among them the legal traditions of the Ancient Near East, with respect to which these texts might prove to be pivotal.[1] Since that time there have appeared several comprehensive treatments of the Aramaic papyri, as though in response to Kutscher's call. The most notable of these are the contributions of Reuven Yaron, Bezalel Porten, and Yochanan Muffs.[2] These three works differ sharply in their approaches to the Aramaic material.

Yaron's study is strictly legal: providing a descriptively systematic analysis of the relevant documents through a breakdown of their schemas and by their classification into the accepted legal categories—marriage and divorce, courts and procedure, law of property, etc. Relatively little attention is paid to historical and comparative considerations.[3] Porten's study, on the other hand, is historical and social, and treatment of the legal system is only incidental to its overall purpose, which was to characterize the Elephantine community.[4] Muffs has done most for a proper assessment of the Elephantine legal system within the perspective of comparative Near Eastern law, pursuing a philological-exegetical method. In the first instance, he sought cuneiform models with which Aramaic

---

* Originally published in Jacob Neusner (ed.), *Christianity, Judaism and Other Greco-Roman Cults: Studies for Morton Smith at Sixty*, part 4: *Judaism after 70* (4 vols.; Studies in Judaism in Late Antiquity 12; Leiden: E. J. Brill, 1975), pp. 37–54. Reprinted with permission from Brill.

[1] E. Y. Kutscher, *JAOS* 74, 1954, 233f., especially 243–48.

[2] R. Yaron, *Introduction to the Law of the Aramaic Papyri*, (= *LAP*), Oxford, 1961; B. Porten, *Archives from Elephantine*, U. of California, 1968; Y. Muffs, *Studies in the Aramaic Legal Papyri from Elephantine*, Leiden, 1969 (= *SALPE*). Less directly relevant, but important, is the contribution of S. Kaufman, *The Akkadian Influences on Aramaic and the Development of the Aramaic Dialects*, Yale U. dissertation, 1971. Also note M. Silverman, *Jewish Personal Names in the Elephantine Documents: A Study in Onomastic Development*, Brandeis U. dissertation, 1967, and cf. *idem*, *JAOS* 89, 1969, 691–709.

[3] Yaron in *LAP*, ch. 9 (99–113) discusses "Some Problems of Comparison," and in ch. 10 (114–18) "Sources and Contacts." As will become evident, Yaron dealt only sketchily with the comparative dimension.

[4] Porten's work is divided into several sections: "Political and Economic Life," "Religion," "Family and Communal Life," etc.

formularies and terms could be associated. He also attempted an historical reconstruction of the origins of Aramaic law.[5]

All of this ferment, which goes beyond Aramaic to include Demotic studies, has had only limited value for the question of the proximate origins of the legal system operative at Elephantine.[6] To identify these origins would require additional source materials in the Aramaic language from the period preceding the Elephantine corpus, and such materials are presently scarce. Our purpose here is to focus attention on the problem of proximate origins, necessarily in a limited way. Certain paradigmatic examples of this problem will be discussed in the hope of clarifying the methodological apparatus available for historical analysis.

I. An Apparent Old Babylonian Survival: The Ṭyb Lbby Complex

The major part of Muff's study is devoted to a clause quite frequent in the Aramaic legal documents: *ṭyb lbby* "My heart is satisfied," and variants of this formula. To understand the problem to which Muffs addresses himself, we cite an example of this clause in context:

> *wʾnt ydnyh wmḥsyh bny ʾsḥwr hwṭbtm lbbn bʾlk nksyʾ wṭyb lbbn bgw mn ywmʾ znh ʿd ʿlm ʾnh mnḥm wʿnnyh rḥyqn ʾnḥnh mnk mn ywmʾ znh ʿd ʿlm*
>
> And you Yedoniah and Mehasiah, sons of Ashor, have satisfied our heart with these goods, and *our heart is satisfied therewith* from this day and forever. We, Menaḥem and Ananiah, are removed from you from this day and forever.[7]

The document in question concerns the disposition of contested goods, i.e. litigation. The defendants "satisfy" the plaintiffs concerning the contested goods, and it is this statement of "satisfaction" which is the core of the matter

---

[5] In *SALPE*, ch. 7, Muffs presents his thoughts on the development of Aramaic law, including some insights on Neo-Assyrian factors relevant to Elephantine law. The relatively brief treatment actually opens up a new line of inquiry for Muffs, and is not entirely consistent with his central findings on the *ṭyb lbby* complex, and its Old Babylonian counterpart, *libbašu ṭāb*. Muffs is actually operating on two levels, which he never fully co-ordinates: a) A study of the philological affinities of an Aramaic and an Old Babylonian formula, and b) The proximate origins of Elephantine law in later cuneiform traditions. For the latter also see his *Addenda and Corrigenda*, 105–208, and n. 38, further.

[6] In *SALPE*, ch. 6, Muffs summarizes the Demotic evidence. His main authority is E. Seidl. See *ibid.* 222, bibliography s.v. Seidl, E. (3 entries). Porten, *op. cit.* 334–43, presents a breakdown of the comparative schemas of the Aramaic and Demotic texts which, although useful, involves some re-positioning of the actual order of Demotic clauses (*ibid.* 340, n. 19). Kutscher, *op. cit.* 247, comments on the limited influence of Demotic on Aramaic law.

[7] *AP* 20:8–10. See Muffs' discussion in *SALPE* 30–31, and see our n. 8. On the notion of removal (*rḥq*), see further, n. 36.

discussed by Muffs. This clause occurs in eleven legal texts.[8] Significantly, it does not occur in documents of gift or grant, but only in contexts where final, binding legal activities are recorded, and not voluntary acts.[9] Muffs demonstrates through separate, independent analysis of the Aramaic and Old Babylonian evidence that Aramaic *ṭyb lbby* and Old Babylonian *libbašu ṭāb* "His heart is satisfied" are functionally and semantically equivalent. Although the third person formulation predominates in Old Babylonian, Muffs was able to find a rare, first person occurrence, as well.[10] As a third factor, Muffs discusses the Demotic counterpart *dj . k-mtj ḥ3tj(.iʾ)* "You have caused my heart to be satisfied," and related forms.[11]

The correspondence of these three clauses had been noticed before Muffs, but it is he who has analyzed them in a new way, and has shown them to be more significant than was previously thought.[12] San Nicolò, and other students of Old Babylonian law had taken *libbašu ṭāb* to be volitional, i.e. a statement which merely expresses agreement or satisfaction with respect to actions already performed.[13]

Essentially, this was Seidl's understanding of the Demotic counterpart.[14] Yaron, writing some years before Muffs' study, considered Elephantine *ṭyb lbby* as merely an expression, devoid of particular legal significance, although he did show some interest in its curious history.[15] Subsequently, when Yaron was faced with Muffs' comprehensive study of this formula, he was forced, as it were, to

---

[8] Cf., in addition to *AP* 20, the following: *AP* 6:11–12, 14:5–6, text 67, *BMAP* 1:4, 3:6–7, 12:6. In contexts other than conveyance, cf. *AP* 2:9, 14:5–6, 15:5–6, 15, *BMAP* 7:5. For convenience, we refer to this clause as *ṭyb lbby*, in the 1st sing. passive construction, although it also occurs in the active + passive construction, and in the 2nd sing., passive construction. All forms are surveyed in *SALPE* 30–5, 51–62.

[9] This is the burden of Muffs' contrast of *ṭyb lbby* with the volitional formula *yhbt ... brḥmn* "I have given in affection", i.e. voluntarily (*SALPE*, 36–50). Cf. our discussion, further in nn. 27–28. Even in those contexts which Muffs considers atypical, as for example *AP* 2, and 14 and 15, where the delivery of goods and dowry litigations are involved, the use of *ṭyb lbby* conveys obligations, and there is nothing voluntary about the legal arrangements projected. Also cf. *SALPE* 56–8.

[10] See *SALPE* 176, and note an Old Babylonian deed from Sippar where we read: *li-*[*i*]*b-bi ṭāb*[ab] "My heart is satisfied" (*CT* IV:7a = M. Schorr, *Urkunden des altbabylonischen Zivil- und Prozessrechts*, 1913, no. 310).

[11] See n. 6, above.

[12] According to Muffs, E. Pritsch was the first to note this correspondence. See *SALPE* 150, nn. 1–4 for literature.

[13] See Muffs' summary of previous work on *libbašu ṭāb* in *SALPE* 63–5.

[14] See *SALPE* 154–7 on views of Seidl and Griffith as to the volitional connotation of the Demotic counterpart of *ṭyb lbby*.

[15] *LAP* 105–6, 108, 122, and especially 123–4.

take it more seriously. Even then, in a critical review of Muffs' book, he persisted in arguing against its legal importance.[16]

The first important step in Muffs' treatment is, therefore, his demonstration that *ṭyb lbby*, along with its Old Babylonian and Demotic counterparts, is a quittance formula, and not merely a statement of satisfaction, in a volitional sense. According to Muffs, *ṭyb lbby* reflects two aspects: 1) Adequate compensation has been received or legal performance accomplished. 2) No further claims will be entertained (= quittance).[17] Muffs arrives at this definition of the provenance of *ṭyb lbby* in several steps. He summarizes its distribution in documents representing the categories of sale and litigation, and in those recording reactions to the receipt of goods and funds.[18] He then proceeds to show the importance of the operative section in the Aramaic texts. In Old Babylonian sale documents, the *Schlussklauseln* are more important than the operative section because these documents were formulated objectively, and little information was provided in the operative section. The Aramaic documents, on the other hand, are formulated subjectively, and the operative section is, therefore, of greater consequence. The failure to take this distinction into account may have impeded a proper appreciation of the function of *ṭyb lbby* as a quittance formula.[19]

In his critical review, Yaron attacks Muffs' interpretation of *ṭyb lbby* as a quittance formula.[20] All of Muffs' analysis would be of considerably less importance if *ṭyb lbby* and its Old Babylonian antecedent turned out to be nothing more than expressions of agreement with no orientation toward the future legal relationship of the parties. Adopting a strictly legal definition of quittance, Yaron sees it as encompassing three factors: 1) Renunciation of rights, 2) Transfer of rights, and 3) Creation of binding obligations between the parties, i.e. the future orientation of quittance. Yaron maintains that in two of the texts cited by Muffs as evidence for taking *ṭyb lbby* as a quittance formula, *AP* 6 and 14, all we actually have is the renunciation of a previous claim, subsequent to the performance of an oath, but not the future-oriented obligations requisite to the concept of quittance. How, asks Yaron, can the provenance of *ṭyb lbby* as a quittance

---

[16] Yaron's important review is in *RB* 77, 1970, 408–16, and see his shorter discussion in *Israel Law Review* 4, 1969, 588–91. Also see the comments of E. Y. Kutscher on the linguistic implications of Muffs' analysis of *ṭyb lbby* in "Aramaic," *Linguistics in South-West Asia and North Africa* (*Current Trends in Linguistics* 6), Mouton, 1969, 363–4, and the review of Muffs by K. R. Veenhof, *Journal for the Study of Judaism*, 5, 1974, 87–90.

[17] *SALPE* 28–9, and particularly 43–50.

[18] *SALPE* 25–6, and survey of usage in other than conveyance documents, 51–62.

[19] See *SALPE* 17–25 where Muffs clarifies the contrast between Old Babylonian and non-Old Babylonian traditions in Akkadian documents from Susa, Kultepe, Assyria, Nuzi, Ugarit, etc. The Aramaic documents are to be identified with the non-Old Babylonian traditions regarding the character of their operative sections.

[20] See Yaron, *RB* 77, pp. 409f.

formula be maintained if such is not provided for in all of the texts cited in evidence?[21]

As a matter of method, Muffs' argument could stand on the rest of his considerable evidence, even if he missed the mark in two texts. The fact is, however, that *ṭyb lbby* does function as a quittance formula in *AP* 6 and 14, if one understands these texts properly. *AP* 6 deals with litigation over a piece of property. Party *A*, currently in possession of the property, swears to *B*, pursuant to a complaint by *B*, that the land is his, and does not belong to *B*. Then *B* states that this oath "satisfies" him on the matter, and he renounces any claim to the land, agreeing not to bring suit against *A* at any future time.

As Muffs explains, based on a positional analysis, the oath of purgation in litigations, such as *AP* 6 and 14, has a function parallel to that of compensation in cases of sale. Thus, *yhbt ly dmwhy wṭyb lbby bgw* "You have paid me its price, and my heart is satisfied therewith" is parallel to: *ymʾt ly ṭyb lbby* "You have taken an oath on my behalf, and my heart is satisfied".[22] In the case of *AP* 6 there is particular indication of binding obligations undertaken for the future, a point earlier noted by Cowley, who cited the provisions *AP* 8:23f. in this connection.[23] From *AP* 8 we learn that when the same property is later transferred by party *A*, the claimant upheld in *AP* 6, to his daughter as a gift, reference is made to the oath taken by *A*, which satisfied *B*, as well as to a *spr mrḥq* "a bill of removal/dissociation" provided by *B* to *A* in the earlier litigation. This is all mentioned in substantiation of *A*'s right to grant said property to his daughter. What emerges is that the oath and the resultant *spr mrḥq* (not explicitly mentioned in *AP* 6, but implied therein in lines 15–16) served as title, and as the basis for the future transfer of rights.[24]

AP 14 concerns the division of property, or more precisely, the settlement of a property dispute following upon a divorce. The oath of purgation is taken by the wife to the effect that the property in question was hers by right, and the husband is "satisfied" by this oath. In practical terms this meant that he agreed to restore the dowry to his estranged wife. So, here as well, the statement of satisfaction goes beyond the renunciation of previous claims to embrace obligations for the future.[25]

In studying legal documents one must always perceive the implicit background involved. In *AP* 6 we observe a situation once removed from an initial transfer, hence oath instead of compensation. In *AP* 14 there is also a background which generates a settlement, and one must ask what the force of a

---

[21] *Ibid.* 409.

[22] Note Muffs' comment on *AP* 6 in *SALPE* 32, and cf. *ibid*., 46. The oath of purgation, so-called, also figures in *AP* 14, and see our discussion of *AP* 14, further, and n. 25.

[23] See *AP* p. 15, introduction to text no. 6, and p. 21, introduction to text no. 8.

[24] *AP* 6:15–16 reads: *wʾnt rḥyq mn kl dynʾ zy yqblwn ʿlyk ʿldbr ʾrʿʾ zk* "And you are *removed* from any claim that they may bring against you in regard to this land."

[25] See *SALPE* 32, 48, 61–2 for Muffs' discussion of *AP* 14.

statement of satisfaction is in such a context. The effect of the oath was to compel further action on the part of the husband.[26]

Yaron also failed to see the point of Muffs' contrast between the volitional clause par excellence, *yhbt ... brḥmn* "I have given in affection (= willingly)" common to the documents of gift, and *ṭyb lbby*, which never occurs in such contexts.[27] The clause *yhbt ... brḥmn* projects the concept of voluntariness. Initial willingness to part with something of value could be cited subsequently as a basis for voiding that act, by stating that it was accomplished without obligation. A change of heart could be a basis for retrieval, and as a consequence deeds of gift normally contain additional statements protecting the recipient from this loophole, and guaranteeing the grant against efforts by the donor or by others to retrieve it. In contrast, the *ṭyb lbby* formula conveys the finality of the transfer, and is not part of the volitional framework, at all.[28]

All in all, we consider Muffs' in-depth analysis of the *ṭyb lbby* complex, and of its Demotic and Old Babylonian counterparts a reliable demonstration of the function of this formulaic complex in the quittance role. In addition, the affinities between the Aramaic and Old Babylonian clauses are precise and compelling. We thus have a central and significant Aramaic formula linked with the diction of an Old Babylonian formula. Ironically, this very conclusion raises a central problem for historical inquiry: Not only is the Old Babylonian period far removed in time from that of the Elephantine documents, which leaves us with no certain link, since the formula *libbašu ṭāb* disappears from legal parlance after the Old Babylonian period, but it seems that it was at least partially replaced by other terms of quittance! As Muffs shows, *zakû* "pure, quit" and related forms, whose usage was quite diffuse down through Neo-Babylonian times, were probably expanded to fill the void left by the disuse of *libbašu ṭāb* after the Old Babylonian period.[29] Strangely enough, Aramaic *zky* does not occur in the legal documents at Elephantine, although it is prominent in later Ara-

[26] See *SALPE* 83.

[27] See R. Yaron, *RB* 77, pp. 415f. for criticism of Muffs' treatment of the volitional clause, and *SALPE* 40–3, for Muffs' interpretation of it.

[28] See *SALPE* 43–50 and note the interaction of *ṭyb lbby* as a quittance formula with notions of *rḥq* "removal." Muffs' point is that even if not followed up by a statement of "removal," which connotes explicit quittance, *ṭyb lbby* has the force of quittance, nonetheless. On the need for additional stipulations in gift documents, see *SALPE* 40–3, and especially discussion on 42–3, and 42, n. 1. Examples of the wish to retrieve a gift, cited by Muffs, are *AP* 18:2–3, *BMAP* 7:41–2, 10:9–10. Thus, in *AP* 18:23 we read: *kzy nksyʾ ʾlh wkspʾ zy ktybn bsprh znh brḥmn yhbt lkm kʿn ṣbyt ʾhnṣl hm* "Whereas I give these goods and silver set forth in this document voluntarily, now I desire to retrieve them." The clause which protects against such an eventuality is: *lʾ nkhl nršh l-* "We shall not be able to institute suit against"- your sons, etc. See *BMAP* 12:26, and discussion by Muffs, *SALPE* 41–3.

[29] See *SALPE* 74, n. 2, and *ibid.*, 123–28. Also cf. *CAD Z*, 23f., s.v. *zakû* (adj.), especially 24–5, s.v. *zakû*, 5. Also cf. *ibid.* 25f., s.v. *zakû* (v.), and 26–9, including D-stem, *zukku*.

maic and Syriac legal formularies as a term of quittance.[30] At Elephantine there are a few attestations of the verb *pṣl* generally taken to connote the "cleansing" of claims.[31]

This, then, is the crux of the historical problem emerging from Muffs' study: How can we account for the legalistic utilization of what appears to be an Aramaic rendition of a formula in Akkadian, which disappears after the Old Babylonian period? Further: How can we account for the fact that the prime successor to Old Babylonian *libbašu ṭāb*, i.e. *zakû*, and related forms, attested down through Neo-Babylonian times, and as well in later Aramaic and Syriac documents as *z/dky*, was not utilized at Elephantine, whereas an older, vanished formula was?

At the present time there is no adequate answer to this question. We can pretty well rule out the Demotic formula as the proximate origin of the Aramaic, a point to which we will return in another connection. Interestingly, Seidl and other students of the Demotic materials had assumed an Old Babylonian antecedent for the Demotic counterpart to *ṭyb lbby*. Whereas this is not likely, the Demotic scholars did perceive the originally non-Demotic character of this quittance formula. The furthest that Muffs can go is to characterize the use of *ṭyb lbby* at Elephantine as archaizing, the conscious imitation of old forms which survived, presumably, in the "fringe" traditions of cuneiform law, and were either known to the Elephantine Aramaic writers, themselves, or transmitted to them by preceding Aramaic writers.[32]

There is, in our opinion, only one possible alternative to Muffs' historical reconstruction: It could be argued that since notions of "satisfaction, agreement", expressed in terms of "goodness of heart" persist in Akkadian in non-legal usage, and in Phoenician and Hebrew, as well, the Aramaic writers might have merely specialized the phrase *ṭyb lbby* from proximate Akkadian or West-Semitic usage, without any awareness on their part that it had a former history as

---

[30] The only attestation of Aramaic *zky* at Elephantine is in Aḥiqar. See *AP* p. 213, s.v. Aḥiqar, col. III, line 46: *ʾp ʾnh ʾḥyqr zy qdmn šzbk mn qṭl zky* "Moreover, I am (that) Aḥiqar who formerly rescued you from an undeserved (= innocent) death." Cf. Deuteronomy 21:8: *dām nāqi* "innocent death." This has nothing to do with the "cleansing" of claims, in a strict sense. The few occurrences of Aramaic *z/dky* at Elephantine have nothing to do with "cleansing" of claims in legal actions, but connote either "pure" in the cultic sense (*AP* 21:6), or "innocent" as in Aḥiqar. See *AP* p. 213, s.v. col. III, line 46: *qṭl zky* "an undeserved (= innocent) death," as in Deuteronomy 21:8: *dām nāqi* "innocent death." The reading *dkyn* in *AP* 27:12 is uncertain, but even if accepted, yields the sense of "free of blame", for damage which occurred during an attack. For a review of literature on *z/dky* in Aramaic and Syriac in legal contexts, sec J. Goldstein, *JNES* 28, 1966, 1f., and *ibid.* 12, s.v. lines 12–15 in the Syriac bill of sale from Dura. Goldstein cites, *inter alia*, E. Y. Kutscher, *Tarbiz* (Hebrew), 19, 1948, 125.

[31] See Kutscher, *JAOS* 74, p. 240, and his earlier study on *pṣh* in *Tarbiz* (Hebrew), 17, 1945–46, 53–6. According to Kutscher, *pṣl* represents: *pṣ*(*h*) + *l* > *pṣl*.

[32] Muffs' awareness of this problem is evidenced in the Addenda, *SALPE* 201, s.v. p. 127.

a legal formula.[33] After all, it is to be assumed that this is what occurred in the first place, in the Old Babylonian period, or even earlier: A general expression assumed a specialized, legal sense without ceasing to function in the non-technical vocabulary, as well. On grounds of method, Muffs should have investigated the non-legal reflexes of the motif of "goodness of heart" as satisfaction (and agreement), and the process by which it had been appropriated as a legal quittance formula. It was, of course, necessary for him to isolate the legal terminology for a proper analysis, and failure to do so had, indeed, hampered earlier attempts to interpret this formula properly. Conversely, however, an awareness of the interaction of general and specialized idioms within a society or culture is basic for historical inquiry. No operative framework within a society can be divorced entirely from the overall idiom of that society.[34]

In this instance, however, there are problems to positing a re-appropriation of general idiom into the legal formulary. In two documents *ṭyb lbby* occurs as part of a more complete quittance formula, with an explicative or complement,

---

[33] As for Hebrew attestations of the notion of satisfaction, see Judges 8:20: *wayyîṭab lēb hakkôhēn* "The priest was satisfied/agreeable." This was noted by Yaron (*LAP* 106) who considered it legal usage, whereas Muffs (*SALPE* 140, n. 1) insists it is not. We agree with Muffs that it is volitional in force, but, on the other hand, it is closer to legal usage than the normal sense in Hebrew of satiety from eating and drinking, or general good cheer (Deuteronomy 28:47). The Danites offer Micah's private priest a better position, which he accepts, and this acceptance is conveyed by the idiom under discussion. Also note the Phoenician equivalent of Hebrew *ṭûb lēb(āb)* in the Karatepe inscription: *nʿm lb*. Thus we read: *wʾp bʾbt pʿln kl mlk bṣdqy wbḥkmty wbnʿm lby* "Moreover, every king elected me to 'fatherhood' by virtue of my justness, wisdom, and *generosity* (*KAI* no. 26, A:I, line 12). The sense here seems to express the quality of one who satisfies others, probably by the material prosperity he brings them. Cf. in the same inscription A:I, line 6: *sbʿ wmnʿn* "plenty and prosperity," or perhaps a sense derived from hendiadys.

Akkadian attests the notion of *ṭûb libbi* in many contexts. Of particular interest to us is the motif of "gladdening the heart" of the gods, characteristic of good kings from Hammurapi (*Code of Hammurapi*, prologue ii:7–9) who is termed: *mu-ṭi-ib li-ib-bi Marduk* (cf. *SALPE* 141, and sources discussed), to Nebuchadnezzar who is called: *mu-ṭi-ib li-ib-bi-šu-un* (i.e. of the gods, his patrons). See S. Langdon, *Die Neubabylonischen Königsinschriften*, 1912, no. 7, col. I:5. Now, if Muffs argues for a quasi-legal interpretation of the Hammurapi characterization, he should be interested in later attestations of the same! Also see the use of *ṭûb libbi* in Neo-Assyrian and Neo-Babylonian epistolary greetings in E. Salonen, *Die Gruss- und Höflichkeitsformulen in Babylonisch-Assyrischen Briefen*, 1967, 86 J, 88, and in the Gilgamesh epic (R. C. Thompson, *The Epic of Gilgamesh*, 1930, 12, s.v. Tablet I, col. II, line 41). I am indebted to my colleague Prof. Stephen Lieberman for pointing out these references to me from post-Old Babylonian sources. Apparently there is much more in omen literature, and in the idiom of hymns and prayers. This requires an exhaustive study.

[34] *SALPE* 28, and n. 4, and *ibid.*, Addenda, 204–5, s.v. p. 141. Muffs surveys some Old Babylonian idiomatic usages related but distinct from *libbašu ṭāb* of quittance terminology.

and it would seem that the entire statement, and not only *ṭyb lbby* can be traced to Old Babylonian usage! Thus we read: *ʿl ʿlyk wṭyb lbbk bgw* "It (= the money) has reached you, and your heart is satisfied therewith".[35] To this, Muffs compares Old Babylonian *apil libbašu ṭāb* "He is paid; his heart is satisfied," and variants of the same formula.[36]

The occurrence of *ṭyb lbby* together with its complement suggests: 1) Demotic is not the probable model for the Aramaic, because the Demotic lacks the complement. 2) The proximate re-appropriation of a non-legal expression into the Aramaic legal formulary is unlikely, because the whole formula, with the complement, bears Old Babylonian affinities. There is, however, another factor to be weighed, and that is the mode in which the Aramaic writers at Elephantine fashioned legal formulas. In their completed form, some of the legal formulas at Elephantine could be analyzed as composites, containing several originally unconnected components, each of which bears close affinities to a different stratum of the legal tradition of the ancient Near East. Thus, for example, we have in *BMAP* 2 three fairly distinct components in the general formulary of the text *ṭyb lbbn* "Our heart is satisfied" (line 6)—Old Babylonian *libbašu ṭāb*; *rḥqn mnh* "We are removed from it" (line 11)—Nuzi *irtēq* "He is removed"; and *hw šlyṭ* "He has jurisdiction" (line 12)—late Neo-Assyrian, and Neo-Babylonian *iššallaṭ* "He has jurisdiction". Even more telling is the fact that in a single statement *ṭyb lbby* may occur with an explicative most similar to a Neo-Assyrian formula. Thus in *BMAP* 12:6 we read: *wṭyb lbbn bgw zy lʾ ʾštʾr ln ʿlyk mn dmyʾ* "And our heart is satisfied therewith, in that for us none of the funds remains outstanding against you." Now, Muffs found some hitherto unnoticed analogues in Neo-Assyrian. Thus, in some texts discussed by Deller we have: x GÍN *lā rēḫe* "x shekels do not remain." Or: *me-me-ni la rēḫe* "Nothing remains." Given the similarities in context between the Aramaic and Neo-Assyrian texts in question, it would appear that here Old Babylonian links up with Neo-Assyrian. The mystery is further deepened by the fact that *zy lʾ ʾštʾr* occurs independently of the formula *ṭyb lbby* in *AP* 11:9.[37]

The possibility exists, therefore, that even in the case of *ʿl ʿlyk wṭyb lbbk* where both components of the clause appear to reflect Old Babylonian diction, we really have a composite created by the Elephantine writer or a proximate precursor, and that we do not have a coherently transmitted formula, any more than we have one in the case of *ṭyb lbby* + *zy lʾ ʾštʾr*. In fact, Muffs himself has

---

[35] The Aramaic formula occurs in *AP* 15:5, *BMAP* 7:5, and see discussion in *SALPE* 51f., 75, 173, n. 4.

[36] In addition to sources cited in n. 35, above, see *CAD A*/II, 157, s.v. *apālu* 1, 7′ (with *leqû*), and 158 for usages in Middle Assyrian, Neo-Assyrian, and Neo-Babylonian.

[37] See *SALPE* 176–9 and B. Eichler, *Indenture at Nuzi: The Personal Tidennutu Contract and Its Mesopotamian Analogues*, Yale Near Eastern Researches 5, 1973, 20, 137–8, s.v. no. 51 on *rēqu*. On *BMAP* 12 see *SALPE* 76, 173, n. 4, and 161–2, where Muffs cites K. Deller, "Zur Terminologie neuassyrischen Urkunden," *Wiener Zeitschrift für die Kunde des Morgenlandes* 57, 1961, 41f.

now lent support to this conclusion. He has shown that although Aramaic *ʿl ʿl* is functionally equivalent to Old Babylonian *apil*, it actually reflects a different diction, wherein "receipt" is expressed as "entrance." According to Muffs, this concept of "entrance", expressed in Elephantine Aramaic as *ʿl ʿl*, is to be identified with biblical Hebrew *bāʾ ʾel* "has come to", used to connote receipt of payment in legal situations.[38]

In summary, it seems likely that as regards *ṭyb lbby* in particular, the Elephantine writers knew an Aramaic, or other West-Semitic rendition of the Old Babylonian formula *libbašu ṭāb*. At the very least, it is clear that we learn most about the meaning and function of Aramaic *ṭyb lbby* from an analysis of Old Babylonian *libbašu ṭāb*. Just how far we are from certainty on the question of proximate origins may be surmised from a comparison of Muffs' complicated study, laden with historical difficulties and a paucity of corollary evidence, with the study on Nuzi indenture by Barry Eichler, who acknowledges his debt to Muffs' earlier endeavor.[39]

Like Muffs, Eichler is attempting to identify legal terminology of a later period with Old Babylonian models. His study deals with a curious term for a type of indenture, peculiar to Nuzi texts, *tidennūtu*. He shows that the legal features and terminology attendant upon the institution of that name are clearly parallel to Old Babylonian *mazzazanūtu*. He is in a position to demonstrate two important facts: 1) The term *mazzazanūtu* falls into disuse at Alalakh, where contracts of similar import from the Old Babylonian level employ this term, whereas those from the Middle Babylonian level replace it with another term. 2) The same institution, under differing names, is widely attested in the Middle Babylonian period, contemporary with the Nuzi documents.[40]

In this case, there is no problem of a significant time lapse, and there is corollary evidence for the replacement of the Old Babylonian term. Most important, Eichler is dealing with one of the probable replacements, and there is no problem of archaizing. He is also dealing with texts written in dialects of the same essential language, Akkadian, and not with two different languages, Aramaic and Akkadian, even though they are related. One reads Eichler's study with the realization that his problem was amenable to solution, whereas one reads Muffs' work with an awareness that he has chosen perhaps the most complicated problem in the Aramaic legal formulary, from an historical point of view, and yet the most exciting one for philological study.

---

[38] Y. Muffs, "Two Comparative Lexical Studies," *JANES* 5, (*The Gaster Festschrift*), 1973, 287f. Muffs calls attention to the usage of *bāʾ ʾel* in Gen 43:23 and Num. 32:19.

[39] B. Eichler, *op. cit.*, and note therein reference to Muffs' study, 10, n. 1 and especially 48, and nos. 2–4.

[40] See Eichler's conclusions summarized *ibid.*, 100–101.

II. Boundary Descriptions in the Aramaic Legal Papyri: The Persistence of a Tradition

The philologian tends to choose materials for study which afford him the greatest opportunity for textual explication. The historian gravitates to materials which afford him the greatest degree of control, holding out the potentiality for a reconstruction of historical situations and developments, and for tracing the history of institutions. Having summarized an unusual example of philological research, let us now attempt to select materials from the Elephantine Aramaic corpus as the historian would, with our objective of identifying proximate origins always in mind.

That feature of the Aramaic legal papyri from Egypt which most adequately meets the demands of the historian is the convention of boundary descriptions applied to parcels of real estate at Elephantine, whereby two of the four directions in the description are expressed as "upper, above", and "lower, below", respectively. We cite an example of the convention under discussion:

> *whʾ ʾlh tḥmy bytʾ zk ... lʿlyh lh A, ltḥtyh lh B, mwʿh šmš lh C, lmʿrb šmš lh D.*
>
> And behold, these are the boundaries of that house ... At the upper end of it (= Northward of it) is *A*, at the lower end of it (= Southward of it) is *B*; to the East of it is *C*, to the West of it is *D*.[41]

In his review of *BMAP*, H. L. Ginsberg sought to clarify the basis for this convention.[42] That "upper" designated North, and "lower" South had been verified on independent grounds by Kraeling, and others, (in contradiction to suggestions emanating from some Demotic scholars that "upper" meant South), based on the identification of buildings and roads adjacent to certain properties so delineated.[43] In such terms, Ginsberg logically sought an explanation for this manner of description in the immediate environment of Elephantine, and tentatively proposed that since islands tend to slope toward the water's edge, and since the fortress at Elephantine was, in fact, situated at the Southern end of the island, "uptown" would be to the North, and "downtown" to the South.[44]

In view of evidence that has since come to light, and upon examination of the evidence referred to only cursorily by Kraeling,[45] it seems to us more likely, even if initially less logical, that the characterization of "upper" as North, and

---

[41] *BMAP* 3:7–10, and cf. in other *BMAP* texts: 4:6–8, 9, 6:5–8, 9:6–9, 13, 10:3–6, 12:7–9, 15–21, 13:5f. and in *AP* 5:4–5 (*ʿlyh* only), 6:7–11, 8:4–8, 14:13–15, 25:5–8. The directions "upper" and "lower" are sometimes also used in the measurements. S. Kaufman, *op. cit.* (above, n. 2) 128–9, regards *taḫūmu* "boundary" as a West-Semitic loanword in Akkadian, rather than the reverse, which is the view of Kraeling (*BMAP* p. 160, s.v. 3:7). The question of origin is still open.

[42] H. L. Ginsberg, *JAOS* 74, 1954, 154, and see *SALPE* 34, n. 3, and literature cited.

[43] For a recent discussion, see Porten, *op. cit.*, 308–10, and also cf. *BMAP* pp. 76–8.

[44] See n. 42.

[45] See *BMAP* p. 78, and nn. 7–10.

"lower" as South at Elephantine in real estate boundary descriptions, is not to be explained as a reflex of the immediate Egyptian environment. Rather it represents the extension into Egyptian Aramaic formulation of an older, non-Egyptian tradition which persisted among the Aramaic writers, and which resisted the usual perceptions of the Egyptian environment common to documents from Egypt in several languages. In effect, Ginsberg's interpretation does not conflict with the evidence to be studied, but there is more to the story. The Elephantine writers were, in fact, being insular about their expressions for directions, but not exactly in the way that Ginsberg suggested!

Fitzmyer, and later Porten, both refer to the fact that in the Old Aramaic inscription from Sefire, dated about the middle of the eighth century B.C.E., we find the descriptive phrase: *ʿly ʾrm wtḥth* "upper Aram and its Lower part."[46] In this geographical reference to Syria, "upper" must certainly refer to the Northern part of Syria, and "lower" to its Southern part. For Porten, the occurrence of this description in an earlier Aramaic source served as corroboration of his independent findings relevant to buildings and roads at Elephantine. Geographical descriptions are not, however, the same as descriptions of individual parcels of real estate, and some comment is necessary on the probable origins of the designation of "upper" as North, and "lower" as South.

This descriptive convention most probably derives from the courses of the central river or rivers in a country or region. In this context, "upper" is related to the sense of "upstream." With the exception of the Nile, which flows in a generally South-to-North direction, the major rivers of the Near East (and elsewhere) flow in a generally North-to-South direction. More precisely, the Tigris and the Euphrates, especially the latter, flow in a Northwest-to-Southeast direction. As a result, in cuneiform traditions from Old Akkadian and Sumerian onward, and down through Neo-Babylonian, some of the nominal, adverbial, and prepositional forms of the verb *elû* "to ascend" may connote "upstream." This is true of *ēlītu* (n.) "upstream", used in contrast to *warittu* "downstream".[47] Similarly, *eliš* (adv.) may mean "upstream", in contrast to *šapliš* "downstream", and the same is true of *elēn* (prep.), and *elēnu* (adv.) [48] Also note the adjective *elû*, used in contrast to *šaplu*, and finite verbal forms of *elû* "to ascend", both of which may convey the notion of "upstream".[49] There is considerable evidence in cuneiform

---

[46] See Porten, *op. cit.*, and J. A. Fitzmyer, *The Aramaic Inscriptions of Sefire*, 1967, s.v. I A:6.

[47] See *CAD E*, 99–100, s.v. *ēlītu* (subst.), attested in Old Babylonian. Especially note: *ana wa-ri-it-ti ša Larsam* "for downstream travel to Larsa" (*TCL* 10, 93:7).

[48] *CAD E*, 95f., s.v. *eliš*, especially 97, s.v. *eliš* 2, b, and note references to particular localities and waterways. For *elēn* (prep.) see *ibid.* 83, s.v. *elēn* 2, and again note references to particular localities, and contrast *šaplānu* "below, downstream." For the form *elēnu*, see *ibid.* 85, s.v. *elēnu* 2 (Nuzi, Neo-Assyrian, Neo-Babylonian), and note references to waterways and rivers.

[49] *CAD E*, 114, s.v. *elû* B (adj.), with reference to the upper (and lower) Zab. Also see *ibid.* 119, s.v. *elû* (v.), 1, c, 3′: "to go upstream."

sources to indicate that "upper, above" was used to designate regions nearer the sources of the Tigris and Euphrates, and of other rivers, as well, and conversely, that "lower, below" designated regions nearer the mouths of these rivers in Southern Mesopotamia. This is, of course, merely the topographical corollary to the river orientation.[50]

In Syria, the river orientation would have been readily understandable and applicable, since the Orontes and the Euphrates flow down through Syria. That Syria should be described in the Aramaic of the Sefire inscriptions much in the same way as was Mesopotamia in cuneiform sources, is not surprising.[51]

Derivative of the river orientation with its topographical implications is the convention of upper = North, lower = South in boundary descriptions of real estate, buildings, etc., going back to Sumerian, where cartographers indicated North as "above", and South as "below".[52] To understand the connection between geographical designations of regions or locales, and boundary descriptions in individual parcels we should mention a peculiarity in some of the Nuzi texts employing the "upper-lower" terminology. One notes the pattern: *Upper, lower, North, South,* as well as: *North, South, upper, lower*. We thus have an East-to-West orientation, not North-South. Perhaps this was a reflex of the Northeast-to-Southwest course of the Diyala River, South of Nuzi, and/or of the Little Zab, North of it. In other words, where local conditions reflected a different direction of river flow, "upper" could mean East or Easterly, and "lower" West or Westerly, the latter indicating, in this instance, the area nearer the point of entry of the Diyala or Little Zab into the Tigris.[53] Other departures from the prevailing equation: upper = North, lower = South, may also be explicable by

---

[50] For geographical references to Northern provinces, upper mountains, upper and lower seas, etc. see the following: *CAD E*, 112–13, s.v. *elû* B (adj.), b) "as topographical indication." Also *ibid.* 113–4: "as geographical name." Also see *ibid.* 115f., s.v. *elû* (v.) for many correlations with the orientation of Mesopotamian rivers. Further, see: *CAD E*, 86, s.v. *elēnû* (adj.), d) 96–7, s.v. *eliš* d) and 3); and 99, s.v. *ēlītu* (subst.), 6.

[51] See M. A. Beek, *Atlas of Mesopotamia*, 1962, map 1 (opposite p. 16) for the course of the Orontes and Euphrates in Syria, and use this map for nn. 47–51, generally, and also for nn. 53–4, which are to follow.

[52] See *CAD E*, 83, s.v. *elēn*, 1, especially noting Nuzi references, and *ibid.* 84–5, s.v. *elēnu* c) and d), again with mostly Nuzi, but some Neo-Babylonian occurrences. Also see *ibid.* 86, s.v. *elēnû* (adj.), with sources in Nuzi, Neo-Assyrian, and Neo-Babylonian, and *ibid.* 113, s.v. *elû* B (adj.), b), for Neo-Babylonian references, and cf. Kraeling in *BMAP* 78, nos. 7–10. Further, see B. A. Levine, W. W. Hallo, *HUCA* 38, 1967, 55–6, glossary, s.v. KISAL.SAG.AN.NA, and literature cited, including E. Unger, *Antiquity* 9, 1935, 318f.

[53] See n. 51. The likelihood that some Nuzi boundary descriptions of real estate parcels were affected by the course of the Little Zab is further suggested by references to "the upper Zab", albeit in later, Neo-Assyrian sources. See *CAD E*, 86, s.v. *elēnû* (adj.), and *ibid.* 114, s.v. *elû* B (adj.), 31. For the pattern at Nuzi under discussion see *HSS* 19 no. 79. In the boundary descriptions (lines 4–7), and in the stipulation of measurements, which follow upon them. This text is edited by B. A. Levine, *JAOS* 88, 1968, 275–6 {*VOL 2, PP. 109–11*}.

this method.[54] These variations mean that in Mesopotamian environments, where the upper-lower terminology was native, local conditions would have affected the orientation even in real estate boundary descriptions. Not so in Elephantine Aramaic, where this terminology was not native.

In documents from Egypt, written in Akkadian and Aramaic, we note a distinction between the geographical description of the country or of its regions, on the one hand, and boundary descriptions of real estate parcels, on the other. In the former, the Egyptian environment determined the manner of description, but in the latter it seems that non-Egyptian traditions persisted. To be more specific: In an Amarna letter from Egypt, a report on the condition of troops reads in part: "From the upper land to the lower land, from East to West, his soldiers are well".[55] As is known from Demotic documents from a later date, Egyptian descriptions always begin with the South.[56] In the Amarna letter, written in Akkadian, use of "upper" and "lower" is accommodated to the Egyptian environment. So, "upper" means South and "lower" North. Similarly, in two Aramaic letters from Egypt, contemporary with the Elephantine legal papyri, we read: *bmṣryn ʿlyt wtḥtyʾ* "In upper Egypt (= Southern Egypt) and its lower (= Northern) region".[57]

On this basis, one would expect that also in boundary descriptions of houses, buildings, etc. the river orientation of Egypt would have prevailed, and yet we see the opposite, i.e. that "upper" means North, and "lower" South, in accord with the non-Egyptian usage. This strongly suggests that whereas one could have hardly ignored the culturally perceived facts of the larger Egyptian environment when speaking of the country and of its two primary regions, such perceptions were not appropriated into the conventional description of individual lots and buildings. Rather was the fairly fixed, non-Egyptian legal and cartographic tradition retained, the very tradition so evident in similar legal contexts in Mesopotamian documents, whereby upper = North, Northerly; and lower = South, Southerly.

It is not important whether or not we can specifically determine the proximate origin of this convention. The occurrence of the geographical characterization of Northern and Southern Syria as "upper and lower Aram" in the Sefire inscriptions allows for the conclusion that it existed already in Old Aramaic, although, as we have noted, a geographical description is not the same thing as a

[54] See *CAD E*, 113, s.v. *elû* B (adj.) for some variations.

[55] See J. A. Knudtzon, *Die El-Amarna Tafeln* I, 1964, 658–9, s.v. 162:80–81 (*apud CAD E*, 113, s.v. *elû* B, b), 1.

[56] See discussion in Porten, *op. cit.* 308–9, and nn. 6–7, and comparative breakdown of the schemas of the Aramaic and Demotic documents, *ibid.* 336, s.v. "Description of Property." This consistency of orientation, starting with the Southerly direction, should reinforce the reasonable conclusion that "upper" in the Amarna letter referred to Southern Egypt.

[57] See G. R. Driver, et al., *Aramaic Documents of the Fifth Century BC*, 1965, 22, s.v. no. 2:2, and cf. *ibid.* 26, s.v. no. 5:5–6.

real estate boundary description. An Akkadian origin, either in Neo-Assyrian or Neo-Babylonian is certainly possible, given the evidence of this convention in cuneiform documents from those periods, and given the overall indebtedness of both the Sefire inscriptions and the Elephantine papyri to cuneiform models.[58] What is paramount is that it is extremely unlikely that this convention at Elephantine is of Egyptian origin, or reflects Demotic usage.

We fully realize that boundary descriptions are not legal formulas in the strict sense, in the sense that a quittance formula or a term of conveyance may be considered legal. Nevertheless, this convention is part of the overall formulary of the legal texts, in the same way as are stipulations of value, descriptions of the objects involved in legal activity, etc. Whatever light can be shed on the probable origins of such elements as these will clearly assist the scholar in the larger task of reconstructing the development of Aramaic legal institutions.[59]

Bibliographical Abbreviations

AP	A. E. Cowley, *Aramaic Papyri of the Fifth Century BC*, Oxford, 1923, University Microfilms, 1964.
BiOr	*Bibliotheca Orientalis*
BMAP	E. G. Kraeling, *The Brooklyn Museum Aramaic Papyri*, Yale, 1953.
CT	*Cuneiform Texts from Babylonian Tablets*
HSS	*Harvard Semitic Series*
HUCA	*Hebrew Union College Annual*
KAI	H. Donner, W. Röllig, *Kanaanäische und Aramäische Inschriften*, Vols I–III, Wiesbaden, 1966.
LAP	R. Yaron, *Introduction to the Law of the Aramaic Papyri*, Oxford, 1961.
SALPE	*Studies in the Aramaic Legal Papyri from Elephantine*. Leiden, 1968, Ktav Publishing House, 1973.
TCL	*Textes cunéiformes du Louvre*
YOS	*Yale Oriental Series*

[58] Note that in Sefire I, C, lines 23–4, *ʿlytk* and *tḥtyth* refer to "its upper story" and "its lower story"—of a house, similar to Akkadian usage, and also Hebrew usage. For a study of some stylistic features of the Sefire inscriptions in a comparative setting, see J. C. Greenfield, *Acta Orientalia* 29, 1963, 1–18, and K. R. Veenhof, *BiOr* 20, 1963, 142–44, especially for Akkadian affinities. On general Old Aramaic-Akkadian affinities, see J. C. Greenfield's study of the Zakir inscription, in *Proceedings of the Fifth World Congress of Jewish Studies*, 1965, 174–91, and *idem*, *Hommages a André Dupont-Sommer*, 1971, 40–59 on the background of Aḥiqar, and n. 46, above.

[59] Prof. Yochanan Muffs was kind enough to discuss his own study, and related matters with me.

On the Role of Aramaic in Transmitting Syro-Mesopotamian Legal Institutions*

I am happy to be returning to one of my very first scholarly interests, the survival of ancient Near Eastern civilization, thanks to the agenda adopted by the initiators of the MELAMMU project. The many-faceted study by S. Alvesen, "The Legacy of Babylon and Nineveh in Aramaic Sources," (1998) has illustrated the possibilities of searching for ancient themes in later sources. My PhD dissertation (Brandeis, 1962) had dealt with a number of technical terms that had skipped, or had almost skipped the Hebrew Bible, and, as well, were absent from the admittedly limited Hebrew epigraphy of the biblical period. These were terms of reference attested in Ugaritic (from Syria of the late Bronze Age), but which reappeared only in the Hebrew (and Aramaic) of the Mishnah and Tannaitic literature, or at the very earliest, in the post-exilic sections of the Hebrew Bible. What fascinated me at the time was the protracted survival of ancient, Northwest Semitic terms. Since that time, the scholarly agenda has been refocused, but some of its original thrust remains. There has also been a great deal of discovery, resulting in the retrieval of Aramaic sources from the Achaemenid and Hellenistic periods, so that it is becoming more feasible to trace the route from ancient Syria-Mesopotamia to later periods via Aramaic.

The agenda that had informed the efforts of Jewish scholars, for the most part, who were acquainted with Talmudic literature and interested in its formation, was to explore an internal, Jewish question. They sought initially to account for the origins of those features of Rabbinic Judaism that did not appear to be the outgrowth either of earlier biblical institutions, nor could they be attributed to contemporary or immediately antecedent Greco-Roman institutions. Such phenomena invited inquiry as to their origins. The likelihood to be explored was that they "came from" the great Syro-Mesopotamian civilizations, mediated through Aramaic, for the most part.

It had long been recognized that much of biblical law bore the Syro-Mesopotamian stamp, as well as that of the Hittites, and of later Persian and/or Zoroastrian culture. I, myself, have devoted considerable effort to illustrating such institutional lineages for biblical cult and ritual. There was also a strong West Semitic component in biblical literature, as one would surely expect. But,

---

* Originally published in A. Panaino and G. Pettinatto (eds.), *Ideologies as Intercultural Phenomena: Proceedings of the Third Annual Symposium of the Assyrian and Babylonian Intellectual Heritage Project, held in Chicago, USA, October 27–31, 2000* (Melammu Symposia 3; Milano: Università di Bologna–IsIAO, 2002), pp. 157–166. Reprinted with permission from the Università di Bologna.

such conclusions were still compatible with A. Leo Oppenheim's telling title of 1964: *Ancient Mesopotamia: Portrait of a Dead Civilization.* After all, biblical law and cult, to name two spheres of inquiry, coincided with the later phases of the cuneiform cultures. But, what of the internally unprecedented ingredients of the Mishnah, compiled and published in Hebrew in Roman Palestine during the early Christian centuries? What of such ingredients in the Babylonian and Palestinian Talmuds of the Roman and early Byzantine/Parthian and Sassanian periods, composed in both Hebrew and Aramaic? All of these postdated the decline of Syro-Mesopotamian civilization (although not by as much time as is generally thought). Modern scholars, and some ancients, as well, have been intrigued by the striking fact that the Babylonian Talmud, in particular, was compiled on the soil of a great ancient Near Eastern civilization, but they have often been frustrated by the seeming inability to show how specific features of Talmudic law might reflect that civilization in both diachronic and synchronic terms. They have tended more often than not to explain features of the Palestinian Talmud, in particular, in terms of Greco-Roman civilization, out of obvious historical and geo-political considerations. But there are growing indications that Palestinian Jewish sources also preserve Syro-Mesopotamian ingredients, and that such were prominent features of Achaemenid and Hellenistic Palestine, not only of Achaemenid and Hellenistic Mesopotamia.

Let me cite two examples of such inquiries, before attempting to analyze how the agenda has changed in recent years, and to explore the significance of that change. I begin with a brilliant and penetrating study by Stephen Lieberman entitled: "A Mesopotamian Background for the So-Called Aggadic 'Measures' of Biblical Hermeneutics?" (1987). Lieberman focuses on several features of Talmudic interpretation, which he studies particularly in light of the earlier efforts by Saul Lieberman, the noted Talmudic scholar, to compare Rabbinic hermeneutic methods to those of the interpreters of the Greek classics, implying that Jewish sages may have learned these from their Greek contemporaries, or proximate predecessors. Stephen Lieberman demonstrates that some of these features are well attested in cuneiform literature, especially in lexical texts. He soon settles into a *tour de force* dealing with two hermeneutic methods. (1) *gematriāh*, the attribution of numerical equivalents to the letters of the alphabets, in the Greek, Hebrew, Arabic and Persian systems, and to syllables and signs in cuneiform, (2) *nôṭārîqôn*, the parsing of a word as being comprised of two homophonic components contracted, or altered in their spellings. He compares the definition of AN = *šamê* "heaven" as *ša*-A-MEŠ (= *mê*) "of water," in a cuneiform text, (CT XXV, pl. 50, line 17) with the midrashic etymologizing of Hebrew שמים as a contraction of שם "there" and מים "water," thus: "where there is water" (Babylonian Talmud, *Ḥagîgāh* 12a).

Stephen Lieberman goes on to explore the broader implications of these methods for an understanding of cuneiform culture, particularly astronomy and mathematics. He poses some pertinent questions of transmission, and argues convincingly that certain hermeneutic methods known in Rabbinic literature were also current in the Neo-Assyrian period and thereafter, and that one need not, as a consequence, conclude that they were adapted synchronically from Greek culture. At one point he has the following to say (1987:219):

> Even with the cuneiform documentation now available, it is possible to get an inkling of the fact that native Near Eastern cultures continued to flourish and contribute to the intellectual and spiritual life of the Hellenistic world long after the death of Alexander in Babylon. With the 'Aggadic' methods of exegesis as an example we can see that a Latin or Greek term could be used for something which was, ultimately, not from Rome or Athens, but from Babylon, Borsippa, or Kalah. We seem to be dealing here with things which acquired a (new) name, but that does not mean that they only came to be used after they had been provided with a Greek terminology.

Even this statement would now have to be revised in light of the recent retrieval of Aramaic texts from Qumran, for example, such as the Aramaic Enoch fragments published by Milik (1976). These add significantly to the Aramaic vocabulary in the area of astronomy, a subject I have explored elsewhere (Levine 1982). It is in the field of law, however, that we are most fortunate in finding extensive terminology in Hebrew and Aramaic that is cognate with Akkadian, as well as calques, and also what I would call Aramaic realizations of Akkadian terms, a classic example being Aramaic נדוניא "dowry," cf. Akkadian *nudunnû,* whose relevance will soon become apparent. It is to the prominent field of law that I turn, therefore, with my second example coming from my own work, a study entitled: "*Mulūgu/Melûg*: The Origins of a Talmudic Legal Institution" (Levine 1968), which represents a reworking of one section of my PhD dissertation. Technically, it has nothing to do with the role of Aramaic, although it will prove to be germane to our understanding of that role, nonetheless. As the title indicates, I was, at the time, asking where a feature of Talmudic law came from. Stephen Kaufman, in *The Akkadian Influences on Aramaic* (1974:71) had the following to say about my study:

> The aim of Levine's study of this word is to prove contemporary Mesopotamian influence on late first Millennium B.C. Palestine, but the history of the term proves no such thing. Its occurrence first at Nuzi, Ugarit and Amarna and only later in Akkadian proper indicates it to be of foreign origin, borrowed into Palestinian and Babylonian culture through separate channels. Most significantly, it cannot be shown that the Hebrew use of the word, or of the cultural institution which it signifies presupposes the development of the term which took place in the Babylonian area.

Kaufman wasn't exactly accurate about my intention, but allowing him some license in return for a degree of equivocation on my part, a more important question is whether he was right about how the term *melûg* found its way into the Mishnah. Let us examine the evidence. Ugaritic poetry attests a term *mlg* which, in context, clearly designates a marriage gift from the prospective groom to the father of his intended bride, occurring in a passage where we also find the synonymous term *mhr* = *mōhar*, and even what appears to be a Ugaritic verbal denominative of Akkadian *tirḫatu,* a frequent term for bridewealth. Elsewhere, this term, written *mulūgu* (also *mulūku,* abstract *mulūgūtu*), is attested in the period fairly contemporary with Ugarit at Nuzi, in an Amarna letter from Mitanni, and in some Middle Babylonian boundary inscriptions. Somewhat later, the transfer of wealth has changed directions, however, which eventually became true of the *mōhar*, as well, so that *mulūgu* came to designate a dowry; namely, paternal assets transferred to the daughter in conjunction with her marriage, namely, "bridewealth" (Greengus 1990). It then reappears in Neo-Babylonian texts, and later its cognate appears in the Mishnah and other Rabbinic sources, always as a Hebrew word. In the Mishnah it is limited to slaves brought by a wife into marriage, which is interesting because slaves are often classified as *mulūgu* in cuneiform documents. In cuneiform documents *mulūgu* often appears alongside *nudunnû*, Aramaic *nedûnyāʾ* "dowry," in Talmudic terminology, and may consist of, in addition to slaves, fields, houses, jewelry, and other unspecified objects. Outside the Mishnah, Tannaitic sources usually employ the combination: נכסי מלוג "*melūg* property." Kaufman lists Akkadian *nikassû* "account" as being realized in Aramaic נכסין, and then appropriated into Late Hebrew. It also appears together with *quppu*, Aramaic *quppāh* "box, wife's funds," listed by Kaufman as an Akkadian loanword in Aramaic, and which is employed in Talmudic literature.

Now, the fact that a cognate of the Hebrew term מלוג reappears in Neo-Babylonian after a long absence, and then as a Hebrew, not an Aramaic word, in Rabbinic literature, raises complex problems of transmission. I agree, of course, that it cannot be considered an Akkadian loanword into Aramaic. But the question remains as to whether Jewish legislators of the 1st or 2nd centuries C.E. knew the term מלוג directly, as a survival of ancient Northwest Semitic (Ugaritic), or whether they knew it because a cognate of the Northwest Semitic term had been preserved in the Neo-Babylonian legal vocabulary, from which it may have been taken into the Late Hebrew of the Mishnah and Talmud.

What I didn't appreciate in the 1960's was the process of the absorption, or integration of peripheral Akkadian culture into the Mesopotamian heartland, a process that began in the Neo-Assyrian period, intensifying in the Neo-Babylonian, and expanding further in the Achaemenid period, in rhythm with the Aramaization of Assryria and Babylonia, and the eventual use of Aramaic as the *lingua franca* of the Persian Empire. Kaufman's study has been of the greatest value in tracing the extent of the appropriation of Akkadian legal terms into Aramaic, generally.

It was Yochanan Muffs' work, *Studies in the Aramaic Legal Papyri from Elephantine* (1968) which brought this very process home to me, so that the occurrence of the term *mulūgu* in Neo-Babylonian legal texts became extremely significant for tracing its survival into the Hebrew, Talmudic vocabulary. Simply stated, Ugaritic *mlg*/Akkadian *mulūgu* is to be classified as a peripheral term. Whether it is a foreign term, as Kaufman maintains, is not certain, because we lack a convincing etymology. I doubt very much if this terminology would have found its way into the Mishnah if it had not first found its way into Neo-Babylonian. I cannot prove this, but I would not dismiss this likelihood, as Kaufman does. If this term should turn up in an Aramaic or Hebrew epigraphic find of the Persian period, or of the pre-Roman, Hellenistic period, for that matter, I would be persuaded that I was right about the background of its attestations in Rabbinic literature.

A. Leo Oppenheim (1955) long ago called attention to the Late Hebrew term צאן ברזל "iron sheep," in the construction: נכסי צאן ברזל "iron sheep property" which is used in Tannaitic literature in contrast to נכסי מלוג. Bridewealth that was classified as "iron sheep" represented an absolute obligation on the part of the husband. He was responsible for the established valuation of the sheep even if they died. They were sheep that could not die, financially speaking. In return, the husband was entitled to shearings, in other words to income accruing from the sheep. As the Talmud puts it: אם מתו חייב באחריותן "if they died, he remains liable for their accountable value" (Tosefta, *Bābā' Meṣī'ā'* 5:6). The same could be said of slaves. If the husband accepted them as "iron sheep" slaves, he would owe his wife their established value, if, as expected, they died while the marriage was in effect. In other words, "iron sheep" became a legal metaphor for guaranteed value, applicable to many sorts of property, just as usufruct, "eating the fruit," became a metaphor for rights to income. Oppenheim cites a number of Neo-Babylonian leases of arable land in which the lessee is to be provided with seed, ploughs and draught animals. There is the stipulation that if any of the bulls die, the lessee can claim them in court. In one contract, BE IX 29 (433/432 B.C.E.), we read: *alpê ša ina libbi imutti izaqqap* "he (the lessor) will claim in court those bulls which will die." There is also reference to *alpê ul imutti, alpê ú* ÁB.GAL *ina libbi ul imutti*. In two such leases, YOS VI 103 and 150 from the reign of Nabonidus, we read as an addition to this statement the explanatory characterization: *ša* AN.BAR (*parzilli*) *šu-nu* "they are (made) of iron."

Oppenheim mentions that San Nicolò had compared these phrases occurring in the Neo-Babylonian texts with similar ones appearing in an Old Babylonian legal document. A man gifted his daughter with the income to accrue from a cow and some sheep, which are characterized as: *ul imutta* "they shall not die." In other words, this income was permanently guaranteed. The context resembles that of Talmudic law in a remarkable way. Oppenheim goes on to mention that Schorr called attention to parallel Greek legal usage of *athanatos* "deathless," referring to a late, sixth century C.E. Egyptian papyrus where the Greek term *zoon sidellion* occurs (no connection between צאן and *zoon*!). To use Oppenheim's phrase, we have here an Old Babylonian metaphor, "coined in Mesopotamia," that reappears in Neo-Babylonian documents and subsequently in Rabbinic Hebrew.

In methodological terms, the most relevant, overall task is to pinpoint the process by which cuneiform legal language was appropriated by Aramaic scribes. Enter the Wadi Daliyeh papyri of the mid-to-late 4th century B.C.E. Douglas Gropp (2001), a major investigator of these papyri, which were found near Jericho but originate from Samaria, can actually tell us when certain clauses, known in Neo-Babylonian contracts, were appropriated and adapted by the writers of Aramaic documents such as the Wadi Daliyeh papyri. There are some remarkable examples of the same. Thus, the Aramaic formula מכיר אטיר "is paid (and) sold/received," occurs in these texts, where it indicates full payment of the sale price (Samaria Papyri 3:3, 7:5). This Aramaic formula corresponds to the Neo-Assyrian and Neo-Babylonian quittance formula: *maḫir nadin eṭir* "received, delivered, paid" (also: *eṭir nadin maḫir*). The verb listed in *CAD E*, 404–406, as *eṭēru* B "to pay" enjoyed wide utilization in Neo-Babylonian. In fact the Aramaic form אטיר is a direct loan word from Neo-Babylonian, realized as an Aramaic passive participle, a Peil form. Aramaic מכיר is more complex, because if, in a similar way, it realizes Akkadian *maḫir* "received" we would have to assume a sound shift of *ḥēṭ* → *kaph*. An alternative would be to assume that Aramaic מכיר is a Peil form of the verb *m-k-r* "to sell," hence: "sold," and represents an adaptation of the Neo-Babylonian formula, which itself represents an adaptation of the earlier formula: *maḫir nadin zaku* "received, delivered, clear." Admittedly, the verbal root *m-k-r* is rare in Aramaic, and best attested in Phoenician-Punic, and in Hebrew (Late Biblical and Post-Biblical).

More recently, J. Oelsner (1997) has discussed the legal formulae of the Wadi Daliyeh papyri in an effort to show specific divergence between Neo-Babylonian and Aramaic syntax, and even between Wadi Daliyeh and the Elephantine corpus, both Aramaic. Clearly, the evolution of legal formulae and terminology was not simply linear, or one-dimensional, with internalization of appropriated phenomena producing variation. And yet, the cuneiform background of much of the Aramaic common law tradition is everywhere evident.

Let us cite the evidence from Wadi Daliyeh. In so doing, it is important to explain that restorations in brackets are virtually certain, being based as they are on internal comparisons.

Samaria Papyrus 3, lines 3–4:

[כספא זנה ש10 דמוהי זי יהו]ענני [עבדה ז]י יקים אטיר מכיר [ויהו]פד[י]ני [בר
דליה ליהוענני זך ע]בד החסן קדמוהי

[This sum of shekels 10, his price, (namely,) of Yeho]ʿanani, [his slave, (namely,) o]f Yaqim, is paid (and) received. [And Yeho]pada[y]ni, [son of Delayah, took possession of this (same) Yehoʿanani as sl]ave, in his presence.

Samaria papyrus 7, lines 5–6:

וכסף מנ[יא 2 ש 4 דמי נישא אלך] אטיר [מכיר ו]יהוטב [לנישא אלך ההחסן
קדמיהם]

And the sum of min[as 2, shekels 4, the price of these personnel] is paid (and) [received, and] Yehoṭab [took possession of these personnel in their presence].

Muffs (1969, 125 [and n. 4]–126 [and n. 5]), called attention, before the Wadi Daliyeh papyri were edited, to the fact that the Babylonian Talmud, in *Bābāʾ Batrāʾ* 29b, and *Bābāʾ Meṣīʿāʾ* 39b, attests a term employed in slave sale agreements, Aramaic ע\איטרא (spelled with *ʾaleph* in manuscripts, with *ʿayin* in printed versions). He assumed that it was cognate with Akkadian *eṭir*, and concluded that an earlier Aramaic equivalent of the relevant Neo-Babylonian formula had probably existed. His surmise has now been corroborated by the Wadi Daliyeh papyri, so that we can pinpoint how a Neo-Babylonian formula entered Aramaic as early as the late fourth century B.C.E., and subsequently survived into the Talmudic legal vocabulary. It would be fascinating to study the Talmudic discussion of law where this term appears. This would show that the understanding of this term was very much in line with its earlier sense in Neo-Babylonian and in Achaemenid Aramaic. So often, scholars do no more than refer to Talmudic sources, and seldom actually examine these sources for what they reveal.

Babylonian Talmud, *Bābāʾ Bātrāʾ* 29b:

רמי בר חמא ורב עוקבא בר חמא זבון ההיא אמתא בהדי הדדי. מר אישתמש בה ראשונה, שלישית, וחמישית, ומר אישתמש בה שניה, רביעית וששית. נפק ערער עילוה. אתו לקמיה דרבא. אמר להו: מאי טעמא עבדיתו הכי? כי היכי דלא תחזקו אהדדי. כי היכי דלדידכו לא הויא חזקה, לעלמא נמי לא הויא חזקה. ולא אמרן אלא דלא כתוב ע/איטרא, אבל כתוב ע/איטרא קלא אית ליה.

Rami, son of Hammaʾ, and Rab ʿUqbaʾ, son of Hammaʾ, bought a slave woman jointly. One made use of her services the first, third, and fifth (years), and the other made use of her the second, fourth, and sixth (years). A claim "went out" against her. They came before Rabaʾ. He said to them: "What is the reason that you acted in this way? (Was it not) so that in this way you would not exercise possession jointly? Just as in this way (the rule of) possession is not in force with respect to you, so, too, with respect to (the rest of) the "world" (the rule of) possession is not in force. We have not so stated except where no "payment received" is written, but if a "payment received" is written, it has a "voice" (= it renders the transaction public).

Commentary

The Late Hebrew term חזקה (*ḥazzāqāh*) "tenure, possession" has several meanings. Here it connotes operative tenure. If one claiming to be the purchaser can offer proof that he has exercised uninterrupted physical tenure over any specific property or slaves for three consecutive years such continuity over time would establish his ownership without the requirement of producing a bill of sale. This rule applies only to property that continuously produces some form of income, on the premise that if the previous owner had a valid challenge, and could disclaim the sale to the current holder, he would have spoken up within the period of three years so as not to lose substantial income (thus, the Mishnah).

So, if the previous owner never came forth, the ownership of the present holder would be deemed valid, even without a bill of sale. Such provisions were necessary in communities that did not maintain title registries. The point of the ruling by the Sage in our case, one of several hypothetical cases discussed in the Talmudic passage, is that these partners could not have it both ways. Since they had staggered utilization of the slave woman so as to avoid the liabilities of uninterrupted joint ownership over the tenure period, they could not turn around and challenge the claim of another against their ownership. They would have to produce a bill of sale.

An exception is made in cases where an **איטרא** "payment received" was written. This means that although a given purchaser could not produce a bill of sale, he had something in writing stating "paid in full," or: "payment received." If the partners could produce such a receipt, their ownership would be presumed to be valid because issuance of the receipt had the effect of publicizing the transaction. This provision implies that receipts may not have been written in every case.

Babylonian Talmud, *Bābāʾ Meṣîʿāʾ* 39a–b:

אמר רב הונא: ״אין מורידין ... ולא קרוב לנכסי קטן.״ כיון דלא מחי, אתי לאחזוקי ביה. אמר רבא: שמע מיניה מדרב הונא ״אין מחזיקין בנכסי קטן ואפילו הגדיל.״ ולא אמרן אלא באחי דאבא, אבל באחי דאמא לית לן בה. ואחי דאבא נמי לא אמרן אלא בארעתא, אבל בבתי לית לן בה. ובארעתא נמי לא אמרן אלא דלא עביד עיטדא, אבל עביד עיטדא קלא אית לה.

Rab Hunaʾ said: We do not bring down [persons to look after real estate left untended after the owner had died, was captured in war, or had fled]... nor (do we bring down) a relative into the property of a minor. Since he (= the minor) does not enter a challenge, the other will end up claiming possession of it (by virtue of inheritance). Rabaʾ said: One may conclude from it, (namely), from (the ruling of) Rab Hunaʾ, (that) "We do not grant *ḥazzāqāh* over the property of a minor even after he has attained majority." We have not said (this) except with respect to brother of the father, but with respect to brothers of the mother we not follow this rule. (In truth,) we have not said (this) even with respect to brothers of the father except with respect to parcels of land, but with respect to houses we do not follow this rule. (Furthermore,) we have not said (this) even with respect to parcels of land except where no "payment received" is executed, but if a "payment received" is executed, it has a voice (= it makes the transaction public).

Commentary

The concern here is that unscrupulous relatives may take advantage of minors if given control over their property when their fathers died. It is assumed that a minor might not know that the property in question belonged to his father, and, for this reason, would not assert his claim to it as an inheritance, or that he would not understand the relevant law, to start with. Three years would therefore pass without a claim, and the relative would own the property. The remedy is to appoint an unrelated person to tend the property, who would have no claim to a share in the inheritance after the three-year period of his service, in any event. Raba᾿ infers from this ruling of Rab Huna᾿ that this Sage was of the view that no one may be granted *ḥazzāqāh* over property initially bequeathed to a minor even if he continued to hold it for three years after that minor had attained majority. Otherwise we might have a situation where even a person unrelated would claim that the heir had sold the property to him, since that heir had never challenged his hold on the property. If the law of *ḥazzāqāh* were in effect, no bill of sale would be necessary. Several qualifications follow, after which the Talmud states that the rule prohibiting granting another *ḥazzāqāh* over the property of minors applies only in cases where it was not the practice to execute receipts of payment, but where such was done, there was no cause for concern, because if the land or other property had been sold to the holder, we would know about it.

It is important to note that in the Samaria Papyri, אטיר מכיר was a provision, or clause written into the bill of sale, itself. The same was true in the Neo-Babylonian documents with respect to the *eṭir maḫir* component. In the Talmudic sources, however, the term אטירא designated a kind of separate receipt.

This may be the place to mention another of Muffs' predictions that was right on the mark. In discussing Aramaic volitional formulae of satisfaction that have Akkadian counterparts, he assumed that *ina ḫud libbišu* "in the joy of his heart," a frequent Neo-Babylonian formula, also had an Aramaic equivalent (Muffs 1969:41, note 1; 128–132). This has now been verified in an Aramaic marriage contract of Edomite provenance from Maresha, the capital of Idumaea, dated 176 B.C.E. and recently published by E. Eshel and A. Kloner (1996). There it is said of the groom that: בחדות לבבה "in the joy of his heart" he declared his intentions to his prospective bride.

Marriage contract from Maresha, lines 1–5:

1. בירח סיון שנת 136 סילב]קוס מלכא
2. קוסרם בר קוסיד הו, בחדות לבבה [... אמר
3. לקוסיד בר קוסיהב: איתי ארסנה [שמה
4. בתולתא. כען בעה אנה מנך זי [
5. מראת בי תנתן לי כנומוס בנת]

1. In the month of Sivan, year 136 (of) Seleu[cus, the king
2. Qosram, son of Qosyad, he, in the joy of his heart, [... declared
3. to Qosyad, son of Qosyehab: There is (a woman), Arsinoe, [her name
4. a previously unmarried woman. Now, then, I am asking of you that [
5. (as) a mistress of the house you give (her) to me, according to the custom of the daughters [

Conclusion

A word is in order about the import of Talmudic literature for the MELAMMU agenda, as I understand it from the published studies of the first meeting, and from statements of purpose issued by the leaders of this group. Talmudic law has had a pervasive role in the life of Jewish communities, east and west, since late antiquity. What is more, that role continues most noticeably in the modern State of Israel, where what has customarily been termed המשפט העברי "the Hebrew law," essentially a way of referring to Rabbinic law, found its way into the new codices that have been, and continue to be compiled to meet the needs of the Israeli legal system. The governing policy in Israel is that, wherever acceptable and applicable (and this is surely not always the case), principles of "the Hebrew law" which serve the desired objective have precedence over those of other systems. To the extent, therefore, that Talmudic law can be shown to preserve elements of ancient Near Eastern law, it constitutes a paradigm for tracing the survival of this important aspect of Syro-Mesopotamian civilization, even to our own time. As more textual evidence, primarily in Aramaic, is retrieved, the path from ancient Syria-Mesopotamia to the Talmudic compendia and thereafter will be charted with ever greater clarity.

Reference Bibliography

Eshel, E. and A. Kloner

1996 An Aramaic Ostracon of an Edomite Marriage Contract from Maresha, Dated 176 B.C.E. *IEJ* 46:1–22.

Greengus, S.

1990 Bridewealth in Sumerian Sources. *HUCA* 61:25–88.

Gropp, D.

2001 *Wadi Daliyeh II: The Samaria Papyri from Wadi Daliyeh*. DJD 28. Oxford.

Kaufman, S. A.

1974 *The Akkadian Influences on Aramaic*. Assyriological Studies 19. Chicago.

Levine, B. A.

1962 *Survivals of Ancient Canaanite in the Mishnah*, PhD Dissertation, Brandeis University.

1968 *Mulūgu/Melûg*: The Origins of a Talmudic Legal Institution. *JAOS* 88:271–285 {*VOL 2, PP. 103–25*}.

1982 From the Aramaic Enoch Fragments: The Semantics of Cosmography. *Journal of Jewish Studies* 33, (Essays in Honor of Yigael Yadin), ed. G. Vermes, J. Neusner, 311–326 {*VOL 2, PP. 379–93*}.

Lieberman, S.

1987 A Mesopotamian Background for the So-Called *Aggadic* 'Measures' of Biblical Hermeneutics? *HUCA* 58:157–225.

Milik, J. T.
1976 *The Books of Enoch: Aramaic Fragments of Qumran Cave 4* (with the collaboration of Matthew Black). Oxford.

Muffs, Y.
1969 *Studies in the Aramaic Legal Papyri from Elephantine*, Leiden. [To be reissued with Prolegomenon by Baruch A. Levine, by E. J. Brill, Leiden].

Oelsner, J.
1997 Neu/spätbabylonische und aramäische Kaufverträge. Pages 307–314 in *Ana šadî Labnāni lū allik* , Festschrift W. Röllig, ed. Beate Pongratz-Leisten, *et al.* AOAT 247. Neükirchen-Vluyn.

Oppenheim, A. L.
1955 Iron Sheep. *IEJ* 5:89–92.
1964 *Ancient Mesopotamia: Portrait of a Dead Civilization*, Chicago.

Salvesen, A.
1998 The Legacy of Babylon and Nineveh in Aramaic Sources. Pages 139–161 in *The Legacy of Mesopotamia*, ed. S. Dalley, *et al.*, Oxford.

The Various Workings of the Aramaic Legal Tradition: Jews and Nabateans in the Naḥal Ḥever Archive*

Language as a cultural base often overrides religion, ethnicity, politics and the social order. Whether functioning within discrete societies or acting as a bridge connecting them, it serves to create a common experience and to express common perceptions. The Jewish-Aramaic and Nabatean-Aramaic documents from Naḥal Ḥever show remarkable affinities alongside their differences. Here we have two communities brought together by the pressures of history, both of which were heirs to the long enduring, broadly expressed and geographically extended Aramaic legal tradition, sometimes referred to as "Aramaic common law." One community was Jewish and the other Nabatean-Arab; one practiced monotheistic Judaism and the other a pagan religion; one was affiliated with the Jews of Roman Palestine whereas the other was part of a far-flung Nabatean network of trading communities that for several centuries constituted a kingdom. And yet, one assumes that a Jew residing or owning property in Maḥoz ʿEglatain (= Maḥozaʾ), a town at the southern tip of the Dead Sea, and his Nabatean neighbor probably would have understood the provisions of each other's legal documents in large part, when read aloud to them. It is more difficult to say whether they would have been able to read each other's script, even if they were literate in their own. The purpose of the present study is to explore aspects of the language and formulation of the Jewish-Aramaic and Nabatean-Aramaic papyri from the Yadin collection, leaving for further inquiry certain structural and compositional features of these legal documents.

The Yadin collection of papyri from Naḥal Ḥever (henceforth: NḤ, registered by number) includes six Nabatean papyri: NḤ 1 [94 CE]; NḤ 2 and 3 [99 CE]; NḤ 4 [99 CE(?)]; NḤ 6 [119 CE]; NḤ 9 [122 CE].[1] They are all legal instru-

---

* Originally published in L. H. Schiffman, E. Tov, and J. C. VanderKam (eds.), *The Dead Sea Scrolls: Fifty Years After their Discovery; Proceedings of the Jerusalem Congress, July 20–25, 1997* (Jerusalem: Israel Exploration Society, 2000), pp. 836–851. Reprinted with permission from the Israel Exploration Society.

[1] The discovery was made and reported by Yigael Yadin ("Les Lettres de Bar Kochba," *Bible et Terre Sainte* 34 [1961] 14–16; "The Expedition to the Judaean Desert, Expedition D: The Cave of the Letters," *IEJ* 12 [1962] 227–257). See also Y. Yadin, *Bar Kokhba* (London and New York: Random House, 1971) 222–253. The publication history is reviewed by Joseph Aviram in N. Lewis, *The Documents from the Bar Kokhba Period in the Cave of Letters: Greek Papyri* (Judean Desert Studies 2; Jerusalem: Israel Exploration Society, 1989) ix–x, and note the Select Bibliography, xii. This volume contains the vast majority of the Greek papyri found in the Cave of Letters, with the Aramaic signatures edited by Jonas C. Greenfield. One also finds in this volume valuable discus-

ments of one sort or another. Papyrus Starcky, a Nabatean-Aramaic document first published in 1954, and known to have come from Naḥal Ḥever, is also of a legal character (Starcky 1954) and may legitimately be studied in conjunction with the Nabatean papyri of the Yadin collection. It is dated between 60–69 CE and, like four of the Nabatean papyri from the Yadin collection was prepared while the Nabatean kingdom, which was to come to an end in 106 CE, still existed. For the information of the reader, the Yadin collection contains twenty-eight Semitic papyri in all, several of them fragmentary, including texts in Hebrew, Jewish-Aramaic and Nabatean-Aramaic. Their publication is being undertaken jointly by Ada Yardeni and Baruch A. Levine, incorporating the earlier efforts of Yigael Yadin and Jonas C. Greenfield.[2]

Taken together, the seven Nabatean documents, several of which are quite lengthy and elaborate and as such unprecedented in Nabatean, testify to close business relations between Jews and Nabateans in the Dead Sea area. One of the principals in the Starcky papyrus is a certain ʾElʿazar, a Jew, and the other a Nabatean named ʾAphtaḥ. The speaker in NḤ 9, a fragmentary Nabatean document, is a certain Yoseph, variously written Yehoseph, but since the name of the other party is missing in a gap it is not known whether he was Jewish or Nabatean. In the same document, the names of the two witnesses that are legible are known to be Jewish: Yehudah, son of Shimʿon and Yoḥanaʾ son of Makkutaʾ. A person named Yehoseph is likewise a principal in NḤ 4, a Nabatean document involving the purchase of land. In NḤ 6, a three-year lease written in Nabatean-Aramaic, both principals are Jews. A certain Yoḥanaʾ, son of Meshullam of Ein Gedi, makes a first-person declaration to another named Yehuda, son of ʾElʿazar Khtusion. In this transaction, the witnesses were also Jews. In NḤ 3, an elaborate Nabatean deed of purchase, the purchaser is a Jew named Shimʿon, and the seller a Nabatean woman named ʾAbiʿadan, daughter of ʾAphtaḥ.

A full review of the onomasticon and prosopography of the Jewish-Aramaic and Nabatean-Aramaic documents from Naḥal Ḥever would further elaborate close business relationships of this sort between Jews and Nabateans, as well as documenting the utilization of Nabatean-Aramaic by Jews. Furthermore, the boundary descriptions of real estate plots involved in some of the business trans-

---

sions of the historical, social, and political setting of the papyri. Instead of registering the papyri as "P.Yadin + number," which has been the general practice, I will here register the papyri "Naḥal Ḥever (NḤ) + number," using the same numeration, and being ever mindful that reference is to the Yadin collection.

[2] After the untimely death of Jonas C. Greenfield in the spring of 1995, the present author undertook to complete his work in collaboration with Ada Yardeni, who had been working with him on these documents, and who has contributed greatly to their decipherment. These texts will be published in a forthcoming volume of the JDS series, and Hannah Cotton has consented to edit several remaining Greek papyri from the collection. As of now, two Jewish-Aramaic documents from the Yadin collection have been published by J. C. Greenfield and A. Yardeni: "Babatha's *Ketubba*," *IEJ* 44 (1994), 75–99 + plates (Papyrus Yadin 10); "A Deed of Gift in Aramaic found in Naḥal Ḥever (Papyrus Yadin 7)," *Eretz-Israel* 25 (Joseph Aviram Volume; 1996) 383–403 (Hebrew).

actions inform us, as we would have expected, that parcels owned or leased by Jews at times bounded on the property of Nabateans. It is likely, of course, that our sample is skewed, so that documents involving Jews, in particular, were preserved in the archive, although two of the total of seven papyri apparently did not involve Jews.[3] In recent publications, Hannah Cotton and Lawrence Schiffman have discussed the implications of such close contact, especially after the termination of the Nabatean kingdom by the Romans in 106 CE, and the establishment of a new border between Judea and *Provincia Arabia*.[4]

The consequences of proximity and the resulting business relations are expressed through cultural interaction as revealed by language. Although unanswered questions remain as to the relative valence of Aramaic and Arabic among the Nabateans, and of Aramaic and Hebrew among the Jews in the late first and early second centuries of the Common Era, it is evident, at the very least, that both communities utilized their own dialects of Aramaic for writing legal documents, and that both had a developed repertoire of scribal conventions for doing so. This is shown for the Nabateans by the legal vocabulary of the Nabatean funerary inscriptions, studied so insightfully by Jonas Greenfield (1974 and now collected in J. F. Healey's valuable monograph (1993). Greenfield and Yardeni, in their discussion of NḤ 7, a Jewish Aramaic deed of grant, and the most elaborate of the Jewish-Aramaic texts from Naḥal Ḥever (except possibly for Babatha's Ketubba), take note of discrete Arabic terms, idioms, and usage which they correctly attribute to the influence of the Nabatean presence in the contemporary environment.[5] As matters stand, this document of grant is exceptional in the collection of Jewish-Aramaic documents for the extent of its Arabic content, making it premature to generalize on the matter of Nabatean influence on Jewish legal formulation. Nevertheless, the Yadin archive adds valuable evidence re-

---

[3] The two Nabatean-Aramaic papyri that do not involve Jews are NḤ 1, a loan document, and NḤ 2, a deed of purchase. It should be noted, however, that NḤ 2 and 3 deal with related business transactions, and that NḤ 3 does, indeed, involve Jews.

[4] See H. M. Cotton, "ἡ νεα επαρχεια ἀραβια: The New Province of Arabia in the Papyri from the Judaean Desert," *Zeitschrift für Papyrologie and Epigraphik* 116 (1997) 204–208; L. Schiffman, "On the Edge of the Diaspora: Jews in the Dead Sea Region in the First Two Centuries CE," *Proceedings, Conference on Israel-Diaspora Relations in Late Antiquity* (Jerusalem: Merkaz Shazar, 1997). Also see the earlier discussion in Y. Yadin, "The Nabatean Kingdom, Provincia Arabia, Petra and Ein Geddi in the Documents from Naḥal Ḥever," *Jaarbericht Ex Oriente Lux* 17 (1964) 227–241.

[5] Arabic terms and idioms occurring in NḤ 7 as transcribed in the Jewish-Aramaic script, and explained by Greenfield and Yardeni, "A Deed of Gift," 383–403 (Hebrew) are the following: (1) וחלף ועללהי, "and date palms and their yield;" (2) די לא וציף, "which is not described;" (3) ארע וערת, "craggy land;" (4) כרבא, "dates near the trunk;" (5) קיס-מא, "measure of water;" (6) אשתרהן, "taken as security;" (7) אצדק, "rightful heir;" (8) ולד, "child, descendant."

garding the linguistic character of Nabatean-Aramaic itself, leaving no doubt as to the extent of its Arabic content.[6]

Apart from the Arabic factor, it is clear from the corpus of Naḥal Ḥever that the current Aramaic legal vocabulary of the Jews, on the one hand, and of the Nabateans, on the other, differed in certain respects. To put it another way: The received Aramaic legal tradition extant among the Jews of the Dead Sea area was in a somewhat different state from that of the contemporary Nabateans. This difference is further demonstrated by the contemporary Jewish-Aramaic papyri from nearby Murabbaʿat published by Milik (1961), and more recently by the Jewish-Aramaic Seiyal Collection II (Naḥal Ṣeʾelim), also from Naḥal Ḥever, published by Ada Yardeni (1997). It should be pointed out that the Aramaic corpus of Jewish documents from the Dead Sea area, dating from the last part of the first century CE through the Bar Kokhba period (132–135 CE), is quite extensive, and that Naḥal Ḥever has emerged as an important locality.

I. The Complexities of a Cultural Continuum: Formulation and Terminology

There are four intersecting and often interlaced lines of inquiry that should be pursued in order to elicit from the Naḥal Ḥever papyri a view of cultural interpenetration between Jews and Nabateans during the period covered by them:

1. The common Aramaic repertoire they reflect—provisions that Jews and Nabateans formulated in the same way, and which normally appear in documents of the same kind executed by both.

2. Aramaic components of the papyri that are distinctively Nabatean and which seldom, if ever, turn up in Jewish-Aramaic documents and vice-versa: Aramaic components distinctive to the Jewish-Aramaic papyri and which do not turn up to any extent in the Nabatean documents.

3. Arabic locutions attested in the Jewish-Aramaic papyri undoubtedly attributable to contemporary Nabatean influence.

4. Arabic elements distinctive to the Nabatean-Aramaic papyri which help us to characterize the current Nabatean scribal repertoire.

Rather than taking up these features *in seriatim*, it is better to begin by discussing some anomalies that do not fit neatly into any of the above four categories, and to see where such analysis leads. A case in point is the term for "connubial payment, dowry," Hebrew מֹהַר, which appears in this same spelling in a Nabatean document of debt or debenture from the year 94 CE (NḤ 1, line 18). The woman whose מהר is mentioned is Nabatean, a certain ʾAmat-ʾIsi, as is her husband who borrows money from it, a certain Muqimu. Now, the term מהר is part of the early West-Semitic vocabulary. It occurs in Ugaritic poetry and in the

[6] M. O'Connor, "The Arabic Loanwords in Nabatean Aramaic," *JNES* (1986) 45, 213–229, tends to downplay the Arabic factor in Nabatean Aramaic, but he wrote before the evidence from the Naḥal Ḥever archive was available. See also the assessment of the Arabic factor in Nabatean-Aramaic by J. F. Healey, *The Nabataean Tomb Inscriptions of Mada'in Salih* (Journal of Semitic Studies, Supplement 1; Oxford /Manchester; Oxford University Press/University of Manchester, 1993), 59–63.

Hebrew Bible[7] and is attested in the fifth-century B.C.E. Jewish-Aramaic papyri from Elephantine.[8] It continues in use in post-biblical Jewish sources, but curiously is not attested in the Mishnah, though elsewhere it exhibits the expected Jewish-Aramaic and Christian-Syriac forms.[9] It is also well attested in Arabic as *mahr*, generating appropriate verbal denominatives.[10] Ironically, it does not, in my view, occur in Babatha's Ketubba, where Yigael Yadin and now, Mordechai Friedman have sought to restore it.[11] Greenfield and Yardeni have disputed its occurrence there, offering a better reading.[12] Nor does this term occur in the Jewish-Aramaic marriage contracts contained in the Murabbaʿat archive, published by Milik.[13]

The question is: How did it get into a Nabatean-Aramaic document of the late first century CE? Did the Nabateans borrow it from their contemporary Jew-

---

[7] For biblical usage see Gen 34:12, Exod 22:15–16, 1 Sam 18:25. In Ugaritic poetry, the *mhr* is paid by the moon god, Yariḫ, to the father of his bride, Nikkal, the moon goddess, at their marriage. See M. Dietrich, O. Loretz, and J. Sanmartín, *The Cuneiform Alphabetic Texts from Ugarit* (KTU: second, enlarged edition; Münster: Ugarit-Verlag, 1995) 70, s.v. text 1.24, lines 19–22. For a general discussion of various types of "wife's property" in Talmudic law, in ancient Near Eastern perspective, see B. A. Levine, "Mulūgu/Melûg: The Origins of a Talmudic Legal Institution, *JAOS* 88 (1968) 271–285, esp. 273 {*VOL 2, PP. 103–25, ESP. 107*}.

[8] For Aramaic usage at Elephantine see B. Porten and A. Yardeni, *Textbook of Aramaic Documents from Ancient Egypt, 2: Contracts* (Jerusalem: Akademon, 1989) 30, B2.6 Cowley 15, lines 4–5: יהבת לך מהר ברתך מפטחיה, "I have remitted to you the mohar of your daughter, Mibtahiah." Also see, ibid, 78, B3.8, Kraeling 7 + 15 etc., lines 15, 25.

[9] See J. Levy, *Wörterbuch über die Talmudim and Midraschim* (4 vols.; Darmstadt: Wissenschaftliche Buchgesellschaft, 1963) 3.40, s.v. מוהר, מוהרא; M. Sokoloff, *A Dictionary of Jewish Palestinian Aramaic of the Byzantine Period* (Ramat-Gan: Bar Ilan University, 1990) 294, s.v. מהר; *LS* 376, s.v. *mahroʾ*, and M. A. Friedman, *Jewish Marriage in Palestine* (2 vols.; Tel-Aviv and New York: The Jewish Theological Seminary of America, 1980) 1.239–311, for a discussion of post-Rabbinic marriage arrangements.

[10] See E. W. Lane, *Arabic-English Lexicon* (4 vols.; Edinburgh: Williams and Norgate, 1863) 2740, s.v. *mahr(un)*, "dowry, bridal gift," and the denominative verb *mahara*, "to give the *mahr*," as well as other denominative forms.

[11] Y. Yadin, "The Expedition to the Judaean Desert, Expedition D: The Cave of the Letters," *IEJ* 12 (1962) 227–257; M. A. Friedman, "Babatha's Ketubba: Some Preliminary Observations," *IEJ* 46 (1996) 55–76.

[12] See the restoration proposed by J. C. Greenfield and A. Yardeni, "Babatha's Ketubba," *IEJ* 44 (1994) 87: וזאננה לך ומכסך "And I will feed you and provide your clothing." But see Friedman, "Babatha's Ketubba," 64, whose restoration, in my view, is unsatisfactory for several reasons, most importantly because the verb יה"ב, "to pay, give," would, according to his reading, have no direct object. One would be left with a clause reading: "And I will pay you as/for your *mohar*" with no stipulation of what the *mohar* would consist of. Formulas of this type uniformly stipulate an amount to be paid as *mohar*, which syntactically represents the object, direct or oblique, of the verb.

[13] J. T. Milik, "Textes Hebreux et Araméens," *Les Grottes de Murabbaʿât* (DJD 2; Oxford: Clarendon Press, 1961) 67–205.

ish neighbors? Did the Nabateans possess it independently, having appropriated it from the Aramaic common law tradition of the Achaemenid period, which probably appropriated it initially from the Israelites/Jews? Or did the Nabateans receive it as part of the early West-Semitic vocabulary, as did the biblical Israelites originally? Are we to read it as an Arabic word in the Nabatean document or as a Hebrew/Aramaic word? In any event, the מהר is not to be considered a consistent earmark of Jewish provenance, nor do all relevant Jewish documents employ it.

A problem of a related sort is presented by the verb נח״ל, "to receive as an inheritance, as a grant," common to the Jewish-Aramaic and Nabatean-Aramaic vocabulary. It occurs both in NḤ 7, the Jewish-Aramaic deed of grant to which reference has already been made, and in two Nabatean documents of purchase (NḤ 2 and 3). In both sets of documents it appears in conventional ownership clauses which specify the ensuing rights of a purchaser, or of one receiving a perpetual grant, as in the case of NḤ 7. It would be well to examine this shared formula in the relevant legal clauses as a method of comparison.

First, the clause as it appears in NḤ 7, lines 17–18/56–57, within the Jewish Aramaic deed of grant. A father confers on his daughter the authority to do the following:

> למקנא ולמזבנו ולמנחל ולמורתו ולמרהן ולמנתן ולמזרע ולמנצב ולמבנא
> ולמפרוע פרענהון ולמעבד בהון כל די תצבין
>
> And to buy and to sell, and to inherit and to bequeath, and to pledge as security and to grant as gift, and to sow and to plant, and to build and to pay their costs, and to do with them (= the parcels of property) whatever you wish.

Then, the clause as it appears in NḤ 2, lines 9/30–31, and NḤ 3, lines 10/33–34, within the Nabatean documents of purchase:

> למקנא ולזבנה ולמרהן ולמנחל ולמנתן ולמעבד בזבניא אלה כל די יצבה
>
> To buy and to sell and to pledge as security, and to inherit and to grant as gift, and to do with these purchases whatever he wishes.

Leaving aside for the moment certain dialectal differences in the morphology of the verb and the redundancy and proliferation of the Jewish-Aramaic formula, we note the following: The common Aramaic repertoire is evident in certain components: (1) קני/זבן, "buy/sell," (2) נתן, "grant as gift," and (3) עבד ב– כל די צבי, "do with X whatever one wishes." The redundant elements in the longer Jewish-Aramaic version are fairly transparent accretions, which will be discussed in due course. The verb רה״ן "to pledge as security" is attested very early in Arabic dialects, and is prominent in the Nabatean tomb inscriptions from Arabia, as Greenfield has shown in his incisive studies. Its occurrence at Naḥal Ḥever, both in the Jewish-Aramaic and the Nabatean-Aramaic documents, clarifies how it entered the Tannaitic vocabulary.[14] Its appropriation is the result of close cultural contact between Jews and Nabateans in the pre-Mishnaic period.

Now we come to the infinitive ולמנחל, "and to inherit." Greenfield and Yardeni note the background of this verb and derived forms at Mari and Ugarit,[15] and in Biblical Hebrew, but have not completely explained its occurrence here, both in its infinitive form, ולמנחל, or in noun form, in the formula שותפו ונחלה, "partnership and estate rights."[16] These lexemes are not part of the Aramaic legal vocabulary, as far as we know. In fact, the noun נחלה does not occur in NḤ 7, the Aramaic document of gift; only the infinitival form occurs in the rights clause. The situation in Arabic is more difficult to assess. Dozy lists a noun *niḫla*^{tun}, "occupation; la manière dont on puvoit à sa susténance; marchandise."[17] The verbal form *naḫala* would express the doing of the same. Wehr lists the same noun, *niḥla*^{tun} with the meaning of "donation, gift, present," and the related verb, *naḫala*, expressing the doing of the same.[18] Though it is conceivable that the infinitive ולמנחל and the noun נחלה were part of the contemporary Arabic legal vocabulary it is unlikely, for the following reasons: Although the meanings attested in Arabic are surely related to the sense of "estate, inheritance," they appear to be derivative, or extended in connotation and lack the connection with land so basic to these documents. Finally, שותפו ונחלה is most probably a variation on Biblical חלק ונחלה, "share and estate" (Deut 10:9; 18:1), pairing an Aramaic term in the absolute construction with a Hebrew term in the absolute, both feminine. In Neh 2:20 we find the combination: חלק וצדקה וזכרון, "a share, and rightful estate, and a record," in which Hebraized צְדָקָה (Aramaic צִדְקַת, צְדָק) replaces Hebrew נחלה. If we retrace our steps to Mari of the early second millennium, we find that the verb *naḫālu*(*m*) in the G-stem means "to hand over, convey" goods and property, and that the noun *niḫlatu*(*m*) designates what was so conveyed. Ugaritic *nḥlt* occurs in mythological contexts where it refers to the domains of deities. In Biblical Hebrew, the verb נח"ל most often expresses receipt of a נחלה, but this change of direction is semantically understandable, especially if we agree that most Biblical Hebrew verbal forms are denominative of נחלה.[19] At Naḥal Ḥever it is the normal Hebrew aspect of the *qal* stem "to re-

---

[14] On the verb רהן in its various forms see the incisive study by J. C. Greenfield, "*Kullu nafsin bima kasabat rahina*: The Use of *rhn* in Aramaic and Arabic," *Arabicus Felix: Luminosis Brittanicus: Essays in Honor of A. F. L. Beeston* (ed. A. Jones; Oxford: Ithaca Press Reading, 1991) 221–226 and literature cited there. See also *m. ʿEduyot* 8:2.

[15] Greenfield and Yardeni, "A Deed of Gift," 398.

[16] Occurring in NḤ 2, line 27; NḤ 3, line 30.

[17] R. Dozy, *Supplement aux Dictionnaires Arabes* (Leiden: Brill, 1881) 646.

[18] H. Wehr, *Arabic-English Dictionary* (ed. J. M. Cowan; 4th edition; Ithaca, N.Y.: Spoken Languages Service, 1994 [1964]) 1112.

[19] On the verb נחל and its various forms, see *ibid*., 398, Papyrus Yadin 7, lines 17–18. Also see B. A. Levine, "Farewell to the Ancient Near East: Evaluating Biblical References to Ownership of Land in Comparative Perspective," *Privatization in the Ancient Near East and Classical World* (ed. M. Hudson, B. A. Levine; Cambridge, MA: Peabody Museum, 1996) 237 {VOL 2, PP. 198F.}, and *CAD N*/I, 126, s.v. *naḫālu* B, and for Ugaritic

ceive as inheritance" that is intended. This analysis is shown most clearly in NḤ 7, where ולמנחל contrasts with ולמורתו, "and to bequeath," just as buying and selling are contrasted in the same clauses (*pace* Greenfield and Yardeni).[20] In light of the above considerations, it would not be unreasonable to conclude that the occurrence of the noun נחלה and of the verb נח"ל in NḤ 2 and 3 reflects biblical and/or Jewish influence on Nabatean legal terminology, although it is also possible that contemporary Arabic already possessed these components on its own, from the ancient West-Semitic vocabulary.

To observe how the common Aramaic tradition is blended with distinctive, often innovative elements, we had best focus on the defension clauses guaranteeing that the property purchased, or granted is free of claims of all sorts, a subject that has also been discussed by Greenfield.[21] In NḤ 7, a representative Jewish-Aramaic formula reads as follows, in one of several versions:

ודין ודבב ומומא כלה לא איתי לירתי ואצדקי ואנוש כלה

> And no suit, or litigation, or oath whatsoever is to be within the power of my heirs and entitled beneficiaries, or of any person whomsoever.

Another version has:

ונדר ומומא ואסר ושבועה לא איתי לבני ולירתי ולאנוש כלה

> And no vow, or adjuration, or binding agreement, or oath is to be within the power of my sons, or my heirs, or of any person whomsoever.

The comparable Nabatean-Aramaic formula reads:

די לא דין ולא דבב ולא מומא כלה

> That there be no suit, or litigation, or adjuration, whatsoever.

Clearly, the basic triad of דין, דבב, מומא, "suit, litigation, adjuration," and idiomatic -ולא איתי ל, "and there is not with respect to / there is not to be within the

---

nḥlt "domain," as in *ǵr nḥlt*, "mountain domain," and *arṣ nḥlt*, "land of domain," see R. E. Whitaker, *A Concordance of the Ugaritic Literature* (Cambridge, MA: Harvard University Press, 1972) 446, s.v. *nḥlt*.

[20] Possible instances in Biblical Hebrew where the *Qal* stem of the verb נח"ל means "to convey, hand over" rather than "to receive" are the following: Exod 34:9: וסלחת לעוננו לחטאתנו ונחלתנו, "May you forgive our sin and our offense and grant us a territory." The context clearly suggests that the issue at stake is the granting of the land by God to Israel, despite their sinfulness. Cf. also Zech 2:16: ונחל יהוה את יהודה חלקו, "And YHWH will grant Judah his share." Finally, cf. Num 34:18: "And one chieftain shall you enlist from each tribe to grant the land (לנחל את הארץ)." This sense seems to be clarified by the postscript in Num 34:29, where the *Piel* infinitival form לְנַחֵל is substituted in order to convey the required sense of "granting" rather than "receiving."

[21] J. C. Greenfield, "The 'Defension Clause' in Some Documents from Naḥal Ḥever and Naḥal Ṣeelim," *Revue de Qumran* 15 (1992) 467–471.

power of," may be classified as part of the received, ancient Aramaic traditions of both Jews and Nabateans. The noun מומא "adjuration" is cognate with Akkadian *mamītu*, which in Mishnah, Nedarim 1:2, appears as: נדר במו[מ]תא, "One who has vowed by adjuration."[22] The Aramaic formula דין ודבב recalls the Akkadian terms *dīnu* and *dabābu*, and in turn, the Hebrew terms דין and דברים.[23] The form אַצְדַק, "rightful heir," discussed by Greenfield and Yardeni (1996),[24] is morphologically the Arabic elative, although the root צד״ק is well attested in Aramaic. This raises the question of whether, in a given instance, a Nabatean scribe was using a form of a common root as Aramaic, or as Arabic. This term is frequent in the Nabatean tomb inscriptions.[25]

What interests me at this point is that the Jewish-Aramaic and the Nabatean-Aramaic documents differ in the way each proliferates legal formulas to embrace all sorts of conceivable, often redundant provisions. Normally, in Jewish-Aramaic documents this is achieved by stringing along Hebrew or Aramaic terms of reference, usually derived from known Jewish sources. We observed this pattern in the very first ownership clause discussed above, and now again in one version of the defension clause, both taken from NḤ 7. In the former instance, the scribe added a series of usual activities: למורתו, למזרע, למנצב, למבנא, למפרוע פרענהון, "to bequeath as an inheritance, to sow, to plant, to build, to defray their costs." In the latter case, the following terms were added: נדר, שבועה, אסר, "vow, oath, binding agreement." The latter case is basically redundant, whereas the former adds specific provisions, which are, however, merely proverbial examples of what a person has the right to do with property he possesses.

The Nabatean legal documents from Naḥal Ḥever afford instructive examples of how a similar sort of proliferation was achieved. Thus, in NḤ 2, lines 25–26, the rights of ownership are outlined as follows:

> וכל די איתי לאביעדן דא בה מן צדק ורשו ותחום וחלק ותקף ותבת וקשם וחדדו\וחרר
>
> And all that this same ʾAbiʿadan possesses in it, by entitlement and jurisdiction, [according to] boundary and share, and valid writ; and firm register, and share, and boundary/free title.

---

[22] See *CAD M/*I, 189–195, s.v. *mamītu*; Sokoloff, *Dictionary*, 295, s.v. מומא, מומתא; Levy, *Wörterbuch*, 3.50, s.v. מומי, מומתא; Greenfield and Yardeni, "A Deed of Gift," 398, lines 18–19; *DNWSI*, 1.459–460, s.v. *ymʾ*, "to swear."

[23] On the Akkadian terms *dīnu*, "lawsuit," and *dabābu*, "litigation" in combination see *CAD D*, 153, s.v. *dīnu* 3, b). For Biblical Hebrew usage, see Deut 17:8 where this combination is approximated: בין דין לדין ... דברי ריבת בשעריכם "whether one civil lawsuit or another ... litigations of dispute within your gates." For earlier Aramaic usage, see *DNWSI*, 1.237, s.v. *dbb*, and Greenfield and Yardeni, "A Deed of Gift," 399, line 21.

[24] Greenfield and Yardeni, "A Deed of Gift."

[25] See *ibid.*; Healey, *The Nabataean Tomb Inscriptions*, 86, H3, line 6, and 91, in the commentary.

The above clause lists five Aramaic legal terms, followed by three Arabic terms. As will be explained in due course, these Arabic terms translate three of the five Aramaic terms, and this is, in fact, the key to their identification. Two of the Arabic terms clearly translate two of the Aramaic terms. Thus Aramaic חלק, "share" is translated by Arabic *qism*, also meaning "part, share." Aramaic תקף, "valid writ, register," is translated by Arabic *ṯabit*, which has a long history in the Arabic legal tradition. Geoffrey Khan cites a recurring statement in Arabic legal documents: *širaʿan ṯābit ṣaḥīḥ la šarṭ*, "as a purchase sound and valid, without condition."[26] This brings us to the last word in the clause, which is Arabic. In the Nabatean script, *daleth* and *resh* are indistinguishable, so that what is written could represent either *ḥ-d-d* or *ḥ-r-r*. Let us take up the latter option, *ḥ-r-r* (= *ḥārīr*) first. It offers two possibilities: It may be taken as a form of the root *ḥrr*, meaning "free, liberated," usually referring to freed persons.[27] This Arabic root, expressed in several forms, is cognate with such Aramaic and Hebrew expressions as חרורי, "freed slaves" (*m. Qid.* IV:1), and the *shafel* שחרר, "to release, manumit," as well as in the abstract noun חרות, "liberation," occurring in the epistolography of the Bar Kokhba period.[28] Although the proposed meaning requires extending the concept of "freedom" to land, so as to produce the sense of "clear, free title," I nevertheless prefer this derivation to the alternative of taking חרר in the sense of "contest," from a meaning "to be heated, hostile," as in the idiomatic formula: מן כל חרר ותגר, "from all contest and claim," known from the Jewish-Aramaic papyri.[29] The reason is that what we have is a sequence of affirmative rights, and it would be more in line with the overall list to take consonantal *ḥrr* as designating yet another of these affirmative rights, rather than interpreting it as a challenge to these rights. Obviously, the two meanings are potentially confusing in Aramaic and Arabic, and even in Hebrew, to a degree, as a perusal of the relevant lexica will show. It is, however, the former option of reading *ḥ-d-d* that offers the simplest, and most precise resolution, because Arabic *ḥada*(*d*) means "border, boundary, as between two things or

---

[26] See G. Khan, *Arabic Legal and Administrative Documents in the Cambridge Genizah Collections* (Cambridge: Cambridge University Press, 1993) 32 and note 96.

[27] See Lane, *Arabic-English Lexicon*, 538–540, s.v. *ḥr*(*r*), and related forms "to be free." Also see Wehr, *Arabic-English Dictionary*, 193–194, s.v. *ḥarra* (*ḥr*). See also J. C. Biella, *Dictionary of Old South Arabic (Sabaean Dialect)* (Harvard Semitic Studies 25; Chico, CA: Scholars Press, 1982) 191–192, s.v. *ḤRR* II, for Old South Arabic *ʾḥrr*(*m*), "freemen."

[28] See Levy, *Wörterbuch*, 4.116, s.v. חרר (*piel*), and the abstract noun חרורי, "freedom." Especially note usage of passive המחוררין, "property free of claims," in *b. Ket.* 51b. For abstract חרו, "liberation" (construct: חרות) in Aramaic letters of the Bar Kokhba period see Milik, "Textes Hebreux et Araméens," 122, papyrus 23:1 and 3 (restored); 135, papyrus 25:1: לחרות ירו[ו]שלם, "of the liberation of Jerusalem."

[29] See Milik, "Textes Hebreux et Araméens," 137, papyrus 26:5; A. Yardeni, "Aramaic and Hebrew Documentary Texts," *Aramaic, Hebrew and Greek Documentary Texts from Nahal Hever and Other Sites* (DJD 27; Oxford: Clarendon Press) 40, no. 9, line 9; Broshi-Qimron (1986), 206, line 7.

places."[30] As such, חדד would translate Aramaic תחום, "border," and we would have precise reverse order:

Aramaic: ותחום וחלק ותקף

Arabic: ותבת וקשם וחדד[31]

It would appear, therefore, that scribes writing in Nabatean-Aramaic proliferated legal formulas by using Arabic equivalents of the Aramaic terms of reference, whereas scribes writing in Jewish Aramaic accomplished the same result with Hebrew and Aramaic synonyms, as we have seen. But there is more to it than that: In the Nabatean Aramaic papyri, the brand of Aramaic utilized in the ownership clause under discussion is characteristically Nabatean. It recalls the formulation of the Nabatean tomb inscriptions, as was shown by Greenfield. Thus, the term חלק "share, estate, territorial rights" appears frequently in the Nabatean tomb inscriptions.[32] Although it occurs in biblical Aramaic (Ezra 4:16), and is attested in other phases of the language, one does not encounter it in the parallel clauses of the contemporary, Jewish-Aramaic documents. More striking is the term תקף (*teqāp*), "valid document," perhaps short for כתב תקף, "writ of validity," which is found in the Nabatean tomb inscriptions. The theme of validity expressed as "force" goes back ultimately to Assyrian legal usage of *dannatu*, as shown by Yochanan Muffs.[33] The form צדק (*ṣedāq*) "entitlement" is particularly challenging. Morphologically, it parallels תקף (*teqāp*), and I take it as Aramaic notwithstanding its relationship to the form אצדק (*ʾaṣdiq*) "rightful heir" discussed above. It does not, however, occur in the same form in the Jewish Aramaic documents from Naḥal Ḥever or Murabbaʿat. Aramaic תחום, "boundary" is, of course, common to both sets of documents, and its considerable significance for tracing the history of the Aramaic legal tradition will be discussed presently. As for רשו, I have not found this exact form in the contemporary Jewish-

[30] Lane, *Lexicon*, 525, col. 2, middle.

[31] My thanks to Geoffrey Khan for pointing these facts out to me.

[32] See J. C. Greenfield, "Studies in the Legal Terminology of the Nabatean Funerary Inscriptions," *Hanoch Yalon Memorial Volume* (Ramat-Gan: Bar Ilan University, 1974) 71–72 (Hebrew) and Healey, *The Nabataean Tomb Inscriptions*, 95, s.v. H4:6–7: *dy lʾ yhwʾ lh bkprʾ dnh ḥlq*, "that he will not have in this tomb any share," and *ibid.* 99, notes to H4, line 7 referring to Biblical Hebrew usage in Deut 10:9: לא היה ללוי חלק ונחלה "Levi had no share or estate." Occurrences in the Nabatean tomb inscriptions are frequent: see Healey, *The Nabataean Tomb Inscriptions*, Glossary, 258, s.v. *ḥlq*.

[33] See Healey, *The Nabataean Tomb Inscriptions*, 86, s.v. H3, lines 3–5: *wlʾršy ʾnwš lmktb bkprh dnh tqp klh*, "And no person has the authority to write for this tomb any [deed of] entitlement whatsoever," and cf. p. 90, notes to H3, lines 4–5, referring to Assyrian *dannatu* (*CAD D*, 90–91, s.v. *dannatu* 8: "valid tablet." Also see Greenfield, "Studies," 73–74, and Y. Muffs, *Studies in the Aramaic Legal Papyri from Elephantine* (Leiden: E. J. Brill, 1969) 193, note 4, who regards *tqp* as a loan translation from the Assyrian.

Aramaic sources, although the verb רש״י is common to the Nabatean tomb inscriptions and to Jewish-Aramaic usage in various constructions.[34]

II. The Persistence of a Near Eastern Legal Convention: Boundary Descriptions in the Naḥal Ḥever Archive

There is perhaps no clearer example of survival and persistence in ancient Near Eastern legal formulation than the convention of delimiting real estate parcels by reference to abutting properties on all four sides, in a directional sequence. We begin the discussion of such boundary descriptions in the Naḥal Ḥever archive by examining an example of the pertinent clause, taken from a Nabatean purchase agreement, NḤ 2, lines 4–5:

ואלה תחומיה: למדנחא – ארחא, ולמערבא – בתי תחא ברת עבדחרתת, ולימינא
– ארע מראנא רבאל מלכא, מלך נבטו, די אחיי ושיזב עמה, ולשמאלא – רקקא

And these are its boundaries: To the East — the road; to the West — the dwellings of Taḥaʾ, daughter of ʿAbad-Ḥaretat; and to the South — the land of Rabʾel, the King, King of the Nabateans, who has revived and delivered his people; and to the North — marshland.

It should be noted at the outset that Aramaic רקקא, "marshland" has now turned up in the fourth century B.C.E. Aramaic ostraca from Idumaea, in the indeterminate form רקק.[35] It is also attested in Talmudic literature in Hebrew texts.[36] As for usage of שמאל, literally "left," to mean "North," the Hebrew Bible (Gen 14:15) attests משמאל לדמשק, "northward of Damascus." This particular way of saying "North" occurs infrequently in Aramaic, and possibly in Phoenician. As for the contrasting ימין, ימינא "right, South," the evidence is, of course, more widespread.[37] It is interesting that in the Jewish-Aramaic papyrus from Naḥal Ḥever, NḤ 7, the terms of reference are different: Aramaic צפונא, "North," and דרומא, "South."

Greenfield and Yardeni provide a brief discussion of the recurring convention of boundary descriptions in their treatment of NḤ 7,[38] the Jewish-Aramaic deed of grant already discussed, as does Yardeni in her publication of the Seiyal Collection II (1997),[39] but there is much more to be said. The convention of specifying the boundaries of real estate parcels in legal documents is very ancient, going back to the Sumerians, and is attested in cuneiform legal documents down through the centuries. It survived in medieval Arabic legal documents as well as in medieval Jewish documents written in Aramaic. Its utilization was wide-

[34] See Healey, *The Nabataean Tomb Inscriptions*, 86, s.v. H3, line 3, and commentary, pp. 88–89 for the present participle *ršy*. See also *DNWSI*, 1086–1087, s.v. *ršy*.

[35] See I. Ephal and J. Naveh, *Aramaic Ostraca of the Fourth Century B.C. from Idumaea* (Jerusalem: Israel Exploration Society, 1996) 86, ostracon no. 191, line 4.

[36] See Levy, *Wörterbuch*, 4.471, s.v. רקק.

[37] See *DNWSI*, 1159–1160, s.v. šmʾl, and pp. 460–461, s.v. ymn_2.

[38] Greenfield and Yardeni, "A Deed of Gift."

[39] A. Yardeni, "Aramaic and Hebrew Documentary Texts," 15.

spread and uninterrupted in many cultures and in different languages. The most proximate parallels to the Naḥal Ḥever papyri, including the Seiyal collection, are from Wadi Marabbaʿat. The same convention informs the Greek papyri from Naḥal Ḥever, which fact is significant but hardly surprising, as we shall see presently. Moving back in history, the Aramaic legal papyri from Elephantine of the fifth century B.C.E. provide extensive evidence as to the currency of this convention in Egypt of the Achaemenid period.

To date, the earliest evidence from Aramaic sources for a North-South geographical perspective comes from the Sefire treaties of eighth century B.C.E. Syria. Following ancient conventions, "above" is North and "below" is South as a reflection of the courses of the Euphrates and the Tigris, which both flow in a southerly direction. Thus, the entire land of Aram is referred to as עלי ארם ותחתה, "upper Aram and its lower part."[40] A similar geographical perception is conveyed in two official Aramaic letters from Egypt of the fifth century B.C.E. The writer refers to lands as זילי זי בעליתא ותחתיתא, "which belong to me, which are in upper [Egypt] and its lower part." The difference is that, given the northerly flow of the Nile, Upper Egypt is its southern part, and Lower Egypt its northern part, as is well known.[41]

For a time, this over-arching geographical perception confused investigators of the Elephantine Aramaic papyri who found directional boundary descriptions in private real estate transactions. But, as determined by E. Kraeling and B. Porten, Aramaic לעליה לה, "above it" in such private documents meant "North," and לתחתיה לה "below it" meant "South," and referred to properties actually lying to the North and South of those listed in the relevant contracts.[42] I have proposed that this divergence indicated resistance to the overall geographical perceptions so basic to Egyptian culture, and meant, in effect, that the conventions employed in drawing up real estate documents were not of Egyptian origin, but were part of the cultural apparatus of the Near Eastern societies from which the residents

---

[40] See J. A. Fitzmyer, *The Aramaic Inscriptions of Sefire* (Biblica et Orientalia 19; Rome: Pontifical Biblical Institute, 1967) Sefire I A, lines 5–6, and p. 31, in the commentary.

[41] See B. Porten and A. Yardeni, *Textbook of Aramaic Documents from Ancient Egypt, 1: Letters* (Jerusalem: Akademon, 1986), 110, A6.7 Driver 5, lines 5–6, and as restored, 104, A6.4 Driver 2, line 2. It may be relevant to mention that the Egyptian perception of "upper" as "South" and "lower" as "North" in a directional context is evidenced in an Amarna letter from the Pharaoh to the king of Amurru. See J. A. Knudtzon, *Die El-Amarna Tafeln* (Aalen: Otto Zeller Verlagsbuchhandlung, 1964) 1.658, s.v. El-Amarna, no.162, lines 80–81, and W. L. Moran, *The Amarna Letters* (Baltimore and London: The Johns Hopkins University Press, 1987) 250: "For his troops and his chariots in multitude, from the Upper Land to the Lower Land, the rising of the sun to the setting of the sun, all goes very well."

[42] For discussion see E. G. Kraeling, *The Brooklyn Museum Aramaic Papyri* (New Haven: Yale University Press, 1953) 76–78; B. Porten, *Archives at Elephantine* (Berkeley: University of California Press, 1968) 308–310.

of Elephantine had come.[43] Although designations meaning "above" and "below" do not occur at Naḥal Ḥever, it is clear that the same, ancient pattern of boundary descriptions was being used there in the Roman period with replacement terminology.

There is considerable flexibility of formulation in the various papyri from Naḥal Ḥever, themselves, including in the Seiyal Collection. The predominant sequence in the Jewish-Aramaic papyri is (1) East-West, (2) North-South, which preserves the traditional precedence of North over South in the ancient Near Eastern conventions as well as the initially easterly perspective. In the Nabatean-Aramaic papyri from Naḥal Ḥever, South consistently precedes North, but the formulary nonetheless begins with East-West. This both resembles and differs from the sequence in Medieval Arabic documents from Egypt which is: South (*giblī*), North (*bahrī*), East (*šarqī*), and West (*ǵarbī*).[44] In the Greek papyri from Naḥal Ḥever, South precedes North, but the sequence still begins with East-West.[45] To put it simply: A Jew or any person at Naḥal Ḥever, writing in Jewish-Aramaic registered North-South, whereas his Nabatean neighbor, or any person writing in Nabatean-Aramaic registered South-North, and this would also pertain to a contemporary Jewish neighbor writing in Greek.

These internal differences also have a long history. The Byzantine papyri from Elephantine, edited by J. Joel Farber,[46] and now conveniently presented in the compendium assembled by Bezalel Porten, *The Elephantine Papyri in English*,[47] consistently express the Egyptian river orientation, beginning with South in the description of boundaries.[48] Conceivably, the Arabic sequence may have been appropriated from the Egyptian Byzantine tradition, or it could be accounted for in other ways. At times, and within a given cultural context, shifts in the sequence of boundaries in specific contracts may reflect the relative importance of the individuals whose properties lay adjacent to those being transacted, as has been suggested by B. Porten.[49] For the most part, however, we are en-

---

[43] See B. A. Levine, "On the Origins of the Aramaic Legal Formulary at Elephantine," *Christianity, Judaism, and other Greco-Roman Cults: Studies for Morton Smith at Sixty* (3 vols.; ed. J. Neusner; Leiden: E. J. Brill, 1975) 3.48–53 {*VOL 2, PP. 57–71*}.

[44] Khan, *Arabic Legal and Administrative Documents*, 31–32.

[45] For discussion see Lewis, *Documents*, 14, III A, iv, and 45, s.v. 11, 4–6 and 17–19.

[46] J. J. Farber, "Greek Texts [D1–52]," *The Elephantine Papyri in English: Three Millennia of Cross-Cultural Continuity and Change* (ed. B. Porten et al.; Leiden: E. J. Brill, 1996).

[47] B. Porten, et al., *The Elephantine Papyri in English: Three Millennia of Cross-Cultural Continuity and Change* (Leiden: E. J. Brill, 1996).

[48] See Farber, "Greek Texts [D1–52]," 431, 014, Recto, lines 7–9, 448, D21, Recto, 15–20; 452, D22, Recto, lines 23–26; 482, D32, Recto, lines 34–40; 510–511, 040, Recto, lines 55–57; 523, 045, Recto, lines 24–25, 31–34 and so forth.

[49] See "Boundary Descriptions in the Bible and in Conveyances from Egypt and the Judean Desert," *The Dead Sea Scrolls: Fifty Years after Their Discovery. Proceedings of the Jerusalem Congress, July 20-25, 1997* (ed. L. H. Schiffman, E. Tov and J. C. Van-

countering cultural differences in perception, not all of which can be explained, and which operated within the broad framework of persistent legal conventions.

Descriptive Provisions of both Common and Distinctive Character

Perhaps the most interesting, and at times enigmatic passages in the Nabatean legal texts are those which describe parcels of land and other possessions germane to the transactions involved, stating the rights of ownership pertaining to them. Often, legal stipulations employing Arabic terms and formulas occur alongside, and even interspersed with physical descriptions registered in Aramaic, so that it is unclear where one feature ends and the other begins. To add to the difficulty, the Nabatean papyri exhibit lacunae and difficult readings precisely in some of these sections.

Whereas comparable formulations in the Jewish-Aramaic legal papyri are more balanced, and descriptions are usually demarcated from legal provisions, the Nabatean scribes tended to braid asymmetrical terminology, as if they were uncertain as to where the various terms would fit in best. These clauses exhibit the greatest extent of divergence between the Jewish and Nabatean documents. Though further investigation will be required, most of the Arabic terms of reference appearing in such clauses have been identified.

The first feature to be considered here pertains to irrigation, a technology highly developed among the Nabateans, as is known. Leases and purchase agreements were required to contain provisions assuring the right of scheduled times of irrigation, and guaranteeing use of irrigation ditches. Greenfield and Yardeni (1996) discuss this subject in their edition of NḤ 7,[50] the Jewish-Aramaic deed of grant which contains such provisions. In a recent study of Greek documents from the archive of a Jewish woman living in Maḥoza, Hannah Cotton discusses the comparable formulary in a similar deed of gift written in Greek, and shows just how widespread was the requirement to stipulate this practice in regions reaching all the way to Kurdistan.[51]

Let us begin by citing NḤ 7, lines 6–7, from the Jewish-Aramaic deed of grant published by Greenfield and Yardeni.[52] There, a father states, in the first person, that he is granting his daughter a grove of date palms, whose boundaries are then delineated. The statement continues as follows:

---

derKam, Jerusalem: Israel Exploration Society in cooperation with the Shrine of the Book, Israel Museum, 2000) 852–861.

[50] Greenfield and Yardeni, "A Deed of Gift."

[51] See H. M. Cotton, "The Archive of Salome Komaise Daughter of Levi: Another Archive from the 'Cave of Letters,'" *Zeitschrift für Papyrologie and Epigraphik* 105 (1995) 193–194 in comments on no. IV, a deed of gift in Greek, lines 8–9/27–28, from the archive of Salome, daughter of Levi, originating from Naḥal Ḥever. See now *idem*, "Aramaic and Hebrew Documentary Texts," 215–216, and R. Katzoff and B. M. Schreiber, "Weekend and Sabbath in Judaean Desert Documents," *Scripta Classica Israelitica* 17 (1998) 102–114.

[52] Greenfield and Yardeni, "A Deed of Gift."

וענימוהי עם ירתי יוסף בר דרמנס לילא חמשא בשבה שעה ופלג מן שעין תלת

> And its [assigned] irrigation times are to be together with the heirs of So-and-So, during the night of the fifth day of the week, an hour and a half out of three hours.

Compare a similar statement from NḤ 3, lines 22–25, a Nabatean deed of purchase:

יומא הו זבן פלוני בר פלוני --- מני, אנה, פלונית ברת פלוני --- גנת תמריא ... על
שקיא וענימיה פלגות שעה חדה ביום חד ב[שבת]א כל שבא [ושב]ה עד עלם

> That day, So-and-So son of So-and-So purchased from me, So-and-So, daughter of So-and-So, etc., a palmery … including its irrigation ditches and its [assigned] times of irrigation, one half hour on the first day of the week, every week, in perpetuity.

The form שבה/א, "week," representing Hebrew שבת, is attested in Elephantine Aramaic in the well-known Sabbath ostracon first published by Dupont-Sommer.[53] Among other things, its usage attests to the meaning "week", but that is another subject.[54] What is of concern here is the fascinating term עני מיה, and variations of the same, which is attested in the Tosefta as עונתו של מים, "his assigned time of irrigation" (*t. Moᶜed* 1:2). As a general rule, irrigation activity was permitted during the intervening days of the festivals, and this extended to the act of leasing out one's assigned times of irrigation to another during those days.[55] I take the form עני to represent the plural construct of ען, hence: "times, periods of-". The projected form ען would represent the masculine of ענת "time, period." Compare the Aramaic adverbs כענת, כען, "now then," and Hebrew עתה (epigraphic עת), and of course Hebrew עת, עתים, "time, times," and the noun עונה, "term"—all cognates.[56] The term עני מיה is best explained as a contribution of Nabatean-Aramaic, which was adopted by contemporary Jews for use in their legal documents and thereby found its way into Talmudic literature.

A recurrent descriptive provision in the Nabatean papyri, of a more general sort, contains both common and distinctive features. It reads as follows:

וכול מנדעם זעיר ושגיא די חזה לה בזבניא אלה שמש וחנה טלל זבן ארכלס דנה

---

[53] A. Dupont-Sommer, "L'ostracon araméen du Sabbat," *Semitica* 2 (1949) 29–39

[54] See J. H. Tigay, "Notes on the Development of the Jewish Week," *Eretz-Israel* 14 (H. L. Ginsberg Volume; Jerusalem: Israel Exploration Society, 1978) 111–121.

[55] See Greenfield and Yardeni, "A Deed of Gift," 395, P. Yadin 7, lines 6–7, referring to S. Lieberman, *Tosefta Ki-fshuṭah, Part V, Order Moᶜed* (New York: Jewish Theological Seminary of America, 1962) 1228–1229, who first interpreted the Talmudic terms on the basis of the reading in the Erfurt manuscript.

[56] See Ezra 4:10–11, and *DNWSI*, 526–527, s.v. *kᶜn* 4. Also see B. A. Levine, "On the Arad Inscriptions," *Shnaton* 3 (1979) 283–294 (Hebrew) for a discussion of epistolary style.

> And every which thing, small or large, which is fitting for him in respect of these purchases, both in sunny areas and where shadow falls, this same Archileus has purchased.

This clause incorporates a well known Aramaic cliché, or merism, referring to everything "small or large." It normally appears in Medieval Arabic documents as: *kull qalīl wa-kaṯīr*, "everything small or large," sometimes as: *ma ... min qalīl wa-kaṯīr*, "whatever ... including small or large."[57] This Semitism is expressed in the Greek papyri at Naḥal Ḥever as: ἐκ πάντος τρόπου μείκρου καὶ μεγάλου, "in every manner (of thing), small or large."[58] It is unnecessary to expand here on the universality of this merism; suffice it to mention its currency in Akkadian, expressed as *ṣiḫir (u) rabi*, "the youngest and the oldest"[59] and in Biblical Hebrew as למקטן ועד גדול, "from small to large/young to old" (2 Kgs 23:2, Jer 42:8 and cf. Gen 19:11, Deut 1:17, 1 Sam 30:19).

The sense of Aramaic שמש וחנה טלל, which we have rendered "both in sunny areas and where shadow falls," had not appeared in the Jewish-Aramaic documents and was unattested until now. Yet, in an Aramaic testament of manumission from Elephantine we find the formula ואנתי שביקה מן טלא לסמשא, "and you are released from shade to sun," namely, anywhere you may be. A line later, the same release stipulation is rephrased as follows: ואנתי שביקה לאלהא, "and you are released to God."[60] The composite term חנה טלל may express the Hebrew/Aramaic verb, חנ"י/חנ"ה, "to encamp, set," as in Jud 19:9: הנה נא רפה היום לערב ... הנה חנות היום, "Behold, the day has grown dim as the sun sets ... behold the setting of the day." The specific form realized in Nabatean-Aramaic חנה is uncertain. We have taken it as a simple-stem participle. Conceivably, חנה טלל might designate a structure of some sort that shaded an area from the sun. In any event, the sense would be that the provisions of the contract covered the entire area of the property.

Conclusions

The Jewish-Aramaic and the Nabatean-Aramaic documents share a common vocabulary of Aramaic "legalese," consisting of idioms and formulas that produce a similar effect on the reader. In fact, the influence of Aramaic on contemporary Hebrew documents, such as those from Naḥal Ḥever and Murabbaʿat, creates a similarity among all three groups. There is, finally, a commonality of compositional structure, with conventional components occurring in routine sequence. And yet, the most challenging task facing scholars is to identify the diversity existing within commonality; to pinpoint the differences, sometimes

57 See Khan, *Arabic Legal and Administrative Documents*, 48.

58 See Lewis, *Documents*, 15, s.v. viii, b, referring to no. 5 a I, lines 11–13, on page 37.

59 See *CAD Ṣ*, 184, s.v. *ṣiḫru*, 2, c).

60 See Porten and Yardeni, *Textbook*, 72, s.v. B3.6 Kraeling 5, lines 9–10.

subtle and at other times blatant, between the ways in which Jews and Nabateans, both heirs to a rich Aramaic tradition, normally expressed themselves.[61]

[61] I am grateful to Hannah Cotton, Simon Hopkins, Alfred Ivry and Ada Yardeni for discussing various aspects of this paper with me.

MULŨGU/MELÛG: The Origins of a Talmudic Legal Institution*

This study is dedicated to the memory of the late Ephraim A. Speiser, wise in law as in life.

The Talmud, in its Palestinian and Babylonian versions, presents a crystallized system of law which developed during the final pre-Christian and early Christian centuries. During that period the Jewish communities of Palestine and Babylonia were open to diverse influences from other Near Eastern cultures. Scholars of Jewish history and law have sought to define and to assess the Hellenistic factor in Jewish law,[1] but relatively little effort has been devoted to a study of the Mesopotamian factor, which may prove to be of great value in understanding the origins of Talmudic institutions.

The channels of influence from the Hellenistic to the Jewish culture were fairly direct, but the course of possible Mesopotamian influence on Jewish Palestine during the first few Christian centuries cannot be so easily traced. It is

---

* Originally published in *JAOS* 88 (1968), pp. 274–277. Reprinted with permission from the American Oriental Society. In the original publication, footnotes 45 and 48 were skipped. To preserve the original numbering, therefore, they have been omitted here as well.

Bibliographical abbreviations are as in *CAD* and *AHw*, with the following additions:

AP = A. E. Cowley, *Aramaic Papyri of the Fifth Century B. C.*, Oxford, 1923.

BMAP = E. Kraeling, *The Brooklyn Museum Aramaic Papyri*, New Haven, 1953.

Genesis Rabbāh = *Midrash Rabbāh, Berēʾšît Rabbāh*, ed. M. A. Mirkin, Tel Aviv, 1956.

hal. = *halākāh*, a section of the chapter in the *Palestinian Talmud.*

P. Koschaker, *RSGH* = P. Koschaker, *Rechtsvergleichende Studien zur Gesetzgebung Hammurapis*, Leipzig, 1917.

J. Levy, *Wörterbuch* = J. Levy, *Wörterbuch über die Talmudim und Midraschim*, Darmstadt, 1963, 4 vols.

Mishnah, The Six Orders of the Mishnah, ed. C. H. Albeck, Tel Aviv, 1952–, 6 vols.

TB = *Talmud, Babylonian*, standard editions, Wilno.

TP = *Talmud, Palestinian*, standard editions, Krotoschin.

UT = C. H. Gordon, *Ugaritic Textbook*, Rome, 1965.

[1] For bibliography see S. Baron, *A Social and Religious History of the Jews*, 2nd ed., New York, 1952, II:427, and note 4; 431–432 and notes 11–14, and especially S. Lieberman, "Rabbinic Interpretation of Scripture," *Hellenism in Jewish Palestine*, New York, 1960, 47–82. A. Gulak, *Das Urkundenwesen im Talmud*, Jerusalem, 1935, explores the connections between the Hellenistic papyrology and Talmudic law. Also see Y. Baer, "The Historical Foundations of the Hallachah," (Hebrew), *Zion*, Jerusalem, 1942, 1–55.

only from the beginning of the third century C.E. that adequate information on the contacts between the Jewries of Palestine and Babylonia becomes available, and by then the Tannaitic institutions had already achieved their definitive form.[2] Thus, though the sages of Babylonia were in a position to transmit Mesopotamian culture to Palestine, their actual role in the creation of early Talmudic Judaism remains uncertain.

There are, however, several facts which support the notion of Mesopotamian influence on Palestinian legal development. The cuneiform script and the Akkadian language continued in use beyond the Seleucid period. The military confrontations between the forces of regional, Mesopotamian rulers and the Romans provided a persisting context for cultural interchange between East and West during the first several Christian centuries. Mesopotamian influence on Hellenistic and Roman law has already received considerable attention from students of antiquity,[3] and the extent of such influence suggests that, as a parallel phenomenon, Palestinian Jewish law was also affected by the enduring impetus of Mesopotamian culture.

With respect to Palestinian society, we should take into account the role of the Aramaic language in preserving and transmitting elements of the Akkadian vocabulary to the eastern shores of the Mediterranean.

The present investigation seeks to contribute only one additional link between cuneiform and Talmudic legal usage. It focuses on a single term, *mulūgu* (consonantal *mlwg*), which is the Hebrew form of the term *mulūgu* (sometimes written *mulūku* in the earlier texts), attested in cuneiform sources. From its first occurrences in the Amarna period, and throughout the period of the Talmud, this term relates to the same complex of legal phenomena. It designates types of dowries bestowed by fathers on their daughters, or by brothers on their sisters, *in loco parentis*.

I

The term *mulūgu* first occurs in the Amarna period—at Ugarit, Nuzi, and at el-Amarna itself. We next encounter it in *kudurru* inscriptions dating from the eleventh and tenth centuries, and then in Neo-Babylonian legal documents. In the form *melûg* it recurs in Talmudic literature.[4]

---

[2] J. Neusner, in discussing the expansion of Tannaitic Judaism, has brought to light certain contacts between the Jewries of Palestine and Babylonia during the first half of the second century C.E. See his *A History of the Jews in Babylonia I*, Leiden, 1965, 113f.

[3] For a recent discussion, see E. A. Speiser, "Cuneiform Law and the History of Civilization," *Proceedings, American Philosophical Society*, 107, Philadelphia, 1963, 536–541, and especially 540, note 20. A. Leo Oppenheim, *Ancient Mesopotamia*, Chicago, 1964, 73, stresses the need for a study of Mesopotamian influence on Hellenistic Egypt.

[4] Sources for the term *mulūgu/melûg*:

a) *mlgh* "her *mulūgu*" *UT* 77:47, p. 183; glossary no. 1480.

b) *mu-lu-u-ki*, pl. *VS* XII 201; p. 57f.; EA 25:col. iii:65 (vol 1, pp. 188f.). *mu-lu-ku*, *ibid.* col. iv:64. *mu-lu-gi*^{meš} pl. *ibid.* col. iv:65.

It has not been possible to relate *mulūgu* to any Semitic root extant in the second or first millennium B.C.E. Suggested etymologies from Sumerian are dubious.[5] A proposed Egypto-Semitic derivation involves considerable phonetic shifting and postulation.[6]

We are no more enlightened by the efforts of lexicographers to provide an etymology for Talmudic *melûg*. The Babylonian Talmud offers no etymology whatsoever in its comments on the Mishnah (*Yebāmôt* 7:1), suggesting that the meaning of the term might have been known in Babylonia. The Palestinian sources relate the term *melûg* to the Hebrew root *mlg/q* "to pluck, break off." As we shall observe, this reflects a central feature of Talmudic legislation regarding the *melûg*, i.e. that the husband had the right of usufruct over *melûg* dowry property, and could "pluck off" its revenue.[7] Similarly, when Talmudic lexico-

---

c) *a-na mu-lu-ku-ti RA XXIII* 31:14, p. 109. *HSS* V 80:13 (*AASOR* X 26:13, p. 59). *a-na mu-lu-ki HSS* V 11:17 (*AASOR* X 31:17, p. 65). LÚ *mu-lu-ku* "a *mulūgu* man" *HSS* XIII 93:17–18, p. 14; *HSS* XIV 2:17–18. *mul-lu-ki, Genava* n.s. XV, 18, no. 10:10.

d) A.ŠÀ *mu-li-gi* "a *mulūgu* field" I Rawlinson 70, col. I:4, KB IV: 78179. A.ŠÀ *ki-i mu-lu-gi* "the field as *mulūgu*" I Rawlinson 70, col. II:17, *KB* IV:82–83.

e) LÚ *mu-lu-gu* "a *mulūgu* man" *VS* IV 46:5. MUNUS *mu-lu-gi-šu* "his *mulūgu* woman" *VS* V 53:9 = Peiser, *Verträge* 26:9, and copy, p. 15. *mu-lu-gu TMH* ii/iii 1:10, *Aegyptus* 27, 1947, 119f.

f) *tamalagum* (?) "a coffer for documents." J. Lewy, *Orientalia* N.S. 19, 1950, 2, note 1f. argues that Old Assyrian *tamalagum* is related to *mulūgu*, which originally meant the container in which the woman kept her valuables. He cites Jewish Babylonian Aramaic *melôgāʾ* "a sack for documents," but this is probably Greek μολγός "leather, skin." He also notes the functional equivalence of *mulūgu* and *quppu* "basket," a point we shall discuss further. Functional equivalence should not be confused, however, with etymology, and we doubt that *tamalagum* is related to *mulūgu*.

g) *ʿabdê melûg* "*melûg* slaves" Mishnah, *Yebāmôt* 7:1–2; *Tôseptāʾ*, *Yebāmôt* 9:1; *TP Yebāmôt* 7:hal. 1; *TB Yebāmôt* 66a–b, *Bābāʾ Qammāʾ* 89b. *šipḥat melûg* "a *melûg* slave-woman" *Genesis Rabbāh* II:155, *TP Yebāmôt* 7:hal. 1, *TB Ketûbôt* 78b, 101a, *Bābāʾ Qammāʾ* 88b–89a, 90a, *Bābāʾ Meṣîʿāʾ* 35a, *Bābāʾ Batrāʾ* 50a–b, 139b. *behemat melûg* "a *mêlug* animal" *TP Yebāmôt* 7:hal. 1; *TB Ketûbôt* 79b–80a. *niksê melûg* "*melûg* property, Goods" *TB Ketûbôt* 78b, *Bābāʾ Qammāʾ*, 88b, *Bābāʾ Meṣîʿāʾ* 35a, 96b, *Bābāʾ Batrāʾ* 50a, 139b. Note that *i-na ma-al-gu-te* (*AHw* 595, s.v. *malgūtu*) is unrelated to *mulūgu*. P. Koschaker, *REGH* 174–175, notes 81–86 discusses the term *mulūgu*, and see Petschow, *Pfandrecht* 58.

[5] Ungnad, *NRV* 89, considers *mulūgu* a Sumerian loanword: MULUK = *ša beli* "of the master, owner (MULU = *amēlu*)," with the original sense of that which the master of the house may dispose of. Cf. *ŠL* 61/188–189, 199, 203. Also suggested is NA_4.MUL.UG = *il-lu-ku* "a precious stone, a sumptuous garment" *CAD I/J*, 86, s.v. *illūku*. A. Falkenstein, *ZA, N.F.* 15, 1949, 326, and note 6 disputes any connection between *illūku* and *mulūgu*.

[6] W. F. Albright, *AJSL* 34, 1918, 92, note 3 suggests that *mulūgu* means "nursing fee" from Egyptian *mnʿt* "nurse." He postulates a verbal form *mnʿ** which, by phonetic shifts, becomes *mnğ/mlg*.

[7] *Genesis Rabbāh* II:155 (section 45:1); *TP Yebāmôt* 7:hal. 1; *kemāʾ detêmāʾ*: *melôg! melôg!* "As you say: 'Pluck! Pluck!'" The root *mlg* was considered a variant of *mlq* "to

graphers recognized the importance of Greek and Latin to their studies, *melûg* was related to Greek ἀμέλγω, Latin *mulgeo* "to milk," again connoting the legal rights of the husband.[8] These derivations are logical rather than etymological, and were adduced without any awareness of the cuneiform evidence. The identity of *mulūgu* with *melûg* is accepted by those Semitists who cite the later usage of the term, and by some Talmudists.[9]

II

Before proceeding to a precise legal analysis, it would be well to offer some general observations on the provenience of the term *mulūgu*/*melûg*. That it designates a type of dowry is evident from the single occurrence of the term in Ugaritic literature. In the marriage of Yariḫ and Nikkal (*UT* 77) the father and brothers of the bride-goddess weigh out on the scales *ṯlḫh wmlgh* "her parting gifts (Hebrew *šillûḥîm*)[10] and her *mulūgu*" (line 47). The *mlg* is here distinguished from the *mhr* (Hebrew *môhar*) mentioned earlier in the text (line 19),[11] which was a payment from the groom to the father of the bride. The Ugaritic evidence does not allow for more than this basic classification.

One document from the Amarna corpus (*VS* XII 201, EA 25) records male and female personnel designated by the term *mulūgu*. They are listed as part of the lavish dowry sent by Tušratta, king of Mitanni, to accompany his daughter, Tatuhepa, on the occasion of her marriage to an Egyptian Pharaoh, most probably Amenophis IV.[12] The text enumerates many gifts, consisting largely of precious materials. In one instance the *mulūgu* personnel came bearing silver on their persons.[13] The list of these gifts concludes as follows:

---

break off," as in Lev. 1:15; 5:8. Cf. *LS* 390, s.v. *mlg*. Levy, *Wörterbuch*, III:123, s.v. *mlg*. D. Feuchtwang, *ZA* 6, 1892, 441.

[8] S. Krauss, *Griechische und Lateinische Lehnwörter im Talmud, Midrasch, und Targum*, Berlin, 1899, II:476. A. Kohut, *Aruch Completum*, Vienna, 1926, s.v. *mlg*.

[9] D. Feuchtwang, *op. cit.*, 441. H. Zimmern, *Akkadische Fremdwörter*, Leipzig, 1917, 46. E. A. Speiser, *AASOR* X, p. 24, note 53. C. H. Gordon, *BASOR* 65, 1937, 30. M. Greenberg, *JAOS* 71, 1951, 172. J. N. Epstein, *Jahrbuch der Jüdisch-Literarischen Gesellschaft* 6, 1908, 360, note 3. V. Marx, *Beiträge zur Assyriologie und semitischen Sprachwissenschaft* 4, 1899–1902, 18, note. Ch. Albeck, *Mishnah*, *Nāšim*, 337, s.v. *Yebāmôt* 7:1. Albeck argues that if *melûg* were a term borrowed from Akkadian it would have been known to the Houses of Hillel and Shammai who, in *Ketûbôt* 8:6 use another formula instead of this term. The variability of technical terminology is admittedly a problem in the study of law, but the absence of a certain term in one source does not allow us to dismiss other textual evidence of considerable weight.

[10] 1 Kings 9:16.

[11] Gen 34:12, Exodus 22:16, 1 Sam 18:25.

[12] See note in EA vol 2, pp. 1057–1058.

[13] *VS* XII 201, EA 25:col. iii:65: *ša* 1 ME MUNUS.MEŠ *mu-lu-ú-ku* 1 *li-im* 4 ME GÍN KÙ.BABBAR *i-na lib-bi-šu-nu na-di* "of 100 *mulūgu* women with 1400 shekels of silver placed on their persons." Col. iv:64: 2 ME MUNUS.MEŠ 30 LÚ.MEŠ *mu-lu-ku* "200 women, 30 men, *mulūgu*."

> *ú-nu*]-*te-e*^{meš} *mu-lu-gi*^{meš} *an-nu-ti gab-ba šu-nu-*[*ma du*]-*uš-rat-ta* LUGAL ^{kur}*mi-i-it-ta-ni*[....]*sa it-ta-di-nu*
> These goods and *mulūgu*'s, all of them, Tušratta, king of Mitanni [.....] which he gave.[14]

These *mulūgu* personnel were, in our view, slaves granted as part of the dowry. Slaves were a logical type of property to be included in a dowry. They were often linked to their original family of owners, and would accompany a bride into her new home, and continue to serve her. This custom is attested in Talmudic sources, where there is legislation governing *mulūgu* slaves (*ʿabdê melûg*), and it seems to be attested as well in several Neo-Babylonian legal texts to be discussed further.[15]

In the Talmudic legal system *mulūgu* slaves were considered the wife's property, primarily. It is, therefore, interesting that in one Nuzi text a man designated *mulūgu* is referred to as belonging to the wife of the man in question, and not to the man himself:

> *a-na* ^{I}*a-pu-uk-ka* LÚ *mu-lu-ki ša* DAM-*at ḫi-iš-mi-te-šup* DUMU.LUGAL *it-ta-din-šu-nu-ti*
> to Apukka, the *mulūgu* man of the wife of Hišmi-tešup, the palace official, he has given them.[16]

The Midrash refers to Hagar, Abraham's "second wife" as a *mulūgu* slave woman (*šipḥat melûg*). In Talmudic legislation this meant that Sarah had the right to dispose of Hagar as she saw fit. This was the legal basis for Abraham's acquiescence to his wife's demands. The Midrash takes its cue from the words of Abraham to his wife: "Your slavewoman is in your hand (= possession); deal with her as you think proper" (Genesis 16:6).[17]

III

Cuneiform legal sources bearing on the term *mulūgu* come primarily from two groups of texts, Nuzi and Neo-Babylonian, with two *kudurru* inscriptions intervening.

---

[14] For the restoration [*ú-nu*]-*te-e*^{meš} cf. EA vol 2, p. 1539, in the index s.v. *unūtu*, and see text 14 iii:8, 45, etc. (EA vol 1, p. 117f.). The fact that here we have a *g* in *mu-lu-gi*, and elsewhere in this text a *k* is probably not significant.

[15] See Mishnah, *Yebāmôt* 7:1–2, and *TMH* ii/iii: 1, *VS* IV 46, *VS* V 53. A woman named Ašte and designated *mu-lu-ki* is mentioned in a text from Kirkuk recently treated by E. R. Lacheman (*Genava*, n.s. XV, 1967, 18, no. 10, line 10, and note, p. 23). From the context it is probable that she was a slave.

[16] *HSS* XIII 93:17–18, p. 14 (*HSS* XIV pl. 2). On the title DUMU.LUGAL = *mār šarri*(*m*) see *Lešônenu* (Hebrew) 31, 1967, 85f.

[17] *Genesis Rabbāh* II:155 (section 45:1): "Hagar was a *melûg* slave woman, and although he (= Abraham) was obligated to provide for her sustenance, he had no right to sell her." Cf. the formulation in Mishnah, *Ketûbôt* 8:1.

The Nuzi material includes more than one type of *mulūgu*. *HSS* V 80 (*AASOR* X 26) is a marriage agreement (*ṭuppi riksi*). Akkulenni agrees to give his daughter as wife to Hurazzi. There is then an exchange of property and silver:

> 7) *ù* ^{I}*ḫu-ra-uz-zi* 1 GUD 10 GÍN KÙ.BABBAR.MEŠ
> 8) *ḫa-ša-ḫu-še-en-nu ki-mu-ú te-ir-ḫa-ti-šu*
> 9) *ša* ^{f}*be-el-ta-ak-ka*$_{4}$*-du-um-me*
> 10) *a-na* ^{I}*ak-ku-li-en-ni i-na-an-din*
> 11) *um-ma* ^{I}*ak-ku-li-en-ni-ma mi-nu-um-me-e*
> 12) KÙ.BABBAR-*šú ri-iḫ-tù ša* ^{f}*be-el-ta-ak-ka*$_{4}$*-du-um-mi*
> 13) *a-na mu-lu-ku-ti ù a-na qa-an-ni-šu*
> 14) *a-na* ^{f}*be-el-ta-ak-ka*$_{4}$*-du-um-me ir-ta-ak-sú-mi*
>
> As for Hurazzi: One herd of large cattle, 10 shekels of silver, in any form desired,[18] as the marriage payment[19] of Belit-Akkad-ummi to Akkulienni he shall pay. Statement of Akkulienni: Moreover, all the remaining silver of Belit-Akkad-ummi as *mulūkūtu* in her sash, for Belit-Akkad-ummi, they have tied.

Several facts are essential for the legal situation presented in this text. The standard amount of the *terḫatu* at Nuzi for a previously unmarried woman was forty shekels.[20] In this text the amounts are not stated explicitly. Speiser called attention, however, to *JEN* I 78[21] where we have a parallel situation which can clarify our text. There, a man accepts twenty shekels for his sister, and states

---

[18] The meaning of *ḫašaḫušennu* is not certain. See *CAD Ḫ*, 136–137. Since the word often occurs in attribution with KÙ.BABBAR, it might describe the form of silver used in marriage payments. E. Lacheman (by verbal communication) has suggested that it means: "in any manner of payment desired," based on the sense of the verb *ḫašāḫu*. The late J. Lewy (by verbal communication) drew attention to Ezra 6:9: *ûmāh ḫašḫān* "In whatever form they desired, whether turtle doves, rams, etc." Also cf. Ezra 7:20.

[19] Although the term *terḫatu* is beyond the scope of this study, some discussion of its sense is required, since in this text, the *mulūgu* was subtracted from the amount paid as *terḫatu*. P. Koschaker, *RSGH*, 130f., and *MVAG* 28, 1921, 56f. renders *terḫatu* "bride price." Dr. H. Lewy has more accurately characterized the *terḫatu* at Nuzi as a payment by the groom and his family to those who reared the young woman, to compensate them for expenses so incurred (*Orientalia* N.S. 10, 1941, 21, note 1). It well may be that *terḫatu* is from the verb *reḫû* "to have sexual intercourse" as Dr. Lewy elsewhere suggests (*Orientalia* N.S. 11, 1942, 342, note 1). Now there is evidence from Neo-Sumerian (A. Falkenstein, *Die Neusumerischen Gerichtsurkunden* I, Munich, 1956, 103f.) that *terḫatu* may never have meant "bride price" at all, but rather payment for the right to have intercourse with the woman, to take her as wife. For the purposes of our discussion, suffice it to say that by taking half of the *terḫatu* and giving it to his daughter, a father was not conveying silver received as payment for an object, i.e. his daughter, but merely continuing to provide for her from funds received.

[20] P. Koschaker, *ZA*, N.F. 7, 1933, 162f.

[21] *AASOR* X, pp.22–23, note 49, and E. Chiera, *JEN* I 78:13. Also P. Koschaker, *ZA*, N.F. 7, 1933, 16f.

that the remaining twenty shekels are to be tied into his sister's *qannu* for her to keep.[22]

This was, then, one of the ways in which the *mulūgu* functioned. From the *terḫatu*, a part was assigned to the bride at the time of her marriage. The purpose was to provide the woman with resources should she leave her husband's home for valid cause. Speiser first noted the provisions of *HSS* V 67 (*AASOR* X 2) in this connection. If the husband were to take a second wife in violation of the marriage agreement stipulated in that document, his wife would have the right to leave his house:

40) *šum-ma* ᶠ*gi-li-ni-nu ú-la-ad ù* ᴵ*še-en-ni-ma*
41) *aš-ša-ta ša-ni-ta i-ḫa-az*
42) *qa-an-na-šú* ŠA-*sag-ma ú-uṣ-ṣi*

"If Gilimninu does bear (a son), and yet Šenima takes a second wife,
she shall *take up* her *qannu* and depart."

Speiser suggested that the problematic ŠA was a miswritten *i-na* and that we have the verb *i-na-sak-ma* "she shall select, take up."[23] This is now rendered certain by the appearance of the same formula in *HSS* XIX 7:47: *qa-an-na-šu i-na-ás-sa-ak-ma ù ú-uz-zi* "She shall take up her *qannu* and depart."[24]

We can therefore conclude that a bride was given silver at the time of her marriage which she would take with her in the event of a proper divorce. At times this silver was designated *ana mulūkūti*.

A recently published Nuzi text, *HSS* XIX 79 presents a different type of *mulūgu*. It records the legal activities of a father who provides for his grandchildren through the instrumentality of the *mulūgu*:

1) *um-ma pa-ik-ku-ma* DUMU *a-ri-iḫ-ḫar-pa*
2) *i-na pa-na-nu-um-ma* DUMU.MUNUS-*ia* ᶠ*aš-ta-a-a*
3) *a-na aš-šu-ti a-na* ᴵ*a-kap-še-en-ni* DUMU *ut-ḫap-ta-e*

---

[22] See H. Lewy, *Orientalia* N.S. 10, 1941, 209–213, for a discussion of other aspects of this transaction.

[23] *AASOR* X, p. 22. Note that the stipulation forbidding the husband to marry another woman in *HSS* V 67 also occurs in our text, *HSS* V 80.

[24] *HSS* XIX 7 is a last will (*ṭuppi šimti*) addressed by Ilaia to his wife Šeltum. He gives her paternal power (*abbūtu*) over his holdings. As long as she lives, she shall be served by Ilaia's sons. When she dies, the sons shall inherit her estate according to usual procedures. Ilaia then discusses what is to be done with his daughter, Unuš-kiaše. He gives her over into his wife's jurisdiction, whom she is to serve. The text then states: KÙ.BABBAR.MEŠ *i-na qa-an-ni-šá-ma ra-*⌈*ki-is*⌉ "Silver has been tied into her sash" (line 26). The father thus provides for his daughter in this traditional way. The *qannu* figured in last wills just as it did in marriage arrangements. The will ends with the clause we are discussing. If as a widow, the daughter were to marry herself to another man, leaving the domicile of her first husband, she would take the contents of her *qannu* with her. Akkadian *aṣû* and Hebrew *yāṣāʾ* both have the technical sense of divorce. Cf. Deut. 24:2 and, in the Mishnah, C. H. Kasofsky, *Thesaurus Mishnae*, Jerusalem, 1960, II:875–876, s.v. *tēṣēʾ*.

4) *at-ta-din ù i-na-an-na* E.MES *i-na e-li-en*
5) E.MES *ša* ^{I}*ki-in-nu-uz-zi i-na šu-pa-al*
6) E.MES *ša* ^{I}*ut-ḫap-ta-e i-na il-ta-an* E.MES
7) *ša* ^{I}*pa-ik-ku-ma i-na su-ta-an* E.MES *ša* ^{I}*pi-iz-zi-ia*
8) 2⸢5⸣ [*i-na*] *am-ma-ti ù i-na il-ta-an* 25 *i-na am-ma-ti*
9) [*i-na su*]*-ta-ni mu-ra-ak-šu-nu* 9 *i-na am-ma-ti*
10) *i-na el-li-ni* 9 *i-na am-ma-ti i-na šu-pa-li*
11) ⸢*ru-pu*⸣*-us-su-nu an-nu-ti* E.MES ^{I}*pa-ik-ku*
12) *a-na mu-lu-ku-*[*ti*] *a-na* DUMU.MUNUS-*šu* ^{f}*aš-ta-a-a*
13) *a-na* ^{I}⸢*a*⸣*-kap-še-en-ni id-din ù* ^{I}*a-kap-še-en-ni*
14) *ki-ma* NIG.BA-*šu ša* ^{I}*pa-ik-ku* 1 ANSE.NITA
15) *ru-*[*bu-tu*]*-ú* SIG$_5$.GA DIŠ-*en-nu-tum ḫul-la-an-nu*
16) *te-ir-te-en-nu* SIG$_5$.GA-*tum* 10 MA.NA.AN.NA.MEŠ
17) *a-na* ^{I}⸢*pa*⸣*-ik-ku id-din šum-ma* É.MEŠ *pa-ki-ra-na*
18) *i-ra-aš-šu-ú ù* ^{I}*pa-ik-ku* É.MEŠ *ša-šu-nu-ma ú-za-ak-ka*$_4$
19) *a-na* ^{I}*a-kap-še-en-ni i-na-an-din šum-ma*
20) É.MEŠ GAL *la i-na-ak-ki-is šum-ma* É.MEŠ
21) [TUR *la ú-*]*ra-ad-da il-ka ša* É.MEŠ
22) *pa-ik-ku na-ši ù* ^{I}*a-kap-še-en-ni*
23) *la na-ši um-ma* ^{I}*pa-ik-ku-ma mi-nu-um-me-e*
24) *iš-tu lib-bi ša* ^{f}*aš-ta-a-a* DUMU.MUNUS-*ia*
25) *ša ú-uṣ-ṣu-ú lu-ú ma-ru*
26) *lu-ú* DUMU.MUNUS É.MEŠ *ša-ad-da-šu-nu*
27) *ù* ^{I}*a-kap-še-en-ni a-na* LU *ša ba-bi*
28) *la i-na-an-din* EME-*šu ša* ^{I}*pa-ik-ku*
29) *iq-ta-bi-i* KU.BABBAR *ša pi-i ṭup-pi el-te-qi*
30) *ma-nu-um-me-e i-na bi-ri-šu-nu*
31) *i-bal-kat* 1 MA.NA KÙ.BABBAR 1 MA.NA KÙ.GI *u-mal-la*
32–38: Witnesses
39) *ṭup-pu i-na* EGIR *šu-du-ti i-na* URU *nu-zi*
40) *i-na ba-ab* ^{d}NÈ.URU$_7$^{nu}.GAL[25]
41) *šá-ṭì-ir*

Translation:

1) Statement of Paikku, son of Arihharpa:
2) Previously, my daughter, Astaia
3) in marriage to Akapšenni, son of Uthaptae
4) I have given. And, now, the houses: above are
5) the houses of Kinnuzzi; below are
6) the houses of Ut-haptae; to the North are the houses
7) of Paikku; to the South are the houses of Pizzia.
8) 25 cubits on the North side; 25 cubits
9) on the South side is their length. 9 cubits
10) on the upper side, 9 cubits on the lower side

[25] The writing of the name Nergal is problematic. What we have is UNU$_7$ as a confusion of UNU = IRI$_{11}$, but the *nu* sign indicates that we are to read UNU and not IRI$_{11}$. On related problems see *MSL* IV: 12, line 5, and comments.

11) is their breadth. These houses Paikku
12) as *mulūkūtu* for his daughter, Aštaia,
13) to Akapšenni has given. As for Akapšenni,
14) as the gift (*qīštu*) of Paikku 1 mule (*mūru*)
15) four years old, of good quality; one outfit of a *ḫullannu*-garment[26]
16) of second quality; 10 minas of tin,
17) to Paikku has given. If the houses a claim
18) acquire, those houses Paikku shall clear;
19) to Akapšenni he will restore them. If
20) the houses are large, he shall not reduce their size; if the houses
21) are small, he shall not enlarge them. The land tax of the houses
22) Paikku bears; Akapšenni
23) does not bear. Statement of Paikku: Whoever
24) from the womb of Astaia, my daughter,
25) issues forth—whether son
26) or daughter—the houses are theirs.
27) As for Akapšenni: to a person of the gate
28) he shall not sell them. The words of Paikku
29) which he spoke: The silver according to the tablet I have taken.
30) Whoever among them
31) breaks the agreement 1 mina of silver 1 mina of gold he shall pay.
32–38) Witnesses.
39) A tablet following upon the announcement in the city of Nuzi
40) in the gate of Nergal
41) has been written.

Paikku had previously given his daughter in marriage. Against this background he now grants a number of houses to his daughter *ana mulūkūti*. This grant is made both to his daughter and to her husband, who gives a *qīštu* to his father-in-law. After a series of common legal provisions, there is the stipulation that children born of Aštaia would come into possession of the houses, and that they may not be sold to someone outside the family. There is then reference to an amount of silver *ša pî ṭuppi*, relating to an aspect of the transaction not recorded in this tablet.[27]

The context here is inheritance. The father of the family takes measures to assure that a part of his estate will accrue to his grandchildren, born of his daughter.

The *qištu* presented by the son-in-law might have been consideration for the "usufruct" of the property, i.e. its income. Under such an arrangement Paikku would continue to pay the taxes, but would receive an immediate payment of sorts, and would be assured that the property would be tended by his son-in-law. The silver mentioned in line 29 might also have been a payment made to Paikku by Akapšenni in this connection. Paikku was, in effect, settling his estate, or part

[26] *CAD I/J*, 282, s.v. *ištenūtu* 1, c. Also see E. R. Lacheman, *op. cit.*, 22, notes to no. 7, lines 2–3.

[27] Cf. *ša pî ṭuppi šanni* in *HSS* V 11:23.

of it, in his lifetime through the instrumentality of the *mulūgu*, granted to his daughter. As we shall note further on, this text has considerable importance for understanding the functions of the *mulūgu* at Nuzi.

The remaining three tablets wherein the term *mulūgu* or its derivative, *mulūgūtu*, occurs have been called "fictitious" *mulūgu* transactions, supposedly a parallel phenomenon to the legal fiction of the sale adoptions at Nuzi.[28] In the sale adoptions the prospective purchaser was adopted into the family so that an otherwise inalienable parcel of land could be sold to him. The *qištu* served as a disguised sale price. It has been proposed that, in similar fashion, a man could bestow a parcel of family land on his daughter under the terms of a *mulūgu* dowry, and in return receive a *qištu* as purchase price. The daughter could subsequently dispose of the property to someone outside the family, thus circumventing the prohibitions against alienating family land.

The argument for a fictitious *mulūgu* is based primarily on the fact that a *qištu* was exchanged for a *mulūgu*, and that such an exchange could be explained best if the *qištu* was actually a purchase price. It is further assumed that a woman would have the right to dispose of *mulūgu* property to someone outside the family, thus making the fiction effective. Both of these assumptions are questionable. We have just noted in *HSS* XIX 79 that a *qištu* was exchanged for a *mulūgu* in a situation where the alienation of family land could not have been the motive. The exchange does not, in and of itself, establish the fiction. Furthermore, it is not always the case that a woman is free to dispose of her *mulūgu* as she wishes. In *HSS* XIX 79 the *mulūgu* was granted to both the daughter and the son-in-law with specific conditions forbidding alienation of the property.

The evidence for the fictitious *mulūgu* actually consists of only two Nuzi texts, *HSS* V 76 and 11 (*AASOR* X 32 and 31), which pertain to aspects of the same transaction. In the former, Paikku granted a parcel of land to his daughter, Arinturi, *ana mulūki*. The daughter gave her father a *qištu* consisting of clothing and a pig-pen stocked with pigs. There is no mention of marriage. In *HSS* V 11, the same Arinturi gives that parcel of land to another woman, Matqašar:

16) *um-ma* ^{I}*a-ri-in-tù-ri-ma*
17) 1 ANŠE A.ŠÀ *a-bi-ia a-na mu-lu-ki*
18) *a-na i-*<*a*>*-ši*[29] *id-din-na-aš-šu*
19) *ù i-na-an-na a-na-ku*
20) *a-na* ^{I}*ma-at-qa-šar-ma*
21) *at-ta-din*
22) *ù* ^{f}*ma-at-qa-šar-ma*
23) *ša pi*$_4$*-i ṭup-pu ša-an-ni*
24) *a-na* DUMU.MEŠ*-šu-nu i-na-an-din*
25) *a-na* LÚ *na-ka*$_4$*-ri la i-na-an-din*

The statement of Arinturi: One *imer* of land my father gave to me as *mulūgu*. And now I have given it to Matqašar. As for Matqašar: In

[28] Note Speiser's comments in *AASOR* X, pp. 13–18, 26–27.

[29] Written: *i-ši*, and corrected by Speiser.

accordance with the other tablet to their (sic!) sons she shall give (it); to a stranger she shall not give (it).

Does this sequence represent the fulfillment of a fictitious *mulūgu* transaction? This *could* be the case if we were sure that Matqašar was not related to Arinturi. No family relationship is mentioned between the two women, and in a Nuzi text of this type it would be strange for such a fact to be overlooked. On the other hand, the stipulation forbidding Matqašar to give the land to someone outside the family would tend to favor a genuine *mulūgu*, and compares with the provisions of *HSS* XIX 79:27–28.

There is, however, a difference. This limitation of Matqašar's rights was once removed from the original granting of the *mulūgu* by Paikku to his daughter, where no such restrictions were mentioned. Also note that this restriction is linked to the provisions of another tablet, and might have been part of a general arrangement between the two women having nothing to do with the particular legal features of the *mulūgu* as such.

It is likely, therefore, that Arinturi was doing business with her *mulūgu* property in association with a woman outside her family, with whom she had other dealings. If this be the case, then the right of the woman to dispose of *mulūgu* property would seem to be corroborated. It is far from certain, however, that this was intended at the outset.

As for the text published by Gadd (*RA XXIII* 31) and considered by C. H. Gordon to be a fictitious *mulūgu*, the legal information provided is not sufficient to allow for a convincing analysis, since we are uncertain of the entire matter of the fictitious *mulūgu* to start with.[30]

To summarize the evidence of the Nuzi texts, we can state the following:

1) A dowry designated *ana mulūgūti*, and consisting of silver, was tied into the sash of the bride at the time of her marriage. The silver comprised one half of the *terḫatu* (*HSS* V 80).

2) Silver placed in the sash could be retained by the woman, and taken with her in the event of proper divorce (*HSS* V 80 + 67).

3) Property designated *ana mulūgūti* was granted by a father to his daughter and son-in-law as a means of assuring an inheritance for children born of the daughter (*HSS* XIX 79).

4) A woman could do business with property designated *ana mulūki* and could apparently give it to someone outside her family (*HSS* V 76 + 11).

IV

The term *mulūgu* is mentioned in two *kudurru* inscriptions. Both are texts of considerable interest in their own right, and their monumental aspects have made them the subject of study by historians of art. They employ the term *mulūgu* only as a synonym for *nudunnu*, and thus shed little light on the distinc-

[30] C. H. Gordon, *ZA* N.F. 10, 1936, 146–169, and literature cited. Also *Extrait de la Révue Babylonica*, Tome 16, *Librairie Orientaliste*, Paris, 1936, 92–93.

tive aspects of this term, serving only to establish the general provenience of the *mulūgu* as a dowry.

I Rawlinson 70 is a text of four columns dated in the reign of Marduk-nadin-ahhe (1098–1081 B.C.E.).[31] The first column describes the land granted as *mulūgu*, and the terms of the grant. Columns II, III, and IV contain, in a style common to *kudurru*'s, dire admonitions aimed at anyone who would abrogate the grant by stating: A.ŠÀ *ki-i mu-lu-gi ul na-din-ma* "The field as *mulūgu* is not given" (II:17). In I:4 the field is termed A.ŠÀ *mu-li-gi*, but there can be no doubt, despite the phonological variation, that reference is to the *mulūgu* field.

Referring to I:4, the text continues:

> 13) ^{Id}SAHAN.ŠEŠ[32] DUMU *ḫab-ban*
> 14) *a-na* ^{fURU}BAD.LUGAL.GI.NA-*a-a-i-ti*[33]
> 15) DUMU.MUNUS-*šú* É.GI_4 DÙG.GA-*a-šab*-^{d}AMAR.UTU[34]
> 16) DUMU *i-na*-É.SAG.ÍL.NUMUN[35]
> 17) LÚ.SUKAL *a-na* u_4*-um ṣa-a-ti* SUM
> 18) *ù* DÙG.GA-*a-šab*-^{d}AMAR.UTU
> 19) DUMU ^{I}*i-na*-É.SAG.ÍL.NUMUN
> 20) *a-na paq-ri la ra-še-e*
> 21) *ni-iš* DINGIR.MES GAL.MES *ù* ^{d}SAHAN
> 22) *i-na* ^{na4}NA.RÚ.A *šu-a-tum iz-kur*

> Ṣer-uṣur, son of Habban to Dur-šarruken-ai-iti, his daughter, the wife (*kallātu*) of Ṭab-ašab-marduk, son of Ina-esagil-zeru, the *sukallu*, he gave forever. As for Ṭab-ašab-marduk, son of Ina-esagila-zeru, against the acquiring of liens he took an oath by the life of the great gods and of Ṣeru[36] at this statue.

It is interesting that the husband remained liable for clearing liens arising against the field, a responsibility usually laid upon the woman's own father or brothers who had effected the *mulūgu* originally.

Another *kudurru* (*BBst* IX) dates from the tenth century, and concerns various transactions between two families, continuing over a period of some twenty years. Arad-sibitti gave a parcel of land to his married daughter: *ik-nu-uk-ma it-ti mu-lu-gi ù nu-dun-ni-e* "He gave under seal, *in the value of* the *mulūgu* and

---

[31] Transcription, translation, and notes in *KB* IV:78f. For bibliography see R. Borger, *Handbuch der Keilschriftliteratur* I, Berlin, 1967, 366.

[32] See W. J. Hinke, *A New Boundary Stone of Nebuchadrezzar* I, Philadelphia, 1907, 213.

[33] See *RLA* II:249 for the name of the city, and *BBst* XXIV: obv. 20 for the personal name, and in W. J. Hinke, *op. cit.*, 204.

[34] See W. J. Hinke, *op. cit.*, 205, 214.

[35] W. J. Hinke, *op. cit.*, 205.

[36] Sumerian SAHAN = MUŠ = *ṣēru* (*CAD Ṣ*, 148, s.v. *ṣēru* B), designating a snake deity, and serving as an element in the personal name. W. J. Hinke, *op. cit.*, 229.

nudunnu" (I:15–18).[37] Twenty years later one of the woman's brothers, who was about to die, made a statement reiterating the father's original grant, and adjured anyone of the family against contesting the validity of the grant.

The writer did not sense any difference between *mulūgu* and *nudunnu*, again indicating the provenience of the term *mulūgu*. In addition, this text reveals to what extent a woman required protection from the attempts of her brothers to deprive her of her estate.

V

Several Neo-Babylonian documents use the term *mulūgu*. The first to be discussed comes from Borsippa (*TMH* ii/iii: 1), and is dated in the sixth year of Nabonidus. San-Nicolò has studied it very carefully, and its principal points of interest have little to do with the specifics of the term *mulūgu*.[38] Nabu-šumu-iškun granted a parcel of land to Nadin as dowry for his daughter, Kabta, on the occasion of her marriage to him. This same man had been previously married to Kabta's sister, and had earlier received the very same land as dowry on that occasion. This document is a reissuing of that land, with the addition of some land termed *babtu* "amount still due."[39] As San-Nicolò suggests, it is probable that Nadin's first wife died without children, or possibly had been divorced under similar conditions, in which case the dowry would revert to the woman's father, and would have to be reissued.

Of interest is the fact that this text lists the *mulūgu* separately from the rest of the dowry, which is termed *nudunnu*, and that the *mulūgu* consisted of household goods (*udê bīti*) and not land. It is likely that in the Neo-Babylonian period the term *mulūgu* was employed more often for movables than for land.

In another text (*VS* IV 46), dated in the tenth year of Nabonidus, we have a legal situation more enlightening for our considerations.[40]

1) 1⅔ MA.NA 2 GÍN KÙ.BABBAR *šá* ᴵDÙG.GA-*ia*[41]
2) A-*šú ša* ᴵᵈAK.A.MU[42] *a-na* LÚ.TUK-*u*ᵐᵉš
3) *ša muḫ-ḫi* ᵈAK.SUR[43] A-*šu šá* ᴵGAR.MU[44] A LÚ.AD.KID
4) *ul-tu rama-ni-šú uṭ-*[*ṭir*]-*ru ku-um* 2.TA
5) *a-me-lut-tu ri-*[*iḫ*]-*tu* LU *mu-*[*lu*]-*gu šá* ᴵᵈAK.SUR

---

[37] Transcription, translation, and notes in *KB* IV:82. Bibliography in R. Borger, *op. cit.*, 220. On the preposition *itti* in the sense of "per, as against" (for the usual *ana muḫḫi*) see *CAD I/J*, 303, s.v. *itti* c. Cf. Akkadian *nudunnu* with Aramaic *nedûnyaᵓ* in J. Levy, *Wörterbuch*, III:334.

[38] M. San-Nicolò, *Aegyptus*, 27, 1947, 118–134.

[39] *CAD B*, 13, s.v. *babtu* 3c, and San-Nicolò, *op. cit.*, 119–120, 124–125, 132.

[40] Ungnad, *NRV*, 280–281 has a translation and notes, but no transcription of *VS* IV 46.

[41] See Tallqvist, *APN*, 236.

[42] Tallqvist, *APN*, 144.

[43] Tallqvist, *APN*, 149.

[44] Tallqvist, *APN*, 208.

6) *ù* ^{f}GEME.^{d}NIN.LIL *šá* DUG.GA-*ia*
7) *id-da-aš-šú-nu-⸢tu⸣* ^{Id}AK.SUR *i-na mi-gi-ir lìb-bi-šú*[45]
8) SES.SES.MU[46] *ù* ^{f}*si-lim-*^{d}*ba-ú*
9) DAM-*šú* LU.UN E-*šu ku-um maš-ka-nu*[47]
10) *ša* ^{f}GEME.^{d}NIN.LIL DUMU.MUNUS-*šú* DUG.GA-*ia*[48]
11) A-*šú šá* ^{Id}AK.A.MU A ^{d}30-DINGIR *ú-ša-aṣ-bit*
12) LÚ.TUK-*ú ša-nam-ma i-na muḫ-ḫi ul i-šal-laṭ*[49]
13) *e-lat* 1 MA.NA 6 GÍN KÙ.BABBAR *šá qú-up-pu*[50]
14) *šá* ^{f}GEME.^{d}NIN.LIL *šá* ŠE.NUMUN *maš-ka-nu*
15) *ṣab-ta-tu*
Witnesses and date: Nabonidus, year 10.

Translation:

1) As for the 1⅔ minas, 2 shekels of silver, which Ṭabia
2) son of Nabu-apal-iddin, to the creditors (*rāšū*)
3) who (held a debt) against Nabu-eṭir, son of Šakin-šum, son of the weaver of reed mats (*atkuppu*)
4) out of his own resources has paid, in place of the two
5) servants, the remainder of the *mulūgu* personnel of Nabu-eṭir
6) and Amat-Ninlil, which Ṭabia
7) had given them. Nabu-eṭir, of his own free will,
8) Ahhe-iddin and Silim-bau,
9) his wife, servants (*nišī*) of his household, in place of the collateral
10) of Amat-Ninlil, daughter of Ṭabia,
11) son of Nabu-apal-iddin, son of Sin-ili, has caused to be seized.
12) No other creditor shall have jurisdiction over them.
13) Excepted (from this prohibition) are the 1 mina, 6 shekels of silver from the "basket"
14) of Amat-Ninlil, for which a grain field as collateral
15) has been seized.

Ṭabia had given his daughter and her husband a *mulūgu* including two slaves. The husband had handed them over to some creditors as collateral for a debt. Ṭabia, the original donor of the *mulūgu*, made a payment from his own funds to his son-in-law's creditors, thus restoring the two slaves. At this point,

---

[45] See the starred note at the beginning of the article.

[46] Tallqvist, *APN*, 15.

[47] Cf. Late Hebrew *maškôn*, and Aramaic *maškônā*ʾ in J. Levy, *Wörterbuch*, III:278–279.

[48] See the starred note at the beginning of the article.

[49] For Aramaic usage of the verb *šlṭ* see C. F. Jean-J. Hoftijzer, *Dictionnaire des Inscriptions Sémitiques de l'Ouest*, Leiden, 1965, 302, s.v. *šlṭ* and *šlyṭ*. This verb figures in the Aramaic contracts from Elephantine. Also see J. Levy, *Wörterbuch* IV:561, s.v. *šālaṭ* for limited Talmudic usage of this verb in contracts.

[50] Cf. Late Hebrew *quppāh* in Mishnah, *Ketûbôt* 6:5. This was a box in which the woman of Mishnaic times kept money to be spent on perfumes and other personal articles.

the son-in-law agreed to substitute two of his own household slaves as collateral, thus retrieving the silver for his father-in-law. It is then stipulated that no other creditor shall have legal control over these *mulūgu* slaves. There is no objection, however, to the lending of some of Amat-Ninlil's *quppu* silver on the security of a grain field.

The issue here is the use of *mulūgu* property as collateral for debts, and we are told that this was not to be permitted. The text reveals the degree of control which a father could continue to exercise over the *mulūgu*. Here, as in several other cases, the *mulūgu* belonged both to the woman and to her husband.

The provision allowing for the lending of *quppu* silver on the security of land indicates that the woman was free to use the resources of her *quppu* so long as proper safeguards were maintained. This is more clearly brought out in the next Neo-Babylonian text to be discussed.

VS V 53 (= Peiser, *Verträge*: 26) records a series of transactions involving wife-owned property. A woman empowered her husband to exchange some of her *quppu* silver for a plot of land, which she then apportioned between her two daughters. To the elder she gave not only land, but the son of her *mulūgu* slave-woman. There follow certain provisions pertaining to the land.

The reference to the *mulūgu* slave is entirely incidental, but nonetheless enlightening. We see how dowry silver was converted into land for greater security,[51] and we observe how the slaves termed *mulūgu* fitted into the system of dowries in Neo-Babylonian times. From the fact that the offspring of *mulūgu* personnel are bequeathed as property, we can conclude that reference is to family slaves, as we suggested earlier.

To summarize the evidence of the *kudurru* inscriptions and the Neo-Babylonian texts, we can state the following:

1) The term *mulūgu* can be used as a synonym for *nudunnu*, and possibly for other terms for dowry (I Rawlinson 70; *BBst*: IX).

2) It can designate movable property given as dowry, and listed separately from land, which is termed *nudunnu* (*TMH* ii/iii: 1).

3) There was objection to the use of *mulūgu* slaves as security for debts (*VS* IV 46), but they and their offspring could be bequeathed as property (*VS* V 53).

4) *Quppu* silver could be lent on the security of land (*VS* IV 46), and could be converted into land and given as such by the woman to her children as an estate (*VS* V 53 = Peiser, *Verträge*: 26).

VI

Thus far, we have presented the available evidence from cuneiform sources on the usage of the term *mulūgu*. It has not been possible to achieve a precise

---

[51] V. Marx, *op. cit.*, 18, and cf. Peiser, *Verträge* 10:27, where a husband replaces the silver he has taken from his wife's *quppu*. The principals are the same as in Peiser, no. 26. Also note the provisions of the Mishnah, *Ketûbôt* 8:3 requiring that money coming into the possession of a married woman be converted into land.

and consistent definition of this term. It is clear, however, that the *mulūgu* was a gift from father to daughter, usually bestowed in the context of marriage, and intended to accomplish the purposes associated with dowries.

Talmudic sources employ the term *melûg* in a more limited sense: *Melûg* is property received by a woman from her father or brothers for which she retains liability after her marriage. Her husband enjoys the usufruct of her *melûg*. In pre-Talmudic and early Talmudic times the woman, by virtue of her control over *melûg* property, retained the right to dispose of it as she saw fit, a right exceptional to her overall status as one subservient to the will of her husband.

In order to understand Talmudic usage a word must be prefaced about the altered role of dowry property in Talmudic law, and about the instrumentalities developed by that system to secure what had been the traditional purposes of the dowry, i.e. the protection of the woman in the event of widowhood or divorce, and the assurance of a proper inheritance for her children. In increasing measure, these devices assumed many of the functions of the dowry.

According to Mishnaic legislation, a husband was required to provide his wife, at the time of their marriage, with a document known as the *ketûbāh*, "writ of settlement," which contained the following provisions: 1. The husband pledged to support his wife and to provide her with domicile, to last during widowhood, if the wife so desired. He also pledged to ransom her if she were captured. 2. The husband set aside a fixed sum, which could be augmented, as settlement in the event of widowhood or divorce. All of the husband's real property was mortgaged to this obligation, which had the force of a prior lien, operating retroactively. Thus, the original amount of the settlement could be recovered, if necessary, from properties sold by the husband subsequent to his marriage. Anyone purchasing land from a married man would have to make provision for this fact. 3. The husband guaranteed that male children born of his wife would inherit the amount of the settlement in the event she died while married to him, and that her female children would remain in his home, and be supported by him until they were married.[52]

The provisions of the *ketûbāh* had the force of "a condition imposed by the court" (*tenâi bêt dîn*).[53] If the husband had, in fact, neglected to provide his wife with the actual writ, the above provisions were in force all the same. A woman

[52] Provisions of the Mishnah, *Ketûbôt* 4:7–12, V:1. Cf. J. T. Milik, *Les Grottes de Murabbaʿât*, DJD 2, Oxford, 1961, no. 21, p. 115, lines 9–16, where, in a marriage contract, almost all of the Mishnaic requirements are included. Also see no. 20, p. 10f. In a deed of sale (no. 30, p. 144f.) the wife of the man effecting the sale states: "I have no claim against this sale forever" (I:6–7; II:27–29). This was undoubtedly necessitated by the fact that all of her husband's real property was mortgaged to the prior lien of the *ketûbāh*, and she had to waive her rights to this parcel of land before the sale could be finalized.

[53] Mishnah, *Ketûbôt*, 4:7f.

had only to supply proper proof of her husband's death, or produce a fit bill of divorce (*gēṭ*)[54] in order to receive these benefits.

Once the *ketûbāh* became obligatory it accomplished the fundamental purposes of the dowry. A woman and her children could look forward to a degree of security whether or not a dowry had been provided. In Jewish communities the practice of settling property was quite ancient,[55] but the obligatory character of the *ketûbāh*, and its special provisions, seem to be the result of early Talmudic legislation.[56]

Another fact of Talmudic law which affected the functioning of dowry property was the legal principle that a husband is his wife's first heir. If a woman died while married, her husband inherited all that she owned as of the moment of death. In such situations, her children were not protected by arrangements guaranteeing them a portion of her dowry, but rather by the *ketûbāh* itself.[57]

With these facts in mind, we can examine the principal Talmudic sources for the term *melûg*:

Mishnah, *Yebāmôt* 8:1:

> In the case of a widow married to a High Priest, or of a divorcée or one rejected from levirate marriage married to an ordinary priest: If the woman brought with her into marriage both *melûg* slaves and "iron sheep" slaves, the *melûg* slaves may not partake of *terûmāh* (of-

---

[54] On the term *gēṭ*, see *CAD G*, 112, s.v. *giṭṭu*.

[55] *AP* 15 is a document of settlement. Also see *BMAP*, papyri nos. 4, 7, 14 for additional examples.

[56] Rabbi Simon son of Šetaḥ, a sage who flourished at the end of the second and at the beginning of the first century B.C.E., is credited with enacting legislation which made the *ketûbāh* into an effective instrument: "Formerly, the *ketûbāh* was issued against her father, with the result that a woman was lightly esteemed in her husband's eyes, and he would be prone to divorce her. Rabbi Simon son of Šetaḥ legislated that the *ketûbāh* be issued against the husband's property, and he was obligated to write in the *ketûbāh*: 'All properties which I own are liable and bound to the sum of money stipulated in your *ketûbāh*'" (*Tôseptāʾ*, *Ketûbôt* 12:1, ed. S. Lieberman, *The Tosefta*, *The Order of Nashim*, 95, and *Tosefta Ki-fshuṭah*, pt. VI, 369–370 and *TB Ketûbôt* 82b). In the second century C.E., Rabbi Meir is credited with making the *ketûbāh* obligatory. We have his view in the Mishnah (*Ketûbôt* 5:1): "Rabbi Meir says: Anyone who provides less than 200 *zuz* for a previously unmarried woman, or less than 100 *zuz* for a widow, is performing a harlotrous union." This implies the requirement of the *ketûbāh* to start with. In the *Bāraîtāʾ* we have a further statement attributed to Rabbi Meir (*TB Ketûbôt* 57a. *Bābāʾ Qammāʾ* 89b): "It is forbidden for a man to allow his wife to remain without a *ketûbāh* even for one hour." Also see *TP Ketûbôt* 5:hal. 2.

[57] Mishnah, *Ketûbôt* 8:1, 9:1f. *Bekôrôt* 8:10, *Tôseptāʾ*, *Bekôrôt* 6:9, ed. Zuckermandel, 541. *TP Bābāʾ Batrāʾ* 8:hal. 5. *TB Bābāʾ Batrāʾ* 111b. There is a dispute as to whether this status is based on Mosaic legislation or not, but opinion tended increasingly to view it as a law of post-biblical origin.

> ferings received by the priests), but the "iron sheep" slaves may partake of it.
>
> What are *melûg* slaves? If they die, they die as hers (i.e. their death represents a loss to her estate), and if they increase in value, the increment accrues to her. Although the husband is obligated to provide their sustenance, they may not partake of *terûmāh*.

In explanation, it should be noted that in Talmudic law a woman eligible for marriage to a man of priestly lineage (*kôhēn*) enjoys the right of partaking of *terûmāh*, even though she may not have come from priestly lineage herself. This is because, as his wife, she is legally classified as his property.[58] On the same principle that one's rights extend to one's property, slaves owned by a priest may share in his *terûmāh*. Now, if a woman ineligible for marriage to a *kôhēn* because of a divorce or rejection from levirate marriage (Leviticus 21:7) did in fact marry a *kôhēn* in violation of the law, she would lose her right to share in the *terûmāh*. The Mishnah is therefore telling us that the slaves of such an ineligible woman, like their mistress, may not partake of *terûmāh*, since they are considered her property, not her husband's, and share her disabilities under the law.[59] This is notwithstanding the fact that *melûg* slaves receive their sustenance as part of the husband's household. The husband is compensated for his expenditures on the *melûg* slaves by benefiting from the revenue of their labors, and not by any rights of ownership over them.

The Mishnah thus clearly defines the legal status of *melûg* slaves. The married woman remained liable for the *melûg*, and any change in value affected her estate. In contrast, the term "iron sheep" (*ṣôn barzel*) refers to dowry property for which the husband bore responsibility. "Iron sheep" is a term of broad application, reflecting the notion of imperishability and guaranteed liability. It appears to be an expression known in Mesopotamian legal usage,[60] and, as another instance of a Mesopotamian usage surviving into Talmudic law, fits in well with our discussion of the term *melûg*. Wealth termed "iron sheep" was available to the husband as capital, whereas *melûg* property was not. "Iron sheep" property was normally inscribed in the *ketûbāh* along with the provisions of the marriage settlement, and could be claimed from the husband or his heirs, just as could the obligatory settlement of the *ketûbāh*.

Mishnah, *Yebāmôt* 7:2:

> A woman of non-priestly lineage who was properly married to a man of priestly lineage, and brought with her into marriage either *melûg* slaves or "iron sheep" slaves—they may partake of *terûmāh*. A wom-

---

[58] Mishnah, *Ketûbôt* 5:2–3, *Terûmôt* 8:1.

[59] Lev. 22:1, *Siprāʾ*, *ʾEmôr* 5:1, ed. I. H. Weiss, Vienna, 1852, p. 97.

[60] See A. Gulak, *op. cit.*, 76f., and *Tarbiz* (Hebrew) 8, 1932, 137–146 on the relevant papyrological evidence. On the Mesopotamian background, see A. Leo Oppenheim, *IEJ*, 1955, 89–92. In cuneiform texts the notion of guaranteed liability was conveyed in the image of deathless animals, and by the formula: *ša* AN.BAR *šu-nu* "They are made of iron."

an of priestly lineage who married a man of non-priestly lineage, and brought with her into marriage either *melûg* slaves or "iron sheep" slaves—they may not partake of *terûmāh.*

In the latter case, the "iron sheep" slaves do not partake of *terûmāh* because they belong to one who is not a priest, i.e. the husband in the situation. The *melûg* slaves, although they remain the property of the woman, who is of priestly lineage, do not partake because they lost the status of property owned by a priestly family, just as the status of their mistress changed when she was married to a man not of the priestly lineage.[61] In the former part of the Mishnah the converse is true.

The legal corollary of this status is the right of the married woman to dispose of her *melûg*. Ownership generally gives to the owner the right to do what he wishes with his possessions. Mishnaic sources dealing with the question of whether a married woman had the right to dispose of her property do not employ the term *melûg* itself, but rather a more inclusive formula: *nekāsîm hanniknāsîm wehayôṣʾîm ʿimmāh* "Goods that enter and depart with her."[62] This formula re-

[61] There are other legal situations which illustrate the status of *melûg* slaves: "*Melûg* slaves gain their freedom by a tooth and an eye with respect to the wife, but not with respect to the husband" (*Bāraîtāʾ* in *TP Yebāmôt* 7:hal. 1, *TB Bābāʾ Qammāʾ* 89b, *Yebāmôt* 66b). According to biblical law (Exodus 21:26–27) a slave gains his freedom if his owner knocks out his tooth or destroys his eye. A *melûg* slave would not come under this law if injured by the husband of his mistress, but only if injured by his mistress, herself. Similarly: "One who steals a *melûg* animal (*behemat melûg*) pays the penalty of twice the amount to the wife" (*Bāraîtāʾ*, *TP Yebāmôt* 7:hal. 1, TB *Ketûbôt* 79b–80a). According to biblical law (Exodus 21:37–22:3), one who steals an animal and disposes of it so that it cannot be retrieved is liable to a fine of twice the value of the animal, sometimes more. The question arises as to who shall receive the amount of the penalty in the case of a *melûg* animal. According to the *Bāraîtāʾ* the woman receives it, since she is considered the owner.

The applications of the formula "goods that enter and depart with her" can also help to define the status of wife-owned property. One situation (Mishnah, *Ketûbôt* 8:6, *Yebāmôt* 4:3) concerns a woman who died while awaiting action by her brother-in-law (Hebrew *yābām*). The uncertainties of her status as one still bound to her husband's family enter into the question of how her property shall be disposed of. Had she lived, and had the *yābām* taken her, her *ketûbāh* settlement would have come under the jurisdiction of her brother-in-law. Had she lived to be rejected by him through the act of *halîṣāh,* she would have collected the amount of the settlement as any widow. In parallel fashion, the *melûg* property would, in the former instance, have remained linked to her brother-in-law, and in the latter instance, would have "departed" with her. Similar problems arise in the case of a woman who was killed in the same accident in which her husband perished, and it was not ascertained which of the two actually died first. If the wife died first the husband was, for a brief moment, his wife's heir. If the husband died first, the heirs of the woman would inherit her *melûg* property (Mishnah, *Bābāʾ Batrāʾ* 9:9).

[62] Mishnah, *Ketûbôt* 8:7, *Yebāmôt* 4:3, *Bābāʾ Batrāʾ* 9:9. Also note the Greek term παράφερνον "above and beyond the dowry," used in Palestinian sources in the same sense as *melûg*. J. Levy, *Wörterbuch* IV:96, s.v. *perā'pûrnôn*, and H. G. Liddell, R. Scott,

flects the fact, referred to above, that such dowry property, in contrast to "iron sheep" dowries, would have to be restored to the woman in acceptable form should she be widowed or divorced. In a literal sense the goods would "depart with her." In the case of "iron sheep" property it was only the value that was guaranteed, but there was no requirement that the objects be retained in their original form, or in any specific form, such as land, etc.

The Mishnah uses this formula rather than the term *melûg* because in Tannaitic texts, the term *melûg* most probably referred only to dowry property, and this passage is dealing with all wife-owned property of whatever source, inherited, granted, or otherwise acquired by the woman. With this terminological problem in mind, we can examine the relevant passage in Mishnah, *Ketûbôt* 8:1:

> In the case of a woman who acquires property before she became betrothed:[63] Both the House of Hillel and the House of Shammai agree that she may sell or grant such property, and that her act is legally binding. If she acquired the property after becoming betrothed, the House of Shammai say: She may sell. The House of Hillel say: She may not sell. Both Houses agree, however, that if she did sell or grant such property, the act is legally binding, after the fact. Rabbi Judah said: They stated before Rabban Gamaliel: In view of the fact that the husband acquired rights over the woman's person, should he not, *ipso facto*, acquire rights over what she owns? He replied to them: We are unreconciled[64] concerning the application of this principle to the more recent acquisitions (i.e. the denial of the woman's rights to dispose of property acquired by her after marriage), and yet you seek to heap upon us even the earlier acquisitions (i.e. to prohibit sale of property acquired before marriage)?
>
> If she acquired the property after her marriage—both Houses agree that if she sold or granted the property, the husband may retrieve his rights to it from the purchasers. If she acquired the property before she was married, and sold it after she was married—Rabban Gamaliel says: If she sold or granted it her act is legally binding. Rabbi Hananiah son of Aqabiah said: They stated before Rabban Gamaliel: In view of the fact that the husband acquired rights over the woman's person, should he not, *ipso facto*, acquire rights over what she owns? He replied to them: We are unreconciled concerning

---

Greek-English Lexicon, 1145, s.v. παράφερνα. On the term *nekes* "property" see *CAD E*, 214, s.v. *nikkassū* (*epēšu*) "to compute, settle accounts," which may be the origin of the Hebrew and Aramaic terms, reflecting a semantic development from the account to its contents, i.e. "wealth, goods." Neo-Babylonian usage knew this sense. Cf. V. Marx, *op. cit.*, 17 (Nbk 283), and also G. Cardascia, *Les Archives des Murašû*, Paris, 1951, 164.

[63] In Talmudic times betrothal (Hebrew *ʾêrûsîn* or *qiddûšîn*) had the force of a quasi marriage, and was usually separated from final marriage (*nissûʾîn*) by twelve months. See Mishnah, *Ketûbôt* 5:2, and *The Talmudic Encyclopedia* (Hebrew), Jerusalem, 1952, II:185–186, s.v. *ʾarûsāh*.

[64] Literally: "We are embarrassed," Hebrew: *ʾānû bôšîm*.

> the application of this principle to the more recent acquisitions, and yet you heap upon us the earlier ones?

It was the late J. N. Epstein who first noted the importance of this passage for the history of the term *melûg*, and the institution of the dowry, generally.[65] Rabban Gamaliel II of Jamnia thought it desirable that a married woman should have the right to dispose of all of her properties, even those acquired after her marriage. He was displeased that this right had been restricted, and wanted the restriction to go no further. He held to the view, therefore, that a married woman may sell property after marriage, so long as it had been acquired before marriage, before the woman had come under the legal jurisdiction of her husband. This is also the view upheld in the *Tôseptāʾ* (*Ketûbôt* 8:1): "Our sages arrived at the conclusion concerning property which she acquired before she was married, and which she sold after her marriage, that the sale or grant of same is legally binding."[66]

What we see here is a trend toward restricting the rights of women over their property. Rabban Gamaliel referred to the practice of former days, when women were free to dispose of their property. In the course of time, the Talmudic sages decided in favor of less economic freedom of action for women, but for more security on their behalf. These decisions were undoubtedly dictated by socio-economic realities, and by the necessity to build upon Mosaic legislation which normally tended to limit the legal activities of women.

The legal principle operative in the Mishnah (*Ketûbôt* 8:1) is that a husband acquires certain rights over his wife's property by having acquired rights over her person.[67] According to the view in this passage, that principle should apply only progressively, to property which the woman will acquire after marriage. All are agreed, therefore, that property acquired after marriage could not be sold by the woman while married. If the woman did so in violation of the law, the husband could recover his rights by confiscating the usufruct to which he was entitled.

---

[65] J. N. Epstein, *op. cit.*, 359–362, and notes 3, 6. Rabban Gamaliel II of Jamnia was head of the Jewish High Court ca. 90 C.E., following the destruction of the Jerusalem Temple, ca. 70 C.E. Rabbi Judah (son of Ilai) was one of the sages of Usha, in the period after the rebellion of Bar Kochba (132–135 C.E.), and Rabbi Hanaiah son of Aqabiah was his contemporary.

[66] Ed. S. Lieberman, *The Tosefta, The Order of Nashim*, 83, and *Tosefta Ki-fshuṭah*, pt. VI, 309–310.

[67] See the discussion on the Mishnah, (*Ketûbôt* 8:1) in *TB Ketûbôt* 78b: "Is the Mishnah teaching us the provisions of the Usha enactment? [No!] The Mishnah is speaking of the law as it applies during the lifetime of the married woman, and concerns the husband's right of usufruct. The Usha enactment is speaking of the law as it applies after the woman's death, and concerns confiscation of the property itself by the husband."

To this notion was added still another legal principle, misrepresentation.[68] An act can be annulled when certain facts essential to it were not transmitted faithfully. As an extension of this principle, it is improper to allow for misunderstanding, even if not explicit. The Talmudic legislators operated on the assumption that a man contracting a marriage with a woman expected to benefit from the "usufruct" of all properties she owned, and that his decision to marry her was based, at least in part, on this expectation. If she were to sell or give away part of her wealth, the husband would be cheated. Once applied to wife-owned property, this principle led to further action aimed at assuring the husband income from all of his wife's property, regardless of when she acquired it, including even what she owned before contracting the marriage initially.[69]

The next clearly documented step taken by the Talmudic legislators in order to bring wife-owned property under the control of the husband was to alter the status of the husband from that of an heir to that of a prior purchaser. This was accomplished in the enactment of Usha, one of a series of laws emanating from that Galilean town. There is some doubt as to when these enactments went into effect. The earliest actual reference to the enactment dealing with *melûg* property is found in the statement of a Palestinian sage of the third century C.E.,[70] but historians have generally tended to date these enactments in the period following the rebellion of Bar Kochba, in the middle of the second century, when the Jewish High Court had its seat in Usha.[71]

The text of the enactment reads: "A woman who sold any of her *melûg* property (*niksê melûg*) during the lifetime of her husband, and subsequently died, the husband may confiscate the property from the purchaser."[72] This was a retroactive statute. Legally speaking, the husband was always the first purchaser, and anyone else who bought *melûg* property from his wife was technically buy-

---

[68] The Talmudic term is: *meqaḥ ṭāʿût* "a mistaken transaction." See Mishnah, *Ketûbôt* 1:6, 7:8, *TB Ketûbôt* 11b, *Giṭṭîn* 14a.

[69] The only exception was property entirely unknown to the husband when he married the woman. Mishnah, *Ketûbôt* 8:2: "Rabbi Simon differentiates between two types of property. Property known to the husband—she may not sell, and if she sold or granted such property the act is not binding. Property unknown to the husband she may likewise not sell, but if she did sell the same, the act is legally binding, after the fact."

[70] H. Mantel, in *Tarbiz* (Hebrew), 34, Jerusalem, 1965, 281–283 correctly identifies the sage as *Judah* son of Haninah, erroneously written *Josi* son of Haninah.

[71] On the history of the Jewish High Court at Usha see G. Alon, *The History of the Jews in Palestine during the Period of the Mishnah and Talmud* (Hebrew), Tel Aviv, 1952, I:291–293, and H. Mantel, *op. cit.* Mantel summarizes all of the sources for the Usha enactments and argues for a third century date. If our analysis of the developments in Talmudic law is correct, it would indeed seem that the enactment of Usha with respect to *melûg* property represents a step beyond Mishnaic legislation, which would suggest a later date.

[72] *TB Ketûbôt* 78b, *Bābāʾ Qammāʾ* 88b, *Bābāʾ Meṣîʿāʾ* 35a, 96b, *Bābāʾ Batrāʾ* 50a, 139b.

ing something not available for purchase. As an heir, the husband would have inherited only what his wife owned as of the moment of her death.

Once accepted, the Usha enactment brought to an end many of the traditional rights of women. We can trace the rights of married women to dispose of their properties back to the Jewish colony at Elephantine, in the fifth century B.C.E. In the Elephantine papyri, on which Epstein had based his study of early Jewish law, there are documents which explicitly guarantee to the married woman the right to dispose of the dowry she had received from her father, or of other grants received from him after her marriage.[73]

Early Jewish practice was altered, and the rights of women over their property were restricted. This restricted view continued to prevail in post-Talmudic Jewish law as well. The term *melûg*, and all that is associated with it, belongs to the heritage upon which Talmudic law was based, rather than to its progressive innovations. It was our purpose here to examine the question of origins, and thus to illustrate one example of the Mesopotamian factor in Talmudic law.[74]

---

[73] *AP* 8 is an example. A man granted his daughter a parcel of land on the occasion of her marriage with the full right to dispose of it as she sees fit: *ʾantî šelîṭāh bēh min yômāʾ zenāh weʿad ʿālam ûbānaîkî ʾaḥaraîkî leman zî reḥîmtî tintenān* "You have jurisdiction over it from this day and forever, and your children after you. To whosoever you desire you may give it" (lines 9–10). *AP* 9 refers to the same transaction and bears the same date. In it, the father modifies the terms of the grant. The son-in-law is told that he may not dispose of the property (line 6). It is to remain for the benefit of children born of their union. In the event of divorce, not more than half of the property can be taken from the grandchildren, and the son-in-law is to act in their behalf. Some of the features of this document are discussed by Epstein, *op. cit. BMAP* 10 has similar provisions. A man granted a house to his daughter: *yehabtēh lāh pas šērît zî lāʾ ketîb ʿal separ ʾintûtāki* "I have given it to you *as a remainder portion* which is not inscribed in your marriage document" (lines 7–8). The right of disposition is then stated in the usual formula. Interesting is the fact that this dowry was not inscribed in the marriage document, and was termed "a remainder portion." This suggests later Talmudic practice according to which the *melûg* was not written into the *ketûbāh*, an indication of its separate status. On *pas šērît* see *BMAP* 253, note to line 7. On Aramaic *pas* "piece" see J. Levy, *Wörterbuch* IV:67–68. Conceivably, *pas* could mean: "tablet, writ," as in a Punic text (H. Donner-W. Röllig, *Kanaanäische und Aramäische Inschriften*, Wiesbaden, 1966, I: 69, line 18). The sense here would be that the house in question was granted on the authority of a separate document. This would also convey the notion of a separate status. Kraeling suggests that the consonantal *šryt* = *šeʾērît*, and reflects the syncope of the *ʾaleph*. He could have cited consonantal *ršyt* for *rēʾšît* in Deut. 11:12, and *šltk* for *šeʾēlātēk* in 1 Sam 1:17.

[74] Aspects of this paper were treated in an address before the Philip W. Lown Institute of Advanced Judaic Studies, Brandeis University. The author is indebted to a number of scholars for their helpful consultations on the varied material included in this study: Profs. E. Lacheman, H. Lewy, W. Moran, J. Neusner, and A. Shaffer. Through the courtesy of Prof. A. L. Oppenheim, Oriental Institute, University of Chicago, the author was able to consult the files of the Chicago Assyrian Dictionary.

The Jewish *Ketūbbāh* as a 'Dialogue Document': The Continuity of a Cuneiform Tradition*

1.1. Pursuing the theme of the continuity of Mesopotamian civilization in the area of law, it is my intention to trace certain formal features of the Jewish *ketūbbāh* "writ of marriage" of Roman times to their Mesopotamian roots. The present investigation follows upon my earlier contribution to MELAMMU III, in which I discussed the important role of Aramaic in the transmission of Mesopotamian legal institutions, examining telling terms and formulas illustrative of this process (Levine 2002). Here, I will focus on a specific component of Rabbinic law, the institution of marriage, and apply the same comparative methodology to a particular type of legal document, the Jewish *ketūbbāh*. This is a subject of extensive scope, and it will be possible to engage only a few of its aspects in the present study. And yet, I hope to reinforce, step by step, the general conclusion that the corpus of Rabbinic literature constitutes, in addition to all else, a repository of Mesopotamian civilization.

1.2. The starting point is the differentiation of two styles, or forms employed in the composition of cuneiform contracts in the first millennium B.C.E., the objective and the subjective, or 'dialogue' form. The objective form records that a legal action has taken place, or will take place, by reference to one or more of the parties in the third-person. The subjective form exhibits a first-person orientation, and in most cases, a second-person address, or reference, as well. Most significant is the fact that it reports (we could say, "quotes") the oral declarations of at least one of the parties. Martha Roth (1989:1–2), in the introduction to her edition of Neo-Babylonian marriage agreements, notes the increasing utilization of the subjective form in various types of cuneiform legal documents, including marriage agreements, during the first millennium B.C.E., replacing the older objective form. In fact, all but six of the forty-five marriage agreements in Roth's collection are of the dialogue type. Now, aside from all else, the Jewish *ketūbbāh* of Roman times is a highly developed example of the 'dialogue document,' since throughout, it records the verbal statements of the prospective husband who proposes marriage to a woman, and states his commitments to her, and to her children.

* Originally published in A. Panaino and A. Piras (eds.), *Schools of Oriental Studies and the Development of Modern Historiography: Proceedings of the Fourth Annual Symposium of the Assyrian and Babylonian Intellectual Heritage Project Held in Ravenna, Italy, October 13–17, 2001* (Melammu Symposia 4; Milano: Mimesis; Bologna: Università di Bologna; Roma: IsIAO, 2004), pp. 169–191. Reprinted with permission from the Università di Bologna.

1.3. It is an appropriate time to discuss the formation of the Jewish *ketūbbāh*, a document prescribed in the Mishnah, the great compendium of Rabbinic law. Recent discoveries in the Judean Desert, at Murabbaʿat and Naḥal Ḥever on the Dead Sea, have made available for the first time several actual documents of this type, dating from the late first to the early second centuries C.E. The best preserved of these is P. Yadin 10, known as "Babatha's *Ketūbbāh*," dated to between 122–125 C.E. In her Textbook, Ada Yardeni (2000, I:119–124) registers the other three as Mur 20 and 21; and P. Hever 11. As for the Mishnah, it was published in Palestine in the early third century C.E., but much of its essential content was extant earlier in various compilations, so that the Judean Desert evidence may be regarded as fairly contemporary with the provisions of the Mishnah. Although composed in Hebrew, the Mishnah cites key passages of the *ketūbbāh* (as well as of the bill of divorce, the *gēṭ*) in the Aramaic that was most often employed for such documents. The complete text of a *ketūbbāh* is not preserved in Rabbinic sources, but we know a good deal about its formulation and provisions from these very citations in the Mishnah, and from other Rabbinic sources. Several Jewish marriage contracts, written in Greek have also been discovered in the Judean Desert, but none of them is of the 'dialogue' type, which may be significant.

In the present study we will not proceed beyond the Tannaitic period, that represented by the Mishnah and Tosefta, but it is important to emphasize that considerable further development of the *ketūbbāh*, as a dialogue document, occurred in the ensuing centuries of the Rabbinic period, continuing into Medieval times. The reader is directed to the comprehensive study of Medieval Palestinian *ketūbbôt* from the Cairo Genizah by Mordechai Friedman (1980), who edits many exemplars, as well as providing an in-depth treatment of the history and formation of the *ketūbbāh*. In fact, the *ketūbbāh* is still in use at the present time, and has been throughout the centuries.

1.4 Once the comparison has been made on a synchronic level between the Judean Desert documents and the Mishnah, we can attempt to trace certain components of the early Rabbinic *ketūbbāh*—terms, formulas, and constitutive provisions—to earlier Aramaic versions of this type of document, and by this route to Mesopotamian sources, as well. Comparative analysis of the several marriage contracts found among the Aramaic legal papyri from the Jewish military colony at Elephantine of the fifth century B.C.E. with Neo-Babylonian, cuneiform marriage agreements will prove instructive in this regard. The Elephantine contracts are well developed examples of the 'dialogue document', and show definite affinities with their Neo-Babylonian counterparts. Our control of the Elephantine materials has been greatly enhanced by the collated editions of B. Porten and A. Yardeni (1989; henceforth: *TAD* II). The forty-five Neo-Babylonian marriage agreements, edited by Roth, date from 635 B.C.E. to 203 B.C.E., and many of them come from the reigns of Nabonidus and Darius I. Their proximity in time to the Aramaic, Elephantine marriage contracts, as well as the features they share with them, make of the latter an important link in the transmission of Mesopotamian legal practices, and may suggest how and when Mesopotamian features were appropriated by Aramaic scribes.

1.5. Our preference for the Neo-Babylonian marriage agreements does not in any way imply that the Aramaic formulary at Elephantine did not draw upon many earlier features of cuneiform law. Brill has recently reissued Yochanan Muffs' pioneering work, *Studies in the Aramaic Legal Papyri from Elephantine*, originally published in 1969, to which I have written a Prolegomenon (Muffs 2003). That work expanded on what Muffs calls "the Assyriological approach," and makes the case for the continuity of the provincial, or peripheral legal traditions of the second millennium into the Achemenid period, and thereafter. Muffs also points to more proximate sources of Aramaic law in the Neo-Assyrian period. Our choice of Neo-Babylonian documents for comparison primarily reflects our present interest in the 'dialogue document.'

1.6. In terms of the Jewish legal tradition, specifically, it is to be noted that whereas Deuteronomy 24 (vv. 1–2), explicitly ordains a writ of divorce, there is no comparable law in the Torah requiring a written contract of marriage. This absence occasioned considerable debate in Rabbinic circles regarding the original authority of the *ketūbbāh*, as to whether it was Mosaic or Rabbinic, and has made it all the more fascinating to search for actual antecedents of the early Rabbinic *ketūbbāh*.

Babatha's Ketūbbāh *(P. Yadin 10)* *and the Mishnah,* Ketūbbôt *4:7–12*

2.1. The best way to begin is through a synchronic comparison of the Judean Desert evidence with the basic Rabbinic prescriptions; more precisely, of P. Yadin 10, with the provisions of the Mishnah, *Ketūbbôt* 4:7–12. A full edition of P. Yadin 10, with epigraphic notes and commentary, is now available in Yadin *et al.* 2002:118–141, and is based on its initial publication by J.C. Greenfield and A. Yardeni (Yadin *et al.* 1994). Some specific readings and issues of legal interpretation remain unresolved, mostly due to lacunae.

2.2. Following is an outline of Babatha's *ketūbbāh*, based on preferred readings and probable restorations, with cross-referencing to other marriage contracts from the Judean Desert assemblage.

1) Date, and names of groom and bride, including the name of the town of Ein Gedi, where one, or both parties resided. This section is poorly preserved, but its content can be reliably surmised (lines 1–4). In line 3 we are able to read the pronoun אנת "you" (second-person, feminine), which indicates that the 'dialogue' pattern commenced with the opening statement. We may assume that the verb אמר "he said" occurred in line 2 or 3. What he says is cited as the formal proposal.

2) The groom proposes to the bride, addressing her in the second-person feminine singular:

[די תהוין לי/הוי לי] לאנת[ה]/לאנת[ו כדי]ן מושה ויה[ו]דאי

> "That you be to me/Be to me as a wife/for wife-hood according to the law of Moses and the Judeans/Jews" (line 4, and cf. Mur 20:3, P. Hever 11:2).

3) The groom pledges support: in the form of food, clothing and domicile for his wife, while referring to the *ketūbbāh* as a binding contract:

ו[זאנ]נה לך ו[מכס]ך ובכתבתך אעלך

> "And I will feed you and clothe you, and pursuant to your *ketūbbāh*, I will bring you into my house" (line 5).

4) The groom acknowledges his wife's claim on him for the sum of 400 denarii, the amount of the dowry (Greek *phernḗ*), on which she may draw at any time, in addition to her basic support (lines 5–9, cf. Mur 20:4–6 [broken], P. Hever 11:3[?]). Further on, first in lines 11 and following, where the text is broken, and then again in lines 17–18, the groom affirms that all that he owns is pledged to the payment of this claim:

וכל נכס]ין [די איתי לי ודי אקנא אחראין וערבין לכתבתך

> "And all properties that I possess and that I will acquire are guaranteed and pledged to (the payment) of your *ketūbbāh*" (cf. Mur 20:11–12; apparently repeated, or resumed in lines 17–18).

5) The groom pledges to ransom his wife if she is captured:

ואם תשבתיי (=תשתביי) אפרקנך מן ביתי מן נכסי [ואתי]בנך לי לאנתה

> "And if you are taken captive, I will redeem you from my 'house' and properties, and I will restore you as a wife" (lines 10–11, cf. Mur 20:6).

6) The groom guarantees the inheritance rights of male children, and support for female children born out of the marriage. The statement regarding male children is missing in the lacuna of lines 12–13, but should be restored there (cf. Mur 20:8–9, 21:12–14). The statement governing female children is reasonably well preserved:

בנ]ן נק[ב]ן [ת]הוא יתבא ומתזנן מן ביתי [ומן נכסי עד] זמן די ית[נסב]ן לבעלין

> "Female children shall reside and continue to be provided for from my 'house,' and from my properties until such time as they are married to husbands" (lines 13–14, cf. Mur 20:7–9 [broken]; Mur 21:10–12).

7) The groom pledges to provide domicile and support for his wife after his death, pending payment of the *ketūbbāh* claim by his heirs:

תהוין יתבא ומתזנן מן ביתי מן נכסי עד זמן די יצבון ירתי למנתן לך כסף כתבתך

> "You will reside, and (continue to be) provided for from my 'house' and from my properties until such time as my heirs will agree to pay you the 'silver' of your *ketūbbāh*" (lines 15–16, cf. Mur 20:9–11, 21:12–14).

8) The groom pledges, addressing his wife in the second person, that he will replace the relevant document on demand (lines 16–17, cf. Mur 20:13–14, 21:19).

9) A resumptive declaration by the groom, in the first-person, that he is bound by the above, stated terms of the agreement (line 18, cf. Mur 21:17 [broken]):

10) Endorsement (line 19). The legible part of the line states:

לבבתה [ב]רת שמעון על יהודה בר אלעזר

"[ ](due) to Babatha, (*vacat*) daughter of Shimᶜon, (incumbent) upon Yehudah, son of Elᶜazar."

This endorsement served as a docket, visible on the fold of the document. It identified the principals, and confirmed the debt that the groom owed the bride.

11) Seal, and signatures of the groom and bride, and of three witnesses (lines 20–26). There is also a partially legible fragment whose function is unclear. In line 23, the entry ממר[ה] "by [her] verbal order" has been reliably restored. In context, this reflects the fact that Babatha was illiterate, and had instructed someone to sign on her behalf. That person's name is illegible.

Comparative Analysis

2.3 Before proceeding, a word of explanation is in order about the term *ketūbbāh*, itself. In the Aramaic of Papyrus Yadin 10, lines 5, 11, 16, the marriage document is repeatedly called כתבתך "your writ of marriage," written defectively without a *waw*, and the same spelling is evident in Mur 21:10, 13 where we find כתבתיך. This defective spelling is also attested in the Aramaic passages from the *ketūbbāh* cited in M. *Ket.* 4:7–12 (see below). When taken as a Hebrew term, it is spelled both *plene* and *defectiva*, depending on manuscript traditions. On the spelling and pointing of the Hebrew term in Jewish literary sources, see Ben-Yehudah, *Thesaurus*, 2552–2553, s.v. כתבה, note 1, by N.H. Tur-Sinai, who explains that in many manuscript traditions this term is consistently written *plene* with a *waw*, even though the *beth* is pointed with a *dagesh*. Its sense is clear: "writ, a written document." It may represent a feminine realization of כתב (= *ketāb*) "writ," which, as an Aramaic term, is well attested in the Official Aramaic of Elephantine (*DNWSI* 546–547, s.v. ktb_2).

Functionally, the term כת(ו)בה often connotes "dowry claim." More precisely, it will refer to the amount in silver, and/or the total value of property written into the *ketūbbāh*, for which the husband incurred financial accountability at the time of marriage, in other words, to the dowry claim against the husband as stated in the *ketūbbāh*, not merely to the document, itself. Thus, in P. Yadin 10:11 [ו]כתב[ת]ך means the same as: כסף כתבתך "the silver of your writ (of marriage)," in line 16.

2.4. Attention should be paid to what is not provided for in Babatha's *ketūbbāh*. As an example, divorce is not explicitly projected as the cause for the eventual dissolution of the marriage, only the husband's demise. Many other contingencies that are frequently anticipated in ancient Near Eastern and Jewish marriage contracts are likewise not addressed explicitly—childlessness, the taking of a second wife, the prior death of the wife, and more. This is actually characteristic of ancient marriage agreements, generally; they vary greatly in their scope and coverage. Notwithstanding, we can establish a considerable number of precise correlations between Babatha's *ketūbbāh* and the Mishnah. Methodologically, it is of great value to be able to correlate scholastic, or canonical texts with actual legal documents of the same period and provenance.

2.5. Five of the provisions from Babatha's *ketūbbāh*, outlined above, are set forth in M. *Ket.* 4:7–12, in almost the exact terms, and in the 'dialogue' form; they are likewise addressed to the intended bride in the second-person feminine. The Mishnah, as a corpus of law, states these provisions conditionally and negatively. Thus: לא כתב לה "If he (= the groom) did not write for her (= the bride)." That is to say: If the *ketūbbāh* document failed to specify any of the several requisite provisions, the court would automatically enforce them. This is because they represent entitlements; in the language of the Mishnah: תנאי בית דין "A condition (imposed) by the court." We may thus reconstruct the main statements of the Rabbinic *ketūbbāh* from the Mishnah's requirements, while conceding that these five provisions do not comprise the entire *ketūbbāh*, only what was considered to be *sine qua non*.

2.6. The Mishnaic provisions are stated as follows:

> a) The pledging of all of the groom's assets to the *ketūbbāh* claim: כל נכסים דאית לי אחראין לכתובתיך "All properties that I possess are guaranteed to (the payment) of your *ketūbbāh*."
> b) Guarantee of ransom and restoration if the wife is captured: אם תשתבאי אפרקניך ואותבניך לי לאנתו "If you are captured I will redeem you and restore you to me in the role of wife."
> c) Guarantee of inheritance rights for male children (cf. no. 6, above, almost certainly to be restored in P. Yadin 10:12–13): בנין דכרין דיהוון ליכי מנאי אנון ירתון כסף כתבתיך יתר על חולקהון דעם אחיהון "(As for) male children whom you will have by me, they shall inherit the sum of your *ketūbbāh*, in addition to their share that is (due them) together with their brothers."
> d) Guarantee of support for female children: בנן נקבן דיהוין ליכי מנאי יהוין יתבן בביתי ומתזנן מנכסי עד דיתנסבן לגברין "Female children whom you will have from me shall be residing in my house and be given sustenance from my properties until they are married to husbands."
> e) Guarantee of widow's right to domicile after the death of her husband: את תהא יתבא בביתי ומתזנא מנכסי כל ימי מגד אלמנותיך בביתי "You shall continue to reside in my house, and be provided for from my properties all the duration of your widowhood, in my house."

In M. *Ket.* 4:12 we read that, in the matter of a widow's right to reside in her late husband's house, the Judeans added the following proviso to the *ketūbbāh*: עד שירצו היורשין ליתן ליך כתבתיך "Until (such time as) the heirs will agree to pay you (the sum of) your *ketūbbāh*." This statement qualifies as a fairly literal Hebrew translation of the Aramaic of P. Yadin 10:16, cited in 2.3, 7), above.

2.7 It may be relevant to mention that in an Aramaic deed of gift from Naḥal Ḥever (P. Yadin 7), dated 120 C.E., a similar residence restriction is imposed on a widow. That document is also a prime example of the 'dialogue' form, since the father of the family speaks in the first person, and addresses his wife in the second person throughout. In that deed, which has the character of a living trust, Babatha's father, Shimᶜon, bestows all of his worldly possessions, present and future, upon his wife, Miryam, such gift to take effect at the time of his death. The gift is granted on condition that so long as Shimᶜon lives, he shall continue to own and derive all benefits accruing from them. An ancillary provision affects the couple's daughter, Babatha, who is referred to as: בבתא ברתנא "Babatha, our daughter." In the event she is widowed in the course of time she may reside in a designated building on the premises, with customary rights of entry and egress. This applies, however, only so long as she remains a widow: ולא רשיה ולא שליטה תהוא למנעלו לביתא הו בעל "But, she shall not have the rightful authority to bring a husband into that house" (P. Yadin 7:26, Yadin *et al.* 2002:85).

2.8. A fascinating subject for study is the groom's proposal, reliably restored in P. Yadin 10:4, and better preserved in Mur 20, and P. Hever 11. The formula [את]י תהוא לא לאנתה "You will be to me as a wife to me" is preserved in Mur 20:3, [accepting the restoration by Milik 1961:120], and in P. Hever 11:2 we can read: די תהוין לי ל[אנתה] "That you be to me as a wife." The reading of the term for "wife" (or: "wifehood") in P. Yadin 10:4 is unclear. Both the noun אנתה "wife," in its various realizations, and the abstract form אנתו "wife-hood, marriage," are possible.

This proposal is not a subject of concern in M. *Ket.* 4:7–12, but was undoubtedly part of the early Rabbinic *ketūbbāh*. Such proposals have a long tradition in the ancient Near East, and are typical of the subjective, or 'dialogue type' of legal documents. They became standard in the later versions of the *ketūbbāh*, and are probably anticipated at Elephantine. (See below, under 3.5).

2.9. The phrase כדין מושה ויהודאי "according to the law of Moses and the Judeans," in Babatha's *ketūbbāh*, developed into the more familiar phrase כדת משה וישראל "according to the law of Moses and Israel," which became standard in the traditional *ketūbbāh*. And yet, reference to "Judean" law was current in the early Rabbinic period It is expressed in the Mishnah by the clause: העוברת על דת משה ויהודית "One who transgresses (fem.) against the law of Moses and Jewish (law)," in M. *Ket.* 7:1. A wife who transgresses in this manner forfeits her *ketūbbāh* settlement, because she has failed to uphold the terms of her marriage.

2.10. There are further comparisons with Rabbinic practice that could be cited, such as the formalities of dating and witnessing. Suffice it to say that P. Yadin 10 and the Mishnah sources correspond with each other to a remarkable degree, both in substance and formulation. This should put to rest any doubts concerning the realism of the Mishnah's *ketūbbāh* provisions; we can now demonstrate that they largely reflect contemporary Jewish practice. We can also attest to the composition of the early Rabbinic *ketūbbāh* as a 'dialogue document'.

2.11. Actually, most of the legal documents discovered in the Judean Desert are of the 'dialogue' type. Restricting ourselves to the Yadin Collection from Naḥal Ḥever, we note that two of the three Hebrew legal texts (P. Yadin 45 and 46) are of the 'dialogue' type, as are all of the Nabatean-Aramaic legal texts (P. Yadin 1, 2, 3, 4, 6, 9), and all but one of the Aramaic legal texts ('dialogue': P. Yadin 7, 8, 42, 47; objective: P. Yadin 43).

Marriage Agreements of the 'Dialogue' Type at Elephantine (Aramaic) and in Neo-Babylonian Cuneiform

3.1. Before taking up the Elephantine marriage contracts, we would do well to explain how we see them as fitting into the ongoing development of later Jewish law. The community whose life is reflected in the Elephantine legal papyri was a Jewish community, to be sure, but an enigmatic one, in some respects. Our approach has been informed by the pioneering study of Jacob N. Epstein, *Notizen zu den jüdisch-aramäischen Papyri von Assuan* (1908). Epstein was one of the great masters of modern Talmud scholarship, and at the same time, a consummate Aramaist, who was one of the first to attempt analysis of the Elephantine legal papyri. His methodology was very uncomplicated: He simply allowed the evidence to speak for itself! The verdict was eminently clear: The terminology and formulary of the Elephantine Aramaic texts are, in fact, replete with analogues to Talmudic law, which, for its part, drew not only on Israelite-Jewish antecedents, but, as it became possible to show, on the Aramaic common law.

3.2. A corollary question pertains to the reception of cuneiform law in first-millennium Israel, during the formative period of biblical law; and in due course, the reception of Aramaic law, as well. In some instances, we may be dealing with cuneiform elements already appropriated into biblical law, so that their presence in the Elephantine papyri was not the result of direct transfer from cuneiform law. It is uncertain as to how much of what we know as biblical law and practice was also known to the Jews of Elephantine. This question certainly applies to our understanding of the Judean Desert contracts and the laws of the Mishnah, which explicitly resonate with Torah law. It is because of such considerations that precise, formal comparisons are so important. It is not merely a matter of the substance of the law, but of the formulation of legal documents, and their composition.

3.3. For Elephantine, we take as our text of reference *TAD* II, B3.8, dated October, 420 B.C.E., while noting that its essential provisions are similar to the other two complete exemplars, B2:6, dated 445 B.C.E., and B3:3, dated 449 B.C.E. Four additional fragments of Aramaic marriage contracts are registered in *TAD* II as B6.1–4. These are all elaborate contracts, containing many derivative and distinctive provisions. Given the extent of the Neo-Babylonian evidence, edited by Martha Roth, it will not be necessary to select a single exemplar for analysis.

I. The formal proposal of marriage and related declarations

3.4. The complexity of this component in 'dialogue documents' has already been commented upon above (*Comparative Analysis*, 2.8). One variable in its formulation pertains to the orientation of the proposal. P. Yadin 10 and the Tannaitic sources express a direct proposal; the groom speaks to the bride, herself, in the second person. It happens that all of the Elephantine contracts that we possess express an indirect proposal, generating third person address. The groom, or one speaking for him, such as his father, addresses one who is legally responsible for the intended bride, her father, mother, brother, or the like. That this was traditional is indicated by the fact that all but two (Roth, nos. 2 and 25) of the dialogue agreements in Roth's collection express an indirect proposal. For purposes of comparison, Roth, no. 25 (Borsippa, 486 B.C.E.), containing one of the exceptional direct proposals, is particularly instructive:

> PN A-*šú* PN *a-na* <f>*tab-lu-*<*ṭu*> DUMU.SAL-*su šá* PN (*ki-a-am*) *iq-bi-im-ma al-*[*k*]*i-im lu* DAM.[*at*]-*ti*
> "PN son of PN to Tablutu spoke (as follows): 'Come to me! May you be a wife!'" (lines 1–3).

The assent of the bride is then recorded:

> (*ár-ki*) <f>*tab-lu-ṭu a-na* PN *taš-me-e a-n*[*a áš-šu-ti*](?) *it-ti* PN *tu-uš-bu*
> "Thereupon, Tablutu to PN consented. She will reside together with PN as wife" (lines 4–5).

In Roth, no. 2, the direct proposal reads in part:

> *lu-ú áš-šá-tum at-*[*ti*] "May you be a wife" (line 6).

3.5. We must realize that we are dealing with a syntactic difference between Akkadian, on the one hand, and Aramaic (and Hebrew, as well), on the other. The latter normally (though not always) employs the verb *h-y-h* / *h-w-h* "to be" in formulas connoting assumption of marital status, whereas Akkadian consistently does not. In the Judean Desert formula, a woman "becomes" a wife (*h-w-h l-*), and further, she belongs to someone, so that we often have "to become a wife to X." A variation on the Aramaic formula can be inferred from the divorce provisions of the Elephantine marriage contracts. Although none of the known Elephantine marriage contracts contains direct address by the groom to the bride, we may infer from the negative statements of the husband and wife in their respective initiations of divorce how a direct proposal of marriage would read. In the negative mode, the husband declares: לא תהוה לי אנתת "She shall not be to me a wife." For her part, the wife declares: לא אהוה לך אנתת "I shall not be to you a wife" (*TAD* II, B3.8:22, 25). A direct proposal from groom to bride, in the positive mode, if we had it, would undoubtedly read: הוי לי אנתת "Be to me a wife." Taking account of the aforementioned syntactic difference, the Neo-Babylonian and the Aramaic formulas are very close to each other.

3.6. In Tannaitic sources, the Mishnah and Tosefta, we find, in place of proposals, a series of oral declarations, which are not part of the written *ketūbbāh, per se*. They state the fact of marriage as *fait accompli*: One of several such declarations states: הרי את לי לאיתא "Behold, you are to me as a wife" (Tosefta, *Qiddûshîn* 1:1, ed. S. Lieberman (1973:276). Lieberman notes the manuscript variant: לאנתו "for wife-hood, in marriage." This is not a proposal of marriage, but a declaration confirming the acceptance of such a proposal. We learn this from documents expressing the indirect proposal. Let us compare the syntax of the indirect marriage proposal at Elephantine with that of most of the Neo-Babylonian marriage agreements:

(a) *TAD* II, B3.8—Elephantine:

> אנה אתית עליך בביתך ושאלת מנך לנשן יהוישמע שמה אחתך לאנתו ויהבתה לי
> הי אנתתי ואנה בעל[ה] מן יומא זנה עד עלם
>
> I came to you, in your house, and I asked from you Ms. Yehoyishma, by name, your sister, for wife-hood, and you gave her to me. She is my wife, and I am her husband from this day and forever (lines 3–4).

(b) Roth, no. 11—Nabonidus (555–539 B.C.E.):

> PN, A-*šú šá* PN, *a-na* IGI PN, A-*šú šá* PN *il-lik-ma ka-a-mu iq-bi um-ma*: [f]*ba-zi-ti* NIN-*ka nu-maš-ti bi in-nam-ma lu-ú* DAM *ši-i* PN *iš-me-šú-ma* [f]*ba-zi-ti* NIN-*su nu-maš-ti a-na* DAM-*ú-tu id-da-áš-šú* [f]*ba-zi-ti* DAM PN *ši-i*.
> PN, son of PN, came before PN, son of PN, and spoke as follows: "Baziti, your sister, the lass, please give to me. Let her be a wife!" PN consented to him, and gave him Baziti, his sister, the lass, for wife-hood. Baziti, she is the wife of PN (lines 1–9).

3.7. Note that in the Aramaic of Elephantine, marriage is declared to exist without recourse to the verb *h-w-h*; the woman in question does not "become" a wife, but is rather declared to be a wife after her hand was sought from her brother. Cf. the negation of this status in Hosea 2:4: כי היא לא אשתי ואנכי לא בעלה "For she is not my wife, and I am not her husband."

3.8. It is interesting to find in one of the Neo-Babylonian marriage agreements a personal elaboration on the usual 'dialogue' statements. Thus, Roth, no. 3:

> DUMU-*ú-a ia-a-nu* DUMU *ú-ba-ʾ* [f]*kul-la-a* DUMU.SAL-*ka bi-nam-ma lu-ú* DAM-*a ši-i*
> "I have no sons. I seek a son. Please give me Kulla, your daughter. Let her be a wife" (lines 4–7).

3.9. As for the status of marriage, itself, it is termed *aššūtu* in Akkadian, and אנתו (*ʾintû*- feminine, absolute) in Aramaic. Thus, on the VERSO (line 45) of B3.8 from Elephantine we read: "The document of wife-hood (ספר אנתו) which ʿAnaniah, son of Meshullam wrote for Yehoyishmaʿ." In the declaration just cited above, from B3.8, the groom states that he is asking for the bride לאנתו "for wife-hood, marriage." Aramaic אנתו has long been recognized as a calque of Akkadian *aššūtu*. In fact, an Aramaic docket of the Neo-Assyrian period from Nineveh, probably to be dated to the early seventh century B.C.E., already attests the Old Aramaic, abstract form *ʾšt* (= *ʾaššût*, *ʾiššût*) "marriage, wife-hood" (Fales 1986:203). Later on, we find the Hebrew term אישות "wife-hood, marriage" in the Mishnah (*Nedārîm* 8:1) and elsewhere in Tannaitic literature.

II. Other elements of dialogue

3.10. In none of the Neo-Babylonian marriage agreements does the 'dialogue' form extend beyond the proposal of marriage, itself, and related declarations. In the Elephantine Aramaic marriage contracts, however, recourse to the dialogue form extends to other provisions. We have already referred to statements initiating divorce so as to clarify their manner of expressing the status of marriage (see above, 4.3). But there is more to such statements. If the husband should rise up in the assembly (עדה) to declare his intention to divorce his wife, he would say:

שנית לאנתתי יהוישמע לא תהוה לי אנתת:

> "I 'hate' my wife, Yehoyishmaᶜ; she shall not be a wife to me" (B3.8:21–22).

In parallel fashion, if the wife should initiate divorce, she would declare:

שניתך לא אהוה לך אנתת

> "I 'hate' you; I will not be a wife to you!" (B3.8:25).

The contrast between the objective form and the 'dialogue document' can be shown by citing an actual third-person formulation of the very same statements in a neo-Assyrian marriage conveyance, which, like the Elephantine marriage contracts, provides for mutual divorce. After recording that a certain man has given his daughter in marriage to a man, the document conditionally projects the initiation of divorce:

> *šum-ma* ᵐⁱ*ṣu-bi-t*[*ú a-n*]*a* (?) PN *ta-ze-e-ra*
> "If Ms. Ṣubītu should hate PN-"
> *šum-ma* PN [MÍ-*šu*] *e-zi-ra*
> "If PN should hate his wife-" (Postgate 1976:105, no. 14, lines 47–50).

3.11. In the Elephantine marriage contracts we also find first person, dialogue statements affirming that the *mōhar* has been paid. This usually follows directly upon the marriage proposal and the declaration of marital status. Thus, B3.8:4–5:

ויהבת לך מהר אחתך יהוישמע כסף... על עליך [וטי]ב [לבב]ך בגו

> "I have paid you the *mōhar* of Yehoyishmaᶜ, your sister, silver in X-amount; it has come into you (= you have received it) and your heart is satisfied with it."

3.12. There are further elements of 'dialogue' at Elephantine. Should the wife's brother, who had initially provided her dowry, ever seek to reclaim it, he would not to be allowed to do so; he remains obligated. The projected statement of the brother to his sister, the wife, reads as follows:

נכס[י]א אלה ברחמן יהבת ליהוישמע כען צבית אהנצל המו

> "These properties I gave to Yehoyishmaᶜ as a gift of affection; Now, I desire to retrieve them!" (B3.8:41–42).

In another instance, the orientation of the document actually shifts to the first person in stating specific provisions, and even contains internal quotations. Thus B2.6:31–35:

ולא אכל אמר: ״איתי לי אנתה אחרה להן מפט<ח>יה ובנן אחרנן להן בנן זי תלד לי מפטחיה״. הן אמר: ״איתי לי ב[נ]ן ואנתה אחרן להן מפטחיה ובניה״ אנתן למפטחיה כסף... ולא אכל [אהנ]תר נכסי וקניני מן מפטחיה. והן העדת המו מנה לקבל ספרא [זנה] אנתן למפטחיה [כס]ף ... באבני מלכא

> And I will be unable to say: "I have another wife besides Miphtaḥiah, and other sons besides the sons Miphtaḥiah may bear me." If I say: "I have a wife and sons other than Miphtaḥiah and her sons," I must pay Miphtaḥiah silver in X-amount, according to the royal standard. And I will be unable to release my properties and possessions from Miphtaḥiah. And should I expropriate them from her in contravention of this document, I must further pay Miphtaḥiah silver in X-amount, according to the royal standard. (Cf. B3.3:13–14).

It would seem, therefore, that the 'dialogue document,' the form that dominates in the Neo-Babylonian cuneiform repertory, underwent significant development in the Elephantine Aramaic marriage contracts. Such development is evident not only in marriage contracts but in other types of Aramaic legal documents, as well. It represents an overall trend, one that has persisted throughout the centuries, and which fully impacted the Jewish *ketūbbāh*.

Abbreviations

Ket.	The tractate *Ketūbbôt* of the Mishnah.
M.	"Mishnah" (when it precedes the name of the tractate). As: M. Ket.
Mur	"Murabbaᶜat," the site of discoveries on the Dead Sea (see under DJD, above).
P. Hever	Naḥal Ṣeʾelim (Wadi Seiyal). Site of discoveries on the Dead Sea.
P.	"Papyrus," as in: "P. Yadin" + no.
TAD II	Porten-Yardeni 1989, below.

Reference Bibliography

Ben-Yehudah, *Thesaurus*
1960 Eliezer Ben-Yehudah, *Dictionary and Thesaurus of the Hebrew Language*, ed. N.H. Tur-Sinai, 8 vols., New York: Thomas Yoseloff.

Epstein, J.N.
1908 Notizen zu den jüdisch-aramäischen Papyri von Assuan. *Jahrbuch der Jüdisch-Literarischen Gesellschaft* 6:359–373.

Fales, F.M.
1986 *Aramaic Epigraphs on Clay Tablets of the Neo-Assyrian Period*. Roma: Università degli Studi "La Sapienza."

Friedman, M.
1980 *Jewish Marriage in Palestine; A Cairo Geniza Study*, 2 vols., Tel-Aviv and New York: Tel-Aviv University and the Jewish Theological Seminary.

Levine, B.A.
2002 On the Role of Aramaic in the Transmission of Mesopotamian Legal Institutions. Pages 157–166 in *Ideologies as Intercultural Phenomena: Proceedings of the Third Annual Symposium of the Assyrian and Babylonian Intellectual Heritage Project, held in Chicago, USA, October 27–31, 2000*. Melammu Symposia 3; Milano: Università di Bologna–IsIAO {*VOL 2, PP. 73–83*}.

Milik, J.T.
1961 Textes hébreux et araméens. Pages 67–205 in *Les Grottes de Murabbaᶜât*. DJD 2. Oxford: Clarendon Press.

Muffs, Y.
2003 *Studies in the Aramaic Legal Papyri from Elephantine*, reissue of 1969 publication, with Prolegomenon by B.A. Levine, Leiden: E.J. Brill.

Porten, B., Yardeni, A.
1989 *Textbook of Aramaic Documents from Ancient Egypt*, vol. 2: *Contracts*. Jerusalem: Hebrew University (abbreviated as TAD II).

Postgate, J.N.
1976 *Fifty Neo-Assyrian Legal Documents*. Warminster.

Roth, M.T.
1989 *Babylonian Marriage Agreements: 7th–3rd Centuries B.C.* AOAT 222. Neukirchen-Vluyn: Verlag Butzon & Becker Kevelaer.

Tosefta
1973 *The Tosefta, The Order of Nashim*, ed. S. Lieberman. New York: The Jewish Theological Seminary.

Yadin, Y., J.C. Greenfield, A. Yardeni
1994 Babatha's Ketubba. *IEJ* 44:75–105.

Yadin, Y., J.C. Greenfield, A. Yardeni, and B.A. Levine
2002 *The Documents from the Bar-Kokhba Period in the Cave of Letters: Hebrew, Aramaic, and Nabatean-Aramaic Papyri*. Judean Desert Studies III. Jerusalem: Israel Exploration Society.

Yardeni, A.
2000 *Textbook of Aramaic, Hebrew, and Nabataean Documentary Texts from the Judaean Desert*, 2 vols., Jerusalem: Hebrew University-Ben-Zion Dinur Center.

On the Semantics of Land Tenure in Biblical Literature: The Term *ʾaḥuzzāh*[*]

Comparative lexicography is a vital pursuit for biblical scholars. Many components of the Biblical Hebrew lexicon remain elusive, and in most cases the avenue of inquiry offering the most enlightenment is exploration of the cognate languages. Unfortunately, biblical scholarship is currently riveted on other objectives, largely to the neglect of philology and lexicography. Perhaps it would help to stimulate interest in the smaller units of biblical literature if it were understood that the results of comparative research in lexicography often have broad significance. Lexicography adds to our understanding of culture and religion, and helps us to define the character of social and legal institutions. Failure to explore the smaller units of knowledge usually leads to unwarranted generalizations and unsubstantiated conclusions about the character of biblical literature and the realities of ancient Israelite society. The discussion to follow will provide several cases in point.

I.

In an earlier study, I investigated the Hebrew term *ʾaḥuzzāh*, which was then translated "land holding." At the time, my primary interest was probing the historical provenance of the priestly writings of the Pentateuch, known as "P." Through a comprehensive review of all occurrences of the term *ʾaḥuzzāh* in biblical literature, it was ascertained that this term of reference expressed the distinctive view of the priestly school and of its later disciples, that the right of the Israelite people to the Land of Israel was established in a certain type of divine grant. It is the God of Israel who ultimately owns the Land of Israel and the Israelites are His tenants, granted the land as an *ʾaḥuzzāh*. They do not own the land outright, a fact which explains the legal provisions of Leviticus 25 prohibiting its permanent alienation. It is not the Israelites' to sell.[1]

In addition to arguing for the lateness of this term relative to others used in the Hebrew Bible to signify possession of land, I pointed out that Hebrew *ʾaḥuzzāh* consistently referred to land that was held legally, pursuant to a grant or charter, or that had been purchased, but never to land possessed, in the first

---

[*] Originally published in M. E. Cohen, D. Snell, and D. Weisberg (eds.), *The Tablet and the Scroll: Near Eastern Studies in Honor of William W. Hallo* (Bethesda, MD: CDL Press, 1993), pp. 134–139. Reprinted with permission from CDL Press.

[1] B.A. Levine, "Late Language in the Priestly Source: Some Literary and Historical Observations," *Proceedings, Eighth World Congress of Jewish Studies, Panel Discussions: Bible Studies and Hebrew Language*, Jerusalem 1983, pp. 69–82.

instance, by conquest or seizure. This distinction is all-important for an appreciation of the priestly versions of the Genesis narratives, which portray the individual Patriarchs as peaceful newcomers to Canaan, purchasing *ʾaḥuzzāh*-land from its legitimate, prior owners. In the same, priestly sections of Genesis the land of Canaan is designated a national *ʾaḥuzzāh* in the words of the covenantal promise.[2]

The term *ʾaḥuzzāh* thus contrasts with other, earlier formulations of land possession in the Hebrew Bible. Forms of the verb *yāraš*, usually translated "to inherit," but quite often connoting actual conquest, would appear to be part of an earlier vocabulary than the term *ʾaḥuzzāh*. Compare the following two formulations:

> Deut. 3:20: *wešabtem ʾîš lîruššātô*
> "Each person may return to his estate."
> Lev. 25:10: *wešabtem ʾîš ʾel ʾaḥuzzātô*
> "Each person may return to his estate."

In effect, *ʾaḥuzzāh* replaces *yeruššāh* as a term for "estate, territory," and curiously, both represent the same morphology. The *Grundbedeutung* of the Hebrew root *y-r-š* and of its cognates (in Ugaritic, for instance) is admittedly somewhat uncertain. It may have primarily connoted inheritance, appropriating the sense of conquest as a predication; or vice versa, it may have progressed from the notion of conquest to that of inheritance. In either case, it is obvious that forms of this verb often connote conquest and its consequences.[3] The term *naḥalāh* "estate, homestead," occurring in fairly early biblical sources, has as its matrix the legal transfer or conveyance of property; this we know from the Mari texts. However, in context biblical *naḥalāh* often designates land that was conquered, in the first instance.[4] The point is that the same contextual connotation is not shared by the term *ʾaḥuzzāh*.

---

[2] See Gen. 17:8, 23:8–9. In Gen. 34:50 the denominative of *ʾaḥuzzāh*, Niphal *hēʾāḥēz*, means "to settle, enjoy the right of settlement." Cf. Gen 47:55, where we read that Pharaoh granted the land of Goshen to the clan of Jacob as an *ʾaḥuzzāh*, with Gen. 47:27, where it is subsequently stated that the Israelites "settled in" (*wayyēʾāḥazû*) there.

[3] The interplay of the two connotations is highlighted in Jer. 49:1–2. The functional sense of conquest is blatant in Num. 13:30, in the context of a planned invasion. Also note Num. 24:18, where the stative form *yerēšāh* means a land "depopulated, dispossessed (by enemies)." Cf. the sense of the Hiphil *hôrîš* "to drive out, dispossess" in Deut. 9:3, 11:23. The infinitive/imperative *rēš* in the first chapters of Deuteronomy (Deut. 1:21, 2:24, 31) clearly connotes possession by conquest. For usage of *yrṯ* "heir" and verbal forms in Ugaritic see J.C.L. Gibson, *Canaanite Myths and Legends*, Edinburgh: T. & T. Clark, Ltd., 2nd Ed., 1977, *Ugaritic Glossary*, p. 148, s.v. *yrṯ*, verb, and *yrṯ*, substantive.

[4] On Mari *naḫālu* "to transfer, convey" see *CAD N*/I, 126, s.v. *naḫālu* B, and *CAD N*/II, 219, s.v. *niḫlatu*. For Ugaritic *nḥlt* "possession, estate," see Gibson, *op. cit.*, *Ugaritic Glossary*, 153, s.v. *nḥlt* and 49, in the text entitled "The Palace of Baal," lines 26–28, and notes 10–11. Hebrew *nāḥal* regularly connotes the receipt of land and property (but see Zech. 2:16), whereas the connotation of Mari *naḫālu* moves in the counter-direction

In discussions with scholarly colleagues, the notion that land designated *ʾaḥuzzāh* was perceived to have been possessed peacefully and consensually, rather than by imposition of conquest, encountered the objection that the verb *ʾāḥaz* most often means the opposite. Although the verb *ʾāḥaz* in Biblical Hebrew in no instance specifically describes military conquest, or the forceful possession of land, it virtually always refers to the use of physical or other force. It speaks of an individual or a group seizing or being seized by others and of being seized by fear and trembling, or by some other powerful emotion.[5]

A dramatic example of the meaning "conquer, occupy territory" for the verb *ʾ-ḥ-z* is found in a proximate epigraphic source. In the Mesha inscription, a ninth-century B.C.E. royal annal, the Moabite king, writing in a Canaanite language akin to Biblical Hebrew, reports as follows:

> "Then Kemosh said to me: 'Proceed to occupy Nebo, which belongs to Israel' (*wyʾmr ly kmš lk ʾḥz ʾt nbh ʿl yśrʾl*)—and I marched through the night and did battle against it from the break of dawn until noon. I then occupied it and killed it off entirely (*wʾḥzh wʾhrg kl*[*h*]) ... For I proscribed it to Ishtar-Kemosh" (Mesha, lines 14–17, with deletions).[6]

There can be little doubt that the verb *ʾ-ḥ-z* here connotes conquest and its consequences. The same connotation is most likely attested in the so-called Adon inscription, sent to Pharaoh Necho II (609–594) by a West-Semitic vassal at the end of the seventh century B.C.E. It is a typical appeal for the Pharaoh's military assistance, in this case against Babylonian forces that have attacked a place named Aphek, for which there are several candidates along the Levantine coast. Notwithstanding serious lacunae, the perfect, plural Aramaic form *ʾḥzw* "they occupied, seized" can be clearly read in line 5 of the inscription, just after a statement recording the arrival of the Babylonian forces:

> [...] *zy mlk bbl ʾtw mṭʾw ʾpq*
> "[Forces?] of the King of Babylonia came, and they reached Aphek __"[7]

---

and signifies transfer to another. It is probable, therefore, that the Hebrew verb *nāḥal* normally functions as a denominative of *naḥalāh* (ultimately Mari *niḫlatu*, Ugaritic *nḥlt*), and means "to receive a *naḥalāh*."

[5] For *ʾāḥaz* in the sense of seizure by violent emotions see Exod. 15:14, Ps. 48:7, and cf. connotations of Akkadian *aḫāzu* in *CAD A*/I, 175 s.v. *aḫāzu*, mng. 1c.

[6] J.C.L. Gibson, *Textbook of Syrian Semitic Inscriptions I, Hebrew and Moabite Inscriptions*. Edinburgh: T. & T. Clark, Ltd., p. 197, lines 14–16, with deletions.

[7] See B. Porten, A. Yardeni, *Textbook of Aramaic Documents from Ancient Egypt, I, Letters*, Jerusalem, Hebrew University (Eisenbrauns), 1986, 6, "The Letter of King Adon." Porten-Yardeni see traces of two additional words in line 5: *wyblw* "they have brought," which is barely legible, and more legible *bkl* "in all, with all," which do not, however, add much clarity to the text.

Given these facts of usage, some have questioned whether a nominal derivative of *ʾ-ḥ-z*, namely *ʾaḥuzzāh*, would exclusively designate land possessed through legal acquisition, and not by conquest. This question only seems logical; in fact, a semantic progression in the meanings of verbs and terms from (a) possession expressed as physical seizure or conquest to (b) some form of contractual possession is typical of many, diverse legal vocabularies. The act of legal possession is normally conveyed in terms expressive of physical holding, or controlling. Often, a symbolic act of physical holding, grasping, or contact of some sort is required to finalize possession.

Biblical Hebrew provides any number of examples of this syndrome, most notably, perhaps, in the verb *lāqaḥ* "to take, seize, conquer," which often means "to acquire"—a wife.[8] The same semantic range characterizes Akkadian *leqû* (Assyrian *laqû*), and perhaps even more emphatically, Akkadian *aḫāzu*, the cognate of Hebrew-Moabite-Aramaic *ʾ-ḥ-z*, which so frequently bears the technical sense "to take a wife."[9] The transactions attested in the cognate, Semitic languages for *lāqaḥ/leqû* and *ʾāḥaz/aḫāzu* are truly fascinating in their own right and testify to the fact that legal acquisition is associated conceptually with physical possession.

I further adduced the analogy of the Old Babylonian term *ṣibtu* "land holding" to illustrate the suggested semantic progression. Deriving from the verb *ṣabātu* "to seize, hold," an equivalent of Hebrew *ʾāḥaz*, it means in Old Babylonian usage pretty much what *ʾaḥuzzāh* means in Biblical Hebrew usage, namely, land held under the terms of a contract. More specifically, *ṣibtu* designates agricultural land held under terms we might call feudal, often among brothers and family relatives. Certain royal officials were granted *ṣibtu* property as reward for their services, and recipients of *ṣibtu* land normally bore the right of usufruct. We read of claims against those who failed to honor the rights of others to *ṣibtu* land, and of rulings that effectively restored such land to those who had lost control over it. All in all, the realistic comparisons in law between Hebrew *ʾaḥuzzāh* and Old Babylonian *ṣibtu* are suggestive.[10] As we shall observe, usage of the Akkadian verb *ṣabātu* will prove relevant to the present discussion in additional respects, as well.

---

[8] The Hebrew verb *lāqaḥ* technically connotes taking in marriage in Gen. 11:29, Exod. 21:10, Lev. 20:17, Deut. 22:13. The sense of forceful seizure for the verb *lāqaḥ* is clearly to be understood in Num. 21:26, 1 Kings 14:26. For a discussion of the connotations attendant upon the verb *lāqaḥ* see Seock-Tae Sohn, *The Divine Election of Israel*, Grand Rapids, MI: William B. Eerdmans, 1991, pp. 11–16.

[9] See *CAD L*, s.v. *leqû*, and *CAD A*/I, 175–177, s.v. *aḫāzu* 2.

[10] See *CAD B*, 164–165, s.v. *ṣibtu* B, mng. 2, and cf. *ibid.*, 14–15, s.v. *ṣabātu*, mng. 3d. It may be relevant to note that in the Bisitun Inscription of Darius the Great, Aramaic *ʾḥdh* "I seized him" is rendered in Akkadian as *iṣṣabatsu*. See A.E. Cowley, *Aramaic Papyri of the Fifth Century B.C.* (henceforth abbreviated *AP*), Oxford, Clarendon Press, 1923, 253, line 47 [Aramaic] and 257, line 47 [Akkadian].

II.

There is, moreover, evidence of a legal character bearing on the verb *ʾ-ḥ-z*, itself, and this evidence makes it possible to identify the source of the unusual connotation of this verb that is reflected in the Biblical Hebrew term *ʾaḥuzzāh*. I failed to observe that in one known Aramaic legal source, the verbal root *ʾ-ḥ-z* actually meant "to acquire, purchase." Reference is to the Aramaic epigraphs, or dockets inscribed in paleo-script on Neo-Assyrian clay tablets recording legal transactions. These inscriptions date from the seventh century B.C.E.; according to S. Lieberman, from the early seventh century B.C.E. They testify to the considerable utilization of Aramaic by the Neo-Assyrian officialdom. The epigraphs have now received a new treatment by Frederick Mario Fales.[11]

Text no. 17 in Fales' collection is a conveyance from Nineveh. Its Assyrian version is almost completely preserved, and it bears an alphabetic-Aramaic docket which admittedly requires some restoration. The obverse of the Assyrian tablet reads as follows:

1) NA$_4$.KIŠIB [
2) NA$_4$.KIŠIB [
3) DUMU *Ḫa-zi-*[
4) EN GE[ME

{seal}

5) SAL *Ḫa-am-bu-su* GE[ME *ú*
6) DUMU.SAL-*ša*(?) *ina* UGU É [
7) *ú-piš-ma* [I]*Lu-qu*
8) LÚ.GAL *ki-ṣir šà* A [
9) *ma lib-bi* 1 MA.NA 8 GÍN KÙ.BABBAR
10) *il-qi kas-pu ga-mur*
11) *ta-din* SAL.MES *šu-a-tú*
12) *zar*$_4$*-pat*(*at*) *laq-qi-ʾu*
13) *tu-a-ru di-nu* DUG$_4$.DUG$_4$
14) *la-aš-šú ...*

Translation:

1) Seal of [
2) Seal of [
3) son of Hazi[
4) owner of the slave-woman

{seal}

5) Ms. Hambusu, the sla[ve-woman and
6) her(?) daughter, from E-[(*PN lost*)

[11] Frederick Mario Fales, *Aramaic Epigraphs on Clay Tablets of the Neo-Assyrian Period*, Roma, Università degli Studi "La Sapienza," 1986, pp. 175–180 [text no. 17]. Also see S. Lieberman, "The Aramaic Argillary Script in the Seventh Century," *BASOR* 192, pp. 25–31.

7) He drew up a contract, [namely], Luqu,
8) the commander of A-[(*PN/GN lost*)];
9) for the price of 1 mina, 8 shekels of silver
10) he made the acquisition. The silver was completely
11) paid for these women;
12) They are purchased and acquired.
13) The right of redress, contest, or litigation
14) does not exist.[12]

Fales suggests reading the Aramaic docket as follows:

1) *dnt ᵓmtᵓ ḥbš zy lqḥ b*
2)] *wbr t h* [
3)] *ḥt mn h* 5 [+ 3 *šqln kspᵓ*]
4) [*mn*(?)] *ᵓḥwh bnwh*
ᵓḥz ᵓmt[ᵓ]

Translation:

"Deed of the slave-woman Habbus, belonging to LQH, and her daughter (?). For one mina(?), eight shekels of silver(?) from her brothers and sons he purchased the slave-woman(?)"[13]

Notwithstanding lacunae and uncertain readings, the verb *ᵓ-ḥ-z* is clearly legible, and Fales is undoubtedly correct in reading it as a 3rd masculine perfect "he purchased." Aramaic *ᵓ-ḥ-z* thus translates the verb *laqû* (= *laqāᵓu*), the Assyrian realization of Akkadian *leqû* "to take, purchase, acquire"; specifically, the preterite, 3rd masculine singular, *ilqi* "he made the acquisition," in line 10 of the Assyrian version.

No less important for understanding the Hebrew term *ᵓaḥuzzāh* are the Assyrian verbal adjectives, *zarpat*(*at*) *laqqiᵓu* "They are purchased and acquired," in line 12 of the Assyrian version, forms that are not present in the briefer Aramaic summary of the transaction. In addition to usage of the verb *laqû* in the active-transitive voice to connote the act of purchase, it emerges that functionally stative forms of the same verb, to be precise, verbal adjectives, were used extensively to signify the completion of the transaction, as if to say: "It is done."[14] It may be relevant that morphologically Hebrew *ᵓaḥuzzāh* is based on

---

[12] J.H. Stevenson, *Assyrian and Babylonian Contracts, with Aramaic Reference Notes*, New York, American Book Company, 1903, pp. 104–105, for hand-copy of the Assyrian text of no. 7 (K. 280, which corresponds to Fales, no. 17.

[13] The present translation is adapted from Fales, *op. cit.* p. 176, where the transcription of the Aramaic is to be found. One is prompted to investigate the concept underlying the biblical, royal names *ᵓāḥāz*, *ᵓaḥazîah/yehôᵓāḥāz/yoᵓāḥāz*, and a few variants of the same. As an alternative to the notion of holding by the hand or as acting in the role of protector perhaps the operative concept is that God acquired or possessed the one so named.

[14] For a discussion of Assyrian *laqû* "to purchase" in legal formularies see J.D. Postgate, *Fifty Neo-Assyrian Legal Documents*, Warminster, England, Aris and Phillips, Ltd.,

the present, passive participial form of the root *ʾ-ḥ-z*, yielding the sense: "she/it is acquired," hence: "something acquired."[15]

There are two, ancillary observations to be made before concluding our discussion of Hebrew *ʾaḥuzzāh*:

a) The Aramaic verb actually occurs in an unusual sale document from Assur of the Neo-Assyrian period, written entirely in Aramaic. In that document, the verb *l-q-ḥ* does not, however, mean "to purchase," but rather "to take up, keep (a tablet)," or perhaps to engage in the process of writing one.[16] We thus observe that in the Aramaic epigraphs Assyrian *laqû* is not translated by the cognate, Aramaic verb *l-q-ḥ*, but by *ʾ-ḥ-z*, whose legal connotations were utilized by Aramaic-writing scribes as we suggest they were by the priestly legislators of the Hebrew Bible.

b) In an Elephantine legal papyrus (*AP* 2, and its duplicate *AP* 3), Aramaic *ʾ-ḥ-d* "to seize, hold" refers to wages "seized" pursuant to the terms of a deed of delivery. This document, incisively analyzed by Y. Muffs, stipulates that failure of suppliers to deliver goods listed in a contract penalizes them with a payment in silver, and gives the officials involved the right to "attach" their wages:

> *wʾnt šlṭ bprsn zy byt mlkʾ ...*
> *wʾnt šlṭ lmʾḥd ʿd ttmlʾ bʾbwr*
>
> "And you have the right to our wages from the Government House ..., and you have the right to *attach* [them] until you are fully [indemnified] for the grain."[17]

"Seizure" of the wages was rightful, for that is consistently the force of the verb *š-l-ṭ* "to have jurisdiction" in these legal papyri. Notwithstanding the difference in the precise, legal connotation between *ʾ-ḥ-z* of the Neo-Assyrian, Aramaic epigraphs and *ʾ-ḥ-d* of the Elephantine legal papyri, it is their common denominator that the verb *ʾ-ḥ-z/d* may signify legal ownership of, or rights to goods and property, and this is significant.

It is our sense, therefore, that the Biblical Hebrew term *ʾaḥuzzāh* would best be translated "acquired land," thus freeing us from the notion of "holding" so often associated with the verb *ʾāḥaz*. It is reasonable to suppose that the priestly

---

1976, pp. 13–17, and see examples, pp. 85–86 [text no. 4], and pp. 86–88 [text no. 5]. Also note numerous examples of the same type of Neo-Assyrian legal documents with the same conventional formulation in Th. Kwasman, S. Parpola, *Legal Transactions of the Royal Court of Nineveh,* SAA 6, Helsinki University Press, 1991. See Glossary, 305, s.v. *laqû* for references.

[15] The *Nominalbildung qeṭullāh* is relatively rare in Biblical Hebrew, but cf. *yeruššāh* "estate, territory" (Deut. 2:5, 9, 19), *kebuddāh* "baggage, load" (Jud. 18:20), *ʿarubbāh* "pledge" (1 Sam. 17:18), *pequddāh* "assignment, watch, order, account," (Hos. 9:7, Isa. 60:17, Num. 3:32), and more.

[16] See Fales, *op. cit.*, pp. 230–232, text no. 49, and especially 232, note 168.

[17] See *AP* 2:16–17; and in the duplicate, 3:18–19 (partially restored). Also see Y. Muffs, *Studies in the Aramaic Legal Papyri from Elephantine*, Leiden: E.J. Brill, 1969, pp. 56–58.

writers of the Torah appropriated a legal connotation of the verb *ʾāḥaz*, otherwise unattested in Biblical Hebrew, from what has come to be known as the "Aramaic common law tradition." This was the very tradition which had informed the Aramaic-writing scribes of the Neo-Assyrian administrative centers during the seventh century B.C.E. The legal arrangements applicable to land designated as *ʾaḥuzzāh* were known in the ancient Near East from early times.

III.

If it is true that Hebrew *ʾaḥuzzāh* replaces forms of the verb *yāraš* and usage of the term *naḥalāh* in the biblical legal vocabulary, then the specialized connotation of the verb *heḥezîq* expressed in Nehemiah 3 represents a still later phase in the semantics of legal possession. By exploring this source we can place the term *ʾaḥuzzāh* in perspective. Interestingly, it is Akkadian *ṣabātu*, as a semantic equivalent, that further informs us as to the distinctive usage of the Hebrew verb *heḥezîq* "to take hold of, grasp" in Nehemiah 3. We will also observe how the Aramaic usage of the Achaemenid period clarifies the functional connotation of Hebrew *heḥezîq*.

Sometime, late in the fifth century B.C.E., Nehemiah undertakes to rebuild the walls and gatehouses of Jerusalem. Jacob Myers has systematically outlined the accomplishment of the project, showing that the text of Nehemiah 3 projects a delineation of activity which proceeds counter-clockwise. We have a long list of families and officials, and craftsmen's guilds and clerics working on contiguous sections of the wall.[18]

The formulas registering the tasks involved in the project are several. In verses 1–3 we have fairly clear terms of reference, most notably, the verb *bānāh* "to build, fortify." But, beginning in verse 4, and continuing throughout most of the chapter, through verse 32, the verb *heḥezîq* is used as a way of introducing the respective efforts of each of the many participating groups. A typical entry reads as follows:

> *weʿal yādām heḥezîq PN ben PN, weneged bêtô*
> "Alongside them, PN son of PN *heḥezîq*, in the area facing his house." (Neh. 3:10a)

Alternative formulations express the direct object. An example is the following:

> *ʾet Šaʿar Haggâiʾ heḥezîq PN weyôšebê Zānôaḥ ...*
> "PN *heḥezîq*, with the inhabitants of Zanoah, the Valley Gate, ..." (Neh. 3:13)

Uniformly, commentators have explained the verb *heḥezîq* in these formulations as "to restore, repair, reconstruct," although nowhere in Biblical Hebrew are such connotations precisely attested. The closest we come in Biblical Hebrew is in the Piel stem *ḥizzēq*, which bears the meaning "to strengthen, rein-

[18] See J.M. Myers, *Ezra, Nehemiah*, AB 14, New York, Doubleday, 1965, pp. 106–120.

force," in contexts descriptive of fortification and reconstruction.[19] Once, in Neh. 3:19, we actually find the Piel form: *wayyeḥazzēq ʿal yādô* PN "So-and-So *ḥizzēq* alongside him." This is either a lapse in the otherwise consistent utilization of the Hiphil stem *heḥezîq*, with no difference in meaning intended, or an intentional usage of Piel *ḥizzēq* to connote reconstruction. There is, of course, the well attested technical idiom *ḥizzēq bedeq* "to repair the breach; renovate," in chronistic records of temple renovation (2 Kings 12:6–9, 13, 2 Kings 22:3). In Ezek. 27:9, 27 similar activity is expressed by the Hiphil: *maḥazîqê bidqēk* "those who repair your breach; maintain your equipment." Reference is to the merchants and sea captains of the Phoenician city states of the early sixth century B.C.E.

It is of interest to note that for itself, Hebrew *ḥizzēq bedeq* compares with Akkadian *bitqa ṣabātu*, which has the same meaning. It is used in similar contexts of reconstruction and temple renovation, and it incorporates the Akkadian cognate of Hebrew *bedeq* "split, breach," namely, Akkadian *bitqu*. Once again, we observe the equivalent transactions of Hebrew and Akkadian verbs meaning "to seize, hold, grasp." Whereas in Akkadian, G-stem *ṣabātu* has active-transitive force, in Hebrew, the simple stem, *ḥāzaq*, has stative force, thus requiring usage of the Piel and Hiphil to convey the active-transitive.[20] It is distinctly possible, therefore, that in Nehemiah 3 *heḥezîq* means what *ḥizzēq* means, namely, "to reconstruct, strengthen," and that it further resonates the technical idiom *ḥizzēq* / *heḥezîq bedeq* "to repair the breach, renovate."

There is, however, an alternative way of understanding the formulations in Nehemiah 3, one which again brings us back to the Akkadian verb *ṣabātu*, and which has implications for the biblical, legal vocabulary. I alluded to this alternative in my earlier study, but failed to explore it in depth. I ventured that verbal *heḥezîq* constituted a late, biblical formula for expressing legal possession, and that in the context of Nehemiah 3, the verb *heḥezîq* had the functional meaning: "to take over, take charge of, possess."

Read in this way, Nehemiah 3 records not only the actual work of building and repair, but an administrative process whereby various families and other sorts of groups as well as ranking officials were assigned contiguous sections of the walls and gatehouses of Jerusalem which they were to repair. These associations accordingly took charge of their assigned quarters, and settled in them, and it is this assumption of responsibility that is conveyed by the verb *heḥezîq*, not the actual work they performed. This interpretation seems to be supported by the fact that in several entries the initial statement that a person or group *heḥezîq* an area is followed by a reference to the work they actually performed (Neh. 3:6–8, 13–15). We further note that in one case, recorded in verse 5, there was a refusal to participate in the reconstruction project. And yet, verse 5 states as follows:

[19] Cf. Ps. 147:13, 2 Kings 12:15, 22:5–6, Isa. 54:2, Nah. 3:14.

[20] See B.A. Levine, "Comments on Some Technical Terms of the Biblical Cult," (Hebrew), *Leshonenu* 30, 1965–66, pp. 3–11.

> "Alongside them, the Tekoites *heḥezîqu*, though their nobles would not bear the burden of their leader's work assignment (*baʿabôdat ʾadônêhem*)."

This would seem to indicate that *heḥezîq* refers to something other than the actual work performed. We are to understand that along with responsibility assumed, there was a potential profit to be realized from participation in the rebuilding of Jerusalem. The participating investors would gain title to housing and workspace in the areas they had reconstructed by their own effort and probably at their own expense. All of this is suggested by the proposed legal-administrative connotation of the verb *heḥezîq*. Nehemiah's master plan was, after all, to resettle Jerusalem and make it the administrative, cultic, and commercial center of a Judea restored.

More persuasive, in my opinion, than the internal, but imprecise evidence suggesting that *heḥezîq* means "to repair, reconstruct" is comparative evidence of a specialized connotation attendant upon the Akkadian verb *ṣabātu*. In the annals of some Neo-Assyrian conquerors, we find statements to the effect that these rulers took over cities and provinces in regions they had occupied for the purpose of rebuilding and reconstituting them under new administration. It is common to find statements containing the clause: GN *ana eššūti aṣbat* "I took over X-place for purposes of renewal," followed by specifications as to the rebuilding of city walls and palaces, the resettlement of the specified town and its renaming or the designation of cubic offerings within it. Or, we may read: URU GN *šuātu ana āl birtūti aṣbat* "I took over that X-town to serve as my fortress city."[21]

What makes the Neo-Assyrian evidence bearing on usage of the verb *ṣabātu* so relevant is the striking similarity of its context with that of Nehemiah 3. The Persians had earlier conquered Jerusalem and Judea in the third quarter of the sixth century B.C.E. and had granted the exiled Judeans a charter allowing them to return. Yet, about a century later, the city was still in ruins. Nehemiah 3 describes in considerable detail how the enterprise known in Assyrian as *eššūtu* "[urban] renewal" was accomplished. In recording that process, the verb *heḥezîq* is employed to signify not the actual work performed, but the prior "take over" of areas and quarters of Jerusalem adjacent to the walls and gates where various families, associations, and officials would accomplish the construction work and eventually reside. Effectively, specialized usage of the verb *heḥezîq* in Nehemiah 3 anticipates the term *ḥazāqāh* "land tenure; possession," and denominative, Hiphil forms (participial *maḥazîq* and perfective *heḥezîq*) in Rabbinic Hebrew.[22]

---

[21] See *CAD Ṣ*, 16–17, s.v. *ṣabātu* mng. 3f. We further note that the sense of "taking charge" suggested for Hebrew *heḥezîq* in Nehemiah 3 may be anticipated in Lev. 25:35: "If your kinsman, being in straits, comes under your authority, and you take charge of him (*weheḥezaqtā bô*) in the manner of a resident alien."

[22] See Mishnah, *Bābāʾ Batrāʾ* 3:2–3, 4:9, *Šebîʿît* 6:1.

In contemporary Aramaic documents we find further evidence bearing on the diction of the late, Biblical Hebrew of Nehemiah 3. We note that in the Aramaic legal papyri from fifth century B.C.E. Egypt, the Haphel participle *mehaḥsin* means "he possesses; he is an owner (of a house or property)." Aramaic *hḥsn* is a semantic equivalent of Hebrew *heḥezîq* "to take hold of." Now, twice we find in the Aramaic papyri that an ethnically identified individual is entitled: *mehaḥsîn beyēb ledigil X* "a landowner in Yeb, the fortress, belonging to the *degel* (detachment) of X."[23] We once read that a *degel* "owns" (*mehaḥsîn*) a field collectively.[24] It would seem, therefore, that contemporary Aramaic legal usage might explain the unusual connotation being suggested for the verb *heḥezîq* in Nehemiah 3, whereas the system projected there was known from earlier times and corresponds with specialized usage of the Akkadian verb *ṣabātu*.

IV.

It has been the purpose of the present study to explore the development of biblical terminology relevant to land tenure, giving the term *ʾaḥuzzāh* center stage. In contrast to the premises of the biblical conquest traditions, the concept of the land of Israel as a national *ʾaḥuzzāh* projects no wars of conquest, but rather the legal acquisition of the land. To us it seems that this recasting of the patriarchal narratives and of the conquest traditions would have been an appropriate response to the edict of Cyrus the Great, and the subsequent Return to Zion and Judea which commenced in the third quarter of the sixth century B.C.E.

Understood in this way, the repossession of the Land of Israel by the people of Israel as a national *ʾaḥuzzāh*, subsequent to the Babylonian exile, gives legal force to the process of *geʾullāh* "restoration" announced in the visions of the exilic Isaiah.[25]

---

[23] See *AP* 7:2–3; 8:2. Also see E.G. Kraeling, *Brooklyn Museum Aramaic Papyri*, Yale University Press, 1953, p. 275, comments on text no. 12, line 5.

[24] See *AP* 16:2. Similar usage of Haphel *haḥsîn* "to possess (kingship)" occurs in the Aramaic of Dan. 8:18, 22.

[25] The God of Israel as *gôʾēl* "redeemer" and the Israelites as *geʾuillîm* "the redeemed" represent major themes in the prophecies of Deutero-Isaiah. See Isa. 43:1, 14, 44:6, 24, 48:17, 49:4, 7, 51:10, 52:3, 59:20, 63:4, 16.

B. Society

The Clan-Based Economy of Biblical Israel*

Introduction

Much has been said about kinship as a dominant feature of the Israelite societies, north and south, of biblical times. The clan, or "sib," as it has been called, was the salient socioeconomic realization of kinship in biblical Israel. One's status, rights, prerogatives, and obligations of all sorts are based on one's affiliation as a member of a family or clan; in other words, they are based on who one's relatives are and who one's forebears were, primarily consanguineously (blood-related), but at times also affinally (related by marriage). When kinship is operative, the larger society is usually configured as a network of kinship groups of various circumferences, and even the nation, in its totality, may be regarded as a single encompassing kinship group. Lineage is the defining diachronic feature of kinship groups, and at least a decided preference for clan endogamy is the defining synchronic feature. The patriarchal narratives of the book of Genesis provide a significant illustration of the kinship principle, because they relate how brides were sought from the ancestral clan back in Haran (Genesis 24; 28–29).

It has been recognized that there is a fictive, or metaphorical, aspect to some of the expressions of kinship in biblical literature, and furthermore, that not every aspect of Israelite societies can be explained in terms of kinship. Yet there are many areas in which real kinship was operative. As an example of contrasts, consider the following: the reference to the Israelite people (*benê Yiśrā᾿ēl*) collectively as one of the *mišpāḥôt*, "clans, sibs, extended families," of the earth strikes us as figurative in Amos 3:1–2, where the prophet imputes collective responsibility to the entire nation and its leaders:

> Heed this oracle that Yahweh has spoken regarding you, O people of Israel; regarding the entire clan (*mišpāḥâ*) that I brought up from the land of Egypt: only you have I acknowledged of all the clans of the earth (*mišpeḥôt hā᾿adāmâ*). This is why I shall call you to account for all your iniquities.

However, other uses of the term *mišpāḥâ* in more discrete frames of reference are surely realistic. The most prominent is the economic context, in which the term relates to land ownership or land tenure in a predominantly agrarian economy; or, as some prefer, in a dimorphic economy, in which pastoral pur-

* Originally published in W. G. Dever and S. Gitin (eds.), *Symbiosis, Symbolism, and the Power of the Past,* (Winona Lake, IN: Eisenbrauns, 2003), pp. 445–453. Reprinted with permission from Eisenbrauns.

suits also produce wealth and goods. There is nothing fictive about the basic role of kinship in biblical legislation governing the inheritance of land, the restriction of its alienation outside the clan, and the pledging of land to debt. Certain narratives involving the disposition of clan property also exhibit a strong element of realism, and the same could be said for biblical prophecy and wisdom in their references to property and wealth.

I. Methodology

Before attempting to describe the clan economy of ancient Israel as we know it, we must clarify a methodological principle: one could (and many do) attempt to explain the economy of biblical societies in terms of traditional tribal, or clannish, patterns of social and political organization—that is, to identify kinship as the organizing social principle, and economic policy as its result. It would be preferable, however, to reverse the priority and explain the predominance of kinship groupings in terms of the economic policies and objectives that they served and abetted. Such kinship patterns, however they originated, persisted because they were suitable to agrarian societies; they were effective in structuring production and consumption. It would be inaccurate, therefore, to view economic policy, in the first instance, as merely the consequence of a set kinship pattern.

It is important to note that the study of ancient economies has generally lagged behind other disciplines, such as archaeology and history, literary-textual study and linguistics, sociology, anthropology, politics, and, especially, when speaking of the Hebrew Bible, the field of religion. This lag is even more observable in any comparison of Western scholarship with Soviet scholarship, which, especially since World War II and mainly for political reasons, focused on economic agendas in the study of ancient societies. The picture is rapidly changing as Western scholars begin to realize the extent of their neglect of these very agendas.

II. The Nature of the Evidence for Biblical Israel

Let me begin by discussing the nature of the available evidence on the clan-based economy of biblical societies, and in so doing, emphasize the severe limitations of this evidence. Generally speaking, we lack external written evidence for the biblical period, which would have to be in the form of Hebrew epigraphy, of which very little has been discovered until now. As a consequence, we are almost totally reliant on the biblical record and on comparative materials from neighboring, and even somewhat distant, lands. Given this situation, the problem becomes one of evaluating the realism of the biblical record; and this is a very subtle scholarly enterprise, since there are considerable inconsistencies and even disagreements within the Bible itself. There is no escaping the need to deal with the literary history of diverse biblical texts through source criticism, although most archaeologists and many of those who currently adduce social models for biblical Israel tend to disregard this caveat.

Material culture must also be studied with a view toward arriving at certain conclusions about society and economy, and indeed archaeologists are of late showing greater interest in the economic implications of their discoveries, although there is a long way to go to effect a proper synthesis. To observe just how the clan operated as a productive and marketing unit, we would need reliable methods for estimating not only population density in local areas, but the sizes of farms and groves under cultivation. We should be able to map agricultural and horticultural patterns on the ground, and to know more about both urban and village life and the demographic intersections of the clan with administrative bureaucracies in population centers. Finally, we should know more about marketing. A new study by Schloen, entitled *The House of the Father as Fact and Symbol* (2001), which synthesizes extensive archaeological, economic, and textual evidence from Ugarit and other areas of the ancient Near East, is of great help in addressing these and related problems. Schloen employs social theory in the process, which, together with an impressive comparative reach, renders his work exceedingly relevant to a realistic understanding of the role of clan-based units in ancient Israel.

III. Biblical Terminology and Historical Reality

Bêt ʾāb as Clan

We begin by offering the judgment that as far as biblical kinship terminology is concerned, *ʿam*, "patrilineal kinship group," *mišpāḥâ*, "clan, sib," *bêt ʾāb*, "patrilineal 'house,'" and *ʾelep*, "clan," represent more-realistic categories for investigation than "tribe," Hebrew *šēbeṭ* and *maṭṭeh*. It is not that there were no tribes in ancient Israel, but rather that the textual sources on the subject of tribes are somewhat confusing and at times exhibit a degree of artificiality. Furthermore, some of the names of the tribes, the etymologies of which often elude us, are more likely to be names of regions and territories in the first instance, rather than eponyms or social groupings. Was *Yehûdâ* (Judah) in the first instance the name of a person or family, or of a region of Canaan? According to Mic 5:1, the inhabitants of Bethlehem of the district of Ephrath are "the youngest (= least) of the clans of Judah" (*ṣāʿîr liheyôt beʾalpê Yehûdâ*), suggesting that Judah was the name of a region, in which other towns and their resident clans were more notable than Bethlehem. This is, after all, the point of the prophecy.

The evidence bearing on clan terminology is less ambiguous. A West Semitic cognate of Hebrew *bêt ʾāb* (*bīt abi*) occurs in the royal inscription of Idrimi, the ruler of Aleppo around the middle of the second millennium B.C.E. (Kempinsky and Naʾaman 1973). Hebrew *ʾelep* is matched by a Ugaritic cognate, *ulp* (*KTU*[2] 1.40), and the root *š-p-ḥ*, from which Hebrew *mišpāḥâ* (and *šipḥâ*, "family slave"?) also occurs in Ugaritic, in clear family contexts (*KTU*[2] 1.16). The term *ʿam* (variant *ḥam*) has cognates in most of the Semitic languages, and the most convincing demonstration of its kinship matrix lies in the fact that it also means "paternal uncle, kinsman" (Koehler and Baumgartner 1983:791–94).

Although we do not have clear and consistent definitions of these socioeconomic units, we are able to define the biblical *mišpāḥâ* maximally as an extended family, often spanning three generations and usually including cousins and uncles, and perhaps others as well. Most of what we know in this regard is in the nature of inferential evidence, coming from what I would classify as late biblical texts, priestly sources such as Leviticus 18 and 20 on marriage and incest; Leviticus 21 on the funerary restriction of priestly families; and Numbers 27 and 36 on inheritance. One could also factor in the somewhat earlier Levirate law of Deuteronomy 25 and its reflex, the story of Ruth. It must be recognized, however, that the reader cannot ascertain from the relevant texts just how extended or how limited the projected *mišpāḥâ* was in each case.

The term *bêt ʾāb* in its early usage is patrilocal, not merely patrilineal, and it is predicated on ownership of a shared clan residence or residences (the strict sense of the term *bayit*), along with shared, arable land often attached or adjacent. Whatever we may conclude about the currency of matriarchal clans in biblical Israel, and there is some evidence of such, it is doubtful whether the construction *bêt ʾimmî*, "my mother's house" (Song 3:4; 8:2), is a genuine counterpart of *bêt ʾābî*. More likely, it merely refers to the home of the young woman; it is where she brings her beloved, and in Song 3:4, *bêt ʾimmî* is parallel with *ḥeder hôratî*, "the chamber of my parent."

It occurs to me that the West Semitic *bêt ʾāb* correlates with what has been termed the "institutional household," a socioeconomic unit of great antiquity, operative most prominently in southern Mesopotamia and elsewhere. It is a socioeconomic structure better accommodated to city-state networks than to centralized kingdoms. This unit, usually referred to in Greek as *ôikos*, has been recently discussed by Lamberg-Karlovsky, who describes the institutional household as follows:

> The household may be defined as a residential group that forms a social as well as an economic unit of production and consumption. Members of the household consisted of kin and clients providing voluntary labor. (Lamberg-Karlovsky 1999:168)

Lamberg-Karlovsky goes on to dispute the often-held notion that such units as the institutional household, which is based on status, inevitably gave way to governmental bureaucracies based on merit, insisting that in fact they not only antedated such centralized structures in many areas of the ancient Near East, but continued to operate fully long after the bureaucracies established their hold. As he puts it:

> It is important to recognize that throughout the vast majority of Near Eastern antiquity the private household remained the primary focus of economic activity. (Lamberg-Karlovsky 1999:183)

Bêt ʾāb as Land-Owner

Whereas the term *mišpāḥâ* is purely relational, or lineage-based, and does not of itself establish whether ownership of land is involved, one would normally apply the term *bêt ʾāb* to a kinship group that did indeed own land on which it resided, as noted above. This is brought out rather subtly by the incident reported in Genesis 31 concerning the daughters of Laban, Rachel and Leah. As is often the case, variations on the theme define the limits of the theme, and this applies with respect to the biblical *naḥalâ*. After Jacob's flocks experience miraculous increment, Jacob decides on immediate flight to Canaan and summons his wives out to the countryside where the flocks are gathered. His two wives have the following to say to him:

> Do we still retain an estate share (*ḥēleq wenaḥalâ*) in our patrilineal "house" (*bĕbêt ʾābînû*)? Have we not been regarded as outsiders (*nokriyyôt*) by him, for he has sold us out! Moreover, he has surely eaten up our silver! So it is that all of the wealth that God has extricated from our father (surely) belongs to us and to our sons. Now, then, all that God has commanded you, do! (Gen 31:14–16)

By way of explanation—we have translated the ambiguous *bêt ʾābînû* as the *terminus technicus* "in our *bêt ʾāb*," in view of the immediate context. By leaving home with their husband, who took all his accumulated flocks with him, Laban's daughters had angered their father to the point of disowning them. We are to understand that at the time of their marriage Laban would have given his daughters silver in place of the usual *naḥalâ*, consisting of clan-owned land, because they were following their husband to another country. However, because of the conflict between Jacob and Laban, Rachel and Leah were dealt out of their *naḥalâ*, so that all of their wealth ended up consisting of the flocks that Jacob had spirited away from Laban's grasp. Rachel and Leah, if they had entertained any qualms about how Jacob had gained control of the flocks, were now free of these qualms and eager to own the flocks. As for the term *ʾelep*, it is harder to define specifically, especially since it is homonymous with the word for "thousand." As a socioeconomic term, Hebrew *ʾelep* represents an extension of the meaning "bull, ox," thus meaning initially "the clan perceived as herd," thereby reflecting a pastoral economy. The Ugaritic evidence, recently investigated by Shedletsky and Levine (1999), correlates well with the biblical, showing how *ʾelep/ulp* came to designate other than kinship groupings as well.

Premonarchic and Monarchic Clan Traditions

To illustrate our judgment that there is more discrete biblical information about clans than there is about tribes, I will compare two sets of biblical traditions. Traditions that relate that the tribes of Israel were allotted territories in the Promised Land at the time of a unified original settlement of the entire land of Canaan are probably less realistic than the Caleb traditions, for example, that relate how a hero was granted a territory in the Judean Hills as a reward for his role in the conquest of that region of the land. This is partially because the Caleb traditions reflect the known practice of royal grants. Thus Joshua, acting in *loco regis*, was said to have granted to this uniquely loyal head of a clan, Caleb, perhaps only secondarily affiliated as a Judean, a sizable territory, some of which Caleb proceeded to grant to his daughter on the occasion of her marriage to a younger conquering hero (Joshua 15; Judges 1). Also note that, in an early biblical source, Judg 17:7, *Yehûdâ* (Judah) is termed a *mišpāḥâ*, not a tribe. This is not the only instance in which the terminology overlaps.

It is important to emphasize that land owned by the *mišpāḥâ* (or the *bêt ʾāb* or *ʾelep*) was private only in the sense that it did not belong collectively to the tribe as a whole, to the realm in the office of the king, or to a temple or town. This land was not individually owned, however, and was not free from clan obligations and restrictions regarding its alienation (Levine 1996). The David stories in the books of Samuel refer to royal grants of land as a means of generating this kind of nonpublic property. A cycle of such stories centers on a steward named Ziba, a man of large family and considerable wealth (2 Samuel 9; 16; 19). In 1 Sam 22:7–8, Saul taunts some of his fellow Benjaminites who had sided with David, as follows:

> Hear me, sons of Benjamin! Will the son of Jesse indeed grant all of you fields and vineyards; will he appoint all of you commanders of thousands and commanders of hundreds? Is this why you have all conspired against me?

There is a similar allusion to royal grants in the words of two insurgents against Moses, whose roles are often modeled after those of a king, in Num 16:14:

> You have not yet brought us to a land flowing with milk and sap, or granted us fields or vineyards as our domain (*naḥalâ*).

The other aspect of the subject, royal attempts to expropriate clan-owned land, is also instructive. The most famous case is that of Naboth of Jezreel in his encounter with Ahab and his queen, Jezebel, as related in 1 Kings 21. The story seems to be predicated on the right of a landowner to refuse to sell to the king his "ancestral estate" (in Hebrew *naḥalat ʾābôt*). Reference to *ʾābôt* holds the clue, and it tells us that clan land was involved. The king of Israel could not simply expropriate such property because he craved it; he had to resort to subterfuge. Yet the prophet Samuel cautions the people regarding the perils of having a king:

> He will confiscate your fields and your best vineyards and olive trees so as to grant them to his courtiers, and he will exact a tithe of your grain and vineyards and give that to his personal guards and courtiers. (1 Sam 8:14–15)

These cases may be classified as inferential evidence because they focus on the rights of the heads of families to their land. In the first instance, land belonged to the head of the family, who could allocate it to his sons and daughters under circumscribed conditions. The conclusion of the 1 Sam 8:14–15 statement refers to the right of a king to impose taxes. The above sources are suggestively monarchic in their configuration, and they illustrate the characteristic conflicts between the prerogatives of royal authority and the rights of families and clans. When the institutional households of a city-state polity came under the hegemony of a more centralized royal authority, there was inevitable tension. Some of this tension is reflected in the sparse Hebrew epigraphy that has come to light, in which estate managers and others complain of tax collectors, magistrates, and administrative/military officials, such as the *śar*. The Lachish and Arad ostraca provide ample evidence of such tension.

A good deal of the information available on the clan in biblical times comes from literature purporting to represent the premonarchic period of Israelite history. Much depends, therefore, on our judgments as to the authenticity of biblical traditions on the so-called tribal confederation of early Israel, as well as those regarding the role of the clan in this context. For example, when Gideon doubts his capacity to lead an army against the Midianites, he expresses himself as follows:

> With what can I rescue Israel? Behold, my clan (*ʾelep*) is the poorest in Manasseh, and I am the youngest in my patrilineal "house" (*bêt ʾābî*). (Judg 6:15)

It is risky to attempt to squeeze socioeconomic information out of this single statement. Here Manasseh could represent either the name of a tribe or of a region, or both. Yet one could take this statement as an indication that the clan participated as a unit in military ventures and bore its own costs; and furthermore, that the leading family of the clan had first access to its wealth. There was a hierarchy of families within the clan, just as there was, presumably, a hierarchy of clans within the tribe (note the reference to *śar hāʾelep*, "commander of the clan," in 1 Sam 17:18). In 1 Sam 9:21, Saul characterizes his own inferior status in terms similar to those used by Gideon. The prophet Samuel tells Saul that he needn't worry about the lost asses, because he and his *bêt ʾāb* are about to come into possession of great wealth. Saul at first doesn't understand what the prophet means and replies:

> I am only a Benjaminite, from the smallest of the Israelite tribes, and my *mišpāḥâ* is the least of all the *mišpāḥôt* of the tribe of Benjamin, so why have you said these things to me?

As we have seen, the early material in the book of Judges, to the extent that we are able to isolate it textually, gives the impression of being realistic regarding the role of the clan. The Song of Deborah speaks of the *ʿammāmîm*, "clans," of Benjamin, *ʿammāmîm* being a diminutive form of the term *ʿam*, which essentially designates a kinship group of consanguineal relatives. When the Israelites are collectively designated *ʿam* by extension, the clear intent is to adduce patrilineal kinship for the entire nation. No matter how fictive or metaphorical the usage of *ʿam* becomes, the original matrix continues to peer through. Thus a study of the term *ʿam hāʾāreṣ* in such contexts as Abraham's purchase of land in Canaan indicates that patrilineal clans are envisioned as owning such lands and that it is up to these heads of clans to approve sales. Similarly, Joseph, after confiscating the produce of the fat years, ends up redistributing it to the Egyptian *ʿam hāʾāreṣ*, namely, the land-owning clans. There is a degree of humor in the fact that biblical narrators assume that other societies are managed in the same way as theirs.

The Song of Deborah also mentions the Machirite clan, well known in the Transjordanian traditions. It is also true, of course, that the same Song of Deborah mentions many names elsewhere known as designating tribes, although most would agree that in the statement "Gilead is settled in Transjordan," the ballad's author is transparently using the name of a known region as an eponym. This probably applies as well to other names occurring in the Song of Deborah. Although the social portrait of premonarchic Israel in Judges is a mixed bag, it is possible to state that it endorses the realism of the clan as a basic unit of society. Mention should be made of a clan celebration called *zebaḥ mišpāḥâ*, "the sacred meal of the clan" (1 Sam 20:20). Jonathan makes excuses for David's absence at a New Moon feast hosted by Saul, saying that David told him he was returning home to Bethlehem for such an occasion to see "my kinsmen" (*ʾeḥḥay*).

Postexilic Clan Fragmentation

It is probably reasonable to assume that the clan continued to serve as the basic economic unit in biblical societies throughout the First Temple period and that clans still owned most of the arable land in common, either within a larger tribal framework or, as suggested above, within an administrative, regional districting system. The clan system seems to have broken down to a degree in the postexilic period, when the individual landowner comes into prominence. This conclusion is based on the stated relationships and duties among members of the same clan toward one another, leading us to reiterate that most of the legal sources on the role of the *mišpāḥâ* and the attendant obligations of clan members are preserved in Torah literature, and at that, in the priestly strata of this corpus. The limited historical indicators present in the historical books are absent from Torah literature, and we are on uncertain ground even in determining whether a given legal or narrative source in the Torah is pre- or postexilic, much less in establishing its precise *Sitz im Leben*.

It is my view, based on independent considerations, that the priestly strata of Torah literature were composed in the postexilic, Achaemenid period and in curious ways reflect the fragmenting of the clan, against the background, still visible in these late sources, of the earlier monarchic periods of preexilic history.

In contrast, an old practice still operative in postexilic times was the sacred duty to restore the blood of a murdered clan relative. There is a remarkable episode reported in 2 Samuel 14 that is relevant to this point. In a melodramatic ruse, a disguised woman entraps King David with a tale of fratricide and clan retaliation. The entire scene is intended to bring home to David the consequences of his continuing refusal to allow the return of his seditious son, Absalom. Following is what the woman has to say:

> Verily, I am a widowed woman, my husband having died. Your servant had two sons who did combat in the field, and there was none to keep them apart, so that one struck the other and killed him. And behold, the entire *mišpāḥâ* rose up against your servant, saying: "Hand over the fratricide and let us put him to death in place of the life of his brother whom he killed." Thus they would eliminate the heir, as well, and extinguish my estate that remained, not affording my husband a surviving name on the face of the earth. (2 Sam 14:5b–7)

If Jeremiah 32 is truly near exilic in provenience and not a later insertion, we have inferential evidence of the duty of a *dôd*, an uncle or perhaps cousin, to redeem the land of his relative that had been pledged to debt. The report is replete with legal terminology, indicating that the practice of clan redemption of mortgaged land was a reality.

A study of debt in biblical Israel once again focuses our attention on the primacy of arable land in the biblical economies. With the exception of debt incurred by craftsmen or merchants, virtually all debt was land related. Landowners would borrow seasonally to acquire seed and implements and to pay laborers, and they hoped to repay their indebtedness after the harvest. A bad harvest, or natural disasters and the effects of war, would often make repayment impossible, leading to indenture and the loss of clan land by foreclosure.

When I say that the clan was fragmented in the postexilic period, I am thinking of the abolition of the sabbatical moratorium on debt and indenture, a change in the law introduced in Leviticus 25 and echoed in Leviticus 27. This change worked in favor of the individual creditor against the interests of the clan. Note the curious provision in Lev 25:47 that the duty to come to the aid of a clan relative facing foreclosure obtained only in cases in which land had been mortgaged to non-Israelites. Otherwise, if he had the resources or if a *gōʾēl* was willing to act as redeemer, he was guaranteed the right to redeem the forfeited land. If not, he had to await the Jubilee, which he might never live to see. Yet one so fortunate as to be able to return to his *ʾaḥuzzâ* would also be returning to his *mišpāḥâ* (Lev 25:10), the people who owned, or had owned, the *ʾaḥuzzâ*. Also noteworthy is the introduction of relationship terms that are not reflective, even fictively, of clan identity. The most notable of these is *ʿamît*, which could very well be rendered "fellow citizen" (namely, a person encountered in daily life), a term that occurs only in the priestly sources of Leviticus and in Zech 13:7, at the tail end of Second Zechariah. We thus observe indications of three successive phases in the economic role of the clan in biblical literature: (1) the premonarchic phase; (2) the monarchic phase; and (3) the post-exilic, imperial phase. Of these, the Persian imperial phase offers the best chance of reconstruction. If only we had biblical information on marketing and trade on the part of the clan … but there is little that can be discerned. It is realistic, in most cases, to assume that the functional, productive unit was also the marketing unit.

Conclusion

It would be wrong to overemphasize the economic role of the clan to the neglect of the economic role of the government, in all its manifestations. The role of temples must also be factored in. Much of the epigraphic evidence that survives is more informative about these societal structures simply because it was produced by such agencies in the first place. The Bible's interest in kinship, clan, and land ownership is understandable, however, in terms of its own agendas, which were primarily social and religious, in affirming the peoplehood of Israel and its common history and destiny in the land. The most prominent feature of biblical traditions in this regard is the primacy of patrilineage in establishing ownership of land. The major variable in the equation is political development, which brought the land owned by families and clans (and maybe tribes) under ever-increasing governmental control. Yet it would be a mistake to underestimate the power of real kinship, or to fail to appreciate the strength of the kinship metaphor applied to all of Israel. If the most powerful affinal metaphor in biblical literature is marital infidelity, the most powerful consanguineal metaphor is the kinship of the clan.

References

Kempinsky, A., and Naʾaman, N.

1973 The Idrimi Inscription Reconsidered. Pp. 211–20 in *Excavations and Studies: Essays in Honor of Professor Shemuel Yeivin*, ed. Y. Aharoni. Ramat Aviv: Tel Aviv University.

Koehler, L., and Baumgartner, W.

1983 *Hebräisches und Aramäisches Lexikon zum Alten Testament* 3. Leiden: Brill.

KTU[2]

1995 *The Cuneiform Alphabetic Texts from Ugarit* (*KTU* 2nd ed.), by M. Dietrich, O. Loretz, and J. Sanmartín. Münster: Ugarit-Verlag.

Lamberg-Karlovsky, C. C.

1999 Households, Land Tenure, and Communications Systems in the 6th–4th Millennia of Greater Mesopotamia. Pp. 167–201 in *Urbanization and Land Ownership in the Ancient Near East*, ed. M. Hudson and B. A. Levine. Cambridge, MA: Peabody Museum of Archaeology and Ethnology.

Levine, B. A.

1996 Farewell to the Ancient Near East: Evaluating Biblical References to Ownership of Land in Comparative Perspective. Pp. 223–46 in *Privatization in the Ancient Near East and Classical World*, ed. M. Hudson and B. A. Levine. Cambridge, MA: Peabody Museum of Archaeology and Ethnology {*VOL 2, PP. 187–208*}.

Schloen, J. D.
2001 *The House of the Father as Fact and Symbol: Patrimonialism in Ugarit and the Ancient Near East*. Studies in the Archaeology and History of the Levant 2. Winona Lake, IN: Eisenbrauns.

Shedletsky, L. and B. A. Levine
1999 The *mšr* of the Sons and Daughters of Ugarit (KTU 1.40). *RB* 100:321–45.

Some Indices of Israelite Ethnicity*

It is my purpose to share some thoughts on Israelite ethnicity as known primarily from the Hebrew Bible, our major source of information about ancient Israel. Throughout the sessions of the Leiden *Rencontre* it was emphasized that it is difficult to define ethnicity to the satisfaction of all. In my view, collective identity based on political and/or territorial cohesion does not qualify as ethnic unless accompanied by a kinship factor. This judgment would apply to the city-states, kingdoms, and empires of the ancient Near East. Some regard a shared language as an index of ethnicity, and language is, indeed, a strong force for cohesion. And yet, one normally expects something more in the way of lasting social affiliation. And so, we search royal documents from the ancient Near East—edicts, correspondence, annals and chronicles, and law codes—as well as private records, and we examine epics and myths and religious texts with certain questions in mind: How are persons and groups addressed in such documents? Are they referred to solely as subjects of the realm, or inhabitants of different locales and lands, as nations and "tongues"? Or, is there more to their reflected identity?

When studying the Hebrew Bible we do not have to seek very far for answers to these sorts of questions. The Hebrew Bible is a celebration of ethnicity; it is, after all, the collected literature of a "people", Hebrew *ʿam*. Biblical laws and rituals, narratives and poetry, prophecy and historiography, even wisdom texts, are infused with a sense of an individual and group identity based on such factors as common ancestry, family and clan affiliation, shared culture and religion, all in addition to a common "tongue" and territorial concentration in a single land. This makes of the Hebrew Bible a classic paradigm of ethnicity, surely distinctive, perhaps even unique in ancient Near Eastern literature. There is a caveat, however. The Hebrew Bible is canonical literature that has been redacted; it speaks for diverse institutions over a fairly protracted period of time. The historian is challenged to develop methods of evaluating the realism and reliability of the biblical record, and that is my methodological objective in this study, relevant to the subject of ethnicity.

Here I will explore in brief several indices of ethnicity applicable to the societies of northern Israel and Judah, primarily during the period preceding the Babylonian exile. They include the question of Israelite origins, the organization of family and clan, the practice of endogamy, and the concept of Israel as a cho-

* Originally published in W.H. van Soldt (ed.), *Ethnicity in Ancient Mesopotamia: Papers Read at the 48th Rencontre Assyriologique Internationale, Leiden 1–4 July 2002* (PIHANS 102; Leiden: Nederlands Instituut voor het Nabije Oosten, 2005), pp. 189–197. Reprinted with permission from the Nederlands Instituut voor het Nabije Oosten.

sen people. All of these themes have been studied extensively by biblical scholars, although seldom from the specific perspective of ethnicity. There will be no attempt to review all of the relevant literature; I will restrict myself to bibliographical references that have a direct bearing on the present discussion.

Ethnicity and the Problem of Israelite Origins

In recent decades, it has become even more difficult than it was previously to engage the subject of Israelite origins in historical terms. There was a time, not too long ago, when the debate concerning Israelite origins centered on the process and character of population shifts in early Iron Age Canaan. Although many issues were in dispute, virtually no one doubted that an Israelite population had, indeed, been introduced into Canaan from outside of it, or questioned that this population had an ethnic basis of cohesion. The operative consensus might have been formulated as follows: A group known as Israelites, bound by ties of clan and kinship, variously conquered large parts of Canaan in rapid or prolonged incursions, settled those areas through migration, or more likely—did both over time. Although biblical traditions differ, or are unclear as to where the Israelites originated, they are consistent in affirming a foreign, non-Canaanite origin for them.

The scholarly atmosphere has changed ever since George Mendenhall (1976, 1996), followed with modifications by Norman Gottwald (1985), and archeologists such as William Dever (1993), began theorizing that biblical authors had transformed what in reality was an internal restructuring of society, resulting from a rural, or peasant revolt against city-states, into a tradition-history of foreign migrations, invasions, and settlement. A broad-based symposium on the subject of the Israelites in Canaan entitled: "Archaeology, History, and the Bible: The Israelite Settlement in Canaan: A Case Study" is presented in *Biblical Archaeology Today* (Biran et al. 1985:31–99). [Gottwald's study of 1985, just mentioned above, originated in that symposium.] These discussions continue in full-force, with more and more scholars joining in as time passes, so that it has become necessary to argue for the reliability of the biblical record on the non-Canaanite origin of the Israelites, in addition to all else. It was a major thrust of Mendenhall's work in general to downplay the role of ethnicity in favor of territorial and political factors, thereby altering the understanding of identifying nomenclature. Thus, for example, Mendenhall (1992) defined the enigmatic biblical term *ʾEmôrî* "Amorite" as territorial, not ethnic, contending that it was employed to identify different persons and groups that came from North Syria. In that case, he was probably correct, but this very identification points to an inconsistency in Mendenhall's proposed reconstruction: He recognized, on the one hand, that Canaan had absorbed foreign populations in the Late Bronze and early Iron Age, but on the other hand, he regarded biblical traditions claiming a non-Canaanite origin for the Israelites, themselves, as unhistorical. The upshot of Mendenhall's analysis is that the Israelites were none other than Canaanites, which *ipso facto* greatly reduces, even eliminates their ethnic distinctiveness.

What separated them from other Canaanites would have been more a matter of class than of ethnicity.

Due primarily to the scarcity of written records and inscribed artifacts from Iron Age I Canaan, it is difficult to determine the identity of those who constructed the buildings and fashioned the artifacts unearthed by archeologists, and who inhabited the settlements that have been surveyed. Archeologists usually point to noticeable changes in architectural and artifactual styles at the beginning of the Iron Age, and examine cult objects in search of identity, but without conclusive results. Destruction levels are likewise elusive. Thus, the Israeli archeologist, Amnon Ben-Tor (1999) can provide evidence for the destruction of Hazor, and suggest a reasonable date for this event, but he cannot substantiate that the Israelites were the ones who destroyed Hazor in the great conflagration he discovered on the site, and which is dramatically depicted in Joshua, chapter 11. One also hears talk of long-term cycles of recurring population change, which would reduce the singularity of whatever shifts that are, indeed, perceptible at the beginning of the Iron Age, and for several centuries thereafter.

It would make things easier if the biblical record, itself, provided a consistent, and less complicated depiction of the arrival of the Israelites in Canaan, but it does not. Nevertheless, there is one cluster of patriarchal traditions that rings true. These traditions regard the earliest Israelites as a clan-based group of common ancestry that migrated from Ḥaran on the Balikh River, southward to Canaan (see Gen 11:31–32, 12:4, for starters). The patriarchal narratives identify Arameans, or other, related West-Semites of the early Iron Age as relatives of the first Israelites. We read of sending back to Ḥaran for brides, and of the recognition of the clan back home as family (Genesis, chapters 24 and 29). These traditions correlate with statements in Deuteronomy 26, which speak of Jacob as *ʾarammî ʾōbēd* "a fugitive Aramean" (Levine 1995). One is also reminded of the historical note in Joshua 24 which reports that the ancestors of the Israelites came from *ʿēber hannāhār*, literally: "the western side of the river", namely, Cis-Euphrates. All of these traditions have in common the tracing of a middle, or upper-Euphrates origin for the first Israelites. A minor point was noted long ago: Abraham's great grandfather is named *Śerûg* (Gen 11:22), which is the name of a town west of Ḥaran, attested in 7th century B.C.E. Assyrian texts, thereby illustrating the overlap of eponyms and toponyms (Hess 1992).

Still another complex of biblical traditions presents the Israelites as being related to the Edomites (or Esavites) of the southern interior, again a theme of the Patriarchal narratives, echoed in other sources, as well. When relations between Israelites and Edomites are hostile, it is considered an act of betrayal on the part of the Edomites, because they are kinsmen (Numbers 20, and cf. Mal 1:2). It is significant that according to Deut 23:8 an Israelite ought not to despise an Edomite "because he is your kinsman". In fact, the tradition of an ethnic relationship with the peoples of the interior extends to the Ammonites and Moabites, as well. These are the children of Lot, Abraham's relative, etiologically cursed in Genesis 19, and often treated with hostility, but nonetheless assured of their rights to their lands (Deut 2:9).

What is perhaps most interesting is that certain biblical traditions present an outline of ethnographic history, recording that many areas of the immediate region underwent population change. The Deuteronomist (Deuteronomy, chapters 2–3) cites what appear to be old records of settlement and conquest. We read that Moab was formerly inhabited by Emim, and Seir by Horim, who were subjugated and displaced by the Moabites (descendants of Lot) and Esavites, respectfully, "just as the Israelite people had done with respect to its conquered territory" (Deut 2:12). The Ammonites overcame and displaced the Zamzumim, and the Philistines from Caphtor displaced the Avites in the coastal region. This is a general pattern, and Israel's domination of large sectors of Canaan was seen as part of a larger phenomenon. In other words, the Levant came to be inhabited by incoming peoples who displaced the indigenous ones; in our case, by Israelites displacing Canaanites, for the most part. Most of these groupings are depicted as ethnic, sharing common ancestry, though some were initially territorial, or territorial in addition to being ethnic. Thus, one assumes that the names Edom and Moab are territorial, in the first instance.

In my commentary on Numbers 21 (Levine 2000:126–133), I discussed the curiosity, noted by many scholars, that the Heshbon ballad projects a north-south route of Transjordanian settlement and conquest by the Israelites. This is in contrast to the accompanying historiography, which routes the Israelites from Kadesh to Transjordan, and then has them proceed in a south-to-north direction. There is every reason to conclude that the north-south route represents historical reality, whereas the south-to-north route may have been introduced so as to accommodate the Egyptian Exodus-saga, which dominates the historiography of Exodus and Numbers, and the early chapters of Deuteronomy. During many periods of history, armies and migrating populations took the north-south route through Transjordan, and legend has it that northern Transjordan was the land of the Rephaim, mentioned in connection with some of the interior peoples. To put it differently: As regards the route that would have been taken by the earliest Israelites, and those who followed, on their way to Canaan and Transjordan, we have reason to project a north-south route originating in Syria. The projected south-to-north route through Transjordan, of which we read in Torah literature and in other biblical references to the Exodus, may have little if anything to do with Israelite origins. It rests on a tradition of an Egyptian sojourn, and of a return to Canaan by the descendants of the Patriarchs, who had dwelled there at an earlier time. The true value of the Egyptian saga may lie elsewhere, in highlighting the ongoing cultural and political contacts between Canaan and Egypt over the course of centuries.

Furthermore, it is likely that at least some of the interior peoples also originated in Syria, and moved southward through Transjordan and northern Canaan, as did the Israelites. It is not necessary, therefore, to conclude that there was separate ethnographic input into the Israelite collective from indigenous peoples of the central and southern interiors, although this is surely possible. It is to be remembered that several Israelite tribes also settled in central Transjordan, and never crossed over into Canaan, proper. The Moabite, Ammonite, and Edomite/Esavite connections may have also resulted from southward migrations originating in Syria. In summary, I identify the first Israelites as one of several groups of immigrants entering Canaan from parts of Syria after the collapse of the Neo-Hittite city-states, and the fall of the kingdom of Amurru. The Israelites may well have entered Canaan in successive waves, and they may also have absorbed certain groups of Canaanites as time passed. As sketchy as it is, this reconstruction accords with general migration patterns, and does not require us to assume "a class struggle" within Canaanite society itself. Moreover, it correlates well with a whole range of persistent cultural features and social patterns characteristic of Syrian societies from early times.

The Israelite Ethos: One Big Family

A key ethnic term in the Hebrew Bible is *mišpāḥâ* "family", more accurately rendered "clan, sib, extended family". A term of fluid usage, and of somewhat uncertain etymology, it can designate social units ranging from an extended family, to a tribe (Jud 17:7), and to an entire nation, conceived as one big family, related through kinship and lineage from common ancestors. An idyllic tale of how the Israelite *mišpāḥâ* operated, when it was at its best, is provided by the book of Ruth (Levine 1987:95–106). It is the larger, national picture that will interest us here, however. The entire people of Israel, or the Judeans and northern Israelites collectively, may be referred to as one, big *mišpāḥâ* (Jer 8:3, Mic 2:3), as can any nation, for that matter, as epitomized by idiomatic *mišpeḥôt hāʾadamâ* "the 'families' of the earth" (Amos 3:2, and cf. Gen 12:3, 28:14). At times, there is blurring of the ethnic-clannish factor with the territorial-political, as is normal with terms of this kind. Thus, in a very late biblical text, Esther 9:28, we have the parallelism *mišpāḥâ* // *medînâ* "province".

The Israelite people is characterized as a patrilineage, composed of tribes and clans, and of patriarchal households, Hebrew *bêt ʾāb*. We now have an in-depth and comprehensive treatment of the 'house of the father' by David Schloen (2001). Although I might not go quite as far as Schloen in basing all societal structures, including monarchies, on the household, I find his methodology in evaluating the realism of biblical narratives thoroughly persuasive. To the extent that this socio-economic unit reflects ethnicity, its investigation proves to be extremely helpful. One is reminded of the Idrimi inscription, dating from the mid-second millennium, wherein this Aleppan leader speaks of his clan and his dealings with them, referring to problems he encountered with É *a-bi-šú*, literally: "the house of his father" (Idrimi inscription, line 10, *apud* Kempinsky & Naʿaman 1973). Once again, we are drawn to ancient Syria for the antecedents of an Israelite social institution.

Taking biblical traditions at face value, a prevalent epitome of the ethnic character of ancient Israel is that of Israel as the "seed" of common ancestors. Among the appellations of the Israelites are: "seed of Israel/Jacob", "seed of Abraham", and variations of the same, "seed of Ephraim" (Isa 7:15), and "seed of the household of Israel" (Jer 23:8). The future of the people is also imaged in this way. Israel is variously promised descendants in the land, or threatened with no seed. We also find usage that is clearly affected by religious themes, such as "the holy seed" (Isa 6:13), and "seed whom YHWH has blessed" (Isaiah 61, cf. Isa 65:23. We even find the image of "Godly seed" (Mal 2:15). In prophetic diatribes we encounter such negative characterizations as "bad seed, seed of evildoers" (Isa 1:14) and "false seed" (Isa 57:4). This proliferation of labels expressive of "seed" indicates how basic was this conception of group cohesion. The same basis defines the royal and priestly lineage, and often characterizes Israelite perceptions of other peoples. It is a *Weltanschauung*.

Was this so in reality, or is this yet another construct, making of kinship through lineage in ancient Israel merely a fiction? There is no doubt that biblical traditions exhibit a fictive character at points. Most likely, the Israelites of north and south took in new groups and families, and, as well, lost some families from their group. Further on, we will also have occasion to observe that endogamy was not as strictly, or consistently practiced as we might have supposed. And yet, there is every indication that identity went by family, and by locale, which intersects with family, and that this pattern continued despite the growth of urban communities and the imposition of the monarchy; it even continued after the Babylonian exile, with some modifications.

There are other terms that apply to the aggregate of Israelites, or more specifically to northern Israelites and Judeans, when these are distinguished from each other. The most relevant to our discussion is Hebrew *ʿam* "people". It is a kinship term, *par excellence*, which may apply to an extended family or clan, as well to the entire people of Israel (Lipiński 2001). As for the frequent designation *benê Yiśrāʾēl*, it identifies, in the first instance, the descendants of an ancestral eponym named Israel/Jacob. But, given the many nuances of the designation *bēn* "son", it is likely that it often connotes something like "member of a group", someone "affiliated" in a loose sense, so that it is not a thoroughly ethnic term. If analyzed carefully, biblical terminology can be sorted out so as to differentiate between the socio-political and the more solidly ethnic.

An enigmatic term of identity is *ʿibrî* "Hebrew". I have no intention of engaging its complexities, being interested here solely in its biblical usage. As noted by various scholars, the designation *ʿibrî* is most appropriate as an identifying tag understood by non-Israelites, and often used by them. Thus, Joseph is identified by his Egyptian captors in this way (Gen 40:15, 41:12), and Pharaoh's daughter is told that little Moses is "one of the Hebrew children" (Exod 2:6). Jonah presents himself to the foreigners on the ship as a Hebrew, from the land of the Hebrews, who worships the God of the Hebrews, which sounds pretty ethnic, come to think of it (Jonah 1:9). This nomenclature is used in the Moses stories (Exod 2:11, 13, 3:18, 5:3), and in relations with Philistines (1 Sam 14:21). We cannot be sure of the derivation of the term *ʿibrî*. For one, I have never been persuaded of its link with Ḫabîru/ʿApîru. It may have originally designated those who came from *ʿēber hannāhār* (Aramaic *ʿabār naharāh*, Akkadian *ebir nāri*), making it more of a territorial term than an ethnic one, after all.

Endogamy and Ethnicity

A common index of ethnicity is the practice of endogamy, the restriction of marriage to one's own group. This practice often accentuates some of the most negative feelings toward the out-groups, and the Hebrew Bible evidences a range of differing attitudes on the subject. Only in the later, post-exilic period do we find a blanket prohibition against marrying *nāšîm nokrîyôt* "foreign wives" (Ezra 10), at a time when specifically religious identity came to the fore. In earlier periods, we usually encounter selective exclusion on other than religious grounds. Thus, it displeases Isaac that Esau had married Canaanite women, so he marries women of his own clan (Gen 28). Abraham and Isaac both send home to Ḥaran to secure brides for their sons, admonishing against marriage with Canaanite women. The relatives in Ḥaran worshipped idols, presumably, so the religious factor was not the basis of acceptability, rather clan affiliation. The preferred marriage was within one's own larger clan, but marriage among the clans, or tribes of Israel was certainly approved. When an internecine conflict broke out between the Benjaminites and the other tribes of Israel, such cross-tribal marriages with Benjaminites were exceptionally interdicted, thereby probing the rule.

Going beyond the Israelites, themselves, we observe an ascending ladder of aversion to non-Israelites, expressed in biblical law and narrative lore. Most rejected are the former inhabitants of the land, the Canaanites, epitomized by the Amalekites, who became objects of eternal enmity (Exodus 17:14, Deut 25:19). But, who was classified as a Canaanite? We have varying lists of Canaanite peoples, some hard to identify. In Deuteronomy 7, the Israelites are admonished not to marry them, or make treaties with them. Next come the Ammonites and Moabites (Deut 23:4), who may never marry into the Israelite community; undoubtedly because of persistent enmity between them and the Israelites. In contrast, Edomites and Egyptians are not to be despised, and children of the third generation may enter the community of YHWH (Deut 23:8–9). In the case of Egyptians seeking to marry into the Israelite fold, gratitude for the sojourn is the reason given for their eventual acceptance. Would that we knew the precise historical reasons for the measured receptivity to Edomites, and the emphasis on their kinship.

It is fascinating to trace the Dinah story at Shechem (Genesis 34) back to the Abimelech cycle in Judges. Abimelech was the son of a Canaanite woman, one of his father Gideon's concubines, who was well connected in Shechem (Jud 9:1–6). In the Patriarchal story, which shows many signs of lateness, the ruse of reconciliation between the Shechemites and the sons of Jacob included an offer of land rights and marriage. This is the tell-tale link: Intermarriage, which was turned down with malice in Genesis 34, is described as an accepted practice in Judges 9, a source dating from a much earlier time. Canaanites are invariably untrustworthy, but in the earlier Judges account, marriage with them is unexceptional, whereas in Genesis 34 it is highly objectionable. In matter of fact, the Hebrew Bible preserves many indications that exogamy was more frequent in pre-exilic times than official statements acknowledge.

Most of our information comes from the lives of kings and other leaders and heroes. Kings were often criticized for marrying many foreign wives. According to 1 Kings 11:1–6 Solomon was condemned for marrying Moabite, Ammonite, Edomite, Sidonian, and Hittite wives from the nations of which YHWH had commanded the Israelites: "None of you shall marry with them, and none of them shall marry with you" (1 Kings 11:2). This report resonates with Deut 7:1–4, 23:4, which, however, omits mention of Edomites, Phoenicians, and Hittites. The reasoning is that foreign wives will lure their Israelite husbands into idolatrous worship, as in the Baal Peor episode of Numbers 25. We read in 1 Kings 14:21 that Rehoboam was the son of Naᶜamah, the Ammonite woman, one of Solomon's wives. We are told that the inhabitants of Maacath and Geshur "dwelled in the midst of the Israelites", which may be a way of saying that they married with them (Jos 13:13), and of course, Ruth was a Moabite woman. Yael of the Song of Deborah was the wife of a Kenite (Jud 5:24). I once proposed, in commenting on Moses and his Midianite relatives, that they were really disguised Kenites (Levine 1993:92–93). The Kenites were excluded from the fate of most Canaanites, because they had befriended the Israelites on their long march to the Promised Land. There may well have been other, similar groups.

Hatred of the Philistines engenders aversion to "the daughters of the uncircumcised" (2 Sam 1:20). The author of the Samson cycle plays on such negative emotions (Jud 14:3), and we read that David, the warrior, was rewarded by Saul for bringing in one hundred Philistine foreskins (1 Sam 18:25, 2 Sam 3:14). Reference to circumcision should not mislead us, however, into thinking that this aversion had any religious basis; it was simply hatred of an enemy, who like the Israelites, had earlier invaded parts of Canaan and subjugated the inhabitants, oppressing the Israelites in the process. I cannot fully explain why being uncircumcised was the feature specifically selected by which to demonize the Philistines, except to speculate that it somehow symbolized other-ness, or extreme foreignness.

We are at a loss to unravel the ethnography reflected in all of these references, which come from different time frames and reflect diverse circumstances. It is fair to say, however, that wars and hostility account to a great degree for the parameters of marriageability, whereas purely religious concerns represent only an added factor in later periods. In virtually every case, the boundaries are what we would truly call "ethnic".

Israelite Ethnicity and the Idea of the Chosen People

There are further indices of ethnicity which might be discussed: law as an ethnic regimen, the role of genealogies in emphasizing lineage, the status of the *gēr*, or resident non-Israelite, and more. But, perhaps, it is worthwhile to deal with the concept of chosen-ness as an expression of ethnicity, even more, of ethnocentrism.

We begin with writings ascribed to Amos, an 8th century prophet who traveled to the Northern Kingdom of Israel to deliver his orations soon before the Assyrian invasions that led to that kingdom's annexation. Amos explicitly challenges the concept of the chosen people by attacking accepted views regarding Northern Israel's position among neighboring peoples, while under the threat of Assyrian invasion. Because of their ethnographic orientation, I have found these prophecies particularly enlightening.

Methodologically, prophetic critiques have been studied as negative inferences. Prophets were criticizing the norm, to be reconstructed from the critique, itself. A prophet who decried land-grabs by the rich and powerful was informing us that such was happening without legal restraint, and one who questioned cultic efficacy was telling us what most Israelites believed to be efficacious. Amos is telling us that most northern Israelites believed that they would be victorious over their enemies, whereas he insisted that *yôm* YHWH, "the day of the Lord", which they awaited so eagerly, would be darkness, not light (Amos 5:18). It is important to point out that the differences in outlook between prophet and community were not differences between official and popular religion; in fact, it is the "official version" that the prophets usually targeted for criticism

Among other things, Amos calls attention to the fact that YHWH has allowed other nations to invade and to take possession of new lands: Cushites (perhaps a veiled reference to the Nubian dynasty in Egypt), Philistines, the last of the Sea Peoples, and Arameans from Kir of Moab (a more problematic reference, historically). Awareness of this pattern should deflate any sense of Israel's unique privilege:

> To me, O Israelites, you are
> Just like the Nubians.
> True, I brought Israel up
> From the Land of Egypt,
> But also the Philistines from Caphtor,
> And the Arameans from Kir. (Amos 9:7).

There is a lesson to be learned from what northern Israelites were being informed about population shifts affecting other peoples and lands: Israel's liberation from Egypt, and the granting of the land of Canaan to their descendants, were not unique demonstrations of divine providence, nor were they unconditional. What God gave, he could take away. In this sense, other nations were also chosen; the *prima facie* evidence of chosen-ness being the possession of a new land. In fact, the book of Amos opens with oracles against neighboring nations, predicting that they would lose their lands because of their sins. Included are Damascus of the Arameans, Gaza of the Philistines, Tyre of the Phoenicians, Edom, the Ammonites, Moab, and even the Kingdom of Judah.

What is remarkable is not that national gods became angry at their chosen peoples, took away their lands and brought about their destruction, but the specific character of the sins of these peoples. It has been noticed that in Amos' oracles, other nations are to be brought down because of their horrendous treatment of conquered lands and peoples—mass deportations, extensive destruction of arable land, atrocities against populations, and major acts of desecration. Even Judah's sins were religious in nature, principally, the worship of false gods. But as for the Northern Kingdom of Israel, the impending destruction will be brought about almost entirely by moral and social sins—oppression of the poor, injustice, and religious hypocrisy. The idea of chosen-ness has thus been enhanced to embrace an ethical teaching, whereby Israel is to be held to a higher standard than other nations.

This brings us to the puzzling declaration in Amos 3:1–2:

> Hear this word that YHWH has spoken concerning you, O Israelites; concerning that entire family (*kol hammišpāḥâ*) that I brought up from the land of Egypt, as follows:
> "You, alone, have I singled out (literally: "known")
> Of all the families of the earth—
> That is why I will call you to account
> For all your iniquities."

The prophet had just finished saying that YHWH had done singular favors for the northern Israelites, bringing them up out of Egypt, granting them victory over the Amorites, and making their sons prophets (Amos 2:9–10). Do these statements mean that Israel is unique among the nations? Do they, in effect, contradict Amos' assertions that what YHWH had done for Israel he had done for other nations, as well? Inevitably, there is a contradiction. In the citation just above, Amos seems to be endorsing the ethnocentric premise instead of challenging it. Perhaps there is an element of irony in the present statement, as if to say that if Israelites want to be considered chosen, they must realize that such privileged status imposes on them a higher standard.

It is of interest that Amos calls the northern Israelites a *mišpāḥâ*, and that he addresses them collectively as a *bayit* "household", thus: *bêt Yaʿaqob*, *bêt Yiśrāʾēl*, *bêt Yôsēp*. The term *bayit*, briefly discussed above as an ingredient in the composite term *bêt ăb*, is initially a term designating a landed household, one that possessed an estate. It then assumed a social connotation, and came to designate a family household, one usually extending over several generations. To refer to all of the northern Israelites as one *bayit* is tantamount to referring to them as being of common "seed", or as belonging to one family, or, as Amos affirms, as belonging to *ʿammî Yiśrāʾēl* "my people Israel" (Amos 7:8, 15; 8:2, 10; 9:14). The entire people were to live together like a household, on its family land.

Bibliography

Ben-Tor, Amnon and Maria T. Rubiato
1999 Excavating Hazor, Part Two: Did the Israelites Destroy the Canaanite City? *Biblical Archeology Review* 25:22–39.

Biran, A. *et al.* (eds.)
1985 *Biblical Archaeology Today*. Jerusalem.

Dever, William G.

1993 Cultural Continuity: Ethnicity in the Archaeological Record and the Question of Israelite Origins. *Eretz-Israel* 24 (Abraham Malamat Volume), 22–33.

Gottwald, Norman K

1985 The Israelite Settlement as a Social Revolutionary Movement. Pages 34–66 in Biran *et al.* 1985.

Hess, Richard S.

1992 Śerûg. *ABD* 5:1117–1118.

Kempinsky, A. & N. Naʿaman

1973 The Idrimi Inscription Reconsidered. Pages 211–220 in *Excavations and Studies* (Studies Sh. Yeivin). Tel Aviv.

Levine, Baruch A.

1987 In Praise of the Israelite *Mišpāḥâ*: Legal Themes in the Book of Ruth. Pages 95–106 in *The Quest for the Kingdom of God* (Studies George E. Mendenhall), H.B. Huffmon et al. (eds.). Winona Lake {*VOL 2, PP. 45–55*}.

1993 *Numbers 1–20*. AB 4. New York.

1995 The Semantics of Loss: Two Exercises in Biblical Hebrew Lexicography. Pages 137–158 in *Solving Riddles and Untying Knots* (Studies Jonas C. Greenfield), Z. Zevit et al. (eds.), Winona Lake {*VOL 2, PP. 281–99*}.

2000 *Numbers 21–36*. AB 4A. New York.

Lipiński, E.

2001 "*ʿam*". Pages 163–177 in *Theological Dictionary of the Old Testament*, vol. XI, G.J. Botterweck *et al.* (eds.), trans. David E. Green, Grand Rapids.

Mendenhall, G.E.

1976 Migration Theories Vs. Culture Change as an Explanation for Early Israel. Pages 135–143 in *SBL Seminar Papers 1976*, G. MacRae (ed.). Missoula.

1992 Amorites. *ABD* 1:199–202.

1996 The Hebrew Conquest of Canaan. Pages 152–169 in *Continuity, Identity, and Ideology: Social Science Approaches to the Hebrew Bible*, Charles E. Carter & Carol Meyers (eds.). Winona Lake.

Schloen, David J.

2001 *The House of the Father as Fact and Symbol*. Winona Lake.

'Seed' versus 'Womb': Expressions of Male Dominance in Biblical Israel*

In recent decades, the field of biblical studies has experienced a thrust of feminist interpretation which has compelled a re-examination of prevailing scholarly attitudes that had been, more often than not, oblivious to women's issues. Considerations of gender have thus come to the forefront, so that many of us are now sensitized to depictions of women in biblical narrative and poetry, to their treatment in law and ritual, and to their somewhat polarized characterizations in biblical wisdom literature. Beyond exhibiting interest in women's issues, we must develop methodologies for representing biblical norms accurately. In discussions with women graduate students, in particular, I have found myself reminded time and again, usually in response to their own reactions, of the predominance of male imagery in the Bible's treatment of the theme of human reproduction, and in its all important social corollaries—the attribution of lineage in Israelite society, and the sharp focus of attention on future generations.

A word of caution is in order before exploring a biblical theme with such obvious socio-historical ramifications: Of late, as questions have been raised about the reliability of the biblical record, it has come to be expected that an investigator issue a disclaimer confessing an awareness that the Hebrew Bible speaks for different sectors of Israelite society, at different times, and hardly for all Israelites at any one, given time. The dating of biblical sources is often open to question, and it is recognized that the received text, in any case, has undergone redaction. All of these factors were realized long before the current climate of opinion. Nothing learned more recently has shaken our view that biblical literature opens a window into the life of a coherent and enduring network of ancient Israelite communities. If this literature is studied critically, and without *a priori* assumptions, its content may enable us to assess prevailing attitudes and policies within those communities with a high degree of realism.

I

In the Hebrew Bible, a man's offspring, less immediately his descendants, are most often referred to collectively as his "seed," *zeraʿ* (זרע), less frequently "the issue of the loins" (*yôṣēʾ ḥalāṣaîm*), or "the issue of the thigh" (*yôṣēʾ yārēk*), or by reference to *mēʿaîm* "intestines, inwards." Such masculine designa-

---

* Originally published in S. Parpola and R. M. Whiting (eds.), *Sex and Gender in the Ancient Near East: Proceedings of the 47th Rencontre Assyriologique Internationale, Helsinki, July 2–6, 2001* (2 vols.; Helsinki: Neo-Assyrian Text Corpus Project, 2002), pp. 2:337–343. Reprinted with permission from the Neo-Assyrian Text Corpus Project.

tions are more frequent, by far, than references to offspring as the fruit of the mother's *reḥem* "womb" (רחם), or in less precise terms her *mēʿaîm* "inwards," or *beṭen* (בטן) "belly." This asymmetry is not merely quantitative since, as we shall see, the Hebrew Bible often seems to be attributing figurative, or virtual childbirth to the father by appropriating feminine terminology to define the relationship between father and child, as if to say that the father produced the child, not the mother! The validity of this assessment will depend on the precise philological and semantic analysis of the relevant terminology, which is often complex and surprising.

In his study of gender in Kabbalistic symbolism entitled *Circle in the Square*, Elliot Wolfson (1995) devotes a lengthy chapter to "Crossing Gender Boundaries in Kabbalistic Ritual and Myth" (pp. 79–121). He shows how the masculine overtook the feminine in many respects, so that so one can identify in Kabbalistic symbolism "the ontic containment of the feminine in the masculine," as well as what he calls "masculine transvaluation of motherhood: the phallic womb." These themes are highly developed in the literature of Kabbalah, whereas in the Hebrew Bible we find only subtle, sometimes cryptic indications of such boundary crossings. And yet, Wolfson's investigations have provided a model for biblical interpretation, as well. As in Kabbalistic literature, so in the Hebrew Bible, we most often observe the female becoming male, although there is some evidence of the male becoming female, as we shall see. These are all cultural perceptions, unbound by the physical facts of sex, and which alter the accepted gender roles of male and female in society. This is the very subject of a recent study by Dorothea Erbele, entitled "Gender Trouble in the Old Testament" (1999), where many of the aspects of male-female relationships to be discussed here are engaged, albeit from a different perspective, and where important issues are raised.

It would be best to survey the female anatomical terms at the outset. Of the three terms used to signify the womb, Hebrew *reḥem* is obviously the most precise, whereas referring to the area in the woman's body where the embryo develops, and from which offspring emerge as *beṭen* "belly" or *mēʿaîm* "intestines, inwards" is imprecise, even by ancient standards. Most often, when speaking of the womb, the Bible will say that offspring issue from the womb, using forms of the verb *y-ṣ-ʾ* "to go out" (Num 12:12; Jer 1:5, 20:18; Job 10:18 [Hiphʿil], 38:8). Less frequently, we read of *peṭer reḥem* literally: "offspring of the womb," expressed by the verb *p-ṭ-r* (cf. Akkadian *paṭāru*) "to dispatch," and the redundant *peṭer šeger reḥem* "dispatched offspring of the womb," which incorporates the Aramaistic root *š-g-r* "to send forth, dispatch." The womb may variously be "closed" (expressed by the verbs *ʿ-ṣ-r, s-g-r*), or "open" (expressed by the verb *p-t-ḥ*), a matter that will be discussed further. In Jer 20:17 a bitter prophet wishes that his mother's womb had been his grave! Adverbial *mēreḥem* connotes a condition that had existed "at, from birth" (Jer 1:6, 29:17).

We should note that the form *raḥam* in the idiom *raḥam raḥămātaîm* expresses the extended meaning of "one nubile woman or two" in Jud 5:30, to which compare the Ugaritic epithet *rḥmt*, said of the nubile goddess Anat. Most likely we have a further attestation of Hebrew *raḥam* in Isa 49:15: *hatiškaḥ ʾiššah ʿûlāh, mēraḥam ben-biṭnāh* "Would a woman forget her suckling infant; by a fertile woman, the son of her belly (be forgotten)?" This would involve reading *mēraḥam* "by a nubile woman," instead of Massoretic *meraḥēm* "from showing pity." In no instance, however, do we find terms like *pĕrî reḥem*, or *ben reḥem*, as we do with respect to the terms *beṭen* and *mēʿaîm*. Of the three terms under discussion, only רחם refers exclusively to the womb of the female. In Jacob's blessing, we read of *birḵōt šādaîm wārāḥem* "blessings of breasts and womb" (Gen 49:5), a statement that, reassuringly, views children as the issue of the mother's womb, who suckle at their mothers' breasts.

In her study, Erbele (1999) discusses the relationship of the noun *reḥem* "womb" to nominal *raḥămîm* "compassion," and verbal forms such as *riḥēm* (Piʿʿel) "to show compassion," drawing on the etymological connection between these several forms. Erbele's understanding of this connection differs from ours, but the point she makes is of great importance, nonetheless: The term for womb reflects emotions that are hardly gender-specific.

Tracing the relevant etymologies involves differentiating between two, originally separate Semitic verbal roots which have interpenetrated in Biblical Hebrew: (1) "to love, befriend" (cognate with Akkadian (*râmu* < *raʾāmu* [*AHw* 951–52]), and (2) "to pity, show mercy" (cognate with Akkadian *rêmu* [*AHw* 970–71]). The Qal stem of the Biblical Hebrew verb *r-ḥ-m* "to love" is uniquely attested Ps 18:2: *ʾerḥomḵā YHWH* "I adore you, YHWH." In a different realization, it is preserved in the unique personal name *Rĕʾûmâh* "Beloved" (Qal, pass. part., fem. in Gen 22:24).

It is likely that in some cases the Piʿʿel forms, which greatly predominate in Biblical Hebrew, also derive from *r-ḥ-m* (1), and the same is true of *raḥămîm*. For example: Hos 2:25: *weriḥamtî ʾet lōʾ ruḥāmāh* "And I will (again) love/befriend the Unloved-One," affirmatively called *ruḥāmāh* "the beloved" earlier in Hosea 2:3. As for nominal *raḥămîm*, it is tempting to conclude that the hendiadys *ḥesed weraḥămîm* is best rendered: "loving loyalty, loving kindness," and that mercy and pity have nothing to do with this locution. Thus, Zech 7:9: "Execute true justice and treat one another with loving kindness."

Now Akkadian *rēmu* "womb" (*AHw* 970) is registered in the lexical lists as a derivative of verbal *rêmu* "to show mercy, have pity," nominal *rēmu* "pity," not of *râmu* "to love." The basis for this identification is not clear to me. I can only conjecture that fertility of the womb was thought to be a blessing motivated by divine mercy, rather than the result of human eroticism! In any event, it is surely valid to associate Biblical Hebrew *reḥem* "womb" with notions of mercy and pity, as Erbele suggests.

What we can say, in agreement with Erbele, is the following: Whereas the terms *reḥem* and *raḥam* are gender specific in Biblical Hebrew, the emotions and behavior underlying these locutions are decidedly not so. It is striking to observe how a verbal root of such inclusive usage generated both a gender-specific anatomical term and an idiomatic way of referring to a nubile woman. This may be taken to mean that the deepest love is realized sexually between male and female, and between mother and child, and that the child is first and foremost the fruit of the mother's womb, not of the father's seed.

How different is the attitude expressed in usage of *mēᶜaîm* "inwards, intestines," and *beṭen* "belly." In speaking of birth (usually with use of the verb *y-ṣ-ᵓ* "to issue forth"), Hebrew *mēᶜaîm* more often refers to the mother's womb, as, for instance *mimmēᶜê ᵓimmî* "from my mother's inwards" (Isa 49:1, Ps 71:6, and cf. Gen 25:23 [*mēᶜaîm* || *beṭen*], Num 5:22, Ruth 1:11). In some cases, however, *mēᶜaîm* (once again, usually with the verb *y-ṣ-ᵓ*) refers to the father's inwards, probably as a replacement for *ḥalāṣaîm* "loins" or perhaps *yārēk* "thigh." Thus Gen 15:4, with reference to Abram: "who shall issue from your inwards," and 2 Sam 16:11, in David's words concerning Absalom: "Behold, my son, who issued from my inwards." 2 Sam 7:12 is especially interesting: "your seed after you, who will issue from your inwards," words said to David in reference to his son, Solomon. Also note the construction *weṣeᵓĕṣāᵓê mēᶜekâ* "the issue of your inwards, your descendants" in Isa 48:19, where it is parallel with *zarᶜăkā* "your seed, descendants." The term *ṣēᵓeṣāᵓ* represents a reduplicative noun form, derived from the root *y-ṣ-ᵓ*.

Whereas a child is never said to be inside the father's inwards, as it is inside the mother's (cf. Ruth 1:11), a child may be said to "issue" from his father's inwards, just as he issues from his "hip" or "loins." This means that in cases where *mēᶜaîm* refers to the father's inwards, the child is being identified primarily as the product of the father's semen, not of the mother's womb.

Unlike *mēᶜaîm*, the term *beṭen*, when used in the context of reproduction, always refers to the mother's womb. Only the constructions *pĕrî beṭen* "fruit of the belly," occasionally *ben/bar beṭen* "son of the belly," are ambiguous in this respect. A case in point is Micah 6:7b where the speaker, presumably a man (as the form of address in verse 8 indicates), poses a rhetorical question: "Shall I offer my first born [*bĕkōrî*] (to expiate) my sin, the fruit of my belly / my 'belly fruit' [*pĕrî biṭnî*] (to expiate) my mortal offense?" In this statement, does *beṭen* refer to the man's loins, in the manner of *mēᶜaîm*, with *pĕrî* "fruit" being a euphemism for semen (cf. Song of Songs 2:3: "and his 'fruit' is sweet to my palate")? If so, *pĕrî biṭnî* would functionally denote "the semen of my belly." Or, is *pĕrî beṭen* to be taken as a bound form, so that *pĕrî biṭnî* connotes "my *pĕrî beṭen*," and *pĕrî biṭneka* "your (masc. sing.) *pĕrî beṭen*" (Deut 7:13, *et passim*)? The same ambiguity occurs in Prov 31:2, where the term used is *bar biṭnî*, however we translate that problematic verse. Also note Job 19:17: "My feeling is hateful to my wife, and my caring *to the sons of my belly* (*libnê biṭnî*)."

It is likely that the latter interpretation is correct, and that *pĕrî beṭen* and *ben/bar beṭen* are bound forms, so that the sense of *pĕrî* is "fruit, child" not "semen." This is strongly suggested by Ps 127:3: "Behold, the estate of YHWH is sons (*bānîm*), the reward—the fruit of the belly (*pĕrî habbāṭen*)." It is also revealing that *pĕrî behemtekā* "the fruit of your cattle" is parallel with *pĕrî biṭnekā* (Deut 7:13, *et passim*). If this interpretation is correct, then we have an appropriation of the mother's status by the father. The mother, and her "belly" belong to the father; her womb and what grows in it have become his "fruit."

This comes close to what Wolfson calls "male containment of the female," and surely illustrates Erbele's point that the relevant inner organs were not regarded as gender specific, as was the case with respect to *reḥem*.

At this point, it would be well to comment on usage of the general term בן, feminine בנת (= *bint*) whose etymology is seldom discussed. In Gen 49:22 Hebrew *bēn*, plural *bānōt*, most probably means "bough, shoot (of a vine)." It is part of a repertoire of botanical imagery used to describe lineage, along with *ḥōṭer* and *nēṣer* "shoot, branch" (Isa 11:1), and *ṣemaḥ* "branch" (Jer 23:5, 33:15). The difference is that *bēn*, from the root *b-n-h*, literally: "what is built, formed," is a morphic term, expressing, in the first instance, the formation of the embryo. Thus, the verb *b-n-h* describes the construction of Adam's rib: "YHWH God constructed (*wayyiḇen*) the rib" (Gen 2:22), and one is reminded of God's words to Jeremiah: "Before I fashioned you (*ʾeṣṣorkā*) in the belly, I had selected you" (Jer 1:5). One can only speculate as to whether an ancient Hebrew writer, or speaker, was aware of the etymology of *bēn*. If such awareness is assumed, then it is remarkable how a term identifying the child as having been formed in the mother's womb is so often used to connote the father's child!

It is also likely that the term *bĕkōr* "firstborn" was similarly appropriated. Jacob refers to Reuben as: "You are my first born (*bĕkōrî ʾattāh*); my strength and the first fruit of my manly vigor" (Gen 49:3). And yet, it would seem that Hebrew *bĕkōr* (Ugaritic *bkr*), refers initially to the first issue of the womb. Thus, Jer 4:31: "For I have heard the voice of a woman in birth pangs; travailing like one giving birth to her first child (*kemabkîrāh*)." There are further indications: Exod 11:5 refers to *bĕkōr haššipḥāh* "the firstborn of the female family slave," and Exodus 13 equates *bĕkōr* with *peṭer kol reḥem* "the first issue of every womb." In most instances, however, we read of the father's *bĕkōr*, suggesting that this relationship has been appropriated; it has been made masculine, so to speak.

There is an instance, however, where the role of the mother is extolled through the very use of the terms *beṭen* and *mēʿaîm*, in parallelism: Thus Gen 25:23, in the oracle to Rebekah: "Two nations are in your belly, and two peoples shall separate from your inwards." Similarly, in God's blessing of Abraham, we find a symmetry between the promise of *zeraʿ* "seed, descendants" to Abraham and the blessing to Sarah (Gen 17:16): "And I will bless her, and I have also given to you from her a son (*mimmennāh lekā*), and I will bless her, and she shall become nations; kings of peoples shall be (born) from her." In the same spirit, Eve was dubbed *ʾēm kol ḥaî* "the mother of all the living" (Gen 3:20), in a folk etymology of her name. Such exceptional highlighting of the maternal role reflects the epic tradition in biblical literature, in its depictions of royal figures, renowned leaders, and heroes, and goes against the overall trend toward masculine dominance in the biblical mentality.

II

The Hebrew word for "seed" is *zeraᶜ* (זרע), a term applicable to the male sperm of humans and animate creatures, as well as to the seed of all vegetation. Its most literal sense, as applied to male sperm, is expressed in priestly texts, where we find the term *šik̲bat zeraᶜ* "a flowing of semen," in the context of rites governing seminal emissions (Lev 15:16). In the sexual legislation of Leviticus 18:20 we find the variation: *šĕk̲ob̲teka lĕzeraᶜ* "your flow of semen" (cf. Lev 20:15).

The 'seed' of the man comes to fullness through the woman. This extended sense is expressed in 1 Sam 1:11, in the words of Hannah's prayer: "May you give to your maid servant the 'seed' of men." Thus 1 Sam 2:20, in the words of the priest to Hannah and her husband, Elkanah: "May YHWH provide you with 'seed' from this woman." Cf. Ruth 4:12, where the good people of Bethlehem bless Boaz as follows: "May your household be like the household of Perez, whom Tamar bore to Judah, from the 'seed' that YHWH will give to you through this young woman."

It is important to emphasize that these references to the role of the woman do not indicate that the woman contributes a life-essence, an egg, to the reproductive process. They mean only that she carries and nourishes the man's seed (see further).

Summarizing the biblical evidence, we can say that the male plants seed in the womb of the female; it is introduced into the vagina through coitus. The womb is like a garden, or a spring. This is intimated in Song of Songs 4:12, in a simile of virginity: "A locked garden is my sister-bride, a locked garden, a sealed spring." The womb provides the same nutrients to the embryo as the mother, earth does to vegetation that grows in it. There is, however, no indication in the Hebrew Bible, as far as we can ascertain, that the female contributes a life-essence, an egg, to the embryo; the role of the female is entirely that of nurturer. The seed is provided by the male, and it grows inside the womb.

Interchanging with the image of seed is that of "root." A barren woman is known as *ᶜaqārāh* "one deprived of a root," in Hebrew *ᶜēqer* "root, descendant" (Lev 25:47). This adjective describes a woman whose womb was closed so that the male seed/root could not enter (Gen 11:30). The male "root" (more frequently *šōreš*) might dry up even after having entered the womb, with the result that the embryo would not grow. Thus, Hos 9:16: Ephraim has been smitten so that: "Their root is dried up; they cannot produce fruit. Even if they give birth, I will kill the choice products of their belly." We read of cases where a woman's womb had been closed to the entry of male seed, and then, through God's kindness, it was opened, as in the case of Leah: "Then YHWH saw that Leah was despised, and he opened her womb, whereas Rachel was barren (*ᶜaqārāh*)" (Gen 29:31).

In discussing the earth, or garden metaphor we encounter a subtlety of biblical idiom that would appear to collide with what has just been said. According to Genesis 1, vegetation contains its own seed, and is self-fertilizing. This is the sense of "vegetation that bears seed (*ʿēśeb mazrîʿa zeraʿ*), the fruit tree that bears fruit of its own species, whose seed is (contained) within it on the earth" (Gen 1:11). What makes this "sexless," and by our standards oversimplified view of vegetative fertility so relevant is that Leviticus 12, which like Genesis 1 is a priestly text, describes conception as follows: *ʾiššāh kî tazrîʿa wĕyālĕdāh zākār*. Now, if the Hiphʿil of Leviticus 12 means the same as it does in Genesis 1, then we would have to conclude that Leviticus 12 is speaking of self-fertilization, and accordingly translate: "When a woman bears seed and gives birth to a male."

It is more likely, however, that the Hiphʿil in Leviticus 12 has the same force as the Niphʿal in Num 5:28: *wĕnizrĕʿah zeraʿ* "she shall be inseminated." In fact, the Samaritan Torah has consonantal *tzrʿ*, indicating that they read *tizzāraʿ*, the Niphʿal form (Levine 1989:73, on Lev 12:2). Although this vocalization indicates an awareness of the problem we are discussing, it is actually unnecessary. The Hiphʿil often has a stative function, rather than a causative one in describing physical conditions. Thus, *yazqîn* "he will grow old" (Prov 2:6), and *yalbînû* "they will turn white," and *yaʾddîmû* "they have become red" (Isa 1:18). We therefore translate Lev 12:2: "When a woman is inseminated and bears a male." There would appear to be no indication of the self-fertilization of humans or animals in the Hebrew Bible, although such notions were certainly current in the ancient world.

The imagery of *zeraʿ*, and its many applications in biblical literature, are well known. This complex of metaphors embodies the future orientation so prominent in the biblical mentality. History became epitome, as real attention turned to future generations. The distinctiveness of this orientation has not been adequately appreciated, nor has its significance as a variable factor affecting operative notions of sex and gender in biblical Israel. Once we determine that in the ancient Israelite mentality fertility, in humans (and animals), depended in substance solely on the male seed, with the role of the woman's womb being regarded as that of a cavity in which the embryo grew and was nourished, it is hardly surprising that those Israelites were so obsessed with sperm. They identified their descendants as their "seed," taking root in the Promised Land, a garden whose nutrients are provided by their God, who brings the rains in due season.

Selected Bibliography

Erbele, Dorothea

1999 Gender Trouble in the Old Testament: Three Models of the Relation between Sex and Gender. *Scandinavian Journal of the Old Testament* 13:131–41.

Levine, Baruch A.

1989 *Leviticus, The JPS Torah Commentary*. Philadelphia: The Jewish Publication Society.

Wolfson, Elliot R.
1995 *Circle in the Square: Studies in the Use of Gender in Kabbalistic Symbolism*. Albany: State University of New York Press.

Farewell to the Ancient Near East: Evaluating Biblical References to Ownership of Land in Comparative Perspective*

The purpose of this study is to inquire into the relevance of biblical literature for the investigation of ancient Near Eastern economic institutions, above all those operative within the biblical societies. My particular concern is with the private ownership of land in Israel in contrast to royal lands, temple estates and other forms of ownership that we would classify as public. In which ways, and to what degree can we mine literature for historical information about private property in the Land of Israel of biblical times?

The Hebrew Bible incorporates within its codes of law, its narratives and court literature, and even in its prophecy and wisdom, extensive references to ancient Near Eastern social, legal and economic practices known to us from comparative cultures. For the most part, scholarly interest in such comparative evidence has been for the purpose of sustaining the authenticity of biblical literature and law, for validating the Bible as a reliable record of what it purports to document, namely, the early history of Israel. There can be no question that the main burden of biblical literature is to tell, in different ways, the salvific history of the Israelite people—their origins, their settlement and habitation of the land of Canaan, their exile and restoration, and the inner development of their social, economic, political and religious way of life.

There are other agendas, however, that warrant scholarly interest. We should seek to understand the Hebrew Bible as a repository of ancient Near Eastern law and lore, literature and culture, religion and myth, economy and government. A relatively late arrival on the ancient scene, the Hebrew Bible may represent (in addition to all else) one of the last major collections of ancient Near Eastern literature, a closing statement on that manifold civilization. The biblical record shows how a small nation, inhabiting a vital crossroad of the world, drew on the institutions of larger Near Eastern societies to structure its life, and to define its collective values and objectives.

---

* Originally published in M. Hudson and B. A. Levine (eds.), *Privatization in the Ancient Near East and Classical World: A Colloquium Held at New York University, November 17–18, 1994* (Peabody Museum Bulletin 5; Cambridge, MA: Peabody Museum of Archaeology and Ethnology, 1996), pp. 223–252. Reprinted with permission from the editors and the Peabody Museum of Archaeology and Ethnology.

The Nature of the Biblical Evidence

Biblical literature does not preserve any actual documents of land conveyance or deeds establishing ownership of land in Israel. Nor do we possess court records, official correspondence or royal edicts from the kingdoms of northern Israel or Judah. Such original documents would have to be provided by ancient Hebrew epigraphy, or by inscriptions found in nearby areas inhabited by Israelites, such as Transjordan. Such extrabiblical evidence is, however, extremely sparse and unusually disappointing in its yield. What we have to work with are canonical law codes, which often approximate original documents in their formulation. These collections of laws, preserved in the Torah (Pentateuch), specify terms of land sale and purchase and impose restrictions on such transactions. They establish liability for damage to crops, levy taxation in various forms, provide for the use of land as security for debt, establish forfeiture procedures and the like. The major problem is that these codes of law cannot be precisely dated or their exact provenance determined. The Bible operates with traditional chronologies, so that we can only approximate the time of promulgation. Torah literature in particular lacks the historical indicators present in the historical books of the Bible and in biblical prophecy.

We also find references to the legalities of land ownership in biblical historiography, in narratives and chronicles, in prophecy and other types of biblical writings, all of which are regularly utilized by scholars to infer the operations of Israelite government and economy. As examples of inferential sources we may include the record of Jeremiah's redemption of land about to be forfeited by a clan relative because of debt (Jeremiah 32), and the record of Abraham's purchase of a field and cave as a burial site from its non-Israelite owners (Genesis 23). The latter is similar to the brief record of Jacob's purchase of a field near Shechem (Genesis 33:18f.).

The biblical evidence for reconstructing the Israelite economy is, therefore, very limited. But there are other complications even with respect to what is available. To illustrate the problem we may refer to comparable questions which persist about the realism of the Code of Hammurapi. It is still unclear whether the Code of Hammurapi was forward looking or retrospective, functional or merely for display. Nevertheless, we are in a position to evaluate it on the basis of numerous court records, royal edicts and official correspondence to and from contemporary Babylon, so that the legal realities of the period and place may be clarified. In evaluating biblical law codes we inevitably find ourselves shifting quickly to comparative evidence from other societies, which though plentiful at times and enlightening in itself, cannot be used as directly as homegrown evidence. Imagine for a moment how the picture would change if 100 court records from Jerusalem of Hezekiah's time were to be uncovered by archaeologists.

Of late, there has been a growing interest in utilizing external theoretical models for the interpretation of biblical literature, which, once again, may be enlightening, although not necessarily historical for the relevant biblical period. If at the very least, the Hebrew Bible had presented a consistent record of the conquest and settlement of Canaan and had characterized the organization of Israelite societies in a consistent way, it would have been simpler to arrive at credible definitions of public and private property, respectively. Our first task is, therefore, to come up with such definitions as the biblical evidence can reasonably sustain.

There is a network of biblical traditions in which tribal origins are projected for the Israelites, and there are intimations of nomadism. The constitution of the Israelite monarchies is said to have come about subsequent to a period of settlement and limited wars, during which a tribal confederation operated without benefit of monarchy or standing armies. Are these traditions realistic, and are they reconcilable with each other?

The archaeological enterprise in Israel and in neighboring Jordan and Lebanon, when assessed with economic concerns in mind, could potentially yield valuable information about the ancient economies of Bible lands. Although archaeologists have of late become more concerned with economic and environmental concerns, we are still far from a proper treatment of the economic ramifications of archaeological discovery, especially with respect to land ownership.

We possess a study by C. H. J. de Geus entitled "Agrarian Communities in Biblical Times: 12th to 10th Centuries B.C.E." (1983). Although it addresses important questions, de Geus' work cannot be compared for historical import with the other chapters in the same volume on agrarian communities in antiquity, precisely because of the severe limitations of biblical evidence outlined above.

De Geus is of the view that the economy of ancient Israel during the early Iron Age (1200–900 B.C.E.) was based primarily on the private ownership of land and cattle, and that many Israelites lived in cities. His evidence for this conclusion is both negative and positive. On the one hand, he shows how flawed are the accepted nomadic theories of Israelite origins. The often assumed processes of Israelite sedentarization don't accord with patterns known elsewhere and at different periods. On the other hand, de Geus (1983:218f.) shows how the introduction of iron into Canaan and advances in the technology of terracing brought about a change from a "dimorphic society" based on both pastoralism and farming, "to an agrarian, urban society with a market economy and private ownership of land."

De Geus goes on to adduce fascinating external models in support of his proposed reconstruction, but he operates with rather loose definitions of "public" and "private," and is scarcely able to document his conclusions, e.g. in his statement that:

> Even when a farmer was not the actual owner of his land, it was he who worked the land in the first place for the benefit of his own family. (de Geus 1983:207).

The principal model de Geus adduces is the "musha" of the modern Near East, a feature of Ottoman administration which, in de Geus' view, harks back to very ancient custom. It is a system of parceling land owned by the Emir to individual farmers, and, at that, is predicated on ownership of such communal lands by the ruler, the Emir. This all sounds familiar to those who have studied biblical traditions regarding the allocation of the land of Canaan to the Israelite tribes and clans by lot, a system alluded to only vaguely in Micah 2:5, Ps 16:5–6, and stipulated in the priestly code of Numbers 26:52–56. However, more study would be required to ascertain in what sense "musha" land can be classified as private.

Although de Geus uses biblical evidence that he assigns to the early period of Israelite history to argue plausibly for the agrarian character of the Israelite economy, he can argue less convincingly for the private status of agrarian property in the usual legal terms. His utilization of the biblical evidence is not systematic, nor is the source material thoroughly analyzed in its own terms.

A more systematic attempt to deal with political, social and economic organization, especially in Judea of the post-exilic Achaemenid period is by Joel Weinberg, some of whose earlier essays have been published in English translation under the title *The Citizen-Temple Community* (1992). At points, Weinberg, who is representative of the Russian school of economic history, touches on questions of land ownership and imperial administration in Judea of the Achaemenid period. Although Weinberg does little with the law codes of the Torah, except to mention a few terms of reference occurring in them, he does utilize the evidence of biblical prophecy, historiography, and identifiably post-exilic writings. Most important of all, he regards the post-exilic experience of the restored Judean community as paradigmatic for an understanding of contemporary Achaemenid societies in other regions of the Persian Empire.

He integrates biblical evidence into the structure of economic and political models drawn from other spheres, where the intent was, initially, to understand the "pre-Hellenistic" socio-political and economic units of the Near East, the antecedents of the Hellenistic *polis*. Weinberg's methodology is valuable in and of itself, although at times it appears that external models have taken over from the biblical sources.

For the purposes of the present study, two of Weinberg's essays are particularly enlightening. "Agricultural Relations of the Citizen-Temple Community" (Weinberg 1992:92–104) deals with the status of arable land and takes account of the changes brought about by the event of the Babylonian exile. The socioeconomic unit which interests him most is the *bêt ʾābôt* "patrilineal 'house'" of the 6th to 4th centuries B.C.E., the subject of another of his essays. His conclusion is that clan lands often were parceled out to individual families, who in a real sense owned and worked these subdivisions.

"Central and Local Administration in the Achaemenid Empire" (Weinberg 1992:105–126) makes the important point that Persian imperial administration was a stable system based on taxation; one which allowed for and even stimulated considerable local and regional autonomy throughout the empire, including of course Judea. This system, which was to influence the Hellenistic *polis*, significantly featured the temple-centered community. Weinberg correctly views the formation of this type of community as the result not of internal development alone, but principally as an outcome of Persian administrative policy. This policy in turn affected the thinking of the Jewish exiles in Babylonia as well as those Judeans who remained in their homeland.

Weinberg's contribution to the subject of the present study is, therefore, considerable. In criticism it can be said that if he had devoted attention to Torah literature he might have seized upon the priestly model of the *ʿēdāh* "community" as correlating with the "citizen-temple community" of Achaemenid times more precisely than the *bêt ʾābôt*. He also would have noted that the sociopolitical term of reference *ʿāmît*, occurring in priestly law, most closely approximates the term "citizen." The failure to place the evidence of Torah law and narrative within the larger context of biblical literature deprives the scholar of valuable sources for the study of biblical economies.

Then, too, Weinberg fails to subject some of the biblical terminology to a precise analysis. As will emerge in due course, there are important legal differences between land designated *ʾaḥuzzāh* and that designated *naḥalāh*. These differences are crucial not only for identifying the *Sitz-im-Leben* of Torah legislation, but also for determining the status of land in reality. Yet Weinberg usually hyphenates the two terms, ignoring the diachronic factor affecting their respective definitions.

The foregoing evaluations of only two of many recent statements on the economic realities of biblical times suggest the desiderata of future research. The challenge is to fashion a methodology for reading the Bible, all of it, with the objective of deriving realistic economic knowledge from its text. In pursuit of this objective, I will begin by probing two examples illustrating the methodological problems involved in mining the Hebrew Bible for economic information: (1) The subject of royal land grants in the pre-exilic period as an instrumentality for generating private property, and (2) The economic effects of war on the ownership of family land.

After thus suggesting methods for reading biblical texts with an economic agenda in mind, I will explore the system of land ownership expressed by the Hebrew term *ʾaḥuzzāh*, "acquired land, domain." I have been studying this system for some years, and the occasion of this conference provides an opportunity to venture some tentative conclusions about its bearing on land ownership in biblical times. In my view, the *ʾaḥuzzāh* system has the greatest bearing on the period of the return to Zion and thereafter, during the Achaemenid period.

Anticipating the discussion to follow, it is here proposed that private land was most often family land in biblical Israel. There is surely nothing unusual about this status, except that we must be clear about what is meant by a "family." The term is ambiguous. It may designate a unit consisting only of parents and children, perhaps of grandparents as well. It also may refer to an extended family, or clan, which includes first cousins and certain affinal relatives extending over several generations. In biblical usage, Hebrew *mišpāḥâ* is best rendered "sib" or "clan," because all indications are that it designated an extended family, if not an even larger unit. In contrast, Hebrew *bayît*, literally "house, household," probably designated, in the first instance, a family sharing the same domicile.

Presumably the head of a family, limited or extended, was the owner of its property, unless he had otherwise disposed of it, which often happened. Family land thus was private in the sense that it did not belong to the tribe as a whole, or to the realm in the office of the king, or to a temple, city or nation collectively. It was not, however, entirely private inasmuch as restrictions usually were placed on its alienation at arm's length, and clan members usually bore obligations with respect to preserving its integrity. These factors will come up for discussion in the description of the *ʾaḥuzzāh* system. There also will be more to say about God, or the gods, as landowners, and how this notion affected private ownership.

Royal Land Grants in Biblical Israel

Biblical literature provides suggestive evidence of royal land grants, indicating that at least some privately owned, .or family owned land was generated in this way. The law codes of the Torah only go so far as to envision a monarchy, and the so-called law of the king in Deuteronomy 17 says nothing about land ownership or land grants. The Torah codes where we logically would seek such information are disguised, one would say. They project the collective as a tribal federation, not a kingdom, so that we read (also in Deuteronomy 17) that the entire tribe of Levi was to be denied a *naḥalāh* "domain" in the projected apportionment of Canaan.

The Hebrew *naḥalāh*, is of basic importance, because it designates property that is conquered, possessed, granted or inherited. More will be said about it as the discussion unfolds. The overall result of the given textual situation is that we must look to nonlegal, biblical sources for information on royal grants of land in pre-exilic Israel and Judah.

In 1 Samuel 22:7–8 we find a telling allusion to such grants. While pursuing David, Saul was informed that some of his fellow Benjamites had defected to his adversary:

> Saul then said to his courtiers, who were in attendance upon him: "Hear me, sons of Benjamin! Will the son of Jesse indeed grant all of you fields and vineyards; will he appoint all of you commanders of thousands and commanders of hundreds that you have all conspired against me?"

A similar allusion to royal grants appears in a tale of two brothers who fomented rebellion against Moses in the wilderness. Moses had summoned to him Dathan and Abiram, sons of Eliab, probably Reubenites, in an effort to quell their rebellion. They refused to appear, and taunted Moses as follows:

> You have not yet brought us to a land flowing with milk and sap, or granted us fields and vineyards as our domain (*naḥalāh*).

The first point to be made is that some of the narratives of the wilderness period, preserved in the synthetic historiography of the Pentateuch known as JE (= Jahwist-Elohist) seem to have been modeled after court history, as it is called. It is entirely possible that they actually derive from the same court circles and portray Moses *in loco regis*. When we read, therefore, that Moses, like David, is taunted about granting the leading warriors of Israel fields and vineyards we are actually being told something about the emergence of private land ownership through royal grants.

As has been noted by any number of scholars, the Caleb traditions fit into this scheme. Caleb conquered the area around Hebron in the Judean hills and was granted these territories by Moses. Subsequently his daughter induced him to give some of his land to her on the occasion of her marriage to a young conqueror as a dowry (Joshua 15, Judges 1). The connection with war, and the granting of land by rulers to returning warriors is, of course, a widely known practice throughout history.

There is a series of narratives strung across 2 Samuel, chapters 9, 16 and 19, about a steward of the house of Saul named Ziba, who was the recipient of a royal land grant. In the first link of the narrative chain, 2 Samuel 9, David summons the steward and questions him about surviving scions of Saul, learning that one of the sons of Jonathan, son of Saul, a certain Mephibosheth (Meribaal), had indeed survived. Mephibosheth, who was lame, was summoned by David and told that he would be installed as a palace retainer to eat at the king's table in Jerusalem. In an effort to act kindly toward the dislodged northern, royal house of Saul and to assist the son of his beloved companion Jonathan, David granted to Mephibosheth all of Saul's lands:

> I shall restore to you all of the fields of Saul, your ancestor (2 Samuel 9:7).

The details of the arrangement are interesting: Ziba and his fifteen sons and twenty servants were to work the arable land and bring forth its yield, which was to go to Mephibosheth as income. What remains unclear is the basis of David's interim ownership of the land, or jurisdiction over it. It would seem from the manner in which the story is told that David had gained ownership over Saul's paternal estate on two related accounts: He succeeded Saul as king, and since no heir to the house of Saul had been found, all heirs having been presumed dead, the former king's estate went to his successor.

The plot thickens as we proceed to 2 Samuel 16. Fleeing from his insurrectionist son, Absalom, David meets up with Ziba in Transjordan. The latter had traveled far to bring David food and drink. Ziba maligns Mephibosheth, charging that the latter had remained in Jerusalem in the hope that David would be overthrown, and the monarchy would return to the House of Saul. Hearing of Mephibosheth's betrayal, David revoked his earlier grant, saying to Ziba: "Behold, everything that is Mephibosheth's [henceforth] belongs to you."

The final phase of business comes in 2 Samuel 19, when David finally is restored to his throne in Jerusalem and Absalom's insurrection is quelled. Appearing in a disheveled state, Mephibosheth comes to plead for his life. He claims that the steward Ziba had deceived David; that he had brought pack animals loaded with food to David only so as to spy on him in Transjordan, and that he, Mephibosheth, had always been loyal. David replied:

> Why do you continue to speak about such of your concerns? I have [already] ordered that you and Ziba should divide the fields between you (2 Samuel 19:30).

Imbedded in this narrative of court intrigue is a complex of legalities. One should not be surprised to discover the blending of more than one legality in the same episode, and a degree of imprecision in the telling. But on the whole we observe the subsequent transfer of land appropriated by David to the heir of Saul, his predecessor, who had died after his dynasty had been deposed. We read further of another transfer of royal land to a king's steward, a man of considerable wealth and status, who is rewarded for his service to the king.

A further allusion to royal land grants is found in 1 Samuel 8, in a passage that has been widely discussed for what it projects as royal prerogatives. In attempting to dissuade the Israelites from constituting a monarchy, the cult prophet, Samuel, warns of the potential cost. The king will conscript Israelites in various ways—as corvée, as a work force to reap his harvest and manufacture weapons, and as members of the royal bureaucracy, while daughters will be summoned to perform domestic chores in the palace. Then Samuel has the following to say:

> He will confiscate (*yiqqaḥ*) your fields, and your best vineyards and olive trees so as to grant (*wenātan*) them to his courtiers, and he will exact a tithe of your grain and vineyards and give that to his personal guards and courtiers.

A case where such expropriation was attempted is recorded in 1 Kings 21. We are told that Ahab, king of northern Israel, sought to purchase a vineyard adjacent to his own fields, but was refused by its owner, Naboth, who told him: "God forbid that I convey my ancestral *naḥalāh* to you."

Initially the king resigned himself to the refusal, which, in fact, has led most commentators to assume that one had the right in the northern Israelite kingdom of the 9th century B.C.E. to refuse to alienate ancestral land, even to the king. It was only by ruse that Ahab's Phoenician wife, Jezebel, had poor Naboth condemned to death for blasphemy and sedition. At this point Ahab simply expropriated the field.

It is likely that a customary right overrode royal authority in land ownership. The king of Israel was expected to respect the *naḥalāh* status of family property. Nevertheless, it would seem that the property of condemned Israelites legally accrued to the state, namely to the king, not to the heirs of the executed person. This process was denounced by the prophet Elijah, but only because Naboth was falsely condemned to death.

We are fortunate to have informative studies pertaining to royal land grants, and royal versus private ownership of land in biblical Israel. Zafrira Ben-Barak has dealt with the principal biblical passages cited above, and has attempted to define the legal and economic realities that inform them. Although she may be accused of supplying much that is not actually said in the text, her methods of textual analysis are carefully reasoned, and she considers every source contextually and systematically.

In the case of Ahab and Naboth it is her view that kings of Israel often purchased private lands in the normal way, without any attempt at coercion (Ben-Barak 1978–9). She cites David's purchase of the threshing floor of Araunah, the Jebusite, as the site for an altar in Jerusalem after its conquest (2 Samuel 24), and Omri's purchase of the property of Shemer for his capital, Samaria (1 Kings 16:24). This is, of course, the reverse of privatization, and reflects the aggrandizement of royal holdings, but it does attest, initially, to the rights of private landowners over their property. The fact is that Ahab, king of Israel, was compelled to circumvent these rights deceitfully; he could not simply issue an order to confiscate Naboth's property.

More to the point of the present study, Ben-Barak's discussion of the Mephibosheth incident is particularly enlightening (Ben-Barak 1981). Adducing parallels from other societies of the ancient Near East, most notably Ugarit, Ben-Barak shows a widespread pattern of royal land grants. The operative formula of conveyance in Akkadian is *našû ... nadānu*, in Hebrew *lāqaḥ ... wenātan* "to take [and] to give." This formula is used in the admonition on royal prerogatives in 1 Samuel 8. The king will predictably take from the populace, and give to his favorites, warriors and courtiers. Ben-Barak notes that the Philistine ruler, Achish of Gath, granted David, his mercenary commander, the town of Ziklag as his fief (1 Samuel 27:6–12).

Ben-Barak isolates three stages in the Mephibosheth transaction: (1) David restores what had been Saul's paternal estate to Saul's sole surviving heir, Mephibosheth. In Ben-Barak's view, David was more or less required to do so because his appropriation of Saul's estate was legal to start with only because there was no living heir of the former king in evidence. Once Mephibosheth was discovered, David could no longer hold on to Saul's ancestral estate. (2) David revokes the grant to Mephibosheth and transfers Saul's original estate to Ziba. Ben-Barak correctly notes ancient Near Eastern parallels, from Alalakh and Ugarit, attesting to the practice of confiscating land as punishment for treason. This is, of course, what we learn from the Naboth incident, and the same legal norms are to be seen in the present narrative. Furthermore, David in this case did just what Samuel warned that kings would do: He handed over an ancestral estate to one of his favorites! (3) David returns half of the estate to Mephibosheth, taking that half from Ziba, after Mephibosheth begged for his life. Such actions on David's part may have been motivated by political considerations, and their only legal import is to suggest that what kings gave, they could take away!

Those investigating royal land grants at Ugarit have original documents at their disposal; students of biblical law and economy have only narratives from the court histories of Judah and Northern Israel. And so, while it appears that the broad pattern of royal land grants operated under kings of Judah and Israel, we have no notion of its extent, and to what degree it actually generated private property in Canaan of biblical times. The sense is that given the dominant concerns of biblical writers, even the few references preserved in biblical literature attest to more widespread practices.

The Economic Effects of War on Ownership of Family Land

A second methodological exercise pertains to the economic effects of war, especially on the status of agricultural land in the country that went to war. In a recent study of 2 Samuel 24 (Levine 1993), I attempted to explain the dynamics of census-taking in biblical Israel so as to understand why the writers of 2 Samuel 24 regarded as sinful David's insistence on taking a census after having fought many wars.

In the history of biblical exegesis; this chapter has been compared to another example of the sinfulness of census-taking, namely, the imposition of a head-tax on all adult Israelite males in support of the Tabernacle project, as recorded in Exodus 30. There it is explained that payment of a *kôper* "ransom," would avert a plague, and in 2 Samuel 24 we read that a plague was the punishment for David's census. It is my view that it was not the taking of a census *per se* that implicated David, but the particular circumstances under which it was conducted.

The use of cultic language to characterize census-taking has directed scholarly attention to another instance of the same usage in the Mari letters. Both J. R. Kupper (1950) and E. A. Speiser (1958) regarded the procedure known at Mari as *tebibtu* to be relevant to our understanding of the biblical fear of the military census. Both these scholars vacillated between the cultic and administrative interpretations of the *tebibtu* process that troops at Mari underwent before going into battle. It is obvious, as both Kupper and Speiser understood at the time, that the Akkadian verb *ebēbu*/D-stem *ubbubu* is often used legally, like other similar verbs connoting cleansing and purification, to refer to clearance from debt and obligation. The question that these scholars should have sought to answer, had their attention been squarely focused on the economic effects of war, can be formulated as follows: Which obligations were incumbent on the troops at Mari, and by comparison, on David's troops as they were mustered throughout Israel to require clearance, and why was securing clearance a hardship, one which David was so strongly advised to avoid imposing?

In 1 Samuel 17:18, where we are told that young David was sent by his father, Jesse, to bring a "care-package" to his brothers who had followed Saul to war and were encamped far from home. There was a package for the military commander, as well, and then we read:

> Inquire after the well-being of your brothers, and take their guarantee (Hebrew *ʿarubbāh*).

Translators of this passage have fudged on the function of the *ʿarubbāh* in this context, notwithstanding the fact that the meaning of this term is hardly in doubt. The Hebrew term *ʿarubbāh* is a cognate of Akkadian *erēbu* "to enter," a verb which often signifies entry into various legal arrangements such as indenture, slavery, and into the role of voucher. In Hebrew, a person designated *ʿārēb* "voucher" literally stands in for another, guaranteeing payment in case of default (Prov 20:17). Hebrew *ʿērābôn*, surviving as Greek *arabôn*, "pledge," is the term used in the curious story of Judah and the harlot for hire. Out of cash at the moment, Judah left the harlot his cylinder seal and its fillet, along with his staff as *ʿērābôn* (Genesis 38). Another related term is Hebrew *maʿarāb* "exchange," in Ezekiel's angry prophecy condemning the profit-hungry merchants of Tyre (Ezekiel 27). Interestingly, a cognate of the same term occurs in a Ugaritic ritual text recently studied by J. M. de Tarragon and B. A. Levine (1993), where it means "gift," literally a gift one brings into the Temple.

In ancient Israel, as elsewhere, the calling up of militias in time of war brought many hardships to the folks back home, and this is just as true today. The absence of many able-bodied men from their farms and vineyards, and from their flocks and herds, for extended periods of time, often seasonally, made it appreciably harder to till the soil, plant and harvest. Large amounts of foodstuffs and other material were used up or lost in war. Who would pay the land taxes and cover the debts of those away from home? Mobilization triggered an economic cycle that was bound to produce hardship. In the best-case scenario the spoils of war might compensate in part for this situation, but domestic production would inevitably go down in the short term. This is why David's brothers were required to pledge that their agrarian obligations had been met, or would be met.

New studies of the Mari documents are required in light of the many additional texts that have recently been published, but it would not be unreasonable to suggest, based on what is already known, that the *ʿērābôn*, like the *tebibtu*, was aimed at assuring that homefront obligations would be met by soldiers going to war. This is why the only son of a family is often exempted from conscription, and why, apart from sentimental reasons, Deuteronomy 20:5–7, exempt from military service one who has just built a home, planted a vineyard, or betrothed a wife. In all three cases the fear expressed is that someone else will gain possession.

And so it is that random references to "pledges" and a highly etiological tale about David serve as vague sources of economic information about the obligations of land ownership in time of war, although it must be conceded that even the explicit letters from Mari have produced their own enigmas!

The ʾaḥuzzāh System of Land Tenure

The only coherent legal code in the Torah that governs land ownership is Leviticus 25, with some corollary provisions appearing in Leviticus 27. These texts are predicated on the *ʾaḥuzzāh* system, and their proper interpretation would add considerably to our knowledge about the private ownership of land in biblical Israel. Some words of introduction are necessary before outlining the *ʾaḥuzzāh* system.

The Hebrew Bible uses three principal terms of reference to denote land ownership; or, to put it another way, to designate the legal status of land. All three terms run the gamut from collective to private ownership. They are: 1) *yeruššāh*, 2) *naḥalāh*, and 3) *ʾaḥuzzāh*. Of the three, *ʾaḥuzzāh* is in my view the latest, or youngest, and its usage is discretely confined to the priestly source of the Pentateuch, and to sources that can be traced to the influence of the priestly school.

The other two terms, *yeruššāh* and *naḥalāh*, are distributed in more than one literary source, or collection of laws. In contrast to *ʾaḥuzzāh*, the terms *yeruššāh* and *naḥalāh* share a semantic range that extends from conquest, to settlement, to legal possession, to inheritance. Although it was undoubtedly true that land owned as *ʾaḥuzzāh* would normally be inherited by the next generation, inheritance is not connoted by the term *ʾaḥuzzāh*, itself, which focuses attention on the initial basis of land acquisition and tenure.

1) The term *yeruššāh* derives from a verb whose primary sense is physical possession by conquest or seizure, and which has the extended meaning of inheritance (Jer 32:8). Cognates of this verb are attested in Ugaritic, where the connotation of inheritance appears to dominate usage. However, one would not use this verb to designate land that was purchased in the first instance, and this is an important point. In the collective dimension, other nations have a *yeruššāh* in God's plan for the world, just as Israel does, because God granted them lands and territories as their *yeruššāh*. Israel therefore must respect their territorial integrity. As for the Israelites, they are commanded to conquer Canaan, a mandate expressed in statements which employ the verb *yāraš*. See Deuteronomy 1:21:

> Behold, the LORD, your God, has placed this land at your disposal; ascend! seize! (*ʿalēh rēš*) just as the LORD, God of your ancestors has commanded you; have no fear nor be dismayed.

The point is that translating *yeruššāh* as "inheritance" masks other realities of land ownership in the first instance. Similarly, the causative stem, *hôrîš*, describes the Israelite takeover of Canaan and the dispossession of its inhabitants; in effect, their reduction to serfdom, sometimes deportation, but consistently their disenfranchisement. By designating family land, tribal lands or national territory as *yeruššāh* the text is defining it as a possession taken, or received, or even redeemed by a clan relative, but not as one purchased or sold.

2) The Hebrew term *naḥalāh* is anticipated by Ugaritic *nḥlt*, which designates the domain of a god in myth. We have such constructions as *ġr nḥlt* "mountain domain" (cf. Hebrew *har naḥalāh*), and *arṣ nḥlt* "sovereign territory." In Ugaritic personnel lists we find what is apparently a participial form, *nḥl*

"heir," although this meaning is uncertain.[1] The basic sense of Hebrew *naḥalāh* is hard to pin down. In Mari usage, studied by D. O. Edzard (1964) the verb *naḫālu* means "to hand over, convey," sometimes by way of inheritance, but not necessarily so. It yielded the denominative *nḥlt*. In Hebrew the cognate verb more often connotes receipt of a possession, not the conveyance of property to another. But this is not always the case. Thus, Zechariah 2:16:

> The LORD shall grant to Judah (*wenāḥal ʾet Yehûdāh*) his portion (*ʾet ḥelqô*) on the sacred soil, and shall again select Jerusalem. (Also Exodus 34:9).

In any event, I doubt if in biblical usage (apparently in contrast to Mari usage) land classified as *naḥalāh* could have been purchased in the first instance; it can only be granted by some authority, human or divine, and consequently received or inherited, as within a family; or, it can be physically possessed as through conquest. The term *naḥalāh* is used extensively, and has many predications.

3) This brings us to the priestly term *ʾaḥuzzāh*. What is the status of arable land designated in this way?

From the very beginnings of modern biblical scholarship it has been accepted as a methodological principle that priestly law on the one hand, and priestly narrative and historiography on the other hand, reflect each other and must be correlated. I am far from comprehending the *ʾaḥuzzāh* system to my satisfaction, but there is some progress to report.

Let us begin with the priestly recasting of the patriarchal period and the Egyptian sojourn as told in the book of Genesis. This literary tradition comes on the heels of earlier historiographic and narrative sources, and characterizes the habitation of Canaan by the patriarchs and their clan in a distinctive way. I understand this retrojection to be the product of post-exilic literary creativity of the early Achaemenid period. In effect, it creates a pre-history of Israel aimed at legitimating the policies of the exilic leadership during the waves of return to Zion subsequent to the Cyrus edict. This is also the *Sitz-im-Leben* of the priestly legislation found in Leviticus 25 and 27, which is retrojected into the wilderness period and the lifetime of Moses and thereby attached to the earlier versions of the Sinaitic theophany.

How does this retrojection work in Genesis? Abraham sets out to purchase a burial site near Hebron for Sarah from the so-called Hittites (Genesis 23). He presents himself as *gēr wetôšāb*, "a resident alien," asking to be sold *ʾaḥuzzāh qeber*, "a grave site as an *ʾaḥuzzāh*."

The status *gēr wetôšāb* usually is taken to indicate a legal disadvantage, as if to imply that Abraham was seeking an exceptional favor. I take it differently: By identifying himself as *gēr wetôšāb*, Abraham was invoking an acknowledged right to negotiate the purchase of land in Canaan. Once he gained ownership of

---

[1] See R. Whittaker, *A Concordance of Ugaritic Literature* (Cambridge, MA: Harvard University Press, 1972), 445f. s.v. *nḥl*, *nḥlt*.

land, his status would be confirmed as a permanent resident. This analysis will receive a degree of confirmation in Genesis 34, the Shechemite episode, as we shall see. The so-called Hittite responded favorably, with honor and respect, and pledged that no person of their community would deny Abraham this right. I dispute the interpretation that this indicates the offer of a gift to Abraham, but that issue is not essential to the present discussion.

The narrative is not entirely consistent in designating the object of purchase. Most of the time, Ephron, the Hittite, is said to be ready to sell Abraham the cave at the edge of his field, but as the negotiations proceed we read of both the cave and the field as having been purchased by Abraham, and this would seem to be more realistic.

Actually, burial practices in biblical Israel bear a relationship to land ownership. In several instances, the Bible records that a leader, such as Joshua, was buried on the border of his *naḥalāh* (Joshua 24:30, Judges 2:9), and Rachel was buried on the border of the territory of the tribe of Benjamin, according to 1 Samuel 10:2. A recent archaeological study of Judahite burial practices by Elizabeth Bloch-Smith (1992) deals briefly with burial sites and land ownership by extended families, showing that the grave or burial cave could often be taken as evidence of ownership by a family, perhaps even as evidence of title.

The terms of reference used in connection with Abraham's purchase of a burial site and a field are also discrete, and fill out the system. Two such terms are found in Genesis 23. Thus, we read that the field and cave and all of its trees "became the property of" Abraham. The Hebrew verb for legal acquisition is *qûm*, "to arise, stand." I have shown, as have others, that this is Aramaistic usage. In Aramaic "to stand" (*qûm*) connotes established ownership, and the binding force of a contract. Its use indicates that the sale has, as we would say, "gone through, has been finalized." The second term, *miqnāh*, from the verb *qānāh*, means "purchase." It defines the status of the *ʾaḥuzzāh*: It has been acquired. Now both these terms, or forms of them, occur in the laws of Leviticus 25 (Levine 1983).

To continue the references to the *ʾaḥuzzāh* system in the priestly recasting of the patriarchal narratives, we turn now to Genesis 34, where we read about the rape of Dinah, Jacob's daughter, by the son of the local ruler of Shechem, a Canaanite. The violent young man told his father that he actually loved Dinah, and so, a delegation approached Jacob to negotiate a marriage, but also to form a new relationship between Jacob's clan and the Canaanite city-state. The proposed terms are spelled out in the following way:

> Become related to us through marriage. Give us your daughters and take our daughters for yourselves. Settle down with us, and the land shall be at your disposal. Settle, and trade it (*ûseḥārûhā*), and acquire land in it (*wehēʾāḥazû bāh*).

Hebrew *hēʾāḥazû* is a denominative verbal form based on the noun *ʾaḥuzzāh*, namely, "to exercise the right of *ʾaḥuzzāh*." What we learn from this tale is that the right to acquire land could be part of an arrangement that included trading rights and exogamous marriage. As the story is set, the clan of Jacob are resident aliens, granted the right to buy land in Canaan from its rightful owners. This right is to be provided for in a treaty, or contract. It is not coincidental that in Genesis 23 the Hittites refer to Abraham as *neśîʾ ʾelôhîm*, which probably means "a headman favored by God," whereas the ruler of Shechem is referred to in Genesis 34 as *neśîʾ hāʾāreṣ*, "the headman of the district."

The final chapter in the Genesis projection of the *ʾaḥuzzāh* system in priestly literature comes in the narrative of the Egyptian sojourn, in chapter 47. There we read that Joseph had brought his father's clan to Egypt, and had presented his father, Jacob, before Pharaoh together with several representatives of his family. This detail is not to be overlooked because it suggests that members of the clan other than the patriarch himself had a voice in its decisions.

Then the following:

> Then Joseph settled his father and his kinsmen, and granted them *ʾaḥuzzāh* in the land of Egypt, in the choice section of the land, in the district of Ramses, as Pharaoh had ordered.

Further in the same chapter we read:

> The Israelites dwelled in the land of Egypt, in the district of Goshen, and they acquired *ʾaḥuzzāh* land in it, and they greatly multiplied.

Bearing the discrete terminology and provisions of the priestly narratives in mind, let us now take up the provisions of Leviticus 25, remembering that they quite possibly reflect conditions in post-exilic Jerusalem and Judah, under Persian administration. I conclude this from Nehemiah 5, where similar economic conditions are reflected. In a sense, Nehemiah 5 may be utilized as an inner-biblical commentary on Leviticus 25, whose provisions may be outlined as follows:

1) *The Jubilee Year.* Every fiftieth year (seven rounds of Sabbaticals) *derôr* (traditionally rendered "liberty," as in the Liberty Bell) shall be proclaimed throughout the land and to all its inhabitants, at which time each person who had lost his *ʾaḥuzzāh* due to debt shall be restored to it and rejoin his clan. That year shall be a fallow year.

There is an extensive literature on the putative relevance of Syro-Mesopotamian *andurāru*, usually a royal edict of debt remission as known from the Old Babylonian and Old Assyrian periods, as well as from Neo-Assyrian and Neo-Babylonian documents, to this biblical law (Levine 1989:171–172, 270–274). Although some have been too eager, perhaps, to adduce extra-biblical parallels, and with questions remaining as to the realism of Jubilees precisely scheduled every fifty years, there is little doubt that the two terms *andurāru* and *derôr*, derive from cognates of the same verb, meaning "to turn, revert," and that they refer to similar legalities. The first biblical reference to *derôr* outside of Torah literature is Jeremiah 34. It correlates with Neo-Babylonian usage in that it refers to the manumission of slaves. With the Chaldeans at the gates of Jerusalem, Judean slave owners are commanded to enact a *derôr*, thereby freeing their slaves who would presumably be conscripted into the army. Deutero (Trito)-Isaiah 61:1 refers to the year of the end of the exile as *šenat derôr*, "the year of release," namely, the year of return from exile and repatriation. In Ezek. 46:17 *šenat-hadderôr* refers to "the Jubilee Year," in a late excursus outlining the powers of the *nāśîʾ* "elected leader," who replaces the king in the prophet's program for the restored community. The passage is interesting in that it limits the prerogatives of the *nāśîʾ*. He may not expropriate the *ʾaḥuzzāh* of the people, though he may bequeath of his own *ʾaḥuzzāh*, delimited in Ezekiel to his own sons. Of particular interest is the provision that if the *nāśîʾ* grants a part of his *ʾaḥuzzāh* to any of his courtiers, it is subject to the law of Jubilee, and reverts to the *nāśîʾ* at that time.

A general statement in the opening section of Lev. 25 guarantees the restoration of land forfeited by debt to its owners at the Jubilee. This is followed by a specific law prohibiting alienation of arable land held as *ʾaḥuzzāh*. An Israelite who sold (the verb *mākar*) or purchased (the verb *qānāh*) arable land to or from his *ʿāmît*, "fellow citizen" must calculate its purchase price on the basis of crop years remaining until the next jubilee, because at that time the field would revert to its original owner. It is to be assumed from what follows in Lev. 25 that such sales were normally compelled by debt. They were more like long-term leases, assuming the law was implemented in practice. Title was not transferred, with only an arrangement resembling usufruct rights coming under contract.

A second term of reference after *derôr*, and which further defines the limitations of ownership, is adverbial *liṣemîtût*, "irretrievably, finally handed over." Land may not be sold under terms that do not allow for its redemption or retrieval. Now, as is known, the stative form *ṣāmit* is attested in the Akkadian documents from Ugarit, where it means "transferred, finally handed over." The terms of sale described in the Akkadian documents from Ugarit refer to real estate, in one case a house, that changed hands, with verbs such as *leqû*, and *nadānu* used to connote purchase and conveyance. It also characterizes royal land grants, by the way. Occurrence of stative *ṣāmit* is always followed by the clause: *a-di da-ri-ti ur*$_5$*-ra še-ra* LÚ *ma-am-ma-an la i-la-qi-šu* "forever, day and night, no person may take it away." The stative verbal form *ṣāmit* may be West Semitic to start with, as has been suggested.[2]

Now, this is precisely what is prohibited in Leviticus 25: Arable, Israelite land may not be sold in this way. A theological basis is adduced for the restriction on alienations: All land belongs to God, and even the Israelites, themselves, do not have title to it! They are like Abraham, *gerîm wetôtāšbîm* "resident aliens," the God of Israel having granted them the land of Israel as an *ʾaḥuzzāh*. In the priestly covenant promise to Abraham after his circumcision, the land of Canaan is granted to his descendents as *ʾaḥuzzāt ʿôlām* "an *ʾaḥuzzāh* forever" (Gen 17:8). In Jacob's blessing to Joseph in Egypt (Gen 48:4), the Patriarch states that the God of Israel has granted their descendents the land of Canaan as

[2] *CAD Ṣ*, 93ff, s.v. *ṣamātu*.

ʾaḥuzzāt ʿôlām. We observe, once again, the correlation of priestly law with priestly narrative.

Exceptions to such restrictions are forfeited urban dwellings, which may be redeemed within a year of sale, and Levitical property, which may always be redeemed and is not subject to the Jubilee.

2) *Land Forfeited because of Debt.* The provisions of Lev. 25 reflect a substantial breakdown of the clan system in favor of private owners, whose rights are being protected at the expense of fellow Israelites, including clan relatives. Revoking the laws of Exodus 21 and of Deuteronomy 15, Israelites no longer will have their debts waived every seventh year. The precise provisions of the *ʾaḥuzzāh* system thus detract somewhat from the heuristic rhetoric surrounding its legislation.

Indenture continues until the Jubilee, although usury is disallowed. Israelites are entitled to redeem forfeited arable land, and the purchaser must comply. But one unable to redeem forfeited land, or whose clan relative won't do it for him, has no alternative but to await the Jubilee. The only exception is in the case where forfeiture was to a non-Israelite resident of the land, a *gēr* or his descendant. In such an event, clan relatives were required by law to come to the aid of the disenfranchised promptly so as to prevent the loss of arable land to non-Israelites (Leviticus 25:47). One senses that this particular provision points to a mixed population under foreign domination rather than to the pre-exilic situation under the Judean monarchy.

There are two curious provisions of the *ʾaḥuzzāh* system stated in Lev. 27:16–24. First is the distinction between one's original *ʾaḥuzzāh* and land one had acquired by purchase, most likely through foreclosure, and which is termed *miqnāh*. This is the same term used in Genesis 23 to define Abraham's acquisition of land. The distinction relates to land that one may devote to the temple, as the text has it "to the LORD (*le*YHWH)."

Then, too, original *ʾaḥuzzāh* land may be permanently devoted as temple property, and becomes subject to various obligations. Such land, unless it is bought back by the original owner with a 20% surcharge, remains temple property and is unaffected by the Jubilee. Its value is assessed according to crop years. It is of interest to note how the status of such land is defined in Leviticus 27: Its status is that of condemned land, *śedēh haḥērem*, such as would be expropriated by the state, or, in this case, the temple from a condemned murderer. In other words, we can now confirm our reading of the tale of Naboth of Jezreel (1 Kings 21) from a different biblical source.

So much for original *ʾaḥuzzāh* property. But what if a man had devoted to the temple land he acquired from a debtor or otherwise, and which had not been part of his original *ʾaḥuzzāh*? The assessment of value is the same, by crop years, but such property remains in the possession of the temple only until the Jubilee; at that time it will revert to its original owner, not to its subsequent purchaser.

We are required to clarify what is meant by original ownership. In all Torah traditions, including the priestly source, the entry of the Israelites in Canaan *en masse* after forty years of wilderness migration is projected as Year One. Very often, legislation is introduced by the formula: "When you enter the land," or variations of the same. In other words, the given laws are presented in terms of what is projected as an original, one-time apportionment of Canaan.

This is the *mise-en-scène*; unhistorical, to be sure, but important to factor into our reading of Torah legislation. As a result, Deut 19:14 states:

> Do not overreach your neighbor's boundary, which the first [settlers] (Hebrew *riʾšônîm*) delimited in your *naḥalāh* that you will receive in the land which the LORD your God is granting you, to take possession of it.

In summary, Leviticus 25 and 27 describe a system of limited, private ownership of arable land in the land of Israel. The Israelite landowner is treated as a firm legal entity in his own right, rather than merely as a clan, or tribal member. The Temple administers dealings in the real estate of the Israelite community. There is an overriding concern with retaining arable land in Israelite hands, so that the clan obligation to act on behalf of a fellow Israelite is stronger in the case of land forfeited to non-Israelites than it would be in the case of foreclosure by another Israelite.

Nehemiah 5: A Biblical Chronicle from the Mid-Achaemenid Period

Another biblical source relevant to our understanding of land ownership as legislated in Leviticus 25 and 27 is Nehemiah 5. In fact, the striking similarities between the two sources argue in favor of assigning Leviticus 25 also to the Achaemenid period.

Early in the second half of the 5th century B.C.E. Nehemiah, a Jew who served as the Persian *peḥāh* in Jerusalem and Judah, was engaged in severe conflict with the Jewish leadership and populace. Nehemiah 5 lists a succession of economic complaints.

> And there are some who say: "We are indenturing our sons and daughters so that we may buy grain and have food to eat and survive."
>
> And there are those who say: "Our fields, vineyards and houses we are mortgaging (the participle *ʿôrebîm*) to be able to buy grain during a famine."
>
> And there are those who say: "We borrowed silver to pay the royal land tax (*middat hammelek*) [mortgaging] our fields and vineyards."
>
> "And now, our flesh is as good as that of our brothers, and our children as good as theirs, and yet we are reducing our sons and daughters to slavery—some of our daughters are already subjected—but we are powerless. Our fields and vineyards belong to others."

What is Nehemiah's response? He censures the *ḥōrîm* and *segānîm*. Between the two of them, these terms of reference have much to tell us about Persian administration. Without entering into great detail, Hebrew *ḥōrîm*, in its cognate, Aramaic form *ḥārēʾ*, corresponds to Akkadian *mār bānē*, most often Old Persian *fratama martiya*, "foremost men," or *fratama amisiya*, "foremost followers" in the trilingual Bisitun inscription of Darius I, as I recently learned from Muhammad Dandamayev by oral communication. As for Hebrew *segān* it is cognate with Akkadian *šaknu* "governor," a term having many meanings. Here it is used with reference to Judeans who may have held official positions or served as land managers. Nehemiah has the following to say to these personages:

> You are foreclosing on debts against one another. We have bought back our Judean kinsmen who had been sold to gentiles, to the extent possible for us, and yet you continue to sell your kinsmen so that they are sold away from us? Even I and my kinsmen have foreclosed against them for silver and grain. Let us abandon this indebtedness. Restore to them as of this day their fields and vineyards, their olive groves and houses, and the hundred [shekels] of silver, and the grain, wine and oil which you are expropriating from them.

The leading Judeans promised to comply, and to dramatize this commitment, Nehemiah shook his sash loose. The ironic reference to buying back fellow Israelites who had suffered foreclosure because of debt incurred to gentiles correlates with Lev 25:47, which requires one's clan relatives to come to his aid in such circumstances. This is one of the telling links between Leviticus 25 and Nehemiah 5.

What is missing in Torah legislation, for reasons already explained, is any reference to royally imposed taxes, or state taxes. All taxes are "to the LORD." The only clue to royally imposed taxation earlier in Scripture is in that old statement on royal prerogatives in 1 Samuel 8, where the intended king would have the authority to impose a tithe on the yield of farm and vineyard. In Nehemiah 5 we find a more realistic reference to the *mandattu* "land tax," (Aramaic *mindāh*, in Ezra 4:13), payable to the Persian authorities. This detail is significant, because it helps to explain the *ʾaḥuzzāh* system.

From Nehemiah 5 it would seem that the *ʾaḥuzzāh* system was not working well. There were undoubtedly external reasons for this situation, having to do with the changing fortunes and policies of the Persian Empire. An internal reason was that Judeans were foreclosing on each other right and left, reducing one another to virtual serfdom, and probably charging usurious interest to boot. In other words, they weren't keeping the commandments of Leviticus 25 and 27. As a result, what the *ʾaḥuzzāh* system had sought to achieve, to protect the rights of individual landowners, was not achieved. This objective also involved retaining Jewish land in the possession of Jews, a theme which resonates loudly in Nehemiah 5. Judeans are losing their land to local creditors, including agents of the Persian rulers. On the basis of such comparisons between Leviticus 25 and

27 and Nehemiah 5 we see preliminary grounds for assigning the former, like the latter, to the Persian period, perhaps to different phases of it.

Determining the Sitz-im-Leben of the ʾaḥuzzāh System: The Comparative Agenda

The preceding discussion illustrates the methodological problems we face in mining the Hebrew Bible for economic information. Referring to the discussion of the *ʾaḥuzzāh* system, the principal subject of this study, and the suggestion that it may reflect the realities of Persian administration in Palestine of Achaemenid times, it must be emphasized that we are still far from any valid understanding of Leviticus 25 and 27 in economic terms. Thus far, it has been possible to describe their provisions as the Hebrew Bible presents them, to place them in biblical context, and to adduce some preliminary comparative references. The only advantage held by Nehemiah 5 over Leviticus 25 and 27 is its discernible historical setting; the economic and administrative realities it reflects need much further investigation.

The hypothesis that Leviticus 25 and 27, and the priestly narratives derive from the Achaemenid period cannot be demonstrated from within. To know what Leviticus 25 and 27 are referring to historically requires knowing when their provisions were instituted and operative; and under which circumstances. In turn, this necessitates the integration of contemporary, comparative evidence that correlates with their provisions and makes sense out of them.

Our task and our method is to study patterns of Persian imperial policy and administration in those regions of the empire which have yielded extensive documentation, especially Babylonia and Egypt. We may learn how land was owned and managed in Judea by learning how it was owned and managed in Babylonia and Egypt during the same historical period, under the same empire.

It is fortunate that this area of inquiry is presently attracting intensive scholarly interest, especially with respect to Mesopotamia. The works of Muhammed Dandamayev, a pioneer in the elucidation of economic systems operative during the Achaemenid period, and of M. W. Stolper, whose study of the Murašû archive deals methodically with economic issues, are prime examples of the kinds of investigations most likely to be of assistance to biblical scholars.[3] Indeed, the biblical period most inviting to comparative investigation in the economic sphere may turn out to be the Achaemenid period after all. Before this harvest can be fully reaped, certain schools of biblical scholars must liberate themselves from theological and other concerns impeding the proper, critical study of Torah literature in all its parts. Attitudes toward Torah literature must change. The Torah must be seen as a collection of sources compiled over many centuries, reach-

---

[3] See Stolper 1985, and Dandamayev 1983, 1987, 1988, for only a few of his recent studies. The *Jahrbuch für Wirtschaftsgeschichte* for 1987, entitled *Das Grundeigentum in Mesopotamien* (Berlin: Akademie Verlag, 1988) contains important studies by J. N. Postgate, M. Dandamayev and Joachim Oelsner on subjects related to the present discussion.

ing from the early monarchic period to the late phases of Achaemenid rule in the Land of Israel. It is part and parcel of the grand farewell to the ancient Near East announced by the Hebrew Bible.

Bibliography

Amusin, J. D.

1979 Śakîr: On the Problem of Hired Labour in the Ancient Near East (in Russian). *Peredneaziatski Sbornik* III:15–25 (English summary, pp. 267f.).

Ben-Barak, Z.

1978–9 The Confiscation of Land in Israel and the Ancient Near East (Hebrew). *Shnaton: An Annual for Biblical and Ancient Near Eastern Studies* 5–6:101–117.

1981 Meribaal and the System of Land Grants in Ancient Israel. *Biblica* 62:73–91.

Bloch-Smith, E.

1992 *Judahite Burial Practices and Beliefs about the Dead.* JSOT/ASOR Monograph Series 7. Sheffield: JSOT Press.

Dandamayev, M.

1983 Aliens and the Community in Babylonia in the 6th–5th Centuries B.C. Pages 133–145 in *Les Communautés rurales*, 2e partie: *Antiquité* (= *Rural Communities,* Second Part: *Antiquity*). Recueils de la Société Jean Bodin 41. Paris: Dessain et Tolra.

1987 Free Hired Labor in Babylonia During the Sixth through Fourth Centuries B.C. Pages 221–27 in *Labor in the Ancient Near East*, ed. M.A. Powell. AOS Series 68. New Haven: American Oriental Society.

1988 Wages and Prices in Babylonia in the 6th and 5th Centuries B.C. *Altorientalische Forschungen* 15:53–58.

de Geus, C. J.

1983 Agrarian Communities in Biblical Times: 12th to 10th Centuries B.C.E. Pages 207–237 in *Les Communautés rurales*, 2e partie: *Antiquité* (= *Rural Communities,* Second Part: *Antiquity*). Recueils de la Société Jean Bodin 41. Paris: Dessain et Tolra.

Edzard, D. O.

1964 Mari und Aramäer. *ZA* 56:142–149.

Kupper, J. R.

1950 Le Recensement dans les textes de Mari. Pages 99–110 in *Studia Mariana*, ed. A. Parrot. Documenta et monumenta Orientis antiqui 4. Leiden: E. J. Brill.

Levine, B. A.

1983 Late Language in the Priestly Source: Some Literary and Historical Observations. Pages 69–82 in *Proceedings of the Eighth World Congress of Jewish Studies*, Panel Sessions: Bible Studies and Hebrew Language. Jerusalem: World Union of Jewish Studies.

1989 *Leviticus*, JPS Torah Commentary. Philadelphia: Jewish Publication Society.

1993 "The Lord your God Accept You" (2 Samuel 24:23): The Altar Erected by David on the Threshing Floor of Araunah. Pages 122–129 in *Eretz-Israel* 24 (Avraham Malamat Volume). Jerusalem: Israel Exploration Society.

Levine, B. A., and J. M. de Tarragon

1993 The King Proclaims the Day: Ugaritic Rites for the Vintage (*KTU* 1.41/1.87). *RB* 100:76–115.

Speiser, E. A.

1958 Census and Expiation in Mari and Israel. *BASOR* 149:17–25.

Stolper, M. W.

1985 *Entrepreneurs and Empire: The Murašû Archive, The Murašû Firm, and Persian Rule in Babylonia*. Uitgaven van het Nederlands Historisch-Archaeologisch Instituut te İstanbul 54. Istanbul: Nederlands Historisch-Archaeologisch Instituut te Istanbul.

Weinberg, J.

1992 *The Citizen-Temple Community*. JSOTSup 151. Sheffield: JSOT Press.

The Biblical "Town" as Reality and Typology: Evaluating Biblical References to Towns and Their Functions*

Genesis 4:16–26 presents an ideological assessment of the components of civilization in capsule form. We read that after his fratricidal murder was exposed, Cain, Adam's surviving son, left God's presence and betook himself to the land of Nod, East of Eden. There, his wife bore him a son named Enoch. Cain then built a town, Hebrew *ʿîr*, and named it after his son, Enoch. This is the Bible's way of enunciating the dynastic principle associated with the early political development of towns. Enoch was slated to rule the town, succeeding his father, Cain. There may even be economic significance in the fact that the first town was constructed outside the horticultural/agricultural "garden," an innuendo that has not been missed in modern scholarship

We read further of Enoch's descendants, to whom are attributed the proverbial occupations—metallurgy, musical instruments, pastoral pursuits, and tent dwelling. Then we are told that Adam had another son named Seth, a replacement for the slain Abel, and that Seth in turn had a son named Enosh, which in Hebrew means "man, human being." The text goes on to state: "It was then that the invocation of Yahweh's name commenced" (Gen 4:26). This refers, of course, to the origin of religion, a feature of civilization that could hardly be attributed to a descendant of Cain! The traditional resolution of this incongruity was to have Adam sire another son, untainted by criminality.

A second primeval genealogy, presented in Genesis 5, presumably introduces another person named Enoch, who, we are told, never died in the normal way, for God took him away. I suspect that this report actually represents the genealogical rehabilitation of the former Enoch, son of Cain. As such it serves to reinforce the awareness that towns and civilization, state and economy, have the potential for violence and oppression, a theme encountered time and again in biblical literature.

The import of the above "myths of origin" is that towns have genealogies as do families and peoples, gods and kings. In Genesis 10, we read of Nimrod, who began to assemble his kingdom in Babylon, and in Uruk and Akkad, and that he

---

* Originally published in M. Hudson and B. A. Levine (eds.), *Urbanization and Land Ownership in the Ancient Near East: A Colloquium Held at New York University, November 1996, and the Oriental Institute, St. Petersburg, Russia, May 1997* (Peabody Museum Bulletin 7; Cambridge, MA: Peabody Museum of Archaeology and Ethnology, Harvard University, 1999), pp. 421–453. Reprinted with permission from the editors and the Peabody Museum of Archaeology and Ethnology.

built Nineveh and Calah, and some other towns we cannot as easily identify. This reflects the heroic strain in the biblical view of urban centers: their attribution to individuals of notable prowess, like Nimrod the "hero," in Hebrew, *gibbôr*. Some of these heroes, themselves, bear the names of towns and lands, as was true of Nimrod/Nimrud, himself.

It is, however, in the story of the so-called Tower of Babel that we encounter a major ideological pronouncement on the potentialities of urbanization (Genesis 11). After leaving the fertile plain of Eden, humankind, then of one language and governed by common laws (for that may be what the Hebrew *ûdebārîm ʾaḥādîm*, literally: "of the same words" truly means) found a valley, and set about baking bricks for the construction of "a town with a tower" (*ʿîr ûmigdāl*), a way of indicating a fortified town. The apprehension expressed by humankind in this narrative is that without a fortified town they would not be able to remain together; that they would be dispersed. The apprehension attributed to the deity in the biblical narrative is that the tower, a sort of ziggurat reaching to heaven, would enable humankind to overthrow God, a recognizable mythological theme. In more clearly political terms, the human urge to aggregate in fortified towns implies that in reverse, the way a conqueror, or ruler can reduce the power of nations and other groups is to disperse their urban populations, to destroy their fortified towns, and thereby prevent regrouping. This is nothing short of an ideological statement on the policy of deportation so widespread in the ancient Near East at various times. In an indirect, and somewhat underhanded way, the biblical author is confirming the function of the town as an aggressive power base.

Here ends the primeval history (Genesis 1–11), except for a routine, priestly genealogy. We have, in effect, a blatantly etiological collection of narratives, beginning with creation, whose agenda and tone prompt a consideration of the conception of the town in biblical literature. The fact that the primeval history, so-called, comes at the beginning of the Bible does not signify that this is the earliest tradition. Its position does suggest, however, that the primeval history, itself comprised of several literary strata, expresses crystallized viewpoints, or representative ones, perhaps, regarding the town as an entity. These viewpoints are charged with apprehension and are suggestively negative in their messages.

Pursuing the method I employed in my contribution to the first volume of proceedings, I propose here to attempt an evaluation of some of what the Hebrew Bible has to say on the subject of towns, with an emphasis on their economic functions. This is part of an effort to fathom the biblical authors' attitudes toward urbanism and to assess the degree of their realism. I am at the beginning of my investigations and remain in great need of external evidence in order to place the biblical record, with all its diversity, into identifiable historical contexts.

Biblical Terms for "Town" and their Implications

The most characteristic Hebrew word for "town" is *ʿîr* (plural *ʿārîm*), which evidences no identifiable etymology. A frequent synonym is Hebrew *qiryāh* and variant forms, like *qeret*, as in Phoenician-Punic *Qrtḥdšt* = "Carthage," meaning something like "Newtown." These terms may derive from a West-Semitic root *q-r-h*, "to cover with a roof, with beams," and may possibly be cognate with Hebrew and West-Semitic *qîr*, "wall."[1] More will be said about these terms further on. Understandably, the connotations of Hebrew *ʿîr* range widely, which further complicates our understanding. The same is true, of course, in many languages, ancient and modern, as we would expect of terminology describing structures, complexes, and delimited areas whose form and extent, as well as political, economic, and social character were subject to continuous change.

From *The Oxford English Dictionary* one learns that classical terms for cities or towns usually express one of two themes: either they connote, in the first instance, the community or citizenry inhabiting the city, which is the case with Latin *civitas*, from which comes English "city;" or, like Latin *urbs*, they connote the place, or constructed complex, within which the citizenry resides, the physical plant. Of course, semantic predications go in both directions (as the connotations attendant upon the Greek term *polis* indicate), but Hebrew *ʿîr* decidedly belongs with Latin *urbs* and genuinely corresponds to the adjective "urban" as we use it in English. The same would be true of Hebrew *qiryāh*. It is for this reason that both of these terms will be translated "town," rather than "city," precisely because English "town" derives from Old English *tuun/tûn*, Old Saxon and Middle Low German *tûn*, Celtic *dun*, with cognates in Danish and Dutch, all connoting a range of physical locales and structures, including "fence, castle, camp, enclosed place, country house or manor, estate," and the like.[2] I know of no biblical Hebrew term that etymologically corresponds to English "city," with its social matrix, unless we consider derivatives of the verb *y-š-b* "to dwell, reside," such as the early and rare term *šebet* and the more frequent *môšāb*, "settlement," (plural *môšābôt*), "settlements," which connote "town" in the priestly literature and its offshoots, especially in Chronicles. Note the compound term *ʿîr môšāb*, "urban settlement."[3]

---

[1] On usage of the verb *q-r-h*, "to cover with a roof, with beams," see Neh 2:8, 3:6, 1 Chron 3:7, 2 Chron 34:11. Also note the noun *qôrāh*, "beam," in 2 Kings 6:2, 5, Song 1:17. On Hebrew *qîr* as a town wall, see Num. 35:4, Jos 2:5.

[2] On English "city," see *The Oxford English Dictionary*, 2nd Edition, Oxford: Clarendon Press, 1989, Volume III, 252–254; on English "town," see *ibid.* Volume XVIII, 319–322.

[3] The term *šebet*, "settlement," occurs in Num 21:15 in an old poetic excerpt, where *lešebet ʿĀr* is best translated "toward the settlement of Ar." Cf. 2 Sam 23:8, an enigmatic passage, where *bešebet Taḥkemônî* probably means: "in the settlement of Tahkemoni/Hakmoni," namely, of a person by that name (Cf. 1 Chron 11:11, 27:32). The more common term *môšāb*, in the sense of "settlement," occurs in Num 24:21, whereas the feminized plural *môšābôt*, "settlements," is frequent in Leviticus 23 and Ezekiel 6. On the

It is true, of course, that the term *bayit*, "house, household," attaches itself to toponyms and as such assumes the functional sense of "manor, town, city," and in this extended meaning would identify a town in initially material terms as the domicile of a family or clan, royal or otherwise. Thus, in Amos 7:13, *miqdāš melek ʿîr mamlākāh* is best translated "royal temple and 'family seat' of the kingdom," synonymous with *ʿîr hammelûkāh/hammamlākāh*, "royal town, capital" in 2 Sam 12:26 and 1 Sam 27:5, respectively. In fact, it might be useful at this point to survey biblical Hebrew usage associated with *ʿîr* and *qiryāh* to learn what we can about the construction and design of towns, with an eye to understanding their functions. It emerges that biblical usage is generally realistic, and for the most part, may be correlated with archaeological evidence from material culture.

Some years ago, Professor Benjamin Mazar opened an archaeological conference in Jerusalem by stating that Num 13:17–20, Moses's charge to the spies dispatched to reconnoiter Canaan, was a remarkable biblical passage because, in fact, it summarized the archaeological agenda. It reads as follows:

> Observe the land: What is its condition? And the people inhabiting it: are they strong or feeble, few or numerous? And what of the land they inhabit: is it bountiful or lacking? And what of the towns where they dwell: are they built as unwalled settlements or as fortified towns?

This excerpt supplies two significant terms of reference: the rare term *maḥanîm*, "unwalled settlements," and the frequent *mibṣārîm*, "fortified towns." The latter, in varying forms, is the most frequent specification of Hebrew *ʿîr*, whereas the most frequent verb associated with *ʿîr* is the verb *b-n-h*, "to build," often nuanced as "to fortify," by building a city wall and/or a watch-tower.[4] This recalls the plan of primeval humankind expressed in Genesis 11. In Ezek 40:2 we encounter the characterization *kemibneh ʿîr*, "like the construction of a town," describing what the prophet saw in his vision atop a mountain, with reference to the temple quarter of the rebuilt Jerusalem. This, in turn, points to a prominent, virtually universal feature of terms for "town" or "city," namely, that they may be understood to designate quarters or precincts within the larger town, much like the French *ville* and *cité*, respectively. This flexibility of usage will prove to be significant in the ensuing discussion.

Similar in meaning to Hebrew *maḥanîm*, "unwalled settlements," are forms such as *perāzôn*, *perāzôt*, and *perāzî*, all of which connote the opposite of fortified towns, which is to say, open, unwalled settlements. Thus, 1 Sam 6:18: *mēʿîr*

---

composite term *ʿîr môšāb*, "urban settlement," see 2 Kings 2:19, Ezek 48:15, Pss 107:4, 7, 36.

[4] Given forms include singular *ʿîr mibṣār*, "fortified town" (2 Kings 3:19, 10:2, Jer 1:18), and plural forms of the same. Especially note 2 Kings 17:9, 18:8: *mimmigdal nôṣerîm ʿad ʿîr mibṣār*, "from guard tower to fortified town." Also frequent is the plural *ʿārîm beṣûrôt*, "fortified towns" (Num 13:28, 2 Sam 20:6). Especially note Deut 3:5: "All of these were fortified towns (*ʿārîm beṣûrôt*), with a high wall, double gates and bar."

mibṣār weʿad koper happerāzî, "from fortified town to open village," introducing the frequent term *koper/kepār*, "village."[5]

A full review of biblical Hebrew usage relevant to the term *ʿîr* would carry us in several directions. In general, it can be said that there is sufficient textual evidence to reconstruct the physical plan of a biblical town, with its gates and towers and access roads, Hebrew *mesillôt* (Jud 20:30–32, 45; 2 Chron 9:11), though hardly enough evidence to speak of economic functions in detail. We may, however, take note of a few special cases in biblical literature that refer to economic and administrative functions. As an example, it is recorded that Solomon constructed *ʿārê hārekeb*, "the towns for chariotry" (1 Kings 9:19, 10:26), where weaponry was stored.

Mentioned alongside such towns are *ʿārê miskenôt*, a term that is more difficult to translate, but that clearly refers to towns designated as storage depots. It is best translated "towns for storage." This function emerges from usage in 2 Chron 32:28, a source from the Achaemenid period, where we read of "storage depots (*miskenôt*) for the grain crop and wine" (cf. 2 Chron 16:4). It was this very type of installation that the Israelites were conscripted to build for Pharaoh (Exod 1:11), and in 2 Chron 17:12 we find an interesting entry: *birāniyyôt weʿārê miskenôt*, "fortresses and towns for storage." Hebrew *birāniyyôt* is cognate with Hebrew/Aramaic *bîrāh binā*ʾ, and Akkadian *birtu*, "fortress," in context "capitol," hence "capital."[6]

Etymologically, the term *ʿārê miskenôt* is yet more revealing. It apparently derives from the noun *sôkēn*, which represents a Hebrew cognate of Akkadian *šaknu*, late biblical Hebrew/Aramaic *segān*, "governor, magistrate, superintendent," a term that flourishes in the Persian period and long thereafter.[7] Allowing for the wide semantic range of this term, which moves from the political to the administrative and managerial context, one could say that towns classified as

---

[5] On the form of the root *p-r-z*, connoting settling in unwalled areas, see Deut 3:5, Jud 5:7, 11, Ezek 38:11, Zech 2:8, Esther 9:19.

[6] On the Hebraized form *bîrāh*, "fortress, capitol," hence "capital," see late sources in Esther and in Dan 1:1, Neh 1:1, 2:8, 7:2, 1 Chron 29:1, 19. The determined Aramaic form *birtā*ʾ occurs in Ezra 6:2 and frequently in the Aramaic of the Achaemenid period and thereafter. See *DNWSI*, I:155–156, s.v. *byrh*. In Akkadian, the cognate *birtu* is attested from Old Babylonian down through Neo-Babylonian, and entered Aramaic from Akkadian. See *CAD B*, 261–263, s.v. *birtu* A.

[7] The title *sôkēn*, a West-Semitic realization of Akkadian *šaknu*, occurs only once in the Hebrew Bible, in a late passage in Isa 22:15: "Betake yourself to this [certain] chancellor (*sôkēn*); to Shebna who is in charge of the palace." In the alternative West-Semitic realization *segān*, known in Hebrew and in Aramaic, this title occurs in contexts suggesting official status, in some cases associated with the royal establishment. Cf. Jer 51:23, where plural *segānîm* occurs alongside Pehah's, or Persian provincial governors. (Also cf. Ezek 23:6, 12, 23.) On Akkadian *šaknu* and its various meanings see *CAD Š*/I, 180–192. On Aramaic *segān*, frequently attested in the Aramaic of the Achaemenid period and thereafter, see *DNWSI*, II:777–778. For usage in post-biblical Jewish sources, including the Mishnah, see Levy 1964, III:475–476, s.v. *segen*, and *ibid.* 476, s.v. *segān, signā*ʾ.

such operated as administrative centers under the control of certain officials, where goods were stored and redistributed. As will be explained in considerable detail, this very designation could apply to Shiloh of the Middle Bronze III and early Iron Age, as well as to other Canaanite, then Israelite towns. Like so many languages, ancient and modern, biblical Hebrew has a category of "large town" (*ʿîr gedôlāh*), applied to Nineveh, Calah, Jerusalem, and Gibeon (Gen 10:12, Jos 10:2, Jer 22:8, Jonah 1:2–3, 2:4), in contrast to a small town with few inhabitants (Koh 9:14).

On Hebrew *qiryāh*, and related *qeret*, the following observations may be offered: a motif associated with this terminology is urban tumult, expressed by the verb *h-m-h*, "to throng, be tumultuous, which suggests population density."[8] The verb *kônēn*, "to set on foundations, to establish," is occasionally employed to describe the founding and/or fortifying of a town (Num 21:28, Hab 2:12). Fortification is also suggested by the description *qiryat ʿôz*, "fortress, bastion" (Prov 10:15, 18:1). We also find that the contrast indicated by *ʿîr-śādeh*, "town-country," is also expressed by *qiryāh-śādeh* in Micah 4:10. According to Lament 2:11, a *qiryāh* has *reḥôbôt*, "plazas, open avenues."

The biblical *qiryāh* is occasionally described as being lofty or as having high urban structures within it (Deut 2:36, Isa 26:5, Prov 9:3), and it has *šeʿārîm*, "gates." (Prov 8:3, Job 29:7). Especially relevant is Isa 25:2–3: "For you (God) have turned a town (*ʿîr*) into a stone heap, a fortified town (*qiryāh beṣûrāh*) into a ruin; the citadel of foreigners from having been a town.... Therefore, a fierce people must honor you; the *qiryāh* of fierce nations must fear you." Finally, there is the characterization of Mount Zion as *qiryat melek rab*, "the capital of the great King," a symbolic reference to the God of Israel (Ps 48:3).

Of etymological significance is the terminology of Neh 2:8 (cf. Neh 3:6, 2 Chron 34:11). The verse in question speaks of a letter to one in charge of orchards ordering him to supply timber "for roofing (*leqārôt*) the gatehouses of the temple fortress (*ʾet šaʿārê habbîrāh ʾašer labbayit*), and for the town wall, and the house where I shall reside." This is a virtual proof-text for the terms *qiryah*, *qeret*—showing their derivation from a verb meaning "to roof over [with beams]." Usage of the Aramaism *bîrāh*, "fortress, capitol," (see above) is also significant (cf. Neh 7:2, 1 Chron 29:1, 19). The overall reference is, of course, to the rebuilt Jerusalem.

Although I am not presently able to present a comprehensive treatment of Nehemiah's memoirs as a source of information about Judean urbanization in the Achaemenid period, it would be interesting to pursue evidence from the book of Nehemiah a bit further. We find in chapter 3 of that book rather detailed descriptions of what we would today call "urban renewal," more precisely, the rebuilding of the outer walls of Jerusalem, which complements data elsewhere provided on the restoration of the Temple and other parts of the city. Some study

---

8 On the Hebrew verb *h-m-h*, "to throng, be in tumult," and the derivative noun *hāmôn*, "throng, tumult," in association with towns, see 1 Kings 1:41, Isa 22:2, Isa 5:14, 32:14.

has been made of the layout of the city of Jerusalem as described in Nehemiah 3, but what is impressive in the present context is the technical terminology available from this single chapter and what we may learn from it about the officialdom and craftsmen residing within Jerusalem's walls.

I have touched upon this matter elsewhere, but only tangentially (Levine 1993). I argued that the Hiphil verb *heḥezîq* "to take hold of," used so frequently in Nehemiah 3, did not connote the actual repairing or construction involved in fortifying Jerusalem, but rather what Akkadian *ṣabātu* means in similar contexts, especially the comparable D- and S-stems, *ṣubbutu* and *šuṣbūtu*, namely, to assume or give control over property for purposes of renewal or as feudal holdings. This becomes significant in the present discussion because it would seem that priests, various local and provincial officials, estate managers, and landowning families from the population centers of Judea were assigned and assumed responsibility for constructing specific sections of the city wall and the gate houses.

Nehemiah 3 enumerates the following groups of craftsmen who were quartered together, usually in a common building: (1) metal workers—*ṣôrepîm*; (2) perfumers—*raqqāḥîm*; (3) small merchants—*rôkelîm*; and (4) professional soldiers—*gibborîm*. Then, there were the priests (*kôhanîm*), Levites (*lewiyyîm*), and temple servitors (*netînîm*); special mention is made of the residence of the High Priest, Eliashib. Repeatedly, we read of officials entitled *śar ḥaṣî pelek*, *śar pelek*, "magistrate of half the district; magistrate of the district."[9] Thus, we read of two persons, each identified as magistrate of half of the district of Jerusalem (Neh 3:9, 12). Similarly, there were two heads of the two half districts of Beth-Zur and Qeʾilah (= Keilah), sites considerably to the south of Jerusalem, north of Hebron. The following locales are designated *pelek*: Beth Hakkerem, just to the south of Jerusalem, and Mizpeh, considerably to the north of Jerusalem.[10] Notwithstanding an inconsistency or two, these designations are employed precisely.

What emerges is a description of Jerusalem as a provincial capital, laid out to accommodate its priesthood, its bureaucracy, and its craftsmen. Officials of outlying towns or districts, as well as prominent landowners from the province of Judea maintained residences or headquarters in the capital. These are registered as "men of X-location." Listed locations of origin include Jericho, near the Dead Sea; Gibeon, not far north of Jerusalem; Tekoa, considerably to the south of Jerusalem just north-east of Beth-Zur; and Zanoah, south-west of Jerusalem.[11] Were these the *ḥôrîm*, "aristocrats," mentioned alongside the *segānîm* (Neh

[9] Cognates of Hebrew *pelek*, "district," possibly occur in Phoenician (*DNWSI*, II:915–916, s.v. plk_1), but surely in Akkadian (*AHw* 863, s.v. *pilku* I) and in later Jewish Aramaic. See Levy 1964, IV:52–53, s.v. *pelāk*, *pilkāʾ*, "district."

[10] The reader is referred to a recent atlas, Aharoni and Avi-Yonah 1993:129, map no. 170, for these locales during the Achaemenid period, in what became the province of Yehud.

[11] Refer to the atlas and map cited in the previous note.

3:16, 4:8, 13, 5:7, 7:5), who may have been landowners and estate managers rather than government officials? In terms of geographical distribution, districts and places of origin listed reach all the way from Mizpeh in the north to Beth-Zur in the south of Judea.

It is unclear from the biblical text who empowered the various officials listed above, whether the Persian authorities or the Jewish leadership, officials like Nehemiah, a Persian Pehah of Judea, who was at the same time a Jew and leader of his people. There is a reference in Neh 3:7 to two men from Gibeon who were somehow associated with the Persian Pehah of ʿAbar Naharah. The wording is enigmatic: "pertaining to/belonging to the 'throne' (*kisseʾ* of the Pehah of ʿEber Hannahar." For the most part, however, it would appear that reference is to the Jewish priesthood and to the internal Jewish administration, serving, in this case, under Nehemiah. As has been noted elsewhere, Nehemiah 5 depicts a confrontation between Nehemiah and other Jewish leaders, and there was, of course, the major conflict between the Judeans and the powerful Jews of Samaria.

There is much more to be learned from Nehemiah 3 about the physical layout of Jerusalem toward the end of the fifth century B.C.E. under Persian rule, and about its economy as well. My purpose here was merely to show that one could initiate a discussion of the urban economy of Achaemenid Jerusalem from the biblical text. It would become apparent early on that without external evidence, proper answers cannot be found to the many questions raised by the biblical text itself.

Against the background of the above review of descriptive terminology, I will explore two models of urbanization in biblical Israel, moving back in time. I will begin in the most recent phase, relatively speaking, by examining the biblical towns of asylum, a model of urbanization that highlights the relationship between temple and town. Although we possess no direct archaeological evidence pertaining to towns of asylum, no town in which an inscription has been found designating it as such, there is reason to regard these biblically projected towns as realistic entities. We will then proceed to discuss biblical Shiloh, a short-lived but fascinating cult-center in the Ephraimite hills, which has been excavated rather extensively in recent years. We have the final report of Israel Finkelstein (1993) and his associates, which deals in considerable detail with economic and political issues. In the case of Shiloh, it is possible to correlate the biblical record with the archaeological history of the site quite persuasively. Comparison of Shiloh with Bethel, another excavated site, will prove to be informative.

Towns of Asylum

The standard Hebrew designation for "town of asylum" is *ʿîr miqlāṭ* (plural, *ʿārê miqlāṭ*). It combines the term *ʿîr* with the verb *q-l-ṭ*, which is virtually restricted to the context of asylum and yields a clear sense from later usage. It means "to draw in, take in, absorb"[12] and suggests that the notion of asylum meant, in fact, that zones had been designated where one would be accepted, or allowed entry under prescribed circumstances, and there protected. The relevance of investigating "towns of asylum" in a general discussion of urbanization lies in the fact that such asylum zones were located at what were or, in most cases, had been cult-centers, with their temples, or less elaborate installations, and that these towns represent the institutionalization of the almost universal notion of "sanctuary." Once inside a temple, or holding onto an altar, or once gaining access to some similarly sanctified environment, a person may not normally be apprehended, put to death, or otherwise punished. One is under the protection of the patron deity. Such towns may thus shed light on at least one of the functions of urban centers. In general, some biblical towns owe, if not their initial formation, their growth and continuity to cultic functions, to the fact that temples and other forms of cult sites had been located within them and had defined their status to a great extent at various periods. Essentially, asylum makes sense only in sacred space.

Most scholarship dealing with the biblical towns of asylum has focused on legal and social issues relating to homicide, as well as questions of dating the biblical evidence. Perhaps the most informative of these studies is by Alexander Rofé (1986) who carefully traces biblical statements in literary-historical sequence. Rofé is on the mark in assigning the Deuteronomic, Deuteronomistic, and priestly prescriptions governing the towns of asylum to schools of authors who accepted the Deuteronomic doctrine of cult centralization, and in regarding them as relatively late. As Rofé explains, and as will be shown here, the reference to the right of asylum in the Book of the Covenant (more precisely Exod 21:12–13) harks back to a time before the doctrine of cult centralization had been promulgated and when all then legitimate cult-sites could absorb fugitive homicides. The need to establish fixed towns of asylum is first indicated in core-Deuteronomy (more precisely Deut 19:1–10) and is to be explained as an expected consequence of the very doctrine of cult centralization. With only one legitimate cult-site in operation (at least officially so), alternative zones of asylum of a noncultic status became necessary to protect manslayers in what Rofé regards as a praiseworthy effort to pursue justice.

But, Rofé limits himself almost entirely to the legal and social aspects of the right of asylum, against the background of the blood feud. Here, a modest attempt will be made to discuss towns of asylum as functioning entities, venturing some speculations as to how the operation of a system of asylum zones may have affected the towns in which they were located and how they reflected the local histories of the relevant towns, themselves.

Several narratives illustrate the right of asylum, as well as the limitations of that right and infringements upon it. Solomon gave orders to seize both his fraternal rival Adonijah and David's powerful general Joab, and put them to death even though each of them, fleeing for his life, had seized the horns of the temple

[12] S.v. *qālaṭ/qelāṭ*, *qelîṭāh*, *qilṭāʾ*, "to absorb; absorption; one detained."

altar (1 Kings 1:50–51, 2:28, and following). These narratives clearly indicate where the right of asylum originates, highlighting its essentially cultic matrix: it is a form of divine protection. Nob, designated *ʿîr hakkôhanîm*, "town of the priests" (in 1 Sam 21 and 22), may have been a veritable town of asylum. It is mentioned in Neh 11:31 as a Benjaminite town, alongside Anathoth, which was Jeremiah's home town. Of Jeremiah it is said that he was "from the priests who are in Anathoth" (Jer 1:1). In fact, although the Samuel narrative does not say so explicitly, David may have sought refuge in Nob while fleeing from Saul precisely because it was a sanctuary town. While there, he was indeed protected. Nonetheless, when it became known to Saul that Ahimelek, the chief-priest of Nob, had given aid and comfort to David, he ordered him and all of his priests slain. In Neh 6:10–11 of a much later period, we read that Nehemiah was advised by a prophet named Shemayah to seek refuge in the Jerusalem temple from those who were coming to kill him. It is questionable, however, whether this has anything to do with asylum, and it is more likely that the temple was a secure place when the doors were bolted. Nehemiah resisted this advice because it would have made him look fearful, arousing scorn against him.

The cultic matrix is evident in some biblical legal statements pertaining to towns of asylum, and to chronicles that refer to their establishment, or their designation in this role. These legal sources can be summarized quite simply and even sequenced in chronological order, at least relatively so. The earliest statements of law occur in Exod 21:12–13 in the context of homicide, as part of what is known as *The Book of the Covenant*, a collection of laws that may well go back to the ninth century B.C.E. and most likely represents a Northern Israelite document.

For one who kills another without premeditation God will provide a "place," Hebrew *māqôm*, to which he may "flee," expressed by the Hebrew verb *n-w-s*, which turns out to be the operative verb in virtually all biblical laws of asylum, and even in the narrative of Joab's flight (1 Kings 2:28). Hebrew *māqôm* is synonymous with *ʿîr* in Deut 21:19, and in Ruth 4:10, *ʿîr* is paralleled by "the gate of his *māqôm*." The statement of Exod 21:12–13 is immediately followed by one governing premeditated murder, which prescribes the following disposition, in contrast: "From My very altar must you apprehend him to face death." There is no town, or *māqôm*, for the outright murderer.

By our reckoning, the next relevant statement of law is in Deut 19:1–13, part of core-Deuteronomy, which may be dated to the mid-eighth century B.C.E. and which even more probably represents a Northern Israelite document. Here we read of the designation, or "setting apart" (the Hebrew verb *hibdîl*), of towns within the land granted by God where the homicide may "flee." The total area of the country is to be divided into three districts, and in each, a town is to be designated for this purpose. The law then proceeds to enumerate projected circumstances under which a homicide would qualify for asylum and concludes with an addendum to the effect that if the land is enlarged, three more towns are to be added to meet the growing needs. The actual term *ʿîr miqlāṭ* does not appear in this statement of law and might well be the invention of later priestly writers who have given us the rather elaborate statement of law on this subject found in Numbers 35. The term *ʿîr* does occur repeatedly, however.

But, we're getting ahead of the story. Chronologically, the next statement comes in the Deuteronomistic introduction to the book of Deuteronomy, most likely a composition of the mid-to-late seventh century B.C.E. originating in Judah. Deut 4:41–43 reports that Moses separated (Hebrew *hibdîl*) three towns in Transjordan to which a homicide might "flee." The list of the towns, which are named, appears schematic, with one town located in the north-Moabite Mishor (Betser), within the territory of the Israelite tribe of Reuben, the second at Ramoth in Gilead of the Gadites, and the third in Golan-Bashan of the Manassites.

To summarize up to this point, we can say that whereas *The Book of the Covenant* suggests a cultic basis for the towns of refuge, the two traditions of Deuteronomy are formulated in an administrative mode, either with general legal emphasis, or more specifically, as a strategy for dealing with the blood feud. This is a striking tendency, and most probably reflects Deuteronomy's adherence to the doctrine of cult centralization, as has been suggested above. Whereas in earlier times there were sanctuaries operating throughout the land, as is inferred by Exodus 21, the subsequent restriction to one central temple would have impeded access to most fleeing homicides. Hence, the need for regional zones of asylum, for which no cultic status is adduced. Conceivably, the actuality that the earlier, regional cult-centers may have survived was suppressed by the authors of the Deuteronomic school so as to deny legitimacy to any other than the central temple. By indirection, the avoidance of cultic references in Deuteronomy endorses the originally cubic basis of asylum.

This brings us to the priestly law of homicide in Numbers 35, which I would date to the Achaemenid period. It is here that a different nexus of cult and asylum is introduced. No legitimate temples stood in the designated towns of asylum, but their administration is given to the Levites, for whom this constituted a reassignment, we could say. Furthermore, the death of the High Priest would occasion an amnesty, as will be noted in due course. Num 35:1–8 prescribe the establishment of Levitical towns, forty-eight in all, including the six towns of asylum specified further on in Num 35:9–34, three on either side of the Jordan. The administration of the towns of asylum is assigned to the Levites. In highly schematic fashion, and through a blending of the earlier statements, a plan for the Levitical towns is laid out, and this would apply as well to the towns of asylum. The towns are to be walled and square, with open areas outside the walls in four directions. The Hebrew term for such open areas is *migrāš*, which we render "town plot," a term occurring as well in Lev 25:32–34 and spun off in the Joshua traditions and in Chronicles. It also figures in the plans for the rebuilt Jerusalem preserved in Ezekiel 45 and 48. Actually, the provisions of Num 35:1–8 are, in this regard, based on the earlier priestly law presented in Leviticus 25. The term *migrāš* would seem to derive from a verb meaning "to drive, corral," thereby suggesting a pastoral origin, but such delimited areas were also used for domestic farming as garden plots adjacent to the towns, as the composite term *śedēh migrāš ʿîr*, "the field of the town plot," indicates. More will be said on this subject in due course.

Numbers 35, in effect, combines the provisions of earlier statements to produce an elaborate law governing the towns of asylum, where one who found refuge could remain, protected from harm by blood avengers, until the death of the incumbent chief priest of Israel, at which time an amnesty would be proclaimed, and he could leave.

Important elaborations are to be found in Joshua 20, also from the Achaemenid period, by my reckoning. The procedures governing the granting of asylum are spelled out in anticipation of the records of the Levitical towns in Joshua 21, and of a statement of policy toward Transjordan that comes in Joshua 22. The fleeing homicide was to make a declaration at the town gate before the elders, who would then "gather him into the town and provide him with a residence," expressed by the Hebrew verb *ʾ-s-p*, a more frequent verb synonymous in this context with *q-l-ṭ*. Upon the death of the High Priest, the homicide was allowed to return to his home town with impunity and there await trial.

What is most interesting is that Joshua 20, while repeating the three Transjordanian towns mentioned in Deuteronomy 4, adds the names of three Cisjordanian towns of asylum: Kedesh in Galilee, Shechem in the Ephraimite hills, and Hebron in the Judean hills. Now, there were many towns named Kedesh, Kadesh, or the like, and their names belie the presence of a cult-site within them at some point in time. As for Shechem and Qiryat-Arbaʿ, that is, Hebron, they certainly had temples located in them in certain periods. Finally, in a late list of towns of asylum preserved in 1 Chron 6:42–45, most likely from the fourth century B.C.E. we read that the towns of asylum, thirteen in number, were granted to the descendants of Aaron. Included are Hebron and Anathoth, and also Debir and Beth-Shemesh, whose very names testify to the presence of a temple at some early period. Clearly, the later, most likely Achaemenid traditions, in Numbers, Joshua, and the evidently Achaemenid writings of Chronicles, in contrast with the preceding Deuteronomic traditions, support, in varying degrees, the hypothesis that towns of asylum were located at cult centers and that initially they had drawn their legal sanction from that reality. Jos 20:9 attests a unique term *ʿārê hammôʿādāh*, "assembly towns," which may refer to religious assemblages, not necessarily held in or around temples.

Biblicists have called attention to the fact that the designation of towns of asylum in Transjordan collides with attitudes stated elsewhere in biblical literature toward the Transjordanian Israelite settlements, and as well, with doctrines denying the sanctity of Transjordan, an area often considered to lie outside the Promised Land. It would take us far afield to attempt an analysis of the differing biblical traditions related to this issue, but some comment can be offered on the Transjordanian question with an eye to the actual character and function of the towns of asylum.

Clearly, the Deuteronomist, represented by Deuteronomy 4, discussed above, was very concerned with the status of the Transjordanian Israelite settlements in central Transjordan, primarily, in the land of Gilead. These were identified in the tribal scheme as the territories of Reuben, Gad, and a clan affiliated with Manasseh. The Deuteronomist took his cue from the JE historiography of Numbers 21–25, 32, where this theme is highlighted. What is presented as a chronicle of the Israelite advance through Transjordan is, underneath it all, a way of relating to the fact that a sizable Israelite community inhabited Transjordan at least as early as the first expansions eastward under the United Monarchy, or soon thereafter, during the Omride period, in the early ninth century B.C.E. It is even possible that Transjordan had been settled by Israelites in the initial stages of that process, in the late twelfth or early eleventh centuries. That is what the JE writers of Numbers would have us believe, and this conclusion may even be suggested by the Moabite stela of Mesha, who, in the mid-ninth century B.C.E., speaks of Gadites inhabiting the north-Moabite Mishor "from before memory," Moabite-Hebrew *mᶜlm*/*mē ᶜôlām*. Historically, it is more likely that the Israelites, like the Arameans after them, would have come down from the North instead of moving up from the South. Those Israelite communities endured and surely prospered at various periods. The expedition of Shishak c. 925 B.C.E. left permanent damage to parts of Gilead, and eventually Tiglath-pileser III depopulated much of that area in the late seventh century (734–721 B.C.E.), as he had done to the population of northern Israel. Tiglath-pileser III did not bring a permanent end to Israelite/Jewish settlement in Transjordan, however, because Jewish settlements persisted there and grew in extent during the Persian and Hellenistic periods, as we know.

In general terms, the question of relationships with and attitudes toward the Transjordanian community appears to have been of much greater concern in certain quarters than we had imagined. Now, Numbers 35, of priestly authorship, takes its cue from the JE historiography and from the Deuteronomist, and accordingly provides for Transjordan the same institutions of asylum as for the land of Israel, proper. This is understandable in the Book of Numbers, since interest in the Transjordanian Israelite community is so intense, and the preserved early traditions, such as are imbedded in Numbers 32, directed attention to that region. In contrast, core-Deuteronomy and Joshua 20–22 provide for towns of asylum only within the land, proper. In fact we find in Joshua 22 a rigorous denunciation of the Transjordanian-Israelite community.

I cannot, at the present time, account for all of these differences in policy, which must surely reflect real, historical situations. All I can say is that it is more realistic to provide for the needs of the Transjordanian community, which existed, after all, whereas doctrinaire exclusion of that community, where we find such attitudes, should be regarded as less realistic and more ideological and tendentious. Such exclusion should be attributed to specific policies that withheld recognition from this actual part of Israelite/Jewish society. I find no difficulty in discovering concern for Transjordan among biblical writers of the Achaemenid period, because Jews lived there in large numbers.

At this point, I would like to backtrack, in order to resume discussion of the plan of the towns of asylum outlined in Joshua 20, and of the Levitical towns, so-called, in Num 35:1–8 and Joshua 21. Attention is also drawn to 1 Chronicles

6, which provides the most specific information we possess on this subject. We must also consider the plan for the rebuilt Jerusalem in Ezekiel 45 and 48. It emerges that there is a complex of biblical traditions in which the extramural *migrāš* is prominent. The term *migrāš* was introduced by the priestly writers and their successors in the Achaemenid period, as I see it. My reasons for suggesting this provenience will be clarified as we proceed.

We begin with Lev 25:29–33. After setting down the law governing arable land, the text makes an exception: urban dwellings may be permanently alienated if not redeemed the first year after their sale, whereas arable land could be redeemed indefinitely. The terminology is complex, yet instructive. We read of *bêt môšāb ʿîr ḥômāh*, "a dwelling in a walled town," and of another type of house referred to as *bātê haḥaṣērîm*, "houses located in unwalled areas." The form *ḥaṣērîm* is elsewhere known only in late biblical sources. In Isa 42:11 reference is to the dwelling of the semi-nomadic Kedarites. More directly relevant are references to the *ḥaṣērîm* in the environs of towns, which we find in late portions of Joshua, such as Joshua 15, perhaps dating from the time of Josiah in the late seventh century or later, and in other parts of Joshua (Jos 13:23, 28, 16:9, 19:8, 21:12). We re-encounter similar references in Nehemiah (11:25, 30; ch. 12) and in 1 Chronicles (4:33, 6:42, 9:22, 25). This permanent feature of towns in the Achaemenid period interacts with references to the *migrāš*, as we shall see presently.

According to Leviticus 25, houses located in such open areas outside the town shared the status of arable land. In a related matter, there is provision for the *migrāš*-property of the Levitical towns. They constitute the permanent *ʾaḥuzzāh*, "acquired estate," of the Levites and may never be alienated, which means that these open areas could never be pledged as security for debt. The point established by this law is that the Levitical town owned the open areas collectively, a fact indicated by the wording of the law. One who acquires an urban dwelling in a Levitical town buys it from the Levites and loses possession of it on the Jubilee, and one may never acquire a Levitical town plot, to start with.

Lev 25:29–33 may be elucidated by 1 Chron 6:35–45, already referred to above. After listing the descendants of Aaron, the text goes on to tell us where they resided:

> And these are their settlements (*môšābôt*), by their circular enclosures (*ṭîrôt*) within their borders. ... They were granted Hebron in the territory of Judah, together with its town plots (*migrāšîm*) all around it. But the field [= arable land] adjacent to the town and its unwalled settlements (*ḥaṣērîm*) they granted to Caleb, son of Jephunneh. (1 Chron 6:39–41,with omissions)

And so, the distinction made in Leviticus 25 between the status of the *migrāšîm* and that of the *ḥaṣērîm* correlates precisely with what 1 Chron 6 states in clearly differentiating between what is owned collectively by the priests, on the one hand, and what went to the tribal leader, Caleb, on the other.

Num 35:1–8 is the next step. The forty-eight Levitical towns, to include the six towns of asylum, were all to have open areas outside their walls, in all four directions, and their precise dimensions are given in a schematic way. There is reference only to cattle and other livestock and similar property, not to gardening, however. I wonder whether this isn't explicable in terms of the projected *mise-en-scène* in Numbers and even in Chronicles, where the text is presumably describing the Israelites when they first entered the land and were engaged in pastoral pursuits. In reality, terms such as *migrāš*, *ḥaṣērîm*, and *ṭîrôt* progress in their connotations from pastoral to agricultural settings and for the most part were introduced in the exilic and postexilic periods.

It seems that the complex *ᶜîr-migrāš* is almost consistently limited to Levitical towns and towns of asylum. This is not where the term originated, of course. In 1 Chron 5:16 we read of "all the *migrāšîm* of Sharon," in a context unrelated to Levitical towns. In other words, the phenomenon of the *migrāš* was more general, but for a complex of reasons, the priestly writers and their successors found in it a category that suited the economic and legal status of cult-based towns. Whoever gave us Ezekiel 45 and 48 utilized this model for the rebuilt Jerusalem, with the Temple at its center, and with *migrāšîm* all around. The biblical *migrāš* may be compared to Akkadian *tawwertum*/*tamirtu*, "surrounding area, surrounding field," designating arable areas in the environs of towns.[13]

Knowing what we do of the welfare function of temples, it is possible that *ᶜîr*, in the composite term *ᶜîr miqlāṭ* originally referred more precisely to a quarter of a town than to the town in its entirety. Thus, in 2 Kings 10:25, *ᶜîr bêt habbaᶜal* is best translated: "the quarter of the Baal temple," located within the town of Samaria. This became clear to me in my study of the Temple Scroll, a document edited by Yigael Yadin, where the term (*ᶜîr hammiqdāš*), which I then translated "Temple City," occurred prominently, referring to the temple quarter of Jerusalem. That document is now dated to the early-to-mid second century B.C.E. Yadin had concluded that the prescriptions of that sectarian scroll applied to all of Jerusalem, and I challenged his view on the grounds that he had misunderstood the sense of the Hebrew *ᶜîr* in context (Levine 1978).

It is likely that fugitives claiming asylum were lodged in a special quarter of town. In effect, forced residence in the town of asylum constituted a form of detention, and detainees would undoubtedly have received rations from the temple or its successor institution. Conceivably, they would have been put to work. There is no evidence as to how long it would take to bring such fugitives to trial, if indeed that was to occur in reality. I suspect that towns of asylum served a penal function, after all. It is generally thought that incarceration was not a penal practice in biblical Israel, but I no longer think the matter is so simple. Detention and penal incarceration cannot be completely disassociated from each other. It is likely that in reality the towns of asylum served as virtual prisons, and that the experience of the homicide resembled that of the indentured servant forced to

---

[13] On Akkadian *tamirtu* see *CAD A*/I, 380–381, s.v. *ālu*, 1, 4, b "surroundings (of the city)."

live on the estate of his creditor and constrained from returning to his own family for a period of years. The indentured "slave" worked on the farm, whereas the fugitive worked in town! In fact, it is likely that not only targeted homicides bided their time in towns of asylum, but those evading taxation and conscription, the homeless, and others.

In the Achaemenid period, the cultic realities had changed in the areas of Jewish settlement. In Judea there were apparently no rivals to the temple of Jerusalem, but in Shechem-Gerizim, in Ephraim, the so-called Samaritan temple stood, a fact that might induce us to take the naming of Shechem as an asylum town in Joshua 20 seriously. In Transjordan there may have been cult sites, as well. But, even if earlier temples no longer functioned in the cultic way, the towns in which they stood might have retained their role as towns of asylum, allowing for some shifting in institutional functions. It may be pure speculation, but quite possibly the Nethinim of whom we read in Ezra-Nehemiah, and who corresponded so singularly to the *širkūtu* of the Neo-Babylonian documents, had some function associated with the asylum quarters, as the Levites surely had. (Levine 1963)

There are those who date the laws governing towns of asylum to an early period or who consider admittedly late references to them to be merely residual memories. The argument is that once a central judicial network is in operation, such legal practices were no longer required. This is simply not true. In tribal or clannish societies, the blood feud persists, and the legal distinctions between premeditated murder and other forms of homicide are seldom as clearly perceived as we think. There is also the consideration that there was more to this biblical institution than merely its judicial aspect, as has been emphasized here. One is left wondering whether a town benefited from being a place of asylum, or whether such was a drain on the local economy. I think probably the former.

The welfare function of ancient temples (and of more recent ones) provides the context for further investigation of the biblical towns of asylum. This conclusion is merely reinforced by their association, in certain biblical traditions, with towns where priests and Levites clustered and points to the economic roles of temples. This is the direction in which I plan to take the inquiry further, searching all the while for external models applicable to the towns of asylum, preferably from the Achaemenid period.

The Case of Shiloh: The Interaction of Economy, Administration, and Cult

The recent archaeological excavations at biblical Shiloh, conducted during the years 1981–1984 and published in a final report by Israel Finkelstein and his associates in 1993, offer an unusual opportunity to undertake a controlled comparison of the biblical and the archaeological evidence.[14]

---

[14] See Finkelstein 1993, especially: "The History and Archaeology of Shiloh from the Middle Bronze Age II to Iron Age II," 371–393.

I begin with the biblical record. We are introduced to Shiloh in Jud 21:19 and following. Without going into a review of the sequence of events that occasioned reference to this town, we learn from the biblical passage that an annual pilgrimage festival, Hebrew *ḥag*, was to take place at Shiloh. There then follows what is perhaps the most precise location given anywhere in the Bible for a particular site: Shiloh is "northward of Bethel, to the east of the road that runs northward from Bethel toward Shechem, and south of Lebonah." The implications of this description will become evident when we review the archaeological evidence, because location and natural environment provide the key to the role of Shiloh. Shiloh stood atop a hill more than 700 m above sea level, with surrounding hills rising about 800 m, at the northern end of a fertile valley. A permanent large water supply came from ʿEin Seilun, about 900 m to its northeast. Shiloh's high position vis-à-vis the surrounding area added to its security.

It was undoubtedly the same sort of annual pilgrimage festival referred to in Judges that prompted a certain Elkanah from the Ephraimite hills to make a trip to Shiloh, where his barren wife, Hannah, vowed to dedicate her to-be-born son, who was to bear the name of Samuel, to temple service. This we read in 1 Samuel 1–3, the most informative source about Shiloh as a regional cult-center. Evading all sorts of narrative concerns and limiting ourselves to information about Shiloh's functions as a cult center, we can state the following: the fact that the sanctuary at Shiloh is designated *bêt YHWH*, literally: "House of Yahweh," a term otherwise reserved for the Jerusalem temple, at least makes it likely that a permanent temple building stood at Shiloh (1 Sam 2:24). It was customary to pronounce vows when on a pilgrimage and to accompany such activity with sacrificial offerings. The occasion of a pilgrimage afforded private access to cult-sites and to the services of their priests. An elaborate cult, served by a clan priesthood, was active at Shiloh, and the Ark, a type of numinous icon carried into battle, was housed there. As a temple, Shiloh was the locus of theophany, as expressed in the story about the voices little Samuel heard during the night. The nexus of prophecy and cult, reflected in the personality of the cult prophet, Samuel, is also brought out in the narratives about Shiloh. In effect, priesthoods, even if clan based, often co-opted new members into their ranks in the very way indicated by the present story and in other ways as well.

The remaining biblical references to Shiloh are less significant for the present discussion and have only suggestive historical importance. They will be taken up when we survey the archaeological evidence, since there are indications that after a period of abandonment following its destruction by the Philistines in the eleventh century B.C.E., Shiloh had a modest afterlife as a cult center.

Were we to speculate on the character of Shiloh and its economic and political functions solely on the basis of the biblical evidence and by drawing on corollary biblical evidence of other cult centers, we might not become at all aware of the initial reasons for the town's existence. Biblical concerns are pretty much restricted to the cultic and the prophetic, with special attention to the military role of the Ark and the ideology of the wars of conquest. In all fairness, however, the biblical record does not present an inaccurate picture, as far as it goes, and in fact correlates well with modern discovery. In fact, the mention of vineyards in the festival narrative of Judges 21 is exceedingly realistic, as we shall see.

Enter the archaeological evidence. The map shows that Shiloh lies between Bethel and Shechem near the South-North road from Jerusalem to Shechem, confirming with only minor modifications the biblical pinpointing of its location. Danish expeditions excavated Shiloh (Seilun) at various times, but their efforts led to less than comprehensive results. The renewed excavations under Israel Finkelstein were able to delineate several principal periods during which Shiloh was operative. The principal early period of massive construction is represented by Stratum VII, covering from approximately 1650–1550 B.C.E., or late MB III. Only ceramic remains were discovered earlier than this phase. There is then a lull during the Late Bronze Age, represented by stratum VI, when, however, large quantities of cult objects were deposited at the site. We then encounter the massive construction of Iron Age I (1150–1050 B.C.E.), Stratum V. This is, of course, the period that concerns us most, because it corresponds to the period of reference in biblical literature. Shiloh enjoyed a continuous, though limited history into the Byzantine period.

The summary to follow is based on the final excavation report. A composite of pre-Israelite Shiloh emerges as we survey discoveries in the principal areas of excavation in Stratum VII, or late MB III. Moving from East to West, the MB III fortification wall has been uncovered from Area D to the northeast, through areas M, K, H, and F, and then southward in the Western sector through area C to area J. There was also a glacis, whose primary purpose was to reinforce the fortification wall. Though no remains of MB III internal construction were discovered in the relevant areas surrounded by the wall, a row of cellars was found in the northern sector running from area F in the west to area M in the east. Information about what lay inside the fortification wall is limited to the northern sector because the southern sector and the summit of the mound were too damaged by later construction. There is no evidence of residential dwellings in this northern sector, though such may have stood in the southern sector. The upshot of these findings is that in late MB III, or stratum VII, a wall encompassed an area of approximately 1.7 hectares, possibly giving up an advantage of standing at the extremity of the northern terrace of the mound, which might have facilitated better defense.

Finkelstein is of the view that a cult site stood at MB III Shiloh. Many cult objects—cult stands, votive bowls, and bull-shaped zoomorphic vessels—were discovered in the storeroom adjacent to the wall in area F, as well as metal objects. There is also the fact that in Late Bronze Age I there was cultic activity at Shiloh, even though the site was uninhabited. Large dumps of cultic debris date to that period, which clearly suggests that worshippers continued to visit the site even while it was uninhabited, because of its earlier importance. This situation was replayed in Iron Age II. Finkelstein supposes that the MB III temple stood on or near the summit of the mound, which was located nearer the northern slope. Such was the case at contemporary Shechem and Bethel. The cultic debris of LB I was found on the northeastern slope, and earthen fills were directed to the summit. There is, however, no evidence of residential dwellings at MB III Shiloh. Finkelstein compares Shiloh with the contemporary remains from nearby Shechem and Bethel, and also from Hebron in the Judean hills. There are many similarities in size, layout, and function that link these MB III towns in a network of sorts.

What unites these towns is their location in mountainous regions. Finkelstein contrasts their functions not only with lowland sites, which were generally larger and included residential areas, but with Samaria, for instance, in the northern highlands. Based on these observable differences, Finkelstein arrives at some important conclusions about the formation and functioning of MB III Shiloh. The walls of lowland towns were essentially for fortification, since these towns were inhabited by sizable populations. In highland towns like Shiloh, the outer wall served as revetment and was placed most advantageously for that purpose. Finkelstein uses the term "highland stronghold." If the MB lowland sites were city-states, how are we to classify the different character of towns like Shiloh, Bethel, Shechem, and more distant Hebron in sociopolitical terms?

Finkelstein attempts to estimate the manpower requisite for the construction of such highland strongholds and concludes that only a leader who held sway over a fairly extensive area, a regional "headman" or chieftain, could have amassed the necessary workforce, estimated at about 3,000 men, to accomplish such construction within a reasonable period of time. Furthermore, it would appear that no more than several dozen persons were present continuously within the small, walled area of the town, most likely officials and priests. Finally, since only eight other satellite villages are located within a radius of 5 km of Shiloh, manpower would have had to be assembled from a much wider radius.

Finkelstein proposes that there were two networks of highland strongholds in the late MB III period: in the North, Shechem was first among towns, exercising some hegemony over Shiloh and Bethel, and in the central mountain range, Jerusalem, holding the same position with respect to Hebron. At each highland stronghold, a chief of sorts held sway, and he administered the storage facilities of his town, represented at Shiloh by the row of cellars inside of the northern wall. As this hill country became populated and horticulture flourished, the lowland areas desired the produce of the vineyards and orchards of Shiloh and its environs, and an administrative structure would have come into being to control such domestic trade or exchange. Without deciding between Alt's differentiation of the lowland city-states and the highland territorial centers, and the views of Kempinsky and Naʾaman, who attribute a higher state of political development to the highland strongholds than Alt or Finkelstein, as discussed by Finkelstein in his report, it is fair to conclude that the reason for Shiloh's early existence was primarily economic, leading to the establishment of storage and redistribution centers. In a word, Shiloh was the seat of a chiefdom, with the title of city-state better reserved for Shechem, to its north.

Lawrence Stager has been studying what he refers to as "port power" in the Levantine coastal societies of the Early Bronze Age, and his insights bear on our understanding of how Shiloh and other highland centers of the Middle Bronze Age operated as redistribution centers, extending their range. Briefly stated, it can be proposed that exchange and redistribution flourished in Canaan of the Middle Bronze Age IIA (c. 2000–1550 B.C.E.) not only between the coastal lowlands and the interior mountain regions, but with the added input of ports, where imported wares and materials were shipped far inland. In the other direction, the produce of the highlands, which included timber, wine, oil, and resin, was in great demand, and was shipped down not only to the coastal lowlands, but also on to the ports for export.[15]

Moving now to the Late Bronze Age, or Stratum VI, approximately 1550–1350 B.C.E., we encounter a sizable dump in area D, associated with a cult place, as the ceramic and other evidence indicates. Finkelstein summarizes the transition from MB to LB at Shiloh in considerable detail. At the end of MB, the fortified towns were destroyed and villages abandoned, bringing an end to the large population increase and to the construction projects of MB II and III. All that remained at Shiloh was a cult place, with all economic and productive administration eliminated. This deterioration may have resulted, in part, from Egyptian activity, but also from internal factors unknown to us.

Finkelstein explains that there was a pattern of isolated cult centers, like Deir ʿAlla in the Jordan Valley at the end of the LB age, which served a nomadic population. In other words, once a site, for reasons more practical than not, had become a cult center and a place of pilgrimage, it might remain in that function even after other functions earlier associated with it had ceased. Nevertheless, indications are that when the Iron Age I settlers, whom the biblical record would classify as Israelites, arrived at Shiloh, the site had been abandoned for about two centuries.

Once again it is probable that the new population was attracted to the site of Shiloh by virtue of the same factors that account for its earlier history. Stratum V is highlighted by the pillared buildings found in area C. These are most reliably dated to the second half of the 12th and early 11th centuries B.C.E. This means that the period of Shiloh's prominence was limited to about fifty years, as the site was destroyed by the Philistines at about the middle of the 11th century. This is supported by the ceramic evidence. Because excavations could not be conducted in the southern sector, we can only speculate that the Iron Age sanctuary stood pretty much where the MB III building had. Most likely, cultic buildings covered most of the area of Stratum V, raising the question as to the extent of other activities at Iron Age I Shiloh.

Finkelstein shares the view of earlier scholars that a stone sanctuary stood at Iron Age I Shiloh, and I strongly agree. The architectural remains elsewhere on the site are representative of early Israelite construction. If Shiloh was not the only Israelite cult center in the Ephraimite hill country of early Iron Age, it was nonetheless singular in its structural indications of public cultic activity. It was a temenos. This is further reinforced by the results of the archaeological surveys

[15] By verbal communication from Lawrence Stager.

in the area, which reveal a great density of villages in the surrounding area, 26 within a radius of 5–6 km, more than in any other part of southern Samaria. What is more, it was Shiloh that promoted settlement in the surrounding area.

Much more could be said about the results of excavation and surveying, but I would rather turn my attention at this point to certain issues that interest me and concern the subject of this conference. The first observation to be made is that Israelite Shiloh had a prehistory that determined its subsequent selection by the Israelites. Initially, MB III Shiloh was selected because of its favorable location and natural and topographical environment, and represented a highland stronghold suitable for regional administration, storage, and distribution of horticultural products, as well as pastoral pursuits. The lowland communities brought agricultural products to Shiloh and received horticultural products from Shiloh, which was not, after all, a real town in the social sense; it was not a community.

We may now venture some concluding observations. There is a cyclic aspect to the archaeological history of Shiloh. As already noted, during the lull of the LB age, large amounts of votive objects were deposited at the site even though it was not in operation. Then, the Israelites came, and there was economic development and significant cultic activity, as well, for a brief period. Soon Shiloh was again destroyed. There followed a period of abandonment, but some activity was resumed at Shiloh in late Iron Age II, during the seventh and possibly eighth century. Buildings were built on the terrace to the north of the mound at the end of the Iron Age, but there is not adequate evidence to determine the extent of activity there. Shiloh was definitely in decline compared with the general increase in settlement in southern Samaria. When Jeremiah taunted his listeners (Jeremiah 7, 26:6) that what had happened to Shiloh would happen to Jerusalem and its temple, his listeners knew whereof he spoke: Shiloh would never rise again, although some cultic activity may have persisted there, as is suggested by the strange incident recounted in Jeremiah 41 about eighty men who came from Shechem, Shiloh, and Samaria to offer incense at the temple in Jerusalem.

What interests me most about the history of Shiloh is that it illustrates the virtual permanence of the sanctity that attaches to cult sites. The iconoclasm commanded by Deuteronomy 12:2–3, aside from the fact that it represents later, eighth century B.C.E. northern Israelite ideology, actually does not require the abandonment of pre-Israelite pagan cult sites, nor probably the razing of cultic edifices. After a general dictum about destroying the *meqômôt*, "cult sites," where the nations worshipped, the text goes on to specify what this meant: "You shall smash their altars, and break down their cultic stelae, and their ʾAsherah-posts shall you burn in fire, and the statues of their gods shall you cut down, and you shall annihilate their name from that site." The specifications do not include the buildings, necessarily, and certainly not the ground.

The question has been debated extensively, but to me it is obvious that sacred ground remained sacred, and that early Israelites repaired to previously operating cult sites like Shiloh and Bethel, and undoubtedly Shechem and Hebron and other sites. Of course, the same economic and administrative factors that had initially determined site selection continued to apply, but prior site-sanctity also figured significantly. What is important is that previous idolatrous activity did not deter Israelites from rebuilding older sites; nothing in their religious outlook kept them away from such sites as Bethel, a notable example of the very cyclic process of which we are speaking. Sanctity of space was not religion-specific.

The *locus classicus* is Jacob's experience at Bethel recounted in Genesis 28, a *hieros logos* of that major, northern Israelite cult center, where in the mid-eighth century the prophet Amos spoke. The tale is told as if Jacob merely happened upon the *māqôm*, "cult site," for that is what this Hebrew term means in certain contexts and probably what it connotes here, not simply "place." In other words, if read carefully, even the biblical version implies that Jacob was aware that the site had been sacred, but was probably unaware initially that Yahweh, his clan deity, was present there.

Admittedly, some ambiguity remains in the narrative, but certain implications seem clear enough. That the author perceived the site to be in ruins when the incident occurred is suggested by relating that Jacob gathered stones to serve as a makeshift shelter. When Jacob awakens, he is overcome with the awareness that Yahweh is present at the cult site, and that he was at the site of a temple, *bêt ʾelôhîm*, a gate to heaven. To be precise, he exclaims as follows: "'In fact, Yahweh is present at this cult site, but I had not known.' He experienced fear, and said: 'How awesome is this cult site. This is none other than a divine temple, and this is the gate to heaven.'" In other words, Jacob knew the site was cultic, but did not realize that his own God was present there until his dream informed him of this.

Jacob proceeds to erect a cultic stela, a *maṣṣēbāh*, which he consecrates by anointing it with oil, and he names the site *bêt ʾĒl*, thereby alluding to his participation in the El cult. Again referring to Elohim instead of Yahweh, Jacob vows a tithe to the temple to be built there, if Elohim protects him and restores him to his home; proclaiming that henceforth Yahweh shall be his Elohim.

Can we synthesize this tale, charged as it is with religious perceptions, with the archaeological history of Bethel? The pre-Israelite background of Bethel differed somewhat from that of Shiloh, though both had an extensive pre-Israelite history as cult centers. According to Albright and Kelso, who published their final report in 1968, Bethel, in contrast to Shiloh, which had been uninhabited for two centuries before the Israelites arrived, was indeed occupied during the Late Bronze Age, more extensively in the earlier phase, prior to the thirteenth century B.C.E.[16] This came after an extensive urban, cultic history during the Middle Bronze Age, at a site whose history reaches back to c. 3200 B.C.E. And yet, excavations show a major conflagration at the end of the Late Bronze Age, as well as what Albright and Kelso call "a cultural break" between LB II and Iron I evidenced in masonry, ceramics, and architecture. Although I sense

[16] See Albright and Kelso 1968, especially: "The History of Bethel," 45–53.

that Albright and Kelso may have attributed too much historicity to the Joshua traditions, it is remarkable to what an extent the account in Jud 1:22–26, telling of the Josephite conquest of Bethel, dovetails with Genesis 28. Whereas the former is more historical in its focus, telling of the conquest of the town by an Israelite tribe, the Genesis account is more religious in its concern with the legitimacy of the cult of Bethel. It is quite possible that the author of Genesis 28 was projecting the pre-Israelite phase after the LB II destruction, when the site lay in ruins, attempting to explain the Israelite rebuilding of the site in cultic perspective by attributing the origin of the major northern Israelite temple at Bethel to one of the Patriarchs.

Quite clearly, Bethel had been one of the major, preexistent cult sites in Canaan, where altars with blood on them have been found and which lay in ruins when the Israelites arrived on the scene. It was, if our reading of the Bethel etiology is correct, a site recognized for its sanctity. It was consequently rebuilt for the same practical reasons that account for its long history as a major town, primarily its location on major roadways, and was concurrently appropriated as an Israelite cult center. I could say more about the El toponymic and the early development of Yahwism as reflected in Genesis 28, but that would carry us far afield.

Here it is relevant to suggest that this is what happened historically in the case of Shiloh, as we now know. In fact, there was a chain of early Israelite cult centers located at sites where MB towns, and in the case of Bethel, an LB town had stood. These had been destroyed and were rebuilt by the Israelites. These sites include Shechem, Bethel, Shiloh, and Hebron (Tel Rumeidah), and probably others.

The subsequent histories of the various sites differed, of course. We are told that the Ark moved to Jerusalem after a Judean named David established that town as his capital, and when the Jerusalem temple was built. Soon after, Judah and Israel again went their separate ways. As Ps 78 puts it: Yahweh became enraged at the religious aberrations of northern Israel, their *bāmôt* and idols, and abandoned the sanctuary of Shiloh in favor of Jerusalem, choosing Judah and the House of David, and manifesting his presence on Mt. Zion, which he loves. In sharp contrast, Bethel enjoyed a period of growth and prominence in Iron Age II and was destroyed only c. 724 B.C.E. by the Assyrians. Near the end of the Assyrian period, after remaining unoccupied, the shrine was apparently put into service again, for whom it is not clear, perhaps for the foreigners settled there. It was the necropolis located at Bethel that Josiah, king of Judah, destroyed after annexing it in 622 B.C.E. (2 Kings 23:15–20).

Conclusions

I would question whether any biblical towns owed their origin to temples, or to some sacred significance originally attached to them, although if we had more information we might find priestly towns with such a history. Even in such instances, we would have to ask why temples were built where they were. Unless we are speaking of far-off peak shrines or distant desert retreats, most temples and smaller cult installations were located where human activity thrived, not the reverse. It occurs to me that Shiloh, before its actual, pre-Israelite history became known, was thought by some to have been selected for other than practical reasons, because it does not lie directly on a main road, like Bethel or Shechem. Now it turns out that it first served as a mountain stronghold and redistribution center governed by a headman, or petty ruler, to whom a network of villages was subservient. For such purposes, it was well situated. The cultic significance of Shiloh derived from its practical significance, but once this sanctification took hold, it survived the practical fortunes of the site in the LB age. It is estimated that cultic functions may have actually predominated in the early Israelite period, and thereafter. The case of Shiloh cautions us against positing a unified theory of the formation of cities, and suggests that there are many interacting factors to be considered. Ultimately, only the archaeological history of a site can tell us how the city was founded. What is most telling about Shiloh is that it was not a city, in the sense of being a community.

From investigating the subject of towns of asylum we learn that the presence of a temple could secondarily determine the character of a town, and make it appropriate for specific functions that would not have accrued to it had no sacred institution been associated with it at a fairly early stage. This nexus is recast in the later alignment of the towns of asylum with the priestly and Levitical towns, which were distributed accessibly in various regions of the country. In a word, local priests, Levites and other cultic functionaries were assigned new tasks.

The city has a future in the biblical plan for a better world society. Nineveh repented, in Jonah's parable if not in reality, and was consequently spared. Isaiah informed the citizens of Jerusalem c. 701 B.C.E. what it would take for that temple city truly to become the City of God, a phase of urban perfection to which we have not yet arrived as the second millennium of the present era draws to a close.

Bibliography

Aharoni, Y., and M. Avi-Yonah

1993 *The Macmillan Bible Atlas*, 3rd Edition, with A. F. Rainey, Z. Safrai. New York: Macmillan Publishing Company; Jerusalem: Carta.

Albright, W. F., and J. Kelso

1968 *The Excavation of Bethel (1934–1960). AASOR* 39. Cambridge, MA: American Schools of Oriental Research.

Finkelstein, I.

1993 *Shiloh: The Archaeology of a Biblical Site*, with Sh. Bunimovitz, Z. Edelman, et al. Monograph Series of the Institute of Archaeology 10. Ramat Aviv: Tel Aviv University.

Levine, B. A.

1963 The Netînîm. *JBL* 82:207–212.

1978 The Temple Scroll: Aspects of its Historical Provenance and Literary Character. *BASOR* 232:4–25 {*VOL 1, PP. 171–200*}.

1993 On the Semantics of Land Tenure in Biblical Literature: The Term *ʾaḥuzzāh*. Pages 134–39 in M. Cohen, *et al.* (eds.), *The Tablet and the Scroll (Near Eastern Studies in Honor of William W Hallo)*. Bethesda, MD: CDL Press {*VOL 2, PP. 141–51*}.

Levy, J.

1963 *Wörterbuch über die Talmudim und Midraschim*. 4 vols. Darmstadt: Wissenschaftliche Buchgesellschaft.

Rofé, A.

1986 The History of the Cities of Refuge in Biblical Law. Pages 205–239 in S. Japhet (ed.), *Studies in Bible*. ScrHier 31. Jerusalem: Hebrew University-Magnes Press.

The View from Jerusalem: Biblical Responses to the Babylonian Presence*

The Hebrew Bible exhibits a strong awareness of the presence of Babylonia on the international scene, and more poignantly, of its direct impact on the destiny of Jerusalem and Judah during a brief, but crucial period of Ancient Near Eastern history.[1] The Neo-Babylonian king, Nebuchadnezzar II, destroyed Jerusalem, devastated major areas of the country, and exiled large numbers of Judeans to Babylonia in a series of military campaigns. These began at the very end of the seventh century B.C.E, and reached their climax in 586 B.C.E. with the complete destruction of Jerusalem and the central Temple. This brought an end to the kingdom of Judah, and to the period of the First Temple, as it is known in biblical studies. It is only to be expected that these historically definitive events, and the circumstances leading up to them, as well as those resulting from them, should have commanded the full attention of biblical writers.

It would have been possible to include in our discussion a review of significant cross-cultural connections between ancient Israel and Mesopotamia, in the areas of law, religion, government, and shared literary genres. To do so in the present instance would, however, require a complex differentiation between specifically Babylonian and more generally Mesopotamian cultural features. It is also to be understood that some of what was thought of as Mesopotamian is actually Syrian, or western, and that the flow of culture was not unidirectional, from east to west. It was decided, therefore, to adopt an historical approach that is structured by identifiable events, leaving an assessment of the extent of Babylonian cultural impact on ancient Israel for another occasion.

The actual history of Babylonia, of its conquests and international policies, its downfall and legacy, are being treated in the various chapters of this volume. The view from Jerusalem deals with responses to, and interpretations of, Babylonian domination in the west, particularly in Judah and the neighboring territories, such as have been preserved in the Hebrew Bible. The current availability of contemporary Babylonian documents, and of other extra-biblical sources, has greatly reduced dependence on information provided by the Hebrew Bible in reconstructing Babylonian history per se, although the Hebrew Bible does, in fact, contain historical information.

---

* Originally published in Gwendolyn Leick (ed.), *The Babylonian World* (New York and London: Routledge, 2007), pp. 541–561. Reprinted with permission from Taylor & Francis Books.

[1] I am grateful to my esteemed colleague, Hayim Tadmor, for his learned critique of an earlier draft of this study.

Biblical literature has a different perspective to offer the historian. In narratives, chronicles, and prophecies we hear the voices of the threatened and beleaguered, of the defeated and conquered; aspects of history that are often absent from the plentiful sources that speak for the major powers, themselves. There is an additional insight to be gained from biblical literature in this regard: it exposes conflicts within the Judean society, itself, usually between prophets and kings (also, "true prophets" versus "false prophets"!), with the true prophets assuming the posture of opposition to royal policy, not that of sanctioning it. The tension of such encounters, in the vortex of national tragedy, is not muted. To the contrary, the relevant issues are dramatized, thereby producing the outlines of a domestic debate on foreign policy.

We will zoom-in on the busy period of twenty-three years, from the death of Josiah, king of Judah, at the hand of Pharaoh Necho II at Megiddo in 609 B.C.E. to the final destruction by the forces of Nebuchadnezzar II, king of Babylonia in 586 B.C.E. The principal biblical sources to be explored here are Second Kings, followed by Jeremiah and Habakkuk, with some attention to other texts, as well. Biblical texts have been subjected to redaction and rearrangement, and contain later and/or secondary material. The interest here is not, however, in the formation of biblical literature, but primarily, in *Sitz-im-Leben*, in the posture and frame of mind that can account for the versions of the events and their interpretation, as these are presented in the Hebrew Bible. The intention is to allow the Hebrew Bible to tell its story, supplying historical information from other sources where available.

The presence of Babylonia continues to be felt in biblical literature covering the period after 586 B.C.E., up to the downfall of Babylonia in the mid-sixth century B.C.E., and during the decades of the Babylonian Exile. In the oracles of Ezekiel and those of the post-exilic period as well as in Chronicles, we encounter a good deal of hindsight and reflection. Thus it is that the life and fate of the last king of Babylonia, Nabonidus, continued to fascinate biblical and post-biblical writers for centuries to come, and tales about the last days of Babylon inform the Book of Daniel.[2]

BABYLONIA IN THE BOOK OF KINGS: HISTORY FILTERED THROUGH IDEOLOGY

Some biblical background

In Genesis, chapters 1–11, the so-called "Primeval History," Babylon is numbered among the most ancient towns in the land of Shinar (*Šinʿār*), a traditional name for Babylonia (Gen 10:10, 11:2; cf. Gen 14:1, 9, Isa 11:11, Zech 5:11, Dan 1:2). Babylon is listed alongside such venerable sites as Akkad, Uruk, Aššur, and Nineveh. We are told that the post-diluvian humans undertook to build a town with a tower in the land of Shinar, which they named Babel, indicating that

[2] Having found no single Bible translation that is, in my view, both felicitous and precise in all instances, I have adopted the practice of translating all citations from the Hebrew Bible afresh, with considerable help from existing translations.

in the Israelite consciousness Babylon symbolized the beginnings of urbanization. Genesis 14:1–17 relate that Amraphel, king of Shinar, was one of four foreign kings, among them the king of Elam, who attacked the five kings with whom Abram was allied. This biblical account, which shows signs of great antiquity, portrays pre-Israelite Canaan as a battleground that attracted foreign armies.

The first historiographic reference to Babylonia, albeit tangential, comes in 2 Kings 17:24, 30–34a, where we read that the king of Assyria, after exiling large numbers of northern Israelites to far-off lands, settled foreigners in Samaria in their place. Among those foreigners were people from Babylon and nearby Cutha, as well as those from towns in Syria. The biblical writer, whenever he wrote, was providing a geographical "spread," as if to say that foreigners from all over the Assyrian Empire had been settled in Samaria.

In Isa 14:4, a caption introducing the famous oracle on the demise of an arrogant imperial king addresses *melek Bābel* "the king of Babylon/Babylonia," but this is misleading. Isa 14:4–23 follow directly upon a late oracle on the downfall of Babylonia, and a prediction of Israel's restoration (Isa 13:1–14:2). This placement may have something to do with the reference to the king of Babylonia in Isa 14:42. However, the content of Isa 14:4–23 suggests that the oracle refers to an Assyrian king, most likely Sargon II, who was killed in battle and left unburied. The oracle of Isa 14:4–23 is not, therefore, directly relevant to Babylonian history, though it does tell us a lot about biblical perceptions of Assyria.

Merodach-Baladan II and Hezekiah

The first official contact registered between the two entities, Babylonia and Judah, was on the diplomatic level. It pertains to a delegation sent by Merodach-Baladan II of Babylonia to Hezekiah, King of Judah in Jerusalem, as reported in 2 Kings 20:12–13 and Isaiah 39:1–2 (cf. 2 Chron 32:31). John Brinkman (1964) has provided a detailed review of the life and role of this Babylonian leader, a veteran fomenter of anti-Assyrian rebellion. The respective passages in 2 Kings 20:12–21 and Isaiah 39, are virtually identical, except for the postscript in 2 Kings 20:20–21, and it is likely that Second Kings was the source for the Isaiah passages. Although there is little reason to question the essential historicity of this report, the precise circumstances surrounding the event are blurred by the larger literary context in which it is imbedded. Both in Second Kings and in Isaiah, the arrival of the Babylonian delegation is placed subsequent to the sparing of Jerusalem and the Assyrian blockade of 701 B.C.E., which makes no sense chronologically. The event surely would have occurred prior to 701 B.C.E., although scholarly opinion has been divided as to precisely when.

Mordechai Cogan and Hayim Tadmor (1988:258–265) argue that the mission sent by Merodach-Baladan II would have arrived in 714/713, the fourteenth year of Hezekiah's reign, which had begun in 727/726 B.C.E. The annals of Sargon II relate that at this very time rebellion was fomenting in Ashdod of Philistia, and Judeans are listed among the groups involved in such activity. Cogan and Tadmor consider it unlikely that Merodach-Baladan would have been able to mount a delegation to Judah in the brief nine months of his later comeback during the early years of Sennacherib. In contrast, John Brinkman (1964:31–35) accepts the view of Sidney Smith, and others, that the delegation from Merodach-Baladan II to Hezekiah arrived about fifteen years before Hezekiah's death, which occurred in 687 B.C.E., hence, between 704–702, precisely during that brief period when Merodach-Baladan staged his comeback. After the death of Sargon II in battle in 705, Hezekiah rebelled, and there were rumblings throughout the empire before Sennacherib's third campaign to Judah and the West, delayed until 701 B.C.E.

How was such an event remembered? The stated occasion for the delegation was Hezekiah's illness; word of which had reached the Babylonian ruler. The Babylonians presented their credentials (Hebrew *sepārîm*), as well as proffering gifts, termed *minḥāh* which is the usual word for "tribute," thereby intimating esteem for Hezekiah's elevated status. Much is made of the fact that Hezekiah showed the legation all of his vast treasures. The Babylonian legation is portrayed as obsequious, and Hezekiah—as boastful.

Enter the prophet Isaiah, who had, according to the narrative sequence, just announced to an ailing Hezekiah that he would be granted a new lease on life. A dubious Isaiah now engages Hezekiah in conversation about the Babylonians visiting from a far-off land. He issues the dire prediction, implicitly critical of Hezekiah, that all of the treasures that the Babylonian messengers had been shown would be transported to Babylon in days to come, and that his princely descendants would become servile courtiers in the palace of the king of Babylonia. The real reason for the delegation to Hezekiah was, ostensibly, Merodach-Baladan's interest in securing Hezekiah's collaboration against Assyria, either against Sargon II or Sennacherib, as the case may be. The message of this narrative, and of Isaiah's prophecy of punishment in kind, is that collaboration with Babylonia in rebellion against Assyria was counter to the will of Yahweh, God of Israel. To whatever extent Hezekiah may have collaborated with Babylonia, and despite his rebellion of 705 B.C.E., he heeded Isaiah's counsel and ultimately submitted to the Assyrian yoke, after all. This accommodation enabled Jerusalem and Judah to survive for a century, albeit in a state of dependency.

In an earlier study (Levine 2005), we argued that this prophetic doctrine, one of submission to Assyria and avoidance of foreign alliances against her, was, indeed, promulgated by First Isaiah in the context of the Assyrian threat to Jerusalem and Judah during the early years of Sennacherib. In response to imperialism on a grand scale, First Isaiah taught that Assyrian world domination was part of Yahweh's plan for the entire earth, and that, eventually, Assyria would also fall (Isa 14:24–27). Assyria was Yahweh's "rod of rage," his instrument for punishing Israel (Isa 10:5–10). A sign that Yahweh controlled the destiny of nations, large and small, was the unexpected sparing of Jerusalem in 701 B.C.E. As will be shown, this doctrine gained acceptance in prophetic circles, and is prominent in the writings of Jeremiah (note, as a prime example, Jeremiah, chapter 27), where it is applied to Babylonia during the reign of Nebuchadnezzar II.

As has been suggested by Cogan and Tadmor, the passages reporting on the Babylonian mission were most probably composed at that later time, between 598–586, during the reign of Zedekiah. This was after the first wave of exile under Jehoiachin, when the temple treasury was actually plundered, and when privileged and skilled elements of the population were deported. In literary terms, what was predicted in 2 Kings 20:12–21 is reported, in similar words, as having been fulfilled in 2 Kings 24:8–17, particularly, in verse 13. Isaiah's "prediction" is thus to be regarded as retrospective, making of the report on the Babylonian mission, itself, a product of the Neo-Babylonian period, when the actual enemy was Babylonia, not Assyria.

This textual analysis would explain the tension between (1) Isaiah's entreaty to Yahweh to grant Hezekiah an extension of life, and his assurance that Jerusalem would be defended against Assyrian destruction (2 Kings 20:1–11), and (2) Isaiah's implied criticism of Hezekiah, expressed in the prediction of the future Babylonian invasion, immediately following (2 Kings 20:12–21). The former announcement bespeaks divine approval of Hezekiah, granting him a reward for his last-minute submission to Assyria in obedience to Yahweh. As such, it may be seen as expressing a contemporary reaction to the sparing of Jerusalem, one consonant with Isaiah's ideology. In contrast, the latter passage reflects the ideology of a later period; specifically, the horrific consequences of Jehoiakim's rebellion (see further). It seizes upon an episode from Hezekiah's reign that had presaged, as it were, the later disaster. Unlike the threat to Judah in Hezekiah's time, it would not be averted. And yet, criticism of Hezekiah is muted; he is not blamed for the future catastrophe, as was his son and successor, Manasseh, because he was a king who had done what was upright in Yahweh's sight.

The mission of Merodach-Baladan II was of little historical importance, as it turned out. And yet, the report in 2 Kings 20 provides a valuable test-case by which to identify the ideological agenda of the biblical writers and redactors who produced the Book of Kings. Rather than fixing on the cultic and moral evaluations of the Judean kings, this report directs our attention to the primary political issue in the prophetic agenda: rebellions against world empires, or alliances and coalitions formed against them, threatened the survival of the Israelites in the land.

Nebuchadnezzar II and the last kings of Judah

The chronicle of events presented in Second Kings pertaining to the reign of Nebuchadnezzar II, and the years leading up to it, is admittedly skeletal. It is fairly accurate as far as it goes, but it is very short on background. The interpretations given to events and the ideology that peers through the narrative are most often stated in brief, formulaic fashion, and give the impression of condensed, prophetic utterances. Thus, Robert Wilson on the overall composition of the Book of Kings:

> Of course, it is always possible that, as a composite work, Kings makes no general points and has no overarching themes ... However, even the most enthusiastic proponents of literary analysis rarely push the argument this far, and almost all scholars see the book as tied together by a complex of overarching themes or motifs. The most frequent account of this thematic unity points to the evaluations made by the editors in the formulaic statements used to introduce and to conclude the reigns of individual Israelite and Judean kings. (Wilson 1995:85)

In reporting the rapidly changing political situation after the fall of the Neo-Assyrian Empire in the late seventh century B.C.E., Second Kings follows the alternating pattern of submission and rebellion on the part of the last Judean kings with respect to both Egypt and Babylonia. To understand this pattern requires knowledge well beyond what the Hebrew Bible provides. An excellent treatment of the shifting international scene, as Judah was caught in the crossfire between Egypt and Babylonia, is that of D.J. Wiseman, *Nebuchadrezzar and Babylon* (1983). Viewing history from the Babylonian perspective, Wiseman fully integrates the biblical data into the overall scheme of things, as he summarizes the valuable information provided by the Babylonian Chronicle Series ("Chronicles of the Chaldean Kings"), which he edited (Wiseman 1956, and see Grayson 1975a). Chronicle 5 records Babylonian military campaigns, and related royal activities, between the years 608–594 B.C.E.

Among other things, the Chronicle highlights the events surrounding 605 B.C.E., and clarifies just how and why Egyptian power waned after the defeat by the armies of Babylonia at the battle of Carchemish; a major event in Ancient Near Eastern history. We now see the importance of the caption in Jeremiah 46:2:

> Against Egypt, against the forces of Pharaoh Necho, king of Egypt, which happened at the river Euphrates, whom Nebuchadnezzar, king of Babylonia defeated (Hebrew: *hikkāh* "struck, destroyed") in the fourth year of Jehoiakim, son of Josiah, king of Judah.
>
> (cf. Jer 47:7)

A penetrating interpretation of the view from Judah and Jerusalem, looking outward, has been contributed by A. Malamat in a series of studies now reappearing in his *History of Biblical Israel* (2001:277–337; 381–386). Here is what Malamat has to say about the political situation affecting Judah towards the end of the seventh century B.C.E. when there was a power vacuum after the Assyrian demise in Hatti, a term used in Babylonian sources to designate the Levant:

> In Political Science terms, Judah was now poignantly caught up in a bi-polar system, meaning that the exclusive control of international politics was concentrated in two powers, solely responsible for preserving peace or making war ... Once the equilibrium is disturbed or

> upset by one of the partners seeking hegemony, the secondary power, lacking sufficient economic and military potential, turns to inexpensive diplomatic means to alleviate its plight ... Such was the fate of Judah. (Malamat 2001:325–326, with deletions)

Malamat goes on to review in detail no less than six shifts in policy, between reliance on Egypt and vassalage to Babylonia, all in the twenty-three-year period from 609 to 586 B.C.E. In the mode of a "maximalist," he elicits from every nuance of the biblical record information that fills in what is missing from it based on our present knowledge. One of the insights deriving from the studies of Malamat, and others, is a better understanding of the persisting tendency on the part of the last kings of Judah to turn to Egypt in the expectation of support against Babylonia. Such support kept coming, although it never held off the Babylonians for very long.

Reading Anthony Spalinger's review of Egyptian history from 620–550 B.C.E. (1977), together with the detailed study by K.S. Freedy and Donald B. Redford (1970), one comes to realize that, although Egyptian power was limited during this period, Egypt remained a major player in Eastern Mediterranean affairs. Freedy and Redford set out to corroborate the dates provided in the Book of Ezekiel, which often refers to events of the reign of Zedekiah but, in the course of doing so, shed light from Egyptian sources on the choices faced by the last Judean king. Babylonia, for all of its power, was far away, as we are constantly reminded, whereas Egypt was very close by. Like other vast empires, the Babylonians were being chronically beset by trouble in other regions, so that "secondary" powers might reasonably hope to break free of domination when a window of opportunity appeared. Emissaries visiting Egypt were bound to be awed by its gold and riches, which far exceeded anything they had seen. After all, Jeremiah 37, among other biblical sources, reports that Egyptian forces, which we know to have been under Pharaoh Apries, brought temporary relief to Jerusalem even during its final, long siege. The Hebrew Bible sees things from the prophetic point of view, which, as it turned out, was validated by subsequent events, but we are not to assume that, at the time, the last kings of Judah were simply acting out of recalcitrance in their repetitive, anti-Babylonian policies.

The reader is directed to other studies that shed light on Judah's tenuous situation. Anson Rainey (1975) brings to bear archaeological evidence, especially that pertaining to Lachish, on the phases of the Babylonian conquest of Judah. The relevance of the sparse, but highly informative epigraphic finds at Lachish and Arad, and of the Adon inscription, has long been recognized, ever since W.F. Albright (1936) called attention to the importance of epigraphy for biblical history. Most recently, Lawrence Stager (1996) has provided preliminary archaeological information on Nebuchadnezzar's campaign of 604–603 B.C.E. on the Levantine coast, particularly at Ashkelon, and Jean-Baptiste Humbert (by verbal communication) has now discovered evidence of Nebuchadnezzar's destruction level at Gaza (cf. Jer 47:1–7). Finally, the historically oriented Anchor Bible commentary on II Kings, by Cogan and Tadmor (1988), provides, along with its careful interpretation of the text, a succinct and detailed review of the events of the period, correlated with the evidence of the Babylonian Chronicle Series, and, as well, with the historical references in the Book of Jeremiah.

Let us then return to the biblical record in Second Kings. Nebuchadnezzar II comes on stage in 2 Kings 24:1, at the point when Jehoiakim, king of Judah, who had been his vassal for three years, probably between 604 and 602, rebelled against him. Previously, Jehoiakim had been a faithful vassal of Pharaoh Necho II for most of his eleven-year reign (2 Kings 23:35). Second Kings 23:29–30 had reported that during the reign of Josiah, Necho set out for the Euphrates to the King of Assyria, ostensibly to assist his ally against the Babylonians by gaining hegemony over areas in Hatti. After the major defeat of the Egyptian forces at the battle of Carchemish in 605 B.C.E., Nebuchadnezzar marched through Judah as part of his larger effort to gain control of the whole area. This is the import of the statement in 2 Kings 24:7 to the effect that the king of Egypt undertook no further campaigns outside of his country, having lost his former hegemony to the king of Babylonia. And so, Jehoiakim switched allegiance to the king of Babylonia.

Several years later, Jehoiakim saw a chance to break free of Nebuchadnezzar after that king's debacle at the hands of the Egyptians in the winter of 601/600, when, as we know from the Babylonian Chronicle Series, Nebuchadnezzar attempted to attack Egypt, proper, and was forced to withdraw to Babylon. After regrouping, Nebuchadnezzar returned and attacked Judah punitively, using diverse troops that were positioned in the west. Jehoiakim may have died in these battles, for there is no credible record of his having been taken to Babylon. In 2 Kings 23:37, Jehoiakim is given the usual, bad report card: he, like his royal ancestors, did what was evil in Yahweh's sight. Here is how the text of 2 Kings 24:2–4 explains the results of Jehoiakim's mistaken strategy:

> Then Yahweh let loose bands of Chaldeans, Arameans, Moabites and Ammonites against him, He let them loose against Judah to destroy it, in accordance with the word of Yahweh spoken though His servants, the prophets. Moreover, it was by Yahweh's command that this happened in Judah, to remove them from his presence because of the sins of Manasseh, because of all that he had done. And as well, the innocent blood that he shed, filling Jerusalem with innocent blood, and Yahweh was unwilling to forgive …

This passage illustrates the two dimensions of the biblical record in Second Kings which will be encountered repeatedly: the political, and the theological, with the former flowing into the latter. Viewed politically, Nebuchadnezzar's attacks against Judah were triggered by Jehoiakim's rebellion, which could mean anything from armed resistance, to refusal to pay tribute, to giving aid and comfort to the Egyptians. The references to rebellion (the Hebrew verb *mārad*), here and subsequently in 2 Kings 24:20 relevant to Zedekiah's later rebellion, relate to the prophetic doctrine outlined above, according to which submission to Babylonia, as to Assyria at an earlier time, was Yahweh's will. In this spirit, we read explicit statements to the effect that it was Yahweh who launched the attacks against Judah, not Nebuchadnezzar and his forces, and that this catastrophe was in fulfillment of the warnings transmitted by Yahweh's servants, the prophets. This prophetic theme is developed to its fullest in Jeremiah, as we shall observe presently. It is tragic to learn that it was already Yahweh's intent during the reign of Jehoiakim to terminate Judah by exiling the people, which is what is meant by saying that Yahweh would "remove (them) from his presence" (2 Kings 24:3; and see Levine 2007).

As regards the theological, or "cultic-moral" dimension of the prophetic ideology, expressed in the above citation, it would be well to comment on the literary function of the cliché "the sins of Manasseh," which occurs in the cited passage. Similar formulaic statements had been interpolated earlier on so as to "foresee," as it were, the loss of the northern kingdom of Israel to the Assyrians (2 Kings 17:7–23, cf. 1 Kings 11:29–39). The link between the two phases, the Assyrian and the Babylonian, is provided, precisely, by Isaiah's prediction to Hezekiah in 2 Kings 20:17–19, discussed above. Such retrospective footnotes served to create an atmosphere of foreboding and anticipation. In 2 Kings 21:10–18, Manasseh, king of Judah and Hezekiah's successor, is effectively blamed for Yahweh's eventual abandonment of his own people, who will be handed over into the power of their enemies (2 Kings 21:14a).

At this point, the enemies are not yet specified as Babylonians, or Chaldeans, but there is no doubt about who is meant. The same motif of abandonment by Yahweh accounts for the brief interpolation in 2 Kings 23:26–27 to the effect that despite Josiah's repentance, his "turning back" (the Hebrew verb *šûb*) from the sins of Manasseh, Yahweh did not "turn back" from his anger at Judah. That statement rationalizes Judah's eventual downfall as punishment for the earlier sins of Manasseh, not those of Josiah, himself. It is as if to say: even Josiah's cultic reforms, religiously correct as they were, could not assuage Yahweh's wrath.

Of both Manasseh (2 Kings 21:16) and Jehoiakim (2 Kings 24:4) it is said that they had shed "innocent blood," a moral and social indictment. Immediately preceding the attribution of Judah's downfall to Manasseh, 2 Kings 21:1–10 enumerate the many cultic, or religious sins of that king. Manasseh's sins comprise a catalogue of almost every kind of paganism, idolatry, and religious disloyalty known in biblical literature! Once these had been enumerated, it became possible to refer generically to "the sins of Manasseh." It is of interest to note that the principal post hoc statements on the earlier fall of the Northern Kingdom of Israel, namely, 1 Kings 11:29–39, 14:5–16, and 2 Kings 17:7–29, characterize Jeroboam I in the same way. He was the "original sinner" of northern Israel, just as Manasseh was of Judah (cf. 2 Kings 16:3–4 regarding the sins of Ahaz).

The present study deals with biblical views of the Babylonians, whereas the cultic-moral agenda is basically a self-critical, internal agenda directed at the Israelites, themselves, and need not occupy us for too long. Suffice it to say that it was a primary thrust of the prophetic movement from its inception to insist that the God of Israel demands a just society, and condemns the shedding of innocent blood. This principle was likewise encoded in biblical law. There is nothing unrealistic about prophetic denunciations of social injustice and lawlessness in Judah, and earlier, in the Northern Israelite society. The rich and powerful were grabbing land from the debt-ridden poor, and were bribing judges, who often condemned the innocent. Nor was there any lack of cultic heterodoxy, for that matter. It was basic to the prophetic doctrine to insist on the exclusive worship of Yahweh, the God of Israel, to eliminate foreign worship, and, as the Deuteronomic movement progressed, even to ban sacrifice at local *bāmôt* "cult sites," When these dictates are violated, the God of Israel becomes angry, so that moral and cultic offenses become part of the explanation of defeat. It bears mention that, like the political agenda, so the cultic-moral agenda speaks primarily of royal policy, fixing accountability on the Judean kings; at an earlier time, on the kings of Northern Israel.

And so, the royal chronicle in Second Kings continues. Jehoiakim was succeeded by another of Josiah's sons, Jechoniah, renamed Jehoiachin, who ruled for only three months. Because Jehoiachin surrendered to Nebuchadnezzar in 597 B.C.E., Jerusalem was not razed to the ground, although the exile to Babylonia began, of the skilled and the professional military, as well as of the king, himself, and his entire court, leaving only the poor peasantry. Except for his idiomatic characterization as a king who did what was evil in Yahweh's sight, Jehoiachin warrants only an oblique reference to disobedience in 2 Kings 24:13–16. In that passage, Isaiah's "prediction" of 2 Kings 20:16–18, that Jerusalem's treasures will be plundered, is fulfilled in Jehoiachin's day, and the description of the plundering resonates clearly with the passage in 2 Kings 20. Nebuchadnezzar then installed Zedekiah, Jehoiachin's uncle, previously named Mattaniah, as king in place of Jehoiachin. His eleven-year reign is introduced in 2 Kings 24:18–20 as follows:

> He did what was evil in Yahweh's sight just like all that Jehoiakim had done. For it was because of Yahweh's wrath that these things happened in Judah and Jerusalem, until he (finally) cast them off from his presence. Then Zedekiah rebelled against the king of Babylonia.

Second Kings 25:1–21 proceeds to chronicle the reign of Zedekiah (compare Jeremiah 39 and 52), employing synchronic regnal years, so that Nebuchadnezzar's siege of Jerusalem extended from the ninth to the eleventh years of Zedekiah, whereas it was in the nineteenth year of Nebuchadnezzar that his commander, Nebuzaradan, completed the destruction of Jerusalem and the burning of the Temple. Before that, when the city was breached, Zedekiah and his entourage had tried to escape by the Arabah road but he was caught, brought to Nebuchadnezzar at Riblah, his sons slaughtered in his presence, and he himself blinded.

One detail of the account warrants special attention. Reference is to 2 Kings 25:6 (cf. Jer 39:5, 52:9), which records Zedekiah's capture in flight. The Chaldean troops overtook Zedekiah near Jericho, and brought him to Nebuchadnezzar at Riblah, where the Babylonian king "laid down the law to him," Hebrew: *wayyedabberû ʾittô mišpāṭ*, literally: "They spoke judgments with him." This distinctive idiom (also in the singular: *wayyedabbēr* "he spoke," and cf. the variant in Jer 1:16) is used elsewhere to characterize how the prophet speaks the harsh truth to the people (Jer 4:12) and to how he demands divine justice (Jer 12:1). Zedekiah had violated his oath of vassalage to Nebuchadnezzar, which accounts for usage of the term *mišpāṭîm* "judgments," and implies punitive action on the part of the suzerain. Hence, Cogan and Tadmor (1988:317) translate: "They passed sentence upon him." The description of the disposition of the temple decorations and furnishings is a litany of plunder in all of its detail, reminiscent of Assyrian and Babylonian royal inscriptions, especially the royal annals. Acts of brutality are recorded graphically, but dispassionately. The chronicle closes in 2 Kings 25:21b with the words: "Then Judah went into exile from his land."

We note that 2 Kings 25:1–21 are free of the cultic-moral ideology, sticking to the tragic consequences of rebellion pursuant to the political agenda of the prophets. That is undoubtedly why, in the preceding passage, 2 Kings 24:18–20, reference to Zedekiah's having done what was evil in Yahweh's sight skips over Jehoiachin, his immediate predecessor, and harks back directly to Jehoiakim, even though momentous events occurred during his very short reign. After all, Jehoiachin had not rebelled; he was, in the view of Second Kings, the victim of the momentum of destruction generated by Jehoiakim, who could have remained a loyal vassal to Nebuchadnezzar, just as he had been to Necho, whom he served dutifully. Although massive damage had been done during the reign of Jehoiachin, survival was still possible under Zedekiah, had he not rebelled, because Jerusalem had not yet been destroyed. The choice that faced Zedekiah is dramatized in Jeremiah 27, to be discussed further on. One has the impression that the author(s) of 2 Kings 25 were experiencing *déjà vu*. Under similarly severe circumstances, Hezekiah had kept the kingdom alive by realizing the futility of rebellion against Assyria. Zedekiah failed to do so with respect to Babylonia.

Assessing the overall character of the biblical record in the Book of Kings it can be said that more interest is shown in the end result of misguided royal policies than in their dynamics, and that it reveals certain ideological inconsistencies. Thus, Josiah met a tragic end notwithstanding his cultic and moral devotion to the God of Israel. In realistic terms, this was because of some offense to, or act against Pharaoh Necho II, or because that Pharaoh had suspected him of such disloyalty. The Hebrew Bible tells us only that he was assassinated on the spot at Megiddo. His son, Jehoahaz, was installed as king by the Judean gentry, but he lasted only three months, at which time the Pharaoh had him arrested and brought to Egypt. The reason given is that he did what was evil in Yahweh's sight, a proverbial way of characterizing cultic heterodoxy. The above are examples of what we find repeatedly in the Book of Kings. The political agenda is often obscure, or it is blurred by explanations of defeat and misfortune that focus on the consequences of religious heterodoxy and moral corruption. Although prophets have a major role in moving the historiography of the Book of Kings forward, Jeremiah, himself, is never mentioned in those sections of Second Kings that cover the period from 609–586 B.C.E. when he was active.

A corollary of the doctrine of submission to Babylonia is the fact that in the Book of Kings, the king of Babylonia is never threatened with divine punishment for what he did to Judah and Jerusalem, or for any of his related acts of cruelty. He is merely carrying out Yahweh's plan. The downfall of Babylonia is a major theme in Jeremiah, as in Deutero-Isaiah and Ezekiel, and elsewhere (such as in Habakkuk), where it is viewed as the fulfillment of Yahweh's plan, and as requisite to the restoration of his people, Israel. The Book of Kings does not see that far ahead. To be sure, the destructive actions of Nebuchadnezzar II and his forces are recounted in Second Kings in their full cruelty and severity, and one senses the impending doom and its attendant hardships. And yet, it is remarkable how impersonal the Babylonian narrative of Second Kings is in contrast to the Assyrian narrative that had preceded it. The king of Assyria engages in debate and he propagandizes; he taunts and displays hubris, just as he is portrayed as doing in Isaiah 10. In contrast, the king of Babylonia, both in Second Kings and in Jeremiah, is configured as an impersonal force, cruel and powerful. He never speaks in public, but only acts; he has no "personality."

"Nebuchadnezzar, My Servant": Jeremiah's Explanation of Defeat

The Book of Jeremiah is, along with Second Kings, a major source of knowledge on the Babylonian presence, as viewed from Jerusalem. It is replete with historical signposts for the reigns of the last three kings of Judah, Jehoiakim, Jehoiachin and Zedekiah, giving some attention to what immediately preceded them, and going on to report on events subsequent to 586 B.C.E.

In the discussion to follow, we will first present graphic images of the Babylonian armies and campaigns as preserved in the book of Jeremiah, because such passages convey the fearful anticipation of impending disaster, and the trauma of the final destruction. We will then proceed to analyze the prophetic outlook on the Babylonian threat, and its consequences for the people of Judah and Jerusalem.

Graphic images of the Babylonian campaigns

In the first nineteen chapters of Jeremiah, before prophecies become linked to the reigns of particular kings of Judah, and connected to specific stages in the destruction, we find numerous characterizations of the Babylonian forces in their advance toward Judah and Jerusalem. Though these prophecies are not sequenced chronologically, we sense how such descriptions assume greater immediacy as the enemy draws nearer. What was far away is soon perilously close! The Babylonians are not explicitly identified as the dreaded enemy until Jer 20:4; prior to that, they are referred to in more relational terms. As noted earlier, the report of the delegation sent to Jerusalem by Merodach-Baladan II (2 Kings 2:14b; Isa 39:3) speaks of the Babylonians as coming "from a far-off land, from

Babylonia." So in Jeremiah, they are first and foremost "a nation from afar" (Jer 4:6, 16; 5:15; cf. Hab 1:8). A variant identification views the Babylonians as coming from the north, reflecting the ancient route of march from Mesopotamia to the Levant (Jer 1:13–15; 3:18; 4:6–7; 6:1; 10:22; 13:20).

The Babylonian forces are described as a lion, a destroyer of nations. His horses are swifter than eagles. He is a powerful nation, speaking a strange tongue; his quiver is an open grave. His stirrings in the northland cause great commotion, a gathering storm (Jer 4:7, 13, 15–16, 20; 5:6; 10:22). Especially poignant is the description in Jer 6:22–25:

> Behold, an army is coming from the northland,
> A vast nation is stirring up from the corners of the earth.
> They hold both bow and lance; he is cruel, they show no mercy.
> The sound of them roars like the sea, and they ride on horses.
> To the man, he is arrayed for battle against you, O daughter Zion.
> When we heard of his doings, our arms went limp;
> Anxiety gripped us; pangs like those of a woman in childbirth.
> Do not go out into the field, nor walk along the road.
> For the enemy has swords; there is terror all around.

In Jer 8:16 the people are urged to take refuge in fortified towns:

> From Dan is heard the neighing of his horses.
> From the shouting sounds of his cavalrymen the whole earth trembled.
> They came and devoured the land and everything in it,
> Every town and those who dwell in her.

As the battle scenes become focused on Jerusalem, we encounter descriptions of conditions in the capital. There are repeated references to the proverbial triad of pestilence, war and famine; to the many dead; to conflagrations, and to the felling of trees. In Jeremiah 39 and 52, both parallels of 2 Kings 25:1–21, the final destruction of Jerusalem is described in graphic detail, and mention is made of Jeremiah's treatment by the conquerors. This dovetails in a curious way with his harsh treatment by Zedekiah and the Judean officials.

Jeremiah's policy toward the Babylonians

Here is what Herbert Huffmon has to say on the subject of Jeremiah's prophetic outlook:

> Jeremiah is not to be characterized as pro-Babylonian, though many of his contemporaries so viewed him, but as pro-Israel. This stance did not demand political independence. The survival of God's people Israel at that time meant, for Jeremiah, submission to God theologically and submission to Babylonia politically ... Jeremiah sought the continuation and revival of God's people. (Huffmon 1999:267, with deletion)

This is the core of the matter, and even those prophecies in Jeremiah that appear to be backward glances at the events are best understood as voicing the doctrine of submission to empires. Huffmon is exceptional in his understanding of the prophet's devotion to his people, notwithstanding his incessant diatribes. It has been an egregious misunderstanding of the classical Hebrew prophets to regard their internationalism as coming at the expense of their loyalty to their own people; not to the kings of Israel and Judah, of course, but to the kinship of the nation. Huffmon continues: "God's people were now making their way in a new international order and needed a unifying theology not linked to political independence, a theology that helped to bring together all that was left of Israel" (Huffmon 1999:268, with deletion).

Now, Huffmon associates the doctrine of political dependency specifically with Jeremiah, suggesting that it was a product of his own age, informed by Josiah's cultic reforms, unsuccessful as they may have been. As we have argued this ideology has a history, and is best understood as an application of First Isaiah's doctrine of a century earlier, coming in response to the Assyrian crisis. If anything, Jeremiah sharpened First Isaiah's doctrine, so that Assyria, (or "the king of Assyria"), the rod of Yahweh's rage, has now become "Nebuchadnezzar, my servant" (Hebrew: *ʿabdî*) in Jeremiah (25:9; 27:6; 43:10).

Jeremiah 27: Nebuchadnezzar II as Yahweh's servant

The clearest exposition of the doctrine of submission to Babylonia as part of Yahweh's plan for the whole earth is to be found in Jeremiah 27, perhaps the most ideologically enlightening of the Zedekiah prophecies. It is likely that Jeremiah 25 represents a reworking of chapter 27, in which we find the prophecy of seventy years that explicitly predicts the downfall of Babylonia, and which morphs into a prophecy of Judean restoration. Both prophecies refer to the king of Babylonia as "my servant," as does Jer 43:50, in a communication to the prophet Jeremiah predicting a Babylonian conquest of Egypt. Without entering into the historical setting of that prophecy, it is important ideologically because the scope of the doctrine that the king of Babylonia is Yahweh's agent is broadened to include Egypt.

The message of Jeremiah 27 is that there is still time to save the people of Judah and Jerusalem, even after the catastrophes that had occurred during the reigns of Jehoiakim and Jehoiachin, if only Zedekiah, king of Judah, "brings his neck under the yoke of the king of Babylonia" (Jer 27:8, 11, and following). Wearing a yoke and reins to dramatize the oracle, the prophet has this to say to Zedekiah:

> I have made the earth, and humans and beasts on the earth, with my great strength and with my outstretched arm, and I have granted it to one who is upright in my sight. And now, I have placed all of these lands into the power of Nebuchadnezzar, king of Babylonia, my servant, and the beasts of the field, as well, have I granted to him, to serve him. All the nations will serve him until the time of his land will come for him, too, and then large nations and great kings will render him subservient (in turn). It shall occur, that the nation or the

> kingdom that will not serve him, namely, Nebuchadnezzar, king of Babylonia, and will not place his neck under the yoke of the king of Babylonia—I will visit punishment on that nation, the word of Yahweh, with war, and with famine and with pestilence, until I hand them over completely into his power.
>
> (Jer 27:5–8)

There is nothing ambiguous about this oracle, which is said to have been delivered at a projected gathering of invited, neighboring nations in Jerusalem—Edom, Moab, Ammon, Tyre, and Zidon—with Zedekiah present. This meeting (some have called it a "summit") would have probably occurred *c.*594 B.C.E. Its background is informatively discussed by David Vanderhooft (2003) in a study of Babylonian "strategies of control." The assembled nations faced a fateful choice, but we may assume that they all made the wrong decision. Jer 27:9–22 expands the core prophecy, warning king and people against being misled by the false prophets and diviners of various sorts who encouraged rebellion, and most likely advocated reliance on Egyptian assistance. Jeremiah's counsel was that the only way to survive was by learning to live under Babylonian domination. There is reference to the temple vessels plundered during the reign of Jehoiachin. These will not be returned until God's own good time, when Babylon, too, will fall. As Tadmor (1999) has shown, the theme of *ʿad bôʾ ʿēt* "until the time has come," basic to Jeremiah 27:7 resonates in Haggai 2 within the post-exilic community. "This people has said: 'It is not the time of coming (*lôʾ ʿēt bôʾ*), the time for the temple of Yahweh to be built'."

A corollary of the doctrine of submission to empire and the notion that Nebuchadnezzar is Yahweh's servant is the idea, already noted above, that it is the God of Israel who is destroying Judah and Jerusalem, not the Babylonians, who are merely doing his will. In fact, one of the themes that links Second Kings to the Book of Jeremiah is usage of the Hebrew Hiphʿil participle *mēbîʾ* "bringing," more precisely the construction: *mēbîʾ ʿal* (alternatively *mēbîʾ ʾel*) "bringing upon, against." Thus, 2 Kings 21:12: "Therefore, thus says Yahweh, God of Israel: Behold, I am bringing a catastrophe upon Jerusalem and Judah, such that anyone who hears of it, both of his ears will tingle!"

The numerous attestations of this discrete idiom are concentrated in the Book of Kings (1 Kings 14:10, with respect to Jeroboam I; 2 Kings 22:16, 20)—with respect to the Babylonian destruction of Judah and Jerusalem; in Jeremiah (Jer 4:6; 5:15; 6:19, 11:11, 19:3; 35:17; 42:17; 45:5; 49:5; 51:64), and in Ezekiel (Ezek 6:3)—against Judah or parts thereof in Ezek 26:7; 28:7—against Tyre; in Ezek 29:8—against Egypt (cf. Lev 26:25; 2 Chron 34:24, 29). It is a virtual *Leitmotif*, which identifies Yahweh as the force bringing misfortune upon his people.

An application of this theme appears in Jeremiah 21:1–10, yet another Zedekiah prophecy, where a horrendous scene is projected: Yahweh will bring the weapons of the defenders of Jerusalem inside the walls, and turn them against the people, themselves. He will do battle with them and destroy them, effectively becoming the enemy! One's attention is immediately drawn to the Book of

Lamentations, traditionally attributed to Jeremiah, and for good reason. "He strung his bow like an enemy; he raised his right arm like an opponent … The Lord was like an enemy; he destroyed Israel" (Lam 2:4–5, with deletions).

Clashes with false prophets: the debate over policy

A close look at Jeremiah's clashes with false prophets and with royal officials, even with kings, especially with Zedekiah, offers an additional perspective on both the political and the cultic-moral agendas of the prophet. The people's first sin is failure to heed the words of the prophets sent by Yahweh. Thus, Jer 25:2–4:

> That which Jeremiah the prophet delivered to the entire people of Judah and to all the residents of Jerusalem, as follows: Since the thirteenth year of Josiah son of Amon, king of Judah, and until this very day, these three and twenty years, the word of Yahweh came to me. And I spoke to you, beginning to speak early in the day, but you did not heed. Indeed, Yahweh sent to you all of his prophets, sending them early on, but you did not heed, nor did you bend your ear to listen.

Admitting some imprecision in both the synchronous, and the internal chronologies, the point of specifying the span of twenty-three years in Jeremiah's speech may be suggestive. It is as if to say that the imminent crisis harks back to the very inception of the Neo-Babylonian Empire in 626/625, which corresponds to the thirteenth year of Josiah. If there is anything to this innuendo, Jeremiah's complaint would qualify as a sage historical hindsight. It is as if to say that, inevitably, the Neo-Babylonian Empire would vie with Egypt for hegemony in the Levant once the Neo-Assyrian Empire lost its power, and that Babylonia would, with occasional setbacks, prevail. Indeed, this speech of Jeremiah is best understood as a reaction to Jehoiakim's rebellion against Nebuchadnezzar.

A related concern is the activism of false prophets who not only tormented Jeremiah, personally, but who grievously misled the people. This is the subject of Jeremiah 23, which expresses several related themes. The one most relevant to the present discussion is the seduction of the people through false prophecies of well being and peace; the notion that the Babylonian "misfortune" will not overtake them (Jer 23:17). Jeremiah had insisted that it would, indeed (Jer 23:12). In language and theme, Jeremiah 23 recalls earlier prophecies of Jeremiah, where we likewise encounter assurances of *šālôm* by false prophets (cf. Jeremiah 6 and 7, as examples).

The most notable episode of conflict with a "false prophet," one of several, is that with Hananiah, recounted in Jeremiah 28, and dated to Zedekiah's fourth year, hence, also in 594 B.C.E. This account may be seen as a take-off on Jeremiah 27, discussed above. In effect, the admonition of Jer 27:9–20 is applied to Hananiah, a prophet from Gibeon, which, we are told, took place in the Temple of Jerusalem, in the presence of the priests and the people assembled. Like Jeremiah, Hananiah officially speaks in the name of Yahweh: he predicts that in two years Yahweh will restore all the vessels and all the exiles taken to Babylon along with Jehoiachin to Jerusalem, for Yahweh will break the yoke of the king of Babylonia, Nebuchadnezzar. Hananiah symbolically breaks off the yoke that Jeremiah was wearing (Jer 27:2). Jeremiah is quick to mock Hananiah, saying that he would wish for nothing better than to see his prophecy fulfilled, but that it was not to be. Some of Jeremiah's words bear repeating:

> The prophets who came before me and before you, from time immemorial, prophesied over many lands and upon great kingdoms—for war, and for misfortune, and for pestilence. (As for) the prophet who prophesies for peace—when the word of the prophet comes about, that prophet will be acknowledged as one whom Yahweh truly sent.
>
> (Jer 28:8–9)

> I have placed an iron yoke on the neck of all these nations to serve Nebuchadnezzar, king of Babylonia, and they shall serve him; even the beasts of the field I have given to him.
>
> (Jer 28:14)

Jeremiah then condemns Hananiah as a false prophet and predicts his imminent death, which actually occurs. Although there have been attempts to historicize this episode, one wonders what realistic assessment of the international situation *c.*594 B.C.E. would have induced Hananiah's prediction. It has been suggested that reference may be to the non-military voyage made by Psammetichus II to Palestine in 592, aimed at showing his presence in the area (see Freedy and Redford 1970:479–480). But, even if Egyptian help was sought and hoped for, it could not under the best circumstances bring about the return of the Judean exiles and of the Temple vessels! That blessed event would have required the defeat of Babylonia, which would not occur until Cyrus the Great conquered Babylon (cf. Ezra 1:7–11). It seems, therefore, that Jeremiah 28 is an allegory of sorts, an epitome on the issue of submission to Nebuchadnezzar, Yahweh's servant, and, as such, is probably of later composition (*pace* Malamat 2001:313–316; for background see Cogan and Tadmor 1988:323, and literature cited). It serves to dramatize the clash with court prophets who always predict victory for the king who sponsors them. It curiously recalls the symbolical clash on the issue of going to war between the prophet of Yahweh, Micaiah, son of Imlah, and the obsequious court prophet Zedekiah, son of Chenaanah, as told in 1 Kings 22.

There is much more that could be said about the image of Babylonia in the Book of Jeremiah. Old themes and references to pre-destruction events continue to crop up in the later chapters, as attention shifts to conditions in Jerusalem and Judah after the final destruction of 586 B.C.E., and to the welfare of the exilic communities in Egypt and Babylonia. We encounter oracles of doom against the nations, and dramatic predictions of the downfall of Babylonia.

Habakkuk Questions the Role of the Chaldeans in Yahweh's Design

A century ago, the great British interpreter of the Hebrew Bible, S.R. Driver (1906) contributed a commentary on Habakkuk to *The Century Bible* which has never been surpassed for insight. Driver was able to pinpoint the difference between Habakkuk and his contemporary, Jeremiah, precisely:

> Jeremiah is so deeply impressed by the spectacle of his people's sin that he regards the Chaldeans almost exclusively as the instruments of judgement … Habakkuk, on the other hand, though not unmindful of Judah's faults (i.2–4), is engrossed chiefly by the thought of the cruelties and inhumanities of the oppressor … Further, Habakkuk is conscious of a problem, a moral difficulty, which is not the case with Jeremiah.[3] The wrongdoing of the Chaldean is more unbearable than the evil it was meant to punish. (Driver 1906:61, with deletions)

In some respects, the vision of Habakkuk is to the Babylonian destruction of Judah and Jerusalem what the vision of Nahum is to the Assyrian scourge, in terms of the rage directed at the oppressive enemy. The difference is that Nahum is talking about past suffering, and is already celebrating the downfall of the oppressor and his long awaited punishment. Habakkuk is at a different point in time, and can only offer assurances regarding the future, when the Chaldeans will be called to account. Then, too, there is no reference to the issue of divine justice for Israel in the vision of Nahum, only to divine vengeance finally unleashed against the enemies of Israel. For his part, Habakkuk parts company with the consensus view that Israel's sins alone are responsible for Israel's suffering by applying the issue of divine justice to the national destiny. As Driver implies in his note, we observe in Habakkuk a subtle transaction. Resonating with Jeremiah's personal complaint, wherein he cites the prosperity of his wicked opponents as a miscarriage of divine justice, Habakkuk accuses Yahweh of the same injustice with respect to the whole people of Israel, who are, after all, more righteous (or at least, less wicked!) than the Chaldeans.

Thus, Jer 12:1 (in the personal context):

> You are (too) righteous, Yahweh, that I should dispute with you!
> But I must lay down the law to you (*mišpāṭîm ʾadabbēr ʾôtāk*)!
> Why does the way of the wicked prosper;
> Why are all the perpetrators of treachery so well off?

Compare Habakkuk 1:12–13 (in the collective context):

> Are you not from of old, O Yahweh,
> My God, my Holy-being; *You do not die*![4]

[3] Driver adds a qualification: "Except, indeed, in so far as it is exemplified in his own personal experience, in the impunity, namely, enjoyed by his own enemies (xii.1–6)."

[4] Roberts, 1991:101 explains that the Masoretic reading *lōʾ nāmût* "We shall not die," represents one of "eighteen corrections of the Scribes," introduced out of reverence.

Yahweh, for imposing justice you appointed him;
O Rock, for disciplining did you establish him
Too pure of sight to look upon evil,
You, who do not countenance wrongdoing—
Why do you countenance the treacherous,
Remain silent as the wicked devours
One more righteous than he?

Yahweh had given power to the Chaldeans for a purpose, to restore order to a lawless Judean society, but that objective was now being compromised by a lawless conqueror who was destroying that very society. Once again we encounter the theme of Babylonia as Yahweh's instrument for punishing Israel, but this time there is prophetic protest against Yahweh's management of the world order.

Habakkuk's antipathy to the Chaldeans pervades his prophecies. References to the cruelty of the invaders also appear in Kings and Jeremiah, but the tone of Habakkuk's oracle rather recalls First Isaiah and Nahum, who condemned the hubris of the Assyrians and their rapacity. Here is Habakkuk's characterization of the Chaldeans, one that goes beyond descriptiveness to voice a strong moral judgment against them:

For behold, I am stirring up the Chaldeans,
That fierce and impetuous nation;
That marches to the broad expanses of the earth;
To seize habitations not his own.
He is terrifying and dreadful.
He makes his own laws and rules.
His horses are swifter than leopards;
They are sharper than wolves of *the steppe*.
His cavalry *is* deployed; his cavalry comes from afar;
They fly like a vulture, in a hurry to devour.
He comes for the sole purpose of violence.
Their course is set like the east wind.
He amasses captives as numerous as the sand!
He trifles with kings; rulers are a plaything for him.
He makes light of every fortified town;
He heaps up earth, and captures it!
Then he passes on like a wind sweeping by;
And ascribes his might to his god

(Hab 1:6–11)[5]

There could be no suggestion that God might die, even if the biblical verse in question actually negates that possibility. Hence, we deduce an original: *lōʾ tāmût* "You do not die."

[5] In Hab 1:7, the given translation: "He makes his own laws and rules" is functional. Literally, the text reads, "From him does his judgment and authority go out." The sense is that the Babylonians have changed the rules of war and government for the worse, and cannot be counted on to behave with decency. In Hab 1:8, read, instead of *zeʾēbêi ʿereb*

One could compose a commentary on Habakkuk's oracle comprised of citations from Babylonian royal inscriptions, showing how the prophecy resonates with their long-held ideology. In the Nabopolassar Epic we read, in an often-quoted passage, how Bel confers sovereignty on Nabopolassar, the founder of the Neo-Babylonian dynasty, at his coronation. The king accepts the charge:

> "With the standard I shall constantly conquer [your] enemies, I shall place [your] throne in Babylon." ... The officers in their joy [exclaimed]: "O lord, O king, may you live forever! [May you conquer] the land of [your] enemies! May the king of the gods, Marduk, rejoice in you ...!" (Grayson 1975:84–85, lines 7–8, 16–18)

In Habakkuk, chapter 2, the prophet receives his answer in the form of a divine assurance that a righteous Israel will survive, while the evil empire will be brought to justice. Thus, Hab 2:2–4, and following:

> Then Yahweh answered me, saying:
> Inscribe a vision; write distinctly on the tablets,
> So that readers may race through it.
> For the prophecy is *a witness* for the set time,
> A testimony for the specified period
> That will not prove false!
> If it should tarry—wait for it!
> It shall surely arrive; it will not be delayed in coming.
> For he is *weak* who is not inwardly upright,
> But the righteous will survive by virtue of his steadfastness.[6]

The prophet's counsel to Judah and Jerusalem would seem to indicate that he was speaking when it was already too late to decide against rebellion, because the destruction of Jerusalem had already occurred. Now, all that can be enlisted in the struggle for survival is to wait upon the God of Israel, and to retain a steadfast commitment to a just society. This message is followed in the continuation of Habakkuk 2, by an open condemnation of the Chaldeans. They sought to oppress all nations and to plunder them, but the time will come when Yahweh of Hosts will bring them down.

"wolves of the evening," *zeʾēbêi ʿarāb{ôt}* "wolves of the steppes," based on the occurrence of this expression in Jer 5:6. The same change would apply to Zeph 3:3 (Roberts 1991:92). Finally, in Hab 1:11 the translation assumes that the persistent subject is the Chaldean enemy. It is he who sweeps by like the wind, assuming an implied comparative. In verse 11b, we rephrase the hemistich and emend to read: *weyāśēm zû kōḥô lʾēlōhô*, literally: "He ascribes that which is his strength to his God." (from Masoretic: *weʾāšēm*—Driver 1906:75). The Hebrew form *zû* is a relative pronoun: "which, whom."

[6] In Hab 2:3 read *ʿēd* "witness," instead of Masoretic *ʿôd* "yet, still." In Hab 2:4, the problematic form *ʿuplāh* (presumably: "puffed up," cf. *ʿopel* "tower"—Micah 4:8), is better taken as a metathesis of *ʿulpeh* "one who is faint." Cf. Ezek 31:15, where this very form describes trees that have withered, expressing the verb *ʿālap* "to be faint, weak." Cf. Isa 51:20: "Your sons have become faint (*ʿulpû*)" What we have is contrasting parallelism: one who is not upright will fail, whereas those who are steadfast will survive.

Epilogue

Genesis 11 relates that Abram (later Abraham), the first Patriarch, hailed from "Ur of Chaldees," Hebrew: *ʾûr kaśdîm*, and that he migrated to Canaan with his extended family. Of his brother, Haran, it is written that he died during his father's lifetime "in the land of his birth, in Ur of Chaldees" (Gen 11:28). In the covenant theophany of Genesis 15, Yahweh informs Abram that it was he who had brought him out of Ur of Chaldees to live in Canaan (cf. Neh 9:7). This is only one of several biblical traditions on the origins of the Israelites, and it is ostensibly anachronistic, and fraught with historical problems. And yet, it testifies to a perception on the part of at least one biblical author that the earliest Israelites originated in southern Mesopotamia.

One can only speculate as to what this identification connotes ethnographically, but it certainly projects a subtle irony. The father of the Israelites abandoned his homeland, Ur of Chaldees, to found a new nation in Canaan, only to be exiled from that land in stages at a later time; first by the Assyrians of northern Mesopotamia, and then by Nebuchadnezzar II, the Chaldean king of Babylonia.

Bibliography

Albright, W.F.
1936 A Supplement to Jeremiah: The Lachish Ostraca. *BASOR* 61:10–16.

Brinkman, J.A.
1964 Merodach-Baladan II. Pages 6–53 in *Studies Presented to A. Leo Oppenheim*. Chicago: University of Chicago Press.

Cogan, M. and Tadmor, H.
1988 *II Kings*. AB 11. New York: Doubleday.

Driver, S.R.
1906 The Minor Prophets: Nahum, Habakkuk, Zephaniah, Haggai, Zechariah, Malachi. (The Century Bible). Edinburgh: T.C. Clark & E.C. Jack.

Freedy, K.S. and Redford, D.B.
1970 The Dates in Ezekiel in Relation to the Biblical, Babylonian and Egyptian Sources. *JAOS* 90:462–485.

Grayson, A.K.
1975 *Babylonian Historical-Literary Texts*. Toronto and Buffalo: University of Toronto Press.
1975a *Assyrian and Babylonian Chronicles*. Locust Valley, NY: J.J. Augustin.

Huffmon, H.B.
1999 Jeremiah of Anathoth: A Prophet for all Israel. Pages 261–271 in R. Chazan *et al.* (eds) *Ki Baruch Hu: Ancient Near Eastern, Biblical, and Judaic Studies in Honor of Baruch A. Levine*, Winona Lake, IN: Eisenbrauns.

Humbert, J.B.
2005 By verbal communication.

Levine, B.A.

2005 Assyrian Ideology and Israelite Monotheism. *Iraq* 67:1 = *RAI* 49.2, 411–427 {*VOL 1, PP. 3–28*}.

2007 The Cultic Scene in Biblical Religion: Hebrew ʿAL PĀNÂI (על פני) and the Ban on Divine Images. Pages 358–369 in *"Up to the Gates of Ekron": Essays on the Archaeology and History of the Eastern Mediterranean in Honor of Seymour Gitin*, eds. Sidnie White Crawford et al. Jerusalem: The W. F. Albright Institute of Archaeological Research; The Israel Exploration Society {*VOL 1, PP. 283–99*}.

Malamat, A.

2001 *History of Biblical Israel: Major Problems and Minor Issues*, Leiden: E.J. Brill. (All of Part IV: Twilight of Judah and the Destruction of the First Temple, 277–337; "The Kingdom of Judah between Egypt and Babylonia," 322–337. Also, Part V: "Jeremiah and the Last Two Kings of Judah," 381–386.)

Rainey, A.

1975 The Fare of Lachish during the Campaigns of Sennacherib and Nebuchadrezzar. Pages 47–60 in Y. Aharoni, *et al.*, *Investigations at Lachish; The Sanctuary and the Residency* (*Lachish V*). Tel Aviv: Gateway Publishers Inc..

Roberts, J.J.M.

1991 *Nahum, Habakkuk and Zephaniah, A Commentary.*The Old Testament Library. Louisville, Kentucky: Westminster/John Knox.

Spalinger, A.

1977 Egypt and Babylonia: A Survey *c.*620 BC–550 BC. *Studien der Altägyptischen Kultur* 5:221–244.

Stager, L.

1996 The Fury of Babylon: Ashkelon and the Archaeology of Destruction. *Biblical Archaeology Review* 22:57–77.

Tadmor, H.

1999 "The Appointed Time Has Not Arrived": The Historical Background of Haggai 1:2. Pages 401–408 in R. Chazan *et al.* (eds) *Ki Baruch Hu: Ancient. Near Eastern, Biblical, and Judaic Studies in Honor of Baruch A. Levine*. Winona Lake, IN: Eisenbrauns.

Vanderhooft, D.

2003 Babylonian Strategies of Imperial Control in the West: Royal Practice and Rhetoric. Pages 235–261 in O. Lipschitz and J. Blenkinsopp (eds) *Judah and the Judeans in the Neo-Babylonian Period.* Winona Lake, IN: Eisenbrauns.

Wilson, R.R.

1995 The Former Prophets: Reading the Books of Kings. Pages 83–96 in J.L. Mays *et al.* (eds) *Old Testament Interpretation, Past Present and Future* (Essays in Honour of Gene M. Tucker). Edinburgh: T&T Clark.

Wiseman, D.J.
1956 *Chronicles of the Chaldean Kings* (626–536 BC). London: The Trustees of the British Museum.
1985 *Nebuchadrezzar and Babylon* (The Schweich Lectures of the British Academy, 1983). Oxford; New York: Published for the British Academy by the Oxford University Press.

C. Language

Assyriology and Hebrew Philology: A Methodological Re-examination*

In the early decades of modern Assyriology, classical Hebrew was utilized as a resource for Akkadian lexicography, on the principle of proceeding from the known to the unknown. Perhaps it would be more accurate to say that Hebrew, along with Aramaic and Syriac, and Arabic, were "misused" in this enterprise. As time passed, the quantity and variety of the Assyriological evidence grew to such dimensions, that Hebraists quite logically turned to cuneiform sources for the clarification of long-standing problems in biblical exegesis. In a sense, Akkadian became the "known" and Hebrew the "unknown," at least in quantitative terms.

Comparative lexicography is hardly uni-directional, and presents complex problems, however approached. And yet, one requires a point of demarcation, and should be clear as to which question he is attempting to answer when having recourse to comparative data. Here, my question is: What is the meaning of certain Hebrew vocables, formulas, etc.? I look to Akkadian for answers where information exists; and more particularly, after the internal evidence of Hebrew has been exhausted without conclusive results. I am guided by Benno Landsberger's brief study, entitled: "Akkadisch-hebräische Wortgleichungen", I would merely invert the order and formulate the present topic as: "Hebräisch-akkadische Wortgleichungen."[1]

Methodologically, it would be best to begin with the *hapax legomena* of the Hebrew Bible, although one cannot stay within that limited framework for too long. Herbert Cohen has produced an informative dissertation, now in published form, on the biblical *hapax legomena* in the light of Ugaritic and Akkadian. Two of his examples will lead us directly into the subject at hand.[2]

---

* Originally published in Hans-Jörg Nissen and Johannes Renger (eds.), *Mesopotamien und seine Nachbarn: politische und kulturelle Wechselbeziehungen im alten Vorderasien vom 4. bis 1. Jahrtausend v. Chr.; XXV. Rencontre assyriologique internationale Berlin, 3. bis 7. Juli 1978* (2 vols.; Berliner Beiträge zum Vorderen Orient 1; Berlin: Dietrich Reimer Verlag, 1982), pp. 521–30. Reprinted with permission from Dietrich Reimer Verlag.

1 B. Landsberger, "Akkadisch-hebräische Wortgleichungen," *Hebräische Wortforschung: Festschrift W. Baumgartner* (VTSup 16; Leiden, 1967) 176–204.

2 *Biblical Hapax Legomena in the Light of Akkadian and Ugaritic* (Columbia University dissertation, 1975) (Missoula, MT, 1978).

Hebrew *ʿᵃḇûr* "harvest, yield," in Josh. 5:12 occurs only once in the Hebrew Bible.[3] From the redundance of this verse, it was clear to Menaḥem ben Saruq of the tenth century that *ʿᵃḇûr* is synonymous with Hebrew *tᵉḇûʾāh* "crop, produce." It was not until 1890, however, that Muss-Arnolt proposed that Akkadian *ebūru* was cognate to Hebrew *ʿᵃḇûr*, as Cohen notes.[4] What is significant in this case is that the precise interpretation of the Hebrew vocable depends very much on the extensive Akkadian evidence pertaining to its usage. The fact that Akkadian *ebūru* is attested in the Old Babylonian period proves, as Cohen notes, that it is not an Aramaic loan-word in Akkadian, as some had erroneously maintained in the past. In his study of the Akkadian influences in Aramaic, Stephen Kaufman concludes that *ʿᵃḇûr* is likewise not an Akkadian loanword in Aramaic, or in Hebrew, either, but rather a genuine cognate.[5]

We now possess more data regarding Hebrew *ʿᵃḇûr*, It occurs in a Hebrew ostracon from Arad, dated to the late seventh or early sixth century B.C.E. The occurrence of the term *ʿᵃḇûr* in an external source of the biblical period is sufficient to suggest that we are dealing with a word of more general usage in Hebrew. Following is a transcription of the ostracon in question:

1) *ḥṭm*		wheat:	
2) *ʾmryhw bn rgʾ*	5	PN son of PN:	5 (ephah)
3) *nḥmyhw bn yhwʿz*	8	PN son of PN:	8
4) *nryhw bn sʿryhw*	5	PN son of PN:	5
5) *ʾḥygm bn šmʿyhw*	7	PN son of PN:	7
6) *gḥm*	5	PN:	5
7) *ydʿyhw*	5	PN:	5
8) *gmryhw*	5	PN:	5
9) [....]*yhw*	6	PN:	6
10) *46 ʿbr*[6]		46 (ephah is the total) yield	

This is a list of allocations of wheat, as the caption in line 1 indicates. Aharoni has shown that the units are *ephah*'s. In Akkadian sources we also encounter *ebūru* as a categorical, or generic term, subsuming specific varieties of grain—wheat, barley, etc. The same generic connotation should be understood

---

[3] Cohen, *op. cit.*, 71f. Attempts to see the term *ʿᵃḇûr* in such forms as *baʿᵃḇûr* are not convincing.

[4] W. Muss-Arnolt, "Notes on the Publications Contained in Volume II of E. Schrader's *Keilschriftliche Bibliothek*. II. The Inscriptions of Esarhaddon," *Hebraica* 7 (1890–91), 82 n. 3. *Apud* Cohen, *op. cit.*, 72 n. 103, s.v. for further biblical references.

[5] S. Kaufman, *The Akkadian Influences on Aramaic* (Chicago, 1974), 99. It is improbable that Ugaritic *ʿbr*, *ʿbrm* in Anat VI:7, 8, and 124:15 of C.H. Gordon, *Ugaritic Textbook* (1965) represent the same vocable we are discussing. See discussion in Cohen, *op. cit.*, 72 n. 105. The possibility of taking Akkadian *ebūru* as a Sumerian loanword from BURU$_{15}$ (EBUR) is also discussed by Cohen, 71 nn. 101–102. Also see *CAD E*, 16, s.v. *ebūru*, in the lexical section.

[6] Y. Aharoni, *The Arad Inscriptions* (Hebrew) (Jerusalem, 1975), 58f., (no. 31): *ad* line 1: *ḥiṭṭîm* = wheat; *ad* line 10: *ʿᵃbûr* = crop, yield.

for Aramaic *ᶜᵃḇûr* in the Elephantine papyri. There is no warrant for rendering this term as "corn", or the like, as has been done almost consistently.[7]

The fact, also noted by Cohen, that Josh. 5:12 has *ᶜᵃḇûr hāʾareṣ* "the crop of the land", analogous to Akkadian *ebūr māti*, adds frosting to the cake, because it is precisely the point of the Joshua passage that, after forty years of migration, the Israelites were finally able to eat food grown in Canaan.[8] In summary, biblical *ᶜᵃḇûr* remains a classic paradigm of the rarely attested Hebrew vocable, whose provenance and precise connotation were established by the cognate evidence from Akkadian. Subsequently, more Hebrew evidence came to light, verifying the earlier conclusions.

A more problematic situation is represented by the Hebrew root *k-p-r*, when compared with Akkadian *kapāru*, and related forms. I have been studying this problem for some years. For Hebrew lexicography the problem has been to determine whether the frequent Piel verb, *kippēr*, and related nominal forms, derive from:

> a) a denominative Qal form, *kāpar* "to coat, smear with, pitch", unique to Gen. 6:14, from Hebrew *kôper* "pitch, bitumen", or
>
> b) a verbal root, cognate to Akkadian *kapāru* "to wipe off", D-stem *kuppuru* "to burnish, cleanse", etc.

Cohen agrees with my proposed classification of three distinct roots in Akkadian:

> 1) *CAD*'s *kapāru* A "to wipe off", minus meanings 2 and 4 under that heading, i.e. "to smear", and N-stem "be smeared", which both belong under meaning 3, below.
>
> 2) *CAD*'s *kapāru* B "to strip, clip, trim down", and extended meanings.
>
> 3) *AHw*'s *kapārum* II, a denominative of *kupru*(*m*), "bitumen", hence: "to smear bitumen", or a similar substance. Meanings 2 and 4 from *CAD*'s *kapāru* A are to be added, and also *kāpiru* "caulker" (*CAD K*, 183–184).[9]

In other words, our resolution posits three, distinct, homonymous roots, a situation one usually attempts to avoid! And yet, this may be the best possible classification. Landsberger's division of *kapāru* "to strip, trim", etc. from *kapāru* "to wipe off", etc. can hardly be refuted, in its own right, and *AHw*'s rejection of it is highly problematic.[10] If we accept *CAD*'s differentiation between *kapāru* A and B we are left with the curious fact that in all but one instance cited either by *CAD* or *AHw*, *kapāru* "to smear" refers in fact to smearing

---

[7] For further discussion see Cohen, *op. cit.*, 71 n. 101.

[8] Cohen, *op. cit.* 71, and n. 100.

[9] A full discussion is provided in B.A. Levine, *In the Presence of the Lord* (Leiden, 1974), 56–63, 123–127, and cf. Cohen, *op. cit.*, 49f.

[10] B. Landsberger, *The Date Palm and its By-products according to the Cuneiform Sources* (Graz, 1967), 30f.

bitumen. In that one case, occurring in a medical text published by Kocher, reference is to smearing a medication on teeth.[11] I hardly think that this is sufficiently remote from smearing pitch as to warrant the discounting of a denominative, *kapāru*, from *kupru*(*m*), which is *CAD*'s conclusion.

It depends on one's overall attitude toward the role of denominatives in the Semitic languages, and in specific Semitic languages. The formation of verbs from existing nouns is attested in Akkadian. Once a denominative is formed, its usage may expand, by analogy, and need not be bound to the cognate accusative.

It is now important to assess what bearing the Akkadian evidence has for Hebrew philology and biblical exegesis. Even Landsberger, who produced the breakthrough regarding the Akkadian vocables coincidentally, while investigating terminology relevant to the date-palm and its byproducts, stopped short of endorsing the identification of Hebrew *kippēr*, the verb most often employed in Biblical Hebrew for expressing expiation and atonement, with Akkadian *kapāru* "to wipe off". I was compelled to dispute his tangential assertion that Hebrew *kippēr* never meant "to wipe out", (= "erase"), as does the verb *māḥāh* in Hebrew. In fact, it does. There was the added fact that Akkadian attests the nominal form *takpertu*, which can specifically connote a rite of purification.[12]

A proper identification of the concept underlying Hebrew *kippēr* and related forms is essential for an understanding of major themes in Israelite religion, most notably purity and atonement. The question that has been debated is whether expiation is to be conceptualized as "covering over, concealment"—of sins and offenses; or "wiping" them off, thus cleansing the offender, or contaminated object.

Both concepts are present in biblical texts dealing with purification and expiation, and this fact complicates the situation. Formerly it was assumed, on the basis of certain derived connotations attested in Arabic, for the most part, that the notion underlying expiation in the biblical view was that of "covering" sins and offenses. This was J. Stamm's view.[13] As the Akkadian evidence became known in greater degree, this view came to be challenged. Thus G.B. Gray, in a posthumous work which appeared in 1922, cites Zimmern on this question, and reports on his discussions with Langdon on the Akkadian evidence.[14] Subsequently, G.R. Driver opted in favor of the Akkadian evidence as against the notion of "covering", but his control over the Akkadian evidence, was, at the time, necessarily limited. Nevertheless, he called attention quite insightfully to Gen. 32:20:

> *ᵓᵃḵapperāh pānau bamminḥāh hahhôleḵeṯ lᵉp̱ānâi*
> That I may wipe off [the wrath] from his countenance, by means of the tribute which goes before me.

---

[11] F. Köcher, BAM 10/13, *apud CAD K*, 179, s.v. *kapāru* A, 2.

[12] *AHw* 1308, s.v. *takpertu*(*m*).

[13] J. Stamm, *Erlösen and Vergeben im alten Testament* (Bern, 1940), 59–66f.

[14] G.B. Gray, *Sacrifice in the Old Testament*, with a Prolegomenon by B.A. Levine (New York, 1971), 67–73.

He further noted that Akkadian in fact attests the idiom *kuppuru pānē* "to rub the face," in omen texts. He failed to note, however, the relevance of Prov. 16:14:

> *ḥamat meleḵ malʾᵃkê māweṯ wᵉʾîš ḥāḵām yᵉḵapperennāh*
> The wrath of a king is like messengers of death, but the skillful person may *wipe it off.*

Referring again to Landsberger's point about *kippēr* and *māḥāh* in biblical usage, it is noteworthy that Driver called attention to Isa. 28:18:

> *weḵuppar bᵉrîṯkem ʾeṯ māweṯ wᵉḥāzûṯkem ʾeṯ šᵉʾôl lōʾ tāqûm*
>
> Your covenant with death will be erased (= annulled),
> Your pact with Sheol shall not endure.[15]

These non-cultic usages of Hebrew *kipper* make the case for its primary connotation, that of "wiping off", a meaning attested in Aramaic usage, as Driver also noted. Thus, the Targum to Prov. 30:20 renders the Hebrew *ûmāḥᵃṯāh pîhāh* "And she wiped off her mouth" by Aramaic *umᵉḵappᵉrāh pummah*. This evidence should reassure us regarding Landsberger's earlier reservations concerning Hebrew *kippēr.*[16]

It would take us beyond the limits of the present discussion to review what, in my opinion, the priestly writers of the Bible did so as to adapt the earlier non-cultic usage of *kippēr*, expressed in the direct-object syntax, to the needs of characterizing religious ideas of atonement and expiation. The fact that Biblical Hebrew preserves, in non-cultic contexts, the more graphic, physical connotations characteristic of Akkadian usage should be enough to sustain the comparison. The alteration of syntax by the biblical writers to predominantly indirect-object constructions (*kippēr* + *ʿal*, etc.) can, I think, be accounted for on internal grounds, once the *Grundbedeutung* of Hebrew *k-p-r* is detached, with respect to the Piel *kippēr* from the denominative *kāpar* of Gen. 6:14. In retrospect, it makes much more sense to view expiation as "cleansing", than it does to associate it with a denominative, connoting the smearing of pitch![17]

Let us now turn to the third, and final example of the method advocated here, the Hebrew term *tᵉrûmāh*, used to designate several types of taxes, levies, and contributions to the priesthood, to temples, and to other authorities. I choose this example for a number of reasons, not the least being that it was an Assyriologist, Prof. W. von Soden who has proposed relating Akkadian *tarīmtu*, and what he classifies in *AHw* as *râmu* III, to this Hebrew term.[18]

---

[15] G.R. Driver, "Studies in the Vocabulary of the Old Testament," *Journal of Theological Studies* 34 (1933), 33–44.

[16] Landsberger, *op. cit.*, 31 n. 95. See Levine, *op. cit.*, 58 n. 9, 61 n. 20.

[17] Levine, *op. cit.*, 64f. J. Milgrom, *Lešônēnû* (Hebrew) 35 (1970–71), 16–17, and *Tarbiz* (Hebrew) 40 (1970–71), 1–8, explains the syntactic adaptation evident in Hebrew usage differently.

[18] W. von Soden, "Mirjām – Maria '(Gottes-)Geschenk'", *UF* 2 (1970), 269–272.

Von Soden maintains that there is an old West Semitic root *r-y-m* which is cognate to Akkadian *râmu* "to bestow a gift", and that some Amorite personal names, usually taken to mean that a certain deity has "exalted" or "raised" the named person, really express this other root. Thus, Amorite *Ia-ri-im-Li-im* is to be rendered: "Lim has bestowed a gift", not: "Lim has exalted".

In Akkadian the situation can be traced fairly well, as von Soden proceeds to do. Circa 1400 B.C.E. forms of *râmu* "to bestow a gift" began to replace other verbal elements, such as *qâšu* "to give a *qīštu*", and *šarāku* "to offer, hand over, devote". In Old Babylonian and Old Akkadian one finds nominal forms such as *rīmu*(*m*) "gift", and *tarīmtu*(*m*) "gift", and Late Babylonian attests *rēmūtu*, with the same meaning.

This situation within Akkadian does not inform us, however, about "Old West Semitic". Von Soden searched for reflexes of the postulated West Semitic verb *r-y-m* in Ugaritic and Hebrew without definitive results, but he came up with the suggestion, albeit tentative, that the Hebrew term *t*^{e}*rûmāh* would not, in these terms, be derived from the root *r-w-m*/*r-y-m* "to be high, raised", as has been assumed. All of this is part of a discussion of the Hebrew personal name *miryām*, in an attempt to arrive at a satisfactory etymology.

This tempting suggestion raises several methodological problems:

1) In *AHw*, von Soden relates *râmu* III "to bestow a gift", to the verb *rêmu*(*m*) "to show kindness". In other words, an extension of the notion of showing kindness[19] is the bestowal of a gift. The problem is that when we consider cognates of Akkadian *rêmu*(*m*) "to show kindness" in Ugaritic, Aramaic, and Hebrew, and even in Arabic, the medial hollow aspect of the verb is expressed as a *Ḥēṭ*, not as a *Waw* or *Yod*. As noted by Y. Muffs, *Reichsaramäisch* attests the noun *rḥmt* (= *reḥēmûṯ*) "gift" (cf. Late Babylonian *rēmūtu*).[20] In Ugaritic, I know of only one instance of the verb *r-ḥ-m* "to show kindness" but it occurs in a firm context, which assures its meaning.[21] In Arabic this root, in contrast with *râmu*(*m*) "to love", which is expressed by an *ʾAlif*, is expressed by *Ḥah*.[22] The situation in Hebrew is admittedly more complex. The personal name *r*^{e}*ʾûmāh* (Gen. 22:24) "the loved one" gives evidence of a similar differentiation in Hebrew.[23] It is also probable that in certain contexts Hebrew *r-ḥ-m* imbeds a cognate of Akkadian *râmu*(*m*) "to love", (*AHw*'s *râmu*(*m*) II).[24]

---

19 *AHw* 952, s.v. *râmu* III, *ibid.* 970, s.v. *rêmu*(*m*),

20 Y. Muffs, *Studies in the Aramaic Legal Papyri from Elephantine* (Leiden, 1969), 132f.

21 Gordon, *op. cit.*, 125–33.

22 See Lane's Arabic-English Lexicon (London, 1867), Parts III and IV, 997: *raʾima* (Stative) "loved, affected, inclined to; to cleave to, make show of affection to". Also, *ibid.*, 1055: *raḥema* "to have mercy, pity, compassion", etc.

23 I owe this reference to Prof. Aaron Shaffer.

24 The best candidate is Ps. 18:2: "I love you / adore you Yahweh, my, strength" (Hebrew: *ʾerḥamḵā*, Qal imperfect). Cf. the rendering in *The Book of Psalms: A New Translation according to the Traditional Hebrew Text* (Philadelphia, 1972), s.v. Ps. 18:2.

It may be relevant to observe that in the Amarna letters we find for the verb meaning "to love" both the reading *ra'âmu*, and the variant *raḫāmu*, which can only be attributed to West Semitic phonetic influence.[25] At the very least, there is a phonetic difficulty in proposing that "Old West Semitic" had a root meaning "to show kindness" which was expressed in Biblical Hebrew as *r-y-m* or *r-w-m*, since one would decidedly expect a *Ḥēṯ* in the medial position.

2) The likelihood that certain Hebrew vocables represent cognates of Akkadian *râmu* "to bestow a gift" depends almost entirely on von Soden's interpretation of certain Amorite personal names. It seems somewhat tenuous to argue from a hypothesis yet to be demonstrated, and to suggest that, for example, the Hebrew personal name *yirmîyāhû* means "Yahweh has bestowed a gift", rather than "Yahweh has exalted". Were more Amorite evidence to emerge, this question would, of course, require re-examination. As regards the personal name *miryām*, which provides the framework for von Soden's study, there are further complications: Ugaritic attests the designation *mrym ṣpn* which, in the immediate context means: "the summit/height of Ṣapān". The writing is probably a variant of *mrwm*.[26] The morphological identity of the Ugaritic designation and the Hebrew personal name argue that Hebrew *miryām* is to be rendered "the exalted one", and that it possibly represents a hypocoristic form of *maryāmyāh*, or the like (cf. the masculine personal name *m^erēmôṯ* in Ezra 8:33, etc.). Names for women in the Bible require much more study, and Prof. von Soden deserves our gratitude for undertaking his investigation.[27]

3) The biblical evidence, when taken on its own, also militates against von Soden's suggested interpretation of the Hebrew term *t^erûmāh*. J. Milgrom hastened to accept von Soden's suggestion. He claimed that it supported his earlier findings, undertaken in all innocence of the evidence adduced by von Soden, that *t^erûmāh* meant "gift", and that the Hiphil *hērîm* in the biblical priestly codes often meant "to set aside", as a gift.[28] Such reasoning confuses etymology and function: In the disposition of the *t^erûmāh*, substances and materials are, indeed, "set aside", but this hardly implies that the term, itself, derives from a root whose primary meaning is: "to bestow a gift",

It is curious that von Soden attempts to draw an analogy from the term *t^enûpāh*, usually rendered "wave offering, heave offering". He suggests that yet another *taqṭûl* nominal form doesn't really derive from a medial *Waw*/*Yod* verb, and must, therefore, be related to Arabic *nauf* "excess, surplus". Ironically, it is J. Milgrom who comes to our rescue here. In another study, he correctly demon-

---

[25] See EA vol. 2, 1493f., in the glossary, s.v. *ra'âmu*.

[26] See Gordon, *op. cit.*, 483, glossary, s.v. *r*(*w*/*y*)*m*. I owe this reference to Prof. H.L. Ginsberg.

[27] See M. Noth, *Die israelitischen Personennamen im Rahmen der gemeinsemitischen Namengebung* (Stuttgart, 1928), 250, (no. 903), for some of the problems associated with the name *miryām*. It occurs to me that other feminine names are also problematic, such as *mîḵal*, *mêraḇ*, etc., which require further investigation.

[28] J. Milgrom, *Tarbiz* (Hebrew) 42 (1973), 1–11; and 44 (1975), 189.

strated that Hebrew *n-w-p*/*n-y-p* had been misunderstood, and that the Hiphil *hēnîp* means "to raise", hence: "to present". Hebrew *t^enûpāh*, if properly understood, is not problematic at all.[29]

To return to the term *t^erûmāh*, itself: The Hiphil *hērîm* may have the connotation "to raise, collect a tax, levy a payment", or the like, (cf. Num. 31:28, Ezra 8:25, 2 Chron. 30:24, 35:7). Furthermore, the semantics of "raising, lifting", are also attested by such terms as *maśʾēṯ* (Punic *mśʾt*) "tariff, tribute" (Amos 5:11, Esther 2:18), and also "ration, allotment" (Gen. 43:34, Jer, 40:5, and probably 2 Sam. 11:8). Also note particularly cultic applications in Ezek. 20:40, and probably Ps. 141:2. Please note that the *t^erûmāh* for the tabernacle project is "taken" from the Israelites (Exod. 25:2–4, etc.).

The precise force of the *taqṭûl* form in Biblical Hebrew is elusive, and yet it seems to express the consequences, or effects of the Hophal, and thus, is predicated on the Hiphil. Literally, *t^erûmāh* means: "that which is lifted, carried away", hence: "collected". The point to be made is that payments, or donations designated *t^erûmāh* are so-called not because they end up as gifts, but because they are "collected", in the first instance.[30]

In the light of the above observations, I must remain skeptical about the proposed relationship between Hebrew *t^erûmāh* and Akkadian *râmu* "to bestow a gift", and related forms such as Akkadian *tarīmtu*(*m*).

As the lexica near completion, it will be possible for Hebraists to secure a more enlightened knowledge of Akkadian lexicography. Hebrew lexicography has a long way to go before it can parallel the progress that has been made in Akkadian lexicography over the last half century. To the extent that lexicography, and its linguistic relative, philology, are valuable in the study of culture, the cross-utilization of Hebrew and Akkadian for comparative inquiry represents a worthy enterprise.

---

[29] J. Milgrom, *IEJ* 22 (1972), 33–38.

[30] It has been objected that in Biblical Hebrew *taqṭûl* forms, which reflect the Hophal, are uniformly late, and that this allegedly militates against viewing the term *t^erûmāh* as a normal, Hebrew *taqṭûl* form. The fact is, however, that in Biblical Hebrew such forms are attested in relatively early sources, as well. Cf. *t^eḇûʾāh*, lit. "that which has been brought forth (by the earth)", hence: "yield" (Lev. 25:15–16, Deut. 16:15, 22:9, 28, 33:14), and *t^eʿûdāh*, lit. "that which has been testified" (Isa. 8:16, 20), and more. As a matter of fact, *t^erûmāh* is no earlier than any other similarly structured forms. The earliest attestation of it is probably in Deut. 12:6, *passim*; most occurrences being in the later priestly sources.

The *CAD* and Biblical Hebrew Lexicography: The Role of Akkadian Cognates*

At the Berlin Rencontre of 1978 I presented a paper bearing the somewhat pretentious title: "Assyriology and Hebrew Lexicography: A Methodological Re-examination."[1] Implicitly, I was inverting the title of Benno Landsberger's 1967 study "Akkadisch-hebräische Wortgleichungen," as if to read: "Hebräisch-akkadische Wortgleichungen."[2] I discussed three examples cited to illustrate how information available from the much more plentiful cuneiform sources had helped to establish the precise meanings of several elusive biblical Hebrew lexemes. The most important of these involved forms of the biblical Hebrew verb *kāpar*, especially Piᶜᶜel *kippēr* "to purify, expiate," which is cognate with Akkadian *kapāru* A "to wipe off," D-stem *kuppuru* "to burnish, clean."[3] This verb was central to my investigation of the phenomenology of biblical ritual. Taken alone, the evidence from biblical Hebrew was inconclusive in defining the principal concept underlying biblical atonement (Hebrew *kippûrîm*). It was the Akkadian evidence that clearly identified that concept as erasing, removing, wiping off impurity.[4] Clarification of the basic sense of the verbal and derived forms in biblical Hebrew had further applications for biblical Hebrew lexicography, as was shown in a preliminary way by G. R. Driver many years earlier.[5]

On this occasion, when we honor the Assyrian Dictionary of the Oriental Institute of the University of Chicago, I wish to pursue the same subject further, focusing on the value of Akkadian cognates, as well as West Semitic cognates known from Akkadian documents, for the elucidation of biblical Hebrew. In this

---

* Originally published in Robert D. Biggs, Jennie Myers, and Martha T. Roth (eds.), *Proceedings of the 51st Rencontre Assyriologique Internationale, Held at the Oriental Institute of the University of Chicago, July 18–22, 2005* (Studies in Ancient Oriental Civilization 62; Chicago: The Oriental Institute, 2008), pp. 111–117. Reprinted with permission from the Oriental Institute of the University of Chicago.

1 Baruch A. Levine, "Assyriology and Hebrew Philology: A Methodological Re-Examination," in *Mesopotamien und seine Nachbarn; 25ᵉ Rencontre Assyriologique Internationale Berlin, 3. bis 7. Juli 1978, Teil 2*, edited by H.-J. Nissen and J. Renger (Berlin: Dietrich Reimer, 1982), pp. 521–30 {*VOL 2, PP. 261–68*}.

2 Benno Landsberger, "Akkadisch-hebräische Wortgleichungen," *Hebräische Wortforschung: Festschrift W. Baumgartner* (VTSup 16; Leiden, 1967), pp. 176–204.

3 See *CAD* s.v. *kapāru* A mngs. 1 and 3.

4 B. A. Levine, *In the Presence of the Lord* (Leiden: Brill, 1974), pp. 56–63, 123–27.

5 G. R. Driver, "Studies in the Vocabulary of the Old Testament," *Journal of Theological Studies* 34 (1933): 22–44.

pursuit, both *CAD* and *AHw* have made vast lexicographical treasures accessible to students of biblical Hebrew.

It needs to be acknowledged that there are those who doubt the value of cognate evidence for biblical Hebrew exegesis. In the first place, so it is argued, such comparisons can be misleading, because each language exhibits its own distinctive connotations, its *Eigenbegrifflichkeit.* Then, too, the meaning of a given biblical Hebrew lexeme can normally be established, or at least divined, without recourse to cognates. This can be accomplished in several ways: from context and usage on an inner-biblical basis, from ancient versions such as the Aramaic Targums, and from the extensive exegetical tradition. Indeed, we encounter few instances where dependence on comparative lexicography is indispensable, where we simply would not know the correct meaning of a biblical Hebrew lexeme without recourse to evidence from a cognate language. Finally, there are etymological and semantic complications that impede the reliable identification of cognates, especially in dealing with biblical Hebrew, a language transcribed by means of a reduced, West Semitic alphabet, a condition that triggers both homonymy and polysemy. Add to this the fact that the biblical text has been transmitted in later "Masoretic" vocalization systems that may mask the true derivation of a given lexeme. This subject was explored in a preliminary fashion by H. L. Ginsberg.[6]

And yet, our understanding of biblical Hebrew can be greatly enhanced through the careful investigation of properly identified Semitic cognates so long as we are clear as to what we seek to learn from them. For the most part, cognates enhance meaning by identifying register, or context. We learn more about what kind of a word it is that we are explaining from the more expansive usage of the cognate. I illustrate the importance of cognates by citing three examples taken from the books of Leviticus and Numbers, on which I have written commentaries.[7] All three cognates had been noted before, and my role has been merely to examine them further and to apply them methodically in biblical exegesis. I am now able to refine my earlier findings, although it is necessary to review the relevant evidence in the process.

An Example of an Akkadian Cognate of a Biblical Hebrew Lexeme

Biblical Hebrew *mūrbeket* (Lev. 6:14, 7:12, 1 Chron. 23:29) means "soaked, mixed," usually in a boiling liquid, such as oil. In all three attestations here cited, which constitute the sum-total of the biblical evidence, this term occurs in prescriptions for processing grain offerings made of semolina flour. Rabbinic sources correctly define *mūrbeket* as "soaked in boiling liquid."[8] Akkadian

---

[6] H. L. Ginsberg, "Behind the Masoret" [in Hebrew], *Tarbiz* 5 (1933/34): 208–23, and "Addenda to 'Behind the Masoret'" [in Hebrew], *Tarbiz* 6 (1934/35): 543.

[7] B. A. Levine, *Leviticus,* JPS Torah Commentary (Philadelphia: Jewish Publication Society, 1989); *idem, Numbers*, AB 4, 4A (New York: Doubleday, 1993 and 2000).

[8] *Sifraʾ, the Tannaitic Midrash on Leviticus*, edited by Isaac Hirsch Weiss (Vienna: Schlossberg, 1856; reprint: New York: Om Publishers, 1946), p. 31b s.v. *Pār. Ṣaw*, 7:6.

attests the verb *rabāku* "to decoct, make an infusion," as in preparing a poultice for healing illness, "to soak in boiling beer or water," yielding nominal *rabīku* and *ribku* "decoction."[9] Distribution (Old Babylonian, Middle Babylonian, Boghazkoi, Emar, Middle Assyrian, Standard Babylonian) suggests that these forms are part of the so-called "peripheral" or "provincial" vocabulary. Arabic attests the verb *rabaka* "to mix," said of mixing dates in melted butter.[10]

Biblical Hebrew conjugates this verb in the Hophʿal stem, passive of the causative, whereas Akkadian attests only G-stem forms, indicating that it was adapted to biblical Hebrew morphology. It is used infrequently in Rabbinic and later Hebrew, in various forms, which may suggest a derivation from earlier Hebrew.[11] The Akkadian cognate establishes the register as medicinal, or as having to do with the processing of food. Typically, the post-biblical exegetical tradition had the meaning right, as one would expect in a case involving ritual praxis. The Akkadian cognates thus serve to add realism to the biblical priestly texts in which Hebrew *mūrbeket* occurs. Biblical Hebrew usage turns out to be practically appropriate and hardly accidental, and the commentator is prompted, therefore, to investigate further Akkadian cognates of biblical Hebrew lexemes that exhibit the same register, for instance, *bālal* (Lev. 2:5, 7:10, 14:21), cognate with Akkadian *balālu* "to mix, brew."[12]

An Example of a West Semitic Cognate of a Biblical Hebrew Lexeme Known from Akkadian Sources

Biblical Hebrew *liṣmitūt* (Lev. 25:23, 30) means "as permanent transfer." This adverbial usage recurs twice, once in a prohibition against the alienation of family-held arable land by Israelites, and then, by contrast, in a statement allowing precisely such alienation—but only exceptionally in the case of urban dwellings. Thus, we read: "But the land must not be sold as permanent transfer (*liṣmitūt*), for the land is mine" (Lev. 25:23). The Aramaic Targum Onkelos translates: *laḥalûṭîn* "irretrievably," which is functionally correct.[13] According to the land-tenure system projected in Leviticus 25 and 27, sales of ancestral land were effectively long-term leases and were usually prompted by unmanageable indebtedness in a system that allowed owners to use land as security for debt. Provision was made for the redemption of land and dwellings lost pursuant to default. It has been my view that these biblical provisions reflect conditions in

[9] See *CAD* s.vv. *rabāku*, *rabīku*, and *ribku*.

[10] See Edward William Lane, *An Arabic-English Lexicon* (Edinburgh: Williams and Norgate, 1867; reprint: Beirut: Librairie du Liban, 1980), Book 1, Part 3, pp. 1021–1923.

[11] See Jacob Levy, *Wörterbuch über die Talmudim und Midraschim* (Darmstadt: Wissenschaftliche Buchgesellschaft, 1963), vol. 4, p. 416 s.v. *rebîkāh*. Also see Eliezer Ben Yehudah, *A Complete Dictionary of Ancient and Modern Hebrew* (New York: Thomas Yoseloff, 1960), vol. 7, pp. 6387–88 s.v. *rābak*.

[12] See *CAD* s.v. *balālu*.

[13] See Alexander Sperber, *The Bible in Aramaic*, vol. 1: *The Pentateuch According to Targum Onkelos* (Leiden: Brill, 1959), p. 210 s.v. Lev. 25:23, 30.

Judea under the Achaemenid imperial system. As early as 1958, J. J. Rabinowitz recognized that biblical Hebrew *ṣemitūt* was an abstract form, cognate with such passive forms as *ṣamit*, or *ṣamat*, attested thus far only in Akkadian documents from Ugarit.[14] *CAD* s.v. *ṣamātu* explains that this verb, at times written out syllabically and in other instances logographically as ŠÀM.TIL.LA.(BI.ŠÈ) (which is also rendered *ina šīmi gamri* "at full value"), is probably West Semitic, not Akkadian, and *CAD* provides an informative discussion of the legal situation described by it.

Leviticus 25:23 first expresses the prohibition of the permanent transfer of arable land, as we have seen, but then, in Leviticus 25:30, parallels the provision of the Akkadian documents from Ugarit with respect to urban dwellings specifically. So it is that Leviticus allows the seller one full year to redeem his urban dwelling, but after that period "the dwelling that is within the walled town shall legally become the property of its purchaser, as permanent transfer (*liṣmitūt*)." In Leviticus 25:30 there is the additional specification: *ledōrōtāw* "unto his generations," to which compare *ana / adi dārīti* (also *addārīti*) "for all generations" at Ugarit. Huehnergard provides a detailed analysis, further clarifying the register of the syllabic Ugaritic forms, and duly noting the biblical Hebrew relationship.[15]

Purely in phonetic terms, there is no problem in regarding forms of *ṣ-m-t* as variants of *ṣ-m-d* "to tie, grasp, hold," variously in Ugaritic and in biblical Hebrew, and this would apply to Ugaritic *mṣmt* "treaty," which calques Akkadian *rikiltu* in expressing the sense of "tying, binding."[16] But the discrete legal usage of stative *ṣamit / ṣamat* in the Akkadian documents from Ugarit argues against its association with *ṣ-m-d* "to tie, bind," a point emphasized by Huehnergard. I cannot, therefore, agree with Muffs, who associates the two and understands the transferred field to be "yoked" to the purchaser.[17] A problem remains with respect to biblical Hebrew and Ugaritic *ṣ-m-t* "to ruin, destroy," and it is likely that we have homonyms.[18] If this analysis is correct, there would be no alphabetic attestation of *ṣamātu* "to transfer" at Ugarit.

The distance in time between the Akkadian documents from Ugarit and Leviticus 25 and 27 (by my calculations about seven hundred years) should not cast doubt on the validity of the cognate relationship. Usage in the Akkadian documents from Ugarit defines the register of the biblical Hebrew forms pre-

---

[14] J. J. Rabinowitz, "A Biblical Parallel to a Legal Formula from Ugarit," *VT* 8 (1958): 95.

[15] John Huehnergard, *Ugaritic Vocabulary in Syllabic Transcription* (Atlanta: Scholars Press, 1987), pp. 171–72 s.v. ṢMT, and literature cited.

[16] G. Del Olmo Lete and J. Sanmartín, *A Dictionary of the Ugaritic Language in the Alphabetic Tradition* (Leiden: Brill, 2003), p. 587 s.v. *mṣmt*.

[17] Yochanan Muffs, *Studies in the Aramaic Legal Papyri from Elephantine*, with Prolegomenon by B. A. Levine (Leiden: Brill, 2003), pp. 20–22.

[18] See Del Olmo Lete and Sanmartín, *Dictionary*, pp. 786–87 s.vv. ṣ-m-t and ṣmt.

cisely, and as the early West Semitic vocabulary in syllabic transcription expands, we will note more and more survivals of this sort in biblical Hebrew.

A Nuance of Biblical Hebrew ṣābāʾ Clarified by the Akkadian Cognate ṣābu

It is not uncommon to find in any number of languages that military, administrative, and social terms overlap, so that we encounter ambiguity in usage and cannot be certain except from immediate context whether reference is to an army or to some other group of personnel. A salient case in point is biblical Hebrew *ṣābāʾ*, which has cognates in Ugaritic, rarely in Punic, and profusely in Akkadian as *ṣābu,* often written logographically as ERIN$_2$, and functioning at certain periods as a collective of *amēlu.*[19]

Numbers 1–4 depict the Israelites encamped in the wilderness after the Exodus from Egypt as a military force on the march to the Land of Canaan, organized by units called *ṣābāʾ,* plural *ṣebāʾôt,* a term best rendered as "corps, division(s)." In certain passages, however, similar terminology is applied to temple personnel, as in Numbers 4:3, 21–49; 8:25: for instance, where Levites are ordered to report for duty, *liṣbōʾ ṣābāʾ* "to do service," and where we read about *kol habbāʾ laṣṣābāʾ* "everyone who reports for service." Such non-military meanings in biblical Hebrew seem all to be clustered in relatively few priestly passages apart from those in Numbers, as for example in Exodus 38:8 (cf. 1 Sam. 2:22) where we find reference to women working in the temple complex who are called *haṣṣōbeʾōt* "the conscripted women," perhaps performing a service similar to the *kisalluḫḫātu* "courtyard sweepers" of the Akkadian sources.[20] Biblical Hebrew also attests a derived meaning for *ṣābāʾ*, namely, "term of service" (Isa. 40:2, Job 7:1).

As is to be expected in the West Semitic sphere, based on the distribution of Akkadian *ṣābu*, the Ugaritic cognates exhibit a predominantly military context; but note the rare Ugaritic *ṣbu anyt* "ship's crew," paralleling ERIN$_2$.MEŠ *ma-la-ḫe-e* "crew of sailors" in the Akkadian documents from Ugarit.[21] Some Ugaritic forms are admittedly difficult to parse. I maintain that Ugaritic developed a denominative *ṣabaʾa* "to march forth, arise," just as did biblical Hebrew.[22] Compare the rare *ṣabāʾu* / *ṣabāḫu* in Old Babylonian and at Mari, occurring in military contexts.[23]

In this case, what we learn from the abundant Akkadian sources where the term *ṣābu* occurs is that the basic sense of this term is "group of people, contingent of workers, population" and that "army, troop of soldiers" is merely one of such groupings. If we were dependent on biblical Hebrew alone, or even on biblical Hebrew with the addition of Ugaritic, we would have a lopsided view.

---

[19] See *CAD* s.v. *ṣābu*, especially usage o.

[20] See *CAD* s.v. *kisalluḫḫatu.*

[21] See Del Olmo Lete and Sanmartín, *Dictionary*, p. 777 s.v. ṣbu (1).

[22] See B. A. Levine, review of *Le Culte à Ugarit*, by J.-M. de Tarragon in *RB* 88 (1981): 245–50.

[23] See *CAD* s.v. *ṣabāʾu.*

Most biblical Hebrew occurrences occur in the divine epithet *YHWH ṣebāʾôt* "Yahweh of the (heavenly) hosts," and *ṣebāʾ haššāmayim* "the host of the heavens," reflecting the theme that the stars and planets are God's army, in what I have called a "military-celestial transaction."[24] The *locus classicus* of this semantic progression is Isaiah 40:26, where it is said of Yahweh, creator of the heavens, that "he deploys their corps (*ṣebāʾām*) by number, calling them all by name."

Next in frequency are the biblical military references, and only in a relatively few texts, such as those of Numbers discussed above, do we find the more general sense of "group of conscripts, personnel." A close review of the sources cited in *CAD* shows fluctuation in usage. I note that the meaning "team of workmen" is frequent in Neo-Babylonian, including in references to temple workers.[25] The Neo-Babylonian texts are contemporary with the priestly texts of Numbers, by my calculations, so that usage in Numbers would reflect contemporary terminology.

Beyond Register: Unmasking Unrecognized Biblical Hebrew Roots via Their Cognates

Another benefit accruing to the lexicographer of biblical Hebrew who chooses to search for Semitic cognates is the possibility of identifying previously unrecognized Hebrew roots, thereby enlarging the biblical Hebrew vocabulary itself. As noted above, it is important to bear in mind that the Hebrew Bible was written in a shortened alphabetic-Canaanite script, which fact makes it probable that separate and distinct Hebrew roots have coalesced or have been obscured, with one or the other being lost to us in the course of time. The first question before the exegete is whether the ancient biblical writers were aware of this graphic process, so that in their usage of the coalesced forms they could have conveyed meanings associated with the previously distinct graphemes. For example: Can we assume that a biblical author, in using the verb *ḥālaq*, would have at times intended the sense of "to pass away, die" rather than the usual sense of "to divide"? It is my view that biblical writers had such awareness. The later Masoretes lacked this same awareness and struggled with the alphabetic script before them to make sense out of difficult lexemes by vocalizing them in special ways.

In a recent study dedicated to the late Jonas Greenfield, I examined two cases in which unrecognized biblical Hebrew roots have been retrieved by adducing evidence from Akkadian and other cognate languages.[26] In another study dedi-

---

[24] B. A. Levine, "From the Aramaic Enoch Fragments: The Semantics of Cosmography," *Journal of Jewish Studies* 33 (Essays in Honor of Yigael Yadin; 1982): pp. 311–26 {*VOL 2, PP. 379–93*}.

[25] See *CAD* s.v. *ṣābu* usage o, "in NB."

[26] B. A. Levine, "The Semantics of Loss: Two Exercises in Biblical Hebrew Lexicography," in *Solving Riddles and Untying Knots: Biblical, Epigraphic, and Semitic Studies*

cated to Yochanan Muffs, I examined a third case illustrating the same process.[27] Here I mention all three, but reserve discussion for the one I consider to be the most consequential for biblical interpretation.

The first case, in the study dedicated to Greenfield, is that of Akkadian *ḫalāqu* "to disappear, vanish, to be missing or lost, to die, perish, to escape, or flee." It was Mitchell Dahood who made the connection with Ugaritic *ḫlq*, whereas Albright took note of West Semitic verbal conjugations of *ḫalāqu* in the El-Amarna documents, a matter further clarified by Anson Rainey.[28] Once again, triangulation with Ugaritic and other western sources has reinforced conclusions that had been arrived at by a direct comparison with Akkadian concerning a biblical Hebrew homograph that had not been recognized prior to modern research. As a result, it is no longer necessary to associate all biblical Hebrew attestations with "dividing, splitting," or alternatively with "smoothness," which often yielded forced translations and resulted in unusual Masoretic vocalizations. I proposed no fewer than eight realizations of this homographic root in the Hebrew Bible. To cite just one example, consider Jeremiah 37:12: "Then, Jeremiah departed from Jerusalem to travel to the territory of Benjamin, so as to flee (Masoretic *laḥaliq*, better vocalized *laḥalōq*) from there in the midst of the people." The Masoretes vocalized the consonants as *laḥaliq*, syncopated for *lehaḥalîq*, the stative Hiphᶜil, meaning "to slip," therefore reflecting the sense of smoothness. I suppose we can still say "to slip away" in idiomatic English, but the verse in Jeremiah is better understood as expressing flight, or escape, rather than slippery smoothness! So, we would have three homographs in biblical Hebrew: (1) *ḥ-l-q* I "to split, divide," (2) *ḥ-l-q* II "to be smooth," and (3) *ḥ-l-q* III "to disappear, vanish." Biblical Hebrew had conflated the two separate *ḥēt*-consonants evident in the unreduced Ugaritic alphabet. In Ugaritic, the sense "to split, divide" was expressed by dotted *ḥēt*, as in the noun *ḥlq* "part, limb," whereas "to vanish, die, be destroyed" was expressed by looped *ḫēt*.[29]

The second case, in the study dedicated to Muffs, is that of Akkadian *damāmu* "to mourn, wail," a meaning which makes better sense for forms of biblical Hebrew *d-m-m* in a number of biblical passages than does "to be still, silent." Here, too, there was evidence from Ugaritic, and also from Eblaite. In a bilingual lexical series edited by Pettinato, logographic SI.DU$_3$ is rendered *t/di-*

in Honor of Jonas C. Greenfield, edited by Z. Zevit et al. (Winona Lake: Eisenbrauns, 1995), pp. 137–58 {*VOL 2, PP. 281–99*}.

[27] B. A. Levine, "Silence, Sound, and the Phenomenology of Mourning in Biblical Israel," *JANES* 22 (*Comparative Studies in Honor of Yochanan Muffs*; 1993): 89–106 {*VOL 1, PP. 335–53*}.

[28] Mitchell Dahood, "Hebrew-Ugaritic Lexicography II," *Biblica* 45 (1964): 408; *idem*, "Hebrew-Ugaritic Lexicography IV," *Biblica* 47 (1966): 406; W. F. Albright, "Two Little-Understood Amarna Letters from the Middle Jordan Valley," *BASOR* 89 (1943): 17 n. 60; Anson F. Rainey, "The Barth-Ginsberg Law in the Amarna Tablets," *Eretz-Israel* 14, *Ginsberg Volume* (1978): 11.

[29] Del Olmo Lete and Sanmartín, *Dictionary*, p. 361 s.v. *ḫlq*, n.m.

mu-mu "lament."[30] Similarly, in an administrative text edited by Archi, we find the noun *da-ma-tu* "lament."[31] What had been known previously by Paul Haupt solely from Akkadian was now attested in early West Semitic.[32] To cite just one biblical Hebrew example, in Isaiah 23:1–2, *hêlîlû ʾoniyyôt Taršîš* "Wail, you ships of Tarshish," is paralleled in the next verse by: *dōmmû yōšebê ʾî* "Moan, you island dwellers."

The third case, once again in the study dedicated to Greenfield, is perhaps the most interesting because it would lend a very different meaning to certain biblical texts that speak of war and conquest, of migration and deportation. There is also the fact that this case reveals a background of homonyms in Akkadian itself. I refer to the biblical Hebrew verb *ʾābad*, which in the simple stem has stative force and is normally taken to mean "to perish, cease to exist," and in the Piᶜᶜel and Hiphᶜil as "to destroy, ruin." Closer examination of both the simple and derived stems reveals that in quite a few instances biblical Hebrew *ʾābad* functions as a verb of motion and does not connote complete or irreversible loss and destruction, but rather disappearance, absence, or distance. A semantic range that reaches from irreversible loss—death, destruction—to absence, disappearance, and distance, is possible, but in certain contexts requires a semantic "stretch" and creates ambiguity.

CAD registers two Akkadian lexemes: (1) *abātu* A, normally an active transitive verb meaning "to destroy, ruin," less frequently stative in the sense of "to collapse, fall down,"[33] and (2) *abātu* B, a stative verb attested only in the G-stem and N-stem meaning "to run away, flee."[34] Not only are the Sumerian lexical equivalents entirely separate, but usage indicates clearly separate meanings. In the lexical series, the synonyms of *abātu* B include *narqû* "remote," *naparkû* "to abscond, escape," and interestingly *ḫalāqu* "to disappear, vanish." Why not consider the possibility that biblical Hebrew *ʾābad* conflates meanings associated with both *abātu* A and *abātu* B in Akkadian? In biblical Hebrew the simple stem of *ʾābad* is stative, so that the active-transitive sense "to destroy" requires either the Piᶜᶜel or Hiphᶜil.

---

[30] See Giovanni Pettinato, *Culto officiale ad Ebla durante il regno di Ibbi-Šipiš* (Rome: Missione Archeologica Italiana in Siria, 1979), p. 47, text 1, rev. ii 25–iii 12, and text 3, rev. xii 21–26; Pettinato, *Testi lexicale bilingui della Biblioteca*: 2769 (Naples: Istituto Universitario Orientale, 1982), p. 320, No. 1116.

[31] See Alfonso Archi, *Asseganzioni di tessuti (Archivo L2769),* Archivi reali di Ebla, Testi 1 (Rome: Missione Archeologica Italiana in Siria, 1985), p. 126, text 13, rev. iv 5–7.

[32] See Paul Haupt, "Some Assyrian Etymologies," *American Journal of Semitic Languages* 26 (1909): 1–26; M. Dahood, "Textual Problems in Isaia," *Catholic Biblical Quarterly* 22 (1960): 400–09. Also see *CAD* s.vv. *damāmu* and *dimmatu*.

[33] See *CAD* s.v. *abātu* A.

[34] See *CAD* s.v. *abātu* B.

Let's try it out. I begin with Deuteronomy 26:5: *ʾArāmmî ʾōbēd ʾābî* translated by Albright as: "a fugitive Aramean was my father."[35] This translation fits, but Albright did not inform us how he arrived at this meaning for the simple stem in biblical Hebrew. Compare the Akkadian N-stem participle *munnabtu* "deportee, fugitive" from *abātu* B, a term discussed by Buccellati in its sociopolitical context.[36] Or compare the reference in an annal of Sennacherib to LÚ *Aramē ḫalqū* "Aramean fugitives," noted by B. Mazar.[37] By the way, Akkadian *abātu* B may also account for the syllabic Ugaritic form *na-ba-di-šu-nu* "their flight," glossed in an Akkadian text from Ugarit and cited by Huehnergard, who does not, however, take cognizance of the existence of both *abātu* A and *abātu* B in Akkadian.[38] He notes that in the same text we also find the comparable Akkadian verbal form *innabbitû* "they fled." In my view, we have two N-stem realizations of *abātu* B at Ugarit, one in Akkadian and the other in syllabic Ugaritic. What has been missed is the attestation of the meaning "to remove, disperse" for the D-stem of Ugaritic *abd* in a magical composition dealing with snake bites, *KTU* 1.100+1.107. Inevitably, that meaning expresses the connotations associated with Akkadian *abātu* B.[39]

This leads directly to another facet of the biblical Hebrew evidence: the application of Akkadian *abātu* B to explain the Piʿʿel and Hiphʿil realizations of the biblical Hebrew root *ʾābad.* In the Piʿʿel, biblical Hebrew *ʾibbēd* often means "to destroy," but in certain passages it means "to disperse, drive away," as applied, for example, to dispersing the flocks (Jer. 23:1). Turning to what may be regarded as Hiphʿil reflexes of Akkadian *abātu* B, we may cite the usage in Numbers 24:19 within an oracle on the Israelite conquest of Moab. There we read that the land will be depopulated and subjugated, and that Jacob "will deport (*weheʾebîd*) survivors from the town (or: 'from Ar')." Similarly, in Zephaniah 2:5 we read that the Philistines will be exiled: "Canaan, land of the Philistines, I shall depopulate you (*wehaʾabadtîk*), leaving no inhabitants." Finally, in Leviticus 23:30 the penalty of banishment, usually expressed by Hebrew *wehikrattî* "I will cut off, banish," is instead expressed by the Hiphʿil of *ʾābad*: "I will banish (*wehaʾabadtî*) that person from among his kinfolk." Most interesting of all is the sequence of Leviticus 26:38–39: In verse 38, as these verses are usually rendered, we read: "You will perish (*waʾabadtem*) among the nations, and the land

[35] W. F. Albright, *From the Stone Age to Christianity: Monotheism and the Historical Process* (Garden City, NY: Doubleday, 1940), p. 181.

[36] Giorgio Buccellati, "Apīrū and Munnabtūtu: The Stateless of the First Cosmopolitan Age," *JNES* 36 (1977): 146–47.

[37] Benjamin Mazar, "The Aramean Empire and Its Relations with Israel," *Biblical Archaeologist* 25 (1962): 98–120. The citation is from the annals of the eighth campaign; see D. David Luckenbill, *The Annals of Sennacherib*, Oriental Institute Publications 2 (Chicago: University of Chicago Press, 1924), p. 42, col. v 22–23.

[38] Huehnergard, *Ugaritic Vocabulary*, p. 104 s.v. ʾBD.

[39] B. A. Levine and J.-M. de Tarragon, "Shapshu Cries Out in Heaven: Dealing with Snake Bites at Ugarit," *RB* 95 (1988): 481–518.

of your enemies will devour you." Verse 39 continues: "Those of you who survive(!) will be heartsick over your iniquities in the land of your enemies." Correct the translation of verse 38 to: "You will *disappear* among the nations; the land of your enemies will consume you," and there is no contradiction between one verse and the next. It turns out that biblical Hebrew *ʾābad*, if understood to reflect Akkadian *abātu* B, is central to understanding responses in biblical literature to the policy of deportation so widely practiced in the ancient Near East.

An Interesting Calque

In Zechariah 4:7 we encounter the construction הר הגדול "the great mountain." In the biblical lexicon this construction is unique. Those familiar with Akkadian epithets will recognize the Hebrew as a calque of Akkadian *šadû rabû* "great mountain," an epithet of gods, notably of Enlil and Aššur, and of temples, such as the Ekur temple.[40]

The passage in Zechariah is cryptic, to be sure, but its immediate context indicates that of temple building. We are told (in verse 9) that the Judean prince, Zerubbabel, laid the foundation of the restored Jerusalem temple during the second year of Darius I and are assured that he would complete the project. Thus, we read:

> What are you, O Great Mountain (*har haggādôl*)?
> Before Zerubbabel you are no more than a plain.
> He shall bring out the first stone to shouts of:
> "It is beautiful, beautiful!"

When we look more closely, we observe that the Hebrew construction *ʾeben hārōʾšāh* "the first stone," which is also unique in biblical Hebrew, suggests Akkadian *libittu maḫrītu* "the first brick," used in foundation rituals, as in the fairly contemporary rituals from Uruk.[41] The point is that what appear to be, on an inner-biblical basis alone, highly unusual constructions become more meaningful when comparative lexicographic evidence from Akkadian is introduced. It is possible to identify the "register" of the biblical vocabulary more knowledgeably.

Conclusion

If I were to ask myself what has changed most since the Berlin Rencontre of 1978 with respect to Semitic lexicography, I would have to say that it is the expansion of the early West Semitic vocabulary in syllabic transcription. This phenomenon is in evidence in many archives, including those from Ebla, Mari, Emar, and Ugarit, and in the Amarna correspondence. Although lateral east-west

---

[40] See *CAD* s.v. *šadû* A mng. 1n.

[41] See Carol L. Meyers and Eric M. Meyers, *Haggai, Zechariah 1–8*, AB 25B (New York: Doubleday, 1987), pp. 227–77, for an extensive discussion of Zechariah 4:1–14. On *libittu maḫrītu*, see *CAD* s.v. *libittu*, especially mng. 1c–2′.

cognates, as between biblical Hebrew and Akkadian, will become less crucial, there will always be instances where such is the only evidence available. More and more, however, we will encounter triangulation and other more complex relationships involving early West Semitic cognates of biblical Hebrew lexemes in syllabic transcription, as has been illustrated here. In any event, this is surely not the time to abandon the search for cognates of biblical Hebrew, eastern or western.

The Semantics of Loss: Two Exercises in Biblical Hebrew Lexicography*

This study examines two Biblical Hebrew lexemes whose meaning has not been fully realized. It is shown that Biblical Hebrew ḥālaq "to be lost, disappear, perish" is a homonym of ḥālaq "to split, divide, apportion". Proper recognition of its nature alters our understanding of a number of biblical passages. It is further shown that the semantic range of Biblical Hebrew ʾābad encompasses the meanings of two probable Akkadian cognates, abātu A "to destroy, ruin" and abātu B, a stative verb connoting absence and flight. Failure to recognize these two sets of meanings for the verb ʾābad has likewise prevented a proper understanding of certain biblical passages.

My first introduction to the scholarship of Jonas Greenfield was in the form of his two early articles, both entitled "Lexicographical Notes."[1] These studies, which have been followed by many similarly enlightening inquiries into the meanings of words, are models of method and analysis and have set a lasting standard of excellence and insight. It is therefore appropriate in a study honoring Jonas Greenfield to engage in further lexicographical inquiry.

Among the problems that complicate the lexicographical analysis of Biblical Hebrew (henceforth BH) is that of homonyms. The first of our two exercises focuses on a proposed homonym, BH *ḥālaq* "to be lost, to disappear, to perish", and it is therefore important to discuss the arguments for and against the acknowledgment of homonyms in a given language. Some lexicographers of the Semitic languages have held that originally homonymous roots tend to coalesce in time, a process sometimes referred to as "contamination," and as a result they lose their distinctive meanings. In this view, biblical writers may no longer have been aware of distinctive roots and meanings, even when they were clearly identifiable. This approach to etymology and semantics hardly encourages the search for or acknowledgment of homonyms in BH; in fact, the very existence of ho-

---

* Originally published in Z. Zevit, S. Gitin, and M. Sokoloff (eds.), *Solving Riddles and Untying Knots: Biblical, Epigraphic and Semitic Studies in Honor of Jonas C. Greenfield* (Winona Lake, IN: Eisenbrauns, 1995), pp. 137–58. Reprinted with permission from Eisenbrauns.

Author's note: I wish to thank my colleague Anson Rainey for discussing the problems treated in this article with me. At one point I even discussed the verb *ḥālaq* with Jonas Greenfield himself; as always, his comments were most enlightening.

[1] J. C. Greenfield, "Lexicographical Notes I," *HUCA* 29 (1958) 159–203; *idem*, "Lexicographical Notes II," *HUCA* 30 (1959) 141–51.

monyms as a phenomenon of language is often downplayed by Semitists in favor of polysemic connotations, all deriving from a single root.

The present investigation proceeds from the assumption that the phonemic inventory produced by speakers of a given language and recorded by its writers in literate societies is actually fairly limited. This situation gives rise to homophones and homographs, words that sound alike and/or are written alike but have no etymological connection to each other.

It would be logical to postulate such a process for BH, which is known to us solely from written documents and whose alphabet represents a shortened version of what was a longer West Semitic orthography. It was inevitable that certain originally distinct phonemes would combine. But, even when no such orthographic or phonic reduction in the writing system is to be assumed, we may have genuinely homonymous roots merely because the phonemic inventory of BH was limited. Furthermore, the dialectology of BH shows a high degree of interpenetration with other Semitic languages, so that lexicographical input from diverse sources may have added to the number of homonyms.

In the case of BH there is yet another factor that tends to impede the identification of homonymous lexemes, namely, the Masoretic vocalization system—the reading of the biblical text as it has been received. Long ago H. L. Ginsberg illustrated by clear examples how this system masks morphological realizations of known roots in BH (such as the internal *Qal* passive, for example) and at times even reads functional lexemes out of existence.[2] It is all well and good to try to understand the basis for the Masoretic pointings, but the lexicographer should not be restrained from considering alternative readings of the same orthographic text that would reveal new meanings.

The second of our examples provides a subtle contrast to the phenomenon of homonyms, representing an instance of what has been called "dialectal interpenetration." We have learned that BH *ʾābad* enjoys a broader semantic range than had been thought, for as it turns out it connotes not only substantial loss, but absence and distance as aspects of loss. As such, BH *ʾābad* comprehends the semantic range of two Akkadian roots, *abātu* A, primarily an active-transitive verb consistently connoting substantial loss, ruin, destruction, death; and *abātu* B, which connotes only absence, flight, vanishing, and the like. In other words, BH *ʾābad* may in some instances mean what Akkadian *abātu* B means. In fact, BH *ʾābad* may be cognate with both of these homonymous Akkadian roots, which are occasionally confused even in Akkadian itself. An awareness of the lexicographical situation in Akkadian suggested that we were missing something in our understanding of the semantic range of BH *ʾābad*. An investigation of Ugaritic *abd* shows that the situation in BH had been anticipated, because Ugaritic *abd* also expresses both meanings: substantial loss as death, and loss as removal and distancing.

It is my overall experience that, more often than not, biblical writers exhibited considerable subtlety in their choice of words and that, consequently, the

[2] H. L. Ginsberg, "Behind the Masoret," *Tarbiz* 5 (1933–4) 208–23 [Hebrew].

modern reader of the Hebrew Bible ought not to be content with surface meanings and leveled translations. Both of the present exercises will, it is hoped, endorse this perception.

Biblical Hebrew ḥlq

Loss as Absence and as Extinction: Biblical Hebrew *ḥālaq* "to disappear, be lost, to perish"; *ḥillēq* "to disperse, drive away, to destroy, to cause the loss of land".

A perusal of the lexica, from Gesenius[3] to *HALAT*,[4] shows that the etymology of the BH root *ḥ-l-q* is complex. Two definitions have dominated the discussion of BH *ḥ-l-q* until relatively recently, as we learn from the presentation of these phenomena in *HALAT*: (1) *ḥ-l-q* I, a stative verb "to be smooth", and in the *Hiphil*, with active-transitive force: "to smoothen", in various ways, ranging from hammering metal (Isa 41:7), to speaking with a smooth tongue. (2) *ḥ-l-q* II, an active-transitive verb "to split, divide, apportion", connotations clearly attested in BH both in the simple stem and in the *Piel*, with intensive force.

HALAT adds *ḥ-l-q* III "to be lost, die, perish", citing cognates in Ugaritic, Akkadian, Ethiopic, and Tigre. However, only Lam 4:16, together with Ps 17:14, itself not a valid example, are singled out as possibly attesting this root in BH, even though more is now known about the workings of this verb.

It is not my purpose here to attempt a full resolution of the etymological problems attendant upon BH *ḥ-l-q* in its various realizations. On the face of it, the meanings listed for both *ḥ-l-q* I and II in *HALAT*'s classification are attested for Arabic *ḫalaqa*, which means both "to smoothen" and "to divide, measure, form".[5] It is customary, however, for Arabic lexicographers to list homographic roots under the same entry, and it is likely that Arabic *ḫalaqa* itself may express more than one original root.

In any event, my concern here is with Ugaritic *ḫlq* and Akkadian *ḫalāqu* and what they have to teach us about BH usage. Whatever we decide about other sets of meanings, this set is clear and unambiguous in Ugaritic and Akkadian. I will now examine the usage of the root that *HALAT* lists as *ḥ-l-q* III and to trace its path in BH. In my view, there is no valid basis for associating BH *ḥ-l-q* III, the cognate of Akkadian *ḫalāqu* and Ugaritic *ḫlq*, with notions of division, apportionment, or smoothness; it is simply a separate root, notwithstanding its phonetic identity with Arabic *ḫalaqa*.

---

[3] H. F. W. Gesenius, *Thesaurus Philologicus* (Leipzig, 1835) 483–85.

[4] L. Koehler and W. Baumgartner, *HALAT* (5 vols.; Leiden, 1967–96) 1.309–10.

[5] *Lane's Arabic-English Lexicon* (London, 1855) 1.799–803, s.v. *ḫalaqa*. Lane lists the first meaning of Arabic *ḫalaqa* as "to measure" and then proceeds to notions of creation, bringing things into existence according to a model. Meaning 12 is "it was, or became smooth", in the sense of being without fractures or being worn smooth. There are nouns such as *ḫalqun* "a share or portion" and adjectives like *aḫlaqun* "smooth".

Comparative Evidence

I begin with the ancient Near Eastern comparative evidence as background. Ugaritic poetry attests *ḫlq* as a parallel word to *mt* "he died, he is dead". This comparative observation on the meaning of BH *ḥ-l-q* was first offered by Dahood,[6] who cited a passage in the myth of Baal and Mot,[7] where we read of the death of Baal:

> *mǵny.lbʿl.*
> *npl.la/rṣ.*
> *mt.aliyn.bʿl*
> *ḫlq.zbl.bʿl.arṣ*
>
> We two arrived at Baal,
> He had fallen to the ground.
> "Dead is Mighty Baal;
> Perished is the prince, lord of earth!"[8]

As noted by Dahood, Ugaritic *ḫlq* is cognate with Akkadian *ḫalāqu* "to disappear, vanish, to become missing or lost, to perish; to escape, flee". The Mesopotamian lexical series list as synonyms of *ḫālaqu* Akkadian *nabūtu* "fled, gone" (from *abātu* B) and *narqū* "distant, away". Sumerian BA.ÚS BA.AN.ZÁḪ is translated *im-tu-ut iḫ-li-iq* "he died, he perished", which immediately recalls the Ugaritic parallelism *mt*//*ḫlq* (*CAD Ḫ*, 36–40). In the D-stem, Akkadian *ḫulluqu* has a wide range of meanings, including "to cause a loss, allow to escape, remove, destroy, ruin".[9]

It is telling that the Semitic root realized as Akkadian *ḫalāqu* and as Ugaritic *ḫlq* also occurs in the El Amarna correspondence. Furthermore, in the El Amarna dialect it develops distinctive connotations and is cast both in the usual Akkadian morphology and in West Semitic verbal patterns. These facts of distribution and morphology demonstrate the rootedness of this verb in West Semitic, quite apart from its occurrence in Ugaritic and BH.

Albright[10] recognized a West Semitic *yiqṭal* form of *ḫalāqu* in EA 274:14, the third-person feminine singular *tiḫlaq*, in a passage later cited by M. Greenberg[11] because of its relevance to the Ḫapiru question:

---

[6] M. Dahood, "Hebrew-Ugaritic Lexicography II," *Biblica* 45 (1964) 408; *idem*, "Hebrew-Ugaritic Lexicography IV," *Biblica* 47 (1966) 406.

[7] J. C. L. Gibson, *Canaanite Myths and Legends* (2d ed.; Edinburgh, 1978) 73 (5 vi 8–10).

[8] Text: *ibid.*; my translation.

[9] F. C. Fensham ("Malediction and Benediction in Ancient Near Eastern Vassal-Treaties and the Old Testament," *ZAW* 74 [1962] 5) calls attention to the use of Akkadian *ḫalāqu* in the curse sections of vassal treaties found at Ugarit, where D-stem *ḫulluqu* may characterize in a general way the specified destruction to be brought upon all who violate the treaty.

[10] W. F. Albright, "Two Little Understood Amarna Letters from the Middle Jordan Valley," *BASOR* 89 (1943) 17 n. 60.

> *yi-ki-im* LUGAL *be-li* KUR-*šu iš-tu qa-te* LÚ.MEŠ SA.GAZ.MEŠ *la-a te-eḫ-la-*[*a*]*q* URU.KI URU *Ṣa-pu-na*
>
> Let the king, my lord, rescue his land from the hands of the SA.GAZ (= Ḫapiru). Let not your city, Sapuna, be lost.

A. F. Rainey explains that the standard Akkadian G-stem of the present future would be *iḫalliq* in the relevant clause, since the thematic vowel of this verb is *-i-* and since in Akkadian *ālu* "city", the antecedent of the verb, is masculine.[12] But in West Semitic languages, words for "city" are feminine, and since the Barth-Ginsberg law applies, the thematic vowel of the G-stem becomes *-a-*. The form *tiḫlaq*, with "city" as antecedent, must therefore represent the third feminine singular.

There are additional attestations of the verb *ḫalāqu* in the West Semitic morphological pattern, including D-stem forms. An example occurs in EA 197:33–34:

> *u an-nu-ú* PN *qa-du* PN *yu-ḫa-li-qu* KUR A-*bi*
>
> And now, whereas PN together with PN caused the loss of the land of Apu …

So much for the verb *ḫalāqu* in West Semitic morphology. Moran, in his discussion of EA 197, offers a further insight concerning usage of the verb *ḫalāqu* in the El Amarna correspondence. It seems that D-stem *ḫulluqu*, however it may be cast morphologically, always has as its direct object a location, a land, or a city. This leads Moran to state: "The 'destruction' is not necessarily material, but most often the loss by the Egyptians of political control."[13] When G-stem *ḫalāqu* has as its subject a place, as is the case in EA 274:14 cited above, this is also the functional sense of the verb.

In summary, we are able to trace the extended history and the wide distribution of cognates of BH *ḥ-l-q* in West Semitic, in Ugaritic, and in the El Amarna dialect. We are not dealing with merely another Akkadian cognate, although even such a situation ought not to deter us from the enterprise of comparative lexicography.

Biblical Evidence

The following suggested attestations of BH *ḥ-l-q* (III) are presented for consideration.

---

[11] M. Greenberg, *The Ḫab/piru* (AOS 39; New Haven, 1955) 46.

[12] A. F. Rainey, "The Barth-Ginsberg Law in the Amarna Tablets," *Eretz-Israel* 14 (Ginsberg Volume; 1978) 11.

[13] W. L. Moran, *Les Lettres d'El Amarna* (Littératures anciennes du Proche-Orient 13; Paris, 1987) 289 n. 1.

ḥālaq libbām (Hos 10:2)

It is this occurrence of a verb *ḥālaq* that first suggested to me the presence in BH of a cognate of Akkadian *ḫalāqu* "to disappear, to vanish, to become missing or lost, to perish", although I was later to learn that others had found the realization of this root elsewhere in the Hebrew Bible. In the course of assessing Ginsberg's theory of Hosean influences on Deuteronomy,[14] I found myself attempting to make sense out of Hos 10:1–8, a powerful critique of northern Israelite religiosity in the third quarter of the eighth century B.C.E.[15]

Hos 10:1–2, which opens the oracle, presents a mixed metaphor in which Northern Israel is compared to a vine that had been fruitful but was now ravaged and broken. The more prosperous this society became, the more altars and cultic stelae were erected. But the lavish endowment of the cult came to an abrupt halt when the fortunes of the society changed dramatically for the worse. The people promptly turned against the royally sponsored cult and tore down their altars. I translate as follows:

> Israel is a ravaged vine;
> His fruit is like him (*piryô yišweh lô*).
> As his fruit increased,
> So did he proliferate altars.
> But their devotion is lost (*ḥālaq libbām*),
> Now that they have experienced misfortune.
> He pulls down their altars,
> Ruins their cultic stelae (Hos 10:1–2).[16]

The Hebrew *ḥālaq libbām* in v. 2 has usually been taken in one of two ways: to some it meant "their heart is deceitful", a notion derived from *HALAT*'s *ḥ-l-q* I "to be smooth, slick". Just as smooth lips, tongues, and mouths speak deceitfully (Ps 55:22; Prov 2:16, 5:10, 7:5, 26:28), so would a "smooth" heart be untrue. Thus, Ps 12:3: *śĕpat ḥălāqôt bĕlēb wālēb yĕdabbērû* "with smoothened lips, they speak with two minds (literally: with one heart and another)". Alternatively, *ḥālaq libbām* has been taken to mean "their heart is divided", in the sense of being uncommitted, disloyal, from *ḥ-l-q* II "to be split, divided". This would, however, constitute a virtually unique case of the stative sense for *ḥ-l-q* "to divide, apportion", which elsewhere has active-transitive force in the simple stem.

[14] H. L. Ginsberg, *The Israelian Heritage of Judaism* (New York, 1982) 19–24.

[15] B. A. Levine, Review of *The Israelian Heritage of Judaism*, by H. L. Ginsberg, in *AJS Review* 12 (1987) 143–57 {*VOL 1, PP. 101–12*}.

[16] In this translation the Hebrew words *ʿattâ yeʾĕšāmû* in Hos 10:2, which follow *hālaq libbām*, are understood as stating the cause for Northern Israel's loss of devotion. Misfortune undermined faith. (In the NJPS, misfortune is conveyed by the words *hālaq libbām* "their boughs are split".) The stative verb *ʾāšēm* may connote the punishment of guilt incurred, not just the guilt itself or feelings of guilt. As a matter of fact, the connotation of punishment seems to be part of Hosea's diction (cf. Hos 4:15, 14:1).

Perusing the concordances and the lexica, one will usually find *ḥālaq libbām* of Hos 10:2 listed under two entries, with a question mark in both! Some have even suggested vocalizing consonantal *ḥlq* as a *Pual* form, *ḥullaq*, to produce the sense of being divided.

Undoubtedly sensitive to the weakness of existing renditions, the translators of the NJPS took this verse differently. The metaphor of the vine was carried over into v. 2, so that it is "the heart" of the vine that is split, not the hearts of the people. A note refers the reader to 2 Sam 18:14, where we read that Absalom was caught by his hair in the branches of an oak tree and remained alive "in the thickness of the oak" (*bĕlēb hāʾēlâ*).

Still others have suggested emending *ḥālaq* to *ḥālap* "to pass away", conveying the sense that the heart of the people, namely, their devotion or affection, had left them. This interpretation is certainly closer to what we would expect in context and, curiously, it is one of the precise connotations conveyed by Akkadian *ḫalāqu*, making it unnecessary and undoubtedly incorrect to emend the Masoretic Text.

There are two principal sets of emotions, attitudes, and resulting relationships expressed by Hebrew *lēb* "heart, mind" that may shed light on the meaning of enigmatic *ḥālaq libbām* in Hos 10:2, once the Akkadian-Semitic meanings of *ḫalāqu* "to pass away, flee, disappear" are brought to bear on the interpretation of this verse. The two are courage and devotion. With respect to both, notions of closeness and distance and of fullness and loss alternate in biblical usage. Hebrew *lēb* as "courage" is not difficult to document. Thus Jer 4:9: "It shall happen on that day, speech of YHWH, that the courage of the king shall be lost and the courage of the princes (*yōʾbad lēb hammelek wĕlēb haśśārîm*); that the priests shall be desolate, and the prophets shall be stunned". This is, of course, the image of "losing heart," and the fact that the stative verb *ʾābad* is used to express this emotional state is significant. After all, Akkadian *abātu* B "to be lost, perish" is a synonym of *ḫalāqu* in the Sumero-Akkadian lexical series, as noted above. The loss of courage is also conveyed by the idiom *nāpal lēb* "the heart fell" (1 Sam 17:32); and "to discourage" others, to nullify their courage, is conveyed by the idiom *hēnîʾ lēb* (Num 32:7, 9; cf. similar images in Josh 14:8; Isa 35:3–4, 46:8; Jer 48:41, 49:22). It is possible, therefore, that *ḥālaq libbām* in Hos 10:2 means "they lost their courage".[17]

But it is probably the loss of devotion that best suits the immediate context of Hos 10:2 after all. In Isa 29:13–14 this state of mind is conveyed by the image of the distant heart:

> The LORD said: Whereas this people draws near in [the words of] of his mouth, and with his lips honors me, he has distanced his heart

[17] *CAD Ḫ*, 37, in the lexical section, cites Old Babylonian LÚ = *ša* part 4:21: LÚ.ŠÀ.ŠU.GUL.AG = *ša li-ib-*[*ba-šu*] *ḫu-ul-*[*lu-qú*] "one whose heart has vanished (perhaps a coward or a weakling)." This is close to being an exact parallel to BH *ḥālaq libbām*, but because there is no context to inform us clearly what "vanished heart" means, we are back where we started.

> from me (*wĕlibbô riḥaq mimmennî*), so that their worship of me is merely the practiced duty of men—for that reason do I persist in dazing this people, dazing them over and again, so that the wisdom of his sages is lost, and the discernment of his analysts is obscured.

Actually, one could just as well read *wĕlibbô rāḥaq mimmennî* "though his heart has become distant from me", introducing the stative sense of the simple stem, instead of the *Piel riḥaq*. In any event, usage of the verb *rāḥaq* "to be distant" recalls the fact, noted above, that one of the synonyms of Akkadian *ḫalāqu* in the Sumero-Akkadian lexical series is *narqū* "distant". One is reminded of Jer 12:2b: "You are near in their mouth, but distant (*wĕrāḥôq*) from their kidneys".

That the image of the distant heart is a way of expressing loss of devotion is reflected in such idioms as "to steal away the heart" (*gānab lēb*) in 2 Sam 15:16 and "to remove the heart" (*hēšîr lēb*) in Job 12:24, as well as "to turn the heart away" (*hēšîb lēb*) in Ezra 6:22. Conversely, restoration of loyalty is expressed as "the heart shall return" (*wĕšāb lēb*), in 1 Kgs 12:27. This idea is expressed most dramatically in Mal 3:24: "He shall 'restore the heart' (*wĕhēšîb lēb*) of fathers to sons, and the heart of sons to their fathers," and so forth.

Come to think of it, Hos 10:1–2 appears to resonate the thought earlier conveyed in Hos 7:11:

> Ephraim behaved like a stray pigeon,
> Showing no fidelity (*ʾên lēb*);
> They called out to Egypt,
> They went to Assyria.

Masoretic *wayyēḥālēq ʿălêhem laylâ* (Gen 14:15)

As the consonants are pointed, this *Niphal* form, derived by the Masoretes from *ḥ-l-q* "to divide", is usually taken to convey the sense of detachment, of deployment in units. I would translate: "He detached himself against them at night, he and his officers, and slew them". Abram had mustered his forces (if that is what *wayyāreq* in the preceding verse means), attacked the invading kings, and routed them, pursuing them to a point all the way north of Damascus.

And yet this rendering is somewhat forced and glosses over a syntactic and a morphological irregularity. We would expect the *Niphal* of *ḥ-l-q* "to divide, apportion" to refer to something that happened to Abram and his forces; that they were themselves split up or divided into units. In similar circumstances, we read that Jacob split up his children (the Hebrew is *wayyaḥaṣ* "he divided in half") when he saw Esau and his forces approaching (Gen 33:1). And yet, the occurrence of the *Niphal* in an indirect object clause, *wayyēhāleq ʿălêhem*, inevitably carries the action to the others, to "them", and the *Niphal* thus loses its reflexive force. The verb now impacts its object, and this is strange for the *Niphal* stem.

If we are free to vocalize the verb as a *Qal* form and accordingly read *wayyehelaq ʿălêhem laylâ*, deriving the resultant form from *ḥ-l-q* III in the sense "to flee", the following translation becomes possible: "He fled past them at night, he and his officers, and slew them". Reference to nighttime is, after all, suggestive of stealth, and we would have a typical maneuver whereby one force moves behind the other and then attacks.

Masoretic *ʾêzeh hadderek yēḥāleq ʾôr* (Job 38:24)

The problems in this descriptive statement are similar to those we encountered in Gen 14:15, where a *Niphal* pointing also occurs. Here it seems almost compelling to vocalize the verb as a *Qal* form and to read *yehĕlaq ʾôr*, deriving the verbal form from *ḥ-l-q* III "to flee, vanish, be lost", which yields the translation: "Where is the path by which light vanishes?" This is the second instance where the Masoretes used a *Niphal* pointing in their effort to elicit meaning, most probably because they did not know of BH *ḥ-l-q* III, the cognate of Akkadian *ḫalāqu* and Ugaritic *ḫlq*.

In anticipation of what will be discussed presently, the complete verse should be translated, because, among other things, it shows the similarity in meaning of *ḥ-l-q* III in the *Piel* stem (*ḥillēq*) and Hebrew *hēpîṣ* "to disperse". I would therefore render Job 38:24 as follows: "Where is the path by which light vanishes, [by which] the East wind is driven (*yāpēṣ*) over the earth?"

I have taken *Hiphil yāpēṣ* as an elliptical stative. Of course, one could also take consonantal *yḥlq* as a *Piel* form and translate: "Where is the path by which 'he' disperses (*yĕḥallēq*) light; [by which] 'he' drives the East wind over the earth?"

Masoretic *laḥăliq miššām bĕtôk hāʿām* (Jer 37:12)

As pointed by the Masoretes, the Hebrew *laḥăliq* would represent a syncopated form of *lĕhaḥăliq*, the *Hiphil* stem. It is inconclusively derived either from *ḥ-l-q* I "to be smooth", hence causative *Hiphil* "to smoothen", or as a *Hiphil* stative, "to slip"; or from the root *ḥ-l-q* "to divide", hence "to break away", or the like. I would accordingly translate "... to slip away from there / to break away from there in the midst of the people". Concordances and lexica often list the unique form *laḥăliq* under more than one entry, with question marks.

Why not vocalize consonantal *lḥlq* as the *Qal* infinitive *laḥălôq* and derive this form from *ḥ-l-q* III "to flee, be lost"? This would yield a clear sense: "Jeremiah departed from Jerusalem to travel to the land of Benjamin, so as to flee (*laḥălôq*) from there in the midst of the people".[18]

Perhaps the most enlightening results of postulating the verbal root *ḥ-l-q* III become evident in the Masoretic *Piel* realizations, which yield connotations very similar to those known for the D-stem *ḫulluqu* "to make disappear, cause a loss,

[18] Actually, Gesenius (*Thesaurus Philologicus*, 483 [under *Hiphil*, 2]) had the meaning of *laḥălîq* in Jer 37:12 right. He quotes Qimḥi, among others, suggesting the Latin translation *evadendi*. He compares *Hiphil heḥĕlîq* to the Hebrew verbs *mālaṭ* and *pālaṭ*, which connote flight and escape. Of course, he was not aware of Akkadian *ḫalāqu*.

ruin, destroy" in Akkadian and West Semitic. In any number of instances, what has usually been understood as an intensive connotation of *ḥālaq* "to divide, cut" should probably be understood as having a causative sense, transmitted by the *Piel* stem, of *ḥ-l-q* III. We have already raised this possibility in the discussion of Jer 37:12. Following are clear examples.

ʾăḥallĕqēm bĕyaʿăqōb waʾăpîṣēm bĕyiśrāʾēl (Gen 49:7)

Assuming the root *ḥ-l-q* I "to divide", this passage has usually been translated along the following lines: "I shall apportion them / divide them up in Jacob, I shall disperse them in Israel". Reference is, of course, to the brothers Simeon and Levi, cursed by their father for their violence (Gen 34:25–31). They were to lose their own territories, only to become pariahs among the tribes of Israel.

Would not Jacob's dire words have more force and the parallelism be closer if we were to derive the *Piel ʾăḥallĕqēm* from *ḥ-l-q* III? We could then translate: "I shall disperse them in Jacob, I shall scatter them in Israel". This was one of the verses cited by Dahood and others as indicating the presence in BH of a cognate of Akkadian *ḫalāqu*, as is Lam 4:16, which follows.

pĕnê YHWH *ḥillēqām lōʾ yôsîp lĕhabbîṭām* (Lam 4:16)

Once again, deriving the *Piel ḥillēqām* from *ḥ-l-q* III would yield a superior translation: "YHWH's countenance has made them disappear / banished them from sight; He will look upon them no more".

Masoretic *ḥăbālîm yĕḥallēq bĕʾappô* (Job 21:17)

Dahood cites this enigmatic clause as an example of *ḥ-l-q* III in BH, and he correctly favors a sense other than "pain, pangs" for Hebrew *ḥăbālîm*. However, the Masoretes probably understood consonantal *ḥblym* to mean just that, "pain (the abstract plural), pangs" (Jer 13:8, 22:23, 49:24; Job 39:3), yielding the translation: "He deals out pain (*ḥăbālîm yĕḥallēq*) in his wrath".

Now, the Masoretes surely knew of a verbal root *ḥ-b-l* "to damage, injure, oppress", which is frequently realized in the *Piel* stem, with intensive force (Isa 13:5, 54:16; Mic 2:10; Ps 140:6[?]; Qoh 5:5). For all we know, the sense of "pain" is itself derived from this very root, as may be the derivation of the name given to Zechariah's second rod, *ḥōbĕlîm* (Zech 11:7, 24). In any event, the Masoretes did not associate *ḥăbālîm* in Job 21:17b with this known root, probably because they did not know of the root we are calling *ḥ-l-q* III. It is quite simple to vocalize consonantal *ḥblym* as *ḥabbālîm*, the *Piel qattāl*-form, "oppressors, robbers" (or possibly as the *Qal* participle *ḥōbĕlîm*). This translation would produce a much better reading of Job 21:17–18:

> How often is the lamp of the wicked extinguished,
> Does their downfall overtake them.

He drives away oppressors (*wĕḥabbālîm yĕḥallēq*) in his wrath;
They shall be as straw before the wind,
Like chaff spirited away by a storm.

wĕʾet ʾarṣî ḥillēqû (Joel 4:2)

It is quite possible that the distinctive connotation of *ḫalāqu* in the El Amarna dialect, that of ruin conceived as deprival of political control over a city or land, is expressed in the oracle of Joel 4:1–9. The context is mixed, with notions of dividing spoils interacting with realities of exile, so that it is difficult to determine the precise sense of *ḥillēqû* in v. 2. To appreciate this ambiguity it is best to translate vv. 1–3 as I understand them:

For, behold, in those days and in that time,
When I shall restore the captivity of Judah and Jerusalem—
I shall assemble all of the nations,
And bring them down to the valley of Jehoshapat.
I shall bring them to trial on the matter of Israel,
  the people who are my possession,
Whom they dispersed (*pizzĕrû*) among the nations;
And [concerning] my land [which] they *expropriated* (*ḥillēqû*).
They cast lots over my people;
They traded the young boy for a harlot,
And the young girl for wine to drink.

The oracle goes on in vv. 4–9 to speak of God's future punishment of the Tyreans and Sidonians, who had occupied Philistia and sold Judeans into slavery to the Ionian Greeks. God will restore his exiled people and, in retribution, the Judeans will then sell young Tyreans and Sidonians to far-off Arabia.

Now, it is certainly proper in context to translate *wĕʾet ʾarṣî ḥillēqû* in Joel 4:2b: "They divided up my land". The reference to casting lots over the people in v. 3 might suggest this rendering: the conquerors divided the land among themselves just as they traded the people as slaves.

And yet it would also yield a harmonious translation if we were to understand *Piel ḥillēqû*, as we have, to convey the sense of Akkadian *ḫulluqu* in the El Amarna correspondence, where a land or a city is the direct object. The Tyreans and Sidonians took control of the land; they "ruined" it by depriving the Judeans of control over it.

Biblical Hebrew ʾbd

Loss, Reversible and Irreversible: *ʾābad* "to flee / to perish"; *ʾibbēd* "to disperse / to ruin"; and *heʾĕbîd* "to banish / to destroy".

The semantic field of BH *ʾābad*, in the simple stem as well as in the *Piel ʾibbēd* and in the *Hiphil heʾĕbîd*, ranges all the way from notions of distance, absence, and separation, "to flee, be lost, exiled", to notions of extinction, "to perish, be lost, die, cease to exist". These sets of meanings are decidedly compatible with each other; they represent a semantic progression or syndrome, and there is therefore no reason to posit two roots in Hebrew. Actually, Akkadian *ḫalāqu*, investigated above, shares a similar semantic range, connoting both loss as disappearing and being missing, and loss as perishing and ceasing to exist. Even in English usage the notion of loss may convey both of these realities.

And yet, Akkadian employs two separate cognates of BH *ʾābad* to comprehend the same semantic range: (1) *abātu* A, basically an active transitive verb meaning "to destroy, ruin", and in less frequent stative realizations, "to collapse, fall down". This verb seems always to connote substantial loss or ruin; (2) *abātu* B, a stative verb attested only in the G-stem and N-stem, which means "to run away, flee", namely, to be "lost" from sight or distant. Its principal synonyms in the Mesopotamian lexical series are adjectival *narqū* "remote", *naparku* "to abscond, escape", and most significantly, *ḫalāqu* "to disappear, vanish". In other words, Akkadian *abātu* A and B, taken together, achieve a semantic range similar in scope to BH *ʾābad*, notwithstanding aspectual differences between BH *ʾābad* and Akkadian *abātu* A (*CAD A*/I, 41–47).

What is being posited for BH *ʾābad* is actually attested, in a less complete way, for Ugaritic *abd*. In the G-stem and its derivatives, Ugaritic *abd* means "to perish, die". Thus, we read in the "Keret Epic" about successive deaths in the hero's family:

> *wbtmhn.špḥ.yitbd*
> *wb.pḫyrh.yrṯ*
>
> So, in its entirety a family perished,
> And from the whole of it—an heir.[19]

What is remarkable in Ugaritic usage is that the D-stem of the verb *abd* has the meaning "to remove, cast off", in the same way that BH generates the *Piel* connotation "to disperse". In a composite Ugaritic magical text, KTU 1.100 + 1.107, recently investigated by Levine and de Tarragon,[20] the infinitive absolute of the D-stem of *abd* recurs in a magical formula for healing venomous snake bites. The gods repeatedly urge the snake charmer on with the following words:

> *lnh.mlḫš.abd*
> *lnh.ydy.ḥmt*
>
> From it (= the snake) let the charmer remove;
> From it—let him cast off venom.

The parallelism of *abd*//*ydy* (from *n-d-y* "to cast off") establishes the sense of D-stem *abd*. The venom was not to be destroyed as such, but rather gathered up in the projected magical procedures of which the magical text speaks.[21]

---

[19] Gibson, *Canaanite Myths*, 82 (4 i 24–25); my translation.

[20] B. A. Levine and J.-M. de Tarragon, "Shapshu Cries Out in Heaven: Dealing with Snake Bites at Ugarit (KTU 1.100 + 1.107)," *RB* 95 (1988) 481–518.

[21] *Ibid.*, 496 nn. to line 8.

An awareness of the existence of two roots in Akkadian and of the Ugaritic evidence allows us to resolve most of the ambiguities of BH usage of *ʾābad*, in all of its realized stems. Such perceptions open the door to a clearer understanding of biblical statements on war and conquest, on divine punishment of Israel and of the nations, and on biblical views of history and destiny. This is so whether one concludes that cognates of both of the Akkadian homonyms have coalesced in BH, or whether one decides that, like Akkadian *ḫalāqu*, BH *ʾābad* had an intrinsically broad semantic range that embraces the connotations expressed by both of the Akkadian homonyms. Armed with comparative information, we can sort out two discrete sets of meanings.

The notion of loss as ruin and extinction is expressed unambiguously in such biblical passages as Joel 1:11, which describes devastated fields and a ruined harvest: *kî ʾābad qĕṣîr śādeh* "for the harvest of fields has perished / is ruined". Similarly, 2 Kgs 9:8 refers to the punitive murder of the wicked house of Ahab: "And the entire house of Ahab shall perish (*wĕʾābad*)!" That is to say, they shall die.

It is the notion of substantial, irreversible loss that generates the causative-factitive reflex "to destroy, ruin, terminate" in the *Piel* and *Hiphil* stems *ʾibbēd* and *heʾĕbîd*, respectively. This unambiguous sense is expressed in many biblical passages that speak of laying waste to physical structures and of killing human beings (including *Piel*: Num 33:52; Deut 12:2; 2 Kgs 19:18//Isa 37:19; 2 Kgs 21:3; Ezek 6:3, and 22:27; and *Hiphil*: 2 Kgs 10:19; Jer 1:10, 18:7, and 31:28).

Contrast the sense of the simple stem in Joel 1:11 and 2 Kgs 9:8 with the sense of participial *ʾôbēd* in Deut 26:5, correctly translated by Albright[22] as follows: *ʾărammî ʾōbēd ʾābî* "my ancestor was a fugitive Aramean" (or, "my ancestor was an Aramean fugitive"). Unfortunately, Albright offered no lexicographical background to explain his rendering. In any event, Jacob's clan did not cease to exist. As Deut 26:5 proceeds to inform us, "and he voyaged southward to Egypt," where he became a large clan.

What recommends seeing a cognate relationship between participial *ʾōbēd* in Deut 26:5 and Akkadian *abātu* B is the occurrence of Akkadian terms meaning "fugitive(s), deportee(s)" that are formed precisely on the N-stem of *abātu* B "to flee", namely, *munnabtu*, *nunnabtūtu*, and related *naʾbūtu*. The phenomenon of the *munnabtūtu* was recently discussed by G. Buccellati, who notes the abundance of references to such uprooted fugitives in Syro-Mesopotamian documents of the Late Bronze Age. Such ancient *deracinés* were a factor in what Buccellati refers to as a cosmopolitan age, before the formation of world empires.[23]

Similar sociopolitical patterns are evident in the Neo-Assyrian Period, a fact that may be more relevant after all to the interpretation of the Deuteronomic creed. In citing the unusual identification, *ʾărammî ʾōbēd* of Deut 26:5, Mazar

[22] W. F. Albright, *From the Stone Age to Christianity* (Baltimore, 1940) 181.

[23] G. Buccellati, "*ʿApīrū* and Munnabtūtu: The Stateless of the First Cosmopolitan Age," *JNES* 36 (1977) 146–47.

calls passing attention to a reference in the annals of Sennacherib to "Aramean fugitives."[24] An investigation of this passage has proved to be most enlightening.

Reviewing his eighth campaign in Babylonia, Sennacherib speaks of a certain Shuzubu, a Chaldean, who had rebelled. In a tone reminiscent of what Judg 9:4 has to say about Abimelech's band and what 1 Sam 22:2 has to say about David's men, Sennacherib characterizes Shuzubu's motley entourage:

> LÚ *A-ra-me ḫal-qu mun-nab-tú a-mir da-me ḫab-bi-lu ṣi-ru-uš-šu ip-ḫu-ru-ma*
>
> Aramean fugitives, the deportee, the murderer, the robber, around him they gathered.[25]

We have, therefore, a parallel in Akkadian of BH *ʾărammî ʾōbēd*, in the plural LÚ *aramē ḫalqū*, an equivalence that once again points to the interaction of Akkadian *ḫalāqu* and *abātu* B in describing forced migration. Furthermore, the passage in Sennacherib's annals groups together the *munnabtu* "the deportee" and the Arameans characterized as *halqū* "fugitives". It is this sociopolitical context that more accurately characterizes Jacob and his clan, rather than the nomadic way of life, an interpretation early attached to Deut 26:5.[26] This context also informs the relatively late oracle preserved in Isa 27:13:

> It shall happen on that day that a great ram's horn shall be blown, and the fugitives in the land of Assyria (*hāʾōbĕdîm bĕʾereṣ ʾaššûr*) and the deportees in the land of Egypt (*wĕhanniddāḥîm bĕʾereṣ miṣrāyim*) shall come and bow down to YHWH at the holy mountain, in Jerusalem.

The parallelism of *ʾōbĕdîm//niddāḥîm* clarifies the functional sense of the verb *ʾābad.* By whatever words they were described, exile and deportation represented a well-tested policy employed by and against Arameans, Philistines, and Phoenicians during the first half of the first millennium B.C.E., if Amos chap. 1 is any indication. Thus, the God of Israel will bring about the exile of Aram (Amos 1:5) and do the same to the Philistines of Gaza, Ashdod, and Ekron, who for their part had sent large local populations into exile to Edom (Amos 1:6–8). In the same way, the Tyreans were to be punished for deporting a large population from the Levantine coast to Edom (Amos 1:9–10).

An expressive biblical metaphor that reflects these ancient realities of exile and deportation is that of stray animals, "lost" from the flock, those whom a good shepherd would never abandon and would seek to round up. The image of

---

[24] B. Mazar, "The Aramean Empire and Its Relations with Israel," *Biblical Archaeologist* 25 (1962) 98–120.

[25] D. Luckenbill, *The Annals of Sennacherib* (Chicago, 1924) 42 (col. V, lines 22–23).

[26] M. A. Beek, "Das Problem des aramäischen Stammvaters (Deut. xxvi, 5)" *Oudtestimentische Studiën* 8 (1950) 193–212.

"stray flocks" (*ṣōʾn ʾōbĕdôt*) became a metaphor for wayward Israel, led astray by their shepherds (Jer 50:6–7). In Ezekiel 34 we find the metaphor of improperly tended flocks, who are allowed to wander off without being rounded up, ultimately to be lost for good:

> Oh son of man, prophesy concerning the shepherds of Israel, and say to them, to the shepherds: Thus says the LORD, YHWH: Oh, shepherds of Israel, who have been tending them: Are not the shepherds supposed to tend the flocks? ... Yet, you failed to strengthen the weak sheep, and the ill one you did not heal, and the one with broken limb you did not bandage, and the outcast (*hanniddaḥat*) you did not bring back, and the stray (*hāʾōbedet*) you did not retrieve (*lōʾ biqqaštem*). So they dispersed (*wattĕpûṣênâ*) without a shepherd (Ezek 34:2–5a, with deletions).

But the God of Israel will rectify the situation and do what a devoted shepherd should:

> I shall tend my flock, and I shall enable them to lie down, says the LORD, YHWH. I shall retrieve the stray (*ʾet hāʾōbedet ʾăbaqqēš*), and the outcast (*hanniddaḥat*) I shall bring back ..." (Ezek 34:15–16; and cf. 1 Sam 9:3, 20; Ps 119:76).

Now, Akkadian attests only the G-stem and the N-stem of *abātu* B, as has been noted. For the meanings "to destroy, lay waste, ruin" Akkadian relies exclusively on *abātu* A, in both the G-stem and the D-stem. But along with meanings we would associate with Akkadian *abātu* A, BH generated another set of *Piel* and *Hiphil* meanings that we would associate semantically with Akkadian *abātu* B. Instead of connoting destruction and ruin, these derived forms convey the sense of expulsion and exile. This semantic development was anticipated in Ugaritic, as we have already observed.

The starting point for a discussion of this set of meanings in BH is Jer 23:1–4, which may be seen as an active, causative reflex of Ezek 34:2–5, 15–16, presented above. There, the simple stem predominates; here, the derived stem. In literary-historical perspective, Jer 23:1–4 undoubtedly antedated Ezekiel 34, but for purposes of analyzing the *Piel* forms in BH, it was logical to discuss the simple stems of Ezek 34:2–5 first. But now, observe how Jer 23:1–4 emerges as a counterpoint to Ezekiel 34, so that *Piel ʾibbēd* conveys the active sense of scattering and dispersing flocks:

> Oh shepherds who disperse and scatter (*mĕʾabbĕdîm ûmĕpiṣîm*) the flock of my pasturing, says YHWH. Therefore, thus says YHWH, God of Israel, concerning the shepherds who tend my people: You have scattered (*hăpiṣōtem*) my flock, and you have driven them out and have not taken account of them. I hereby hold you to account for the evil of your deeds, says YHWH. I shall gather in the remnant of my flock from all of the lands to which I have banished them and I shall restore them to their sheepfolds, and they shall be fruitful and increase. I shall place over them shepherds who will tend them, so that

> they will no longer be afraid or terrified, nor shall they be unaccounted for.

Now, *abātu* B is a synonym of *ḫalāqu* "to be lost, disappear" in the Mesopotamian lexical series, and, indeed, the parallelism of *ʾibbēd//hēpîṣ* in Ezekiel 34 recalls the synonymous parallelism of *hillēq//hēpîṣ* in Gen 49:7, where the objects of the verbs were tribes of people, not flocks.

In view of the repeated use of the verb *biqqēš* "to seek out, retrieve" as a contrast to *ʾibbēd* "to disperse, drive out" in the metaphor of the shepherd and his flock, it occurs to me that we have been missing something in our understanding of Qoh 3:5–6, which, inter alia, resonates this very metaphor:

> A time to cast away stones,
> and a time to gather stones.
> A time to embrace,
> and a time to hold back from embracing.
> A time to seek out (*ʿēt lĕbaqqēš*),
> and a time to drive away (*ʿēt lĕʾabbēd*).
> A time to retain,
> and a time to throw away.

So much for the *Piel*, *ʾibbēd* "to drive away, exile, deport, disperse". Let us now examine attestations of the *Hiphil*, *heʾĕbîd* in the sense of "deport, banish, expel", reflecting the same sociopolitical realities that informed the *Piel*.

In writing a commentary on Leviticus, I encountered a problem in Lev 26:41, part of the protracted admonition that serves as an epilogue to the Holiness Code. This modified execration text heaps disaster upon disaster in projecting the consequences of Israel's repeated failure to submit to the divine will. Finally, God decrees exile for his people. As received in the Masoretic Text, Lev 26:41 reads:

> I, moreover, will act with hostility toward them, and I will bring them (*wĕhēbēʾtî ʾōtām*) into the land of their enemies. Perhaps then at last will their thickened heart submit, and they will expiate their transgression.

Since late antiquity it has been recognized that the threatened punishment of exile would not likely be expressed as bringing a people into the land of their enemies, since the verb *hēbîʾ* in BH so often connotes restoration and the attainment of a sought-after destination. Furthermore, the usual syntax is *hēbîʾ ʾel* or *hēbîʾ l-* "to bring to", *hēbîʾ* + a locative accusative, or even *hēbîʾ min* "to bring back from", but not *hēbîʾ b-*. The Septuagint translates: καὶ ἀπολῶ αὐτοὺς "and I will destroy them", undoubtedly reflecting a Hebrew text that read *wĕhaʾăbadtî ʾōtām* instead of *wĕhēbēʾtî ʾōtām*. On this basis, the original text would have threatened that God will bring about the destruction of his own exiled people. Some have postulated that the Hebrew text was consciously emended in antiquity so as to avoid this very idea, thereby producing the text that reads *wĕhēbēʾtî*.

A question remains, however: How is it that the Hebrew text, read and translated by the Septuagint authors and emended by late redactors, would have contained such thoughts in the first place? The truth is that it did not! Most likely, the Septuagint translators misunderstood the meaning of *wĕhaʾăbadtî* in their Hebrew text and failed to perceive the nexus of vv. 38 and 41 precisely because they did not know of an alternate set of meanings borne by the *Qal ʾābad*, namely, "to flee, wander away", or of the *Hiphil hĕʾebîd* "to banish, scatter, cause to flee". They knew only the meaning "to destroy, ruin" for the *Hiphil* of BH *ʾābad* and, indeed, translated the *Qal* form *waʾabadtem baggōyim* in Lev 26:38 as καὶ ἀπολεῖσθε ἐν τοῖς ἔθνεσιν "and you will perish among the nations".

The same limitation of knowledge was what stimulated the redactors to emend the text from *wĕhaʾăbadtî* to *wĕhēbēʾtî*, if, indeed, this is what occurred. Had they correctly understood what the biblical author intended to say, they would not have been troubled by the *Hiphil* of BH *ʾābad*.

More accurately, the text used by the Septuagint translators meant the following:

> You will vanish (*waʾăbadtem*) among the nations, and the land of your enemies will consume you (v. 38).
>
> And I will disperse them (*wĕhaʾăbadtî ʾōtām*) in the land of their enemies (v. 41).

In effect, Lev 26:41 is an alternate way of expressing the thoughts conveyed in Lev 26:33 within an earlier section of the admonition: "And you—I shall scatter (*ʾĕzāreh*) among the nations," and so forth. The present interpretation has the advantage of removing the apparent contradiction between v. 38 and the verses that follow. If *waʾăbadtem* in v. 38 connotes actual extinction, how is it that vv. 39–41 speak of survivors who are contrite and confess their transgressions? One is more or less compelled to assume a process of redaction whereby the severity of an earlier statement was subsequently mitigated. However, if properly understood, the simple stem *ʾābad* in v. 38 and original *Hiphil wĕhaʾăbadtî* in v. 41 both connote exile or deportation, not extinction, and so it is relevant to speak subsequently of exiled remnants and their ultimate fate.[27]

Soon after my work on the final chapters of Leviticus, I found myself studying the poetic sections of Numbers. Bearing in mind what I had learned, namely, that Akkadian *abātu* B connoted flight and remoteness, I expected that in contexts of conquest and war the BH *Hiphil heʾĕbîd*, might convey something like the *Piel ʾibbēd*, namely, "to banish, deport, disperse".

[27] In my commentary (*Leviticus* [JPS Torah Commentary; Philadelphia, 1989] 190–92, 275–81), I was still groping with the semantics of BH *ʾābad* and could only suggest, logically, that this verb might not connote total destruction but only a stage in the process. In the light of what has been learned since, the literary interpretation of the Epilogue to the Holiness Code (Lev 26:3–26) will have to be revised.

In Balaam's fourth oration (Num 24:15–19) we are told that in the future a mighty Israelite warrior-king will conquer Moab and Edom-Seir. The following will be the consequences for Edom-Seir:

> Edom shall be a dispossessed land (*yĕrēšâ*),
> Seir—a land dispossessed by its enemies (*yĕrēšâ ʾōyĕbāyw*);
> While Israel is triumphant.
> Jacob will subjugate them (*wi[y]rōdēm yaʿăqōb*),
> And deport survivors (*wĕheʾĕbîd śārîd*) from ʿAr.

The overall context indicates the pattern of conquest and dispossession—of subjugation, not of annihilation per se. In a similar vein, Zeph 2:5 is probably predicting that the God of Israel will exile the Philistines from the coastal region:

> Oh, inhabitants of the coastal strip,
> the nation of Cretans;
> The oracle of YHWH [is spoken] against you,
> Canaan, land of the Philistines:
> "I shall depopulate you (*wĕhaʾăbadtîk*),
> Leaving no inhabitants!"

The concluding statement quotes the actual oracle. The prophet goes on to describe how the coastal strip will be reduced to grazing land and to predict how the God of Israel will in due time resettle the remnant of Judah in the former territory of the Philistines.

The question of whether, in any given statement, *Hiphil heʾĕbîd* connotes destruction or whether it connotes exile is consequential for our understanding of biblical notions of conquest and of biblical policies for the treatment of native populations. Included as relevant is the Deuteronomist's program for the conquest of Canaan, where such language is employed (Deut 8:20, 9:3). The same ambiguity surrounding *Hiphil heʾĕbîd* affects our understanding of the verb *hikrît* "to cut off", used by Deuteronomy in speaking of what the God of Israel will do to the Canaanite peoples (Deut 12:29, 19:1). Were the Canaanites to be killed off systematically, or were they to be systematically deported, exiled from the land? It also remains to explore, with the same question in mind, the oracles of Ezekiel 25 against the interior peoples—Ammon, Moab and Edom—where *heʾĕbîd* and *hikrît* occur both separately and in parallelism (Ezek 25:7; and cf. Jer 49:38). Based on my understanding of the semantic range of BH *ʾābad*, it is my view that *Hiphil* forms functioned as part of the political vocabulary and, like such verbs as *Hiphil hôrîš* "to dispossess" (Deut 9:1, 18:12) and *riḥēq* (Isa 6:12), *hirḥîq* (Ezek 11:16) "to expel afar", realistically connote deportation rather than annihilation. The same would be true of God's admonition to Israel: exile, not extinction is the threatened punishment.

The interaction of *hikrît* and *heʾĕbîd* also comes into play in the formulation of the penalty of banishment in priestly law. In almost all cases, the law will state: (a) "that person shall be cut off (*wĕnikrĕtâ hannepeš hahîʾ*) from among "her" kinfolk" (Gen 17:14; Exod 12:15, 19; Lev 7:20); or (b) "I will cause to be cut off (*wĕhikrattî*)" that person (Lev 17:10, 20:3–6). There is little doubt that banishment or ostracism, rather than death, was originally intended as the punishment for the relevant religious offenses. And so, when we encounter a unique instance in Lev 23:30, where instead of *wĕhikrattî*, we read *wĕhaʾăbadtî ʾet hannepeš hahîʾ miqqereb ʿammāh*, we are prompted to translate: "I will banish that person from among 'her' kinfolk". Banishment is the exile of the individual and his family.

Conclusion

The two exercises here presented illustrate, in a small way, the abundant possibilities afforded by comparative lexicography for adding to our understanding of the Hebrew Bible. Beyond lexicography and philology, the investigation of unrecognized meanings helps to clarify major themes in biblical literature and to bring into focus biblical perceptions of human experience.

The connotations attendant upon the BH roots *ḥ-l-q* and *ʾ-b-d* relate predominantly to the dire, catastrophic aspect of history and to the down side of human experience. These two roots connote loss, but their precise interpretation reveals that such loss is not always perceived as absolute. These roots also embrace more hopeful connotations: a people exiled may be restored, and those who are distant may return.

Hebrew (Postbiblical)*

1. *The Language*

Literature in the Hebrew language has been composed uninterruptedly from the biblical period until the present day, and virtually every phase of Hebrew creativity is relevant to biblical studies. It is necessary, therefore, to define how the term "postbiblical Hebrew" (PBH) is being employed so as to clarify the necessarily limited scope of this introduction. As used here, "postbiblical," in contrast to "biblical Hebrew" (BH), refers to that phase of the Hebrew language expressed in written sources from Palestine of the prerabbinic and rabbinic period; in chronological terms, from the late first century C.E. until approximately 400 C.E. Certain linguistic features that later became pronounced in PBH are earlier attested in late-biblical writings of the Persian period (538–312 B.C.E., e.g., Chronicles and Ezra-Nehemiah) and continue to appear increasingly in biblical writings of the early Hellenistic period (Ecclesiastes, Esther, and Song of Songs).

1.1. *History*

The most extensive repository of PBH consists of the Tannaitic writings: the Mishnah, Tosefta, the collections of halakhic midrash (*Mekhilta*, *Sifra*, and *Sifre*), and Tannaitic baraitot (talmudic passages that are "external" to the Mishnah). Also included are writings of the Palestinian Amoraim (who succeeded the Tannaim) preserved in the Jerusalem Talmud and the primary collections of haggadic midrash (the *Midrash Rabbah*, the *Pesiqta* collections, and the like). Surely, the basic passages of the Passover Haggadah, and certain early prayer texts, qualify as exemplars of PBH. In their canonical form, most of these sources do not antedate the early third century C.E., although much of their content was undoubtedly composed earlier. The Hebrew of these sources is referred to as *ləšôn ḥăkāmîm*, "the language of the sages," namely, rabbinic Hebrew.

As a result of intensive efforts at retrieval and study of early manuscripts of the rabbinic Hebrew texts, some of which are vocalized entirely or in part, it has been possible to correct many of the errors that were imbedded in printed editions (and even in poor handwritten copies), thereby allowing for a more accurate assessment of the orthography, phonology, and morphology of PBH and all that proceeds from such knowledge. In other words, it is now possible to have a

* Originally published in J. Klatner and S. L. McKenzie (eds.), *Beyond Babel: A Handbook for Biblical Hebrew and Related Languages* (Resources for Biblical Study 42; Atlanta: Society of Biblical Literature, 2002), pp. 157–182. Reprinted with permission from the Society of Biblical Literature.

better sense of how PBH sounded and to identify forms of the language with greater certainty. It has also been possible to take note of differences between the readings in Palestinian and in Babylonian manuscripts, suggesting that there may have been dialects of PBH.

The corpus of PBH has been augmented in recent decades by the discovery of texts in postbiblical epigraphic Hebrew (PBEH), consisting mostly of inscriptions, legal documents, and letters dating to the first two Christian centuries. These texts speak for Palestinian Jewish communities of the period immediately preceding the publication of the Mishnah and other Tannaitic writings. In addition to the independent value of their contents, they enable us to assess the realism of the language employed in the rabbinic writings themselves. The verdict is indisputable: rabbinic Hebrew is representative of prevalent forms of the contemporary written language. In fact, the epigraphic sources often make it possible to trace the formation of rabbinic Hebrew. As an example, a lease of arable land written in Hebrew during the years of the Bar Kokhba revolt (132–135+ C.E.) sounds remarkably like legal passages of the Mishnah dealing with similar matters (see below, §2.3).

For purposes of this discussion, writings in what has come to be known as "Qumran Hebrew" will not be included. Most scholars would classify the Hebrew of the sect's canonical writings, and of other literary and hermeneutic texts found at Qumran, as the "last branch" of biblical Hebrew. Qumran Hebrew had some impact on rabbinic Hebrew but not as much as might have been expected. Some examples of continuity will be noted.

Abba Bendavid authored a voluminous and meticulous work in Hebrew entitled *Biblical Hebrew and Mishnaic Hebrew*. In it he compared biblical and rabbinic Hebrew in exhaustive detail and was able to show that rabbinic Hebrew is a natural outgrowth of earlier phases of the language.[1] In fact, he proposed that it reflects the spoken Hebrew of Palestinian Jews, later adopted as the formal, written language by sages of the early Christian centuries. E. Y. Kutscher agreed with his assessment and further refined it in his valuable article in the *Encyclopaedia Judaica*.[2]

According to Kutscher's reconstruction, it was the destruction of the Second Temple that led to the demise of biblical Hebrew as a literary language and the

---

[1] Abba Bendavid, *Biblical Hebrew and Mishnaic Hebrew* (2 vols.; Tel Aviv: Dvir, 1967).

[2] E. Y. Kutscher, "Mishnaic Hebrew," *Encyclopaedia Judaica* 16:1590–1608. This article was later revised and published as chapter 6 in E. Y. Kutscher, *A History of the Hebrew Language* (ed. Raphael Kutscher; Jerusalem: Magnes, 1982). Those desiring in-depth treatments of specific problems in PBH should consult the studies in M. Bar-Asher, ed., *Studies in Mishnaic Hebrew* (ScrHier 37; Jerusalem: Magnes, Hebrew University, 1998). Included are chapters on some aspects of PBH to be discussed here, including determination, purpose, and result clauses and the development of new conjugations from biblical roots. The collection opens with a review of previous studies of Mishnaic Hebrew grammar and an assessment of the available evidence.

rise of the current vernacular as the written language. Although the precise character of spoken Hebrew in that period is obscure, as is the nature of spoken Hebrew in earlier biblical times, it is possible in certain instances to trace the early development of specific PBH forms. It is Kutscher's view that spoken PBH flourished mostly in Judea, whereas in Galilee Aramaic had taken over. However, after the destruction of the Jerusalem temple, and following the later Bar Kokhba revolt (132–135+ C.E.), many Jews from the central and southern parts of the country, including the academic leadership, migrated to Galilee, bringing with them their version of Hebrew and the Tannaitic writings already composed in it. They still spoke Hebrew, but their children, growing up in an Aramaic-speaking environment, did not continue to do so. Consequently, PBH survived primarily as a written language.

Most modern research in PBH has been published in academic Hebrew, and in the past it has been a subject of interest primarily to Jewish scholars trained in reading Hebrew texts of all historical periods. Now that the importance of PBH for the study of the Hebrew Bible, as well as for the understanding of Judaism in late antiquity, is being increasingly realized by a wider scholarly audience, more studies in English and the European languages have begun to appear. At the same time, biblical scholars of all backgrounds are being motivated to gain competency in modern, academic Hebrew. In this connection, it bears mention that modern Hebrew itself owes much of its tone and vocabulary to PBH.

Jewish sources written in PBH constitute a vast and varied library of biblical interpretation, just as do those preserved in Aramaic. In fact, much of the haggadic midrash and the talmudic material (including the baraitot) preserved in PBH is interspersed with Aramaic passages and is often imbedded in Aramaic texts. The contents of such interpretation range in scope and character from precise lexicography to legal hermeneutic and from the semantics of diction to structural analysis of literary form. One who has not mastered PBH, like one who has not studied Aramaic, would find all of these sources, which reveal Jewish understandings of the Hebrew Bible at crucial periods in the history of religions, inaccessible in their original language.

Medieval Jewish luminaries such as Saadyah Gaon and Maimonides turned to rabbinic Hebrew for information on the direct meaning of biblical texts, finding it especially valuable for explaining biblical *hapax legomena*. It was their view that the sages preserved reliable traditions on the meaning of biblical Hebrew, deriving from the time when it was a living language. The semantics of biblical Hebrew are greatly illuminated in haggadic midrash, as an example, and, generally speaking, the intertextual method is basic to rabbinic interpretation. On the thematic level, once we leave philology and exegesis, rabbinic sources open a window into the later development of Judaism by dwelling on issues relating to the human-divine dialogue and the future of the Jewish people and their ongoing mandate to fulfill Mosaic law. One finds expansive discussions and disputations on Jewish self-definition, exile and restoration, this world and the next, virtue and faith, and suffering and divine justice.

Finally, the voluminous halakhic materials preserved in PBH serve to reveal how Jewish communities in Palestine of the Roman period developed the requisite institutional structures and formulated legal and ritual procedures through a hermeneutic that enabled them to anchor their creativity in the text of the Hebrew Bible, principally in Torah literature. Quantitatively, most of what has been preserved in PBH consists of commentary on the text of the Hebrew Bible. Viewing the Hebrew Bible as the crystallization of a long process of formation has drawn scholars to the languages of the ancient Near East. Viewing the Hebrew Bible as the beginning of a continuous process of commentary and interpretation should recommend the study of PBH.

1.2. Grammatical Features

Without a doubt, the most salient feature of PBH is the pervasive infusion of Aramaic, affecting phonology, morphology, tense system, syntax, and vocabulary. As an example, analysis of PBH shows that its tense system parallels that of Galilean Aramaic (largely preserved in Tannaitic writings) and also that of Christian-Palestinian and Samaritan Aramaic. The infusion of Aramaic is already apparent in PBEH and, as Kutscher intimates, might even allow us to classify PBH as a fusion language. Knowledge of ancient Aramaic is, therefore, prerequisite to a proper appreciation of PBH. It would be mistaken, however, to ignore other sources of input, such as Phoenician-Punic, early West Semitic, and dialects of Hebrew other than BH.

The grammatical outline that follows is intended merely to focus on some of the distinctive characteristics of PBH, drawing comparisons and, more often, contrasts with BH. It is based on Kutscher's treatments, cited above, using many of his illustrative examples and further elaborating on certain features of the language that he treated only cursorily. It hardly presumes to be comprehensive and is intended to facilitate the comprehension of PBH texts on the part of those whose competence lies primarily in the area of BH and the West Semitic languages, especially ancient Aramaic.

1.2.1. Orthography

PBH demonstrates a marked tendency toward plene spelling, already noticeable in PBEH, while still retaining defective spelling in many instances. Such fluctuations occur to a lesser extent in BH, especially in late BH. Thus, in PBH, long *ū* and *ō* vowels are often spelled with *wāw*. Even short and half vowels may on occasion be signified with *wāw* and *yôd* (and even *ʾālep*), yielding forms such as *ʿômôrîm* "sheaves" (cf. BH *ʿomārîm*) and *lîqrôt* "to read, call," where the short *i* vowel of the prefixed *lāmed* is written with *yôd*. Certain plene spellings found in Qumran Hebrew texts are also attested in PBH.

1.2.2. Phonology

Both the consonants and vowels of PBH are identical with those of BH, with some drifting and shifting discernible in the later phase. There was a degree of interchange between *ʾālep* and *hê*, and *ʾālep* and *ʿayin*. Laryngeals and pharyngeals, in general, were often confused, perhaps under the influence of Greek, but these did not completely lose their sound value. Spirantized *bêt* and *wāw* also merged at times. Other sound shifts are likewise known. Thus we find *ḥêt* > *ʿayin*, producing *ʿāg ʿûgâ* for *ḥāg ḥûgâ* "he drew a circle." Similarly, *qôp* and *kāp* were occasionally interchanged, and more frequently *bêt* > *pê*, so that a verbal form such as *ləhabqîaʿ* would be realized as *ləhapqîaʿ* "to break through." Final *mêm* in undeclined nouns often shifts to *nûn*, such as in *ʾādām* > *ʾādān* "person, man."

Most of these shifts are paralleled in Galilean Aramaic but were often hyper-corrected by copyists and printers of the rabbinic texts to conform to BH. A degree of shifting is also discernible with respect to vowels, as from *i* to *e* and from *ā* to *ō*, in line with Galilean Aramaic and with Septuagint transcriptions. We find metathesis and dissimilation, as from *rêš* to *lāmed* (e.g., *margālît* > *margārît* "pearl"). There are also clues in the rabbinic sources to different pronunciations in various regions of the country, akin to the *shibboleth* phenomenon. As a rule, these observable changes follow well-known sound shifts and and do not obscure the intended meaning. Yet, it is likely that in its day PBH probably sounded considerably different from BH.

1.2.3. Morphology

1.2.3.1. *Independent Personal Pronouns*. BH *ʾānōkî* "I" disappears from PBH and is fully replaced by *ʾănî*, a process that had already begun in late BH. Biblical Hebrew *ʾănaḥnû* (rarely *naḥnû*) "we" is replaced by *ʾānû*, which represents an internal Hebrew development. Under the influence of Aramaic *ʾant*, the second-person masculine singular independent pronoun is often expressed as *ʾatt*, alongside *ʾattâ* "you." In the second- and third-person plural, the casting of the independent pronouns is fluid, so that the forms *ʾatten* and *ʾattem*, as well as *hēn* and *hēm*, can signify both masculine and feminine. As noted by Kutscher, the situation with respect to independent personal pronouns is symptomatic of the character of PBH in general and is the result of three forces: (1) the background of BH, (2) the infusion of Aramaic, and (3) internal Hebrew developments.

1.2.3.2. *Pronominal Suffixes*. Vocalized manuscripts of the Mishnah reveal that the second-person masculine singular suffix in PBH is realized as *-āk*, not BH *-ekā*, and that the feminine is *-ik*, not BH *-ēk*, yielding forms such as *dəbārāk* and *dəbārik*, respectively. In the plural, the casting of the suffixes is fluid, as between final *mêm* and *nûn*, just as it is in the independent personal pronouns.

1.2.3.3. *Demonstrative Pronouns*. For the near deictic, PBH discards the feminine *zōʾt* "this" and carries over late BH *zô* (also written *zōh* in BH), which did not likely develop from *zōʾt* but rather represents a different dialect of late BH. Instead of epicene BH *ʾēleh* "these" PBH has *ʾēlû* for both masculine and feminine.

For the distant deictic, PBH uses, in addition to *hahûʾ* (masculine) and *hahîʾ* (feminine) "that," the forms *hallāz* (masculine) and *hallâ* (feminine) "that" and the plurals *hāʾēlû* and *hallālû* (*hēlêlû*) "those" (epicene). PBEH attests the variation *hallazo* "that." The function of the distant deictic can be expressed by declined forms of the particle *ʾt* plus a determined noun form, such as *ʾôtô hayyôm* "that day." The reflexive pronominal function can be expressed with *ʿeṣem* "bone" used in the sense of "self," such as in *hûʾ ʿaṣmô* "he, himself," or as an accusative: *qôneh ʾet ʿaṣmô* "he acquires himself, secures his own freedom."

1.2.3.4. *Relative and Possessive Pronouns.* Instead of the predominant BH relative *ʾăšer* "which, that," PBH employs prefixed *še*, already known in late BH and which bears no relation to *ʾăšer*, whose basic meaning is "where." It also generated an independent possessive pronoun by combining the relative *še* with possessive *lāmed*, resulting in *šel* (with geminated *lāmed*) "of, belonging to," which is declined as *šellî* "mine," and so on. The principal impact of these innovations is realized in the syntax of PBH, where their origin and early development will be discussed against the background of late BH.

1.2.3.5. *The Verb.* PBH generated the *a-b-a* consonantal pattern (e.g., *kārôk* "to wrap"), and it carries over from late BH reduplicative forms such as *lənaʿănēaʿ* "to shake" and *ʿarbēb* "to mix." Significant changes appear with respect to the verbal stems. The *puʿal* has virtually disappeared in PBH, except for the participle (e.g., *məquddāš* "is sanctified"). The perfect of the *hitpaʿel* has given way to a form *nitpaʿel* (this is the correct form), which conveys similar force. Thus, *nitʿôrār* "he awakened" instead of *hitʿôrēr* (see further). There are other developments also due to the influence of Aramaic. Thus, the *hipʿil* coexists with the *šapʿel*, whose role is greatly expanded in PBH. There are rare traces of the internal *qal* passive, especially in *primae nûn* roots.

There are differences in the force and functions of the verbal stems between BH and PBH. In PBH, the *qal* can often express a denominative function, such as in *pārāh ḥôlebet* "a milking cow." In intransitive and stative verbs, the *qal* may convey a more active sense than in BH. Thus, in PBH *gādal* means "he grew, became great," whereas to express the state of being one would say *hāyâ gādôl* "he was large." In PBH the *nipʿal* is utilized extensively and lends itself to diverse functions (see below). It tends to express reflexivity, not merely passivity, to a greater degree than in BH and often signifies incipient (inchoate) action.

The functions of the *piʿel* are expansive in PBH. Apart from the intensive and causative functions, one notes many *piʿel* denominatives. The *piʿel* can also have the force of an intransitive, signifying inchoate action, such as *bikkərû* (consonantal *bykrw*) "they began to ripen." It would appear that the *piʿel* replaced the *qal* in some instances. The *hipʿil* retains its earlier functions and, as noted, coexists with the Aramaistic *šapʿel*, which is conjugated like a *piʿel*. The *hopʿal* carries on, and the *nitpaʿel*, which has all but replaced the perfect of the *hitpaʿel*, has several functions. These include inchoative: *ništaṭṭâ* "he went mad"; reciprocal: *ništaṭṭəpû* "they became partners"; and passive: *nitgallâ* "it was uncovered, it appeared." The *hitpaʿel* remains operative in participial, imperfect, and imperative forms, where it often has virtually transitive force. Thus, *hitqabbēl lî giṭṭî* means "receive my bill of divorce on my behalf" (*m. Giṭ.* 6:2). Certain verb forms characteristic of BH disappeared, like the cohortative, the short imperfect, and inverted forms with *wāw*-consecutive. Of the infinitives, only the construction with prefixed *lāmed* survived, and clusters composed with it, such as *millômar* (consonantal *mlwmr*) "from saying."

Conjugation of the perfect differs from BH in two respects. The second-person plural is the same for masculine and feminine, so that the forms *kətabtem* and *kətabten* "you wrote," for example, are epicene. The second-person masculine singular is realized as *kātabtâ* in the same long form as is found in Qumran Hebrew. As in Qumran Hebrew, there is a penchant in PBH for regularly employing the pausal form. The imperfect follows BH, except that the second- and third-person feminine plurals of BH have disappeared. The participle favors the *qôṭelet* form, although there are also instances of the *qôṭəlâ* form. The masculine plural alternates between the endings *-îm* and *-în*, under the influence of Aramaic. The plural feminine imperative of BH (*šəmôrnâ* "watch, guard") has disappeared. Kutscher notes that in PBH the participle can be negated by *lōʾ*, not only by *ʾên*, as in BH. The infinitive may be negated by *šəllōʾ* plus the infinitive construct with prefixed *lāmed*, such as in *šəllōʾ lišmôr* "not to watch."

Certain forms disappear from the written sources, whereas new vocalizations are generated. In the *qal* perfect of strong verbs, the *qāṭôl* form has disappeared, whereas the participial *qāṭôl* form has proliferated in the singular case of anomalous *yākôl* "to be able," yielding the feminine and plural forms *yəkôlâ*, *yəkôlîn*, and *yəkôlôt*. There is a general tendency to favor the *yiqṭôl* imperfect over the *yiqṭal*, even with respect to intransitive verbs. This pattern appears to be consistent in the case of *mediae ḥêt* verbs, such as in *yišḥôṭ* "he will slaughter" instead of BH *yišḥaṭ*. At times, the imperfect of the *hitpaʿel* is vocalized like Aramaic (e.g., *titḥabbar*). *Primae ʾālep* verbs may exhibit elision of the *ʾālep*, yielding forms such as the infinitive *lômar* (consonantal *lwmr*) "to say" and *lôkal* (consonantal *lwkl*) "to eat." *Primae ʿayin* verbs in the *nipʿal* may be vocalized with *səgōl*, such as *neʿĕśâ* "it was done."

Third weak verbs show considerable change in PBH. *Tertiae ʾālep* verbs are usually treated as *tertiae yôd* such as *qārînû* "we called, read," although the imperfect is still *yiqrāʾ* and infinitival *liqrôt* "to read" coexists with the less-frequent conflate form *liqrôʾt* (cf. Qumran Hebrew). The feminine ending with *tāw* is frequent in *nipʿal* perfect forms of third weak verbs, such as *niṭmêt* "she became impure" (*tertiae ʾālep*), *nikwêt* "she was burned," and *nišbêt* "she was taken captive" (*tertiae yôd*). Of considerable interest is the PBH form *hāyāt* "she/it was," the third feminine singular of the third weak verbal root *h-y-h*, which in BH appears as *hāyətâ*. Since the later form did not likely develop from the earlier, and since it cannot be traced to Aramaic influence, it probably derived from a different dialect of Hebrew. Aramaic influence accounts for forms such as *hĕwēh* (masculine) and *hĕwî* (feminine) imperative "be" and the plural imperative *hĕwû*. PBH also attests forms of this verb such as imperfect *yəhēʾ* instead of *yihyeh*. Also attested are participial forms with *qāmēṣ*, such as *zākeh* "he gains possession, merits" and *ḥāyeh* "he lives," alongside the more normal form, *qôneh* "he acquires." PBEH may well attest similar participial forms, even in strong verbs, perhaps under the influence of Aramaic.

The infinitive constructs of *primae yôd* and *primae nûn* verbs are patterned after the imperfect on the masculine model: *lêrēd* "to descend" rather than *lāredet*, and *lîtēn* "to give, pay" rather than *lātēt*. Also note the form *lîṭṭôl* "to take," with the assimilation of initial *nûn* and plene vocalization with *yôd*. Certain fluctuations are evident in the case of middle weak verbs, whereby *mediae yôd* verbs are often realized as *mediae wāw* and whereby the *nipʿal* participle and perfect of middle weak verbs coalesce, so that a form like *nîdôn* can mean both "he/it is judged" and "he/it was judged." We also encounter, for instance, a *hipʿil* participle *mēśîm* "he assigns," reflecting the *qal* imperfect *yāśîm* "he will put, place." PBH seems to favor geminate forms in the case of both transitive and intransitive verbs.

PBH exhibits a much more developed tense system than BH, undoubtedly due to the influence of Aramaic, as has been noted above. One finds the following tenses:

(a) The perfect, which also serves as a preterite.

(b) A modal imperfect, expressing intention or wish, or the imperative, or the negation of same. Thus, *ləʿôlām yōʾmār ʾādām* "A person ought always to say" or *lōʾ yōʾmār ʾādām* "A person ought not to say." The imperfect is not employed to convey the indicative future, that function having been appropriated by the participial present. This being the case, there was no longer need for the inverted perfect (*wəqāṭal*) or the inverted imperfect (*wayyiqṭōl*).

(c) Periphrastic tenses, compounded with the verb *hāyâ* + the participle. Thus, we find a progressive perfect *hāyâ ʾômēr* (also *ʾômēr hāyâ*) "he used to say, was saying," a future *yəhēʾ yārēʾ* "he shall be in awe" (subjunctive), and an imperative *hĕwēh ʾômēr* "be saying, say."

(d) A true present tense conveyed by the participle, which also conveys the force of a present-future. Thus, hypothetically, *hûʾ nôsēaʿ* may mean "he is traveling" and also "he will be going away."

(e) The imperative, which carries on from BH.

(f) A new anticipatory future tense with *ʿātîd* ("expecting, in readiness") + infinitive construct with prefixed *lāmed*: *ʾattâ ʿātîd lîtēn* "You will be expected to give; you will ultimately give." Also note use of *sôp* "end," declined + infinitive construct *šessôpēnû libdôq* "that in the end, we will examine" (literally, "that our end is to examine").

(g) The passive participle, mainly of intransitive verbs, functioning as a present prefect, such as *məqubbāl ʾănî* "I am in receipt, I have received."

The overall effect of the above developments is to enable PBH to express more elaborate sequences of tenses and to place actions and situations in a punctive relation to each other, resulting in greater narrative freedom and an enhanced capacity for description. They also had an impact on the syntax of PBH, as will be shown below.

1.2.3.6. *The Noun and Verbal Nouns*. PBH exhibits considerable morphological creativity in generating or expanding usage of verbal nouns based on the *qal* and other stems. Kutscher counts about fifteen different forms based on the *qal* alone. Thus, the stative *qəṭîlâ* form is used extensively in PBH, such as *ʾăkîlâ* "eating" (130 attestations in the Mishnah alone). Other stative forms are recast as *qəṭîlâ*, so that we encounter a form such as *śərîpâ* "burning" for BH *śərēpâ*. We also find Aramaistic masculine forms such as *kəlāl* "general rule" and *pərāṭ* "specification" alongside feminine *qəṭālâ* "death, execution." New *qal* forms are *gāzēl* "robbery" and *ḥānēq* "strangulation." Finally, the *nomen agentis* of the *qal* comes into its own in PBH in such forms as *lāqôaḥ* "purchaser."

Turning to other stems, we find additional verbal noun forms. The *piʿel* yields forms such as *haddibbēr* "the *logos*" alongside *haddibbûr*, and feminine *kappārâ* "expiation," from Aramaic. There are also *piʿel*-based forms such as *wîddûy* "confession" (lit., "exposing oneself") that express the reflexive sense and *kārēt* "the penalty of being 'cut off,'" also expressed as *hikkārēt* in the *nipʿal*. The *hipʿil* yields both masculine and feminine verbal nouns configured like the infinitive, such as *heqṭēr* "burning" ("an offering on the altar") and *hôrāyâ*/*hôrāʾâ* "instruction." Verbal nouns based on the *qal* with affixes also occur, such as *gôzəlān* "robber" and *rôṣəḥān* "murderer" (in Babylonian sources *gazlān* and *raṣḥān*). These are Aramaistic forms, yet they hark back to the Akkadian affix *-ānu*. PBH developed new plurals in addition to masculine *-îm* and *-în* and feminine *-ôt*, such as *merḥăṣāʾôt* (in Babylonian sources) and *merḥăṣîyôt* (in Palestinian sources) "bath-houses." The plural of nouns ending in *-ût* is seen in *malkût*, *malkûyôt* "kingdom, kingdoms." PBH attests double plurals that yield combinations such as *rəʾšê šānîm* "New Years" and *bātê kənēsîyôt* "synagogues."

1.2.3.7. *Particles*. PBH exhibits some new particles, although as a rule the BH prepositions have remained. The following are noteworthy: *bintayim* "meanwhile, in the interim," *ʿakšāyw* "now," *kədê* "in order to, so as to," and *kêsad* "how, in what manner." Prefixed *ʾālep* can function as prepositional *bêt*, such as in *ʾabayit* "in the house of, at the house of." There are cases where prefixed *lāmed* serves as the accusative particle, as in Aramaic, and the prepositions *ʿad* "up to, to" and *ʿal* "on, to" interchange, as they do in Galilean and Samaritan Aramaic. Negation is indicated by *ʾên*, which is declined as in *ʾênî* "I am not" and so forth, and the participle may also be negated by *lōʾ*, as already noted. We find constructions such as *ʾim lōʾ* (in PBEH *ʾîlōʾ*) "if not" and the shortened negative *ʾî* plus the independent pronoun, as in *ʾî ʾattâ* "you do not" or the interrogative "don't you?" We also find the affirmative *hēn* "yes" and *hēk* "how," taken from Aramaic. One notes a general fluidity in the use of prepositions.

1.2.4. Syntax

The distinctive character of PBH as a written language is perhaps determined more by syntax than by any other feature, with the possible exception of vocabulary. Before summarizing predominant syntactic features of PBH in some detail with a view to their background, a general observation is in order. In PBH the subject usually precedes the verb in the sentence. This is not consistently so, but is more of a prevalent pattern than in BH and is due to the influence of Aramaic syntax.

1.2.4.1. *Verbal Complements*. PBH favors various constructions, including the finite verb plus the participle as in *hitḥîl bôkeh* "he began crying," a combination only rarely attested in BH.

1.2.4.2. *Subordination*. The prominence in PBH of subordinate clauses, especially relative clauses, contrasts with the prevalence in BH of coordinate clauses joined by conjunctive *wāw*. A major consequence of this marked trend is seen in the manner of expressing possession, with subordination virtually replacing the declension of nouns with pronominal suffixes. Thus, instead of hypothetical *bêtî* "my house," we would find *habbayit šellî* (replacing *habbayit ʾăšer lî*). Although these marked changes are clearly due to the influence of Aramaic, it is curious that the actual way of signifying relative subordination in PBH (and PBEH) is with the particle (or prefix) *še* "that, which." As will be shown, this particle derives from contemporary Phoenician-Punic and is itself virtually unknown in Aramaic, where the particle *dî*, earlier *zî*, performs this function.

In fact, it would be practical to begin a discussion of the syntactic character of PBH as a whole by using the particle *še* as a probe, because its functions and utilization are so far reaching. B. A. Levine has traced the history of the particle in BH through Phoenician *ăše* (= prosthetic *ʾālep* + *še*) and prefixed *še* in Punic (rarely in Ammonite).[3] In an earlier study of spoken Hebrew in biblical times, Levine summarizes the utilization of relative *še* in late BH, most extensively in the Song of Songs and Ecclesiastes.[4] Noting that there is, of course, no etymological connection between *še* and *ʾăšer*, the relative pronoun in standard BH, Levine concludes that usage of the particle *še* in Hebrew in late BH is due to the presence of Phoenician-speaking communities during the Persian period all along the Levantine coast, from Acco in the north, via Dor, to Ashdod in the south, and even reaching inland in some areas.

In Nehemiah 13:23–24 we read of contemporary Judeans speaking "Ashdodite" (*ʾašdôdît*), a likely reference to Phoenician, and who no longer know how to speak Judean Hebrew (*yəhûdît*). It was about then that a form of the Phoenician-Punic relative pronoun began to be utilized in biblical writing. One notes that in the Lachish and Arad ostraca, which date to the very last decades of the

---

[3] B. A. Levine, "The Prefix *še* in Biblical Hebrew in the Light of Ancient Epigraphy" (Hebrew), *Eretz-Israel* 18 (N. Avidgad Volume; 1985): 145–52.

[4] B. A. Levine, "Chapters in the History of Spoken Hebrew" (Hebrew), *Eretz-Israel* 14 (H. L. Ginsberg Volume; 1978): 155–60.

period of the First Temple, the relative pronoun *ʾăšer* still dominated, which helps to pinpoint the time when its replacement, the prefix *še*, was introduced. It is not necessary here to dwell on the one definitely early attestation of *še* in BH, in the Song of Deborah (Judg 5:7), which probably reflects Akkadian *ša*.

In earlier Phoenician inscriptions, we find the form *ʾš* (*separatim*), whereas in Punic the prefixed form *š* is attested, as in the Nora inscription from Sardinia, dated to the sixth century B.C.E. at the latest. There we have such constructions as *šhʾ* (= *šehûʾ*) "that he/it is, which is" and *šbn* (= *šebbānâ*) "which he built." In later Punic we find constructions with genitive *lāmed*, such as *hʾš šlh* (= *hāʾîš šellāh*) "her husband" and the Latin transcription in Poenilus, *syllohom* (cf. *šellāhem*) "which is theirs," with the *lāmed* geminated.

In summary, it can be stated that under Phoenician-Punic influence, late BH absorbed the relative particle *še* just as it was also coming under intense Aramaic influence. The result was that its syntax tended toward subordinate clauses, principally relative clauses, which were signified by prefixed *še*. Thus it was that the written Hebrew of the postexilic period, and the spoken Hebrew of the time, were affected in a way that laid the groundwork for the syntax of PBH. We now survey the workings of the particle *še* in PBH (and PBEH).

1.2.4.2.1. Syntactic Subordination. Before a possessive *lāmed*, the particle *še* expresses syntactic subordination. There are several possible constructions for this.

(a) When the subject and object are both determined: *hayyayin wəhaḥōmeṣ šellaggôyîm* "the wine and the vinegar of the Gentiles" (the prefix *še*, plus the geminated possessive *lāmed*, plus the noun with the definite article, which produces further gemination).

(b) When the subject and object are indeterminate: *lāšôn šellîzəhôrît* "a thread that is of crimson wool."

(c) Anticipatory genitive, with the independent possessive pronoun *šel* (*separatim*): *ribbônô šel hāʿôlām* "Its Master, (namely,) who is of the world." A variant is the *junctim* construction: *ribbônô šellāʿôlām*, with the prefix *še* plus the possessive *lāmed*, geminated. This construction actually occurs in LBH, in Song 3:7: *hinnēh miṭṭātô šellišlōmōh* "Behold, his bed, (namely) which is of Solomon." The tendency in PBH to imply determination without using the definite article has produced the construction: *ribbônô šel ʿôlām*. In PBEH and in early manuscripts of the Talmud we find, instead of gemination, plene renderings of prefixed *še* with *hê* and *ʾālep* plus possessive *lāmed*. Thus, in a Hebrew inscription from Dabbura in the Golan, dating to the late second or early third century C.E., incised on a basalt lintel, we read *zh byt mdršw šhlrby ʾlʿzr hqpr*, literally: "This is his House of Study, (namely) of Rabbi ʾElʿazar Haqqappar." For the plene orthography itself, in differing syntactic roles, note the Ketib in Eccl 6:10 *ʿim šehattaqîp mimmennû* ("with one who is stronger than he" [Qere:

šettaqîp]).[5] In P. Yadin 51:2, a Hebrew letter of Bar Kokhba (132–135 C.E.), we find the form *ša*(*h*)*tišləḥû* "that you send.

(d) The independent possessive pronoun *šel* and its subject may be declined, producing possession through subordination. This already occurs in Song 1:6: *karmî šellî* "My vineyard, which is mine." It should be noted that Aramaic is the language that generated declined relative-genitives such as *dî lî*/*zî lî* "which is mine," combined as *dîlî*/*zîlî*.

1.2.4.2.2. Introducing a Relative Clause. The particle *še* may be prefixed to verbal and nominal forms, as well as to independent pronouns, to generate relative clauses. Following are illustrative passages, all coming from the very first chapter of the Mishnah, *Ber.* 1, translated literally for effect.

(a) *miššāʿâ šehakkôhănîm niknāsîm leʾĕkôl bitərûmātān*: From the time that/when the priests come in to partake of their offering" (participial present with temporal sense).

(b) *maʿăśeh šebbāʾû bānāyw mibbêt hammišteh*: "So it happened that his sons returned from a house of feasting"; *kol mah šeʾāmərû ḥăkāmîm*: "In every case that/where the sages said"; *happeh šeʾāmar hûʾ happeh šehittîr*: "The mouth that prohibited, it is the very mouth that permitted" (with the perfect).

(c) *šeʿābartā ʿal dibrê bêt hillēl*: "Because [literally, 'it is for the reason that'] you transgressed against the words of the House of Hillel."

(d) *šeneʾĕmar*: "That it is said (in Scripture)"—introduces biblical citation (with the *nipʿal* perfect).

It is to be noted that the particle *še* is often combined with prepositional elements, either independent or prefixed, as some of the above passages illustrate. Most of these combinations are modeled on Aramaic usage. Following are some further examples: *mippənê še-* "because, for the reason that"; *ʿal šûm še-* "because, for the reason that" (also, *miššûm še-*); *kəšem še-* "in the same way that"; *kədê še-* "in order that." One could list scores of similar idiomatic constructions. Often the particle *še* clusters with prepositions prefixed to nouns, as in *śəʾōr šebbāʿîsâ* "the leaven that is in the dough."

1.2.4.2.3. Prefixed to an Imperfect Verb. When attached to a following verb in the imperfect, the particle *še* can function modally and as a virtual imperative or jussive.

(a) In the modal function: *ʿad šeyyaʿăleh ʿamûd haššaḥar* "until it is that the pillar of dawn shall rise"; *miššeyyakkîr bên təkēlet ləlābān* "from (the time) that he could differentiate between royal blue and white." (Note the clustering of prepositions in the latter example.)

(b) As a virtual imperative: In the example given above, from P. Yadin 51:2, a Bar Kokhba letter, the form *ša*(*h*)*tišləḥû* is best translated "that you send; you will send." This function is characteristic of Aramaic. Compare the following examples from the Mishnah: *šeyyəhēʾ* "that he/it should be,

[5] D. Urman, "Jewish Inscriptions from Dabbura in the Golan," *IEJ* 22 (1972): 16-23.

let him/it be"; and *šellōʾ yihyu ʾēlû bənê bêtî* "Let these not be members of my household."

Before leaving the subject of subordinate clauses, note should be taken of the function of the definite article, prefixed *hê*, as a relative pronoun in the sense "the one who." This phenomenon is already attested in late BH. In Exod 16:17–18, we read *hammarbeh wəhammamʿîṭ* "the one who (gleaned) much and the one who (gleaned) little." It is much more frequent, however, in PBH, and often introduces general statements. Thus, *haššôḥēṭ ʾet happārâ* "The one who/whoever slaughters a cow"; *hammitkawwēn lômar tərûmâ wəʾāmar maʿăśēr* "The one who/whoever intends to say 'priestly offering' but says 'tithe.'" Also note *kol hamməšallēm qeren wəḥōmeš* "Anyone who pays the principal, plus (the penalty of) one-fifth."

1.2.4.3. *Ellipsis*. PBH favors elliptical statements. This is one of the special nuances of the participle-present, especially the masculine plural participle functioning as a present-future tense. Thus, *pôdîn maʿăśēr šēnî kəšaʿar hazzôl* "They/we redeem (may redeem) the 'second tithe' according to the low price." Similarly, *mēʾêmātay ʾôkəlîn pērôt hāʾîlān?* "From what point do (may) they/we eat the fruit (of trees) that grew during the seventh year?" This works in the negative as well. Thus, *ʾên qôšərîn ʾet hassûs* "They/we do not hitch up the horse." The sense is that the participle is prescriptive, not merely descriptive, and that it is conveying what is customary, proper, or even required. Negatively, it can express what is improper or even forbidden. In the singular, we find statements such as *nôṭēaʿ ʾādām qiššût ûdəlaʿat* "A person 'plants' (may plant) cucumbers and pumpkins." For itself, ellipsis is also expressed by the third-person perfect plural, such as *gāzərû ʿal yiḥûd happənûyâ* "They decreed against uniting with an unmarried woman." It is also seen in a limited way with the imperfect. Ellipsis is further expressed by the periphrastic tenses. An example of this is seen in *m. Sanh.* 4:5: *kêṣad məʾayyəmîn ʿal ʿēdê nəpāšôt? maknîsîn ʾôtān ûməʾayyəmîn ʿălêhen* "How do they/we issue the charge to witnesses in a capital case? They/we would bring them in and issue the charge to them."

1.2.4.4. *Agreement*. Allowing for some fluidity, agreement as to number and gender is preserved in PBH, but there is less consistent agreement in respect of determination. Thus, we find constructions such as *kōhēn haggādôl* "the high priest" (instead of *hakkōhēn haggādôl*) and even virtual, or implied, agreement whereby the construction *kōhēn gādôl* would be rendered "the high priest." Thus, *m. Yoma* 1:1 reads *maprîšîn kōhēn gādôl* "They/we separate the high priest," and 1:3 has *ʾîšî kōhēn gādôl* "My sire, the high priest."

1.2.4.5. *Determination of the Direct Object*. In BH it is fairly consistent for the determined direct object of the transitive verb to be introduced by the accusative particle *ʾet* plus the definite article *hê*. Although this syntax is well attested in PBH, it is only one of several ways of signifying the determined direct object. Thus, *m. Bik.* 3:1: *kêṣad maprîšîn habbikkûrîm* "How do they/we set aside the offerings of firstfruits?" (without *ʾet*). But, see *m. ʾAbot* 2:9, *hārôʾeh ʾet hannôlād* "The one who sees what is being born [i.e., who is forward looking]." Normally, the accusative particle introduces the declined, direct object, which is, by definition, also determined. Thus, *hammôkēr ʾet śādēhû* "The one who/whoever sells his field." Also note usage of the accusative particle to introduce functional, determined direct objects, as in *məʿaśśēr ʾet šehûʾ nôtēn lâ* "He tithes that which he is giving her" (*m. Demai* 3:5). It is significant that PBH, more often than not, fails to signify determination in the direct object where we might expect it. To put it another way, determination is often implied with respect to the direct object, just as it is in some cases with respect to the subject. It has already been noted that declined forms of *ʾet* serve as distant demonstratives.

1.2.5. Lexicon and Diction

The following factors have figured in the formation of the lexicon of PBH and have affected its diction.

1.2.5.1. *Disuse and Replacement*. Certain BH words disappeared from PBH, even terms for family relationships and body parts, semantic areas that are usually regarded as being resistant to linguistic change. Examples cited by Kutscher are BH *dôd* "uncle" and *beṭen* "belly." It is inconceivable that even a single word occurring in the Hebrew Bible was unknown in the PBH period, surely to those who wrote the canonical works in rabbinic Hebrew. Consequently, considerable weight must be given to conscious replacement and responsiveness to new vocabulary, coming primarily from spoken Hebrew and Aramaic. In this connection, it is important to emphasize, as Kutscher does, that BH does not represent the total repertoire of the Hebrew language, written and spoken, of the biblical period. Even the very sparse amount of Hebrew epigraphy now available from the biblical period has revealed vocabulary unknown from canonical sources, and one supposes there was much more. Qumran Hebrew further endorses this conclusion. Some of what is new in the vocabulary of PBH is, therefore, attributable to dialects other than BH. It has also been pointed out that Phoenician and Punic may have contributed to the vocabulary of PBH to some degree. In the same vein, it is also likely that PBH preserves old West Semitic vocabulary, going back as early as Ugaritic, which is absent from the BH lexicon.

1.2.5.2. *Changes in Meaning and Aspect*. At times, BH vocabulary persists in PBH, but the meaning undergoes change. Kutscher points out the example of the Hebrew verb *n-h-g* "to lead," which is active-transitive in BH, whereas in PBH it exhibits a stative-reflexive aspect, meaning "to conduct oneself, to behave." To secure the force of the active-transitive in PBH one would have to use the *piʿel*, such as *hammənahēg ʿolāmô bəḥesed* "the one [i.e., God] who conducts his world with kindness," or even the *hipʿil*. There is also evidence of semantic progression. In this way, the BH verb *g-z-r* "to cut" comes to convey in PBH the meaning "to decide, issue an edict," in line with a well-known semantic syndrome. Connotations may become specialized, so that the BH term *ʿăṣeret* "recessional, sacred convocation" is used in PBH with special reference to the Pentecost festival. Similarly, a term of wide connotations like BH *ṣədāqâ* comes, in PBH, to connote gifts to the poor, specifically.

1.2.5.3. *Morphological Changes*. New lexemes were generated from known Hebrew roots, as is generally true in the ongoing development of agglutinated languages. In the case of PBH, many of these new morphologies were appropriated from Aramaic, which had already developed them. Some examples of this process have already been cited above, under the heading "Morphology" (§1.2.3).

1.2.5.4. *Denominatives*. Aramaic is known for its extensive denominatives, and this undoubtedly affected PBH, along with other factors, in its proliferation of denominative forms. For example, late BH developed a secondary form, *tərûmâ* "levy, priestly offering" from the root *r-w-m* "to be high," with *tāw* preformative (Exod 25:2). Subsequently, PBH generated the denominative *tāram* "to donate."

1.2.5.5. *Borrowings from Aramaic and Other Languages*. There are many lexemes that are best known in Aramaic and that may be assumed to have entered PBH from that language. This process began, for the most part, in the late BH of the Persian period and accelerated with time. An example from late BH is consonantal *ʾsr* "binding agreement, edict" (vocalized both as Aramaic *ʾesar* and as late BH *ʾissar* in Num 30). Quite possibly, this Aramaic term is a calque of Akkadian *riksu* "contract, binding agreement" and related forms, from the Akkadian root *rakāsu* "to tie, bind." In fact, rabbinic sources are replete with legal and administrative terms that ultimately derive from Akkadian (sometimes even Sumerian). Consider such terms as the following: *dap* "tablet," from Akkadian *ṭ/duppu*; *taggār* "merchant," from Akkadian *tamkāru*; *ʾûmān* "artisan, craftsman," from Akkadian *ummānu*. A term like *šəṭār* "written document" resonates with the Akkadian verb *šaṭāru* "to write" but is itself an Aramaic creation, appropriated into Hebrew. Somewhat differently, the noun *kətāb* in the sense of "writ" enters PBH from Aramaic, although it is based on a common Semitic root. A typically Aramaic verb like *b-ṭ-l* "to cease, be idle," occurring once in Eccl 12:3, a late biblical book infused with Aramaisms, expands in PBH, generating various nominal and verbal forms.

There are surprisingly few Arabic words in PBH. Recent investigations have revealed a series of Arabic legal terms in PBEH, in the Judean Desert documents, some of which are written in Nabatean-Aramaic. A rare example is the Arabic verb *rahina* "to pledge," which, in the Judean Desert documents, is used in the simple stem and occurs in the Mishnah in the *hopʿal* of the Hebrew: *ʿal hattînôqet šehūrhănâ bəʾašqəlôn* "concerning the female infant who was pledged as security in Ashkelon" (*m. ʿEd.* 8:4).

There are quite a few Greek words appropriated into PBH. They are mostly administrative, mercantile, religious, and cultic terms and names of items from the material culture. Simply put, a type of building or gate, vessel, or the status of a person would often be expressed in Greek. Latin words in PBH lie mostly in the military or administrative spheres. Examples are *ligyôn* "legion," *liblār* "scribe," and the like. For purposes of recognition, it is important to note that many Greek and Latin loanwords underwent a degree of phonetic adjustment as they were appropriated into PBH and Aramaic. Thus, for example, a Greek term that began with a cluster of voiceless consonants would take on a prefixed, prosthetic *ʾālep*, as in *ʾisṭəraṭêgôs* "commander," from *strategós*. In certain cases, Greek words became so much a part of the Hebrew language that they generated denominatives. A good example is *zîwwēg* "to join," as in marriage, and nominal *zîwwûg* "match, pair," from the Greek *zygón*, "pair."

A number of Persian words entered PBH, usually via Aramaic. A classic example is *gizbār* "treasurer," frequently attested in Aramaic and ultimately deriving from Elamite and Old Persian *ganza barra* "bearer of the treasury."[6]

2. Selections from Postbiblical Hebrew

2.1. From Mishnah Sanhedrin *4:5*

כיצד מאיימין על עדי נפשות? היו מכניסין אותן ומאימין עליהן: שמא תאמרו מאמד, ומשמועה, עד מפי עד, ומפי אדם נאמן שמענו; או שמא שאין אתם יודעין שסופנו לבדוק אתכם בדרישה וחקירה. הוו יודעין, שלא כדיני ממונות דיני נפשות: דיני ממונות—אדם נותן ממון ומתכפר לו; דיני נפשות—דמו ודם זרעיותיו תלוין בו עד סוף העולם. שכן מצינו בקין שהרג את אחיו, שנאמר "דמי אחיך צעקים"; אינו אומר "דם אחיך" אלא "דמי אחיך." דמו ודם זרעיותיו ... לפיכך נברא האדם יחידי, ללמדך, שכל המאבד נפש אחת מישראל מעלה עליו הכתוב, כאילו אבד עולם מלא; וכל המקים נפש אחת מישראל כאילו קים עולם מלא. ומפני שלום הבריות, שלא יאמר אדם אבא גדול מאביך; ושלא יהו מינין אומרים: שתי רשויות בשמים. ולהגיד גדלתו שלהקדוש ברוך הוא: שאדם טובע כמה מטבעות בחותם אחד, וכלן דומים זה לזה; ומלך מלכי המלכים הקדוש ברוך הוא טבע כל אדם בחותמו שלאדם הראשון, ואין אחד מהן דומה לחברו. לפיכך כל אחד ואחד חיב לומר: בשבילי נברא העולם ...

2.1.1. Transliteration

kêṣad məʾayyəmîn ʿal ʿēdê nəpāšôt? hāyû maknîsîn ʾôtān ûməʾayyĕmîn ʿălêhen: šemmāʾ tōʾmərû mēʾōmed ûmiššemûʿâ; ʿēd mippî ʿēd ʿûmippî ʾādām neʾemān šāmaʿnû. ʾô šemmāʾ ʾî ʾattem yôdəʿîn šessôpēnû libdôq ʾetkem bidərîšâ waḥăqîrâ. hewû yôdəʿîn šellōʾ kədînê māmônôt dînê nəpāšôt. dînê māmônôt—ʾādām nôtēn māmôn ûmitkappēr lô. dînê nəpāšôt —damô wədam zarʿîyôtāyw təlûyîn bô ʿad sôp hāʿôlām. šekkēn māṣînû bəqayyin šehārag ʾet ʾāḥîw, šenneʾĕmar: "dəmê ʾaḥîkā ṣōʿăqîm." ʾênô ʾômēr 'dam ʾāḥîkā.' ʾellaʾ 'dəmê ʾāḥîkā'; dāmô wədam zarʿîyôtāyw. ləpîkāk nibrāʾ hāʾādam yəḥîdî, ləlammədāk šekkol hamməʾabbēd nepeš ʾaḥat miyyiśrāʾēl maʿăleh ʿālāyw hakkātûb lə ʾîlû ʾibbad ʿôlām mālēʾ; wəkol hamməqayyēm nepeš ʾaḥat miyyiśrāʾēl kə ʾîlû qiyyam ʿôlām mālēʾ. ûmippənê šəlôm habbərîyôt, šellōʾ yōʾmar ʾādām: "ʾabbaʾ gādôl mē ʾābîkā." wəšellōʾ yəhû mînîn ʾômərîm: "šatê rəšuyôt baššāmayim." ûləhaggîd gədūlatô

[6] The classic dictionary of Greek and Latin loanwords in rabbinic literature was published more than a century ago: Samuel Krauss, *Griechische und Lateinische Lehnwörter in Talmud, Midrasch und Targum* (Berlin: S. Calvary, 1898). An in-depth treatment, albeit of more limited scope, is Daniel Sperber, *A Dictionary of Greek and Latin Legal Terms in Rabbinic Literature* (Ramat-Gan: Bar Ilan University, 1984).

šellhaqqādôš bārûk hû ʾ. šeʾādām ṭôbēaʿ kammâ maṭbəʿôt bə ḥôtām ʾeḥād, wəkūllan dômîm zeh lāzeh, ûmelek malkê hamməlākîm, haqqādôš bārûk hûʾ, ṭābaʿ kol ʾādām bə ḥôtāmô šellʾādām hāriʾšôn wə ʾēn ʾeḥād mēhen dômeh laḥăbērô. ləpîkāk kol ʾeḥād wəʾeḥād ḥayyāb lômar: "bišbîlî nibrāʾ hāʿôlām."

2.1.2. Translation

How do they issue the charge to witnesses in capital cases? They would bring them in and issue the charge to them: Perhaps you are making approximate statements, from hearsay, (that) one witness heard from another, or (stating that), "We heard (this) from a trustworthy person," or perhaps you do not know that in the end we will examine you with thorough interrogation. Be it known to you that capital cases are not like civil cases. In civil cases a person makes monetary compensation and is exonerated. In capital cases the blood (of the victim) and the blood of his descendants "are hanging" upon him (= the witness) to the end of time. This is what we find (written) regarding Cain, who killed his brother, as it is said (Genesis 4), "The bloods of your brother cry out." The (verse) does not say "the blood of your brother," but rather "the bloods of your brother," (both) his blood and the blood of his descendants. It is for this reason that only a single human being was created, to teach you that anyone who destroys one living soul from within Israel, Scripture weighs (the scales) against him as if he had destroyed the entire human population. Whereas anyone who preserves the life of one soul within Israel, it is as though he had preserved the life of the entire human population. And to promote harmony among people, so that one person will not be able to say, "My father was greater than your father." And so that the sectarians will not be able to say, "There are two authorities in heaven." And to relate the greatness of the Holy One, blessed be He. For when a person mints several coins with one stamp, they are all alike. But the King of the Kings of Kings, the Holy One, blessed be He, minted every person in the stamp of the first human being, and yet not one of them is like the other! It is for this reason that every person should say: "It is for me that the world was created!"

2.1.3. Notes

1. The opening sentence is elliptic, using the masculine plural participle-present.

2. The plural masculine *piʿel* participle *məʾayyəmîn* "they charge" is a denominative from *ʾêmâ* "dread, fear" (Gen 15:12; Isa 33:18), adjectival *ʾāyōm* "awesome" (Hab 1:7). Note in this form that the masculine plural is signified by *nûn*, an Aramaistic feature common in PBH. The same thing is seen in the forms *yôdəʿîn* "know," *təlûyîn* "are hanging," and *mînîn* "sectarians." Yet other masculine plurals end in *mêm*.

3. In this selection, we find some of the periphrastic tenses characteristic of PBH. For example, *hāyû maknîsîn ʾôtān* "They would bring them in" (perfect of the verb *h-y-h* plus the participle); *hĕyû yôdəʿīn* "Be it known to you" (imperative of the verb *h-y-h* plus the participle).

4. To a considerable degree, the syntax is dominated by relative clauses introduced by prefixed *še*.

5. Other features reflected in this passage include: (a) double plurals, e.g., *dînê nəpāšôt* "capital cases" and *dînê māmônôt* "civil cases"; (b) fluctuations between plene and defective orthography; (c) repeated use of the definite article *hê* as a relative, e.g., *kol hamməqayyēm* "anyone who preserves"; (d) anticipatory genitive, e.g., *bəḥôtāmô šellʾādām hāriʾšôn* "in the stamp of the first human being." In the latter case, note that there is no agreement with respect to determination (it is not written *hāʾādām hāriʾšôn*) and also that the possessive pronoun is prefixed (*junctim*).

6. The conditional adverb *šemmāʾ* "if, perhaps" is Aramaic and is cognate with Akkadian *šumma*. At times it is negatively suggestive and best rendered "lest."

7. Note the convention of referring to the Hebrew Bible as *hakkātûb* "the written word, Scripture." This appellation is an active entity; it makes pronouncements and judgments!

2.2. Sifra, QEDÔŠÎM, *Introduction*[7]

״וידבר ה׳ אל משה לאמר דבר אל בני ישראל ואמרת אליהם קדושים תהיו״ (ויקרא יט) מלמד שהפרשה נאמרה בהקהל. ומפני מה נאמרה בהקהל? מפני שרוב גופי תורה תלוים בה. ״קדושים תהיו״—פרושים היו. ״קדושים תהיו כי קדוש אני ה׳ אלהיכם.״ לומר: אם מקדישים אתם עצמיכם, מעלה אני עליכם כאילו קידשתם אותי; ואם אין אתם מקדישים עצמיכם, מעלה אני עליכם כאילו לא קידשתם אותי. או אינו אומר אלא: אם מקדישים אתם אותי, הריני מקודש; ואם לאו—איני מקודש ת״ל (= תלמוד לומר) ״כי קדוש אני.״ בקדושתי אני בין מקדשים אותי ובין אין מקדשים אותי. אבא שאול אומר: פמליא למלך. ומה עליה להיות? מחקה למלך.

2.2.1. TRANSLITERATION

"wayyədabbēr ʾădônāy ʾel mōšeh lēʾmōr: dabbēr ʾēl bənê yiśrāʾēl wəʾāmartā ʾălêhem: qədôšîm tihyû" (wayyiqrāʾ 19). məlammēd šehappārāšâ neʾĕmrâ bəhaqhēl. ûmippənê mah neʾĕmĕrâ bəhaqəhēl? mippənē šerôb gûpē tôrâ təlûyîm bâ. "qədôšîm, tihyû"—pārôšîm hĕyû. "qədôšîm tihyû kî qādôšʾ ʾănî ʾădônāy ʾĕlōhêkem." lômar: ʾim maqdîšîm ʾattem ʿaṣmêkem maʿăleh ʾăni ʿălêkem kəʾîlû qîddaštem ʾôtî; wəʾim ʾên ʾattem maqdîšîm ʿaṣmêkem maʿăleh ʾănî ʿălêkem kəʾîlû lōʾ qîddaštem ʾôtî. ʾô ʾênô ʾômēr ʾellaʾ: ʾim maqdîšîm ʾattem ʾôtî hărênî məquddāš, wəʾim lōʾ—ʾênî məquddāš. tilmôd lômar: "kî qādôš ʾănî" biqədûšāti ʾănî, bên məqaddəšîm ʾôtî. ûbên ʾên məqaddəšîm ʾôtî. ʾabbāʾ šāʾûl ʾômēr: pammelyâ lammelek. ûmâ ʿālêhā lihyôt? meḥaqqâ lammelek.

[7] Isaac Hirsch Weiss, ed., *Sifrāʾ Dĕbê Rab, Qedôšîm* (Vienna: Schlossberg, 1857; repr., New York, Om, 1946), 86b, col. 1.

2.2.2. *Translation*

Then YHWH spoke to Moses as follows: "Speak to the Israelite people and say to them, 'You shall be holy'" (Lev 19). It teaches that this parashah was spoken in the full assembly (of the people). And for what reason was it spoken in the full assembly (of the people)? Because most of the fundamental principles of the Torah "are hanging" upon it. "You shall be holy." Be separatists! "You shall be holy because I, YHWH, your God, am holy." That is to say, if you sanctify yourselves, I will weigh (the scales) in your favor as if you sanctified me, but if you do not sanctify yourselves, I will count it against you as if you had not sanctified me. Or is it that he is saying that (only) if you sanctify me am I sanctified, but if not—I am not sanctified? You should learn to say "for I am holy"—I am in my (state of) holiness whether they sanctify me, or whether they do not sanctify me. Abbaʾ Shaʾul says: "(It is like) the entourage (in relation) to the king. And what is it obliged to be (doing)? Emulating the king!"

2.2.3. *Notes*

1. Elliptical *məlammēd* "it teaches" often introduces commentary on a specific biblical verse (cf. infinitival *ləlammədāk* "to teach you" in the passage cited above from *m. Sanh.* 4:5). A further example of ellipsis, with virtual stative force, comes further on with *bēn ʾim maqdîšîm ʾōtî* "Whether they sanctify me," etc.

2. The form *təlûyîm* "are hanging" ("are contingent") reflects the widespread use of passive participles with stative force. The same locution occurs above in the selection from *m. Sanh.* 4:5.

3. The correct form is *pārôšîm* "separatists," which represents the *nomen agentis*, quite frequent in PBH, and has active force. It is also the name for the sect known as the Pharisees!

4. The phrase *tilmôd lômar* "You shall learn to say" is a formula that introduces biblical citations being adduced as proof texts.

5. The idiom *maʿăleh ʾănî ʿălêkem* "I will weigh (the scales) in your favor" is the positive reflex of the same idiom as appeared in the selection from *m. Sanh.* 4:5, where *ʿālāyw* meant "against him."

2.3. *An Example of PBEH: P. Yadin 46, Lines 1–12 (135 C.E.)*[8]

1 בשנים לכסלו שנת שלוש לשמעון בן כוסבא נשיא ישראל בעין גדי ישוע קבי[ש]
2 בן שמעון מן עין גדי אמר לאלעזר בן אלעזר בן חיטא ולאליעזר בן שמואל שניהם
3 משם מודא אני לכם היום שחכרתי מכם תמקום שנקרה הסלם ותמקום שנקרה
4 הב*ר תללו חכרתי מכם תדקלים ותשאר האילן שבהם ותעפר הלבן ותדקל
5 הטוב ותחצד שבכפר תכל שהחזיק חנניה בן חיטא מלפני מזה שאזרע
6 תעפר הלבן ואגה תדקלים כנומוס ואכנוס לנפשי כל המה פירות והבאה

[8] From Y. Yadin et al., eds., *The Documents from the Bar Kokhba Period in the Cave of Letters: Hebrew, Aramaic and Nabatean-Aramaic Papyri* (JDS 3; Jerusalem: Israel Exploration Society, 2002), 66.

7 שיהיה שבמקום הלז עד זמן שישלם זמן הפירות של עין גדי של הירק
8 ושל האילן היך נומוס לעומת ככה אחכרתום לי בכסף זוזין מאה וששים
9 שהם סלעים ארבעין תללו אשקול לכם ואטול מכם קשרים אילא יתקבל לי
10 ועליכם לשפות לפני מן חרר ותגר עד ס[וף] הזמן הלז ועליך אתה אלעזר
11 לקרב לי מן החכור הלז[ולשקו]ל[כסף]דינרין עשרה שהם סלעים שתים ושקל
12 חד וקים עלי לעמת ככה ישוע [בר]שמעון ענפשה

2.3.1. Transliteration

1. *bišənayim ləkislēw šənat šālôš ləšimᶜôn ben kôsibbâ nəśîʾ yiśrāʾēl bəᶜên gedî yēšûaᶜ QBY*[*Š*]
2. *ben šimᶜôn min ᶜên gedî ʾāmar ləʾelᶜāzār ben ʾelᶜāzār ben ḥayyāṭāʾ wəʾĕlîᶜezer ben šəmûʾēl, šənêhem*
3. *miššam: môdeʾ ʾănî lākem hayyôm šeḥākartî mikkem tammāqôm šenniqrâ hassulām wətammāqôm šenniqrâ*
4. *habbōr. tallālû ḥākartî mikkem; taddəqālîm wətaššəʾār hāʾîlān šebbāhem, wətaᶜāpār hallābān wətaddeqel*
5. *haṭṭôb wətaḥăṣād šebbakkepar: takkol šeheḥĕzîq ḥănanyâ ben ḥayyāṭāʾ millipnê mizzeh. šeʾezraᶜ*
6. *taᶜāpār hallābān wəʾaggēh taddəqālîm kənômôs wəʾeknôs lənapšî kol hammâ pêrôt wəhăbāʾâ*
7. *šeyyihyeh šebbammāqôm hallāz ᶜad zəman šeyyišlam zəman happêrôt šel ᶜên gedî šel hayyārāq*
8. *wəšel hāʾîlān hêk nômôs ləᶜummat kākâ ʾaḥkartûm lî bəkesep zûzîn mēʾah wəšiššîm*
9. *šehēm səlāᶜîm ʾarbāᶜîn tallālû ʾešqôl lākem wəʾeṭṭôl mikkem qəšārîm ʾîlōʾ yitqabbēl lî*
10. *waᶜălêkem ləšappôt ləpānay min ḥărār wətiggār ᶜad s*[*ôp*] *hazzəman hallāz wəᶜālêkā ʾattâ ʾelᶜāzār*
11. *ləqāreb lî min haḥăkôr hallāz* [*wəlišqô*]*l* [*kesep*] *dînārîn ᶜăśārâ šehēm səlāᶜîm šəttayim wəšeqel*
12. *ḥad wəqayyām ʾālay ləᶜummat kākâ yēšûaᶜ* [*bar*] *šimᶜôn ᶜannapšēh*

(three witnesses)

2.3.2. Translation

1. On the second of Kislev, year three of Shimᶜon, son of Kosiba, Premier of Israel, in Ein Gedi, Yeshuᶜa QBY[Š]
2. son of Shimᶜon, from Ein Gedi, stated to ʾElᶜazar, son of ʾElᶜazar, son of Ḥayyaṭaʾ, and to ʾEliᶜezer, son of Shemuʾel, both of them
3. from there: I acknowledge to you this day that I have leased from you (both) the site that is called the *Sullam* and the site that is called
4. the *Bor*. Those have I leased from you (including) the date palms and the rest of the trees within them, as well as the cropland and the date palms
5. of first quality, and the (*ḥṣd*-date crop) that is in the village; all that Hananiah, son of Ḥayyaṭaʾ held prior to this. I (undertake) to sow

6. the cropland, and I will pick (or: prune) the date palms as is customary. And I shall gather in for my use all of those fruits and the crop
7. that will come into existence in that site, until such time as the fruit season at Ein Gedi will reach its end, both of vegetables
8. and of trees, as is customary. On this account, you have leased them to me for silver (in the sum of) 160 *zuz*,
9. which are (equivalent to) forty *selaᶜ*. Those I shall count out to you (both), and I will take from you "ties." If not, (another) may be in receipt for me.
10. And it is incumbent upon you (or: [9] If it will not be received by me, [10] then it is incumbent upon you) to silence (all objections) before me (or: to provide clearance before me), against any grievance or contest, until the e[nd] of that season. And it is incumbent upon you, ʾElᶜazar,
11. to deliver to me from (the amount of) that lease [and to weigh o]ut [silver] ten denarii, which are (equivalent to) two *selaᶜ*, plus [12] one [11] shekel.
12. I am legally bound on this account. Yeshuᶜa, [son of] Shimᶜon, on his own behalf.

(three witnesses)

2.3.3. Notes

1. The determined accusative is affected by syncopation. Examples of this phenomenon are seen in *tammāqôm* "the site," reduced from *ʾet hammāqôm*, and *tallālû* "those," from *ʾet hallālû*. This appears to represent how Hebrew was spoken.

2. Note the fluidity of *ʾālep* and *hê*, whereby we have participial *môdeʾ* (instead of *môdeh*) "(I) acknowledge," but *šenniqrâ* (instead of *šenniqrāʾ*) "that is called."

3. The text exhibits Aramaistic features. Examples are: (a) the verbal stem *ʾāpᶜel* instead of *hipᶜil*, as in *ʾaḥkartûm* "you have leased them"; (b) Aramaic *ʾîlōʾ* "if not," *hêk* "how," and *taddeqel, taddəqālîm* "the palm tree, trees"; (c) the form *ᶜannapšēh* (assimilated from *ᶜal napšēh*) "on his own behalf," exhibits the Aramaic third masculine singular suffix, *-ēh*.

4. We find back-translations from Aramaic. Thus, *kol hammâ*, literally "all the what," reflecting Aramaic *kol mandəᶜam*, and *ləᶜummat kākâ*, literally "facing this," reflecting Aramaic *loqŏbēl dāk*.

5. The term *nômôs* is Greek *nomos* "custom, law," often occurring in PBH as *nîmûs*. The construction *kĕnômôs* "like the custom" is often found.

6. Note the unusual *hipᶜil* based form, *hăbāʾâ* "crop" in place of the expected form *təbûʾâ*.

3. *Ancient Sources, Modern Resources*

3.1. *Postbiblical Epigraphic Hebrew*

An excellent resource is Ada Yardeni's *Textbook of Aramaic, Hebrew and Nabataean Documentary Texts from the Judaean Desert, Parts A and B*. Part B contains an English section with translations of the texts and information on the script traditions. This compendium makes it possible to engage the overall corpus of epigraphic finds with the advantage of collated readings, an analysis of scripts, background information on various groups of texts, and reliable translations. Yardeni's hand drawings are an added benefit, enabling the reader to see an accurate image of a text as it was written in antiquity. Texts written in PBEH are usually executed in clear scripts that, in and of themselves, present few problems of decipherment, allowing for lacunae, fading ink, and the condition of the papyrus or other material on which the inscriptions are written.

3.2. *Postbiblical Hebrew*

The resources available to someone seeking to master PBH are plentiful in certain respects and yet lacking in others. There is as yet no scholarly grammar of rabbinic (or Mishnaic) Hebrew that is based on reliable manuscripts, nor is there yet a good dictionary of rabbinic Hebrew. The best talmudic dictionary, including both Hebrew and Aramaic, is that of Jacob Levy, *Wörterbuch über die Talmudim und Midraschim*. The Academy of the Hebrew Language in Jerusalem is preparing *The Historical Dictionary of the Hebrew Language* as a long-term project, and from time to time it issues computerized lexical materials that are very useful. Concordances of the Mishnah, Tosefta, Tannaitic literature, and the midrashic collections are also available.

The corpus of PBH is very extensive, and it is recommended that those new to the field acquaint themselves with its many collections before engaging the original sources. A good place to start is Jacob Neusner's article on the formative canon in rabbinic Judaism found in *The Encyclopedia of Judaism*. Unfortunately, no bibliography is provided for these entries, but they are succinctly formulated and highly informative. As a follow-up, see *Reader's Guide to Judaism*, a publication of the New York Public Library, under the appropriate topics, especially the "Booklist Index." Although published several decades ago, and therefore not entirely up to date, the *Encyclopaedia Judaica* and its supplements contain authoritative articles on all of the rabbinic collections.

New translations of the rabbinic corpus are readily available, thanks mostly to the unprecedented efforts of Neusner and his associates. They have literally unlocked the vast body of rabbinic literature by providing multivolume English translations of both the Babylonian and Jerusalem Talmuds, the major midrashic texts, the Mishnah, and the Tosefta. All of these works contain valuable information on the contents and history of the relevant rabbinic collections.

The best study edition of the Mishnah is Hanoch Albeck, *Šiššāh Sidrê Mišnāh* (*The Six Orders of the Mishnah*). The text was vocalized by Hanoch

Yalon, an eminent Semitist who pioneered the investigation of Mishnah manuscripts. This edition provides Hebrew introductions to each order and tractate, lists the relevant Torah passages, and includes a succinct Hebrew commentary to the text.

The Tosefta has been edited by the distinguished talmudist Saul Lieberman in *Tosefta Ki-fshuṭah: A Comprehensive Commentary on the Tosefta*. This is a multivolume work with a critical edition of the unvocalized text of the Tosefta based on the Erfurt manuscript with a short running commentary in Hebrew and an extensive, separate Hebrew commentary. There are many critical editions of the midrashic collections. A reliably vocalized edition of *Midrash Rabbah* with Hebrew commentary is that by Moshe Aryeh Mirkin.

4. Bibliography

Albeck, Hanoch
1958 *Šiššāh Sidrê Mišnāh*. 6 vols. Jerusalem: Bialik Institute and Dvir.

Bar-Asher, M.
1998 *Studies in Mishnaic Hebrew*. ScrHier 37. Jerusalem: Magnes, Hebrew University.

Bendavid, Abba
1967 *Biblical Hebrew and Mishnaic Hebrew*. 2 vols. Tel Aviv: Dvir.

Krauss, Samuel
1898 *Griechische und Lateinische Lehnwörter in Talmud, Midrasch und Targum*. Berlin: S. Calvary.

Kutscher, E. Y.
1972 Mishnaic Hebrew. *Encyclopaedia Judaica* 16:1590–1608.
1982 *A History of the Hebrew Language*. Edited by Raphael Kutscher. Jerusalem: Magnes.

Lieberman, Saul, ed.
1955–88 *Tosefta Ki-fshuṭah: A Comprehensive Commentary on the Tosefta*. 15 vols. New York: The Jewish Theological Seminary of America.

Levine, B. A.
1978 Chapters in the History of Spoken Hebrew (Hebrew). *Eretz-Israel* 14 (H.L. Ginsberg Volume):155–60.
1985 The Prefix *še* in Biblical Hebrew in the Light of Ancient Epigraphy (Hebrew). *Eretz-Israel* 18 (N. Avigad Volume):145–52.

Levy, Jacob
1924 *Wörterbuch über die Talmudim und Midraschim*. Berlin and Vienna: B. Harz.

Mirkin, Moshe Aryeh, ed.
1967 *Midraš Rabbāh*. 11 vols. Tel Aviv: Yavneh.

Neusner, Jacob
1999 Rabbinic Judaism: Formative Canon of. Pages 1132–75 in vol. 3 of *The Encyclopedia of Judaism*. Edited by Jacob Neusner, Alan J. Avery-Peck, and William S. Green. 3 vols. New York: Continuum.

Sperber, Daniel.
1984 *A Dictionary of Greek and Latin Legal Terms in Rabbinic Literature*. Ramat-Gan: Bar Ilan University.

Terry, Michael, ed.
2000 *Reader's Guide to Judaism*. Chicago: Fitzroy Dearborn.

Urman, D.
1972 Jewish Inscriptions from Dabbura in the Golan. *IEJ* 22:16–23.

Weiss, Isaac Hirsch, ed.
1857 *Sifrāʾ Dĕbê Rab, Qedôšîm*. Vienna: Schlossberg. Repr., New York: Om, 1946.

Yadin, Y., J. C. Greenfield, A. Yardeni, and B. A. Levine, eds.
2002 *The Documents from the Bar Kokhba Period in the Cave of Letters: Hebrew, Aramaic, and Nabatean-Aramaic Papyri*. Judean Desert Studies 3. Jerusalem: Israel Exploration Society.

Yardeni, Ada.
2000 *Textbook of Aramaic, Hebrew and Nabataean Documentary Texts from the Judaean Desert and Related Material*. 2 vols. Jerusalem: Dinur Center, Hebrew University.

The Language of the Magical Bowls*

The notes and comments to follow are appended to Chapter Six.* In Vol. IV, pp. 110–113, Neusner stressed the role of magic in the life of Babylonian Jewry during parts of the Talmudic period, especially as reflected in the image of the Talmudic sage as one possessed of magical knowledge, and even magical powers. Neusner's discussion of a selected group of Aramaic magical bowl inscriptions adds to his earlier insights in this area.[1]

For purposes of this study there is no need to enter into the question of establishing Jewish provenience for each and every magical text. In this respect, Neusner's assignment is probably conservative. In his glosses to Montgomery's collection of texts J. N. Epstein tended to assign more texts to Jewish authorship than was normally thought to be the case. It is clear, in any event, that Jewish and non-Jewish inscriptions of this type do not represent separate phenomena, but rather variations on the same theme; and, at that, not far reaching variations. Jewish stereotypes were employed by Mandeans, and Jews might well have used the Mandean script and dialect on occasion, and invoked Christian and pagan divine powers as well. What we have is a common idiom and mentality, and little typological distinctiveness. Jewish influence on Babylonian magic of the period in question should not be understated.

The magical bowl inscriptions, written primarily in Aramaic, Syriac, and Mandaic have been uncovered in what was ancient Babylonia, many in the ruins of ancient Nippur. They bear clear linguistic and cultural affinities to the Babylonian Talmud, to Rabbinic literature in general, and to ancient Jewish mystical literature. Whatever questions remain as to the exact dating of these texts, there is no doubt that they reflect, as a corpus, a type of magical praxis extant among Jews in Talmudic times. The cuneiform Aramaic incantation should allay any doubts as to the extended currency enjoyed by Aramaic incantations in Babylonia.[2]

Generically, the bowl inscriptions belong to a large body of literature produced in late antiquity and in the Medieval period dealing with the acquisition of mystical knowledge and its utilization either in theurgic or mystical activities This literature drew from diverse sources. Our primary concern here is to ex-

---

* Originally published in J. Neusner, *A History of the Jews in Babylonia*, vol. 5: *Later Sasanian Times* (Studia post-Biblica 15; Leiden: E.J. Brill, 1970), pp. 343–375. Reprinted with permission from Brill. Note that the footnote numbering here does not match that of the original publication.

[1] Also see J. Neusner, *Numen* 16, 1969,1–20

[2] C. H. Gordon, *AfO* 12, 1937–39, 115–117, B. Landsberger, *ibid.* 247–257, and C. H. Gordon, *Orientalia* 9, 1940, 29–38.

amine contemporary Jewish sources relevant to the Babylonian magical bowls. We take our cue from a treatise by Gershom Scholem, *Jewish Gnosticism, Merkabah Mysticism, and Talmudic Tradition* (Jewish Theological Seminary, 1960) in which Scholem inquired into the relationship of the Talmudic and mystical literatures. In an appendix to that volume (D, 118–126), Professor Saul Lieberman demonstrated the extensive dissemination of mystical literature within the community of Talmudic sages. Though Scholem was concerned primarily with the history of religious thought, he devoted considerable attention to theurgy and to its interactions with mystical experience. He presents a valuable edition of an Aramaic incantation, and examines the halakhic character of mystical literature, indicating to what extent the noted Talmudic sages were involved in mystical speculation.

Scholem's methodology is valuable in studying theurgy. We must, for the moment, refrain from treating the more mystical aspects of the magical bowls—the angelology, divine nomenclature in general, and the cosmorama projected in the texts, though these be matters of great significance in themselves. Here we will concentrate on comparative philology, attempting to assess, from the specific to the more general, the extent of affinity borne by these texts to other sources on Jewish theurgy and religio-legal practice in Talmudic times. This study hardly pretends to be comprehensive, and is intended only to be representative. Philologically speaking, our guide is J. N. Epstein, who brought to bear on some of these texts his incisive knowledge of the Aramaic dialects, and of the whole of Talmudic literature. J. A. Montgomery, C. H. Gordon, J. Obermann, and W. C. McCullough have provided us with most of the primary material.[3] The recent monograph on the Mandaic magical texts by E. M. Yamauchi (*AOS* 49) renders the examination of the comparative material easier, and we owe him no small debt.

In 1966 the late Mordecai Margalioth pieced together the hitherto lost treatise on ancient Jewish theurgy, *Sepher Ha-Razim* "The Book of Mysteries" (Hebrew) (henceforth *ShR*). This Hebrew compilation presents a systematic manual of magical praxis. It was written in Palestine sometime between the first and fourth centuries, with the linguistic criteria favoring a date nearer the beginning of that period. In *ShR* we have a type of "*Ritualtafel*", to borrow a term used to classify Mesopotamian magical texts.[4] The *Ritualtafel* prescribed the order of magical rites, and indicated at which points invocations and incantations should be recited. These, in turn, were presented separately, and constituted the large bulk of the magical series. The magical bowl inscriptions are the recitational texts, but we cannot ascertain from them, except by oblique reference, the exact procedures which constituted the coherent praxis of magic. *ShR* includes both the recitational material and the praxis, in more or less operational sequence. In terms of its own composition it differs, therefore, from the Mesopotamian pat-

[3] See in the list of bibliographical abbreviations pp. 374–5, and miscellaneous notes, a, for publications.

[4] Cf. as an example E. Reiner, *Šurpu*, in *AfO*, Beiheft 11, Graz, 1958.

tern; but with respect to the magical bowl inscriptions it serves as a kind of *Ritualtafel*. We shall, therefore, exploit the rich material of *ShR* in an attempt to clarify what the incantations meant in magical terms.

Our plan is to present philological notes to a selected number of magical texts which we found particularly inviting for comparative study. The notes will be followed by comments on central themes related to the corpus of bowl inscriptions as a whole.

I. Philological Notes

1. McCullough, A.

This is the brief text of a spell for the expulsion of evil spirits who have been afflicting a household. Our translation of the text differs from that of McCullough in several instances.
Consonantal transcription:[5]

1. *hlzyʾ ʾlyʾl dylryʿyʾl sryʾl wšlyšyʾl ʾzlwn ʾtwn hmšh mlʾkyn*
2. *dy mmryn ʿl byth dbʾby br mhlptʾ ʾwbyn wykbšwn yt qyymthd mʾbrzyn brhyʾ*
3. *yrwšylmʾy bt mrwdwk tht rygylh dbʾby br mhlptʾ qrystyʾ rbt dbʾby br mhlptʾ*
4. *dṣyr whtm bʿzqth ḏʾl šdy dbʾby br mhlptʾ*

Translation:

1. Girded are El-el, Dilriʿiel, Sariel, and Shlishiel. You begone, oh five angels
2. who are acting defiantly against the house of Babai, son of Maḥlapta; spirits of the dead! Let them (i.e. the four angels named above) grind QYYMTHD MʾBRZYN with millstones!
3. Yerushalmai, daughter of Mruduch, is under the power of Babai, son of Maḥlapta, (and of) Qristia, the lady of Babai, son of Maḥlapta.
4. This is tied and sealed with the signet ring of El-Shaddai, belonging to Babai, son of Maḥlapta.

Notes:

Line 1: The four angels are girded to do battle against evil forces. Aramaic *ḥlz* is a variant of *ḥlṣ*. In the sense of "to gird" *ḥlṣ/z* I should be differentiated

[5] Notes on our method of transcription in this study:

ḏ = the Mandaic ligature *adu* (*AOS* 49, 68, and 70, no. 2.4).

h = *Heh*. In the Aramaic script of the Babylonian magical bowls there is no difference in written form between *Heh* and *Ḥet* (AIT 29). With some exceptions, unattested in this study, the same is true in the script of the Mandaic bowls (*AOS* 49, 68, and 70, no. 2.3). Therefore:

h = *Heh* and *Ḥet* in *all actual textual transcriptions* from Babylonian Aramaic and Mandaic magical bowls.

ḥ = *Ḥet* in transcriptions from Syriac and other Semitic scripts which differentiate between *Heh* and *Ḥet*, and in all transcriptions of any language presented for purposes of linguistic analysis, vocalization, etc. (Also note the phoneme *ḫ* in transcriptions of Akkadian).

from *ḥlṣ* II "to press, squeeze out," hence: "extract, remove" (Lev. 14:40, 43, Deut. 25:9–10, Isaiah 20:2, Lam. 4:3, and cf. Talmudic *ḥălîṣāh* "the removal of the shoe" in Levy II, 64, s.v.). By extension, this verb appropriates the sense of deliverance from danger (*HuAL*, 308–309, s.v. *ḥlṣ*), and this root is cognate to Akkadian *ḫalāṣu* (*CAD Ḫ*, 40, s.v. *ḫalāṣu*, and adj. *ḫalṣu*, *ibid.* 51–52) which was originally applied to pressing out oil from seeds and fruits, for which compare Talmudic usage of this verb in Levy II, 63, s.v. *ḥlṣ*.

Biblical Hebrew *ḥālûṣ*, as a military term for an advanced unit, represents a different root, and derives, apparently, from the noun *ḥalāṣayim* "loins", probably cognate to Akkadian *ḫanṣātu* (*CAD Ḫ*, 81, s.v.). It means: "one whose loins are girded." A relationship to Akkadian *ḫalṣu*, "fortress" etc. is possible, but problematic (*CAD Ḫ*, 51). Despite the contrast of *ḥālûṣ* and *meʾasēp* "rear guard" in Joshua 6:9, 13, which suggests that the *ḥālûṣ* was a unit detached in advance of the main army, and thus "extracted" (a connotation fitting *ḥlṣ* II), the distinction between the two roots must be maintained. The sense of "gird" is logically extended to mean "strengthen", as in Isaiah 58:11: "YHWH will continually lead you, and sate your throat when it is dry with thirst, and add strength to your bones" (Hebrew *yaḥalîṣ*, and cf. Talmudic *ḥillûṣ ʿaṣāmôt* "strengthening of bones" in *TB Berākôt* 13b). The sense of "strength" is also attested in Syriac (*LS* 237, s.v. *ḥālîṣāʾ* and *ḥālîṣûtāʾ*). This is also the sense we have in McCullough C:20: *hlyṣʾ dhlyṣyʾ* "the strongest of the strong."

The biblical *ḥālûṣ*, was so called because of his state of preparation for battle, his equipment, etc., and not because he was part of a unit that was detached from the main body. In our magical inscriptions the verb *ḥlṣ/z* is often joined to *ʾsr* and *zrz*, and other verbs expressing preparedness for battle, and the related trapping of magical agents (*ʾsr*). In *AIT* 19:13, we have the following combination:

> *ʾtwn ʾsyry whlyṣy wzryzy ʿl kl šydy wsṭny byšy*
> "You are bound, girded, and belted against all demons, daevas, and evil devils."

The verb *zrz* (which may be a variant of *ʾzr*) has as its most concrete sense "gird, arm", witness the Aramaic noun *zarzāʾ* in Levy I, 552–553, s.v. *zarzāʾ*. In effect, we have a description of magical agents portrayed as warriors prepared to do battle, after having been bound (*ʾsr*) and pressed into the service of the person seeking magical assistance. Also cf. *AIT* 2:1–3, and see the comments.

All of the four angels named here are attested from other sources. *ShR* has three of them: *ʾlʾl* (variant: *ʾlyʾl*), *dlrʾl* (variant: *dylyryʿyʾl*, as here) and *sryʾl*. All three are placed in the sixth firmament (*ShR* VI:14, 19, 23), and are related to the magical objective of gaining victory in battle.

Line 2: *dy mmryn ʿl byth d-*. In Talmudic usage, *hamrēh* + *ʿal* has the sense of defying juridical authority (Levy III, 251, s.v. *mry*). Demons defy the authority of God. Cf. *AIT* 1:9: *wymrdwn wʿbryn ʿl gzyrtʾ dmryhwn*. "They rebel, and transgress against the decree of their master." Perhaps the raging of demons, associated with defiance, is also implied here.

ʾwbyn. Hebrew *ʾôb*. In Isaiah 19:3 *ʾôbôt* and *ʾiṭṭîm* are used in the parallel sense of spirits conjured up by necromancy (*CAD E*, 397, s.v. *eṭemmu*). Akkadian *eṭemmu* occurs frequently as a cause of affliction in Mesopotamian magical incantations, and perhaps *ʾwbyn* in the Aramaic texts is a translation of *eṭemmu*.

wykbšwn yt X. brhyʾ. Forms of the verb *kbš* are used frequently in the magical bowls to describe the action of God and his servants on inimical forces, or upon the natural world (Cf. note on *AIT* 16:6). The Paᶜel of *kbš* is used with respect to millstones in *TB Môᶜēd Qāṭān* 10a, in the sense of denting stones so as to have them grind the flour more finely. It is also said of placing heavy stones on an object, as in pressing down the ashes at the bottom of an oven (*TB Bêṣāh* 32b).

Line 3: *tht rygylh d-*. Assuming that Yerushalmai was a member of the afflicted household, or perhaps the one more particularly afflicted, McCullough is essentially correct in rendering the phrase: "under the protection of -." A more precise nuance would be afforded by: "under the power of -", which is the sense of *taḥat raglê-* in biblical usage (2 Kings 5:17, Malachi 3:21, Psalms 8:7, 47:4, Lam. 3:34). The intent here is that this person is one of Babai's household and is consequently under his jurisdiction, or legal authority. Such a person thereby enjoys the protection of the master of the household, who is responsible for him.

Line 4: *ṣyr whtm* (= *ṣîr weḥātîm*). Cf. Isaiah 8:16. *Ṣîr* is the Peᶜil of either *ṣwr* or *ṣrr*, with little appreciable difference in meaning, and some probable confusion of roots. In *TB Ḥullin* 105b the phrase *ṣîr weḥātîm* is applied to the condition of a lost article, which may allow us to presume that it was owned by someone prior to being lost. *Ṣîr weḥātîm* is here a legal formula, in the sense of: "signed, sealed, and delivered." As a result of the inscribing of the magical bowl and its disposition, the magical spell is completely binding. It is doubtful that the actual sealing up or closing of the bowl is intended, but of that we cannot be certain.

2. AIT, no. 8

This is an exorcism. It contains reference to the *gēṭ*, the Jewish writ of divorce, and is consequently of great significance for comparative study.

Line 3: Read, with Epstein: *ᶜrṭyl šlyhytyn wlʾ lbyšytyn* "You are disrobed naked, and not clad." Epstein cites sources showing that *šlḥ* has the sense of loosening clothing, disrobing. Cf. *ArOr* 9, 1937, 92, K:3. Also cf. in Mandaic, *AOS* 49, 359–360, s.v. *šlḥ*, and A. Sperber, *The Bible in Aramaic*, Leiden, 1959, 62, Targum Onkelos to Genesis 37:23 where Hebrew *wayyapšîṭû* is translated into Aramaic *waʾašleḥû*. Also see our note to *AIT* 13:16. In Nuzi Akkadian the verb *mašāru* "to send" is applied to the loosening of clothing. Thus: *qannāšu imtašar* "He loosened his belt/sash" (*AHw* 624, s.v. *mašāru*). Also see Levy IV, 558, s.v. *šelaḥ* for additional sources. Perhaps the biblical Hebrew usage of the Piᶜel in the phrase: *šallēaḥ peraᶜ* "let the hair grow loose/long" (Ezekiel 44:20) is related to this connotation of the root *šlḥ*. On the form of consonantal *šlyhytyn* see Rossell, 51, 7:16, where it is explained that the masc. part. pl. is occasionally used for the feminine. Here we have *šelîḥîn* (masc. passive part, pl) + *tên* (fem. pl. 2nd person pronominal element) which shifts to *šelîḥittên* with the assimilation of the final Nun of the part. Similarly: *lebîšittên* (line 11) and *ḥatîmittê*(*n*), in the same line.

wstyr sʿrykyn wrmy ʾhwr gbykyn. "And your hair is disheveled, and cast behind your back." See our note to *AIT* 13:7, and cf. *ArOr* 9, 1937, 92, K:3, and note on p. 93 to lines 3–4. Also cf. in a Mandaic incantation recently published by E. M. Yamauchi in *Berytus* 17, 1967, 52–54, line 10, and note, s.v. *lagdlia* "do not plait the hair." Cf. *TB Yebāmôt* 116b: *setîrê mazyayik* "your locks are disheveled."

Line 6: Read, with Epstein: *ʾwmyty ʿlykyn bryqʾ* (= *byqrʾ*) *dʾbwkwn*, etc. "I adjure you by the honor of your father and by the honor of your mother." We have in the magical bowls several forms of the verb *w/ymʾ*, which are related to the noun *mômātāʾ* "ban" (in our text, line 14). See Levy III, 50, s.v. *mômātāʾ*; which, in the Mishnah, *Nedārîm* 1:2 is corrupted to *môtāʾ*. In a similar sense we have *šammēt* "to place a ban", a denominative of *šammātāʾ* (Levy IV, 583). Aramaic *mômātāʾ* is cognate to Akkadian *māmītu* (*AHw* 599, s.v.). In line 12 we have: *mšbʿnʾ ʿlykyn* "I forswear you," the usual Hebrew formulary. Cf. *ShR* I, 74, *et passim*, and S. Lieberman, *Greek in Jewish Palestine*, New York, 1942, 121, and note 53.

In the Aramaic bowls we have the following forms: a) *ʾwmyty* (*ʾômîtî*) "I have adjured," the Apʿel perfect, 1st sing. Cf. the older Aramaic *hwmytk* (= *hômîtkā*) "I have adjured you", Hipʿil perf. 1st sing. + 2nd pronoun, in the Aramaic inscription from Daskyleion, dated ca. 400 B.C.E. (F. M. Cross Jr., *BASOR* 184, Dec. 1964, 9, and note 19; further R. S. Hanson, *ibid.* 192, Dec. 1968, 3, and notes 1–3). Also see *AIT* 3:3. Read with Epstein: *ʾwmwʾy mwmynʾ lk wʾšbwʿy mšbʿnʾ ʿlk* (= *ʾômôʾê mômînāʾ lāk waʾašbôʿê mešbaʿnāʾ ʿalāk*) "I surely adjure you, and I surely forswear you." Also cf. *AIT* 14:3 and in Syriac, *Orientalia* 18, 1949, 338–339, line 7.

The demons were adjured in the name of their father and mother, whose names are specified. Cf. *AIT* 17:8–9. This feature of the exorcistic oath has an interesting background. In the Mishnah, *Nedārîm* 9:1, we read:

> Rabbi Eliezer said: We may seek a way out (Hebrew: *petaḥ*) of vows on behalf of a person by invoking the honor of his father and his mother (*kebôd ʾābîw weʾimmô*)."

This is taken to mean that one seeking release from a regrettable vow would be asked if he would have so committed himself had he realized, at the time, that the fulfillment of such a vow would reflect dishonor or disgrace on his parents. The Palestinian Talmud, *ad loc.* clarifies the legal presumptions involved. If we are to presume that one would perjure himself to spare his parents, then we dare not allow for such "openings". The majority of sages disputed Rabbi Eliezer's view, stated above.

By naming the parents of Lilith at the time of the exorcistic oath the practitioner was eliminating subsequent appeal to the legal principle expressed in the

Mishnah, should the demons attempt to effect release from the ban to which they had acceded under potent pressure. Joshua, son of Perahiah, as a legitimate sage, would have had to take such an appeal into account, and so it is eliminated at the very outset. Though the parents of demons would have undoubtedly been put to shame by the acceptance of such bans by their children, the ban would remain in force. It should also be noted that according to Mosaic law there were situations in which the father held jurisdiction over his daughter's vows (Numbers 30:4f.).

dšlh ʿlykyn šmtaʾ. "For he has dispatched to you (or: against you) a ban." In some Aramaic usages, *šlḥ* has the technical sense of dispatching a written communication. In *AIT* 32:4 we have: "as when R. Joshua s. Perahiah was in court session and wrote a restraining ban," etc. There, *ketab* is in place of *šelaḥ*. À propos the banishment of demons cf. *TB Šabbāt* 67a: *lîṭ tebîr ûmešammat* "cursed, broken, and placed under a ban." Also cf. *ArOr* 6, 1934, 322, A:2, *ibid.* 9, 1937, 100, N:8, and parallel. For the legal force of the ban known as *šammātāʾ* see Mishnah, *Nedārîm* 1:1, and *TB ibid.* 7a–b.

Line 7: On the formulary of the Jewish *gēṭ* see Epstein 37, and *AIT* 159. Cf. *AIT* 9:5f., 10; 11:8, 17:9f., 18:8–9f., and *ArOr* 6, 1934, 469, G:5–6, 7, 9; *AASOR* xiv, 1934, 141, lines 5–7, *AOS* 49, 21:10–11.

In line 16 of our text we have still another part of the formulary of the *gēṭ*: *mn ywmʾ dnn wlʿlm* "from this day forward and forever." Cf. *Orientalia* 10, 1941, 117, 1:4: *mn ywmʾ dnn wšʿtʾ dh wlʿlm* "from this day and from this hour forward and forever." See C. Albeck, *The Six Orders of the Mishnah, The Order Nāšim* (Hebrew), Jerusalem, 1954, 267–268 for the Aramaic text of the *gēṭ*. Also cf. *ArOr* 6, 1934, 326, C:8, and our note to lines 15–16, below.

wlhyrwdykyn. Montgomery renders: "for your terrification." Perhaps read: *wltyrwdykyn* (= *ûletirrûdêkên*) "for driving you out." In Talmudic Aramaic we have *trd* with a *Tau*, as a variant of *ṭrd*, as evidenced in the nominal form *ṭardāʾ* "an unsettled person", a variant of *ṭārôdāʾ* (Levy IV, 669 and II, 186, respectively). On the various meanings of *ṭrd* see J. Greenfield, *HUCA* 29, 1958, 210–212.

Line 8: *wšlnytʾ whṭpytʾ*. The latter term for a type of female demon clearly drives from *ḥṭp*, and means something like: "the rapacious one." Aramaic *ḥaṭpîtāʾ*, is the translation of Hebrew *taḥmās* "falcon" in the Targum to Lev. 11:16 and Deut. 14:15. The verb *ḥṭp* elsewhere serves as the translation of *ḥāmās* "violence" (Targum to Jeremiah 51:46), which is taken to be the etymology of the name of the bird of prey. See Levy II, 40, s.v. *ḥāṭôpāʾ* and Levy, *TW* 251, s.v. *ḥaṭpîtāʾ* and *LS* 227 s.v. *ḥāṭôpāʾ*. Demons are portrayed as birds of prey, especially female demons. As for *šlnytʾ* we propose to take it from the root *šlh/y* "to draw out," which, in Talmudic usage is said of fishing; as when the fisherman pulls out fish from the water (Levy IV, 557 s.v. *šlh/y*). We therefore suggest: *šallānîtāʾ*, a Paʿel nominalized formation with the characterizing *-ān* and the fem. gentilic: "the snatcher."

Lines 9–10: See P.S. in Epstein, 42.

Line 11: On the signet ring, see the comments.

Lines 15–16: *ʾp ʾnty lylytʾ byštʾ qbwly gyṭ p[ṭw]ryky wʾgrt šybwqky mn hdyn X. br Y., wmn Z. ʾyttyh bt A. wtwb lʾ tyhdryn ʿlyhwn mn ywmʾ dnn wlʿlm*. "Moreover, you, evil Lilith, receive the writ of your dismissal and the document of your abandonment from one, X. son of Y., and from Z. his wife, daughter of A., and never again return to them from this day forward and forever."

The sense is that once banished, divorced, so to speak, the female demons, principally Lilith herself, were adjured never to return to the household. This is consonant with the legal theory of the *gēṭ* according to which the husband dismisses his wife (*pṭr*), and expels her (*trk*) from his domicile, and leaves her outside of it, forbidden to return (*šbq*). In Talmudic terminology, it is always the woman who is spoken of as returning to the man, or not returning. Thus, one who remarries his divorced wife is termed: *hammaḥazîr gerûšātô* "one who brings back, restores his divorced wife" (Mishnah, *Yebāmôt* 4:12, etc.). The definition of a woman mentally incompetent and therefore unable to receive a *gēṭ* is: *šemegārešāh wehî ḥôzeret* "for he divorces her, but she keeps coming back" (*TB Yebāmôt* 113b). This is also the notion of the graphics of divorce in those magical texts wherein we have reference to the formulary of the *gēṭ* (see note to line 7). The demons are divorced in legalistic terms, and warned not to return. This is also the basic notion of divorce in Mosaic legislation:

> A man takes a wife and possesses her. She fails to please him because he finds something obnoxious about her, and he writes her a bill of divorcement, hands it to her, and sends her away (Hebrew: *šlḥ*, Piᶜel) from his house; she leaves his household," etc. (Deuteronomy 24:1–2a).

It is therefore puzzling that a statement concerning the practice of demons in divorcing their wives would seem to project a situation wherein the husband, once having divorced his wife, does not return to her!

Thus, we read in *AIT* 11:7–8:

> *kmᵓ dktbyn šydyn gyṭyn wyhbyn lynšyhwn wtwb lᵓ hdryn ᶜlyhyn*
> "As demons write and issue writs of divorce to their wives, and do not again return to them" (fem. pl.).

Epstein 47–48, notes to *AIT* 32; lines 9–10, discusses this clause in another connection, and concludes that *hdr* + *ᶜl* = *hdr* + *b*, a Talmudic idiom meaning: "to retract, reverse one's view, or action." The resulting interpretation would then be that the demons, once having divorced their wives, never change their mind; which apparently does happen in the case of humans! The verb *hdr* would refer to one's decisions and to his views, and not to the motion of returning.

This clause occurs a number of times in these inscriptions (*AIT* 18:8–9, 26:6, *AASOR* xiv, 1934, 141, line 6, *Orientalia* 10, 1941, 351, no. 11113, and also *ArOr* 6, 1934, 469, L5:6, and *AOS* 49, 21:10–11). Some of the occurrences cannot help us determine the referent of the returning, since they have abbreviated versions of the clause without the preposition *ᶜal* + suffix.

We cannot accept Epstein's ingenious suggestion, because of several considerations: a) the Paᶜel *haddēr* + *ᶜal* clearly has the sense of returning to some place or person in *AIT* 8:16, 11:7–8. It is possible, of course, that the Qal has a different sense. On the other hand the sense of retraction occurs only in the Qal, whereas the root *hdr* + *ʿal* occurs in both stems. b) Judging from Talmudic Hebrew, it is clear that *ḥāzar* + *b-* "to retract" is distinct from both *ḥāzar* + *ʿal* and *ḥizzēr* + *ʿal*, both of which relate to the sense of motion. Levy II, 32–33. Levy cites one instance, (*TP ʿAbôdāh Zārāh* I, 39a), in which the idiom *ḥāzar* + *b-* seems to have the sense of motion, but we doubt if the reverse is true, i.e. that *ḥāzar* + *ʿal* could mean: "to retract".

We must, therefore, seek another solution to the meaning of the clause. In *ArOr* 6, 1934, text G, we have two occurrences of this clause, one in line 6, and the other in line 11. In line 6 the clause is written normally, as far as the orthography of the part. of *hdr* is concerned: *wtwbw*(!) *lʾ hdryn ʿlyhyn*. In line 11, however, it is written: *hdrn*, without a *Yod*. See plate xxv for verification. Gordon inserted a *Yod* in parentheses (= *hdr-y-n*) to make the clause conform to other occurrences.

Actually, it is perhaps this orthography which reflects the original clause! When we bear in mind that *Waw* and *Yod* are often indistinguishable in this orthography (Rossell, 14, 2:3), we see that *ʿlyhyn* could just as well be read *ʿlyhwn* (= *ʿalêhôn*), the masc. pl. 3rd person preposition, instead of the feminine. We would then have, in this instance, the following reading in line 11: *welāʾ hādrān* (fem. part. pl.) *ʿalêhôn* "They (= the divorced wives) do not return to them (= the former husbands)." A perusal of the copy of *AIT* 11:8 (plate xii) shows that there the scribe at first wrote *hdrn* and then inserted a *Yod* above the line, producing *hdryn*.

It is our proposal that the original clause was as we have interpreted *ArOr* 6, 1934, line 11, i.e. that the wives do not return to their former husbands once divorced, but that the precise sense of this was misunderstood or confused. Scribes saw other masc. pl. participles in the clause, such as *kātebîn*, *yāhabîn*, and erroneously wrote *hdryn* (= *hāderîn*). Along came modern scholars, and logically read *ʿlyhyn* (*ʿalêhên*), the fem. pl. instead of *ʿlyhwn*. The scribes who wrote these inscriptions were much less than scholars!

3. AIT, no. 13

This is an incantation against barrenness. The principals are the same as in *AIT*, no. 1, and if our text is considered Jewish, so must no. 1. We have prepared a revised translation, incorporating Epstein's corrections.

Interior

1. Closed be the mouths of all the peoples, armies,
2. and tongues, from before B. d. S.
3. The angel Rahmiel, the angel Habbiel, and the angel Hananiel-
4. They, the angels shall love and hold dear and embrace B.
5. d. S. Before all of the sons of Adam whom he begat by Eve, let us enter into their presence.

6. With their garment they will clothe her, and with their covering they will cover her; with the robe of God's kindness.
7. They sit with her. They pleat her hair as is fitting. In the name of YHWH, in-YH(?), El-El, the great
8. and the terrifying one, whose word is all healing. This incantation is true and legally binding forever. (Hark! the sound of-).

Exterior

9. Hark! The sound of a woman. The sound of a woman who travails but does not give birth. Hush! Quietly,
10. let E. s. S enter into his house (= wife), and into the body of B. d. S.,
11. his wife. For she is a woman closed up, travailing but not giving birth. May she be like fresh myrtle for crowns. Amen. Amen.
12. True and binding. Healing from heaven for B. d. S. May mighty Afarof (= Hermes), trampling and repulsing (?)... Amen. Amen. Selah. Healing and wellbeing from heaven, forever and ever.

Notes:

Line 1: With Montgomery vocalize: *sekîrê pûmêhôn*. Cf. C. H. Gordon, *Orientalia* 10, 1941, 125–126, Text 6:1f.

Line 4: Read with Epstein: *yrhmwn wyhbbwn wyhbqwn*, removing the word mistakenly added by Montgomery (*wyhnwn*). It seems that the angels are portrayed as impregnating the woman, or at least as arousing her passions by bodily contact.

Line 5: "the sons of Adam whom he begat by Eve." Cf. *ShR* II:22: "of the sons of Adam and Eve." This specification was undoubtedly necessitated by the fact that certain would-be humans are actually the offspring of one human and one demonic parent. According to Jewish legend, Eve was impregnated by the reptile Satan, from which union the fratricide, Cain, was born. In reverse, Lilith acted as Adam's succubus, from which unions demons were born (*Legends*, I, 105, 118, and notes). Also note *AIT* 1:8–9; "I adjure you, all sorts of Liliths, in the name of your seed, who bear Lilis and Liliths. They seduce the sons of light (*benê nûrāʾ*)." See our note to *AIT* 16:7.

Line 6: "The robe of God's kindness." Cf. in the cuneiform Aramaic incantation, lines 30–31 (*AfO* 12, 1937–39, 107f.): *áš-làḫ-te-e šá-am-lat r*[*u*]*-ga-z*[*a*]-(*a*)*-a-ʾi-*[*i*] [*a*]*l-bi-iš-te-e šá-am-lat š*[*a*]*l-ma-a-ʾ*[*i-i*] "I stripped him of the garb of his ragings and I clothed him with the garb of his wellbeing." Also cf. lines 20, 22–23. Zechariah 3:1–5 projects some of the same imagery.

Line 7: Read with Epstein: *myzyh* (*myzy*) *myzyyhyn*. The word in parentheses is a dittography. On *mazyāhā* "her hair" cf. Talmudic *mazyāʾ* in Levy III, 62 s.v. Epstein suggests that *myzyyhyn* is Syriac *zḥ* "to arrange hair" (*LS* 192, s.v.). He calls attention to the Talmudic legend which tells that God pleated Eve's hair before presenting her to Adam (*TB Berākôt* 61a, and see Genesis Rabbah, ed. Mirkin, Tel-Aviv, 1956, par. 18, 127f., to Gen. 2:22. Cf. Levy, I, 220, s.v. *bintāʾ* II, and vol. IV, 316, s.v. *qelîʿāh*).

Line 8: "whose word is all healing." Cf. in the Mandaic bowls, *ArOr* 9, 1937, Text M:16–17: "Who heals all illnesses with the word. Heal with the word -", and in *AOS* 49, no. 9:19, and see glossary, 309, s.v. *ʾsʾ*. Also cf. *ShR* II:180–181: "Their tongue is healing, their speaking binds the wound, and wherever their names are mentioned you will find success."

qlql. Coming at the end of the interior section, this anticipates the beginning of the next section, beginning with our line 9. Cf. in *AIT* 1, end of line 11, in anticipation of line 12. This is a frequent scribal practice in Jewish texts.

Line 9: *qāl*! *qālāʾ d-*. Cf. in Mandaic (*AOS* 49, glossary, 350, s.v. *qʾlʾ*, and Epstein, 46).

Line 10: Our translation follows Epstein who takes *byth* as connoting wife, in line with Talmudic notions (*TB Šabbāt* 118b: "I refer to my wife as 'my house'"). The text in line 10 reads: *lgwb byth*, an error for *lgw* "inside", as noted by Epstein.

Line 11: Montgomery read: *ʾblyty*, but was at a loss to explain the word. Epstein reads: *ʾdlyty*, which is probably correct. He noted Mandaic usage of *ʾ/ydl* metathetically for *ʾ/yld* "to give birth". We thus have: "a woman lying in." Another possibility would be to take *ʾdlyty* from Akkadian *edēlu* "to lock", and related forms (*CAD E*, 25–26, s.v. *edēlu*, and *ibid*. 33, s.v. *edlu*, adj.). Our form *ʾedlîtî* would be a feminine adj., meaning "the locked one," a traditional way of describing a barren woman as one whose womb is closed up (Gen. 20:18, 1 Sam. 1:5–6). In omen texts, Akkadian *edēlu* is applied to physical conditions wherein limbs and organs are closed (*CAD E*, 26, s.v. *edēlu* a, 4, and b, 4).

Line 12: *ʾprprp*, rather than Montgomery's incorrect reading *ʾprprṭ*. See Epstein's note, *ad loc.*, 46.

ʾṣy qwhy. (As corrected by Epstein). The former word, a verbal form, occurs in *AIT* 1:11, in a series of words meaning "to inflict damage, trample." See Levy I, 6, s.v. *ʾîṣāʾ* II "to injure, trample." The latter word might be the verb *qhh/y*, which in the Paʿel means: "to push away, cast off." (Cf. Levy IV, 256, s.v. *qihhāh*). The question is what forms of the verbal roots are represented here. The former could be a Qal part., but the latter could not be a Paʿel part, and so this problem remains. The sense seems clearly to be that Hermes is beseeched to expel the evil forces. Cf. *AIT*, no. 2, where the robe of Hermes is donned by one coming to destroy the forces of evil.

4. AIT, no. 16

This is an incantation for the healing of a family. It provides what amounts to a catalogue of evil forces. We present a revised translation, as in no. 13.

Translation:

1. Healing from heaven for D. s. A.
2. and for S. d. D., his wife, and for H. and Y.
3. and K. and M. and P. and A. and S., the children of S.,
4. and for their houses and property; that they may have children, and that they may live and endure, and that

5. no "injurer" who exists in the world may plague them. And in the great name of the holy one, the holy God, whose name is one
6. who subdues darkness under light, disease under healing, wrecking
7. under construction, violence under order, disturbance under tranquility. Subdued are all the sons of darkness under the throne of God, whose name is one.
8. Bound and subdued are the daevas. Refuge is taken away from evil spirits and malicious pebble-spirits and bans, and the rulers
9. of darkness, and the evil spirit and Naʾalah demon, and the demons who chain, of the night and the day; and the curses, and the necklace charms and counter-charms; and spells (lit: words) and bans,
10. and demons who rap, and those who deliver to evil forces; male and female forces of misfortune, and the mysterious voice that cries out; and the prince of poverty, and demons and daevas and devils
11. and idol-spirits, and Liliths, and workers of black magic, and potent magicians, and the seven demons who chain, of the night and the day. They are bound, subdued and pressed down,
12. away from D. s. A. (names of members of his family)
13. and from their entire household, and from their possessions, and from their entire courtyard, from this day and forever. Amen.
14. Amen. Selah. "God said to Satan: God is enraged at you, Satan! God is enraged at you; (enraged is) He who has chosen Jerusalem. Is this not a coal plucked from the fire?" (Zach. 3:2).

Notes:

Line 5: *mzyq*. For Talmudic usage see Levy III, 66–67, s.v. *mazzîq* (2). Read with Epstein: *wbyšmyh rbh dgdy*(!) *ʾlhʾ qdyšʾ dhd šmyh*. The word *qdy* is simply an error for *qdyšʾ*.

Line 6: *dkbyš* (= *dekābēš*, part.). On the Paʿel of this verb see note to McCullough A:2. The root *kbš* actually has several distinct connotations in these bowls:

1. The verb *kbš* in its usual sense of "to press down, subdue, and technically": "to pave a road." (See no. 2).

2. The noun *kibšāʾ* (variant: *kebîš*) "paved road." Cf. *kebeš* "a ramp."

3. The noun *kibšā* variant: *kbyšʾ*, "esoteric knowledge," hence: "spell." Literally: "that which is covered, hidden."

4. The denominative verb *kbš*, from *kibšāʾ*: "to cast a spell."

Each connotation requires some explanation:

1. For the normal verbal usage see Epstein, 38–39, note to *AIT* 9:6–7. He observes that Aramaic *knʿ* used here is equivalent to Mandaic *kbš* in the parallel imagery of *AIT* 32:6–7. Also see Epstein's note to line 11 of our text, where we have metathetical *mškbn* for *mkbšn*. Also cf. *AIT* 6:7, 9(?).

2. The term *kibšāʾ* "paved road" occurs in *AIT* 28:2 *kybšy ʿlmʾ lʾ ʾytkbyšw ʾylʾ ʿl* "The eternal roads were not paved except by means of [this spell](?)" This phrase is probably an Aramaic rendering of the biblical phrase *netîbôt ʿôlām* in

Jeremiah 6:16. These paths are understandably hidden. Cf. Levy II, 292, s.v. *kebeš* and 293, s.v. *kibšāʾ*.

3. The noun *kibšāʾ* "esoteric knowledge" occurs in the Talmud (*TB Berākôt* 10a): *bahadê kibšê deraḥamānāʾ lemāʾ lāk*? "What business have you with the Allmerciful's mysteries?" Cf. Levy II, 293, s.v. *kibšāʾ* 4 and *kibšôn*. Hebrew mystical literature uses the term *kebûšîm*. Thus, the frequent noun *kibšāʾ* does not mean "press" or the like, and does not refer primarily to the subjugation of the demons as such, or of the natural world, but to the covered and hidden quality of the spell. It is synonymous with *rāzāʾ*, and other similar terms.

4. The denominative verb *kbš* (Paʿel), from *kibšāʾ* means: "to cast a spell", just as *ʾšp*, from *ʾyšpʾ*, means: "to conjure." (Cf. *AIT* 2:3–4, *ArOr* 6, 1934, 378, D:14–15).

We have a variance of usage which can be confusing. Often several connotations are employed in the same passage, alongside one another. For example, *AIT* 6:7: *wkybšʾ hdyn kbyšnʾ lhwn bšwm hdyn šbʿ mylyn dy šmyʾ wʾrʿh kbyšyn bhwn* "And this spell (no. 3) I cast (no. 4) for them in the name of the seven magic spells (lit.: words) by which heaven and earth were subdued (no. 1)." Cf. *Orientalia* 20, 1951, 307, 6–8.

All of the four connotations are clearly derivative from the same root, but must be differentiated in the process of interpretation.

hbltʾ thwt šwytʾ. This is Epstein's correction of Montgomery's reading: *šmtʾ*, which does not at all fit the context. The word *šewîtāʾ* means: "equilibrium, accord, tranquility." The semantics are as follows: What is equal (the root *šwy*) is balanced and in accord. It is also worth something, with which it is equal. Thus, it is dignified (Syriac usage, cf. *LS* 760–761, s.v. *šewāʾ*, and the adj. *šewēʾ*, and related forms). This is a logical contrast to *ḥabbaltāʾ* which characterizes a condition of disorder. This may be the sense of *šāweh* in the Talmudic designation *bêt dîn šāweh* "a unanimous court," i.e. one in accord (*TP Qiddûšîn* III, hal. 4, and cf. J. Neusner, *A History of the Jews in Babylonia* I, Leiden, 1965, 152–153, and note 5). In the light of the sense of *šewîtāʾ* in this incantation, we must question Scholem's reading of the opening formula of an Aramaic incantation (Scholem, 85, and note, 87). See our note to Scholem, Incantation, line 1.

Line 7: "Subdued are all the sons of darkness under God's throne." The Aramaic is: *benê ḥašōkāʾ*. Cf. *benê ḥôšek* in the *Manual of Discipline* I:10–11 in J. Licht, *The Rule Scroll*, (Hebrew) Jerusalem, 1965, 61: "to love all the sons of light (*benê ʾôr*)... and to despise all the sons of darkness." This pair of terms is quite frequent in the Dead Sea literature. The occurrence of *benê ḥašōkāʾ* in our text makes us question Epstein's reading in *AIT* 1:9, where he reads: *lbny nyrʾ sṭyn* "They entice the bearers of the yoke (= the devout)." The word *nyrʾ* could just as well be read *nwrʾ*, and, in fact, *bar nîrāʾ* does not mean one who bears the yoke of God's commandments, but rather "slave, slavery" (Levy III, 392, s.v. *nîr* IV, 2). Demons continually attempt to seduce the chosen sons of light, and many of them, we are told, fall away from the sect. This is a notion endemic to the Dead Sea literature, and suits us here as well. Cf. *br nhwrʾ* "son of light" in *Orientalia* 10, 1941, 345, Fitzwilliam, line 35, as an epithet.

It would seem, therefore, that we have reference in the magical bowl inscriptions to the two contrasting categories so prominent in the Dead Sea literature. This terminology is, of course, related to the notion that light envelopes the righteous and darkness engulfs the wicked (1 Enoch 1:8, 64:11, 108:11–15). This originally meant that the righteous would reside near God in the upper firmaments where there is brilliant light, and the wicked in the netherworld where darkness reigns. The terminology is quite specialized, however, and it is interesting to find it in the magical bowls.

Line 8: *nqyṭn kdnʾ rwhy byštʾ*. Epstein notes Syriac *kedan* "refuge, protection" (*LS* 318, s.v.), which is cognate to Akkadian *kidinnu* and related forms (*AHw* 472–473, s.v. *kidi/ennu(m)*, *kidinnu* I, and *kidinnūtu*).

šwmhtʾ "names". Cf. *AIT* 8:9–10, according to Epstein's reading: *mlʾkyn šwmyn byšyn* "angels, evil names."

wrbrby dhšwkʾ "the rulers of darkness". Cf. *Orientalia* 10, 1941, 356, Princeton, lines 15, 21: *rwrbʾtʾ dhyšwkʾ*, and *AOS* 49, 1:11, *et passim*. In the Dead Sea literature we have the term *malʾak ḥôsek*. See in the *Manual of Discipline*, III:20–22, in J. Licht, *op. cit.*, 92; in the *Thanksgiving Scroll*, XII:5–6, in J. Licht, *The Thanksgiving Scroll* (Hebrew), Jerusalem, 1957; *memšelet ḥôsek* "the jurisdiction of darkness." Also cf. in the *War Scroll*, I:15, XIII:12.

In Talmudic legend "the ruler of darkness" (*śar šel ḥôsek*) was banished by God before creation (*Legends*, I, 13, V, 16, notes 41–42).

Line 9: *wnʾly*. See Levy III, 332, s.v. *naʾalāh*. Cf. *ArOr* 6, 1934, A:3. *wmbkltʾ dlylyh wdymmʾ* "and the demons who chain, of the night and the day." Cf. in line 11: *wšbᶜ mbkltʾ dlylyh wdymmʾ* "and the seven demons who chain," etc. Also cf. *ArOr* 6, 1934, 322, A:2; 9, 1937, 92, K:2, *Orientalia* 10, 1941, 120, 3:2. Take *mbkltʾ* as metathetical for *mkbltʾ* an Apᶜel part. from *kbl*. See Levy II, 288, s.v. *kablāʾ* for the Talmudic curse: *ʾarᶜāʾ dimekabbelāʾ welāʾ ᶜābdāʾ pērê* "a chained land which does not produce fruit." Also see S. Lieberman, *Greek in Jewish Palestine*, N.Y., 1942, 119–120 for Talmudic usages of *kbl*. *qyblyʾ* "counter-charms". See Levy IV, 238 s.v. *qebal*.

wmlltʾ "imprecations." This is an Aramaic fem. pl. Cf. *AIT* 6:9. On the term *millāh* in the sense of "magical spell" see D. Sperber, *REJ* 125, 1966, 385–389, who cites pertinent Talmudic and post-Talmudic Jewish sources, and comments on the magical bowl edited by C. H. Gordon, *Orientalia* 10, 1941, 339–340 wherein the term *millāh/miltāʾ* has this sense. Also cf. *ibid.* 345, Fitzwilliam, line 43, and *AIT* 34:6. See *AIT* 293, s.v. *mllʾ*. In the cuneiform Aramaic inscription we have the idiom: *ma-li-e mi-il-li-ni* "full of words," i.e. spells. Sperber also refers to Scholem, 85, line 14: *lrqyᶜh mlyh slqh bstr krsyh dʾlh rbh*, etc. "The spells ascended to heaven, at the side of the throne of the great God," etc. The point is that the evil magical spells were summoned up to God's throne and there subdued and reversed so that their targets would no longer be afflicted by them. In line 7 it is said that the sons of darkness are subdued under God's throne. See our note to Scholem, Incantation.

Line 10: *wʾyštqwptʾ* "demons who rap". Cf. variant *šyqwptʾ* (*AIT* 86, and note 114, and *ArOr* 6, 1934, 324, B:6, and *ibid.* 9, 1937, 93, K:3. Cf. *AOS* 49, 28, and note 62.

btqlʾ dqryh "a mysterious voice that cries out." S. Lieberman, *Hellenism in Jewish Palestine*, N.Y., 1942, 194–199 points out that very often what was meant by *bat qôl* was an unusual or unexpected sound or voice, perhaps the coincidental recitation of a biblical verse by a school child that had particular bearing on one's own situation and could therefore be seen as an omen. It was not necessarily a heavenly voice, or divine in any sense. This term occurs in Syriac incantations. See J. Teixidor, *Sumer* 18, 1962, 52, no. 59098, line 6, and variant: *bytqlʾ*, 54, no. 44107, line 3. Teixidor apparently misunderstands the provenience of this term, which he renders in one instance: "the word pronounced." He considers it a type of invocation, which it can hardly be!

wʾšlmtʾ "deliverance spell/spirit", i.e. that which delivers one into the hands of evil. Cf. *Orientalia*, 10, 1941, 117, 1:1; 127, 7:9. This is the usual sense of the Apʿel of *šlm* in Syriac and Mandaic (*LS* 783, s.v. *šelem*, Af., and *AOS* 49, 360, in the glossary, s.v. *šlm*). Montgomery (*AIT* 85–86, and notes 109–111) rejects this interpretation, probably because he misunderstood the cultic evidence. Hebrew *šelāmîm* was understood, at times, to derive from the sense of "complete, perfect", and it was rendered τελείαι in some versions of the Septuagint. Similarly, we have Mandaic *šlmʾnʾ*. On this basis, the Targum used *ʾašlēm* denominatively in the sense of offering a sacrifice (Cf. *Orientalia* 10, 1941, 121, 4:3–5; and *ibid.* 117, 1:3). On the various Septuagint renderings of *šelāmîm* see S. Daniel, *Le Vocabulaire du Culte dans le Septante*, Paris, 1966, 287f. Montgomery's reasons for rejecting the rendering "deliverance spell/spirit" were, therefore, incorrect.

wʾsrh dmyskynwtʾ "the prince of poverty." The term *ʾisārāh/ʾ* is a variant of *sārāh/ʾ*. See Scholem, 48, and note 17. Cf. *ArOr* 9, 1937, 94, L:12–14: *wbyšmyh dmṭṭrwy*(!) *ʾysrʾ rbh dklyh ʿlmʾ wbyšmyh drpʾl ʾysrʾ dʾswtʾ* "In the name of Metatron, prince of the entire world, and in the name of Raphael, prince of healing." Also cf. *ArOr* 6, 1934, 328, D:11; *Orientalia* 10, 1941, 280, line 10: *ʾysrʾ rbʾ* "the great prince," and *Orientalia* 20, 1951, 307, line 5: *srʾ rbʾ* (all epithets of Metatron). Also cf. *Orientalia* 10, 1941, 123, 5:10: *ʾysrh ṭbʾ* "the good prince", an epithet of some magical agent. For similar epithets, cf. *ArOr* 6, 1934, 331–332, texts E, F, and Hyvernat. See *AIT* 79, note 70, and 86, note 112 for Montgomery's misunderstanding of this term.

Line 14: Cf. *Orientalia* 10, 1941, 127, 7:10–11, and Levy, I, 351, s.v. *gʿr*.

5. Miscellaneous Notes

a) Obermann, text II (AJSL 57, 1940, 15–28, and plate, 31)

This incantation is unusual in our corpus because it has as its purpose inflicting pain on someone, and can be considered black magic, rather than prophylactic magic; which is normally the case in these Aramaic inscriptions.

Lines 1–2: *wlʾ lytybwn lh šyntʾ lʿnyh wlʾ lytybwn lh nwmʾ bpgrh* "Let them not restore sleep to her eyes, and let them not restore slumber in her body." Obermann noted the biblical overtones of the pair: "sleep-slumber", for which see Psalms 132:4. The Jewish liturgy expresses the same imagery, in the blessings of the morning service (*birkôt haššaḥar*), which were current in Talmudic times. The final blessing reads, in part: *hammaʿbîr (ḥeblê) šēnāh mēʿênaî ûtenûmāh mēʿapʿapaî* "who removes (the bonds of) slumber from my eyes, and drowsing from my eyeballs." In Talmudic usage, Hebrew and Aramaic, the verb *nwm* often connotes a state less than complete sleep. For the text of the blessing see *TB Berākôt* 60b, and *Talmudic Encyclopedia* (Hebrew), Jerusalem, 1952, IV, 363f., and especially 370.

Of particular interest is the use of the term *peger* here and in some Mandaic magical inscriptions to designate a living body. Here it is said of the body of a sleeping or recumbent person. Jewish liturgy may add to our appreciation of the magical factors involved in the sleeping state. In the morning service there is a prayer of gratitude for the re-awakening to life on a new day. It speaks of the soul, of its purity and divine origin, and of its destiny. It will be taken away from man at death, and restored to him at the resurrection. The prayer concludes with the words: "I give thanks before you my God, and God of my fathers," *ribbôn kol hammaʿaśîm, ʾadôn kol hannešāmôt, ... hammaḥazîr nešāmôt lipegārîm mētîm* "Ruler of all created beings, master of all souls, ... who restores souls to dead bodies." Traditional interpretation has seen two dimensions in this conclusion of the prayer, i.e. the future resurrection, and also the sense that being awakened through God's kindness every morning is a kind of resurrection, since while asleep the person is without his breath of life (*nešāmāh*) and has a foretaste of death. One may sleep the sleep of death (Psalms 13:4) if God does not restore his soul to him. Since the purpose of the magical incantation we are examining was to disturb sleep, appeal was made to the power which controls sleep, i.e. to God, in his image as "the great judge of the souls of the dead" *dynʾ rbʾ dnyšmtʾ dmytyn* (line 15). In a reverse reflex, we see that the liturgical blessing appeals to God in the same dimension. In other words, the power sovereign over sleep, whether to disturb it, or awaken the slumberer, is the power sovereign over the soul and over life itself, because sleep is a kind of death or expiration.

Obermann was at a loss to know the identity of the antecedent of the 3rd pl. verb *lytybwn* "let *them* restore." In *ShR* we have what may have been the type of praxis associated with the recitation of an incantation such as this one:

"If you seek to cause your enemy to be disturbed in sleep, take the head of a black dog who has never seen light as long as he has lived; and take a slice of a water-pipe and write on it the names of these angels (i.e. those mentioned above in line 61, 'who keep sleep away from men') and recite as follows: 'I submit to you, angels of disturbance (*malʾakê rôgez*), who stand on the fourth rung, the life and soul and breath (*ʾet napšô weʾet nišmātô weʾet rûḥô*) of X. son of Y., that you may bind him with chains of iron and tie him to posts of bronze. Do not give his eyeballs sleep, or drowsing, or deep slumber. May he cry out and scream like a woman in childbirth. Allow no one to release him.' Write this, and place the slice of metal into the mouth of the dog, and place wax over its mouth, and seal it with a signet ring which bears a lion on it. Hide the dog's head behind his house, or in a place where he comes and goes."

There then follows the procedure for the release of the spell. We propose that demonic beings something like "the angels of disturbance" are the likely antecedent for the verb: *lytybwn* "let them (not) restore". This suggestion also relates to the apparitions which are supposed to trouble the sleep of the woman to be afflicted: *bhylmᵓ wbhyzwnh dmyyhw nqyᶜwn lh* "In her dreams and her apparitions may their forms awaken her" (Line 3). See my comments on the word *ḥzw* in *JAOS* 84, 1964, 19, note 4. Cf. Epstein, 35, to *AIT* 7:14, on the verb *dmy*, and *AIT* 1:12–13, *ArOr* 6, 1934, 49, G:8, *Orientalia* 10, 1941, 119, 2:3, 8: *hyzwnyn snyyn* "hateful apparitions." Also see *Orientalia* 20, 1951, 306, lines 3–4: *lylytᵓ byštᵓ dmtᶜyᵓ lybᵓ dbny ᵓynšᵓ wmythzyᵓ bhylmᵓ dlylyᵓ wmythzyᵓ bhyzwnᵓ dymmᵓ* "Evil Liliths who lead the hearts of men astray, and who appear in nocturnal dreams and daytime apparitions." Also cf. Mandaic usage in *AOS* 49, 24:9–10, *et passim*. The imagery of these incantations is strongly reminiscent of the descriptions of troubled sleep in the book of Daniel.

Thus it is that the black magic of the incantation and of *ShR*, on the one hand, and the grateful prayers of the morning ritual, on the other, represent contrasting reflexes of the same intrinsic conceptions.

Line 9: *dᵓhdr ᶜl* "Concerning this curse which X. *has caused to* encircle Y." Cf. *AIT* 4:6: *wšwrᵓ rbᵓ dnhšᵓ ᵓhdryt ᶜlyh* "I encircled him with a large wall of bronze." In that text, the purpose was to protect the person encircled. Also cf. *AIT* 34:4.

Lines 11–12: *wlᵓ tyhwy lh lX. bt Y. tqntᵓ lᶜlm wlᵓ pšrtᵓ lᶜlm* "And may there never be for X. daughter of Y. a remedy or solution." On Talmudic usages of *taqqantāᵓ* see Levy IV, 664, s.v., and s.v. Hebrew *taqqānāh*. On *pešartāᵓ* see Levy IV, 152, s.v. *pešar*, 2, as relevant to the unraveling of the meanings of dreams, etc., and cf. *AIT*, glossary, 299, s.v. *pišrāᵓ*, and Mandaic forms in *AOS* 49, glossary, s.v. *pšr*.

Line 14: *whyᵓ šlyṭnᵓ wbrynᵓ* "And the living one (= God), the ruler and creator." The sense of *ḥayyāᵓ* as an epithet of God is well known in Jewish mystical literature. On the epithet *ḥaî hāᶜôlāmîm* "the one who lives eternally" see Scholem, 110, no. 16, and *Major Trends in Jewish Mysticism*, New York, 1946, 58–59, and note 65. Also see *ShR* VI:39, and *AIT* 38:7: *brᵓzywn wpᵓqtwn dᵓlhᵓ hyᵓ* "By the mysteries and ordinance of the living God."

b) McCullough, D.

Lines 5–6: *wbšwmᵓ dmṭṭrwn hldh dhw mšᵓmyš qdym brgwdᵓ* "And in the name of Metatron *ḥldh*, who ministers in front of the curtain." Here, *brgwdᵓ* = *pargôdāᵓ* of Talmudic and mystical provenience (Levy IV, 98–99, s.v.) i.e. the curtain hanging at the entrance to God's heavenly abode. In Jewish mystical literature, one of Metatron's titles is: *šammāšāᵓ reḥîmāᵓ* "the beloved attendant"

(Scholem, 50, and note 23). He is also known as *sar happānîm* "prince of the countenance" (Scholem, 52) because of his station in the presence of God.

The word *hldh* is problematic. Since Metatron is also known by the title *sar šel ʿôlām* "prince of the world" (Scholem, 48), and in an Aramaic magical bowl inscription as *ʾisārāh rabbāʾ dekûlēh ʿālemāʾ* "the great prince of all the world" (see note to *AIT* 16:10), it may not be incorrect to suggest that *hldh* is biblical *ḥeled* "eternity," hence: "the world" (*HuAL* 303, s.v. *ḥld* I). The final *Heh* is problematic, because determination (if that's what it's supposed to represent), is expressed by ʾAleph in this text. The conclusion of the description of Metatron is difficult, and we are not convinced by McCullough's interpretation, though we have nothing definitive to suggest, either. The clause reads: *whw rhym ʿl mʾdʾ whw rhym ʿl bʾryʾ*. In *Orientalia* 20, 1951, 307, line 5 we read: *bhwmrtyh dmyṭṭrwn srʾ rbʾ dmytqry ʾsyh rbʾ drhmy* "By the talisman of Metatron, the great prince, who is called the great healer of mercy." Now *bʾryʾ* can mean: "the healthy ones," (Levy I, 264, s.v. *bārî*(ʾ), 1), and so we would expect that *mʾdʾ* would yield a meaning for disease, in contrast. The closest we can come is Hebrew *madwēh*, Aramaic-Syriac *madwāʾ* "weakness, sickness" (Levy, III, 28, s.v., and *LS* 143, s.v. *medawaî*, 2) one afflicted," from *dwy*).

Line 9: *ʾnʾtwn šbtyn* (McCullough: *šbtwn*, imperative, pl.) *wmbṭlyn* McCullough renders: "Cease, and frustrated go trembling," etc. Despite the absence of the *Yod*, it would be preferable to take *šbtyn* as a Peʿil form: *šebîtîn*, and render: "You are void and annulled." Cf. in *ArOr* 6, 1934, 328, D:10: *kwlhwn šbytyn wbṭlyn* "They are all void and annulled." Also cf. *Orientalia* 10, 1941, 341, 91751:9: *mṭpr* (= *mpṭr*) *yt nydry ʾdm wgzr dyn šl mʿlʾ hwʾ ybṭyl yt nydry ʾylyn* "He who cancels the vows of man, and the decree of heaven, may he annul all of these vows", and *ibid*. 123, 5:1.

This phraseology is known from an Aramaic post-Talmudic composition, the Kol Nidre, traditionally recited on the eve of Yom Kippur (See *Talmudic Encyclopedia* (Hebrew) II, 390, s.v. *hattārāt nedārîm*, 16). This liturgical text is formulated legally out of the intent either to annul vows made during the prior year or to seek forgiveness in anticipation for those probable in the year to come. The terms *ʾissar*, *ḥērem*, *šebûʿāh*, etc. occur in it. Most relevant is the following passage: *kolhôn yehôn šerîyîn*; *šebîqîn*, *šebîtîn*, *beṭēlîn ûmebaṭṭelîn* "All of them (i.e. the vows, etc.) are released; they are abandoned, inoperative, null and nullified." All of the terms used in this clause are attested in the Aramaic magical bowl inscriptions as part of a legalistic vocabulary transposed into a magical key. It is therefore preferable to retain the phrase *šebîtîn ûmebaṭṭelîn* (Paʿel, passive part. masc. pl.) in our text, in the very sense it has in the Kol Nidre, but in a magical context. Also cf. the force of *bṭl* in Mandaic incantations (*AOS* 49, 22:229–231, and glossary, 313, s.v. *bṭl*). This is also the sense of the Paʿel *tybṭlwn* (= *tibaṭṭelûn*) in line 10 of our text.

c) Scholem, Incantation

Scholem (84f.) presents a new interpretation of an Aramaic amulet incantation originally published by A. Dupont-Sommer (*Jahrbuch für Kleinasiatische Forschung* I, 1951, 201–215, Lamelle A), together with a second amulet text (B) of which only fragments of several lines remain. In the opening formula (line 1) Dupont-Sommer had read: *šwy wrḥmyn mn šmyh*, but he didn't understand the sense of *šwy* here, knowing only the sense of price and value. Scholem saw traces of a *Lamed* in the opening formula of amulet B published by Dupont-Sommer, and consequently separated the words differently, and read: *šyyl rḥmyn mn šmyh* "Begging mercy from heaven." It is probable, however, that *šwy wrḥmyn* should be retained. The *Waw* of *wrḥmyn* differs appreciably from the apparent *Lamed* at the beginning of B. Furthermore, the formula of B is different from that of A. There is also the fact that the Aramaic idiom for begging mercy is *beʿāh/ʾ raḥamîn* (Hebrew: *biqqēš raḥamîm*) and not with the verb *šʾl/šyyl* which means rather: "to inquire about-." Actually *šwy* constitutes the indetermined counterpart to *šwytʾ* in *AIT* 16:6, and see our note to that passage for the semantics involved. Thus: *šwy wrḥmyn mn šmyh* is to be rendered: "Accord and mercy/love from heaven." On the indetermined state of fem. nouns ending in *-î* see F. Rosenthal, *A Grammar of Biblical Aramaic*, Wiesbaden, 1963, 29, no. 57. Note that both *šwy* and *rḥmyn* are indetermined here. (Whereas I had made the identification of *šwy* with already attested *šwytʾ*, it was Prof. H. L. Ginsberg who pointed out to me relevant grammatical data, for which I am grateful).

The text continues to speak of Metatron at the side of God's throne, and contains a passage that is clear in its simple sense, yet rather puzzling in terms of its meaning within the magical context of the incantation. The passage portrays a scene in which three female demons are questioned concerning their needs for food, drink and sleep:

> *hmwn tlthyn ḥdh kpnh wlʾ ʾklh ḥdh ṣḥyh wlʾ štyh wḥdh nymh wlʾ dmkh ʾmrt lkpntʾ lmt kpnh wlʾ ʾklh lṣḥyḥh lmt ṣḥyh wlʾ štyh lnʾmt lmt nymh wlʾ dmkh ḥzy tlthyn wʾmr ndʾn* (lines 16–22).
>
> "The three of them—One is hungry but does not eat. One is thirsty but does not drink. One drowses but does not slumber. You say to the hungry one: 'Why do you hunger and yet don't eat?' To the thirsty one: 'Why do you thirst and yet don't drink?' To the one who drowses: 'Why do you just drowse and not slumber?' He views the three of them and says: 'Get out!'"

The graphics of this scene can be better perceived by citing a passage from another Aramaic incantation, apparently unnoticed by Scholem, who states that "no exact equivalent to the present formula is yet known." We refer to the text published by C. H. Gordon, *Orientalia* 10, 1941, 349 (Iraq Museum, no. 9731:8–10).

> *slyqyt lʾygrʾ blylyh wʾmryt lhwn ʾm kpnytwn ʾytw ʾyklw wʾm ṣhtwn ʾytw ʾyštw wʾm hrbytwn ʾytw ʾydhnw wʾm lʾ kpnytwn wlʾ ṣhtwn*

> *wlʾ hrbytwn hdrw wʾz ylw bʾwrhʾ dʾttwn bh wʿwlw lbytʾ dnpqtwn mynh wʿwlw bpwmʾ dnpqtwn mynh*
>
> "I ascended to the roof at night and said to them (i.e. the demons): 'If you are hungry, come, eat! And if you are thirsty come, drink! And if you are dried up, come, be oiled! But, if you aren't hungry, or thirsty, or dried up, go back by the way you came! Enter the house from which you departed, and the mouth from which you emitted!'"

Disregarding much that is intrinsic to this passage, such as the significance of the roof, etc. we immediately realize that providing hospitality for demons was a duty that could not be overlooked. Like many hosts, the exorcist is saying, in effect, that unless there is more coming to the demons in the way of official hospitality, they had better be on their way! Their presence is no longer desired. In other words: "Is there something else I can get you, demons?" (Cf. in Syriac, *Orientalia* 18, 1949, 338–339, line 3).

In Scholem's incantation, it is undoubtedly Metatron addressing the demons, who ascended to the side of God's throne (line 12f.). Metatron is addressed in line 8. In an Aramaic magical bowl he is called: *wmyṭṭrwn ʾysrʾ rbʾ dkwrsyh* "And Metatron, the great prince of His throne" (*ArOr* 6, 1934, 328, D:11).

The verbal form *ʾmrt* in line 19 could be taken as the *krasis* of the imperative + 2nd person pronoun (= *ʾēmar* + *att*) or more probably as the participle masc. sing. + the pronoun (= *ʾāmeret*/*ʾāmerat*). See J. N. Epstein, *Grammar*, 62, 64, respectively). We prefer the latter, and similarly have taken *ḥzy* in line 22 as a participle, masc. sing., and not an imperative. Thus *ḥzy* = *ḥāzê* and not *ḥazî* (Epstein, *Grammar*, 97, 96, respectively). Cf. the indicative in the parallel clauses of Gordon's text.

In interpreting this text, line 14 is crucial. We have already discussed the sense of the term *millāh*/*miltāʾ*, and related forms in our note to *AIT* 16:9, observing that its sense is not simply "word" but "spell, imprecation, curse," etc. Thus, *lrqyʿʾ mlyh slqh*, translated by Scholem as: "The *words* ascended to heaven," would better be rendered: "The *spells* ascended to heaven." The spells or curses ascended with the demons who bore them, or who authored them to start with. In sending the demons packing, Metatron is acting to nullify the spells which the demons brought. Most probably they were summoned on high to be subdued and commanded to return whence they had come.

II. Central Themes in the Magical Bowl Inscriptions

1. Magical Warriors

We have seen that magical agents, principally angels, are girded and armed for battle against the forces of evil, according to the mentality operative in the magical bowl inscriptions. This was expressed in McCullough A, where we noted the sense of the verb *ḥlṣ/z* "to gird" in this connection, calling attention as well to other ways of expressing the same notion.

In *AIT* 2:1–3 (cf. *Orientalia* 10, 1941, 273–274, text 11) we have a first person description of the engagement of the enemy by a sorcerer who portrays himself in imagery characteristic of propitious angels:

> *twb ᵓzlnᵓ ᵓnh X. br Y. bhyly dnpšy bqwmty qṣyṣᵓ dprzlᵓ qrqpty dprzlᵓ qwmt dnwrᵓ dkyᵓ wlbyšnᵓ lbwšᵓ dᵓrmsᵓ dkyᵓ wmmllᵓ whlynᵓ bmn dbrᵓ šmyᵓ wᵓrᶜh ᵓzlyt wpgᶜyt bhwn bsny byšy* etc.
>
> "Again I come, I, X. son of Y., with my own might. On my body are arms (or: hands) of iron, a head of iron, a body of pure fire. I don the pure-white and simmering robe of Hermes. My might is from Him who created heaven and earth. I have come to strike against the evil enemies," etc.

We have followed Epstein in reading this passage (30–31, and cf. his notes to *AIT* 27:5, 55). Montgomery misread this passage, reading *dbyᵓ* for *dkyᵓ* "pure, white," thus missing the point about the description of Hermes' robe. Cf. *Orientalia* 10, 1941, 125, 6:5: *mlᵓkyn bhyryn dkyn wqdyšyn* "Bright, pure, and holy angels." The word *wmmllᵓ* (= *ûmemallelāᵓ*) is also descriptive of the robe. It is said of the hissing of coals (Levy III, 134, s.v. *melel*, II). This obviates Montgomery's questionable speculations on the Logos (supposedly associated with the verb *mll* "to speak") and the connections between Hermes and the Logos (*AIT* 95f., 123–124). Also contrast Montgomery's interpretation of *AIT* 19:7 with that of Epstein, 49, *ad loc.* The description of the bellicose image of the sorcerer is continued in 2:4–5. (Cf. *AOS* 49, 22:178–181):

> *by qštᵓ gbynᵓ lkwn wby ytrᵓ psyṭnᵓ lkwn*
>
> "I bend the bow against you, and I stretch the bow-string against you."

Such descriptions of propitious magical agents have their roots in early antiquity, and Yamauchi's discussion, though somewhat superficial, has the benefit of stressing the Mesopotamian background of Babylonian magic in the early Christian centuries (*AOS* 49, 62f., and in the bibliography). For an understanding of the role of such imagery in Jewish magic, *ShR* is an enlightening source. The garments and the aspects of angels are subjects we cannot treat properly in this study, but some discussion of the bellicose image of these angels can be attempted here (See *ShR* I:46f.). The "pure-white and simmering robe of Hermes" is paralleled by similar garments described in *ShR*. Thus, *ShR* II:92: "their garments (Hebrew: *lebûš*, = Aramaic *lebûšāᵓ* in *AIT* 2:2) are garments of white, like light." Also, *ShR* II:14–15:

> "They stand dreadful, wrapped in wrath, girded with awesomeness, surrounded by trembling. Their covering (Hebrew: *kesût*) is like the pattern of fire (*ketabnît ᵓēš*), their countenance like the appearance of lightning.

> "And in it (i.e. the third firmament) are three archangels seated on their thrones. Both they and their clothing (*lebûš*) have the form of fire (*bidemût ʾēš*)... and, as for them, their valor is like fire" (*ShR* III:3–4).

As one ascends the seven firmaments, the environment becomes more purified. Thus, in the seventh and highest firmament we have the following description:

> "They (i.e. the "beasts" and "wheels" of the Merkabah) stand in front of Him, group by group, and immerse themselves in rivers of purity, and wrap themselves with a covering (*kesût*) of white fire" (VII:16–17).

In Jewish mystical literature, the garment of God (variously *lebûš* and *ḥālûq*) is similarly described (Scholem, 56–64). Ultimately, Jewish utilization of this motif derives from the book of Daniel, 7:9f.

Lightning is connected with fire in these descriptions. It is both a weapon and the epitome of the speed of the angels:

> "These are the ones whose station is on the fourth rung. They are girded (*ʾazûrîm*) with the whirlwind, and the sound of their marching is like the clash of bronze. They fly from the East, and turn from the West to the gate. They are as swift as lightning, and fire is around them" (II:59–61, and cf. III:1–2. Also cf. *ShR* VII:4, 36).

This description from *ShR* brings us back to the Aramaic magical bowls, to *AIT* 12:6–9, especially 7f.:

> *dqymyn wmṭhryn mn ywmy ʿlmʾ wnygryhwn lʾ mythzyn brqdyhwn lyh lʿlmʾ kwlyh wytbyn wqymyn bʾtrhwn nšpyn ky zyqʾ brqyn ky brqʾ ʾynwn ybṭlwn wyšmtwn kl gysy* etc.
>
> "They stand (Aramaic *qʾm* = Hebrew *ʿmd*, frequent in *ShR*) and purify themselves, from days of yore. Their feet are invisible to the entire world when they dance about. They are seated, and then stand up in their places. They blow like the storm; they flash like lightning. They are the ones who will nullify and place a ban over all spirits," etc.

Perhaps the best way of summarizing the bellicose image of the propitious angels is by reference to their deployment in the various firmaments, usually portrayed in military terminology:

> "In charge of them are seven *šôṭerîm* (the chief angels of each firmament), and they (i.e. the angels) surround them in camps upon camps (Hebrew: *maḥanôt*), from both sides" (I:2–3).
>
> "For in it are angels without number, arrayed in armies (*ʿasûyîm ṣebāʾôt ṣebāʾôt*)" (II:3).
>
> "And they are stationed by units (*ḥayyālôt ḥayyālôt*)" (V:2).
>
> "And armies and camps (*ûṣebāʾôt ûmaḥanôt*) stand in dread... Army regiments march in its midst (i.e. in the midst of the sixth fir-

mament) ... and preceding the units of the spirits (*ḥayyalê hārûḥôt*) are myriads of angels, fashioned from the tongue of flame; burning like fire, their body like embers of fire! They are stationed on embers of fire," etc. (VI:2f.).

The role of the bellicose angels is epitomized in the following invocation:

> "That you may come and stand near me to help me in this time, wherever I may go, and may you be seen alongside me, a great army (*ḥayil gādôl*) in all of your valor, and with the might of your lances. May those who behold me, from near and far, and all who come to do battle against me and to seize me, be shattered before me by the great fear of your dreadfulness; and may they be unable to do me harm," etc. (VI:41–45).

Particularly reminiscent of the magical bowls is the following description of warrior angels in *ShR* (II:130–133):

> "These are the ones whose station is on the ninth rung. They are armed with might (Hebrew: *zerîzîm beḥayil*). They fly through the air. Their valor is strength, and the form of swords is in their hand. They are prepared for battle(s), grasping the bow, holding the javelin. They dance about like tongues of flame (*meqappeṣîm mēʾēš*). They have horses of fire, and the harness of their chariots is fire. They terrify wherever they turn!
>
> "These are the ones whose station is on the fifth rung. They bear shield and lance. A bronze helmet is on their head, and scaled armor is their garb" (II:75–76).

These descriptions undoubtedly have their origin in myth and epic, but they have found their way into magical incantations as a result of the particular role assigned to certain of the gods in magical praxis. The clearest example is the weaving of the Ea-Marduk mythology into the Neo-Assyrian magical texts (B. Levine, *Eretz-Israel* 9, 1969, 92, and note 33, and *AOS* 49, 62f.). Since gods were entreated for assistance in combating demons, their images of valor and might carried over into the magical literature. In a monotheistic setting, gods become angels, and the pantheon is converted into a court ruled over by God and replete with angel-gods who do his bidding. This often necessitates the use of weapons, cosmic and metallic. The magical bowls reflect a mentality wherein some gods continued to be operative, (at least by reference to their characteristics), but with the main tasks assigned to angels.

Before leaving the subject of magical warriors, a word is in order about the utilization of magical figurines, portrayed as warriors and so fashioned. Reference to such magical tools is extremely rare in the Aramaic bowls. One possible reference to a sculptured figurine occurs in *AIT* 12:5–6, which we take to be the description of an amulet rather than an actual figurine.

The use of figurines did, however, have its place in Jewish magic and again *ShR* may fill in what is not told of the praxis in the bowl inscriptions:

> "If you seek to expel from the city any sort of wild beast, whether lion, bear, or tiger; or to restrain a river or body of water that is rising and threatening to flood the houses of the city, fashion a figurine of bronze in the form of one of them (i.e. a lion, etc.). Prepare a thin sheet (Hebrew: *ṭas*) of iron and inscribe on it, inside and out, the names of the angels (i.e. those previously enumerated), and gird it onto (*haḥgēr*) the figurine. Bury the figurine at the entrance to the city, and let it be facing North.
>
> "If it is a river or body of water upon which you seek to cast a spell, so that it will not inundate the city, fashion a figurine of stone and inscribe on it the names of these same angels, on two thin sheets of bronze, and place the thin sheets under the heels of the figurine. Fashion a rod of marble and place it on its shoulder. Let its right hand hold the rod, and its left hand be open. Let the figurine be facing toward the water" (II:110–117).

Here, again, the Mesopotamian prototype glares through the later usage, and we have further documentation of the warlike image of the propitious magical agent (See B. Levine, *op. cit.*, 94f.).

2. The Signet-ring (ʿizqetāʾ) and its Uses

In the Aramaic magical bowls the signet ring is often employed in affixing a seal to a writ of divorce being issued against Lilith and her cohorts (*AIT* 8:11, 11:8–9, // Ellis I and in Mandaic, Lidzbarski V, = *AOS* 49, text 21, 17:12, 18:11, and in Syriac 34:8.) Also cf. *AIT* 9:11, and *ArOr* 6, 1934, 469–470, G:9 where *ḥtmʾ* is used in this function instead of *ʿizqetāʾ*. In McCullough A the writ of divorce is not included, but the objective was the expulsion of demons from a household.

In a few instances we have a more basically magical utilization of the signet ring, i.e. the placing of a magical seal on demons, or on the chains that bind them, to prevent their escape. In *AIT* 15:7 this notion is expressed, although probably merely as imagery:

> *ʾsryt ytkwn bʾyswry nhšʾ wprzlʾ wḥtmyt ytkwn bṣwrt ʿyzqtʾ dnwrʾ*
> "I have bound you (i.e. the demons) with bonds of bronze and iron, and sealed you with the form of a signet ring of fire."

This application is more clearly expressed in a Mandaic text (*AOS* 49, 24:10–11) where the actual seal of the signet ring is affixed to the demons themselves. A signet ring may be also be used to affix a seal to a house, its threshold, etc. that are to be protected. Thus, in the Syriac of *AIT* 21(//22, 23):

> *dyḥtym bytlth ʿzqyn wmḥtm bšbʿh ḥtmyn*
> "Which (i.e. the house, etc.) is stamped with three signet rings and sealed with seven seals." (Cf. *Orientalia* 10, 1941, 120, 3:3).

Similar passages occur in other texts, where, at times, prodigious numbers of differing seals are used. Cf. *ArOr* 6, 1934, 321, A:1–2; 324, B:4–5; 331–332, texts E, F, and Hyvernat; *Orientalia* 10, 1941, 279, 1932.619:14, 1932.620:13–14.

The signet rings are variously described. Thus, we have those inscribed: *ʾēl šaddaî* (McCullough A:4, *AIT* 8:11, 17:12, *ArOr* 6, 1934, 324, B:4). There are also those inscribed with the "specific" name of God, *šēm* (*ham*) *mepôrāš* (*AIT* 11:8–9//Ellis I, and Lidzbarski 5 = *AOS* 49, 21:20; *AIT* 18:11, and 34:8, a Syriac text. *AIT* 11 and its parallels require some clarification, because they have often been misunderstood.

The Aramaic in *AIT* 11:8–9 reads:

> *bʿyzqth dṣyr wglyp ʿlh šm mpwrš mn ywmy ʿlmʾ ymy ššt ymy brʾšyt*
> "With the signet ring upon which is drawn and imprinted the 'specific' name from the days of yore, from the days of the six days of creation."

The Aramaic parallel, Ellis I, has:

> *wbʿyzqtʾ dšlymwn dʿlwhy šm mprš rbh-*
> "And with the signet ring of Solomon upon which is the great 'specific' name-."

The Mandaic parallel, Lidzbarski 5 (= *AOS* 49, 21) has an amplified, and somewhat corrupt rendering (21:20–21):

> *bʿyzqtʾ d̲šlymwn mlkʾ br dʾwyd d̲ṣyr glyp ʾlhʾ*(!, corruption of Aramaic *ʿlh* "upon it") *šwmʾ rbʾ wyqyrʾ glyp ʾlhʾ* (again, a corruption of *ʿlh*) *šymʾ mpršʾ mršʿšʾyt šyt ywmʾ bryšyt*
>
> "With the signet ring of Solomon, the king, son of David, upon which is drawn and imprinted the great and honored name; imprinted on it is the 'specific' name from the beginning, from the six days of creation."

A similar corruption of the formula occurs in line 17 of the text:

> *bʿzqtʾ d̲ṣyr glyp ʾlʾhʾ* (corruption of *ʿlwhy*) *bšwmyk ʾmʾtʿmʾ*
> "With the signet ring which is drawn and imprinted with your name, oh X."

Yamauchi lists *ṣyr glyp* in his glossary of "Angels, Gods, and Demons." (*AOS* 49, 367), thinking that it was a proper name of some sort. There is no evidence of such a divine being! What happened was that the scribe misunderstood his Aramaic models, confusing *ʿlh* with *ʾlhʾ* because they are homophonic, though not homographic, and because in Mandaic ʿAyin often shifts to ʾAleph. On Aramaic *ṣyr* "to draw" see Levy IV, 180, s.v. *ṣwr*, 2, and *ibid.* 187, s.v. *ṣyr*. Despite the almost parallel idiom *ṣyr whtm* "tied and sealed" (see note to McCullough A:4), we prefer to take *ṣyr* in this clause to mean "draw" rather than "tie", because reference is not to the affixing of the seal, which may involve tying, but rather to what is imprinted on the signet ring itself, and tying seems not to belong in this context. On Aramaic *glp* see Levy I, 337, s.v. *glp*, and note usage of this verb pertaining to the imprinting of God's name on the diadem of the High Priest. Also see the review of *AOS* 49 by M. Smith, *AJA* 73, 1969, 95f. who notes the same misunderstanding of *ṣyr glyp* on Yamauchi's part.

The signet ring of Solomon, mentioned above, is referred to frequently in these texts. Cf. *AOS* 49, 24:10, *ArOr* 6, 1934, 331–332, *Orientalia* 10, 1941, 279, 1932.619:14, 1932.620:13–14. Also cf. *Orientalia* 10, 1941, 274, 11:17–18, and especially *ArOr* 6, 1934, A:1–2:

> *hdʾ hyʾ ʿyzqtʾ dšlmh br dwyd dʾnyš* (= *dʾynš*) *lʾ mṣy mzylh lʾtm* (= *lhtm*) *wʾynš qdmh lʾ qʾym*
>
> This is the signet ring of Solomon, son of David, to which no one can go, and before which no one can stand.
>
> *bʿzqtʾ dʾlšdy bryk hwʾ wbʿzqtʾ dšlmwh mlkʾ br dwyd dʿbyd ʿwbwdtʾ bšydy dykry wblylytʾ nwqbtʾ*
>
> With the signet ring of El-Saddai, blessed be he, and with the signet ring of Solomon, the king, son of David, who performed acts of magic against male devils and female Liliths.

In addition to Solomon of old, signet rings are mentioned as being in the possession of other personages, such as Rabbi Joshua son of Perahiah (*AIT* 8:11, 17:12), and a certain *byt hnwm* (See *AIT* 19:17, and 47f.). In McCullough A:4 we have reference to a signet ring in the possession of the master of the household, undoubtedly supplied him by the magical practitioner. Texts E, F, and Hyvernat in *ArOr* 6, 1934, 331–332 speak of many signet rings, among them those of Michael, Gabriel, Kasdiel, etc. Two other names mentioned are: Yokabar-Ziwa, son of Rabbê, and Aspanadas-Dêwa, the jinnee of king Solomon. We cannot be certain of the identity of the personages and spirits involved.

The signet ring of Rabbi Joshua son of Perahiah, in particular, was employed in affixing the seal to writs of divorce; and this derived from Joshua's reputation, in his time, as a wonder-worker and a sage. In the latter role, he issued bans, and held court to banish demons, and consequently it was his signet ring that became proverbial in this regard.

Both the Asmadeus legend of the Talmud and *ShR* have much to tell us about the utilization of signet rings in magical praxis. The use of such rings to seal documents requires no explanation. It is their use to hold down demons that invites inquiry here.

The Asmadeus legend, in its Talmudic version, relates how Solomon sought to obtain secret information known only to Asmadeus, king of the demons, concerning the whereabouts of *šāmîr waššayit*, miraculous worms that could cut through stone. Solomon dispatched one of his trusted officers, Benayahu, to wrest this valuable information from Asmadeus. By means of a ruse, Benayahu succeeded in putting Asamdeus to sleep, and while the archdemon lay unconscious, he bound him with chains upon which was engraved "the name", and with the signet ring of Solomon bearing the same engravure on it.

Along with the chains and the signet ring, Benayahu also employs shearings of wool and flasks of wine. When Asmadeus awakens, Benayahu casts a spell on him, by saying: "The name of your master is upon you," which he repeats. This renders it impossible for Asmadeus to break the chains, ordinarily no difficult task for one so mighty!

In the continuation of the account, Asmadeus tricked Solomon into handing him the signet ring, which he instantly swallowed, thus preventing its further use against him.

Our primary interest in this legend is the function of the signet ring. In the Talmudic story it was employed to subdue a demon so as to coerce him to divulge magical information. One who possesses the ring can incarcerate and coerce magical agents. Of particular value is an understanding of the practice of inserting such rings into one's mouth. Whereas it is clear that Asmadeus wanted to prevent further use of the ring and therefore swallowed it as a way of rendering it inaccessible to anyone else, it is also clear that this particular method of holding on to the ring had still another meaning. In fact, it was a means of releasing spells. This becomes quite clear from several passages in *ShR*.

Thus, one who seeks to return home safely from war, or to avoid conscription initially, fashions a ring of iron, and a flower of pure gold upon which are written the names of the appropriate angels. On the third of the month he inserts the flower into the ring and then engraves on the outside of the ring, at the place where the flower rests, the images of a man and a lion. The text then continues:

> "And when you seek to depart from the place whence you were to leave for the war, and you observe that men are coming after you to seize you, take the ring and place it in your month, and lift your eyes to heaven, etc.... and pronounce the names of the guardian angels" (*ShR* VI:29–34f.).

The person then entreats the angels, after which he is supposed to observe smoke and thick darkness in front of him. At this point he removes the ring from his mouth, and replaces it on his finger. Subsequently, when he arrives at his home safely and can reasonably assume that the angels whom he had pressed into his service are no longer needed, he releases them by again placing the ring into his mouth and pronouncing the following formula of release:

> "I have released you. Go on your way." (*ShR* VI:51).

He may then replace the ring on his finger.

Asmadeus had done precisely what one is instructed to do according to the "Book of Mysteries." Placing a ring in one's mouth was a way of releasing a spell, perhaps because it could be swallowed and kept from anyone else. It was not so disposed of, however, when further use was anticipated. Asmadeus releases Solomon's spell by swallowing the ring, and the follower of the Book of Mysteries similarly releases the spell he had cast over propitious angels by the same method he uses to prevent his enemies from seizing him. In other words, the spell is released much in the same way that it is cast. (Also cf. *ShR* V:19–42).

3. The Reversing and Releasing of Spells

The reversing of spells, usually connoted by a form of the verb *hpk*, Aramaic *h/ʾpk*, Mandaic *ʿpk*, is integrally related to the releasing of spells. As we will attempt to show, reversal was often a prerequisite step toward final release. The Mandaic bowls provide the best starting point for a discussion of these two related dimensions of theurgic praxis.

In his review of Yamauchi's monograph (*AOS* 49) Prof. Morton Smith corrects Yamauchi's rendering of the verb *ʿpk* from "repulse" to: "turn backwards" (M. Smith, *op. cit.*). In the same vein, Smith further discusses Yamauchi's interpretation of a formulary relevant to the disposition of spells. With variations, it reads as follows:

> *ʾmrynyn gbrʾ tqypʾ d̲šryʾ lwṭtʾ d̲lṭnyn bšwm ʾyhwn d̲hlyn mlʾky* etc.

Yamauchi renders:

> "We say: 'O mighty being who dissolves the curses which we have cursed in the name of these angels,'" etc. (*AOS* 49, 5:14–15, 17–18, cf. *ibid.* 6:14f.).

The crucial word is *šryʾ*. Yamauchi takes it as an active part. masc. sing. (= *šārēʾ*), the antecedent being the mighty one who is addressed. Smith took this word as a passive part. fem. pl. (*šāreyāʾ*) with *lwṭtʾ* "curses" as the antecedent. The passage would then be rendered:

> "We say: 'O mighty one! Released are the curses which we have pronounced,'" etc.

The preceding lines set the scene for the dialogue. A powerful sorcerer has brought tribulation on those who had cast the spells and curses. It is clear that *gabrāʾ teqîpāʾ* designates the sorcerer (and not some divine being), by analogy to *meʿabedāʾ teqîpā*, "powerful practitioner of magic" which is so frequent in these bowls.

The situation in this text is duplicated in a number of others (See *AOS* 49, 361, in the glossary, s.v. *šrʾ*). On the heels of the tribulations, the authors of the curses inquire of the sorcerer what has caused their misfortune. He replies that if they recant and retract their curses, all will be well:

> "Release that which you have cursed, and remove that you have which spat" (lines 13–14).

The authors then make a legal statement (the formulary we are discussing presently), addressing the sorcerer. Smith contends that since the sorcerer clearly commands the authors to retract, their reply to him should convey their acquiescence, i.e. that they had retracted their curses. To render the word *šryʾ* as referring to the action of the sorcerer would contradict the terms of the encounter, making it seem as though he, and not the authors of the curses, could dissolve them. Logically, Smith is correct. There are, however, counter indications.

In *Orientalia* 10, 1941, 117, 1:2–3 we have a formulary which definitely assigns the dissolution of spells to an angel in much the same terms as were employed in the Mandaic text, with equivalent Aramaic usage:

> *bšwm hpkyʾl mlʾkwʾ dhpyk lwṭtʾ wʾšlmtʾ* etc.... *dʿbdw lyh* etc.
> "In the name of Hapkiel (= the divine reverser), the angel who reverses curses and deliverance spells, etc. that are performed against him," etc.

And further, in line 4:

> *ʾtwn ˣbrw dynʾ wlwṭtʾ wšyqwptʾ myn X. br Y.* etc.
> "You, remove the evil sentence, and the curse, and rapping spirit from X. son of Y." etc.

It is therefore preferable to allow for a degree of inconsistency in the Mandaic texts. On the one hand, the authors of spells must release them, and the sorcerer uses his powers to get them to do so. On the other hand, the sorcerer, or in other instances the angel, is one whose potent magic has given him the reputation of being able to bring about the desired result, and he is subsequently called the one who reverses or releases spells. He is so called in terms of the results he produces, though technically the authors are the ones who retract their spells under his pressure. Perhaps this is one of the reasons why spells must be "brought back" to their authors, or reversed. It is so that their authors may retract them, thus liberating those who suffer from them. It is thus that we have the dialogue between the sorcerer working on behalf of the afflicted and the authors of the spell.

In *ArOr* 6, 1934, 326, C:7–8 we have the following description of the process of reversal:

> *wytʿqrwn kl hršyn byšyn mn hdyn X. br Y.* (= his mother),... *wythpkwn lʾhwryhwn wyhdrwn wyʾzlwn ʿl ʿbdyhwn wʿl mšrdrnyhwn* etc.
> "May all the evil magical acts be removed from one, X. son of Y.... May they be turned backwards, and return, and go *to* those who performed them and *to* those who sent them forth," etc. (Cf. *Orientalia* 10, 1941, 123, 5:5, *ibid.* 125, 6:8 and E. Yamauchi, *JAOS*, 85, 1965, 515, line 17).

The preposition *ʿal* is here the crucial factor. Does it mean: "against" (so Smith, *op. cit.*), or is it directional? In other words: What is here the force of the reversal of spells? Is it to bring down upon the authors of spells that which they sought to bring upon their targets? Perhaps! A good case can be made, however, for concluding that the spells are returned to their authors primarily so that they would renounce them. The authors are punished not by the boomeranging curses, but by the actions of the propitious magician who uses his skills to bring about the renunciation of the spell by its author. Cf. *AASOR* xiv, 1934, 141, line 1.

The magical texts contain frequent references to the reversal of spells. See *AIT* 23, *AOS* 49, 348, s.v. *pk*, and *Orientalia* 10, 1941, 117, 1:1; 339, no. 19745:1f.; 348, no. 9726:1–3; 350, no. 9736:8–10.

These observations apply as well to the evidence of *ShR*, for there we have several good illustrations of how spells were released by those who had cast them initially. The orientation is different, in some cases, from what we have observed in the magical bowls. Most often, in *ShR*, we are dealing with one who had pressed a propitious magical agent into service on his behalf, and then released him when his work was completed. The dynamics are the same as those projected in many of the magical bowls, even if there we are viewing the situation from the position of the one afflicted, and not from the corner of the afflicter, as in *ShR*.

We have already discussed the use of the signet ring in releasing spells. Now we turn to a more precise analysis of what happened, magically speaking, when a spell was released. In *ShR* I:176–186 we are instructed on how to communicate with the departed. One stations himself opposite a grave, pronounces the names of the appropriate angels, while carrying with him a mixture of oil and honey in a new glass jar. He then offers these materials to the spirit of Hermes with the entreaty that he bring a certain person to him from the dead, so that he might speak with him in mutual freedom from fear:

> "Let him speak with me without fear and tell me the truth without fear, and may I not fear him. And let him tell me my request, that which I require of him...
>
> "When the dead person comes out, place the glass jar before him and speak your piece. Hold a staff of myrtle in your hand. If subsequently you seek to release him (i.e. the dead person who was summoned), strike him three times with the myrtle staff, pour out the oil and honey, break the jar, and cast the myrtle from your hand. Return to your home by a different route."

In our notes to Obermann II we discussed *ShR* II:59f., the magical objective of disturbing someone's sleep. The release involves undoing, essentially, what had been done to cast the spell. The "angels of disturbance" are released by exhuming the dog's head which had been buried, removing the wax seal from its mouth, removing the message that had been placed in it, and casting it into the fire (*ShR* 62–72).

At times, releasing a spell necessitates the recitation of a release formula in addition to the performance of magical acts like those just described. Thus, a person desiring to divine what someone else is planning or dreaming up concerning him invokes the particular guardian angel in charge of such matters, to the accompaniment of magical acts. He then foreswears the angel in mythological terms to reveal to him what is in the heart of the other person. This procedure is repeated on three successive nights. If all goes well, one will behold "a column of fire and cloud, upon which there is the form of a man." At that point, the angel will divulge to him what he seeks to know.

Subsequently, when one seeks to release the guardian angel he throws water heavenward. (He was standing all the while near a body of water.) He then mutters:

> "Oh lord Boʾel (cf. line 209), the invisible! He is a refuge for us, the perfect shield-bearer. I have released! I have released! Sink down and return to your way!"

This is to be repeated seven times, after which success is assured (*ShR* I:234–235). On the invocation itself see *ShR*, p. 80 *ad loc*. Another release formula occurs in IV:71–72.

There are instances where releasing a spell involves changing the orders originally issued to the propitious angels and the detailed repetition of procedures employed in casting the spell (III:16–31). In III:47–56 release was effected primarily by the repetition of the original adjuration, with the addition of a release formula. The same is the case in IV:25–40, release: 40–42.

In *ShR* the verb *hattēr*, used as an antonym of *ʾsr*, is parallel to Talmudic *šry* (Levy IV, 610–611, s.v. *šry* II), also employed in the magical bowl inscriptions. Thus, in *AIT* 19:4–5 we have the phrase: *bšybʿʾ ʾysryn dylʾ myšltryn wbtmnyh htmyn dylʾ mytbryn* "With seven bonds that cannot be released, and with eight seals that cannot be broken." Further, in line 14, we have: *dʾynš myn ʾyswryh lʾ npyq wmn thwt ydwhy lʾ šwr* (with Epstein) "That no man from its bond may depart, or from under its hands be freed." Also see *ArOr* 6, 1934, 332, text E (and parallels): 5, 8:

> *wbhtmʾ rbʾ dmry ʿlmʾ dlʾ qytryh myštry wlʾ htmyh mytbr*
> "And with the great seal of the master of the universe, whose "knot" cannot be loosed, nor his seal broken."

In a similar vein, Obermann II:11–12 reads:

> "And may there never be for X, daughter of Y. a remedy or solution."

(See our note to Obermann II:11–12).

4. *The Mythological Substratum in Magical Incantations*

We have already noted, in several connections, that mythological motifs are woven into magical praxis. This is primarily a result of the fact that the divine beings who are the protagonists of myth are often the very same powers to whom humans turn when they are in need of help in fighting evil forces (See our comment "Magical Warriors", and our note to *AIT* 16:6).

Mythological motifs enter into theurgy in yet another way. The binding power of the spell may be epitomized by identifying it with the creation of the world, the bringing of order out of chaos, and the continuing maintenance of an orderly universe. Momentous feats of divine power on earth may also serve the same purpose. For the practitioner of theurgy, these motifs had a primarily magical character, and, indeed, there is an inherently magical dimension to myth. As for Jewish magic, the biblical account of creation, and the Genesis record of primeval history strongly suggested magical interpretations, stressing as they do the power of God's spoken word in the creational sequence. Whereas normative Jewish tradition tended to interpret the acts of creation and the features of divine rule as expressions of God's will more than as magical cause and effect, as the casting of spells and the like, the interpretations of the theurgist were not in direct opposition to the "mythological" traditions of the Bible. These interpretations are an understandable variation on the theme of divine power utilized to bind the forces of nature, as well as to effect proper control over the destiny of man, and over his works.

Scholem (82–83) presents a text from an as yet unpublished manuscript of the Lesser Hekhaloth (MS Oxford 1531, fol. 42b) which describes the binding force of a spell (*ʾysrʾ wḥytmʾ*) in cosmic and natural terms. Almost every one of the attributes there ascribed to the spell can be documented from similar characteristics associated with spells in the Babylonian magical bowl inscriptions.

AIT 34 is a Syriac incantation whose composition and content are most unusual within the corpus of these texts. Epstein (49–53) affords a clear reading and interpretation of the text, leaving very few difficulties in the wake of his ingenious notes and corrections. We shall not present a transcription of the entire text, but only a schematic representation of it, eliminating certain detailed listings of demons, etc. unnecessary for our purposes here.

The composition of the text reflects a definite format, as will be seen. There are four successive passages, each beginning with the formula: *ʾāsîr weḥātîm* "bound and sealed." This sequence is followed in turn by two passages, the former beginning with the formula: *weḥatîmāʾ beḥitmāʾ d-* "And we seal with the seal of-", and the latter with the formula: *ʾit(ʾ)asar beʾissûr* "bound with the bond."

ʾsyr wḥtym ʾyk dʾmr mwšʾ lymʾ dswp wqmw ʾyk šwrʾ dmn trwyhwn gysn, ʾsyr wḥtym
ʾsyr wḥtym bhdʾ mltʾ dʾškbh (= *dʾkbšh*) *ʾlhʾ lʾrʿh wlʾylnʾ* etc.
ʾsyr wḥtym bʾswr ṭwrʾ drmʾtʾ
ʾsyr wḥtym bgw šmyʾ wʾrʿʾ šmšʾ wshrʾ kwkbʾ wmzlʾ wbmltʾ ʾsyryn wbpqdnʾ qymyn bšwm etc.
ʾsyrʾ wḥtymʾ kwlh byšwtʾ dʾyt (dittog. *dʾyt*) *bpgrh dX.* etc. *bḥtmh d X.* etc. *wbʿzqth dšlymwn br dwyd dbh ḥtymym* (list of various demons).
wḥtymnʾ bḥtmʾ dʾylšdy wʾbrkss mryʾ tqypʾ wḥtmʾ rbʾ dḥtymyn bh šmyʾ wʾrʿʾ wkl šydʾ etc.
ʾtsr bʾswr nwrʾ wbšyšln myʾ ʿdmʾ lmyšrʾ šmyʾ wʾrʿʾ ʾmyn ʾmyn (lines 3–11, with deletions)

Translation:

Bound and sealed; just as Moses spoke to the Red Sea and (the waters) rose like a wall on both sides. (So is it) bound and sealed.
Bound and sealed; with that spell by which God subdued the earth and the trees etc.
Bound and sealed; with the bond of the high mountains.

Bound and sealed; like heaven and earth, sun, moon, stars and constellations. For they are bound by the spell, and stationed by the ordinance. In the name of etc.

Bound and sealed is all of the demonic evil that exists in the body of X. etc.—by the seal of X. etc. and by the signet ring of Solomon, son of David, by which are sealed (list of various demons).

For we seal with the seal of El-Shaddai and Abracsas, the powerful lord, and with the great seal by which are sealed heaven and earth, and all the demons etc.

Bound by the bond of fire and by the ferrets of water until such time as heaven and earth will be released! Amen. Amen.

Scholem's text begins with the formula:

dyn hwʾ ʾysrʾ wḥytmʾ dʾsyryn byh ʾrʿʾ wʾsryn byh šmyʾ
"This is the 'bond' and the seal by which the earth is bound and by which the heavens are bound."

This is more poetic than what we have in *AIT* 34, but the terms are much the same.

Scholem's text continues on the cosmic theme:

wʾrʿʾ nyydʾ mnyh/wtbl mtrʿšʾ mqdmwhy
"And the earth moves away from before it, and the universe is upset at its approach."

Cf. *AIT* 7:12:

dmn qdmwhy zʿ ymʾ wmn btrwhy zyʿyn ṭwryn
"At whose approach the sea moves, and in whose aftermath the mountains quake."

(We have not come across the word *tebel* in any of the Babylonian magical bowl inscriptions, to designate the natural world.)

The remainder of the text reads:

ptḥ pwm ymʾ wstm my rqyʿʾ
ptḥ šmyʾ wmrwwy ltbl ʿqr ʾrʿʾ wmʿrb ltbl

"It opens up the mouth of the sea, and closes up the waters of the firmament. It opens the heavens and waters the earth. It heaves the earth and confounds the universe."

Cf. *AIT* 9:6:

dybhwn ʾytknʿw šmyʾ wʾrʿh ṭwryʾ ʾytʿqrw wrmtʾ bhwm ʾytmsrʾh
"By means of which heaven and earth were humiliated, the mountains heaved about, and by means of which the heights were brought low." (See Epstein 38–39).

The mystical text would appear to be referring to the primeval flood; the beginning and the end of it, to be more precise. It could also be referring to the contrast of divine beneficence in providing water for the earth and divine punishment in withholding rain, as an ongoing feature of the natural world.

The mystical compilation is patterned after magical incantations, with the introduction of religious themes absent in the magical texts. The theme which here expresses itself is divine beneficence. Whereas magical texts refer to the mythological dimension in terms of potency over evil forces, of victory over that which is inimical, the mystical literature carries the logic of divine power several steps further, and speaks of God's blessings in more religious terms.

Other expressions of similar mythological motifs are to be found in *AIT* 2:3, (//*Orientalia* 10, 1941, 273, text 11), 4:3 (with Epstein's corrections), 6:4–5, 7:12, 9:6//32:6–7, 33:7–8; 10:3–5, 19:15, *AASOR* xiv, 1934, 141, line 8, *Orientalia* 10, 1941, 125, 6:3–4, 343, and 347, h:23–28; *ibid.* 18, 1949, 339, 1–7f., *ibid.* 20, 1951, 307, line 8. These allusions really warrant a more comprehensive treatment than we are giving them here. Similarly, *AIT* 14 contains important parallels to the other text from Lesser Hekhaloth presented by Scholem (82).

*Bibliographical Abbreviations**

AASOR	*Annual of the American Schools of Oriental Research*
AfO	*Archiv für Orientforschung*
AIT	J. A. Montgomery, *Aramaic Incantation Texts from Nippur*, Philadelphia, 1913.
AJA	*American Journal of Archaeology*
AJSL	*American Journal of Semitic Languages and Literatures*
AOS 49	E. M. Yamauchi, *Mandaic Incantation Texts, American Oriental Series*, vol. 49, New Haven, 1967.
ArOr	*Archiv Orientální*
Epstein	J. N. Epstein, "Gloses Babylo-Araméenes," *REJ* 73, 1921, 27–58; 74, 1922, 40–72.
Epstein, *Grammar*	J. N. Epstein, *A Grammar of Babylonian Aramaic* (Hebrew), Jerusalem, 1960.
hal.	*halākāh*, a section of a chapter in the Palestinian Talmud
HuAL	W. Baumgartner, *Hebräisches und Aramäisches Lexikon*, Leiden, 1967.
Legends	Louis Ginzberg, *Legends of the Jews*, VII vols. Philadelphia, 1954.
Levy	J. Levy, *Wörterbuch über die Talmudim und Midraschim*, 4 vols., Darmstadt, 1963.
Levy, *TW*	J. Levy, *Targumisches Wörterbuch*
McCullough	W. S. McCullough, *Jewish and Mandaean Incantation Texts in the Royal Ontario Museum*, Toronto, 1967 (Texts are designated A–E).
par.	*pārāšāh*, a section in the Midrash.
REJ	*Revue des Études Juives*
Rossell	W. H. Rossell, *A Handbook of Aramaic Magical Texts, Shelton Semitic Series* II, Ringwood Borough, NJ, 1953.

Scholem	G. Scholem, *Jewish Gnosticism, Merkabah Mysticism and Talmudic Tradition*, New York, 1960
ShR	M. Margalioth, *Sepher Ha-Razim, A Newly Recovered Book of Magic from the Talmudic Period*, (Hebrew), Jerusalem, 1966.
TB	*Talmud, Babylonian*, standard editions, Wilno
TP	*Talmud, Palestinian*, standard editions, Krotoschin

* Note: The following publications by C. H. Gordon will be referred to only by source, without the name of the author:

"An Aramaic Incantation" *AASOR* xiv, 1933–34, 141–144.

"Aramaic Magical Bowls in the Istanbul and Baghdad Museums," *ArOr* 6, 1934, 319–334.

"An Aramaic Exorcism," *ArOr* 6, 1934, 466–474.

"Aramaic and Mandaic Magical Bowls," *ArOr* 9, 1937, 84–106.

"The Aramaic Incantation in Cuneiform," *AfO* 12, 1937–1939, 105–117.

"Aramaic Incantation Bowls," *Orientalia* 10, 1941, 116–141, 272–284, 339–360.

"An Incantation in Estrangelo Script," *Orientalia* 18, 1949, 336–341.

"Two Magic Bowls in Teheran." *Orientalia* 20, 1951, 306–315.

Aramaic Texts from Persepolis*

Dedicated to the memory of
my departed father, Dôb-Baer Hallēwî;
the first to teach me Torah.

Bowman considers the Aramaic texts from Persepolis as ritual records, describing aspects of the haoma ceremony, and recording the names of the celebrants. We conclude that they are administrative notations, recording the names of the donors of the objects on which the texts are inscribed. The arguments on the meaning of the key verb *ʿbd*, presented by Bowman, are criticized, and new material is also brought to bear on the terms *srk* and *ʾškr*.

We now have Raymond Bowman's long awaited edition of the Aramaic texts from Persepolis, unearthed during the expedition by the University of Chicago under Erich F. Schmidt between 1936 and 1938.[1] Bowman has assembled important data on the chronology of Persepolis during the first half of the fifth century B.C.E., from the personal names and official titles listed in the Aramaic texts. He shows acumen in attacking certain textual problems, and his commentary and introduction provide the scholar with information necessary for a proper understanding of this corpus of some two hundred brief, formulaic inscrip-

* Originally published in *JAOS* 92 (1972), pp. 70–79. Reprinted with permission from the American Oriental Society.

[1] *Aramaic Ritual Texts from Persepolis*. By Raymond A. Bowman. (Oriental Institute Publications vol. 91.) Pp. 194, pl. 36. Chicago: Chicago University Press, 1970. $25.—(Henceforth abbreviated as Bowman.)

Abbreviations are as in *The Assyrian Dictionary*, University of Chicago (*CAD*), with the following additions:

Jean-Hoftijzer = C. F. Jean, J. Hoftijzer, *Dictionnaire des Inscriptions Sémitiques de l'Ouest*, 1965.

Koehler-Baumgartner = L. Koehler, W. Baumgartner, *Lexicon in Veteris Testamenti Libros*, 1958.

Levy, *Wörterbuch* = J. Levy, *Wörterbuch über die Talmudim und Midraschim*, 1963, vols. I–IV.

Persepolis I, II, III = Erich F. Schmidt, *Persepolis I* (OIP 68), 1953; *Persepolis II* (OIP 69), 1957; *Persepolis III* (OIP 70), 1970.

PFT = R. T. Hallock, *Persepolis Fortification Tablets* (OIP 92), 1969.

PTT = G. G. Cameron, *Persepolis Treasury Tablets* (OIP 65), 1948.

TB = Talmud, Babylonian, standard editions, Wilno.

TP = Talmud, Palestinian, standard editions, Krotoschin.

Yadin, *War Scroll* = Y. Yadin, *The Scroll of the Sons of Light against the Sons of Darkness*, trans. Chaim and Batya Rabin, 1962.—

tions written on various stone implements—mortars and pestles, plates and trays—found in the treasury at Persepolis. It is our opinion, nevertheless, that Bowman wandered far from the correct interpretation of these texts as a result of a philological methodology which imposed on them a provenience not their own.

We consider a fresh examination of these Aramaic inscriptions necessary. This writer is not an Iranologist, and the principal interest in this study is to treat the Aramaic of the Persepolis texts.

We are greatly aided by Bowman, himself, who carefully identified Iranian elements in these inscriptions.[2] In 1948, George G. Cameron published an important volume on the discoveries in the Persepolis treasury, dealing primarily with the Elamite texts, but including a discussion of the Persepolis treasury finds, as a whole, projecting their significance for historical, linguistic, and religious studies.[3] Erich Schmidt's three volumes on the Persepolis expedition contain a wealth of relevant material, including contributions by Cameron in which he presented his view on the Aramaic texts.[4] Cameron's understanding of these texts was, in our opinion, essentially valid, although certain serious problems in the texts remained unexplored.[5] Now we have R. T. Hallock's voluminous publication of the Elamite fortification tablets from Persepolis, which add considerably to extant knowledge of the Elamite language, and, in a more general way, to our view of life and administration in the Achaemenid capital.[6]

The Aramaic inscriptions, which all represent variations of the same formulary, can hardly compare in linguistic importance with the Elamite finds, but they can, if properly understood, yield some new information of value to the Aramaist and to the historian.

Bowman took his cue for interpreting the Aramaic inscriptions from a scene depicted in several seal impressions on clay, also found in the treasury.[7] In the opinion of most scholars, this scene portrays a part of the haoma ceremony. The seal shows objects like those which bear the Aramaic inscriptions—mortars, pestles, etc. It also shows several persons in distinctive garb positioned around a table, or altar of sorts. This seal has an Aramaic caption: *ḥtm dtm* [("the seal of *Dtm*[“). Bowman restores this name as *dtmtr*, which frequently occurs in these inscriptions as that of a treasurer.[8] Bowman's restoration is convincing, and

---

[2] *Bowman* 63, s.v. loan words, and cf. discussion, 41.

[3] *PTT* Especially note discussion entitled: “The Significance of the Persepolis Treasury Tablets,” 1–23. Additional Elamite materials, edited and discussed by Cameron, appear in *JNES* 17 (1958) 172–76; 24 (1965) 170–85. Also see R. T. Hallock, *JNES* 19 (1960) 90–100.

[4] *Persepolis I, II, III*. For contributions by Cameron relevant to the Aramaic texts, see *Persepolis II*, 55–55b.

[5] See note 14.

[6] *PFT*.

[7] *Bowman* plate 1, A and B, and cf. discussion, 6f.

[8] *Bowman* 197, index, s.v. *dtmtr*, and cf. discussion 28f. Also consult the chronological tables, 58–60.

leaves little doubt, when joined to the evidence of the seal impressions, that the Aramaic texts refer to the use of the same objects as those portrayed in the seal impressions. The question is: How are we to understand the relatedness of the seal impressions to the Aramaic texts, and what are the implications of the seal impressions for their interpretation?

Bowman contends that the texts convey in words what the seal impressions depict graphically, i.e. "the action", the performance of a ritual, or of part of it. In other words: The texts are "ritual" because they record rites actually performed, telling, *inter alia*, where certain officials stood in relation to one another at a point in the haoma ceremony, and who was the celebrant who employed the utensils during the ceremony.[9] Corollary to this interpretation of the texts, Bowman presents an elaborate discussion of the haoma ceremony itself; its history, and the role it played in Iranian military and religious life.[10] All of this material, including descriptions of the haoma rituals from literary sources, bears more direct relevance to the seal impressions than it does to the Aramaic inscriptions, themselves.

To illustrate Bowman's methodology, we present here a sample text (no. 10), accompanied by Bowman's translation:

1 *bsrk byrtʾ*
2 *lyd mtrpt sgnʾ*
3 *whprn ʿbd ʾbšwn zy*
4 *gll rb znh ʿm hwn rb*
5 *lyd dtmtr gnzbrʾ*
6 *ʾškr šnt* 10(?) + 3.
1 In the ritual of the fortress
2 beside Mithra-pāta, the *segan*,
3 Vahu-farnah used this
4 large pestle of stone with a large mortar
5 beside Dāta-Mithra the treasurer.
6 *ʾškr* of year 13 (?)[11]

Our attention is drawn to Bowman's rendering of the verb *ʿbd* in line 3 as: "used," where one would expect: "made, had made." In Bowman's view, this verb describes the activity of the celebrant who *used* the utensils, and not of the person who devoted them to the fortress. The preposition *lyd* in lines 2 and 5 is understood in the strict, locative sense. In those texts where *lyd* is replaced by *qdm* in line 5, *qdm* is rendered "before", in the same terms. These prepositions

[9] *Bowman* 38–43.

[10] *Ibid.* 6–15.

[11] Superlinear dots used by Bowman to indicate unclear readings are omitted from the transliteration, since readings are fairly certain in text no. 10. For the same reason, brackets have been omitted from our transliteration.

supposedly describe where the participants in the ritual were standing in relation to one another. In line 1 the term *srk* is translated "ritual."[12]

Preliminary to a detailed analysis of the formulary common to these texts, Bowman's interpretation may be questioned on two grounds: 1) Aramaic *ʿbd* does not have the meaning "to use". This verb is central to the formulary, and to Bowman's entire interpretation. As we shall show, he fails to prove that it means "to use," and fails, as well, to explain why it should not be taken in its accepted sense. 2) Texts such as these cannot suffer an interpretation imposed on them by external evidence. A distinction must be drawn between two aspects of textual interpretation: a) The text *qua* text; its content, and reason for having been written. b) That which may be derived from the texts, in other respects.

We learn from these inscriptions that the objects on which they were written were provided to the fortress at Persepolis for use in a ritual, in part depicted on seal impressions. The objects are ritual objects, but the texts, themselves, are not ritual texts. They are administrative notations. They record data pertinent to the donation of the objects, including the following information: 1) The name of the donor who had the objects made (the verb *ʿbd*). 2) To whom, or to what agency the objects were presented. 3) When the objects were delivered. 4) Identification of the objects by name as mortars, etc., sometimes including the specification of size, materials of manufacture, etc. 5) Occasionally, specification of the use intended for the objects.

In substance, Cameron held this view of the texts.[13] Bowman made the critical error of allowing the problems raised by Cameron's philological treatment to obscure the basic soundness of his overall understanding of the texts.[14] Here, then, is our proposed translation of text no. 10, which we present as an alternative to Bowman's translation:

1 In the administration of "The Fortress,"
2 Under the authority of Mithra-pāta, the *segan*,
3 Vahu-farnah made this large pestle
4 of stone, with one large mortar.
5 Under the authority of Dāta-Mithra, the treasurer.
6 Delivery of year 13(?).

The philological notes which follow may serve as documentation: Line 1: *bsrk byrtʾ*. We agree with Bowman that *srk* stands in a construct relation to *byrtʾ*,

[12] *Bowman* 192, index, s.v. *qdm*. Also see the chapter entitled "The Action," 38–43, Cf. 32, 68, and n. 44.

[13] See note 4.

[14] Cameron took *srk*, *prkn*, and *hst* in the opening formula as place names (*Bowman* 20–1), which turns out to be problematic. He also saw Persian influence in the alleged construction *ʿbd ... lyd*, whereas it is doubtful that this construction actually occurs in our texts. Cameron correctly identified *ʾškr* with Akkadian *iškaru*, Hebrew *ʾeškār* but did not complete his investigation of this term. (See note 60.) Bowman noted a number of probable incorrect readings on the part of Cameron, and revised Cameron's chronology. (See note 8.)

and is not a place name, as one might expect if the formula were read: "In X, the fortress." We further agree that, all factors considered, the objects bearing the inscriptions were probably manufactured at Persepolis, and that the inscriptions refer to donations made to the Persepolis fortress, and not to several different establishments.[15]

À propos the term *byrtʾ* we should note Cameron's earlier suggestion that Elamite *pir-ra-tam$_4$-ma* was an Aramaic loan-word to be normalized *birta-ma* "at the fortress", and that it replaced the usual name for Persepolis in several of the Elamite texts from the treasury.[16] On this basis, one could have supposed that in our Aramaic texts *byrtʾ* was a way of identifying Persepolis. In that case, there would be no question about *srk*, or the variants, *prkn* and *hst*, in the opening formula. The real place name would have been represented by *byrtʾ*, itself, i.e. "The Fortress," and not by these preceding words. In a subsequent study by W. Eilers, Cameron's suggestion was convincingly invalidated. Eilers showed that pir-ra-tam$_4$-ma was Old Persian *fratama* "noble," an official title, and an epithet of persons of rank.[17] It seems that Cameron, himself, may have given up his earlier proposal, since, in a later publication of some treasury texts, he translated *pir-ra-tam$_4$-ma PN* as: "The distinguished PN", without commenting on this word.[18] Now that we have Hallock's edition of the Elamite fortification tablets we learn of a related form *pirratammiyaš* "of prime quality". This removes any lingering doubts about the etymology of *pirratamma* in Cameron's texts, or in the fortification tablets.[19]

It is still reasonable, however, to take *byrtʾ* in our Aramaic texts as a way of referring to Persepolis, idiomatic in Aramaic.[20] We therefore translate *byrtʾ* with capitals: "The Fortress," i.e. Persepolis.

---

[15] *Bowman* 20f., and nn. 1–4. On place names preceding names of fortified cities and capitals in Akkadian usage see *CAD B*, 261f., s.v. *birtu* A, 1. In Aramaic, see *Jean-Hoftijzer* 35, s.v. *byrh*. Also cf. Esther 1:2, *et passim*: *bešûšān habbîrāh* "in Susa, the capital," and possibly Ezra 6:2: "In Hamadan, the capital, which is in Media, the province."

[16] *PTT* 23, 141 (notes to text 36:2). Also cf. 153–4 (notes to 44:2, 44a:2).

[17] W. Eilers, *ZA* 51 (1955) 225–36. On Persian *fratama* cf. Biblical Hebrew *partemîm* (Esther 1:3, 6:9, Daniel 1:3). Eilers showed that *pir-ra-tam$_4$-ma* did not, in fact, stand in exactly the same position as did *Ba-ir-šá*, the usual name of Persepolis in Elamite. There were also problems of a phonetic character in attempting to normalize the Elamite *pir-ra-tam$_4$-ma* as *birta-ma*.

[18] Cameron, *JNES* 17 (1958) 174, in text 1957:2:6.

[19] *PFT* 745, glossary, s.v. *pirratamma*, *pirratammiyaš*.

[20] In 1 Chronicles 29:1 *habbîrāh* refers to the Jerusalem temple. The sense of "temple" for *byrh* is known in Nabataean (*Jean-Hoftijzer* 35, s.v. *byrh*, 2). This is also true of Talmudic usage (Levy, *Wörterbuch* I:222 s.v. *bîrāh*, I). In the same terms, Hebrew *ʿîr*/*hāʿîr* "(the) city" can refer to Jerusalem without further specification (Isaiah 66:6, Ezekiel 7:23, and cf. Isaiah 32:13, in which both *ʿîr* and *qiryāh* "city" are used in this way).

Bowman cites some of the relevant sources on the term *srk*, basing his treatment on Yadin's study of *serek* in the *War Scroll*, and noting that this term also occurs in Talmudic literature.[21] Before discussing whether or not *srk* can mean "ritual" in the Persepolis texts, a systematic re-examination of the evidence is necessary. What evidence do we have relevant to *srk/serek*?

1) The verbal root *ś/srk* is attested in Hebrew and Aramaic, and is cognate to Arabic *šarika*. The basic sense of this root is: "to adhere to, follow, tie, wind one's way", etc. Biblical Hebrew has *śerôk* "shoelace" and the *Piel* part. *meśāreket* in Jeremiah 2:23, describing the "winding" movements of a doe.[22] In Talmudic and post-Talmudic sources we find *srk*, and nominal forms, having similar connotations. This verb may refer to tying a shoelace, and to the movements of animals, like goats, who skip about. The *Qal* part. *śārek* may mean: "to adhere to-" as one may "stick" to his previous statements; or: "to stick to-", as one substance "sticks" to another. The *Aphel* part. *masrêk* may also mean: "to adhere to-" in a physical sense.[23] The *Aphel* part. is also attested in a Greek-Aramaic bilingual form Mtskheta, in Georgia, (line 9), where the context is geographical, speaking of the locations of conquered cities. The clause: *dhwʾ msryk* means: "on which it borders, to which it is joined," or the like.[24] In Talmudic usage we also have nominal *serek/sirkāʾ* "an adhesion (of the lung, skin)."[25]

As already suggested by some lexicographers, *ś/srk* is probably a phonetic variant of *ś/srg* "to weave, intertwine." Biblical Hebrew has *sārîg* "a tendril of a vine" (Genesis 40:10, etc.), and verbal forms meaning: "to climb over, intertwine" (as said of vines). In Late Hebrew and Aramaic we find the verb *sārag* "to weave"—cloth, etc., and also the extended usage: "to delete, skip over" (cf. the verbal noun *sērûg*).[26]

2) In Talmudic and post-Talmudic sources we have the nominal *serek/sirkāʾ*, meaning: "custom, practice, rule", etc. Traditionally, this form has been derived from the verbal root *ś/srk*, and has been explained as "that which one adheres to, which one follows," hence: "custom," etc. Semantically, there are analogues to such a derivation. Thus, *minhāg* "custom" derives from the verb *nāhag* "to conduct, lead", and means "that by which one is led, conducted."

---

[21] *Bowman* 22–4, and notes and see Yadin, *War Scroll* 148–52.

[22] *Koehler-Baumgartner* 931, s.v. *śrk*, and 930. s.v. *śerôk*.

[23] See Levy, *Wörterbuch* III:592–3, s.v. *serak*, and *serek/sirkāʾ*, and cf. E. Ben-Yehudah, *Dictionary and Thesaurus of the Hebrew Language* (Hebrew) (1960) V:4219–21, s.v. *sārak*, and A. Kohut, *Aruch Completum* VI (1926), 137–8, s.v. *serak*; S. Krauss, *Addidamenta ad Librum Aruch Completum* (1937), 305, s.v. *serek*, 2. For Syriac, see *LS* 499, s.v. *serak*, and see our note 34.

[24] F. Altheim and R. Stiehl, *Die aramäische Sprache unter den Achaemeniden* (1963), 244–55, and notes to line 9.

[25] For sources, see note 23.

[26] On forms with final *k*, see notes 22–23. On *ś-r-g* in Biblical Hebrew see *Koehler-Baumgartner* 930, s.v., and 931 s.v. *sārîg*. On Late Hebrew *sārag* "to weave," see Levy, *Wörterbuch* III:585–6, s.v. *serag/sārag* and *sērûg*, and related forms. For Syriac, see *LS* 496, s.v. *serag*, and related forms.

In fact, Rashi explains the term *serek* as *minhāg* in his comments to several Talmudic passages.[27]

Derivation from the verb *ś/srk* is commonly accepted for Dead Sea *serek* and related forms, as it is for the Talmudic and post-Talmudic term. Until the discovery of some Jewish sectarian documents, published by Solomon Schechter in 1910, this etymology probably went unquestioned. Subsequently, in the completed Ben-Yehudah lexicon, we find the following comment, appended by the editor, N. H. Tur-Sinai, to the entry *srk* (v.), à propos the suggestive phrase: *keserek hattôrāh*, occurring in the Schechter document: "And perhaps it (i.e., *serek*) is related to Aramaic *sārekāʾ* "commissioner" (Hebrew: *šôṭēr*), and its meaning is something like "administration" (Hebrew *mišṭar*), hence: "statute."[28]

In our opinion, this suggestion can now be substantiated. Now that we have more Dead Sea sources for study, it can be shown that the term *serek*, and related forms, convey the basic sense of governance and administration, and not the notion of "following, adhering" or the like. The same is also probably true for some Talmudic occurrences of *serek/sirkāʾ*.

The Aramaic title *sārāk* "chief commissioner" occurs in the book of Daniel (6:3, 5), in Talmudic literature and in the Targumim as *sārekāʾ*, where it sometimes serves as the Aramaic rendering of Hebrew *šôṭēr*, a point noted by lexicographers. This title most certainly does not derive from a Semitic verbal root. It is based on Avestan *sāra* "head", a concept underlying many titles given to leaders.[29] Daniel, chapter 6, relates that three *sārekîn* were in charge of all the satraps during the reign of Darius, and that Daniel was one of the three.

Returning to the passage containing the phrase: *keserek hattôrāh* in the source we now call *The Zadokite Document* (VII:8), we note that Chaim Rabin translates: "according to the *order* of the Law." The passage is really not speaking of any particular "order", but of laws and statutes. The phrase *keserek hattôrāh* means: "according to the prescription of the Torah." In X:4 we read: "And this is the *serek* for the judges of the congregation." Again, Rabin renders *serek* "order", where we would suggest: "procedure", or the like. The point is that "order" implies "following", thus relating the term *serek* to the verbal root *ś/srk*, and that accounts, most likely, for Rabin's consistent translations of *serek*

[27] See Rashi *ad TB ʿAbôdāh Zārāh* 30a, *Niddāh* 67 and *Sanhedrîn* 51b.

[28] See S. Schechter, *Documents of Jewish Sectaries* I (1910), Hebrew text, 7, line 8. For most references to *serek* in Dead Sea literature see A. Haberman, *The Scrolls from the Judean Desert* (Hebrew) (1959), concordance, 107.

[29] See F. Rosenthal, *A Grammar of Biblical Aramaic* (1963), 58 (no. 189), and *Koehler-Baumgartner* 1104, s.v. *sārak*. On occurrences of Aramaic *sārekāʾ* as a translation of Hebrew *šôṭēr* see Yadin, *War Scroll* 151, n. 4, and A. Kohut, *op. cit.* VI:138, s.v. *sārekāʾ*. Yadin probably considered the Aramaic title *sārāk* as cognate to the verb *srk*. Problematic *srwkyʾ* in the Aramaic of the Sardis bilingual (line 4), dated 5–4th cent. B.C.E., may represent the title *sārāk*. If so, this title would be attested earlier than Daniel, and nearer the period of the Perespolis texts. See H. Donner, W. Rollig, *Kanaanische und aramäische Inschriften* (1966), I:50, no. 260 B:4, and II:307.

as "order."[30] We do not dispute the fact that *serek* connotes "order", as our subsequent discussion of the *War Scroll* will demonstrate. There, it is clear that the battle array itself was referred to as *serek*. Our contention is that the notion of "order" conveyed by usages of the term *serek* does not derive from the idea of "following, adhering to-", or the like, but from the exercise of authority and leadership, as a result of which military units, as well as courts, and ritual procedures, were constituted or prescribed, and their order determined. To rule or administer is, primarily, to establish the order of things.

This conclusion is further borne out by usages of the term *serek* in the *Rule Scroll*, most comprehensively studied by J. Licht in a Hebrew volume. The term *serek hayyaḥad* means: "the code/jurisdiction of the *Yaḥad*", as in I:16: "All who come under the code/jurisdiction of the *Yaḥad*." Here the term *serek* is probably not part of the name of the group, as it seems to be in certain passages of the War Scroll. (See further.) Similarly, V:1 should be translated: "This is the *statute/code* for the men of the *Yaḥad*."[31]

It is in the *War Scroll*, however, that the true meaning of *serek* most clearly emerges. Yadin almost consistently translates the term: "disposition." In II:1 we read: "Fathers of the congregation, fifty-two. The chiefs of the priests *they shall dispose* (*yisrôkû*) after the chief priest and his deputy," etc. Again in line 6 we read: "All these *they shall dispose* at the time of the Sabbatical year." Thus, Yadin. We submit that the finite verbal form *yisrôkû*, unique to this section of the *War Scroll*, should be translated: "they shall appoint." That is what the text is talking about.

In VII:1 we find a unique occurrence of the title *sôrekê hammaḥanôt* "camp prefects". In this title we have either an internal Hebrew denominative of the term *serek*, or, possibly, a direct translation of the Aramaic title *sārāk*. Other occurrences of the term *serek* also cause us to doubt that this term has anything to do with "following." Thus, in IX:10 Yadin renders: "The *disposition* for changing the array of the battle." We submit: "the rule/procedure for changing the array of the battle."

Yadin notes that the term *serek* can, of itself, designate a military unit, and even the entire force, comprising the men of the *Yaḥad*.[32] Our question is: Does *serek* designate the unit or force because the men are deployed in a certain order or position, or is it so called because the unit, together with its tactics and array, was constituted according to a plan, which was in turn instituted by command? Note that the document containing the battle plans was also termed *serek*.[33] All of this points to the exercise of authority and command.

---

[30] See C. Rabin, *The Zadokite Document* (1954), and n. 2 to line 6a; also 49, etc.

[31] J. Licht, *The Rule Scroll* (Hebrew) (1965), 66, and references cited in the index, 314, s.v. *serek*. Licht seems to favor the sense of "order, arrangement" to that of "code."

[32] Yadin, *War Scroll* 148, and n. 10; 149, and n. 1.

[33] Yadin, *War Scroll* 331, *ad* XV:5: "In the book Serekh ʿIttô." Thus, Yadin. We submit: "In the book 'The Code of *ʿIttô*'." Reference is perhaps to Isaiah 60:22.

Yadin devotes considerable attention to the Greek term *taxis*, discussing its remarkable equivalence to *serek* in Dead Sea Literature, and noting that an Aramaic fragment of *The Testament of Levi* has *beserek* where the Greek has *en taxei*. This had been previously noted by Saul Lieberman some years before the recent discoveries. He cited the occurrence of the term *serek* in Schechter's documents, and stated that *taxis* was the precise translation of Talmudic *serek.*[34] The similarities in application of these two terms are, indeed, striking. These comparisons do not, however, endorse the derivation of *serek* from the verb *ś/srk*! The noun *taxis* is cognate to the verb *tassô*, and to the noun *tagma*. The verb *tassô* has several related meanings: 1. "to arrange, put in order, array, marshal," etc. 2. "to appoint, to assign a task, to order one to do a thing." 3. "to place in a certain order, to lay down rule; to impose laws." The term *tagma* means: "that which has been ordered or arranged," especially: "an ordinance, command." Common to all of these connotations is an orientation from the sources of authority to those subject to it. "Order" is a function of authority. Thus, Greek *tagma* also means: "a regular body of soldiers, a division; an order or rank."[35] We submit that a similar orientation underlies the term *serek*, and that this further suggests its derivation from an official title.

On the basis of the evidence surveyed thus far, we posit two, separate lexical entries for Talmudic usage: a) *serek/sirkāʾ* I, and related forms, from the verb *ś/s-r-k*, a variant of *ś/s-r-g*. These forms clearly convey the sense of "adhering, following," etc. Thus, the nominal form *sirkāʾ* means "an adhesion." b) *serek/sirkāʾ* II "custom, rule," thus: "procedure, order." Evidently, a degree of confusion entered into Talmudic usages of *serek/sirkāʾ*, but once we allow for the existence of two, separate derivations we observe that Talmudic usage, itself, seems to support this predication. Several examples from Talmudic literature will serve to clarify this conclusion:

1. *TB Ḥullin* 106a: *neṭîlat yadaîm leḥullîn mippenê serek terûmāh* "The washing of the hands for *ḥullîn* (profane food) is because of the rule of *terûmāh* (priestly gifts)." Impure hands render *terûmāh* impure by contact, but not *ḥullîn*. Nevertheless, "so as to habituate those who partake of *terûmāh* to wash their hands, they instituted it (i.e. the washing of the hands) for *ḥullîn*, as well." (Rashi, *ad loc.*). Idioms of similar import are: *neṭîlat serek* "procedural washing" (*TP Bikkûrîm* 2:2), and its variant in the Babylonian Talmud, *serek ṭebîlāh* "the rule of immersion" (*TB Yômāʾ* 30a), and *ṭebîlat serek* "procedural immersion" (*TP Yoma* 3:3). In this context *serek* connotes the required procedure.

2. *TB Niddāh* 67b: *miššûm serek bittāh* "because of her daughter's procedure." That is to say: A menstruating woman whose period ends on the eighth day should, technically speaking, be permitted to immerse herself on that day, and yet the sages instructed her to wait until the night following that day, so as

[34] *Ibid.* 149, and n. 2. Also see S. Lieberman, *Tosefet Rishonim* (Hebrew), (1936–7), I:188, no. 14, and Talmudic sources discussed. (See further).

[35] Yadin, *War Scroll* 150, and n. 4. See Liddell-Scott, *Greek-English Lexicon*, 8th ed., 1526, s.v. *taxis*, 1528–29, s.v. *tassô*, and 1522 s.v. *tagma*.

to prevent her daughter from violating the law. Her daughter, thinking that the day in question was her mother's seventh, would interpret her immersion on that day, if allowed, as permission for her to immerse herself on the seventh day, which is forbidden by law. Traditionally, *serek bittāh* has been taken to mean the tendency of a daughter to "follow" her mother's practices. Actually, it relates to what the daughter, herself, does; to whether or not she upholds the law. The notion of "following" is not actually present in the term *serek*, itself. The referent of *serek* is the daughter, not the mother!

Similarly, in the idiom *sirkāʾ* ... *neqaṭ* "to adopt a practice, custom" (*TB Sanhedrin* 51b, *ʿAbôdāh Zārah* 30a), the term *sirkāʾ*, itself, does not imply "following." It is the verb *neqaṭ* which conveys that notion.

We may summarize our findings on Persepolis *srk* as follows:

1. Dead Sea usage of the term *serek* and related forms fits in well with a derivation from an official title, known in the book of Daniel, Aramaic *sārāk*. The occurrence of the nominal form *srk* in an Aramaic text from the fifth century B.C.E. is an important item of evidence, because it indicates that in Empire Aramaic the nominal form *srk* already existed, and that it meant "administration, jurisdiction."

This nominal form would have been available to the Dead Sea writers, and would have been admirably suited for designating their rule of conduct, the arraying of their military forces in the projected battle against the Sons of Darkness, as well as for designating the sect, itself, as a group bound by authoritative leadership.

2. What we have classified as Talmudic *serek/sirkāʾ* II also derives from the Aramaic title *sārāk*, and continues the tradition of Dead Sea usage. In Talmudic sources the term *serek/sirkaʾ* II became confused with forms of the verb *ś/srk*, an etymology consistently pursued by the traditional commentaries.

3. As for the sense of *serek*, it is clear that Bowman misunderstood Yadin's point about this term in the War Scroll. *serek* does not, in and of itself, mean "ritual," no matter how we understand its derivation. It is the immediate context which sometimes applies the notion of "rule, custom, order," etc., to ritual matters. Similarly, the terms *maʿarākāh*, *sēder*, and *ḥôq*, connoting features of the battle array, may be applied to matters ritual, in various contexts.[36] We have, therefore, proposed translating the opening formula *bsrk byrtʾ* "In the administration of 'The Fortress'."

The variants of *srk* in the opening formula of the Persepolis texts, *prkn* and *hst*, are difficult to identify, and the discussion to follow is inconclusive. Bowman renders *bprkn byrtʾ* "In the (haoma-)crushing ceremony of the fortress," taking *prkn* from Semitic *prk* + the affix *-ān*. The word *prkn* can be Semitic, Iranian, or a hybrid. As a Semitic root, the problem lies in the affixed formation *prkn*, and not in the root meaning. The formation *prkn* could mean one of the following: a) "crushing, pounding," or the effects of such actions. The formation *prkn* (*porkān/purkān*, in Aramaic) actually occurs in *Frahang-i-Pahlavik*, where

[36] Yadin, *War Scroll* 142f., 179f., and 374, index, s.v. *ʿrk*.

it appears to have the meaning: "destruction, distress," i.e. the effects of crushing or pounding.[37] b) "the crusher" (Aramaic *parkān*).[38] c) Possibly: "that which is, or has been crushed."[39] Thus, *bprkn byrtʾ* would most likely mean: "In the crushing of the fortress," i.e. in the destruction of the fortress! As a Semitic word *prkn* is, therefore, problematic.

In several texts we have the construction *ʾbšwn pyrk*, which Bowman renders: "crushing pestle."[40] The form *pyrk* is admittedly difficult. Furthermore, in text no. 8:3 we have: *hwn znh lḥšl* (reading probable) "this mortar for crushing," representing a more characteristically Aramaic way of indicating the use intended for the object in question, and employing an old Aramaic form of the *Qal* infinitive. In text no. 5:3 we have: *bprk rb*, which Bowman translates: "In the great (haoma-)crushing ceremony.'[41]

Searching for other possibilities, we note Akkadian *parakku* "dais, throne room, sanctuary," etc.[42] The affix *-ān* would remain problematic, of course, but the meanings of *parakku* would suit our context. Especially suggestive is the Sumerian loan word in Akkadian *para(m)māḫu* "great, eminent *parakku*," since Sumerian MAḪ has the Akkadian value *rabû* "great, large." This would correlate with *bprk rb*, which we would then render: "In the great chamber/sanctuary."[43] We cannot be certain, however, that at Persepolis, during the period in question, a chamber would be called *parakku*.

Bowman cites a suggestion that *prkn* is a hybrid, representing Semitic *prk* + Old Persian *-ana*, an affix denoting place, and yielding the sense: "a place of crushing."[44] We have no other clear indications, however, that hybrids were extant in the Aramaic of Persepolis.

As an Iranian word, *prkn* has been identified with Persian *paragnah*, a term describing a part of the haoma ceremony.[45] Bowman rejects this suggestion on

---

[37] *Bowman* 22, and nn. 25–7. On Aramaic *perak* see *Jean-Hoftijzer* 235, s.v. *prk*, I, and Levy, *Wörterbuch* IV:114–115, s.v. *perak*, and related forms. On Akkadian *parakku(m)* see *AHw* 828–9, s.v., especially mng. 7. On the formation *prkn* see *Jean-Hoftijzer* 235, s.v. For the formation *porkān*/*purkān* cf. biblical Aramaic *polḥān* (Late Hebrew *pulḥān*) "cultic service, worship," literally: "serving." See *Koehler-Baumgartner* 1113, s.v. *polḥān*.

[38] Cf. *gazlān*/*gazlānāʾ* "robber" is Aramaic and Late Hebrew. See J. N. Epstein, *A Grammar of Babylonian Aramaic* (Hebrew) (1960), 112–113, s.v. quadriliterals III, adj., for other examples.

[39] A formation *pûrekān* is possible, though in this orthography we would expect a *waw*. See J. N. Epstein, *op. cit.* 113, c.

[40] *Bowman* 81 (text no. 9:3). The reading *pyrk* is clearly legible in text no. 17:5. Also cf. nos. 13:3, 14:3.

[41] *Ibid.*, 77–8, and comments to line 3 of the text.

[42] See *AHw* 827–8, s.v. *parakku(m)*, especially mng. 2.

[43] *Ibid.* 829, s.v. *para(m)māḫu*. On Akkadian values of Sumerian MAḪ see A. Deimel, *Sumerisches Lexikon* II/2, 104, no. 57:10, MAḪ.

[44] *Bowman* 22, and n. 27.

[45] *Ibid.* 22, and n. 23.

the grounds that Persian *g* would not come into Aramaic as *k*. The phonetic problem is probably not crucial, and this suggestion should be studied further by Iranologists. Bowman cites two suggestions by Professors Emmerick and Harmatta, respectively, that the third variant, *hst*, relates to the act of crushing. Emmerick renders *hst* "place of crushing."[46]

It is clear that most of the above suggestions regarding *prkn* and *hst* betray the search for a meaning associated directly with the haoma ceremony. It is possible, of course, that the context favors a different concept entirely, i.e. an administrative term like *serek*, or an accounting term. After all, these texts are talking about the conveyance of *materiel*, according to our view. In his glossary to the Elamite tablets, Hallock lists the term *paraka* (variant: *parak*) which he translates "issued," from the verb *pari-* "to go to, to issue."[47] Relevant to *hst* in our texts, we note Elamite *hasatiš*, and related forms, composed of *ha* + *sat* + pronominal element. Elamite *sat*, from the verb *sati-* "to feed," means: "ration." Thus, *hasatuk* means: "to them it was given as *sat*."[48] Whether or not the above Elamite forms bear any relation to *prkn* or *hst* is a question which can best be decided by students of Elamite.

In summary: The term *hst* is clearly non-Semitic, and *prkn* is probably non-Semitic, as well. The context seems to us to favor terms designating a place, or agency within the fortress, or possibly administrative terms.

Line 2: *lyd* PN *sgnʾ*. Bowman renders: "beside PN, the *segan*." He briefly discusses earlier suggestions by Cameron, Henning, and Diakonoff on the sense of *lyd* in certain Aramaic texts, but rejects them all. Diakonoff, in his studies of the Nisā inscriptions from Turkmenistan, correctly understood the functional sense of *lyd*, which he there rendered: "under the authority of —." Diakonoff cites a few texts where he found the formula: *lyd* + official title. This is essentially the same formula as we have in our Aramaic texts.[49] One could also cite Esther 2:3, *passim*. Thus, Esther was remanded "under the authority of Hegai, the royal official/eunuch, keeper of the women", with Hebrew *ʾel yad*, equivalent to *leyad*. Bowman failed to note that in an Aramaic letter from Elephantine, the preposition *lyd* has the sense required in our texts. Aršam complains that

---

[46] *Ibid.* 24, and nn. 42–4.

[47] *PFT* 740, glossary, s.v. *paraka*.

[48] *Ibid.* 693, s.v. *hasatis*, *hasatuk*, etc., and 751, s.v. *sat*, and *sati* (2 entries).

[49] *Bowman* 39, n. 9. See I. M. Diakonoff, V. A. Livshitz, *Documenty iz Nizy*, Moscow (1960), for examples. Thus: *lyd pḥtʾ* in nos. 1068:2, 1379:3, 1708:4, 1891:4, 2120:3–4, etc. (Cf. W. B. Henning, "Mitteliranisch, 7: Parthien: Nisa," *Iranistik: 1. Linguistik*, HdO [1958], 27f.) Also note *lyd ḥštrp* in nos. 31:4, 74:2, 76:3, 78:4, 649:2–3, 1188:2, 1673–2:2, and *lyd dyzpty* in nos. 652:1–2, 1511:1, etc. Actually, in the Nisā texts we also have the full formula: *lyd PN* + official title, identical to the Persepolis texts. Thus: *lyd kwpyzt ḥštrp* in nos. 590:2–3, 890:3–4, *lyd Mtprn dyzpty* in nos. 636:2–3, 1654:2–3, 1730:2, 2042:2, and probably *lyd Mtrssnk mrzwpn* in no. 1899:203. Also note the construction *hyty PN ... lydyh* in no. 2167:3. For German translations of some studies by I. M. Diakonoff, et al. see O. Mehlitz, *Sowjetwissenschaft* 4 (1954) 557f, especially 580, the note to b, 2.

another officer with "the troops under his command" (Aramaic: *ḥylʾ zy lydh*) did not obey him. Driver notes that *lyd* can have the same force as *byd*.[50] Thus, the preposition *lyd* need not be taken in the strictly locative sense, implying physical proximity or direction, but is to be understood in our texts as relational.

Similarly, the preposition *qdm* for *lyd* (cf. text no. 14:5, as an example) may also have extended usages, based on the locative sense. Thus, one may present a report or complaint "before" one in authority or address a petition to him, without the implication that using the preposition *qdm* actually placed one person in physical proximity to the other. Likewise, one may speak of activities carried on under the purview of another, in a figurative sense.[51] The objects bearing the inscriptions were presented to the fortress "before" the treasurer, i.e. into his charge or purview.

Before proceeding to the critical verb *ʿbd* in line 3, we should note that both Cameron and Bowman assumed a greater degree of syntactic coherence in these formulaic texts than is the case. The formulary is composed of disparate phrases and clauses, to be separated by commas and periods. There is no syntactic continuity between line 2 and 3; or between lines 3 and 4, and line 5. We do not have in these texts the construction: *ʿbd ... lyd*. Both in line 2, and in line 5 of text no. 10, for example, *lyd* introduces a prepositional phrase that stands by itself as a laconic, formulaic entry. From the looks of it, our formulary should not be compared to the literary idiom "made into the hand of" in Persian, as suggested by Cameron, nor should Bowman have been concerned with the question of whether or not such an idiom is attested in Aramaic sources.[52]

Line 3: PN *ʿbd*. Bowman renders: "PN used." He argues for this translation on the following grounds: 1) The Akkadian verb *epēšu* "to do, make", can have the specialized connotation: "to use."[53] 2) Biblical Hebrew *ʿbd* can mean: "to work (a field)", a connotation which Bowman considers akin to the sense of using. There is a problem in suggesting this comparison: Biblical Hebrew *ʿbd* is semantically differentiated from Aramaic *ʿbd*. The semantic equivalents of Aramaic *ʿbd* in standard, Biblical Hebrew are *ʿśh*, and occasionally *pʿl*, which is also the Phoenician equivalent of *ʿśh/ʿbd*. What Hebrew *ʿbd* may or may not mean in Genesis 2:5 or 2 Samuel 9:10, sources cited by Bowman, has no bearing on its meanings in Aramaic.[54] In late Biblical Hebrew we begin to have Aramaistic usages of *ʿbd*.[55] This brings us directly to Bowman's next argument.

---

[50] See G. R. Driver, *Aramaic Documents of the Fifth Century B.C.* (1968), 16, s.v. text no. 4:1.

[51] See *Jean-Hoftijzer* 251–2, s.v. *qdm* III, especially no. 1, a; and F. Rosenthal, *op. cit.* 37, no. 84.

[52] *Bowman* 39–40.

[53] See *CAD E*, 230, s.v. *epēšu* 2f., 6.

[54] On usages of Phoenician *pʿl* see *Jean-Hoftijzer* 231–2, s.v.

[55] An example is *waʿabādêhem* "and their deeds, actions," in Koheleth 9:1. Thus, H. L. Ginsberg in *The Five Megilloth and Jonah* (1969), 71, and cf. in the introduction, *ibid.* 52f., and literature cited.

3) Bowman contends that in post-Biblical Hebrew the verb *ʿbd*, especially in the *Niphal* stem, can mean: "to use (something);" as, for instance, to use an object for idolatrous purposes.[56] The fact is, of course, that Late Hebrew has both the Hebrew and Aramaic usages of *ʿbd*. When the Mishnah speaks of an object: *šeneʿebdāh bô ʿabêrāh* "with which a transgression has been committed" (Mishnah, *Bekôrôt* 6:12), it is clearly employing Aramaic *ʿbd*, and not Hebrew *ʿbd*. In any event, Aramaic *ʿbd* in such contexts does not mean "to use" at all!

4) According to Bowman, the *Peshitta* to Ezra 7:23 may be employing *ʿbd* in the sense of "to use." This is probably incorrect. The Aramaic of the biblical passage may be translated as follows: "All that is commanded by the God of heaven shall be done diligently (*yitʿabēd ʾadrazdāʾ*) for the temple of the God of heaven", etc. — The *Peshitta* has: "All that is in the edict shall be given. Give to him in accordance with the law of the God of heaven. Let him get about doing (it)!" — In Syriac, the last part of the passage reads: *nissab weneʿebēd*, literally: "Let him take, and do." Our rendering (above) reflects the fact that the verb *nissab* (3rd masc. sing. imperf.) functions here as an auxiliary verb, joined to *neʿebēd*, producing a temporal sense. This construction in Syriac represents the *Peshitta*'s understanding of Aramaic *yitʿabēd ʾadrazdāʾ*, replacing the adverb with a verb.[57]

It is of interest to note one late Punic text from Tripoli in which *ʿbd* apparently has the sense of "to use."[58] The most that can be said is that a verb with the meaning "to do, make" can occasionally have the specialized connotation: "to use," as is true of Akkadian *epēšu*. The evidence for such a connotation is virtually non-existent in Aramaic. In addition to arguing in favor of the sense: "to use", Bowman attempts to argue against the expected sense: "to do, make, have made" for the verb *ʿbd*. Since our texts are not speaking of craftsmen who actually "made" the objects in question, we would have to take *ʿbd* as having a factitive connotation, i.e. "to have made." This connotation, Bowman maintains, would require the causative stem, the *Haphel*; but the orthography does not allow for such a form.[59]

This is patently incorrect. We are dealing here with a cultural concept, and not primarily with a grammatical feature of the language. According to this concept, the donor or sponsor is credited with the actual accomplishment of a worthwhile project, as if he, himself, had done the work involved. In certain contexts this is true of Aramaic *ʿbd*, as it is of Hebrew *ʿśh* "to do, make," Phoenician *ṭnʾ* "to erect" (?), and Akkadian *epēšu* "to do, make," in the *G.* stem.[60] In

[56] Levy, *Wörterbuch* III:604, s.v. *ʿābad*/*ʿabad*, and related forms. Also cf. Ch. Y. Kasofsky, *Thesaurus Mishnae* (Hebrew) III (1958), 1297, s.v. *ʿbd*, b.

[57] See C. Brockelmann, *Syrische Grammatik* (1962), 119–120, no. 225.

[58] See *Jean-Hoftijzer* 200, s.v. *ʿbd*, 5.

[59] *Bowman* 38, and n. 3.

[60] On Phoenician *ṭnʾ* see *Jean-Hoftijzer* 101.

Akkadian we have the *Š* stem, *šūpušu* with the factitive connotation, but this is in addition to G stem *epēšu*, which also has this general sense.[61]

In a manner similar to Akkadian, Late Hebrew has *haʿaśēh*, the *Hiphil* of *ʿśh/y* "to do, make," in the factitive sense: "to have made, bring about, cause another to do," etc.[62] This is, however, late usage, and does not invalidate what has been said about the factitive force of the *Qal* stem, *ʿśh*. We find no *Hiphil* for Hebrew *bnh* "to build," or for Phoenician/Hebrew *pʿl* in ancient sources. What is most telling is the fact that Aramaic *ʿbd* seems unattested in the causative stem, although Hebrew *ʿbd* "to work" comes into Aramaic and Late Hebrew usage in the *Šaphel* stem as *šaʿabēd* "to impose work upon-, to enslave."[63]

The verb *ʿbd* can, of course, refer directly to the manufacturer, as in many Nabataean inscriptions;[64] but where do we find, in Aramaic, that the verb *ʿbd* has as its subject the user of an object in a ritual? What we find is the verb *ʿbd* describing the activities of kings, gods, and men in sponsoring, donating, and providing objects, as well as in actually making them. In our context *ʿbd* could just as well be translated "present, donate, provide," but we have retained the rendering "he made."

Line 6: *ʾškr šnt* x. Bowman leaves the word *ʾškr* untranslated, but sees it as deriving from the root *škr* "to be intoxicated," and related forms. He analyzes it as a nominal form with the prosthetic *ʾaleph*, on the analogy of *ʾiṭbaʿ* "coin", a variant of *ṭebaʿ*, attested in text no. 43:4.[65] Such an interpretation is possible, but highly improbable in view of Akkadian *iškaru*. Cameron was correct in identifying *ʾškr* of our texts with Akkadian *iškaru*, Hebrew *ʾeškār* (Ezekiel 27:15; Psalms 72:10).[66]A careful study of *CAD I/J*, s.v. *iškaru* A, indicates that the basic sense of this term is: "work assigned."[67] Meaning 3 in *CAD* is especially relevant to our Aramaic texts: "finished products, staples, or material to be deli-

[61] See *CAD E*, 232f., s.v. *epēšu*, 5, *šūpušu*.

[62] See Levy, *Wörterbuch* III:708, s.v. *ʿśh*, Hiphil. Cf. the *Piel ʿiśśāh* "to force, compel" (*ibid.*)

[63] See Levy, *Wörterbuch* IV:558, s.v. *šaʿabēd*, and related forms. The *Piel* of *ʿbd* means: "to work, treat," as said of hides or parchment, in Late Hebrew usage (Levy, *Wörterbuch* III:604, s.v. *ʿābad*).

[64] See *Jean-Hoftijzer* 199, s.v. *ʿbd* I, 1.

[65] *Bowman* 53–5, especially 54, and n. 19.

[66] *Ibid.* 54, and nn. 10–12. Bowman assumes that biblical *ʾeškār* means "tax," the Neo-Assyrian usage of the term (*CAD I/J*, 248 mng. 4). This is accurate as far as Psalm 72:10 is concerned, because there *ʾeškār* is parallel to *minḥāh* "tribute." But, in Ezekiel 27:15 it is more likely that *ʾeškār* refers to trade and exchange and not to tribute or tax. The synonyms of *ʾeškār* in that passage, part of an oracle on the commercial city-state of Tyre, are *maʿarāb* "surety, exchange" (cf. vv. 9, 27) and *ʿizbônîm* "goods, stores," literally: "that which is left behind," to be sold or traded. See *Koehler-Baumgartner* 694, s.v. *ʿizbônîm*, and 731–2, s.v. *ʿrb*, I. The context in Ezekiel actually favors the very sense of "staples, finished products to be delivered," which applies to our Aramaic texts, or at least a meaning approximating that sense.

[67] See *CAD I/J*, 244f., s.v. *iškaru* A.

vered." This meaning seems to be particularly evident in Neo-Babylonian sources, although it is based on older usage. Most of the citations in *CAD*, under this meaning, come from the reigns of Cyrus and Cambyses. We read of deliveries made by named persons on specific dates. Materials to be delivered included agricultural products, garments, and bricks. The texts employ the verbs *nadānu* "to give, pay," and *šūrubu* "to bring in, deliver," in connection with *iškaru* goods.[68]

Further support for taking *ʾškr* in our texts as Akkadian *iškaru* (Hebrew *ʾeškār*) comes from the Nisā texts, where we have what may be an Aramaic equivalent of *iškaru*. In most of the Nisā texts we find a concluding formula, which follows upon the delineation of commodities included in a particular delivery: *hnʿlt ʿl šnt X. hyty PN mdwbr*, etc. "Delivery for the year X. *PN*, the transporter, brought (it)."[69] Sznycer is correct in taking *hnʿlt* not as a finite verbal form, in the *Haphel* stem, but either as an infinitive construct, *hanʿālat*, or as a nominalized form, *hanʿālût*; in either case yielding the sense: "delivery, revenue," literally: "that which is brought in." The infinitive construct is probably preferable, and is to be compared with biblical Aramaic *hanzāqat* "pain, detriment," in Ezra 4:22. Thus, Nisā *hnʿlt* is functionally equivalent to Persepolis *ʾškr*.[70]

This completes our analysis of the formulary. Several terms occurring in variations of the formulary require further study.[71] Our interpretation obviously

---

[68] *Ibid.* 246–8, mng. 3, f, 1–4′. Akkadian *šūrubu* is semantically equivalent to Aramaic *hnʿlh*, the *Haphel* infinitive used in the Nisā texts (See further, in notes 69–70.) Also see S. Kaufman, *The Akkadian Influences on Aramaic* and *the Development of the Aramaic Dialects*, Yale Dissertation (1970) 67, s.v. *iškaru*. Kaufman suggests the meaning "quota" for Persepolis *ʾškr*, and stresses that *iškaru* would have been borrowed by Aramaic from Babylonian, and not from Assyrian.

[69] M. Sznycer, *Semitica* 5 (1955) 73 (text 1, lines 7–9), and 77, notes to the text. The formula recurs in subsequent texts. Other scholars had taken consonantal *hnʿlt* as a finite verbal form, as is the case in the Elephantine papyri, where this verb also occurs. Also see I. M. Diakonoff, *op. cit.* for numerous examples of this formula, and note the variant *hnʿlt šnt*, *ibid.*, text no. 264:5.

[70] *Koehler-Baumgartner* 1099, s.v. *nzq*.

[71] The word *sḥr* is problematic (*Bowman* 91). On the title *gnzbrʾ*, Persian *ganzabara* "treasurer", note its occurrence in Elamite as *kanzabara*. See *PTT* 42, s.v. *ga^n-za-bara*, and 43, n. 9. Cf. *PFT* 738, glossary, s.v. *kanzabara*. The title is composed of *ganza* "treasure," plus *bara* "bearer." The former element occurs in biblical and post-biblical sources (cf. 1 Chronicles 28:11, Ezra 5:17, 6:1, Esther 1:3, Ezekiel 27:24). The noun bore a denominative verb, *gānaz* "to store away, keep safe" (Levy, *Wörterbuch* I:346–7, s.v.). For later usages see Ben-Yehudah, *Dictionary and Thesaurus of the Hebrew Language*, II:812–813, s.v. *gēnez*, a, b, and related forms, and the verb *ganaz*. The doubts expressed there (*ibid.* 812, n. 1) about the Persian derivation of these forms can pretty well be dismissed. Also note the verbal noun *genîzāh* "storing," which can refer either to the act of storing, or to a place of storage. These usages attained considerable importance in Jewish history and religion.

requires us to alter Bowman's treatment of official titles, since we would not see them as designating religious functionaries in these inscriptions.[72]

Bowman's comparative inquiry into the Dead Sea literature also requires serious modification. We are not competent to offer a critique on his treatment of such subjects as the haoma ceremony, and the developing character of Iranian religious life.[73]

ADDENDUM: A large part of the discussion centered on the word *srk* on the assumption that it is a term meaning "administration," or the like, so that the formula *bsrk byrtʾ* would mean: "in the administration of the capital." It turns out that *srk* may rather be the name of a town, like the variant *bprkn byrtʾ*, for instance. On this basis the inscribed objects would have been brought to Persepolis from elsewhere, as some suggested. If so, the entire discussion of *srk* would be irrelevant with respect to the Persepolis texts, themselves, but hopefully instructive in explaining its meaning elsewhere!

The probable reading *lḥšl* in text no. 8:3 requires some comment. Akkadian *ḫašalu* is often used with reference to the husking and pounding of grains and herbs (*CAD Ḫ*, 137–8, s.v.). Cf. Talmudic usage in Levy, *Wörterbuch* II:124, s.v. *ḥešal/ḥăšal*, and *ḥûšlaʾ* "husked barley corn"). Also note biblical Aramaic *ḥāšel* (part.) in Daniel 2:40, and possibly Hebrew *neḥešālîm* in Deuteronomy 25:18.

On *bz/bzy*, note Bowman's discussion (*Bowman* 149, and n. 315, and in the Glossary, 191). Bowman leaves the term untranslated, stating that it appears to be a modifier of *gll* "stone", perhaps a type of stone. Of possible relevance is Old Persian *baji*, Elamite *baziš* "tribute, tax" (See Kent, *Old Persian* 199, lexicon, s.v. *baji*, and *PFT* 677, glossary, s.v. *baziš*). Another possibility is mentioned by Hallock in the name of Gershevitch (*PFT* 16). It seems that Elamite *bazikarra* designates the manufacturer of a type of container. Thus, *baziš*, in certain passages, could mean: "container." We present these references only as a suggestion for further inquiry.

[72] *Bowman* 25–32, 34. Bowman's treatment of *ʾlp plg* should have been the paradigm for his discussion of other titles, where he erroneously converts administrative officials into religious functionaries.

[73] Professors E. Y. Kutscher, Y. Muffs and H. Paper called this writer's attention to useful reference material. Aspects of this study were presented in an address before the American Oriental Society in April, 1971.

From the Aramaic Enoch Fragments: The Semantics of Cosmography*

The caves of Qumran continue to yield exciting new literary materials, not the least significant of which are preserved in Aramaic. J. T. Milik, with the assistance of Matthew Black, has now provided us with a careful and learned edition of the Aramaic Enoch fragments from Qumran cave 4.[1] His analysis shows that they derive from different copies, written at different times. This fact explains the differences in orthography and morphology observable among the fragments as a whole, as well as paleographic distinctions. In Milik's view, most of the fragments antedate the Herodian period, though a few exhibit the Herodian script.

Whether or not Aramaic was the original language of the Enochic corpus, in whole or in part, these recently discovered fragments put us in possession of a new Aramaic vocabulary particularly relevant to astronomical and mythological themes. The Enochic corpus is a major repository of both. Given the wide diffusion of the Aramaic language in the Hellenistic and Roman periods, and its role as a conduit of Near Eastern and Hellenistic culture, this new vocabulary may enable us to establish literary-historical links not previously attainable.

The comments to follow are based on the diplomatic transcription of the fragments, collated with the photographs. In a few instances, virtually certain restorations of individual words will be accepted, but the specific terms of reference to be investigated here all appear in integral form and require no restoration.[2]

I

It is curious how the philologian often returns to the same words and phrases, and therefore to the same concepts, from quite divergent perspectives. In recent years, I have had occasion to study two Hebrew-Aramaic terms belonging to the military and administrative vocabulary of the Achaemenid and Greco-Roman periods. Now I find these same terms occurring in the Aramaic Enoch fragments in an astronomical or celestial context. (1) The term *dgl* (*degel*, in

---

* Originally published in *Journal of Jewish Studies* 33 (*Essays in Honour of Yigael Yadin*; 1982), pp. 311–326. Reprinted with permission from Oxford University Press.

[1] J. T. Milik, *The Books of Enoch, Aramaic Fragments of Qumran Cave 4* (with the collaboration of Matthew Black), Oxford, 1976.

[2] Milik's protracted reconstructions of ancient Aramaic are justified because they provide a textual environment for the fragments, which are not all that extensive. Nevertheless, they present certain problems for the Aramaist.

Hebrew) designates a socio-military unit. Mentioned in the book of Numbers it is well attested in Aramaic documents of the Achaemenid period, originating in Egypt, and elsewhere. It also occurs in certain Qumran texts, mostly as a military designation but once in a celestial context.[3] In the Aramaic Enoch fragments, it refers to constellations, in heaven. (2) The term *srk* (*sereḵ*, in Hebrew) connotes "rule, administration; a jurisdictional unit". It is one way of designating the Qumran sect itself and is used with reference to codes of procedure and rituals. It occurs in Targumic and Rabbinic literature and possibly in the Aramaic texts from Persepolis.[4] In the Aramaic Enoch fragments, it appears once, in a clearly celestial context associated with the courses of heavenly bodies.

A third term also belongs to this group, exhibiting the same range of connotations: *msrt*/*msrh* (Both the form and vocalization of the singular absolute of this noun are difficult to establish). In view of the complexities involved, and because I have not had occasion to satisfy myself as to its problematics in earlier studies, more attention will be devoted to it here. The later terms, *māsôrāh*, sometimes written *massôrāh*, and *masôreṯ*, sometimes written *massôreṯ*, designate *The Tradition*, both Scriptural and oral, in a variety of literary contexts; and whatever light can be shed on the early development of these terms may prove to be relevant to their later usage.[5]

All three terms, two of which go back to biblical language, express what may be called the *military-celestial transaction*. To explain the semantics, let me cite three examples of this in the Near Eastern languages.

Hebrew *ṣāḇāʾ* signifies "personnel, labor force, army". It is given these meanings in certain biblical sources, most notably perhaps in the priestly wilderness traditions of the book of Numbers. In other contexts, *ṣāḇāʾ* more often characterizes the heavenly "hosts", the stars and luminaries. One of the epithets of God is YHWH *ṣᵉḇāʾôṯ* "LORD of the heavenly hosts". The Akkadian cognate *ṣābu*, furnishes extensive comparative evidence on the military and administrative connotations of Hebrew *ṣāḇāʾ*, although the transaction to the heavenly sphere is best documented in the Hebrew Bible, and in literature influenced by it.[6]

A full-blown transaction, in Akkadian proper, is represented by usages of the term *manzaltu*, which attests a range of meanings from "a position at court", to "an array of battle", to "the location of a star". It derives from the root *uzuzzu*

---

[3] See B. A. Levine, "Research in the Priestly Source: The Linguistic Dimension" (Hebrew), *Eretz-Israel* 16 (*Studies in Honor of H. M. Orlinsky*), 1982.

[4] B. A. Levine, "Aramaic Texts from Persepolis", *JAOS* 102 (1972), 70f. {*VOL 2, PP. 361–77*}. This was a review article of R. A. Bowman, *Aramaic Ritual Texts from Persepolis* (*Oriental Institute Publications*, vol. 91), University of Chicago Press, 1970.

[5] Hebrew *māsôreṯ* in Ezek. 20:37 is a special problem to be discussed further on. As written, it is singular; but it may reflect an original plural. All other early pre-Rabbinic forms are plurals.

[6] See *CAD Ṣ*, 46f., s.v. *ṣābu*, for Akkadian usage.

"to stand".[7] In Hebrew, Phoenician-Punic and Aramaic we find the form *mazzal*, and in Arabic, *manzal*, all with astronomical (or astrological!) connotations.[8]

A precise semantic equivalent of Akkadian *manzaltu* is Hebrew *maᶜᵃmād* "station, rank", from the verb *ᶜ-m-d*, "to stand". It means "a position at court" (1 Kings 10:5//2 Chron. 9:4), "a rank of priests and Levites or worshippers, a military unit" (as in the War Scroll from Qumran), but also "a station of angels or heavenly bodies".[9]

Underlying this transaction is a cosmography in which earth and heaven are parallel in structure and organization, and the same would extend to the netherworld, which is a "heaven" of sorts. This concept is embodied in the Akkadian word *tamšīlu*.[10] Earth is the replica of heaven; which, of course, reflects an inversion of reality. Terrestrial structures and forms are projected into other domains of the cosmos. Heavenly temples and palaces, and cities as well, are described in literature as resembling what is real on earth. In a similar way, luminaries and planets are projected as battle arrays and stations of troops. This military and administrative transaction is especially appropriate because it conveys the atmosphere of obedience, order and subservience to authority typical of divine rule over the cosmos.

In the case of each of these three terms, and the concepts conveyed by them, the Aramaic Enoch fragments add significantly to the completeness of the semantic transaction, and also help to clarify other aspects of meaning and usage.

II

I would like to summarize what I was able to learn concerning the two terms, *degel* and *sereḵ*, in my earlier studies so as to focus on the contribution of the Aramaic Enoch fragments in each case. Subsequently, the third term, *msrh*/*msrt*, will be investigated in the light of the evidence of these fragments.

(1) *Degel*

In a Hebrew study of the language of the priestly source within Torah literature, the descriptions of Numbers 2 and 10 (cf. Num. 1:52) were discussed. These texts portray the Israelite encampments in Sinai by means of the term *degel*, which replaces the more normal designation *maḥᵃneh* for a unit of three

[7] See *CAD M*/I, 228f., s.v. *manzaltu*. Milik mentions this transaction on p. 187f.

[8] See the plural *mazzālôṯ* in 2 Kings 23:5, written *mazzārôṯ* in Job 38:32. For Phoenician-Punic, see R. Tomback, *A Comparative Semitic Lexicon of the Phoenician and Punic Languages* (SBL Dissertation Series 32), Scholars Press, 1978, 168. s.v. *MZL*. This term occurs in later Jewish literature, quite frequently.

[9] Y. Yadin, *The Scroll of the War of the Sons of Light against the Sons of Darkness* (Hebrew), Jerusalem, 1957, 184f., for a discussion of the cultic usage, and 135f., for military usage.

[10] See W. L. Moran, *Analecta Biblica* 12 (1959), 257–265, for a discussion of the typology expressed in the term *tamšīlu*.

tribes. Professor Yigael Yadin was able to define the "strength" of the *degel* in the Qumran War Scroll, where it is used to designate certain units in the military array of the sect as it goes to battle, as Prof. Yadin compares it to the Roman *cohors*.[11]

Hebrew-Aramaic *degel* (*dᵉgal*, in Aramaic) is a West-Semitism which probably entered Hebrew from the Imperial Aramaic of the Achaemenid period. (This derivation has implications for dating the wilderness traditions of Numbers, but that matter need not concern us here.) To understand the term itself, it is important to know that in the Persian mercenary colonies at Elephantine and elsewhere it indicated the basic unit of organization. It was a Persian, not a particularly Jewish organizational term. The Qumran writers clearly modeled their descriptions of military organization on the traditions of the book of Numbers and use the term *degel* alongside an entire complex of terminology taken from that biblical source.

The etymology of *degel* is less clear than its functional meanings. It has usually been derived from the verb *d-g-l*, cognate to Akkadian *dagālu* "to see, look upon", and has been explained as: "emblem, standard", i.e., "something looked upon". Closer study led me to propose that *degel* was related to *migdāl*, "watch-tower", which represents *mdgl* by metathesis. In this way, the *degel* can be defined as a military unit functioning under the command of the tower or fortress, whose chief is known as *bēl madgalti*, "the tower-commander", in ancient Hittite texts. Once it was clarified that *degel* refers in the first instance to the unit, not to emblems of the unit, certain problems were resolved. This applies to the traditions of Numbers, as well as to the dynamics of organization projected in the War Scroll.

My colleague Lawrence Schiffman directed my attention to the occurrence of *degel* in a celestial context in the liturgical composition known as *Serekh Shirot ᶜOlat ha-Shabbat*, first edited and published by John Strugnell, and which Schiffman has now studied anew.[12] The relevant passage reads in Schiffman's translation:

> (8) The quiet voice of songs of joy and the quiet blessing of God (are heard) in all the *camps* of the angels … And the voice of praises … (9) and from among all their cohorts, *dglyh*[*m*], *as they pass by*(?); all their *troops*, singing one after another, *in their position*".

Schiffman explains that the angels are "divided into military units, like Israel in the wilderness, and the sect in the War Scroll".[13] Now we have in the

---

[11] See Yadin, *op. cit.*, 46f.

[12] L. H. Schiffman, "Merkabah Speculation at Qumran: The 4Q Serekh Shirot ᶜOlat haShabbat", *Mystics, Philosophers, and Politicians, Essays in Jewish Intellectual History in Honor of Alexander Altmann*, Duke University Press (1982), 15–47.

[13] Schiffman, *op. cit.*, 35, 44, in comments to line 8f. I have restored *bᶜb*[*rm*] in line 9 on my own responsibility. It is not part of Schiffman's rendering of the passage. I have also added a final *Mēm* to *bmᶜm*[*dm*].

Aramaic Enoch fragments attestations of further semantic development, in the astronomical context.

(2) *Sere<u>k</u>*

In a study of the Aramaic inscriptions from Persepolis, found in the treasury of that fortress, and dated by the late Raymond Bowman to the first half of the fifth century B.C.E., I was able to suggest a new classification of the various vocables and forms deriving from orthographic *s-r-k*. Many of the Persepolis inscriptions begin with the formula *bsrk byrtʾ*, which at the time I translated: "In the *administration* of the Fortress". The alternative interpretation was to take *srk* as a place-name, so that we would have the common syntax, "In the fortress of GN." If all the stone utensils on which the inscriptions appear had been either manufactured or even inscribed in Persepolis, the former interpretation could be sustained; but if not, *srk* might be the name of a province or city. In any event, the comments, relevant to the meaning of *srk*, as presented in that context, are still pertinent to our discussion.

I posited two separate vocables. (a) *sere<u>k</u>*, late Aramaic *sir<u>k</u>āʾ*, "adhesion"—of the lungs etc. This term is unrelated to the one occurring in Qumran literature, and now in the Aramaic Enoch fragments. It derives from the Hebrew and Aramaic root, *ś/s-r-k*, a variation of *ś/s-r-k*, "to weave, intertwine", and hence, "to follow closely", etc. (b) *sere<u>k</u>* (*s*[e]*ra<u>k</u>*, in Aramaic), "rule, procedure, a unit constituted by command, a code," etc. This term is to be derived from Avestan *sāra*, "head, chief", related to the Aramaic official title *sārāk* in Dan. 6:3, 5. Hebrew-Aramaic *sere<u>k</u>* is translated by Greek *taxis*, which has a similar semantic range. To my knowledge, the Aramaic Enoch fragments provide the earliest celestial attestation of this term.

(3) *Msrt/msrh*

Almost everything about the verb *m-s-r* and its nominal forms, in Hebrew and Aramaic, is uncertain. As mentioned, the intricacies of this terminological complex are new to me. I was led to study it because it appears alongside, or in similar contexts with, the other two terms with which I was familiar, *degel* and *sere<u>k</u>*. Now in the Aramaic Enoch fragments, the astronomical connotation, "station, position", is confirmed for the orthographic forms *mswrt* and *msrthwn*, each of which occurs once.

In the War Scroll from Qumran, the plural *m*[e]*sôrô<u>t</u>*(?) is found twice. In 3:2–4 we read:

> And upon the trumpets of the assembly of the princes let them inscribe: "The Princes of God".
> And upon the trumpets of the divisions (*hmswrwt*) let them inscribe: "The Forces of God".

In the War Scroll 3:12 we read:

> The rule for the standards of the entire community, according to their divisions (*lmswrwtm*).

In his commentary, Professor Yadin suggests at one point that *m^{e}sôrôṯām* is parallel to *ṣiḇʾôṯam*, "their forces", in the book of Numbers and is thus a generic term for military units of various strengths, applying to all eight gradations recorded for the forces of the sect, all the way from the combined forces of the entire community to the small units of one hundred and of ten fighting men. They may all be called *m^{e}sôrôṯ*.[14]

In the Manual of Discipline (10:2f.), the plural *m^{e}sôrôṯām* exhibits the celestial transaction and refers to the positions of the constellations of the Zodiac, most probably as they make their circuit on the days of the new moon. Milik translates as follows:

> When the lights shine forth from the Holy Dwelling-Place and when they also retire to the Place of Glory, when the constellations (of the Zodiac) make (their) entrance on the days of the new moon, and their *circuit at their positions* (*msrwtm*) every new moon succeeding one after another.[15]

This passage is part of a doxology in which God, who established the order of the heavenly bodies and thereby determined the seasons and divisions of the year, is praised as ruler of the cosmos. It should be noted that most scholars found this passage unintelligible until Milik was able to interpret it on the basis of the Aramaic Enoch fragments where the celestial connotation is attested.

Before encountering the two occurrences of the verb *m-s-r* in Numbers (31:5, 16) and the possible nominal form *māsôreṯ* in Ezek. 20:37, it would be best to tackle the question of etymology head-on. The biblical forms do not occur in such clear contexts that we can translate them accurately without knowing what the verb *m-s-r* means.

This problem has been addressed by Professor Z. Ben-Ḥayyim, who attempts to explain the root-meaning of *m-s-r* in Hebrew and Aramaic on the basis of Samaritan-Aramaic evidence.[16] It is Professor Ben-Ḥayyim who has shown us just how important the Samaritan literature is for our knowledge of the Aramaic language, and our present inquiry is a case in point.

Ben-Ḥayyim finds that Rabbinic and later usages of *m^{e}sôrāh* and *m^{e}sôreṯ*, and of finite forms of the verb *m-s-r* in the sense of "tradition, to transmit, hand down", do not reflect the original root-meaning of this verb. Hoping to retrieve the earlier significance from the Samaritan Targum, from the literary composi-

---

[14] See Yadin, *op. cit.*, p. 38, n. 6; p. 40 (chart); and p. 272, in comments to War Scroll 3:3.

[15] Milik, *op. cit.*, 187. The term *t^{e}qûpāh*, "circuit", helps to define the context of the passage. It enjoys wide usage in Rabbinic literature.

[16] Z. Ben-Ḥayyim, "*Māsôrāh and Māsôre ṯ*" (Hebrew), *Leshonenu* 21 (1957–58), 283–292. An English summary appears in Z. Ben-Ḥayyim, "Tradition in the Hebrew Language", *Aspects of the Dead Sea Scrolls*, ScrHier 4, Jerusalem (1958), 211f.

tion known as *Mēmar Markā*ʾ, and from a tenth-century C.E. dictionary, *Hammēlîṣ*, with its three columns—Biblical Hebrew, Arabic and Aramaic[17]—he concludes that the root-meaning of *m-s-r* is "to count, number". He posits a semantic development parallel to that of *m-n-y*, "to count", in Aramaic. In derived forms, *m-n-y* appropriates meanings such as "to appoint", and this becomes important, because Aramaic *m-s-r* translates Hebrew *p-q-d* in the Samaritan sources, in alternation with *m-n-y*. It seems to be Ben-Ḥayyim's view that *p-q-d* signifies "to count", and that its other meanings are predicated on this basic sense. I quote from his own statement of his views:

> Even in the Aramaic of the Samaritans, the connotation of "counting" and "numbering" is not regularly expressed by the root *m-s-r*. It is reasonable to suppose that *m-s-r* was replaced, in most instances, by *m-n-y*, once its meaning as "counting" became rare; but it was not replaced wherever there was a need for two, synonymous terms for "counting", and it was not possible to suffice with the root *m-n-y* alone.[18]

This analysis is illustrated, for example, by Num. 3:22 and its rendering in the Samaritan Targum:

Samaritan version of the text:

> *up̱ᵉqûdêhem bᵉmispar kol zāḵār mibben ḥôdeš wāmāʿlāh pᵉqudêhem.*

Samaritan Targum:

> *wmswrtwn bmnyʾn kl dkr mbr yrḥ wlʿl mnyʾnyhwn.*

Professor Ben-Ḥayyim thinks that a form of *m-s-r* occurs here because in this verse, Hebrew *pᵉqûdîm* occurs twice, and contrast was required so as to avoid using the same verb, *m-n-y*, for both occurrences of that Hebrew word.

There is, of course, much more to Ben-Ḥayyim's analysis, but in principle, he derives the meaning "to count" for the verb *m-s-r* from Samaritan Aramaic, where *m-s-r* alternates with *m-n-y* to translate various forms of Hebrew *p-q-d*. On this basis, he works out a semantic theory to account for such meanings as "military unit", for *mᵉsôrāh*, from the sense of "list, register", which is predicated on the notion of counting. He claims to account for the later senses such as "transmit, hand down", by drawing on the semantic connection between "counting" and "recounting, relating", etc. He notes that Aramaic *m-s-r*, as the translation for Hebrew *p-q-d*, is translated by Arabic *jarada*, which in the form *jarīda*ᵗᵘⁿ, can mean both "a military detachment" and "a list, register, tally". Note also the Septuagint's rendering of *p-q-d* by *arithmeō*, "to count", in Num. 3:22.

---

[17] The dictionary, *Hammēlîṣ* was edited by Professor Ben-Ḥayyim. *The Literary and Oral Tradition of Hebrew and Aramaic amongst the Samaritans*, Jerusalem (1957), vol. II, 437–622.

[18] See Ben-Ḥayyim, *Leshonenu* 21 (1957–58), 287. (The translation is mine.)

There are many analogues to the semantic development posited by Ben-Ḥayyim with respect to the verb *m-s-r*, but a close examination of his own sources of evidence raises questions in our case.[19] I wish to state an alternative etymology for Aramaic and Hebrew *m-s-r* which may affect the outcome of our investigation considerably, though it may appear to focus on a subtle detail.

(1) In my opinion the root-meaning of *m-s-r* is "to detach, separate, divide". This yields nominal forms signifying: "division, position, station". I have in mind a semantic development similar to that found in such verbs as *ḥ-l-q*, *p-r-q*, *p-l-g*, *p-s-q*, *p-r-s/ś/š*, signifying "to divide, cut off, separate", all of which yield nominal forms meaning "division, section", etc.[20] On this basis, the term *m*^e^*sôrāh*/*m*^e^*sôreṯ* would be interpreted "division", as contrasted with "unit", technically speaking. In other words, the root *m-s-r* does not mean "to tie, bind", as some have explained it, but conveys the notion of achieving coherence through being *separated* from something else!

Methodologically, we should first ask ourselves how the Samaritan writers and lexicographers understood the verb *m-s-r* in Num. 31:5 and 16, the only two Torah passages where it occurs in Hebrew. I cite from *Hammēlîṣ*, letter *Mēm*, lines 384–385:

limsor	*ltgryd*	*lmmsr*
wayyimmās^e^*rû*	*wtgrdw*	*wʾbyʾrw*

Comments:

As noted by Ben-Ḥayyim, Aramaic *wʾbʾrw* in line 385 reflects the verb *b-ḥ-r*, "to select", and yields the meaning, "They were selected, recruited". The Arabic of line 385 has a V-form of the Arabic verb, *jarada*, *watajarradū*, signifying: "They were detached, set apart"—from the rest. This verb, *jarada*, especially in the II-form, and in forms derived from it, is used several times in the middle column of *Hammēlîṣ* when forms of Aramaic *m-s-r* occur in the third column, and it would be best to consider it before proceeding further.

The basic sense of Arabic *jarada* is "to denude, strip"—i.e. the land of its herbage, etc. In the II-form, this verb has a variety of connotations—"to peel off, divest (someone of clothing), prune (a tree)", etc. Most interesting in the context of the present discussion is the sense, "to detach a company (from an army)". The nominal-adjectival passive form, *jarīda*^tun^, therefore connotes "a detachment", i.e. of horsemen or the like, so-called because it was separated from another force. Arabic *jarīda*^tun^ also indicates "a palm-branch *stripped* of its leaves". This yields the sense of "tally", because palm-sticks were used for tally-

---

[19] An excellent example is Akkadian *manû*, which attests in the simple stem all the meanings of the Aramaic *m-n-y* in the derived stems. See *CAD M*/I, 221f. s.v. *manû* (v.).

[20] From *ḥ-l-q* we have *maḥlāqāh*, "division"—of priests or of soldiers (in the War Scroll) etc. From *p-l-g*, we have Late Hebrew and Aramaic *p*^e^*lûgāh*, "division of opinion, unit". From *p-r-q*, we have *pereq*, denoting a literary division and a season of the year. From *p-s-q*, we have Hebrew *pasûq* and Aramaic *pisqāʾ*, "verse, citation, pericope", etc.

ing, with notches cut into them for this purpose. The dual meaning of Arabic *jarīda*^{tun} will become relevant to our discussion of the Hebrew term, *p*^{e}*qûdîm*. Nevertheless, I find no indication that finite forms of the verb *jarada* mean "to tally, count".[21]

When we correlate all the columns of line 385, we achieve a reliable translation of Hebrew *wayyimmās*^{e}*rû*: "They were *recruited*".

Line 384 refers to Num. 31:16, where we find the enigmatic phrase *limsor maᶜal*, which has often been emended to read, *limᶜol maᶜal*, the normal usage. Precisely because the verb *m-s-r* occurs twice in Numbers 31, and only there, I prefer to resist the temptation to normalize usage and would retain the infinitive, *limsor*, in this verse. The Aramaic of line 384 merely has a simple-stem infinitive of *m-s-r*, but the Arabic has a verbal noun of the II-form, *litajrīd*. I would translate v. 16 as follows:

> These are the very ones who were involved in the Balaam incident, seceding in rebellion against the LORD.[22]

(2) Perhaps we may become more comfortable with the root-meaning, "to detach", for Aramaic *m-s-r* by reference to *Hammēlîṣ*, letter *ᶜAyin*, lines 329–330:

waᶜ^{a}*raptô*	*pltqw(!)dh*	*wtqdlnh*
waᶜ^{a}*raptô*	*pltgrdh*	*wtmsrnh*

Comments

The references are Exod.13:13, 34:20, where the clause recurs:

> *w*^{e}*ᵓim loᵓ tipdeh waᶜ*^{a}*raptô*
> If you fail to redeem (the firstling of an ass), you must sever its neck, at the back.

As Ben-Ḥayyim proposes on the basis of other sources, the Arabic verb in line 329 is *qaddaᵓ*, "to cut off, chop off", and not a form of *q-w-d*, "to lead, conduct".[23] The Aramaic of that line seems to fit exactly. It has a denominative from Aramaic *q*^{e}*dāl*, "neck", just as the biblical text has a denominative from *ᶜôrep*, "the back of the neck". It is line 330 that puzzled Ben-Ḥayyim, as it had earlier scholars. The Arabic has a II-form of the verb *jarada*: *faltujarrīdhu* "You shall sever it", i.e. the neck. If, then, the Aramaic has *wtmsrnh*, this clearly indi-

---

[21] On the verb *jarada* see *Lane's Arabic Dictionary, Book I*, 405–407. The meaning "newspaper" for *jarida* is modern. Note the Late Hebrew and Aramaic cognate, *g-r-d* (Job 2:8), and see J. Levy, *Wörterbuch über die Talmudim und Midraschim*, Darmstadt (1965), 1:356f.

[22] Hebrew *maᶜal* is used herein an extended sense of "rebellion", not merely with respect to cultic offences, although the sacral association remains even in later usage. Cf. Deut. 32:51, Ezek. 17:20, *passim*, and Ezra 10:2, 10, etc.

[23] Conceivably, the copyist wrote a *Waw* for a correct *Daleth*. The correct form is *faltuqaddidhu*.

cates that the verb *m-s-r* was taken also to signify, "detach, sever". So before engaging the ambiguities of the Hebrew verb *p-q-d* in its various forms, it is important to note that *m-s-r* and finite forms of Arabic *jarada* correlate effectively.

(3) The Hebrew verb *p-q-d* presents us with two ambiguities. In the first place, it enjoys a variety of connotations in the simple, and in derived, stems. Its root-meaning is most certainly not "to count", but clearly something like "to hand over, deliver, assign", and hence, "to turn one's thoughts to, take notice of", etc. This range of significances correlates with the extensive evidence available for the Akkadian cognate *paqādu*, in all stems where it occurs.[24] In certain contexts, Hebrew *p-q-d* can mean "to count", for the simple reason that counting is part of the process of arraying forces, recording, appointing, etc. That *p-q-d* is sometimes rendered by the Aramaic verb *m-n-y*, "to count" does not indicate that the root-meanings of the verbs are the same. It is necessary only to examine where *p-q-d* is in fact translated *m-n-y* in the Samaritan Targum, and in *Hammēlîṣ*, to see the difference. (See further.)

The second ambiguity concerns Arabic *jarīda*^{tun} which translates Hebrew *p*^{e}*qûdîm* in one instance. Does it denote "tally" or "detachment" in Num. 3:22, a passage already cited as part of Ben-Ḥayyim's argument? Let us examine *Hammēlîṣ*, letter *Pēh*, lines 259–260, and correlate them with the Samaritan Targum:

p^{e}*qûdêhem*	*ʿdthm*	*mnyʾyhwn*
p^{e}*qûdêhem*	*grydthm*	*mshrtwn*

Comments:

The term *p*^{e}*qûdîm* occurs twice in this verse, and we know from the Samaritan Targum that in the first instance it is translated, *mshrtwn*, and in the second, *mnyʾyhwn*, "their totals". The Arabic for the second is, as expected, a form of the verb *ʿadda* "to count", *ʿiddatuhum*, whereas the Arabic rendering of the first is *jarīdatuhum*. The difference can be explained, in my view, by the fact that the second *p*^{e}*qûdîm* introduces a numerical total and could properly be interpreted as "their totals". The first *p*^{e}*qûdîm* is more accurately rendered, "their divisions, arrays". I think, therefore, that *jarīda*^{tun} does not mean "tally" here, but "detachment". This would produce the meaning for Aramaic, *mshrtwn*, of "their divisions".

In the dictionary I note another occasion where a form of *p-q-d* is translated by the verb *m-n-y* because, in the context, the sense of counting would be appropriate. In that entry, the Arabic is not expressed by the verb *jarada*! I refer to letter *Pēh*, line 103:

bip̱qod	*ʿnd ʾḥṣ*	*bmnyn*

[24] See *AHw* 824ff., s.v. *paqādu*.

Comments

The reference is Exod. 30:12, in a passage speaking of a census. The Aramaic has *bmnyn* "while/at counting", whereas the Arabic has *ʿinda ʾiḥṣāʾ*, "upon counting" (a verbal noun of the IV-form).

Thus far, we have observed that treating *m-s-r* as having a meaning different from *m-n-y* rather than one synonymous with it has enabled us to make good sense of a number of entries in *Hammēlîṣ* by establishing correlations between the Arabic and Aramaic columns.

A strong point in Ben-Ḥayyim's argument is that in the derived stems, Hebrew *p-q-d* is translated alternatively by derived forms of *m-s-r* and *m-n-y*. The connotations in either case are equivalent: "to appoint, be appointed", etc. Does this mean, however, that the root-meanings of *m-s-r* and *m-n-y* are the same? It is often the case, after all, that similar ultimate connotations can be arrived at by different semantic routes. For example, Hebrew *p-q-d* ends by signifying "to count" in certain contexts, while Aramaic *m-n-y* begins with that meaning; the same is true of Akkadian *manû*. Unless it can be shown that the root-meaning of *m-s-r* is "to count", who is to say whether its semantic development parallels that of *m-n-y*/*manû* or that of *p-q-d*?

A certain amount of "drift" is to be expected in various manuscripts of the dictionary and of the Samaritan Targum. True, one observes an alternation between *m-s-r* and *m-n-y* as translations of Hebrew *p-q-d*. This is not because the sense of "counting", which Ben-Ḥayyim claims is basic to the root *m-s-r*, became rare and was replaced by *m-n-y*. Rather it is because the more basic sense of *p-q-d*, conveyed more fully by *m-s-r*, has given way to a more uniform rendering, by analogy; so that more often than not *p-q-d* is understood to mean "to count". It is the virtue of the Samaritan Targum and of *Hammēlîṣ* that they do not give way to these tendencies as much as some other Targumim. I might add that in *Hammēlîṣ*, Hebrew *s-p-r*, "to count", is not translated by *m-s-r* but only by *m-n-y*.[25]

Together, the Samaritan Targum and *Hammēlîṣ* preserve the etymology of the Aramaic verb *m-s-r*, which is "to detach, divide, separate", and of the pluralized nominal form **msrt* (in various spellings), which means "divisions". It is this derivation which makes sense of the term *mᵉsôrôṯ* in the Qumran texts, including the Aramaic Enoch texts. All attestations of this term encountered thus far are plurals, just as Hebrew *pᵉqûdîm* occurs only in the plural. Plurality seems to be endemic to the term.

III

A word should be said, at this point, about the ancient crux, *māsôreṯ* in Ezek. 20:37. Some modern scholars, including Ben-Ḥayyim, would exclude it from consideration of the verb *m-s-r* and related nominal forms because of the

[25] See *Hammēlîṣ*, letter *Samekh*, lines 117–120.

morphology indicated by its pointing. They find no analogies in Hebrew for a passive form *qāṭôleṯ*.

There is a tradition in Jewish exegesis which derives *māsôreṯ* from the root *ʾ-s-r* "to bind", and posits the syncopation of the *Aleph*, *ma*(^{ʾa})*soreṯ* > *māsôreṯ*.[26] There are also variant readings posited in the versions.

I have never been satisfied with any of these approaches, especially the replacing of one otherwise unattested form by another! The pointings in the Hebrew text of the Bible, as we have it, should not always be accorded the status of originality and cannot always serve as evidence for actual morphologies. Certainly there is in this case a real possibility that the pointing *māsôreṯ* reflects later attempts to understand the word reflecting the notion of "tradition". If we are permitted to regard the pointing as secondary and concentrate on the consonantal text, it is reasonable to associate *māsôreṯ* with the verb *m-s-r*, and with the nominal form *m*^{e}*sôrôṯ*, found in the Qumran texts and in the Samaritan Aramaic sources surveyed thus far. I would therefore suggest reading *bimsôrôṯ* in Ezek. 20:37, and I would translate vs. 37–38 as follows:

> I shall make you pass under the rod, and *form you into the ranks of the covenant*. I shall purge you of those who rebel and revolt against me. I shall take them out of the lands of their sojourning, but they shall not enter the land of Israel, so that you may realize that I am the LORD.

Comments:

For those willing to accept the presence of a dittogram, I would recommend deleting *habb*^{e}*rîṯ* at the end of v. 37. This has of course been suggested many times, since that word shares no less than three consonants with the verb which opens v. 38, and it is even possible that the *Yod* in *habb*^{e}*rîṯ* represents the *Waw* in *ūbārōṯī*. I have indicated this option in separating some sections of the translation by hyphens. But the proposed translation will work either way. The pastoral metaphor of counting the flocks (Lev. 27:32) is mixed with the military-administrative organization of the people arrayed as divisions or ranks. In ch. 34, Ezekiel uses a similar pastoral metaphor, but in the context of redemption, not of divine punishment. Hebrew *hēḇîʾ b-* means, "to insert, place", and hence, "to cause to enter" ranks.

Ezekiel 20 projects a replay of the wilderness experience following the exodus from Egypt. In that early age, most of those who had come out of Egypt perished in the Sinai wilderness because of their rebellion against God. This time, the exile being over and the people liberated from the lands of their captivity, God will again deny entry into the land of Israel to most, who have also rebelled by practicing idolatry, etc. Vv. 35–36 set the scene for vv. 37–38, which

---

[26] See E. Ben-Yehudah, *Thesaurus and Lexicon of the Hebrew Language*, New York (1960), 4:3117, s.v. *māsôrāh*, and n. 1; 3140, s.v. *māsôreṯ* and note 1. Summaries of the exegesis are provided.

are climactic. The people shall be assembled in the wilderness, where God shall enter into judgment on them. V. 37 tells how the selection of the worthy and the rejection of the unworthy will take place. The exiles shall be mustered like sheep and formed into *m*ᵉ*sôrô*ṯ, "divisions, ranks", as their ancestors had been arrayed in *p*ᵉ*qûdîm*! Only this time the ranks shall not be those of a marching order for a people on the way to its land, but a method for separating the sinful from the relatively few who are to be restored to their land.

If this interpretation is acceptable, the plural *m*ᵉ*sôrô*ṯ (as I read consonantal *msrt* in Ezek. 20:27) is further and indeed earlier attestation of the term found in the Qumran texts. Also it provides another link with Num. 31:5, 16.

IV

The Aramaic Enoch fragments attest all three of the terms under discussion: (1) *degel*, (2) *sere*ḵ, and (3) *m*ᵉ*sôrô*ṯ, in Aramaic forms. We will cite the relevant passages in the order most conducive to their interpretation.

(1) I En. I, ii, I (pl. II):

Line (2)

> *wlʾ mʿb[ryn] bsrkn*
> They do not deviate from their *ordained course*.

Comments:

As Milik notes, *bsrkn* represents: *b*ᵉ*sirk*ᵉ*[hô]n*, a singular noun, with pronominal suffix. The verb as restored is a Pael participle of the root *ʿ-b-r*, which has the sense of "going beyond, deviating from". The Greek has *taxis* for Aramaic *s*ᵉ*ra*ḵ, again confirming the equivalence of the two terms. It is likely that *s*ᵉ*ra*ḵ occurs many times in the Aramaic Enoch. In this astronomical context, the notion of position is paramount. The text speaks of the regularity of the heavenly bodies which announce the seasons of the year.

Line (3)

> *ḥzw ldgly [qyṭh] ... wbdgly śtwʾ*
> Observe the signs (of the constellations) [of summer] and the signs (of the constellations) of winter.

Comments:

For Aramaic *d*ᵉ*gal* the Greek has *semēion*, which especially refers to the signs of the constellations. This translation reflects metonymy, whereby the term for the military unit is used to designate the standard, or emblem, of the unit. This particular usage occurs in a number of languages and has confused some scholars, who translate *degel* in Numbers and in the War Scroll as "standards". Yadin has shown that this is not accurate. The word for "standard" is *ʾôṯ*.

Whereas in the Qumran liturgy, 4Q *Serekh Shirot ʿOlat ha-Shabbat*, discussed above, the term *degel* designates a group of angels, a meaning more consonant with the military context, the usage here is more properly astronomical and again stresses the positions of the constellations as they appear at various seasons, months and days.

(2) 4Q Enastr.[b] 28 – En. 82:9–13 (pl. XXX):

Milik translates:

> [... with regard] to their Zodiacal periods, their new moons, their (daily) signs (*ldglyhwn*) ... and according to] their authority with regard to all *their stations* (*lkl msrthwn*) ... chiefs of thousands ... dividing the days ... and these are the names.[27]

Comments:

In this unfortunately fragmented passage, we find two of the terms under discussion: *dᵉgal*, and the plural form *mᵉsorāṯhôn*, "their stations". Milik renders *dᵉgal* in its immediate context as "daily signs", since the progression is from seasons, to months, to days. The sense of the text is that the periods of time as indicated by the heavenly signs are named by their jurisdiction (Aramaic: *šolṭan*—Milik translates: "authority") in their respective "stations", or one might even say "divisions". The sense is of position, as in the passage of the Manual of Discipline cited earlier.

(3) 4Q En[c] 1, i – En. 1:9 – 5:1 (Pl. IX)

> *bmswrt* [*nh*]*wryhwn*
> In the *stations* of their lights.

This is the plural construct form *bimsôrāṯ-*. The immediate context tells us that the luminaries do not alter their courses but remain in their proper positions. This further illustrates the spatial emphasis.

V

The later terms, *māsôrāh* and *māsôreṯ*, in their various spellings and vocalizations, deserve a separate study. I have the impression that one semantic predication cannot account for all the meanings these terms have appropriated over the centuries. I nevertheless conclude with the observation that a root-meaning, "to separate, divide", for the verb *m-s-r* could develop into the sense of transfer

[27] The military dimension of the transaction is apparent here in the term *rēʾsîn dᵉʾalpīn*, "chiefs of thousands", which is an Aramaic rendering of the Hebrew *śārê ʾᵃlāpîm* in Exod. 19:21–25.

and transmission normally associated with the late nominal forms, *māsôrāh* and *māsôreṯ*. The semantic link is conveyed in the notion of *sharing*, of *extending* something of one's own to another. Perhaps the text of the Bible was fixed in this way, according to its *divisions*, large and small; and the oral teachings of masters were *apportioned* to disciples, who received and accepted them. The linear progression of tradition parallels the semantics of cosmography, which are more than uni-dimensional. God is ruler of the cosmos, and we perceive Him as ordering the heavens in much the same way as an earthly ruler arrays his forces.

In a certain sense, however, the inversion of reality in ancient literature may have more meaning than semantics! May He who establishes peace in His higher spheres, also establish peace on earth![28]

[28] I am grateful to my colleague at New York University, Professor David King, for his assistance with the Arabic materials. The interpretation of the Arabic sources is, however, entirely my own responsibility. I am also grateful to another of my colleagues, Professor Lawrence Schiffman, for allowing me to consult his study in advance of publication. Professor Franz Rosenthal was kind enough to read the manuscript and offer criticism. Aspects of this article were presented in the form of a paper at an international conference on Aramaic Studies held at Bar-Ilan University in January, 1980.

Lexicographical and Grammatical Notes on the Palmyrene Aramaic Texts*

Some of my recent studies have brought home to me the power of language to transcend religion, national and ethnic identity, history and political affiliation. A classic paradigm is the Aramaic language, in all its dialects and phases. During its long history, Aramaic has preserved the documented legacies of diverse communities in a common language, with the result that they all exhibit shared cultural features in vocabulary, diction, composition, typology, and substance. This is clearly demonstrated by the *Palmyrene Aramaic Texts*,[1] edited by the late Delbert Hillers, in collaboration with Eleonora Cussini, his former student and editor of the present volume dedicated to his memory. It is, therefore, appropriate to offer some notes on the Palmyrene inscriptions in honoring a cherished colleague and friend, who excelled as a Semitist with a special interest in Aramaic, and who was a prominent scholar of the Hebrew Bible.

Published as part of *The Comprehensive Aramaic Lexicon Project*, PAT greatly facilitates further investigation of the Palmyrene texts, themselves, and by extension, of other, fairly contemporary Aramaic sources. Most of the datable Palmyrene Aramaic texts are from the first three Christian centuries, and consist of honorific and funerary inscriptions, with a few legal texts, most notably the great Tariff from Palmyra. As in the case of the Tariff, many other inscriptions exhibit both Aramaic and Greek versions.

I was stimulated to embark on the present study after completing, in collaboration with Ada Yardeni, the edition of the Hebrew, Aramaic, and Nabatean-Aramaic papyri from Naḥal Ḥever on the Dead Sea (*JDS* 3), which include a large number of the so-called Bar Kokhba letters, as well as six, exceptional Nabatean legal documents.[2] Several important connections with the Palmyrene inscriptions were noted in the Commentary to the Naḥal Ḥever texts, and in hindsight, I have noticed additional points of comparison. Further study of primary Aramaic sources of the early Roman period, of all varieties, has been greatly stimulated by the publication of the comprehensive corpus of Judean Desert texts. This corpus is now available in Ada Yardeni's *Textbook of Aramaic, Hebrew, and Nabatean Texts from the Judaean Desert.*[3] Yardeni has

---

* Originally published in E. Cussini (ed.), *A Journey to Palmyra: Collected Essays to Remember Delbert R. Hillers* (CHANE 22; Leiden: Brill, 2005), pp. 103–117. Reprinted with permission from Brill.

[1] Hillers-Cussini 1996.

[2] See Yadin *et al.* 2002; henceforth *JDS* 3.

[3] Yardeni 2000; henceforth: *TDT*.

edited the corpus, providing a Glossary-Concordance, Bibliography, analysis of script traditions, and translations of texts. The reader is further directed to the recent editions of Greek papyri from the Judean Desert, mostly of a legal character, prepared by Naphtali Lewis (1989), and Hannah M. Cotton (1997). The Palmyrene Aramaic inscriptions also reveal considerable affinity to literary sources composed in the contemporary Jewish languages, Post-Biblical Hebrew, and Jewish Aramaic, Palestinian and Babylonian, as preserved in the vast corpus of Rabbinic literature. There are even connections with Late Biblical Hebrew that should be brought to light. As we know, Post-Biblical Hebrew is infused with Aramaic features, not the least in its vocabulary, and yet its value as a resource for the study of Aramaic language and literature in late antiquity has not been fully utilized. The brief comments to follow are a product of a fresh, albeit brief look at the Palmyrene Aramaic inscriptions, with a view toward highlighting certain of their comparative links. The richness of the Palmyrene inscriptions invites much further investigation.

Grammatical Notes

I. Use of the Paᶜᶜel *(D-Stem) in Palmyrene Aramaic*

The D-stem appears to be well attested at Palmyra, as evidenced by the examples listed here of verbs in the D stem, or forms based on it, culled from the PAT Glossary. Quite possibly, several additional forms which have been parsed as G-stems (= *Peᶜal*), could just as well be taken as D-stems (= *Paᶜᶜel*).This option is by no means compelling, and is merely offered for consideration. If, however, these possibilities are accepted, the list of forms based on the D-stem at Palmyra would be significantly augmented. Surveying usage of the D-stem at Palmyra will afford, in any event, an opportunity to comment on the meanings of the forms, themselves.

a) D-stem verbs

[Note: This list is not complete. Several unclear forms, and forms of uncertain meaning are omitted].

(1) *brk* v. "to bless." Comparative Semitic evidence indicates the D-stem, even though this root evidences etymological and morphological problems. The Aramaic G-stem passive participle, *bryk* "blessed," frequent at Palmyra, predicates a G-stem.

(2) *zbn* v. "to sell. The D-stem is confirmed by immediate context and general Aramaic usage, as well as by morphology in some instances. For Judean Desert legal texts, see Yardeni 2000, *TDT* II:47–48, s.v. *zbn*, *Paᶜᶜel.*

(3) *ḥdt* v. "to renew, restore, install." The sense is confirmed by immediate context, and by parallel usage in the cognate Semitic languages, which share a common typology. In East Semitic, cf. Akkadian D-stem *uddušu* "to renew" and derived forms (*CAD E*, 30–33), often in the context of building repairs and renovations. A similar typology is evident in West Semitic, and is at home in

Phoenician-Punic *ḥdš* (*Piʿʿel*). Cf. *DNWSI*, 350; Krahmalkov 2000:176; and in Late Biblical Hebrew, where the *Piʿʿel ḥiddēš* likewise occurs in the context of renovation (2 Chron 15:8 [altar], 24:4, 12 [temple]).

(4) *ṭll* v. "to roof over"—a chamber. Cf. *ṭṭlyl* "ceiling" (below, under III, a), probably also: *mṭlh* "portico." The D-stem is denominative of *ṭll* (=*ṭĕlāl*) "shade, protection," thus: "to provide shade." Perhaps cf. the Ugaritic substantive *mẓll*, based on the D-stem participle; a parallel word for *bt* "dwelling," and *mṯb* "seat, dwelling," deriving from *ẓl* "shadow, protection," hence: "covered structure" (Whittaker 1972:287). Also note the Akkadian D-stem *ṣullulu* "to roof (a building)," and related forms, attested from Old Babylonian on (*CAD Ṣ*, 239–240, s.v. *ṣullulu* A), and cf. rare JPA *ṭll* "to cover, screen" (*DJPA*, 225).

(5) *ṣbt* v. "to ornament." Presumably, this is denominative of the verb *ṣby* "to desire," nominal: *ṣbw* "object, desired object," yielding Palmyrene *tṣby*, *tṣbw* "ornament," literally, "a desired object" (see under III, a). This meaning reflects a well known typology, whereby what is desired comes to mean almost any object, or affair, for that matter. Hence, *ṣbt* is a D-stem form, meaning literally: "to render desirable," with causative force.

(6) *qdš* v. "to consecrate." Common Semitic usage of D-stem, confirmed by morphology.

(7) *qrb* v. " to offer." The D-stem is characteristic of Palmyrene Aramaic, in cultic context, and is attested in other Aramaic dialects (*DJPA*, 502, Levy IV:369), in Achemenid Aramaic and at Hatra (*DNWSI*, 1028), whereas Hebrew most often employs the *Hiphʿil* for this meaning.

(8) *šmš* v. "to serve." See below, under Comparative Vocabulary with the Judean Desert Texts.

(9) *tqn* v. "to prepare, set up." See below, under Comparative Vocabulary with the Judean Desert Texts.

b) Nouns and adjectives based on the D-stem

[Note: Normally, the forms listed here are not explicitly identified as D-stem in the PAT Glossary.]

(1) *ḥṭyʾ* n. "fine, penalty." This term occurs in the same clause as the verb *ḥwb* "to owe." Thus, *dy yḥwb ḥṭyʾ* "that he shall owe a penalty." (See the next entry for references). The literal meaning is: "that which removes the offense," expressing the privative function of the D-stem. The same term occurs in the Nabataean tomb inscriptions (Healey 1993:219), s.v. H 34, line 11: *dy ʾyty ʿlwhy ḥṭyʾh* "that he shall bear a fine" (literally: "That there shall be upon/against him a fine"). Healey (*ibid.*, 224) discusses this term, calling attention to Ezra 6:17 where we have the *Paʿʿel* infinitive construct *leḥaṭṭāyāʾ* (*Qere*: *lĕḥaṭṭāʾāh*) "to expiate," literally: "to remove the sin." The point of stressing the literal meanings is to establish that *ḥṭyʾ* is, indeed, based on the D-stem. It is probable that Arabic forms of the cognate root derive from Aramaic.

(2) *ḥyb* adj. "owing, obliged." This adjective (= *ḥayyāb*) is constructed on the *qaṭṭāl* formation, from the root *ḥ-w-b*. (See below under Comparative Vocabulary with the Judean Desert Texts, s.v. *ḥwb* v.).

(3) *mmzgn* n. "mixer," n. The *Paᶜᶜel* participle + the affix: *ān*, serves as *nomen agentis*.

(4) *mpmsy* n. "guardian, foster parent." See below, under Comparative Vocabulary with the Judean Desert Texts.

(5) *mšmš* n. "officiant." See above, under D-stem Verbs, *šmš* v.

(6) *qšt* n. "archer." This is the *qaṭṭāl* form (= *qaššāt*), known in Biblical Hebrew (Gen 21:20), and generally in the Semitic languages, and serves as a *nomen agentis*.

(7) *tyr* adj. "compassionate" (= *tayyār*), the *qaṭṭāl* form based on the D-stem, from *t-w/y-r* "to turn, return." Hence: "the one who turns back"—from his wrath; namely, the compassionate God (as suggested by Y. Muffs, in a personal communication). For the Akkadian background see further in Muffs (1969:132). Note the composite divine epithet *rḥmnᵓ wtyrᵓ* "merciful and compassionate (PAT 1911, line 2).

c) Possible D-stem forms

(1) *ḥsr* v. "to spend, spend on." The context is that of a donation, where it is said of the donor: *wḥsr lhwn mn kysh* "and he spent on them from his (own) purse." *DNWSI*, 394, ḥsr$_1$, correctly questions whether this isn't really a *Paᶜᶜel* form after all. The sense of "spending" derives from the notion of incurring loss, of diminishing a quantity, or volume. We would literally translate: "And he incurred loss for them from his own purse." JPA attests the D-stem in the sense of "removing, decreasing" (*DJPA*, 211), and the Rabbinic sources, in Post-Biblical Hebrew and Aramaic, attest many examples of the D-stem in the sense of "creating a lack, leaving something out" (Levy II:91).

(2) *ḥšb* v. "to reckon, compute." The form that occurs is infinitival *lmtḥšbw*, more likely reflexive of the D-stem than of the G-stem, hence, the *Ithpaᶜᶜal* rather than the *Ithpeᶜel*. The immediate context is the assessment of taxes. Biblical Hebrew attests the D-stem in the required sense. Thus, Lev 25:27: *weḥiššab ᵓet šĕnê mimkārô* "He shall reckon the years since his sale," and also cf. 2 Kings 12:16: *wĕlōᵓ yĕhaššĕḇû ᵓet hāᵓănāšîm* "They did not keep check on the men." Also note the operative D-stem in JPA (*DJPA*, 216), and in Post-Biblical Hebrew, where we also find nominal *ḥiššûb* "calculation," in an astronomical context (Levy II:120–121). SA is revealing in this case, where both the *Paᶜᶜel* and the *Ithpaᶜᶜal* are attested (*DSA*, 298); in fact, the SA *Paᶜᶜel* translates the Hebrew *Piᶜᶜel* of Lev 25:27, cited just above. CPA also attests the *Ithpaᶜᶜal* (*CCPA* I, Glossary, 258).

(3) *nṣb* v. "to erect." The G-stem in verbal forms, if actually attested, would likely be stative in meaning, namely "to stand, stand erect" rather than active-transitive/causative-factitive "to erect, set up." The frequent Hebrew *Niphᶜal*, *niṣṣāb* "standing" reflects this. To express the sense of "to erect, set up" Phoeni-

cian-Punic uses the *Yiphʿil* (Krahmalkov 2000, 334; s.v. *NṢB* I), and Biblical Hebrew uses the *Hiphʿil*. The Hebrew nominal forms *maṣṣāb*, "station," and *maṣṣēbâ* "stele," are based on the *Hiphʿil*, and designate what has been erected, whereas such forms as Phoenician-Punic *NṢB*, Hebrew *nĕṣîḇ*, Syriac and Palmyrene *nṣbh*, are based on the G-stem, and designate what is "standing." So, there are noun forms based on the G-stem. The presentation in *DNWSI*, 749–750 is non-committal. I have taken the Deir ʿAlla passage (Combination I, line 14), cited in *DNWSI*, as representing the *Piʿʿel*: *wnṣbw šdyn mwʿd* "And the Shadday-gods have set up a council" (Levine 1993:244, 249). This has not been accepted by most investigators who suggest that *wnṣbw* is a *Niphʿal* form: "and they were standing in an assembly," or the like. El-Amarna *naṣābu* (*CAD N*, 33) "to settle (?)" [Gt] reflects the stative sense of "being situated, standing." The problem is that the *Piʿʿel*/*Paʿʿel* of the verb *nṣb* is otherwise unattested, unless we include Deir ʿAlla and Palmyrene *nṣb* in this category. Interestingly, A. Tal (*DSA*, 541–542) attributes all meanings attested for *n-ṣ-b* in Samaritan to a root meaning "to plant, set up, establish, collect." This is unlikely; it is more likely that there has been contamination with the homophonic Aramaic verb *nṣb* "to plant" (*DJPA*, 358–359; *LS*, 442; *CCPA* I, Glossary, 276). It is better to preserve the distinctness of the two roots. There is also the matter of how to classify forms of the *primae-yod* realization of the same root, namely, *yṣb*. G-stem forms of *y-ṣ-b* are stative in force in Jewish Babylonian Aramaic, whereas the same dialect, together with Biblical Hebrew, attest *Paʿʿel* and *Piʿʿel*. *Hithpaʿʿel* forms (Baumgartner 1967–, 408; Levy I:256). Dan 7:19 attests an Aramaic *Paʿʿel* infinitive construct *lĕyaṣṣāḇāʾ* "to make firm," hence: "ascertain (the meaning)." Notwithstanding the many problems raised by *nṣb* and its alternate realization, *yṣb*, I would argue for the *Paʿʿel* stem in Palmyrene, and at Deir ʿAlla, and seek to make certain that we haven't overlooked it elsewhere.

(4) *špr* v. "to be good to, to do good to." See below, under Comparative Vocabulary with the Judean Desert Texts.

d) A possible G-stem form identified as D-stem

pšq v. "to make clear, show, explain." This verb is expressed in most other Aramaic dialects and in Post-Biblical Hebrew in the G-stem, and is realized phonetically as *psq*. The sense in Palmyrene is established by the Greek of the Tariff text: *diasaphēsantos*, from *diasapheou* "to explain." At Hatra we find the G-stem in the sense of "to decide" (*DNWSI*, 946). Actually, the *Grundbedeutung* of this verbal root in Aramaic is "to cut," which typologically may connote "deciding." (Cf. the legal connotations of the root *g-z-r* "to cut"). I therefore question the basis for classifying *psq* as a *Paʿʿel* form in Palmyrene, since G-stem forms (and noun forms based on the G-stem) abound in Post-Biblical Hebrew and in other dialects of Aramaic, where we encounter meanings such as: "to specify, determine" allocations, rulings in law, and the like (Levy IV:77–81; *DSA*, 603). In fact, SA attests a noun form based on the G-stem: *pĕšîkû* (feminine absolute) "allocation." Semantically, "to explain, make clear" is a reasonable predication of "to cut, decide, specify," especially in the context of a tariff where the subject is the computing of a tax liability. Having said this, SA does attest a D-stem with the sense of "to split, divide," translating Hebrew *nittaḥ* "to dismember, cut up-" said of animals (Gen 29:17), and *bātar* "to cut up-" said of birds (Gen 15:10). There is, however, no apparent need to use the intensive D-stem in order to secure the sense of "clarify, explain."

II. An example of aspectual change

The Palmyrene causative *ybn*[*w*]*n* "they will determine" is unusual in Aramaic, and in Biblical Hebrew, where the verbal root *b-y-n* enjoys wide distribution. In Biblical Hebrew the verbal root *b-y-n* normally means "to discern, understand, comprehend." As such, it anticipates a result that accrues to the subject of the verb, who achieves understanding, not to its object. Understanding something thus affects the one who understands, not what is understood. This aspect applies whether the verb is conjugated in the simple (*Qal*), passive-reflexive (*Nipḥʿal*), or causative (*Hipḥʿil*) stems. How interesting it is, therefore, that in Palmyrene Aramaic the causative stem is once attested with an active-transitive meaning: "to cause to understand, to lay down in rules" (*DNWSI*, 152, s.v *byn*$_1$). This is so in the Tariff (PAT 0259), Aramaic text, I, line 8: *dy ybn*[*w*]*n mdʿm dy lʾ msq nmws* "who are to determine anything that is not entered in the law." The meaning is confirmed by the Greek version, which has: *diakreinontas*, and comes in the charge to the council, who must clarify rulings in cases not covered by existing written laws.

Actually, the active-transitive sense is quite well attested in Late Biblical Hebrew, undoubtedly under the influence of Aramaic, except that, in this case, Hebrew preserves more than Aramaic does! Thus, Dan 8:16: *Gaḇrîʾēl! hāḇēn lĕhallāz ʾet hammarʾeh* "Gabriel! Explain to that person the vision" (literally: "enable that person to understand," with accusative *lamed*). Daniel had just been relating that he sought to understand (*waʾăbaqqĕšâ bînâ* "and I sought understanding") the vision, when he heard a voice commanding the angel to explain it to him! Also, Dan 11:33 *ûmaśkîlê ʿam yāḇînû lārabbîm* "And the knowledgeable among the people will teach the public (accusative *lamed*)." This is the role of the Levites, according to 2 Chron 35:3: "Then he (Josiah) said to the Levites who are the teachers of all Israel (*hammebinim lekol Yisraʾel*)." Cf. 1 Chron 25:8: *mēḇîn ʿim talmîd* "teacher with student." In Nehemiah (8:3, 7–9) there is further mention of such *mēḇînîm*, for the most part Levites (and cf. 1 Chron 27:32). Psalm 119 attests the *Hipḥʿil* imperative, *haḇînēnî* "Make me understand," a call addressed to God, no less than six times! Jewish Aramaic, Palestinian and Babylonian, attest a modulated *ʾApḥʿel* form: *ʾănî ʾôḇîn wĕʾādûn lĕpānêkā* "I will give (you) to understand and rule (on the matter) before you (*apud* Levy I:219, citing BT *ʿAbodah Zarah* 41a, and see *DJPA*, 96).

III. Some Interesting Morphologies in Palmyrene Aramaic

a) Nouns with Tau*-preformative (taqṭîl)*

Three *taqṭîl* forms occurring in the Palmyrene texts have already been noted: *ṭṭlyl* (= *taṭlîl*) "ceiling"; *tšmyš* (= *tašmîš*) "use"; and *tṣby*/*tṣbw* (= *taṣbî*/*taṣbû*) "ornament." Of the three, it is the form *tšmyš* that invites discussion, occurring twice in the Tariff, in an administrative context. The D-stem of this verb has already been discussed above. Actually, the meaning "administration" suggested by Teixidor is compatible with known Aramaic usage. Syriac attests a similar *tau*-form: feminine *tešmeštāʾ* "service, ministration" (*LS*, 788). Also note SA *tšmyš*, and feminine *tšmy*(*š*)*h*, and even abstract *tšmy*(*š*)*w* in the sense of "work, labor" (*DSA*, 913–914). Post-Biblical Hebrew and the Jewish dialects of Aramaic attest a specialized meaning: "sexual relations" but also the more common sense of "utility", hence: "a useful object, utensil" (*DJPA*, 593). Thus, we find such terms as *tašmîšê miṣwâ* "articles used in the performance of a religious commandment," and *tašmîšê qĕdûšâ* "articles used in the performance of the cult, or worship" (Levy IV:676).

b) The title rbn "chief; leader"

The form *rbn* (*rabbān*) represents *rabb* + *ān*, the affix, generating a *nomen agentis*. Palmyrene attests meanings probably having to do with the priesthood, and clearly with the market place. Thus, *rbnšqw* "term as *agoranomos*;" namely, "term as chief of the market." We also encounter other roles, including caravan leader, one in charge of water sources, and leader of the *symposium*, the *mrzḥ*, a very honored position. Palmyrene shows a trend toward abstract forms, in this case absolute *rbnw*, construct *rbnwt-* "term of leadership; office of leader" (cf. Post-Biblical Hebrew *rabbānût* "position of leadership)." The form *rabbānāʾ* is attested in Syriac (*LS*, 707), and *rabbān* in JPA (*DJPA*, 514) with the meaning of "teacher, scholar." In the Rabbinic sources, this title is used to designate several of the Patriarchs of Palestinian Jewry, and serves as a title introducing the personal name. Examples are: *Rabbān Gamlîʾēl* (the Elder), *Rabbān Šimʿôn ben Gamlîʾēl, Rabbān Yôḥānān ben Zakkāʾy*, and for academic leaders of similar status in Babylonia: *Rabbānāʾ ʾAšši, Rabbān ʿUqbāʾ*. Levy (IV:416–417) outlines the information for the Palestinian and Babylonian sources.

There are also plural forms: *rābbānîn* (generally Palestinian Aramaic), and *rabbānān* (generally Babylonian Aramaic), often used collectively to designate the collegium of Sages. Titles compounded with *rab* (Common Semitic) exhibit a wide range of meanings, as noted by Hillers and Cussini, all expressing the basic sense of "chief, master." Characteristically, religious communities, Jewish and Christian, appropriated guild terminology, and administrative titles to designate religious offices.

Comparative Vocabulary with the Judean Desert Texts

Following are several terms common to Palmyrene Aramaic and the Judean Desert texts. In each case, we observe how one group of sources illuminates the other.

(1) *ʾsr* v. "to bind, obligate one's self." The one occurrence at Palmyra is in a broken funerary inscription, PAT 2774, which, for the most part, consists of personal names. In its final preserved line, line 12, it reads: [...] *wʾsrw whqymw byny*[*hwn*] "[...] and they made a binding agreement between them (literally: "and they bound and they established between them"). The two verbs in sequence, *wʾsrw whqymw*, are best taken as hendiadys. This reading is suggested by the formulary of the Samaria Papyri found at Wadi Daliyeh, dating from the fourth century B.C.E.[4] In those slave sales, we find standard provisions, stated as follows: (1) *wrʿw ḥd mn ḥd ʾsrʾ bynyhm wznh ʾsrʾ hqymw bynyhm* "And they were mutually satisfied with the binding agreement between them. And this is the binding agreement (which) they established between them" (Papyrus 1, lines 4–6). (2) *ʾw ʾšnh bʾsrʾ znh zy hqymt ʿmk* "Or, if I renege on this binding agreement that I have established with you" (*ibid.*, lines 6–8). (3) *lqbl ʾsrʾ znh hqymw bybyhm* "In accordance with this binding agreement (which) they established between them.[5] In effect, the Palmyrene formulary is merely a variant of the formulas occurring in the Samaria Papyri, wherein the causative *hqym* "to establish, enact" is the operative verb. The term *ʾsr* "binding agreement" (also: "edict") has a long history, and occurs in the Hebrew, Aramaic, and Nabatean-Aramaic documents from Naḥal Ḥever (*JDS* 3, 50–51). In Numbers 30, the Torah chapter dealing with vows, it occurs as *ʾĕsār*, the normal Aramaic form (Dan 6:8, *et passim*), but is also vocalized *ʾissār* (Levine 2000:427–430; Levine 1999; *DNWSI*, 90–92, s.v. $ʾsr_1$ and $ʾsr_2$).

Mirabile dictu, this is the first time that I have taken the Palmyrene attestation into consideration! What is most interesting about the Palmyrene formulary is that it employs a finite verbal form, G-stem, *wʾsrw* "and they bound," which fact makes it directly relevant to the interpretation of Numbers, chapter 30, where we also have finite verbal forms. Thus Num 30:5: *weʾĕsārāh ʾašer ʾāsĕrâ ʿal napšāh* "and any binding agreement by which she had bound herself." The root *ʾ-s-r* in Aramaic is thus attested in Aramaic documents of the Achemenid period, at Elephantine, Saqqara and Wadi Daliyeh, Post-Biblical Hebrew and Aramaic, in texts of the Greco-Roman period, including at Palmyra. It seems to develop a primarily negative connotation in Rabbinic literature and in Christian texts (see *DJPA*, 67, s.v. *ʾsyr* "forbidden, prohibited," and *ibid.* 68, s.v. *ʾsr* v. "to prohibit").

(2) *br*/*b*(*r*)*t ḥry* n. "freedman, freedwoman." Cussini discusses the feminine designation *bt ḥry*, rendered in Latin as *liberta*, "freedwoman" in PAT 0246.[6]

---

[4] Cross 1985, pp. 7–17; Cross 1988, pp. 17–26; Gropp *et al.* 2001.

[5] *Ibid.*, lines 10–11; and see Cussini 1993, pp. 245–246.

[6] Cussini 2004.

The Latin identifies the deceased woman in question, Regina, as *liberta et coniuge* "freedwoman and wife" of the named man Barates, whereas the Aramaic mentions only that she is *bt ḥry*. Clearly, Regina was the wife of Barates. Cussini takes note of the difficulty in regarding Regina as a manumitted slave woman, and yet that is what Latin *liberta* has been taken to mean, and undoubtedly does mean, in many cases. Although the Latin terms *libertus* and *liberta* are of wide use, the equation: *bt ḥry* = *liberta* is unique to this inscription. A similar problem confronted the editors in interpreting P.Yadin 10 from Naḥal Ḥever, the marriage contract (*kĕtubbâ*) of the well known Babatha, executed at her second marriage and dated in the early second century C.E. In that document the precise formula is: *mzwn ʾnth brt ḥwryn*, which is translated "the (fitting) sustenance of a free (= married) woman." In commenting on P.Yadin 10, the editors called attention to a highly unusual feature of a Greek marriage contract, dated 310 B.C.E., from Elephantine, in Egypt, wherein the husband is designated *eleuthéros* "free man," and the wife *eleuthéra*, and it is further stated: "Let Heracles provide to Demetria everything pertaining to a free wife (*gunaikì eleuthérai*)."[7] The sense is not entirely clear, but "free" may mean "free born," rather than "freed, manumitted." Or, it may mean that the man and woman in question were free and unencumbered to marry; in the case of the woman, that she was no longer under the jurisdiction of her father, or pledged to another man. In any event, "free woman" is preferable to "freedwoman," its having no necessary connotation of prior slave status. A possible resolution of the difficulty may be to equate all three designations: thus, Aramaic *ʾnth brt ḥwryn* = Greek *gŭné eleuthéra* = Latin *liberta et coniuge* "a free wife" (taking the Latin as hendiadys).

This leads one to propose that in PAT 0095, *brt ḥry* also means "free wife," and implies no previous condition of servitude. There we read that two women cede a number of burial niches. One of the women is designated *brt ḥry* PN, and it is stated that she is *mprnsytʾ* "the executor" of that man's son. Here, too, the sense may be "free wife," namely that she was simply his wife. See the discussion in *JDS* 3, 48, and also see below, no. 5, *mprnsy*.[8]

(3) *ḥwb* v. "to owe" adjectival *ḥyb* "owing, obligated." The adjectival form has already been noted above. The verbal form in the G-stem occurs in two clear contexts (a) in the rules of the symposium, PAT 0991, line 11: *dy yḥwb ḥṭyʾ dd*[*ynrn* ...] "that he shall owe the penalty of denarii X-number." (b) A provision in a funerary inscription: "Anyone who installs any outsider in the tomb" *yḥwb lpsqws zwzyn ʾ*[*lp*...] "shall owe the treasury 1[000] zuz." In a Nabatean-Aramaic sale contract from Naḥal Ḥever (dated in the twenty-eighth year of Rabʾel II = 97/98 C.E.) one of the parties states, in the 1st person: "And if I, PN ... will deviate from this (agreement) without authority" *ʾḥwb lk ʾnt* PN *dnh* ... *kl dmy zbnyʾ ʾlh* "I shall owe you, this same PN the entire price of these purchases"

---

[7] *JDS* 3, p. 135, and cf. Farber 1996, p. 409 [D2 = P. Elephantine 1, lines 4–5], and note 1.

[8] This interpretation of P. Yadin 10 and of PAT 0095 had been suggested by Hannah M. Cotton.

(*JDS* 3, 209–210, s.v. P.Yadin 2:14–15). The *ʾAphʿel* participle, masculine singular occurs in P.Yadin 4, line 14 (*JDS* 3, 250–251) in a legal agreement: *mwdʾ wmtḥyb ʾnh* "I acknowledge liability" (hendiadys). Also note the *Ithpaʿʿal* participle in CPA (*CCPA* I, Glossary, 1, 255). Various forms of this root occur frequently in later phases of Aramaic.

(4) *mwdʾ* v. "declare, acknowledge" (the *ʾAphʿel* participle). This verb, in several related forms, characteristically introduces binding statements in legal documents that serve to verify sales, leases, loans, debt obligations, receipts of payment, and the like. Hillers and Cussini (PAT, Glossary, p. 369, s.v. *ydy* v.) cite the occurrence of this term in the Syriac Bill of Sale from Dura Europos, studied by J. Goldstein (1966), and others. This document is now available in Drijvers and Healey 1999:232–236, as P1, along with two, additional Syriac legal texts (as P2, P3), studied by J. Teixidor and S. Brock, all of which employ this terminology. What is more, the Judean Desert texts, in Hebrew, Aramaic, and Nabatean-Aramaic, attest this terminology quite regularly, as do their Greek counterparts, where the operative form is *homologéô* "I acknowledge," a feature of the Greek papyri from Naḥal Ḥever, edited by N. Lewis (1989) and by Hannah M. Cotton (1997).

This is a case where the editors of the Naḥal Ḥever papyri failed to adduce the relevant evidence from Palmyra, or from the Syriac legal papyri from Dura Europos, for that matter. See *JDS* 3, p. 60, in the Commentary on P.Yadin 45: line 6; and cf. P.Yadin 4, line 14; *JDS* 3, pp. 250–251. Notwithstanding these omissions, the discussion provided in *JDS* 3 directs the reader to provisions in Rabbinic law which are of considerable interest. The single, clear attestation of this typology in the Palmyrene texts comes in a document of cession, wherein a woman "declares" (feminine participle) to a certain person (*mwdyʾ l*PN), a Nabatean, to judge by his name and patronymic, that she has received a specified payment from him, in return for which she has ceded to him a half of her share of a burial cave (PAT 1791). Interestingly, P1 from Dura Europus also concerns receipt of payment by a woman who states: "I acknowledge (*mwdynʾ*) ... that I have received (*dqblt*)" a sum of silver, in consideration of which she has sold her female slave to a certain man. P2 concerns a loan, and P3—an acknowledgement of a lease, which is the very subject of P.Yadin 44–46 at Naḥal Ḥever!

(5) *mprnsy* n. "guardian, foster mother," and the denominative verb, *prns* "to provide." The given noun form, feminine, determined: *mprnsytʾ* is based on the *Paʿʿel* participle. As explained just above, in connection with the designation *bt ḥry*, the woman in question was most likely a guardian over her husband's son. Palmyrene also attests a denominative. Of the good deeds of a certain man it is said: *wprns brmnhwn bkl [s]bw klh rbʾ wzʿrʾ* "And he provided, apart from these (matters), for every possible need, great or small" (PAT 0261, lines 3–4). The quadriliteral, *parnās* "executor, administrator," occurs in the Hebrew and Aramaic texts from Naḥal Ḥever and Murabbaʿât, as well as on lead weights, and is discussed in considerable detail in *JDS* 3, 48, in the Commentary on P.Yadin 44, a Hebrew legal text. This evidence relates to administrators who operated as part of the Bar Kokhba regime in Judea during the period of the re-

volt against Rome in 132–135+ C.E. The information provided by the Palmyrene texts was helpful, pointing to the private role of such agents, who have status in Rabbinic law, whereas the Judean Desert evidence reflected a public role, for the most part. An Aramaic deed of gift from Naḥal Ḥever, P.Yadin 7:16 attests the denominative, D-stem form *pirnûs* "support," and Rabbinic sources attest, in addition, feminine *parnāsâ*, with the same meaning (*DJPA*, 448; Levy IV:120–121). J. Naveh (1978:97, no. 63:2), discusses an Aramaic synagogue mosaic from Noarah, near Jericho, probably dating to the fifth or sixth century C.E, where we read: [*d*]*kyr lṭb bnymyn prns*[*h*] *br ywsh* "May he be [rem]embered for good, Binyamin, the administrator, son of Yose."

(6) *šmš* v. "to serve." Cf. above, the noun *mšmš* "officiant," based on the D-stem participle. In P.Yadin 7, lines 28–29, an Aramaic deed of gift from Naḥal Ḥever, we read that a wife, the recipient of the gift, was required to serve her husband: *wmšmšh yty mn qṣt mtnt*ʾ *d*ʾ "and she shall be serving me from part of this gift." (*JDS* 3, 84–85, Commentary, *ibid.* 107). One questions Krahmalkov (2000, 472), who lists Phoenician-Punic *ŠMŠ*, v., as a G-stem. D-stem verbal forms are frequent at Hatra (*DNWSI*, 1168), and, along with forms derived from the D-stem, abound in JPA and CPA (*CCPA* I, Glossary, 295; *DJPA*, 558–559), as well as in Post-Biblical Hebrew (Levy IV:582), and in SA (*DSA*, 912–913). A Syriac lease found near Dura Europos (Drijvers and Healey 1999:244, s.v. P3:17) has the *Nithpa*ʿʿ*al* form *wnštmš* (= *wĕništammāš*) "he will have use of."

(7) *špr* v. "to do good to, to be good to." The *Pa*ʿʿ*el* participle is attested in P.Yadin 6, line 9, in a Nabatean tenancy agreement: *wmšpr wmh*ʾ "and making improvements and *keeping fruitful*" (*JDS* 3, pp. 260–261, Commentary, p. 265). Reference is to the obligation of a tenant to maintain the land he has undertaken to work. The unique instance of the G-stem in Biblical Hebrew has stative force. Thus Ps 16:6: ʾ*ap naḥălātî šapĕrâ lî* "Indeed, my estate is lovely to me." Note the personal name, *Šiprāh* (Exod 1:15). (The *Pi*ʿʿ*el* may be attested once in Job 26:13, with direct object, but this remains uncertain). Forms of this verbal root probably represent early Aramaic input in Biblical Hebrew. Also cf. adjectival Phoenician-Punic: *špr* (defective for *šappîr*; Krahmalkov 2000:479). In most dialects of Aramaic, the G-stem has stative force, whereas to express the factitive-causative, Jewish Aramaic dialects employ the ʾ*Aph*ʿ*el* (Levy IV:599; *DJPA*, 564), as the Samaritan clearly does (*DSA*, 924), in forms like ʾ*ašpîr* "he did well, acted correctly" (ʾ*Aph*ʿ*el*, 3rd masculine singular perfect). In any event, the G-stem for the Palmyrene is less likely in context.

(8) *tqn* v. "to prepare, set up." As used, we certainly have a D-stem, not a G-stem, if comparative evidence is any indication. In the funerary inscription we read that any of the sons or cousins of the builder of the enclosed burial place "may dig and install for himself a grave (*yḥpr wytqn lh mqbrt*ʾ)." This root in the D-stem is also attested in an Aramaic letter of the Bar Kokhba period from Murabbaʿât: *wttqn* (= *wĕtĕtaqqēn*) *lhn mqwm pnw* "and set up for them a vacant place." Reference is to the storage of a delivery of wheat.[9] The D-stem also oc-

[9] Milik 1961, p. 162, s.v. Mur 44, lines 4–5; new edition in *TDT* I, 159.

curs in another Aramaic Bar Kokhba letter, P.Yadin 57, line 4: *wtqn* (= *wĕtaqqēn*) *ythn wšlḥ ythn lmḥnyh* "And prepare them, and deliver them to the encampment" (*JDS* 3, 326–327). Reference is to the myrtle, willow, and palm branches, and the citrons used in the celebration of the Tabernacles festival. The three kinds of branches had to be bundled, and that is the precise sense of "prepare" in this case. These are all simple, physical meanings.

This verb is also current in Post-Biblical Hebrew as well as in Syriac, SA, JPA, CPA, and notably in Rabbinic literature, generally (*DNWSI*, 1228; *LS*, 831–833; *DJPA*, 559–590; *DSA*, 960–961; *CCPA* I, Glossary, 297; Levy IV:663–664). What is remarkable is that the various dialects of Aramaic and Post-Biblical Hebrew developed quite a number of nominal forms with applied meanings. Of particular interest are legal terms connoting "enactment, ordinance," e.g. Post-Biblical Hebrew *taqqānâ*. The etymology of *t-q-n* remains somewhat uncertain, although it is likely that it represents a secondary formation, with *tau*-preformative, from *k-w-n* "to stand," with *kaph* expressed emphatically as *qoph*. This suggests that *t-q-n* may have served as a replacement for the verb *q-w-m* "to rise, stand," which in Aramaic legal parlance appropriates the sense of "be valid," and in the intensive and causative stems, the sense of "establish, validate, fulfill." An indication of this is the CPA form *ᵓtqnw* "rule" (*CCPA* I, Glossary, 244) which translates Hebrew *bĕrît* "covenant" in 1 Kings 8:23. In Syriac we find that *qeyomoᵓ* is the word for Hebrew *bĕrît* (*LS*, 653, s.v. *qeyomoᵓ*, meaning 5).

* * *

At Palmyra, as in other communities where Aramaic served at least as a written language, mourners of diverse backgrounds expressed the pain of loss using the same, powerful exclamation: *ḥbl* (=*ḥăḇāl*!) "Woe! Alas!" What is more, the hope for consolation was also expressed in pretty much the same way by all concerned: *dkyr bṭb* "(Be he) remembered for good/with goodness." If we were to trace the isoglosses of these locutions, and their derivatives, in Aramaic sources of Late Antiquity and subsequent periods, we would become intensely aware of the common responses of many peoples during critical passages of the life cycle. Such is the power of a shared language.

Bibliography

Baumgartner, W. *et al.*

1967– *Hebräisches und Aramäisches Lexikon zum alten Testament*, 4 vols., and Supplement. Leiden: E. J. Brill.

Cotton, Hannah M.

1997 Greek Documentary Texts. Pages 133–279 in H. M. Cotton and A. Yardeni, *Aramaic, Hebrew and Greek Documentary Texts from Naḥal Ḥever and Other Sites*. DJD 27. Oxford: Clarendon Press.

Cross, Frank Moore, Jr.

1985 Samaria Papyrus 1: An Aramaic Slave Conveyance of 335 B.C.E. Found in the Wâdi ed-Dâliyeh. Pages *7–*17 in *Nahman Avigad Volume*. Eretz Israel 18. Jerusalem: Israel Exploration Society.

1988 A Report on the Samaria Papyri. Pages 17–26 in *Congress Volume: Jerusalem 1986*. Edited by J. A. Emerton. VTSup 40. Leiden: Brill.

Cussini, Eleonora

1993 The Aramaic Law of Sale and the Cuneiform Legal Tradition. Johns Hopkins University PhD. Dissertation.

2004 Regina, Martay and the Others: Stories of Palmyrene Women. *Orientalia* 73:235–244, pl XXIII, XXIV.

Drijvers, H. J. W. and John F. Healey

1999 *The Old Syriac Inscriptions of Edessa and Osrhoene: Texts, Translations, and Commentary*. HdO 42. Leiden: Brill.

Farber, J. Joel

1996 Greek Texts. Pages 386–568 in Bezalel Porten *et al.*, *The Elephantine Papyri in English: Three Millennia of Cross-Cultural Continuity and Change*. Leiden: Brill.

Goldstein, Jonathan A.

1966 The Syriac Bill of Sale from Dura-Europos. *JNES* 25:1–16.

Gropp, Douglas M. *et al.*

2001 Wadi Daliyeh II: The Samaria Papyri from Wadi Daliyeh. DJD 28. Oxford: Clarendon Press.

Hillers, Delbert and Eleonora Cussini

1996 *Palmyrene Aramaic Texts*. Publications of the Comprehensive Aramaic Lexicon Project. Baltimore: The Johns Hopkins University Press.

Krahmalkov, Charles R.

2000 *Phoenician-Punic Dictionary*. Orientalia Lovaniensia analecta 90. Leuven: Peeters.

Levine, Baruch A.

1993 *Numbers 1–20: A New Translation with Introduction and Commentary*. AB 4. New York: Doubleday.

1999 Vowing, Oaths, and Binding Agreements: The Section on Vows in the light of the Aramaic Inscriptions (Hebrew). Pages 84–90 in *Frank Moore Cross, Jr. Volume*. Eretz Israel 26. Jerusalem: Israel Exploration Society.

2000 *Numbers 21–36: A New Translation with Introduction and Commentary*. AB 4A. New York: Doubleday.

Levy, Jacob

1963 *Wörterbuch über die Talmudim und Midraschim*. 4 vols. Darmstadt: Wissenschaftliche Buchgesellschaft.

Lewis, Naphtali
1989 *The Documents from the Bar Kokhba Period in the Cave of Letters — Greek Papyri*. Judean Desert Studies 2. Jerusalem: Israel Exploration Society, The Hebrew University of Jerusalem, The Shrine of the Book.

Milik, Jozef T.
1961 Textes hébreux et araméens. Pages 67–205 in *Les Grottes de Murabbaʿât*. DJD 2. Oxford: Clarendon Press.

Muffs, Yochanan
1969 *Studies in the Aramaic Legal Papyri from Elephantine*. Studia et documenta ad iura Orientis antiqui pertinentia 8. Leiden: Brill. Reprint: with Prolegomenon by Baruch A. Levine. HdO 66. Leiden; Boston: Brill, 2003.

Naveh, Joseph
1978 *On Stone and Mosaic* (Hebrew). Jerusalem: Israel Exploration Society.

Whittaker, Richard E.
1972 *Concordance of the Ugaritic Language*. Cambridge, MA: Harvard University Press.

Yardeni, Ada
2000 *Textbook of Aramaic, Hebrew and Nabataean Texts for the Judaean Desert*. 2 vols. Jerusalem: Hebrew University, Ben-Zion Dinur Center for Research in Jewish History.

Scholarly Dictionaries of Two Dialects of Jewish Aramaic*

Michael Sokoloff, *A Dictionary of Jewish Palestinian Aramaic of the Byzantine Period*. Second Edition. Ramat-Gan, Israel: Bar Ilan University Press; Baltimore and London: The Johns Hopkins University Press, 2002. 847 p. (1st ed. by Bar Ilan University Press, 1990)

Michael Sokoloff, *A Dictionary of Jewish Babylonian Aramaic of the Talmudic and Geonic Periods*. Ramat-Gan, Israel: Bar Ilan University Press; Baltimore and London: The Johns Hopkins University Press, 2002. 1582 pp.

The two dictionaries under review represent the product of decades of assiduous research and persistent effort on the part of Professor Michael Sokoloff of Bar Ilan University. Previously, he has contributed major works in the Aramaic field in collaboration with other scholars. There is, first of all, *A Corpus of Christian Palestinian Aramaic* (Groningen: Styx Publications, 1997), a multivolume edition of texts prepared in collaboration with Christa Müller-Kessler. This was followed by a Hebrew work, שירת בני מערבא [*Jewish Palestinian Aramaic Poetry from Late Antiquity*] (Jerusalem: Israel Academy of the Sciences and Humanities, 1999), prepared in collaboration with Joseph Yahalom. However, the dictionaries reviewed here, which represent his most ambitious projects, bear his name alone, with only technical and electronic assistance in their actual preparation provided on the part of others. Sokoloff has also published *A Dictionary of Judean Aramaic* (Ramat-Gan: Bar Ilan University, 2003), covering sources from 150 B.C.E. to 200 C.E., which includes the rich material preserved in the Aramaic papyri from the Judean Desert.

The immense scope of Michael Sokoloff's scholarly productivity, most clearly exemplified in the publication of the two dictionaries, strains the limits of comprehension. All students of the Judaic heritage owe him a special debt for facilitating the mastery of talmudic and related texts, Palestinian and Babylonian. All Semitists, of whatever area of interest, are indebted to him for affording them better access to the rich treasures of Aramaic. The present dictionaries are affiliated with the *Comprehensive Aramaic Dictionary Project*, whose editor is Professor Stephen Kaufman, a noted Aramaist on the faculty of Hebrew Union College. In the Preface to the second edition of the *Dictionary of Jewish*

* Originally published in *AJS Review* 29 (2005), pp. 131–144. Reprinted with permission from Cambridge University Press.

Palestinian Aramaic of the Byzantine Period (*DJPA*) Sokoloff lists reviews of the first edition of that volume, published in 1990, including the penetrating piece by Stephen Kaufman.[1] Another brief, largely descriptive review of *DJPA* by Siam Bhayro has just appeared.[2]

Sokoloff's two dictionaries are part and parcel of the current surge of new compendia, a development driven by computer technology, which now makes it possible to process the vast, requisite data in less than a full lifetime! In this regard, Bar Ilan University deserves much credit for its pioneering efforts in computerizing archives of Judaica, most notably the responsa literature; and these technical facilities were of great help to Sokoloff, as well. It is also important to recognize that behind Michael Sokoloff stand generations of scholars who pored over manuscripts, discovered buried epigraphy and edited their finds, and advanced our understanding of linguistic phenomena. Their efforts enabled Michael Sokoloff to compile dictionaries based on the sound readings preserved in talmudic and other manuscripts rather than on the often corrupt readings of the printed editions that had been utilized in previous dictionaries. New discoveries expanded the lexicographical corpus beyond its earlier limits, and research in Aramaic dialectology clarified long-standing problems in Aramaic lexicography. Because both of the dictionaries under review follow the same methodology, are the work of the same scholar, and cover related Aramaic dialects and textual collections, they will be reviewed jointly.

The Expanding Corpus and Dialectal Integrity

In his respective introductions, Michael Sokoloff sets forth his purpose and methodology against the background of extant dictionaries, the best of which is Jacob Levy's four-volume dictionary, *Wörterbuch über die Talmudim und Midraschim*, first published in 1875, with a second edition published in 1924 and reprinted in 1963. (Levy also contributed a principally targumic dictionary entitled *Chaldäisches Wörterbuch über die Targumim und einen grossen Theil des rabbinischen Schriftthums* [2 vols., Leipzig, 1867–68].) Levy's talmudic dictionary contains both Hebrew and Aramaic entries, so that the same root, if common to Hebrew and Aramaic, will be listed twice, once as Hebrew and once as Aramaic. As for the Aramaic entries, themselves: they are undifferentiated by dialect, as between Palestinian and Babylonian. One can be guided only by the textual sources that are cited. Sokoloff often refers to the well-known dictionary by Marcus Jastrow, *A Dictionary of the Targumim, the Talmud Babli and Yerushalmi and the Midrashic Literature* (New York, 1903). Levy's dictionaries were never translated into English, whereas Jastrow's dictionary was widely used in North America and elsewhere.

The basis for inclusion in Levy's talmudic dictionary was textual, namely, the attestation of a lexeme in the literary sources. This is not to say that Levy

[1] *JAOS* 114 (1994): 239–48.

[2] *JBL* 123 (2004): 382–85.

failed to register linguistic information pertaining to the textual entries. In fact, he did very well at this, providing suggested cognates in Syriac, Biblical Hebrew, Arabic, and of course listed loanwords from Greek and Persian. It is just that by purpose, and within the limits of critical progress in the mid-nineteenth century, his corpus of reference consisted entirely of the traditional textual sources. Indeed, the virtue of his dictionary is that it is textually complete.

The two present dictionaries are language-dialect based. Two dialects of Aramaic have been defined, Jewish Palestinian Aramaic (JPA), and Jewish Babylonian Aramaic (JBA), on an ethno-linguistic basis. This is to say that JPA is the Aramaic dialect of the Jews of Palestine during certain periods, which differed in identifiable respects from the Aramaic dialect employed, for example, by Christians of the same periods who were living in the same or nearby areas. Similarly, JBA is the dialect of Aramaic employed by Jews in Mesopotamia during certain periods. We can identify additional dialects, in both Palestine and Mesopotamia, for example, in Samaritan Aramaic, Nabatean Aramaic, Syriac, and Mandaic. Such demarcations are not only real in linguistic terms, but also reflect the realities of group existence in the Near East of late antiquity. Religious and ethnic communities lived closely together, creating a social construct; they were bound by intersecting religious, economic, and historical factors, all of which impacted the distinctiveness of their respective languages to the dialectal level. Furthermore, their various canonical literatures exhibited distinctive features. There are, of course, elements that the various dialects have in common, and much can be learned from the overlapping of dialects. There was also interaction among the larger communities themselves, and considerable cultural borrowing. In broader perspective, all communities who spoke and/or wrote Aramaic shared aspects of common culture. Often, dialects formed as a result of political and demographic changes, with sub-groups branching off from the parent community and going their separate ways.

Adopting a dialectal approach requires the lexicographer, in this case, the lexicographer of Aramaic, to include in the corpus of sources all written materials emanating from the designated groups, within the specified periods, whatever their status in canonical terms or their genres. Sokoloff carefully lists his sources for both dictionaries, many of which are of recent discovery, being the result of archeological excavation and archival research. The provenance of a given noncanonical source, as to whether it is Jewish or not, can usually be established on the basis of reliable criteria. In lexicographical terms, the value of a verb, or term of reference occurring in a noncanonical text for our comprehension of a talmudic verb or term, may be considerable. Henceforth, our perception of talmudic language will change from what it was, because we can now view a word or phrase in its ethno-linguistic context and often in its quotidian usage.

The extra-talmudic sources that Sokoloff cites for Jewish Palestinian Aramaic are from the Byzantine period in Palestine, which he dates from the third century C.E. until the Arab conquest in the seventh century C.E. He does not stop at that point, however, but goes on to include sources from the Geonic, post-talmudic period. Sokoloff has utilized the sixteenth-century Venice manuscript of the Palestinian Talmud and other partial manuscripts, and has cited manuscripts of similar authenticity for midrashic and targumic texts. Sokoloff has included all of the Palestinian midrashim of the period, and Palestinian targumic texts, including the *Targum Neophyti* (TN), which is of recent publication.[3]

He also cites Geonic halakhic literature, inscriptions (including amulets), *ketubot* (Jewish marriage contracts), papyri from Egypt, evidence from the Tiberian *masorah*, and even Aramaic liturgical poetry. The dictionary represents, for the first time, an impressive exercise in dialectal completeness, especially in its inclusion of Geonic literature, which is a rich source of Aramaic.

The sources that Sokoloff cites for the *Dictionary of Jewish Babylonian Aramaic of the Talmudic and Geonic Periods* (*DJBA*) are equally authentic. In addition to the Babylonian Talmud, cited from preferred manuscripts of the various tractates, the dictionary includes data provided by the more extensive Geonic literature of Babylonia, which is of several genres: responsa, legal compendia, formularies and documents, historical and lexical texts, and liturgy. Sokoloff also counted among his sources the exegetical writings of Anan ben David (ca. 800 C.E.), the founder of a precursor of the Karaite sect. Also included are some Masoretic texts. Of great significance are the hundreds of Aramaic magical texts, most inscribed on the insides of bowls (known as "magical bowls"), from Iraq and Iran, dating from the fifth to the eighth centuries C.E.. There are many more where these came from, yet to be published. Not only Jews utilized such bowls, but also Christians and Mandaeans, using their respective dialects of Aramaic. It is usually possible to identify Jewish provenance, although argument on this issue continues to occupy specialists in the field.

The assembling of a dialectal corpus for both JPA and JBA is a great achievement, in itself. Michael Sokoloff's two dictionaries are unprecedented in kind, and introduce a new model of lexicography applicable to two major dialects of ancient-to-early Medieval Aramaic. If it is a proper goal of the humanities in higher education to assure that every Semitist be knowledgeable in the languages of the Talmud, and that every Talmudist qualify as a Semitist, then Michael Sokoloff has made the attainment of these goals possible for more and more scholars.

Methodology and Meaning

Ultimately, a dictionary is only as good as the meanings ("glosses") it provides. A corollary to determining the meaning of a given lexeme is the sequence in which multiple meanings are listed. Sequencing is the usual way of indicating the relative roles of such meanings, lending special importance to the meaning listed first. In the case of the present dictionaries, which provide English translations of Aramaic lexemes, determinations of meaning and sequence require not

[3] *The Neophyti Targum of the Pentateuch*, ed. A. Diez-Macho (Madrid-Barcelona, 1968–1978) (text corrected from a photograph provided by the Hebrew University).

only a thorough knowledge of the Aramaic dialects themselves, but also of the English language and its usage. The lexicographer is, after all, a translator as well, and must find the most felicitous rendering. Great effort is required to resolve the inevitable tension between fidelity to the original language and comprehensibility in the language of translation.

Every lexicographer has an approach to the phenomenon of meaning, itself, even if this approach is not articulated. One who operates with the concept of *Grundbedeutung* "base meaning" will register different meanings to start with, and will undoubtedly develop a different sequence for listing the meanings than one who has less interest in etymology than in contextual, or functional connotation. In the latter case, sequence might be determined on the basis of the frequency, or distribution of one meaning over another. There are further translation issues: How far can one stretch the semantic field of a given lexeme? How prevalent is polysemy, and how frequent are homonyms?

The advantage of a base-meaning approach is that it can lead to a better sense of the etymology and semantics of the original language, as to how lexemes extend their meanings within a given language. This is especially true of agglutinative languages, like the Semitic languages, which are based overall on a relatively small number of roots, whose meanings are modulated, in turn, by morphological and phonetic alternations. One who can trace a given form back to its root, and who knows the patterns of change affecting it, is on the road to discerning meaning in all of its diversity The disadvantage of the etymological approach is that it may not do justice to functional meaning in immediate context, which is what the user of the dictionary is seeking. With acumen, a way can be found to balance these competing interests.

Regarding the "lemma," or the given form in the entry, Sokoloff has chosen "the most basic form of the lexeme, e.g. the triradical root of a verb or the absolute state of a noun" (*DJPA* 6; in *DJBA* 22–23, "an emphatic form of a noun." [Actually, Sokoloff often lists absolute noun forms in *DJBA*, as well]). Regarding "gloss," here, the English translation of the lexeme, Sokoloff states: "The English gloss is intended to convey a general meaning for the lexeme, whereas its more specific nuances are detailed in the lexical section" (*DJPA* 6). In *DJBA* 23 this is merely reformulated: "The English gloss given at the beginning of the entry is intended to give a general idea of the meaning of the lexeme, while more exact nuances are given in detail in the semantic section." In other words, Sokoloff is more attuned to etymology in his presentation of the Aramaic lemma, which provides "the most basic form," than he is with respect to the English gloss, where he first lists "a general meaning" or "a general idea of the meaning." As will become evident in the discussion to follow, it is my sense that Sokoloff's policy on meaning can potentially detract from both the precision and the utility of the two dictionaries. It might be preferable to list the most basic meaning first.

Another factor affecting the determination of meaning is the lexicographer's view of the interrelatedness of the Semitic languages and the significance of cognates. A corollary to this is the presumed relationship of dialects and phases within Aramaic. Sokoloff conforms to the current trend away from emphasis on "common Semitic" derivations, and he clearly seeks to identify the most applicable usage within the specific dialect covered by each of the present dictionaries. This is as it should be, but if he were to weigh alternative meanings solely within a given dialect, or even within Aramaic as a whole, without reference to the larger linguistic environment, such a policy would shut out relevant evidence. Now, Sokoloff consistently provides comparative references to other dialects of Aramaic, and selectively does the same for Hebrew, especially the contemporary Middle Hebrew. On occasion he cites Akkadian and other cognates, as well. And yet, it is my sense that at times he fails to factor in relevant comparative evidence that would be useful in determining the contextual meaning.

Decisions regarding which information should be presented in a given entry, and which need not be, involve both synchronic and diachronic factors. A dictionary, unless it is intended to be an historical dictionary; is synchronic in its thrust. Its primary objective is to explain the words of a language or dialect in use during the designated period. In the process it is often useful, however, to provide data from earlier periods so as to be clear as to how a given meaning developed. In this respect, as well, Sokoloff might have been more inclusive.

In evaluating the present dictionaries, so vast in their content, it would be best to take up the issues just discussed by citing specific examples that illustrate them. Here are a few:

Format and Apparatus

Format is all-important in presenting data, because it determines what hits the eye of the reader most directly. As an example, the recent *Dictionary of the North-West Semitic Inscriptions*, by J. Hoftijzer and K. Jongeling (2 vols., Leiden: E.J. Brill, 1995) is comprehensive in its coverage and masterful in its lexicographical determinations. It is a boon to scholarship, reliably directing the researcher to diffuse sources. Yet, its format is so cumbersome that at times it comes close to obscuring the glosses themselves in a mangled thicket of profuse abbreviations, fragmentary citations, and bibliographical data! In this respect, Sokoloff has done an excellent job of standardizing *sigla*, of using bold-face type and other helpful formatting mechanisms, and of organizing the data comprehensibly. In his introductions, he clearly explains the scope of the lexicographic data he provides in each entry. There is an immense variety of collateral information crammed into small spaces without impeding reader comprehension.

There is one improvement in format that I would have liked to see: an initial register of all attested meanings, listed according to their occurrence in the several stems. Let's look at a sample entry: *DJPA* 477: קדש vb. **to sanctify, betroth, dedicate**.

These glosses are followed by the lexical section, which lists all of the attested forms derivative of this verbal root. Only then do we find all of the glosses registered by stems. Somewhat altering Sokoloff's translations in form, though not in substance, I would rearrange the opening section as follows

> קדש vb. Pe. (unattested in JPA) Pa. **1. to sanctify, consecrate. 2. to sanctify (wash) the hands and feet** (before a sacred act). **3. to proclaim the new moon as sacred. 4. to betroth a woman.** Af. **to dedicate.** Itpa. **1. to be sanctified. 2. to sanctify one's self by washing the hands and feet** (before a sacred act). **3. to be proclaimed as sacred** (said of the new moon).

This rearrangement provides an immediate overview of the full role of the verb in JPA. A similar revision of format would apply to the same verb in JBA (*DJBA* 987–988). The resulting format would resemble the system employed in *The Assyrian Dictionary of the University of Chicago*, which I have always found helpful when searching for derivative meanings. As the matter stands, one reading an entry in either of the present dictionaries is not immediately informed as to which stems attest each of the given meanings.

Translation and Sequence

We will examine a sample entry in which accurate translation and proper sequence constitute the primary issues:

> *DJPA* 138–139: דבר vb. **to take, lead, move**. [Complete list of meanings as given in *DJPA*: Pa. **to lead, guide**. Itpe. **to be taken**. Itpa. 1. **to move, travel**. 2. **to be guided**.]

Critique: The case for registering "to take" as the first meaning is, presumably, that Aramaic דבר translates Hebrew לקח in TN, which is a major source for defining usage of the verb דבר in JPA. This rendering is not consistent, however, because elsewhere TN renders Hebrew לקח by the Aramaic verb נסב, whose primary meaning is, indeed, "to take." An examination of the citations shows that TN consistently employs Aramaic דבר in the Peʿal and Itpeʿel stems in cases where BH לקח means "to take out, away; to bring" in context, but where BH לקח means "to take hold," it is more appropriately rendered by נסב. Contrast the following in TN: (a) Gen 24:7: "YHWH, the God of heaven, who led me out / took me out from (לקחני מ-) the household of my father." TN: דבר יתי. Here, as in most of the cited instances, the BH syntax is modulated by prepositions, such as מן "from," or אל "to:" In some instances, motion may be signified by the locative accusative. (b) Gen 43:15: "And the double portion of silver they took (לקחו/TN: נסבו) in their hand, together with Benjamin" (*DJPA* 352–353). In this case, BH לקח indeed means "to take in one's hand." Such sensitivity to nuance in TN accords surprisingly well with English usage, where "to take," by itself, more precisely means "to hold, seize, take to one's self."

The base-meaning of Aramaic דבר is "to lead," hence: "to bring forth, lead out, conduct, take out, away" and so forth. The core image is that of shepherding, of tending flocks—an image that is translocated to the human sphere. In fact, Sokoloff lists "to lead" as the first meaning of the Paʿʿel of JPA דבר (= *dab-*

bir). He cites a Palestinian Targum fragment on Gen 48:15, with reads (in my translation):

> אלהים הרעה אתי מעודי
> TN:די דבר יתי מן טל[יותי]
> "The God who has been shepherding/tending me from my birth"
> TN: "who has guided me since my youth."

One of Sokoloff's citations for Itpaᶜᶜal (perhaps Itpeᶜel), meaning 1 "**to move, travel**" further illustrates the pastoral matrix of the verb דבר. TN on Exod 12:42 presents a brief excursus on the Exodus theme, taking its cue from the reference to large flocks and herds earlier on in the biblical passage (Exod 12:38). Exod 12:41–42 read in part:

> All of the ranks of YHWH (צבאות יהוה) departed from the Land of Egypt. That was for YHWH a night of vigil (ליל שמרים) to bring them out from the Land of Egypt.

Here is how TN describes the scene:

> דין ידבר בריש ענה ודין ידבר בריש ענה ומימריה מדבר ביני תריהון
>
> **Sokoloff's translation**: "This one will move at the head of the sheep, and that one will move at the head of the sheep, and his *memar* will move between them."
>
> **Proposed translation**: "One will take the lead at the head of (some of) the flocks, and another will take the lead at the head of (some of) the flocks, while his Logos takes the lead between them."

The Itpaᶜᶜal (possibly Itpeᶜel) ידבר is assimilated from יתדבר. [I would opt for the Itpaᶜᶜal, which would yield an iterative sense that is appropriate in immediate context.] A vigilant God, identified as the *memar* "the Word, Logos" (*DJPA* 305), leads the flocks from his forward position between them.

In JBA, usage of the verb דבר is less linked to translations of Scripture, and consequently yields more nuances. One who consults *DJBA* 312–313 will note that Sokoloff lists for the verb דבר a meaning **to apply** (meaning no. 4), which, citing Morris Jastrow, he regards as a calque of MH נהג. As realized long ago, an aspectual change occurred in usage of Hebrew נהג. In BH, verbal forms are transitive "to lead, drive, conduct" whereas in MH the force is stative/reflexive: "to conduct one's self, to behave." In fact, one could combine Sokoloff's meaning number 2 **to act** with his meaning number 4 **to apply**. Thus, the citation from B. *ᶜEruvin* 45a: פוק חזי מאי עמא נהג; "Go out and see how the people conduct (themselves)/behave."

It is entirely possible, however, that the above analysis has it in reverse! The stative/reflexive meaning "to behave, conduct one's self" in MH may, itself, represent a reflex of Aramaic נהג "to behave, conduct one's self," an aspectual change likewise expressed in the noun מנהג[א] "custom, practice" (*DJPA* 317; *DJBA* 685–86), most likely original to Aramaic. If so, Aramaic נהג (*DJPA* 342; *DJBA* 731–32) may not be denominative מנהג, after all. In any event, there is a semantic relationship, perhaps even an equivalence between Aramaic דבר and Hebrew נהג, and this, in addition to all else, argues for a first meaning: "to lead, take out" in the Peʿal stem. It may be relevant to note that Targum Onkelos regularly renders BH נהג by Aramaic דבר. Finally, Aramaic and West-Semitic מדבר[א] "desert" (*DJPA* 291; *DJBA* 642) is, etymologically speaking, the place where flocks are "led, driven"—to graze, as we would gather from Exod 3:1b: וינהג את הצאן אחר המדבר, "He drove the flocks into the steppe." On this basis, the Paʿʿel of דבר extends the base-meaning, yielding the sense: "to guide, direct."

In summary, the verb "to take," if not modulated syntactically—for example "to take out, away"—clashes with proper English usage and also skews the precise import of the translations of BH לקח in TN, and other sources. The first gloss of Aramaic דבר should be the English verb **"to lead,"** and the translations of all forms of this verb can, and should be formulated so as to reflect this base-meaning, which was undoubtedly understood by ancient writers of Aramaic.

Polysemy versus Homonymy

Very often, the issue in the translating process is one of semantic theory: Polysemy finds a multiplicity of meanings in a single root, whereas homonymy acknowledges the presence of separate roots within a given language with different meanings, which are orthographically identical ("homographs") or phonetically identical ("homophones"), or both. Judgments in this regard are unavoidably subjective. It is my sense that Sokoloff does well on polysemy; he doesn't usually strain the semantic range. I have, however, found numerous instances where he may have assumed homonyms unnecessarily, and has, as a result, generated two or more entries where only one was called for. This tendency on his part is undoubtedly related to his preference for contextual over etymological meanings. The root נגע may serve as an example where polysemy is more likely than homonymy; *pace* Sokoloff:

a) *DJBA* 729–730: 1# נגע vb. **to touch, deal with something**. 2# נגע vb. **to be afflicted with leprosy**. *DJBA* 747: ניגעא, נגעא n.m. **a sore**.

b) *DJPA* 341: נגע n.m. **plague**; נגע vb. **to touch, strike**.

Critique: There was a widespread belief in Near Eastern antiquity that disease, injuries to the body, plagues, and other misfortunes resulted from the "touch" or "strike" of a deity. This notion is reflected in the narrative of Jacob's bout with the angel of YHWH, where we read that the angel "touched, struck" (ויגע ב-) Jacob's hip socket, with the result that Jacob was incapacitated (Genesis 32:26). Most interesting is the fact that the Akkadian verb *lapātu* "to touch" also means "to afflict," with the derived nouns, *lipittu* and *liptu* connoting "disease."[4] Hebrew and Aramaic נגע would seem to exhibit the same semantic field as Akkadian *lapātu*. If so, Sokoloff's JBA 2# נגע "to be afflicted" would derive from the same root as 1# נגע "to touch." Furthermore, with regard to Sokoloff's 2# נגע, it

[4] *CAD L*, 87, s.v. mng. 1; 199, 201–202, s.v. mng. 2.

is more likely attested only in one stem, contrary to the way it is registered in *DJBA*, as occurring in two stems. Thus, we have an Itpeʿel or Itpaʿʿal participle, מינגעה (assimilated from מתנגעה) "is afflicted," and an Itpeʿel or Itpaʿʿal perfect, אינגעה (assimilated from אתנגעה) "was afflicted." Actually, Sokoloff notes that the verbal stem in evidence is uncertain. The association with leprosy (if that's what it was) is contextual, resonating with BH נגע צרעה (Lev 13:2). The same would be true of the JBA noun ניגעא "sore," which is simply a contextual connotation (*DJBA* 747). In view of the above analysis, I would subsume Sokoloff's JBA 1# נגע and his 2# נגע under one entry; and would also reject the notion that the latter is denominative of nominal ניגעא "a sore," which seems forced. This analysis would yield the following rearrangements:

> a) JBA: נגע vb. Pe. **1. to touch, 2. to touch upon** (a question), **to deal with**. Af. **to bring into contact**. Itpe./ Itpa. **to be afflicted**. n.m. ניגעא **sore**.
>
> b) JPA: נגע vb. Pe. **1. to touch, 2. to strike**; Af. **to strike**. נגע n.m. **plague**, lit. **the "touch" of God**.

A second case where polysemy is more likely than homonymy is the root ענ׳. According to Sokoloff, we have the following separate entries in JPA and JBA:

> a) In JPA (*DJPA* 412–413):
> **#1**. ענ׳ vb. **to answer, respond**. **#2**. ענ׳ vb. **to be late**. **#3**. ענ׳ vb. **to afflict**. **#4**. ענ׳ vb. **to be poor**.
>
> b) In JBA (*DJBA* 871–872):
> **#1**. ענ׳ vb. **to respond, answer**, **#2**. ענ׳ vb. **to become poor**, **#3**. ענ׳ vb. **to afflict, torture, delay**.

Critique: We know a great deal about the root ענ׳ (variants: ענה and ענו) from West-Semitic, including Old Aramaic and other Aramaic dialects, Moabite, Phoenician-Punic, BH and Ugaritic. There are two undisputed homonymous roots in the West-Semitic languages: (1) "to address, sing, respond, answer" (in the simple stem and its reflexes) and (2) "to be reduced to poverty, be poor" (in the simple stem and its reflexes); D-stem and its reflexes: "to subjugate (BH 'to rape'), oppress, reduce to poverty, afflict." Both roots are of wide usage, and attest a broad range of meanings.

In comparative perspective, there is good reason to conclude that the notions of "poverty" on the one hand and "affliction, subjugation" on the other derive from the same root, and yet Sokoloff separates them in both JPA and JBA. The notion of poverty and deprivation is a stative function of the simple stem and its reflexes, whereas the Paʿʿel generates an active-transitive aspect, conveying the notion of subjugation, of afflicting, or oppressing others. This mutually exclusive distribution of aspects in the respective stems is complementary, and is normal for the semantic range of a single root.

The meaning "to be late" (Peᶜal) and "to delay, postpone" (Paᶜᶜel) is another matter. Sokoloff lists the meaning "to delay" under #3 עני in *DJBA*, together with "to afflict, torture," whereas in *DJPA* he lists the same meaning as a function of #2 עני "to be late," attested in the Peᶜal stem and its reflexes, and separately from #3 עני "to afflict," attested in the Paᶜᶜel. Confusing the registration is a relationship with the MH legal term ענוי הדין "the postponement of a verdict," or "the delaying of judgment" (Mishnah, *ʾAbot* 5:8). Sokoloff apparently disassociated this set of meanings from the noun ענה, det. ענתה **time** (*DJPA* 412), where Sokoloff refers to MH עונה "period of time."

The fact is that the lexeme ענה, though indeed cognate with Hebrew עונה, is very much at home in Aramaic itself! In the Nahal Hever papyri from Palestine of the late first and early second centuries C.E.,[5] an unusual Aramaic and Nabatean Aramaic term was encountered: עני מיה, also ענימין, literally "times of water," and functionally "assigned times of irrigation." A Hebrew term, probably a calque of Nabatean Aramaic, namely, עונות של מים, is attested in the Tosefta.[6] Now, the component ענה and, as suggested in the *editio princeps* of the Nahal Hever papyri,[7] a posited masculine form *ען, are the very elements encountered in the Aramaic enclitic particle כען **as of now, now** (*DJPA* 266; *DJBA* 594), feminine כענת (cf. Imperial Aramaic; Biblical Aramaic). I was not fully aware of all of these connections until the preparation of this review.

I now propose that the JPA/JBA verb עני is denominative of ענה "time" (masculine ען), and that its meaning is: "to exceed the time, to be late:" Paᶜᶜel: "to postpone, delay" On this basis, the MH legal term ענוי הדין and related verbal forms, would reflect the Aramaic meaning, not *vice versa*. In any event, the meanings "to be late; to postpone" would be unrelated to the root that means "to be poor; to afflict, oppress."

A more complex case is that of the Aramaic verbal root גבר, where several entries come into play:

> 1) In JPA: a) *DJPA* 132: nm. גמר **completion**; vb. גמר **to complete, destroy**. b) *DJPA* 131: גמיר adj. **perfect, complete**; גמירה **destruction**.
>
> 2) In JBA: a) *DJBA* 290–292: גמר vb. **to finish, learn, decide**; vb **1**. Pe. intr. **to be finished, completed**. Af. **to teach**. b) *DJBA* 289: גמיר adj. **complete**. c) *DJBA* 289: גמירא nm. **one who has learnt**. d) *DJBA* 292: גמרא, גמארא nm. **tradition, *gemara*, completion**; לגמרי, לגמארי **entirely, completely**; עד גמרא **entirely, completely**.

---

[5] *The Documents from the Bar-Kokhba Period in the Cave of Letters: Hebrew, Aramaic, and Nabatean-Aramaic Papyri*, ed. Y. Yadin, J.C. Greenfield, A. Yardeni, B.A. Levine, (JDS 3; Jerusalem: Israel Exploration Society, 2002): 6, 95–96, 218.

[6] *Moᶜed* 1:2; see Saul Lieberman, *Tosefta Ki-fshuṭah: A Comprehensive Commentary on the Tosefta* (Hebrew), (New York: Jewish Theological Seminary of America): 5:1228–29.

[7] *The Documents from the Bar-Kokhba Period in the Cave of Letters*, 6.

Critique: The issue here is whether (a) "to finish, complete" and (b) "to learn, study," Afʿel "to teach, train," can be regarded as sharing the same semantic field, in which case they can all be derived from a single root. The other given meanings can be reconciled. Thus, "to destroy, annihilate" is to bring to an end, "to decide" is to conclude, finalize. (As for the meaning "to ripen," it probably expresses a different root, גמל, assuming a conditioned sound shift: *lamed* <> *resh*). Can we say, however, that "to learn, study" is "to complete"—a process? Does the Afʿel "to teach" mean to bring someone to completion? How are we to account for the JBA term גמרא "corpus of knowledge/interpretation/tradition," which is the equivalent of Hebraic תלמוד[א] "corpus of instruction," likewise occurring in JBA (*DJBA* 1209–10), and even once in JPA (*DJPA* 583)? The only difference between the two terms is that Hebraic תלמוד, with *tau*-preformative, means "what has been taught, instruction" whereas Aramaic גמרא means "what has been learned, knowledge." It would be forced to conclude that the term גמרא means "the completion," namely, what was added on to the Mishnah, or the oral tradition (*pace* Ben-Yehudah: 605–606, s.v. גמרה),[8] because such a meaning would not parallel Hebraic תלמוד, as we would expect it to do.

Complicating the problem is the fact that the meaning "to finish, complete" is well attested outside of Aramaic. BH attests the stative meaning "to be at an end"[9] and West-Semitic provides only sparse evidence,[10] but Akkadian *gamāru*[11] is a frequent verb, realized in many forms, and which shares the semantic range of Aramaic גמר to a remarkable extent. Aramaic גמר "to finish, complete" is also cognate with Arabic *kamala* "to be complete, entire, finished" (stative); II-form "to perfect, to make complete, to finish".[12] It is less clear, however, that Arabic *jamara* "to put away, aside": II-form "to collect together, assemble, to knot, or plait the hair"[13] is cognate with the Aramaic and/or the Akkadian verb under discussion.

In contrast, the notion of "learning, studying," unless it can be connected semantically with the notion of "finishing, completing," seems to be restricted to JBA, and to infrequent attestations in Palestinian Hebrew sources of the talmudic period, and as such is listed in the *Complete Dictionary of Ancient and Mod-*

---

[8] *Complete Dictionary of Ancient and Modern Hebrew* (Hebrew), by E. Ben-Yehudah, Jerusalem: Rafael Hayim Hakohen, 1958 (reprint by Thomas Yosseloff, New York, 1960): 605–806, s.v. גמרה.

[9] L. Koehler, W. Baumgartner, J.J. Stamm, *Hebräisches und aramäisches Lexikon zum Alten Testament* (Leiden: E.J. Brill, 1967–1995): 190.

[10] *DNWSI*, 226–27.

[11] *CAD G*, 24–32, and see derived forms.

[12] Manfred Ullmann, ed., *Wörterbuch der klassischen arabischen Sprache* (Wiesbaden: Otto Harrassowitz, 1970): 358, and following.

[13] *An Arabic-English Lexicon*, by E.W. Lane (London: Williams and Norgate. Reprint Beirut: Librairie du Liban, 1980): 452–54.

ern Hebrew (Hebrew)[14] as a separate entry. Sokoloff lists only two attestations with this meaning in JPA, which are probably JBA forms, after all. The case is very weak for classifying finite, and certain nominal forms of Aramaic גמר as denominatives of גמרא, the corpus of tradition and law, as if to say that they mean "to learn the גמרא" (*pace* Levy, I:343, and with Ben-Yehudah: 805, s.v. גמר, c., and note 1, by N.H. Tur-Sinai).[15] This derivation would put us back where we started, unsure of what the term גמרא, itself, means. (There is one clear homonym, namely, the noun גומרה [*DJPA* 123], גומרתא [*DJBA* 269] **live coal**, and similar forms in SA.[16] Compare Akkadian *gumaru* "ember" in *The Assyrian Dictionary of the University of Chicago* G:133, where reference is made to the Aramaic cognates, and also to Arabic *jamratun* "a live, or burning coal."[17] Also note MH מוגמר "incense placed on coals to fumigate" [Mishnah, *Berakot* 6:6, etc.]. These lexemes need not concern us here.)

There may possibly be a semantic bridge linking the two sets of meaning in the notion of "deciding, concluding," but there is always the pervasive notion of "totality" in one set of meanings, whereas this notion is not endemic to the other set. I confess that I cannot trace the origin of the meaning "to study, learn." It may turn out to be a spinoff of 1# גמר, after all, and not a genuine homonym. Perhaps further investigation will clarify this issue. For now, I would, in the interest of clarity, opt for two entries in *DJBA*, and classify the principal meanings as follows, somewhat differently from Sokoloff:

> 1# גמר vb. Pe. **1**. intr. **to be finished, completed**. **2**. tr. **to finish, complete, decide**. Pa. **to destroy, bring to an end**. adj. גמיר **complete**. adv. לגמרי, לגמארי **entirely**; עד גמרא **to completion, entirely**.
>
> 2# גמר vb. Pe. **to be knowledgeable, to study, learn, interpret; derive a law hermeneutically**. Af. **to teach, to engender an interpretation**. Itpe. **to be learned**. nm. גמירא **a learned person**. nm. גמרא, גמארא **interpretation, received tradition, body of interpretation**; As a proper noun: **the corpus known as the Gemara**.

Conclusion

The present review has hardly done justice to the vast scope of the two dictionaries produced by Michael Sokoloff. My intention was to convey something of the historic significance of his contribution, which cannot be overestimated.

---

14 *Complete Dictionary of Ancient and Modern Hebrew* (Hebrew), by E. Ben-Yehudah (Jerusalem: Rafael Hayim Hakohen, 1958; reprint by Thomas Yosseloff, New York, 1960): 805.

15 Jacob Levy, *Wörterbuch über die Talmudim und Midraschim*, first published in 1875, second edition in 1924 (reprinted in 1963), I:343; and with the *Complete Dictionary of Ancient and Modern Hebrew* (Hebrew), by E. Ben-Yehudah, 805, s.v. גמר, c., and note 1, by N.H. Tur-Sinai.

16 A. Tal, *A Dictionary of Samaritan Aramaic* (Leiden: Brill, 2000): 151.

17 *An Arabic-English Lexicon*: 453.

By focusing on several cases in point, I sought to address some basic issues that face the lexicographer of an ancient language, one with a very long history and which embodies numerous dialects and phases. Second to Hebrew, Aramaic is the Semitic language most intimately associated with Jewish tradition and culture, and it has been drawn upon extensively in the modem revival of Hebrew as a spoken and written language. In another dimension, the treasures of the Jewish Aramaic dialects represent if not the greatest then surely one of the greatest repositories of written Aramaic in existence, a repository that is rapidly losing its erstwhile esoteric image thanks to the persistent efforts of Michael Sokoloff.

Abbreviations

Af.	Afʿel, the parallel of Old Aramaic/ Hebrew Hafʿel/ Hifʿil
BH	Biblical Hebrew
DJBA	*A Dictionary of Jewish Babylonian Aramaic*
DJPA	*A Dictionary of Jewish Palestinian Aramaic*
Itpa.	Itpaʿʿal, reflex of the Paʿʿel in Aramaic
Itpe.	Itpeʿel, passive reflex of the simple stem in Aramaic
JBA	Jewish Babylonian Aramaic
JPA	Jewish Palestinian Aramaic
MH	Middle Hebrew
Pa.	Paʿʿel, the Aramaic D-stem
Pe.	Peʿal, the Aramaic simple stem
TB	Talmud, Babylonian
TN	Targum Neophyti